MERCHANTS AND TRADING IN THE SIXTEENTH CENTURY: THE GOLDEN AGE OF ANTWERP

T0382910

PERSPECTIVES IN ECONOMIC AND SOCIAL HISTORY

Series Editors: Andrew August
Jari Eloranta

TITLES IN THIS SERIES

Forthcoming Titles

MERCHANTS AND TRADING IN THE SIXTEENTH CENTURY: THE GOLDEN AGE OF ANTWERP

BY

Jeroen Puttevils

Routledge
Taylor & Francis Group

LONDON AND NEW YORK

First published 2015 by Pickering & Chatto (Publishers) Limited

2 Park Square, Milton Park, Abingdon, Oxfordshire OX14 4RN
52 Vanderbilt Avenue, New York, NY 10017

Routledge is an imprint of the Taylor & Francis Group, an informa business

First issued in paperback 2020

Copyright © Taylor & Francis 2015
Copyright © Jeroen Puttevils 2015

To the best of the Publisher's knowledge every effort has been made to contact
relevant copyright holders and to clear any relevant copyright issues.
Any omissions that come to their attention will be remedied in future editions.

All rights reserved, including those of translation into foreign languages. No part of this book
may be reprinted or reproduced or utilised in any form or by any electronic, mechanical, or
other means, now known or hereafter invented, including photocopying and recording, or in
any information storage or retrieval system, without permission in writing from the publishers.

Notice:
Product or corporate names may be trademarks or registered trademarks, and
are used only for identification and explanation without intent to infringe.

BRITISH LIBRARY CATALOGUING IN PUBLICATION DATA

Puttevils, Jeroen, author.
Merchants and trading in the sixteenth century: the golden age of Antwerp. –
(Perspectives in economic and social history)
1. Antwerp (Belgium) – Commerce – Europe – History – 16th century. 2.
Europe – Commerce – Belgium – Antwerp – History – 16th century. 3. Merchants – Belgium – Antwerp – History – 16th century. I. Title II. Series
382'.09493222'04-dc23

ISBN-13: 978-1-84893-576-1 (hbk)
ISBN-13: 978-0-367-66878-5 (pbk)

Typeset by Pickering & Chatto (Publishers) Limited

CONTENTS

Voor Leonie, mijn ouders en mijn familie

ACKNOWLEDGEMENTS

This book would not have rolled off the press without the support of many people and institutions. I would like to thank the Research Foundation Flanders (FWO), the University of Antwerp, Utrecht University, the University of Pennsylvania and Fulbright Belgium–Luxembourg: the financial support of these agencies allowed me to do the research for this book in excellent conditions. Sophie Rudland and Miranda Kitchener of Pickering & Chatto Publishers were especially helpful in the final stages of the preparation of this book.

Peter Stabel and Oscar Gelderblom acted as supervisors of the PhD dissertation (written at the University of Antwerp) on which this book is based. It was a true pleasure to learn the art of writing history from both of them, each with his own intellectual strengths and emphases. Their continuous questions and suggestions are at the core of this book. I could not have wished for better mentors. I would like to express my gratitude to the other members of my dissertation committee: Hilde Greefs, Bruno Blondé, Hugo Soly and Thomas Safley. I particularly enjoyed the ongoing discussion of my research with all of them. Special thanks goes out to Thomas Safley for being such an excellent and congenial host at the University of Pennsylvania during my stay there in the spring of 2013. Herman Van der Wee and Richard Goldthwaite's constructive criticisms have made this a better book, as did the anonymous referees on behalf of Pickering & Chatto.

Several others have read and commented on individual chapters: Bert De Munck, Dave De ruysscher, Bart Lambert, Wouter Ryckbosch and Botho Verbist. I particularly enjoyed sharing an office with Jelle De Rock and Wouter Ryckbosch for several years. When they were not there, Dries Raeymaekers, a couple of offices down the hall, proved to be an equally pleasant alternative to talk about history and life. I was fortunate to present many bits and pieces of this book over the years at the seminars of the Centre for Urban History (University of Antwerp), the Financial History Workshop (Utrecht University), the N. W. Posthumus Institute and the Economic History Forum (University of Pennsylvania). Jeremy Schreiber single-handedly corrected my English in the dissertation version of this book. Tim Bisschops, Jan De Meester, Michel

Oosterbosch and Irène Leydecker-Brackx were so kind to share their data with me. Lastly, and in the end most importantly, I want to thank Leonie, my parents and my family for their continuous support and love. Without them, there would be no book, so I dedicate all these pages to them.

LIST OF FIGURES AND TABLES

INTRODUCTION

In 1601 John Wheeler's *Treatise of Commerce* was published in London by the printer John Harison. As secretary of the English Merchant Adventurers, Wheeler set out to glorify the society and to convince its opponents of the necessity of the society. The treatise depicts merchants from the Low Countries, and in particular those of Antwerp, in a notably poor light; these merchants were allegedly going 'to eat out the Adventurers out of their trade, as they of Antwerpe therefore did the Merchants of other nations, Portugals, Italians, Dutches or Germans, and others, whereby they greatly enriched themselves, their prince and countrey'. Wheeler goes on to detail how the Antwerp merchants had ousted their competitors from international commerce. They had bought spices from the Portuguese, sometimes paying beforehand, and managed to establish a 'plaine Monopoly whereby they only gained, and all other nations lost; for that being in few mens handes, were sold at such a rate, as they lifted to their owne private lucre and gaine, and to the hurt and damage of all others'. A few years before the beginnings of the Dutch Revolt Antwerp merchants had taken over the profitable export of English kerseys to Italy and the Levant from their Italian, English and German colleagues and 'were to become the greatest dealers in that way ... with linen cloth, Worsteds, Sayes, Tapestrie, & other Netherlandish wares, by meanes whereof the said Italians, English and Germanes were forced to leave that trade, or to doe very little'. The German merchants let their Antwerp counterparts 'eat, as it were, the bread out of their mouth': Antwerp merchants took over the export of both merchandise from the Low Countries and transit products to the German hinterland. The Hanseatic Easterlings 'beganne not alitle to be diminished by those of Amsterdam, and other, but new upstarte townes in Holand, with their great number of Hulkes, and other shippes'. The more creditworthy Antwerp merchants were able to indebt Spanish merchants and sell them their worst wares, while exporting the good ones to Spain on their own accounts.

Wheeler wrote that around 1520 there were but sixteen merchants from the Low Countries in London 'and amongst them not past foure of any credite, or estimation'; these merchants brought to the city mere knick-knacks, such as 'stone pottes, brushes, puppets, and toyes for children, bristles for shoomakers, and such other pedlery ware of small valew, and sometimes a little fish, and three or foure peeces of linen cloth'. By 1560:

> there were in London, at least one hundred Netherlandish Merchantes, the most part whereof were of Antwerpe, and thither they brought all kinde of wares, which the Merchantes of Italie, Germanie, Spaine, France, and Eastland (of which all nations there were before that time divers famous and notable rich Merchants and Compa- nies) used to bring into England out of their own Countries directly, to the great damage of the said strangers, and of the naturall borne English Marchants.[1]

In short, Portuguese, Italian, German, Hanseatic, Spanish and English merchants all eventually found themselves holding the short end of the stick in the com- petition with Netherlandish merchants. Only the political troubles in the Low Countries and the powerful opposition of the Merchant Adventurers – accord- ing to their secretary – stopped this rise of the Netherlanders to commercial power. This account of the ascent of Antwerp merchants on the European mar- kets can hardly be called neutral and is of course part and parcel of the political agenda and discourse of the Merchant Adventurers in preserving their commer- cial privileges. Nonetheless, the fact that the secretary of the English Merchant Adventurers was so worried about the activities of Low Countries, and especially Antwerp, merchants is highly significant. These Low Countries traders were not only displacing the Merchant Adventurers from trade but were also threatening the commercial interests of the Portuguese, the Hanseats, Spanish and Italian merchants throughout Europe during the sixteenth century. This commercial emancipation of Low Countries merchants, often operating from Antwerp, dur- ing the sixteenth century (1480–5) is the subject of this book.

Why is the commercial ascent of this particular group of Low Countries merchants historically relevant? Attention to particular groups of merchants by economic historians can hardly be called new. Extensive research on the eleventh- and twelfth-century Maghribi or Geniza merchants who left a large corpus of fragmentary sources in the Cairo Geniza and who operated trading enterprises within the Mediterranean, on Genoese and Venetian merchants, on their Florentine colleagues, the Hanseatic League, the south German merchant-financiers who became active on the European market in the fifteenth century, on the Spanish and the Portuguese who stood to gain from their world empires, on the English Wool Staplers, the Merchant Adventurers and the great trading companies, on the Dutch in the seventeenth century and on merchant diasporas such as the Sephardic Jews and the Armenians, has put forward a plethora of possible explanations for the rise and dominance of these respective merchant groups. Key advantages of these groups consisted of: an access to strategic, often home-grown, commodities which were in demand in other markets; a reliance on and access to efficient transportation; the rapid appropriation of advanced commercial know-how and accounting; a capability to attract sufficient working capital; a participation in princely and state finance; the support of networks based on family and/or religion which enhance intra-group trust; and, finally, the role of institutions, both private and public order. This book verifies how far these explanations take us in accounting for the rise of a new group of merchants: those of the Low Countries. No single factor singularly explains the ascent of this group; it is the cumulative combination of the above factors which provides the most complete answer. This may be perhaps a somewhat dull and anticlimactic answer at first sight, but it does justice to historical reality. Still, this book argues that some factors matter more than others and that other factors had unexpected consequences.

Between 1480 and 1585, Antwerp's golden sixteenth century, Low Countries merchants cashed in on the general demand for Low Countries products on European markets which they easily obtained in Antwerp's hinterland, close to the production side. Yet, this specialization in homegrown goods was not very outspoken; Low Countries traders were also very active in the flow of re-exports running through Antwerp. The sixteenth-century economic upsurge allowed these merchants to position themselves as important intermediaries for both exports out of the Low Countries, and imports of foodstuffs, raw materials and finished goods to the Low Countries. The concentration of European trade in one node, the city of Antwerp, accelerated the ascent of native traders by bringing them into close contact with merchants from other regions, from whom they appropriated commercial techniques and learned of new commercial opportunities. The city of Antwerp did not restrict access to trade; every individual could participate, provided he or she (many female traders were active in Antwerp) had the necessary capital and know-how. As such, Antwerp hosted open-access institutions.[2] Positive discrimination by the city was extended only to particular groups of foreign traders; native merchants did not receive any preferential treatment or support and this may have resulted in a lack of organization and privileges of the group abroad. Despite this, Low Countries merchants still managed to establish themselves as important players which casts light on the role played by merchant guilds and institutions. The flexibility and contractual security of partnerships and short-term credit through bills obligatory would surely have increased the financial competitiveness of Low Countries traders.

This analysis of the operations of Low Countries merchants answers several important questions. First, their activities and entrepreneurship provide insight into the economic and institutional factors underpinning economic development of the region of the Low Countries, a densely urbanized and commercialized area in preindustrial Europe.[3] Second, the entry of new merchants into long-distance commerce is an issue that has been largely ignored in the historiography on European long-distance trade and thus requires explication. This book is a comparative study of the phenomenon of new merchants appearing in international markets, notably in the sixteenth century, a period of world-wide expansion of the European economy. Third, sixteenth-century Antwerp, the commercial hub for this group of traders, figures as an important protagonist in recent accounts of the role of institutional development in European commerce; Antwerp was one of the first cities of commerce which generated open-access institutions and did not favour one group of merchants over another. This book, by focusing on the Low Countries' native merchants, argues that these accounts are only partially true. This goes to show that although institutions definitely matter, they are always only part of a larger story.

The object of study, a particular group of merchants, requires a careful defini-tion. As will become clear in the following chapters, only merchants from the Southern Low Countries who had migrated to Antwerp or had very close ties with the Scheldt town are analysed in depth. Antwerp was the dominant com-mercial gateway but there were several other towns, both in the Northern and in the Southern Low Countries, with extensive connections to European mar-kets.[4] This dissertation does not take into account merchants from those other cities without ties to Antwerp – although not having contact with Antwerp and trading abroad was virtually impossible in this period, as we will see. What we understand as trade also requires clarification. The dissertation does not take retail into account; only the trade between producers and wholesalers who collected the products and exported them or who supplied producers with raw or semi-finished materials they had imported are considered.[5] Low Countries merchants were very active in the collection of Low Countries products for export. The men and women who were active in trading goods between the commercial gateway of Antwerp and its hinterland and/or in marketing these goods in European centres of commerce had to rely on their own judgemental decision about buying and selling and can be defined as entrepreneurs.[6] These men and women could rely on capital, favourable institutions and commercial opportunities and that they were incentivized by the substantial profits which could be obtained in commerce.

Today, the attention to Low Countries merchants will not come as a surprise to most scholars of the late medieval and early modern Low Countries. But his-toriographical attention for this group of merchants was to develop slowly. In the first quarter of the previous century, Henri Pirenne and Richard Ehrenberg mar-ginalized the role of these native traders in the sixteenth-century development of the Antwerp market and reserved the leading part for the foreign merchants who established their businesses in the Scheldt town in the late fifteenth and early sixteenth centuries; in this view, it was Portuguese traders and their spices, English merchants bringing textiles and South Germans offering silver and cop-per who built the Antwerp market.[7] The Ghent historian Hans Van Werveke argued that important Antwerp merchant houses, such as the Schetz, Pruynen and Van Dale, should not be neglected, yet still ascribed Antwerp's commercial flourishing mainly to the presence of foreign merchants.[8] Gradually, Antwerp historians such as Léon Van der Essen, Jan-Albert Goris, Oskar de Smedt, Jan Denucé and Floris Prims started to observe the contribution of native merchants to long-distance commerce in sixteenth-century Antwerp.[9]

In the late 1950s and early sixties this view was fundamentally adjusted by the work of Wilfrid Brulez and Herman Van der Wee. Jan Craeybeckx in 1957 brought together anecdotal information on several sixteenth-century Low Countries commercial and industrial entrepreneurs.[10] Two years later, Wilfrid Brulez published his excellent in-depth analysis of one important native merchant family, whose enterprising *pater familias*, Jan Della Faille, originated from the Courtrai countryside and migrated to Venice and later to Antwerp, where he set himself up as an independent merchant.[11] Brulez used the history of the Della Faille as a *pars pro toto* for the wider emancipation of Low Countries merchants and the democratization of long-distance commerce out of Antwerp. Brulez extended his analysis to those merchants who were related to the Della Faille and/or worked for them and to those who were also active in the trade with Italy, one of the main businesses of the merchant house. Brulez attributed this emancipation to the adoption of advanced Mediterranean (mainly Italian) commercial techniques. Marine insurance, commission trade, bills of exchange and double entry bookkeeping which the Low Countries traders are believed to have picked up quickly, facilitated their participation in European commerce.[12] Four years later, Herman Van der Wee's magisterial study of the growth of the Antwerp market equally stressed the importance of native merchants and tied them explicitly to the growth of the Low Countries export industry, whose produce they marketed throughout Europe.[13] From the 1530s native merchants acquired more and more skills and capital to compete with the foreign merchants in Antwerp.

Since Brulez's and Van der Wee's pivotal studies a large number of case studies have added to our understanding of this group.[14] Some of these case studies considered individual entrepreneurs[15] while others dealt with several generations of traders within a family.[16] There were also studies of groups specializing in particular trades.[17] Of particular note is Eric Wijnroks's detailed study of Antwerp merchants' participation in the Russia trade in the second half of the sixteenth century.[18] Oscar Gelderblom came to the conclusion that merchants who had emigrated from the Low Countries were important for the growth of the Amsterdam market at the end of the sixteenth century, but notes that this could not have happened without the close symbiosis with Amsterdam and Holland traders.[19] In a sense, this book offers a prequel to Gelderblom's research on Amsterdam. The research for this book started with a modest analysis of the participation of Low Countries merchants in the trade with Italy in the middle of the sixteenth century.[20] Building further on Brulez, I showed that Low Countries merchants were able to fill a vacant commercial niche, left by the Venetian merchants when they decided to make use of the services of Low Countries agents and buy Low Countries products brought by Antwerp merchants to Venice.

Explaining the Ascent of Merchants from the Low Countries

This book verifies the explanatory power of four major potential comparative advantages enjoyed by Low Countries merchants. The first two chapters deal with the access these merchants had to strategic commodities and the resultant relations they had with Antwerp's industrialized hinterland, the economy of the Low Countries and European markets. Low Countries merchants could assume different roles and profiles: they could focus on trade between Antwerp, the Low Countries' commercial gateway, and European markets, or they could redistribute imports to the hinterland for industrial production and local consumption and carry the industrial output of the Low Countries to Antwerp. Of course, different combinations, specializations and variations were possible within this frame. Changes in the marketing landscape – the commercial maelstrom of Antwerp attracting more and more trade and its development from a fair-based, seasonal market into a permanent trading venue – also created opportunities for commercial middlemen, some of whom would morph into wholesale, long-distance traders.

The products of the Low Countries industry, having been restructured in the fourteenth and fifteenth centuries, were among the main European export products of the Antwerp market. In Herman Van der Wee's eyes merchants from the Low Countries were responsible for the marketing of home-grown commodities such as light textiles, linen, tapestries, copper items and other metal wares, etc., and thus were riding the wave of economic development of the Low Countries during a phase of export-driven growth.[21]

Low Countries merchants also benefited from a general upsurge of European trade in the sixteenth century, a process fuelled by the re-opening of continental trading routes. At the end of the 1960s Herman Van der Wee and Theo Peeters argued that the revival, spread and intensification of overland trade went hand in glove with economic prosperity.[22] The revival of this trade flux between the eleventh and the early fourteenth centuries was followed by a depression because continental Europe lost its access to long-distance trade. While the Atlantic port towns benefited from maritime trade, these benefits did not outweigh the general economic contraction on the continental hinterland.[23] From the second half of the fifteenth century and well into the sixteenth century, a general upsurge of the European economy was mirrored by the revival of continental trade. John Munro has confirmed that continuous warfare from the 1290s until the first half of the fifteenth century weighed heavily on continental trade routes to southern

Europe (mainly to Italy).[24] Maritime routes displaced continental transport but maritime transport was relatively more costly; in fact, it was too costly for the cheap textiles which were integral to the export package of the Low Countries at that time. Low Countries industry re-oriented to luxury woollens for which higher transportation costs were not prohibitive to export. When the continental route became safe again in the middle of the fifteenth century, huge volumes of cheap Low Countries textiles again flowed north and south, often through the continental fairs of Frankfurt, Geneva and Lyon.[25]

Antwerp was perfectly able to reap the benefits of the revival of trade: situated in north-western Europe in a region which for centuries had functioned as the commercial meeting place for north and south, with direct access to the North Sea and close to Cologne and the continental trade routes. The Brabant Land Toll and the Water Toll were rising steadily from the second half of the fifteenth century onwards until the 1560s.[26] The growing volumes of trade through a combination of intensive maritime and continental trade can occur only when the group of traders expands or the existing group manages to control the larger volume of trade. Moreover, when continental trade became available again, cheaper textiles could once more be exported alongside luxury textiles, thereby increasing the trade volume even more.

In the first chapter I will show that the group of native merchants operating out of Antwerp was increasing throughout the sixteenth century and effectively capturing this growing volume of trade. Contrary to their contemporaries, the English Merchant Adventurers and their commercial successors, the merchants of the Dutch Republic founded during the Dutch Revolt, sixteenth-century Low Countries traders could not boast a commercial navy; for marine transportation they relied on the shipping services of others, especially skippers from the northern parts of the Low Countries, whose cost efficiency was becoming clear throughout the sixteenth century.[27] Continental transportation went through a similar revolution in the sixteenth century: professional carriers and transport firms (mainly Italians and south Germans) became active in transport between the Low Countries and Italy at least as early as the 1540s, which enabled merchants to outsource the burdensome planning and managing of overland transportation; this professionalization gradually extended to France as well.[28] Hence, Low Countries traders had to rely on the shipping services of others and lacked their own means of transportation.

The first chapter establishes, based on detailed taxes on imports to and exports from Antwerp, that Low Countries merchants did not display a marked preference for the trade in home-grown goods; their foreign counterparts operating out of Antwerp were equally active in this trade. Moreover, Low Countries merchants were as active in the re-export of important products traded at Antwerp, such as English textiles, spices and sugar. Clearly, Low Countries traders did not translate their home advantage of trading in home-grown products into a comparative advantages, something which other merchant groups such as the English Wool Staplers and Merchant Adventurers did. The chapter sketches the growth of the group of Low Countries merchants, their relative position vis-à-vis their foreign colleagues in Antwerp, the relative weights of trade between Antwerp and various European markets, and the volumes of and characteristics of goods which circulated between Antwerp and these markets. Finally, the commercial attractiveness of Antwerp is described in this chapter. The presence of Low Countries merchants in European trading centres is documented in the second part of chapter one. This presence abroad allowed them to seize important commercial opportunities such as filling in the commercial vacuum caused by the withdrawal of the Venetians from the Low Countries markets or their early investments in the exploitation of the Canary and Azores Islands which provided them with a sought-after commodity, sugar.

Chapter two deals with the relationships between Low Countries traders, Antwerp and its hinterland on the one hand and between Antwerp and the groups of Low Countries merchants active in different European trading centres. The chapter builds further on the first chapter's observation that native merchants were not significantly more specialized in Low Countries products than foreign traders active in Antwerp. The chapter shows that Low Countries merchants did have strong relations with the production side of the Low Countries, Antwerp's hinterland. Many had migrated from the industrial towns and the countryside to set up a trading house in Antwerp. This did result in comparative advantages: they were able to acquire commodities at the source, assuring that they would be in tune with the latest tastes on European markets; they spoke the same language as producers and middlemen; and they were familiar with the technicalities of production and local customs. Hence, different strategies were possible: to engage in long-distance trade with several other European markets or to visit local markets and producers and take their commodities to the commercial gateway. For the latter option, thorough knowledge of the local products and local connection mattered. According to Jessica Goldberg, eleventh- and twelfth-century Jewish traders in Fustat and Cairo faced a similar trade-off between localism and cosmopolitanism. The choice for one strategy or the other was determined by resources, family ties, training and personality.[29] This resulted in different roles to be played by various Geniza merchants – but also by Low Countries merchants operating centuries later: they could act on a local, a regional or a long-distance basis.[30]

Capital forms a second factor of comparative advantage. To market their goods and put their commercial skills to work, merchants needed access to finance and contemporary observers argued that Low Countries traders were remarkably able to raise such capital. The remarkable scope and depth of financial markets in the Low Countries has been noted by several historians.[31] Involvement in government finance explains (part of) the success of many commercial groups: the Augsburg, Nuremberg and Genoese bankers who financed the Habsburg state serve as an example.[32] The role of Low Countries traders in sixteenth-century government finance has largely been overlooked. Similar to their south German and Italian colleagues, bankrolling European crowns does explain the rise of individual merchants; yet, not every merchant had the capital and daring to engage in this risky, yet potentially rewarding, activity. The introduction to chapters four and five briefly deals with the understudied participation of Low Countries merchants in government finance. Chapters three and four elaborate how Low Countries traders relied on both equity (credit in return for a part of the profit) and debt finance (credit at a fixed interest) to finance their commercial enterprises. Chapter three is based on the analysis of a sample of Antwerp partnership contracts – the first systematic collection of such contracts – and reveals many details about partnership contract design. It compares Antwerp partnerships with those of other merchant groups (especially those of the south Germans and of merchants from Medina del Campo). Partnership contracts were firmly embedded in customary law and their registration allowed Low Countries merchants to attract capital from outsiders and non-family members. Partnerships offered merchants a solution to several problems at once: attracting capital, arranging liabilities, incentivizing partners (through a share of the profit) not to cheat, streamlining the organization's workings and acquiring partners' useful commercial knowledge and skills for the firm. Antwerp law foresaw legal guarantees, contract registration and enforcement for these outside investors. Technically, commission trading is of course not an equity-based activity, but the profit realized by the commission agent will prove vital for potential transactions in the future. Through commission trade, Low Countries merchants bought and sold commodities in the Low Countries on behalf of others, which integrated them into European trade.

Chapter four focuses on the bill obligatory. This is not to deny the role of other types of debt financing such as annuities, bills of exchange and deposits; merchants used all these financial instruments at the same time to spread their risks. The bill obligatory was very popular and both the law and commercial practices allowed for such bills to circulate from one party to another. Historiography has acknowledged the rules of this circulation but has not really explored the opportunities and the dangers of this circulation for Low Countries merchants.[33] While circulation created a useful financial instrument for economic growth, the growing intensity of its use undermined its efficiency, because the growing anonymity within the growing merchant community required additional guarantees for payment of the bill obligatory which put a burden on the instrument's initial flexibility. Native merchants in particular, and especially the smaller ones, used such bills to obtain credit to finance their commercial enterprises.

Until now, the history of the ascent of Low Countries traders operating out of Antwerp seems to have progressed very smoothly: they had access to products sought after throughout Europe; could obtain the necessary commercial skills to operate in long-distance trade; and they had access to the various financial instruments. This is not necessarily a matter of course. Sheilagh Ogilvie has demonstrated that institutions such as European merchant guilds could exclude large segments of society from long-distance trade. Institutions are the subject of the fifth and last chapter. Douglass North has defined institutions as the 'rules of the game in society or, more formally, ... the humanly devised constraints that shape human interaction'.[34] Greif takes a different approach and labels institutions as 'a system of rules, beliefs, norms and organizations that together generate a regularity of (social) behaviour'.[35] This book takes a more pragmatic approach to institutions by narrowing them down to agency relationships governed by family ties, norms and beliefs, laws, organizations such as merchant guilds or city governments and the services provided by these organizations such as justice and contract registration. The last two types of institutions (organizations, i.e., merchant guilds and the city government, and the services provided by these organizations) form the core of the Conclusion.

Because of their geographical dispersal throughout Europe, particularly after the Fall of Antwerp in 1585, the group of Low Countries traders might be categorized as a diaspora surpassing geographical and political boundaries.[36] Related through family ties and the same religion, diaspora communities are seen as setting in which commercial transactions can be executed, relying on communal control, shared norms and values.[37] Merchants have always relied on others through private order mechanisms. In particular, Avner Greif has shown – concentrating on the Maghribi traders, a group of Jewish merchants active in the eleventh- and twelfth-century Mediterranean ports under Muslim control – how private order solutions could sufficiently structure intra-group transactions.[38] A multilateral reputation mechanism or traders' coalition assured that a Maghribi merchant would not cheat his colleagues, since such action would result in reputation damage and expulsion from the commercial network (foregoing, as a *persona non grata*, all future transactions within the network). Such a private order organization, according to Greif, reduced the need of Maghribi merchants to turn to courts and the state, which were Muslim in that period and region, for contract enforcement. Personal relations between merchants were crucial to organize transactions and several merchant diasporas, such as the Sephardim and the Armenian Christian merchants from New Julfa, relied on extensive commercial networks without backing from any state.[39] The reliance of merchants on these informal networks has not escaped historians: kinship, friendship, shared cultural beliefs, social norms and mutual interdependence made such commercial relations work.[40]

A characterization of the Low Countries merchants as a merchant diaspora might be one step too far, for Low Countries traders did not display a shared sense of community and members of the group could be Catholic or Protestant. Yet, as in all commercial groups, Low Countries merchants did share family ties and intermarried. The book also documents countless instances of other ways which made co-operation between merchants possible: the prospect of future transactions, the observation and communication of past behaviour, the central-ity of reputation, the discourse and practice of friendship, peer pressure and the threat of ostracism (being shut out of the family or a particular group of traders). Reputation was important to all merchants but even more so to new entrants on the market. Many Low Countries merchants became active in long-distance trade and faced the challenges of setting themselves up as reputed and honest traders. As did other merchants, Low Countries traders relied on signals which would render them trustworthy in the eyes of their established colleagues and potential clients: owning real estate, being backed by people who stood surety for them, using a discourse of confidence and trust in their daily dealings and correspondence and acquiring merchant manners or a commercial habitus in the Bourdieuian sense.[41] Then as now, reputation only works when information flows freely and is available to those requiring it and when memories are good.[42]

On top of informal solutions, ironclad contracts and courts as potential deterrents and actual punishment mechanisms structured commercial transac-tions as well. Contracts and courts are obviously not private order solutions; they are supported by a state apparatus. Recent evaluations of Greif's claims and an alternative reading of Maghribi Geniza documents show that the above-mentioned private order institutions relied equally on courts and states. The Maghribi traders made use of the services of Islamic courts; merchant guilds relied on state support; and their community responsibility system was struc-tured by courts and laws.[43] Hence, as always strict dichotomies do not do justice to historical complexities. Gelderblom rephrases the complementarity of pri-vate and public solutions into 'the embeddedness of private solutions in a wider framework of public institutions.'[44] Moreover, European merchants combined formal and informal sanctions.[45] They overcame the difficulties of long-distance trade in a politically and legally fragmented pre-modern Europe by relying on informal networks and on the formal institutions created by cities and states. We will see that informal debt instruments, a financial means favoured by Low Countries traders, became the subject of a meticulous legislation and could be formalized and enforced when requested. In general, Low Countries traders, as all other merchants, relied both on private solutions in the form of networks of family, friends and countrymen, and on public institutions which could enforce both agreements made in these networks and transactions with strangers.

Low Countries merchants also relied on the services offered by the city. Sixteenth-century Antwerp gradually developed open-access institutions and services which were available to all traders, both foreigners and natives, incorporated or guild-less merchants. Ogilvie's account of merchant guilds foregrounds the importance of local urban and central governments which could choose to extend privileges and rights not to particular merchant guilds but to all economic agents within their realm, which created much more potential for economic development.[46] This was associated, according to Ogilvie, with the gradual emergence of impersonal markets and impartial states that provided security and contract enforcement to all, regardless of their identities or guild membership. Such open-access institutions, as impartial mediators, generated uniform institutional trust. Ogilvie proves through her analysis of merchant guilds in medieval and early modern Europe that the Low Countries was one of the first regions to develop generalized trust through impersonal markets and impartial states which furthered economic development.[47] Oscar Gelderblom comes to similar conclusions in his comparative study of the commercial successor cities of Bruges, Antwerp and Amsterdam through the framework of political economy.[48] Gelderblom argues that in these cities open-access or generalized institutions were created which granted access to markets, finance, contract registration and enforcement and protection from violence.[49] Commercial cities were pushed to install such regimes by inter-city competition and rivalry, both of which were especially dense in the Low Countries. This rivalry could result in the installation of legal and/or fiscal barriers between cities by which one city wanted to contain another, as S. R. Epstein has shown to have happened in late medieval Tuscany.[50] This could even result in outright inter-city warfare. However, commercial cities profited from the fiscal and financial gains of trade. These cities were eager to preserve this treasure and consequently tried to avoid costly and harmful rivalries, especially those in the forms of war and legal and/or fiscal barriers. This was mostly the case in the Low Countries, according to Gelderblom, despite the occasional disruptive revolt or war. To do so, cities such as Antwerp had to invest heavily in commercial infrastructure and markets which allowed buyers and sellers who did not know each other to trade in a transparent manner, directly or through intermediaries such as hostellers and brokers, professions which the city sought to regulate carefully.[51] This transparent commercial infrastructure was petrified for example in Antwerp's New Bourse building.[52] Commercial cities also accepted commercial customs and rules and introduced them in the urban laws. Sixteenth-century Antwerp lawmakers combined and integrated learned Roman law, city customs and mercantile practices from foreign traders into a coherent body of urban law.[53] Commercial cities such as Antwerp set competitive and transparent tariffs and taxes and opened the market to all economic agents. These cities feared the departure of merchants, both because of the resulting loss of income and because the merchants would move to one of their competitor cities instead. Sixteenth-century Antwerp increasingly moved towards such an inclusive regime. The last chapter documents one such service which the city of Antwerp offered to all merchants: courts of law.

It is beyond question that Low Countries traders reaped the benefits of the inter-urban competition which led to the creation of open-access institutions. These institutions allowed them to organize their trade and transactions; as such, the ascent of Low Countries traders can partially be explained as a consequence of institutional change. The final chapter of this book demonstrates that this was only true to a certain extent. Low Countries merchants may have profited from the generation of open-access institutions, but their colleagues did so as well. Ironically, the Antwerp city government did not favour its own merchants. At the end of the fifteenth and in the beginning of the sixteenth centuries the Antwerp and central governments had granted new privileges – and reconfirmed older ones – to groups of foreign merchants. The presence of foreign merchant guilds and their privileged position in sixteenth-century Antwerp worked against native merchants trying to establish themselves on European markets. The English Merchant Adventurers, who had received extensive privileges, were a formidable force to be reckoned with, both in Antwerp and in London where Low Countries traders were also operating. Responding to the influx of foreign merchants at the beginning of Antwerp's commercial growth (1480s and 1490s) and to the fierce competition of incorporated foreign merchants, Low Countries traders exhibited a corporate reflex. However, the Antwerp urban government was very reluctant in approving these merchant guild propositions because they feared to offend the foreign traders, who, in their eyes, were crucial for Antwerp's commercial wealth. Even in the few cases when establishment of a native merchant guild was approved, the guild was kept under firm control of the urban government. Low Countries traders had to make do without strong merchant guilds in Antwerp. Partially as the result of the lack of strong merchant power in their home base Low Countries traders lacked a merchant guild and privileges in other European commercial cities where the climate was sometimes hostile towards them. Despite all this, they were still very active on these markets and were not especially hindered by not having their own merchant guilds. This proves that when profits were bountiful, merchants could still be active in places which had 'bad' institutions, much like contemporary mining companies looking for rare metals for electronics do in Africa where less-than-desirable institutions persist.[54]

The existence of open-access institutions in Antwerp notwithstanding, this history shows that political economy matters. Sixteenth-century Antwerp was very different from other trading European centres where trade – or at least the most lucrative parts of it – was largely in the hands of natives, whether city authorities were dominated by these very merchants such as Lübeck or Venice.[55]

In these cities native merchants were directly responsible for the commercial success of the city or not; only in a second phase did these cities' trade attract outsiders. Antwerp's commercial origin as a fair market, open for everyone, and the forced move of the foreign merchants from Bruges to Antwerp in 1488 contributed to the fact that there was not a considerable group of politically entrenched merchant-citizens. Throughout the sixteenth century few merchants joined the aldermen who ruled the city. The city magistrate and central authorities were eager to attract foreign merchants for the revenue they would generate and later did not dare to antagonize them in the climate of inter-city commercial competition as described by Gelderblom.

Antwerp's particularity is not only located in its political economy; its commercial trajectory had an equally profound impact on institutional development. The ups and downs of commerce and the expansion in the number of merchants active in the city had effects of their own. Firstly, the group of Low Countries merchants grew in tandem with the volume of trade handled by Antwerp. They and other merchant groups were able to share the growing pie. Yet, when Antwerp started to experience commercial difficulties during the beginning of the Dutch Revolt, the shrinking pie gave way to (unsuccessful) protective reflexes of the by-then established group of Low Countries traders. A second challenge was the growth of the mercantile and the total urban population: by the middle of the sixteenth century, around 1,500 merchants resided in the Scheldt city and Antwerp's total population tripled between 1480 and 1568.[56] This concentration resulted into anonimization. Janet Landa has shown, based on her case of Chinese commercial middlemen in Southeast Asia, that 'as the trading group expands, personal relations, and hence trust among group members become attenuated'. Two possibilities determine the subsequent evolution of the group: either the trading group will erect barriers to limit the number of members; or, if contract law is sufficiently developed, the trading group dissolves because it can transact with strangers.[57] When the economy develops a better legal infrastructure, particularistic exchange networks based on mutual trust within such closed groups are replaced by impersonal exchange networks based on contracts. Sixteenth-century Antwerp faced a similar choice. Antwerp opted to keep open trade for all and as a result it developed ways, clear contracting rules to name but one, to deal with the challenge of a growing group of traders. This is evidenced by chapter four on bills obligatory: these bills kept circulating freely within Antwerp's economy; they could be custom made but were underpinned by clear contract rules and enforced in court when necessary, using the document and other accounts of it as evidence.

This book is based on the scarce evidence available on Low Countries merchants. The sources include account books, correspondence, merchant manuals, certifications and acts registered by the Antwerp aldermen, civil sentences and trial case files, notarial acts, probate inventories, inventories of bankrupt traders,

taxes on import and export and notes by city and central government administrators. A prosopography of the entire group proved impossible given the sparse
references to most individual merchants besides the more extensive data on a few
important players. Separately, all these documents give only scraps of evidence,
but taken together the ascent of merchants from the Low Countries onto the
European markets becomes clear. It is my hope that this analysis of the trade
done by Low Countries merchants contributes as a necessary and effective *pars
pro toto* to the current debate on the underlying institutions and mechanisms
of commerce which fuelled the economic development of pre-modern Europe.

Setting the Scene

The city of Antwerp, on the banks of the river Scheldt, experienced high levels of
population and economic development during the sixteenth century, the city's
Golden Age, as economic historians have often termed it. According to Fernand
Braudel the activities of the world economy, controlled by Western Europe, were
concentrated in one dominant node of the urban network, the *pôle urbaine*,
where the important international trade flows merged and thus allowed for
transactions on a large scale.[58] Antwerp assumed this function after Bruges and,
to a lesser extent, Venice, becoming the most important centre in West European commerce and one of the largest cities north of the Alps.[59] This brief sketch
serves to guide the reader through the complex history of the Antwerp market.

Antwerp's initial success and growth in the fifteenth century was closely inter-
twined with the annual Brabant fairs held in the city and in Bergen-op-Zoom,
another Scheldt port. The Antwerp fairs (Whitsun and St. Bavo (1st of October))
were established in the late 1310s and early 1320s; those of Bergen-op-Zoom were
of a later date (1337–59) and fell on Easter and All Saints.[60] The establishment of
the fairs were preceded by the granting of privileges by the duke of Brabant, first
to English merchants in 1296 and then to all foreigners in 1315.[61] The fairs and
the city flowered for a short time, but the city was then captured by the count of
Flanders, who enforced the market primacy of Bruges, much to the detriment of
the Antwerp fairs.[62] From 1405, the Brabant fairs started to flower again; during
these fairs the produce of the young but dynamic Brabant textile industry was
sold, as well as English wools and products from the nearby Rhineland. The fairs
became ever more attractive to international merchants – including Englishmen,
Germans, and traders from the Mediterranean – and locals alike.[63] Merchants
in Bruges frequently visited the Brabant fairs.[64] Bruges' commercial role was
not entirely eliminated: the Spanish wool staple remained in the city and for a
while Bruges retained importance as the major financial centre of the Low Countries.[65] The period 1490–1520 is characterized by what Herman Van der Wee has
described as the 'tripod of English textiles, South German metals and Portuguese

spices' which fuelled the growth of the Antwerp market.[66] Besides English, south German and Portuguese traders, Germans from the Rhineland, Italians, French merchants, Spaniards, and Dutch and Flemish traders were to be noticed in the city. Initially, transactions took place mostly during the fairs, where it was mainly transit products, i. e., merchandize that was not produced in the Netherlands that changed hands. Thus during its first phase of growth the Antwerp market hosted a fair-based commercial system.

Political conflicts, such as the wars between the Habsburg emperor Charles V and the French king Francis I and between the Holy Roman Empire and Denmark, paralysed international trade during the 1530s. The Central European economy was seriously weakened by the *Deutscher Bauernkrieg* which swept through the Holy Roman Empire. These political conflicts triggered a financial and monetary crisis and a price rise of foodstuffs. Moreover, the Portuguese spice monopoly, one of the three major foundations of Antwerp's trade 'tripod', was enfeebled by Venice's and Marseille's (re-)entrances into the spice trade.[67]

The second growth phase, roughly from 1530 until 1566, was marked by the increasing importance of exports of Netherlandish products, the transit market being impaired by the crisis. Trade with southern Europe, the Iberian colonies and the Levant especially grew in importance. Italy exported silk and bought English textiles and products from the Low Countries. Spain supplied agricultural products and bought various commodities for its colonies; the deficit was paid in American silver. This fertile international trade created opportunities for the sales of products from the Low Countries: tapestries, expensive cloth, jewellery, paintings and also manufactures from rural industries such as Hondschote says. Antwerp became the top gateway for its strongly industrialized and urbanized hinterland: the Netherlands. By the middle of the sixteenth century Antwerp controlled more than seventy-five per cent of the international trade that flowed through the Low Countries (by sea and by land).[68] The economy of the Low Countries was highly dependent on international trade: one historian has estimated the total imports of the Netherlands at 7 guilders per capita in the middle of the sixteenth century. When compared to France and England (1.5 guilders per capita), the importance of these imports quickly becomes clear.[69] Moreover, a quarter of the industrial production of the Netherlands was destined for export. During this second growth phase, the Antwerp market achieved a permanent character and international trade in the city was conducted year-round, to the detriment of the Bergen-op-Zoom fairs which quickly faded in importance.[70] Besides its commercial and industrial primacy, Antwerp was also an important financial centre. Charles V and his bankers, amongst them the Fugger, used the Antwerp capital market to loan large amounts of capital, thereby integrating Antwerp into the Habsburg financial system and becoming connected with the financial markets of Lyon, the Castile fairs and Genoa.

Given its connections with government finance the Antwerp financial market suffered during the series of Spanish state bankruptcies.

The Iconoclasm of 1566 and the subsequent Dutch Revolt caused rising taxation, military destruction, blockades, etc., and gradually ended the Scheldt town's commercial hegemony. Population more than halved in a few decades; in 1585, when the city was reconquered by Alessandro Farnese, duke of Parma and the Spanish governor of the Netherlands, after a fourteen-month siege, the population had dropped to a mere 42,000 inhabitants. Antwerp became isolated, not due to the alleged full closure of the Scheldt, but through the erection of fiscal barriers on the river's trade.[71] A trade diaspora of Antwerp merchants was the result. The merchants initially spread all over Europe but gradually coalesced in Amsterdam.[72] Yet Antwerp did experience an 'Indian Summer' at the end of the sixteenth and the first half of the seventeenth centuries (in 1615 the city's population had slightly recovered, numbering 61,000 souls). The Southern Netherlands were still exporting textiles and other merchandise to the Iberian Peninsula and to its dependencies in the New World. Antwerp was also a centre of the Counter Reformation and the resulting artistic bloom, personified by Peter-Paul Rubens and Anthony Van Dijck.[73]

1 ANTWERP, ITS MERCHANTS AND THEIR TRADE

Introduction

The aim of this chapter and the next is quite straightforward: establish the key facts about the businesses of Low Countries merchants operating out of Antwerp.[1] It endeavours to prove the ascent of Low Countries merchants on the Antwerp market and in various other European commercial cities. In this chapter the Antwerp market, its trade and merchants are dealt with. Using different sources, the growing number of native merchants active in Antwerp will be sketched. In the middle of the sixteenth century, the central government taxed imports to and exports from the Low Countries. The accounts of these taxes allow for a careful evaluation of the types and volumes of goods traded. The preferences of different groups of merchants for specific types of products and their destinations also become clear in this part of the analysis. Low Countries merchants were not more active in the marketing of home-grown products than were their foreign colleagues. This partially refutes the hypothesis by Herman Van der Wee that the Low Countries' industrial success propelled Low Countries merchants onto European markets.[2] Moreover, this chapter proves the democratization of trade in sixteenth-century Antwerp: smaller traders were equally active on distant markets and traded similar goods to their bigger colleagues. Sixteenth-century Antwerp was one of the first cities to develop generalized or open-access institutions allowing all merchants to participate in commerce.[3] The observed democratization indeed demonstrates that all merchants could participate.

Counting Antwerp's Merchants

With the growth of the permanent market, the community of merchants grew. The inflow of new merchants in Antwerp is hard to quantify, as is the total number of merchants operating out of Antwerp, and especially the number of native, Low Countries merchants. Ludovico Guicciardini fawned over the wealth and the social and linguistic skills of Antwerp's native merchants but did not gauge their number.[4] Unfortunately, no source is known which allows for the careful and direct reconstruction of this number and its growth throughout the sixteenth century. Hence, historians must rely on indirect sources and rough estimates.

None of these sources, because of their respective biases, informs us about the actual number of Low Countries merchants operating in sixteenth-century Antwerp, the evolution of that number or its relative magnitude as compared with that of the foreign merchant population. However, in putting these various numbers together, a picture emerges of the growth of the group of native merchants. By the end of Antwerp's Golden Age in 1585, when Antwerp fell back to the Spanish crown, the indigenous merchants had become a sizeable group and outnumbered their foreign colleagues.

The Antwerp magistracy produced certificates, written declarations on behalf of private persons, often local and foreign merchants, concerning various commercial and/or juridical issues. These so-called certificates consist of a declaration made under oath, sometimes in the presence of a witness, and provide the identity of the applicant, the nature of the issue, the types of goods, the time and place of the transaction, the means of transport and all persons involved in the transaction. Some of the certificates deal with seizure of goods, arrests, theft and loss of merchandise. The certificates did not adhere to a strict style, but they were considered legal evidence. People applied for certificates mostly to establish property rights and in cases of problems with transactions, as well as for many other reasons. This heterogeneity characterizes the certification books and, because of this broad scope and legal validity, certificates were often used by merchants.[5] The applicant received an official version and the text was copied into the ledgers of the urban administration; these ledgers survived the fire of the city hall during the Spanish Fury in 1576. The (on average) 160 certificates per year were clearly insufficient to record all the daily transactions of the hundreds of merchants in the Scheldt town.[6] As such, these certificates provide only an imperfect image of Antwerp's trade at the end of the fifteenth and early sixteenth centuries (1488–1513).[7]

To establish the presence of foreign and native merchants in the early trade of Antwerp, we have analysed the Antwerp certificates for two entire years: 1492 and 1512–13.[8] In the 1492 and 1512 sample years respectively 259 and 499 certifications and aldermen's deeds were selected from the Doehaerd corpus.[9] These supplied data on 124 merchants and commercial personnel operating in Antwerp[10] for 1492 and 165 for 1512 for whom data of origin were available. In 1492 sixty-nine foreign merchants and fifty-five native merchants had certificates registered; in 1512 there were seventy-seven foreigners and eighty-eight natives.[11]

Although these certificates are unlikely to include all merchants in Antwerp at the time, they nonetheless provide an idea about the relative proportions of the groups of foreign and native merchants. These groups were about the same size in the late fifteenth and early sixteenth centuries. Yet, these numbers, around 150 merchants each, do not do justice to the entire merchant population which was surely far more numerous, especially during the fairs.

Roughly twenty years later, the Antwerp notarial records provide hundreds of deeds requested by local and foreign merchants. The records of Zeger Adriaan 's-Hertogen for 1540 were selected to count the number of foreign and local merchants using his services.[12] His deeds show that the collective of foreign traders may have outnumbered native merchants, but native traders were the largest group among 's-Hertoghen's clients.

In 1543 the central government imposed a one per cent export tax (Hundredth Penny) on the value of the goods. For export to France the tariff was set at six per cent. The proceeds of the tax were earmarked to finance the Habsburg war against France and its allies.[13] This taxation took place in the second growth period of the Antwerp market which started at the end of the 1530s and lasted until 1566. This growth was mainly fuelled by trade with southern Europe.[14] The accounts provide a highly detailed insight into the exports of the Low Countries in these years. However, because of the on-going war, these numbers should be considered as minima. The most complete data are those for exports to Italy. These registers contain the names of the exporters; their nationalities can be deduced from their names and the occasional geographic references.

In 1544–5, almost 4,000 merchants were engaged in Antwerp export: the largest groups were Low Countries and German traders (1,499 and 1,475 respectively). French, Iberian and Italian merchants were less numerous (453, 252 and 229; the English were exempt from the tax).[15] A similar two per cent tax on imports from and exports to the Iberian Peninsula and its colonies was imposed form April 1552 through June 1553.[16] These tax revenues were destined for the protection and arming of the merchant fleet in the Atlantic and North Sea.[17] In the 1550s the merchants active in the trade with Spain and Portugal vastly outnumbered those in the trade with Italy ten years earlier. It is possible to count 875 exporters and 453 importers. Iberian merchants were the most numerous group, both in exports (432) and imports (221); however, the Low Countries merchants were a commercial force to be reckoned with (370 exporters and 184 importers).[18] Historians of Antwerp have used these numbers and other bits and pieces of information to estimate the numbers of foreign and native merchants in Antwerp around the 1560s.

Table 1.1: Estimations of merchant group size in the middle of the sixteenth century

Place of origin	Number (Brulez)	Number (Gelderblom)
Italy	200	100
Portugal	150	100
France	100	150
Spain	300	150
Germany	300	300
Hanseatic Germany	150	–
South Germany	150	–
England	300–600 (during fairs)	300
Total foreign merchants	1,350–1,650	1,100
Low Countries	400–500	400

Source: *Brulez*, 'De Handel', pp. 128–31; Gelderblom, *Cities of Commerce*, p. 33.

Brulez's and Gelderblom's estimates confirm the previous findings: Low Countries merchants were outnumbered by the foreign merchant community but were the largest merchant group active in Antwerp. In the second half of the sixteenth century a series of voluntary loans and taxes provides (partial) insights into the numbers of Antwerp merchants. In 1552 the Antwerp magistracy requested a voluntary loan from the city's inhabitants and merchants.[19] Although the deposits of the lenders reflect individual generosity rather than personal wealth, the list itself provides an indication of the relative contribution of the native merchants: the sixty-eight Low Countries traders active in Antwerp accounted for 17.64 per cent of the total loan input.[20] In comparison, the Italians and their nations raised 13.55 per cent of the loan. In 1574 Antwerp was forced to raise a compulsory 400,000 guilders loan in order to pay off mutinying Spanish soldiers. The 2,036 contributors, who accounted for between 12 and 15 per cent of the city's heads of household, lent between two thousand and eight thousand guilders.[21] Three hundred and thirty native merchants contributed more than 240,000 guilders. However, this dominance of the native merchants as compared to their foreign colleagues is probably biased: the city government may have spared the foreign merchants in an effort to keep them in the city, and the Hanseats and English were exempt from the compulsory loan.[22]

In October 1579 new money was needed to pay for troops to fight Habsburg general Alessandro Farnese who had just conquered the town of Maastricht.[23] Three hundred citizens each had to lend between 50 and 1,000 guilders on a monthly basis, secured on the revenues of several taxes.[24] The loan was to be repaid within six months. A commission of current and former aldermen and members from the shippers', retailers' and cloth-workers' guilds were appointed to draw up a list of the three hundred lenders. At least fifty-seven of the three hundred assessed persons were well-known native merchants; collectively they paid 36.15 per cent of the 52,000 guilders monthly loan.

In 1584 and 1585 the beleaguered city of Antwerp organized a monthly tax on 4,687 heads of household with means (23.8 per cent of the total number of heads of household).[25] Roughly 1,400 native merchants (not all of whom were assessed for the tax) can be counted in the tax registers, along with a meagre 130 foreign merchants.[26] The Dutch Revolt definitely distorts these numbers: merchants from all over the Low Countries fled from the advancing Spanish armies to Antwerp (thereby inflating their number), while foreign merchants unsure about the political and commercial future of the region departed the city.[27] On average, the foreign merchants still residing in Antwerp paid a higher monthly tax than their much more numerous native counterparts (29.30 guilders versus 18.19).[28] This does not necessarily mean that the foreign merchants still outcompeted the locals: the foreigners could have been taxed more and there were many local merchants who paid more tax than even the highest amount paid by the foreign merchants.

The numbers for the second half of the sixteenth century show the reversal of the fortunes of the foreign and native merchants active in Antwerp. The group of native merchants continued to grow and the number of foreigners (relatively) declined, mostly due to wars, religious persecution and the Dutch Revolt. Ironically, when Antwerp fell in 1585, the number of Low Countries traders may have reached its zenith. The same push factors which had driven the foreigners away caused the Low Countries merchants' diaspora at the end of the sixteenth century.[29]

Migration to the Commercial Gateway

The numbers presented above provide stock insights into the number of merchants and the respective shares of each group. The *Poortersboeken* or citizens registers can be used to reconstruct ups and downs over time, i. e., a flow view.[30] In order to grow at such a high rate (the city's population had reached 100,000 inhabitants in 1568), Antwerp had to rely on massive immigration. Many (aspiring) merchants migrated to Antwerp in search of commercial success, commercial infrastructure and contacts with European markets and Antwerp's hinterland, the Low Countries. The citizens' registers as a source have many flaws, however, only citizens who had purchased citizenship rights were registered; all persons who were *poorter* by birth or who had been granted the rights by the city government are not mentioned in the books.[31] Citizenship was not obligatory for merchants and many preferred to maintain the status of inhabitant, or *ingezetene* (obtained automatically by living one year and a day in the city).[32]

Sixteenth-century Antwerp attracted most of its immigrants (as measured in the Poortersboeken) from the duchy of Brabant (41.7 per cent), the county of Flanders (13.6 per cent) and the prince bishopric of Liège (7.4 per cent). The percentage of all new citizens who came from outside the Low Countries was 13.6 per cent.[33] After 1585, the city's migration recruitment area diminished drastically. Some foreign merchants, such as the English Merchant Adventurers, would not even have considered of becoming a citizen since Antwerp citizenship could not be combined with their foreign merchant guild membership.[34] Registering as an Antwerp citizen would thereby result in loss of fiscal, financial and legal privileges. This renders it risky to use the Poortersboeken to assess the size of Antwerp's foreign merchant population. Merchants from the Low Countries and those lacking privileges in Antwerp had more incentives to buy citizenship rights, and so the Poortersboeken are more accurate for estimating the merchants' numbers and evolution over time. Between 1533 and 1608, 1,089 merchants registered as new citizens.[35]

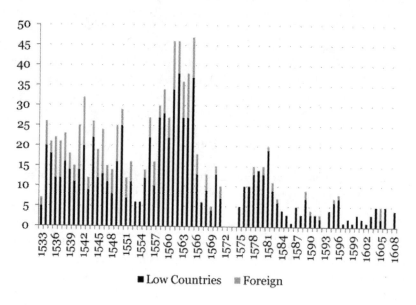

Figure 1.1: Number of merchants registering as new Antwerp citizens, by origin
Source: **Calculations based on Poortersboeken database Jan De Meester.**

Especially in the peak years – the second half of the 1550s and the first half of the 1560s – Antwerp citizenship proved to be highly attractive to many merchants who had settled in Antwerp.[36] The prosperous second half of the 1530s and the 1540s and the crisis of the early 1550s are also indicated in the records of new merchants.[37] In the late 1570s and early 1580s many merchants fled the war and went to Antwerp; this is also reflected in the small rise of new citizens registering as merchants.[38] Between 1533 and 1608, more than three-quarters of the immigrating merchants came from the Low Countries regions (including Liège); less than 25 per cent immigrated from outside the Low Countries. Before 1566, more foreigners were registered as new citizens than after that date (26 per cent versus 12 per cent). Their share amounted to 37 per cent in the 1540s and 29 per cent in the 1560s, but dropped between these periods and after the 1560s.[39]

Trade between Antwerp and Europe

Unfortunately, no sources exist by which to develop a quantitative diachronic understanding of the entire import and export flows into and out of the Low Countries throughout the entire sixteenth century and the commodities within them.[40] As always, the historian has to make do with biased and small slices of evidence. What share did merchants of the Low Countries have in commodity flows running through the Netherlands? And what type of commodities were they dealing in: products from the Low Countries or imports and transit goods as well? Using several snapshots on the imports and exports and the identities of the merchants involved we can qualify the argument of Herman Van der Wee. He asserts that the development of export industries in the Low Countries led to the growing importance of native merchants.[41] Native merchants were also involved in the redistribution of imported foodstuffs, colonial products and raw materials for industrial activity in the Low Countries. The following section will determine which were the major import and export products in the trade of the Low Countries. The commercial preferences of foreign and native merchants will also be determined (did native merchants favour Low Countries products more than their foreign counterparts?). Finally, the distribution of the imported and exported values within these groups and between merchants will be evaluated where the data allows such insight.

Antwerp's Dominant Position in Low Countries Commerce around the Middle of the Sixteenth Century

The concentration of trade in Antwerp is clearly revealed in the proceeds from the Hundredth Penny tax on export in 1543–5.[42] As expected, Antwerp had a large share in the exports of the Low Countries, both over land as by sea: Antwerp's total exports in the period August 1544 to August 1545 amounted to

£1,010,877 gr. Fl. (76.6 per cent of the Low Countries' total exports). Antwerp was less dominant as a maritime port (70.02 per cent) than as a hub for road transport (80.60 per cent of total continental exports).[43] Amsterdam (11.98 per cent) and Arnemuiden (6.42 per cent) occupied a distant second and third position in the port hierarchy, as did the land-locked border towns of Arras (7.31 per cent) and Valenciennes (3.77 per cent) for which the trade with France was surely affected by the war. Antwerp as an inland port relied on satellite ports, of which Arnemuiden was the most important (36.01 per cent of all Antwerp maritime exports in 1544–5), followed by Amsterdam (5.73 per cent) and Dordrecht (2.82 per cent). Commodities sent from (and taxed in) Antwerp for export to the deeper Zeeland ports of Arnemuiden, Middelburg and Veere, the port of Amsterdam and Dordrecht are included in the above table.[44] Antwerp together with all these Low Countries towns was part of an integrated port system constituted by the Zuiderzee coast, the IJ bay, the Zeeland delta and the Meuse and Rhine areas with Antwerp firmly at the top.[45]

Landlocked border towns in the Southern Low Countries, such as Arras (4.56 per cent), Valenciennes (2.21 per cent) and Namur (1.19 per cent) still managed to grasp some portion of international trade (in this case, exports to other countries in 1543–5) to France, Germany and the prince-bishopric Liège. In Arras and Valenciennes, Antwerp merchants were involved in exports to France.[46] In 1552–3, Antwerp was less dominant in imports from the Iberian Peninsula to the Low Countries: Antwerp had a share of 68.1 per cent (and 77.9 per cent of the exports to Spain and Portugal). Bruges' share in the imports accounted for 24.9 per cent, especially because Bruges still hosted the staple for the imports of Spanish wool (and 12.1 per cent exports). Thus, Bruges was more an importing city than an exporting one and, given these numbers, it remained an important centre.[47]

Antwerp Exports in 1544–5

The rich data from the 1544–5 Hundredth Penny tax on export out of the Low Countries allows a detailed breakdown of the region's export by destination. Because of the war with France, an analysis of the exports to France has been omitted, since trade with France would have been heavily depressed. The accounts provide highly detailed insight into the exports of the Low Countries in these years. However, because of the war, these numbers should be considered as minima. The English Merchant Adventurers were exempt from the Hundredth Penny. Hence, exports to England are under-reported. De Smedt estimates that the Merchant Adventurers were responsible for 30 per cent of all export to England; in that case, £41,787 gr. Fl. should be added to Antwerp's export to England, increasing the share of England export to 17.09 per cent.[48]

Trade over land with Germany and Italy was crucial for Antwerp, amounting to almost 60 per cent of all its export activity.

Table 1.2: Antwerp exports in 1544–5 by destination

Destination	Total value of exports in £ gr. Fl.	Per cent of total value of exports
Germany	364,499	36.60
North Germany and the Baltic	79,339	7.85
Central Germany	177,873	17.60
South Germany (incl. Switzerland and Austria)	96,161	9.51
Germany (unspecified)	11,126	1.10
Italy	223,791	22.14
England	138,130	13.66
Spain	102,126	10.10
France	77,053	7.62
Unknown	66,614	6.59
Portugal	20,127	1.99
Liège	11,844	1.17
Levant	6,692	0.66
Total	1,010,877	100.00

Source: **Author database Hundredth Penny tax on export.**

The Holy Roman Empire was Antwerp's biggest client. The cities of Nuremberg, Cologne, Frankfurt and Leipzig were the main recipients of the Antwerp export flows.[49] Many goods were sent to Nuremberg and redistributed from there throughout central and eastern Europe (probably via the Nördlingen fairs[50]), as were those dispatched to Frankfurt, which hosted well-attended fairs. The Antwerp–Cologne trade nexus involved far more merchants than that of any other German city, due to Cologne's proximity to the Netherlands and its function as a redistribution centre.[51] From Cologne, Antwerp imported 619,124 litres of Rhine wine in 1543 and more than one million litres in 1560, as well as clothing, metals and Westphalian linen. According to the proceeds of the Hundredth Penny, besides Antwerp, other ports were responsible for the exports to northern Germany and the Baltic including Amsterdam, Arnemuiden and Veere; on a much smaller scale Delfshaven, Enkhuizen and Monnickendam exported to the Lesser East and the Baltic.[52]

Which commodities were exported from Antwerp? As noted above, the tax records meticulously report the types of goods exiting Antwerp's gates and docks as well as their value. Even so, 41 per cent of all commodity references consist of an amalgamated, mixed series of goods (some English kerseys, a couple of pounds of sugar and two Hondschoote sayes or serges, for example). Consequently, the remainder of this article firstly draws on commodities with individually defined values, in addition to goods for which a quantity was available and for which the average value per quantity could be derived, from at least fifty other references with values (for example, two pounds of São Tomé sugar). These goods still amount to 67.83 per cent of all Antwerp export trade. All calculations based on commodity categories are executed in a second way by using instances of commodity categories (exploiting the entire dataset).[53] The typology of goods by Lesger is used here.[54]

Table 1.3: Antwerp exports in 1544–5 by product category

Product category	Taxed value in £ gr. Fl.	Per cent of total	Times mentioned
Textile products, semi-finished goods	479,272	69.89	7,147
Sugar and spices	97,019	14.15	1,950
Mercery goods	23,443	3.42	3,091
Oil, wax, soap	19,389	2.83	895
Textile raw materials	12,274	1.79	418
Chemicals, dyestuffs, ashes, tar	10,176	1.48	1,143
Metals: raw materials and semi-finished products	6,322	0.92	448
Hides, skins, leather, fur	4,654	0.68	524
Miscellaneous	4,149	0.61	316
Fish	2,466	0.36	511
Wine	2,299	0.34	362
Metals: finished products	2,198	0.32	376
Grain/crops (unprocessed)	1,794	0.26	408
Dairy products and animal fats	1,641	0.24	697
Fruit	1,230	0.19	553
Books, paper	851	0.12	241
Cattle, meat and bacon	660	0.10	47
Articles for general use	582	0.08	310
Paintings	512	0.07	105

Product category	Taxed value in £ gr. Fl.	Per cent of total	Times mentioned
Timber	361	0.05	205
Building materials (exc. timber)	162	0.02	128
Weapons	159	0.02	37
Fuel and lighting products	97	0.01	53
Beer	96	0.01	76
Salt	57	0.01	109
Foodstuffs	32	0.00	35
Total	685,720	100.00	21,090

Source: **Author database Hundredth Penny tax on export.**

The bulk of Antwerp's exports consisted of (semi-finished) textile products, spices and sugar. Especially the first category contains many different types of products (in order of magnitude): English and Low Countries woollen cloth, English kerseys, Flemish sayes[55] and linen, silk cloth, frisettes,[56] ostades,[57] tapestries, satin[58] and fustians.[59] Sugar and spices mainly consist of re-exported sugar and pepper.[60] The third most important category are merceries, *kremerijen*, or 'mercery goods'. In his *Description of the Low Countries* Ludovico Guicciardini frequently mentions 'mercery goods of all sorts and prices distributed not only in Europe but mostly to Africa and the West and East Indies through Spain and Portugal', often in conjunction with household goods, 'made of gold, silver, silk, thread, wool and a number of metals'.[61] Presumably, mercery goods were fashionable, certainly not inexpensive items, often produced in the Low Countries.[62]

Cloth includes English cloth and cloth from Low Countries production centres such as Flanders and Holland and, more specifically, from Amsterdam, Mechelen, Leuven, Weert and Haarlem. Sayes came (when explicitly mentioned) from Hondschote and Arras. Linen was mostly produced in Brabant and Flanders. Many of the English textiles were finished (dyed) in Antwerp, which had become a dyeing centre where foreign trends and fashion were known quickly. Around 1539, 1,350 labourers were active in this industry.[63] A large part of the wool probably came from England. Two of three 'classic Antwerp tripod' products (English textiles and pepper) amounted to an important share of Antwerp's export.

The exported commodities can also be ordered by destination. English cloth and kerseys, Low Countries textiles and pepper, again, occupy key positions in the exports of most regions. Striking figures are the silk cloth sent to England (a transit product which exporters purchased in Italy and the Levant), the pepper sent to Italy (since Italian merchants had been pepper exporters for centuries), and the Baltic wax sent to the Iberian Peninsula (for the production of candles).[64] Portuguese pepper was exported from Antwerp to Italian cities, including the ancient spice market, Venice. However, one should not conclude on the basis of these exports that Venice's role as a spice market was completely played out when it started to attract Portuguese pepper itself. Venetian merchants were still sending large quantities of other spices (such as cinnamon, ginger, camphor, mace, cumin and the like) to their Antwerp agents.[65] Transit goods (such as English kerseys, English cloth, pepper and sugar) make up 70.90 per cent of all Antwerp's (re-)exports, while Low Countries products account for 29.10 per cent. These figures corroborate the hypothesis that Antwerp was a fortuitous combination of mostly foreign commodity chains, a meeting centre that could just as well be replaced.[66] In this sense Antwerp differed from its predecessor Bruges. Bruges was less dependent on such re-export and transit trade. Bruges was foremost a gateway for the Flemish textile industry and its strong home market (urbanized Flanders and other parts of the Low Countries) absorbed imports from northern and southern Europe. Direct trade between those two regions may have been less strongly developed at Bruges.[67] As such, Bruges was a strong gateway, which was only toppled by the political disturbances at the end of the fifteenth century.

Antwerp Imports and Exports from and to the Iberian Peninsula 1552–3

The most complete statistical overview of Low Countries commerce, including both imports and exports, is provided by the two per cent tax on trade with Spain and Portugal in April 1552–June 1553 (a period of twenty-one months).[68] The tax revenues were destined for the protection and arming of the merchant fleet in the Atlantic and North Sea.[69] Linen was the main export commodity from the Low Countries (30.2 per cent of total exports).[70] Most of this linen was produced in the Oudenaarde area and to a lesser extent in Holland, Rouen, Brabant and Hainaut. Much of it was destined for re-export to the colonies. Spain was the most important linen buyer, both for its own home consumption and for re-export to the Americas.[71] In 1552–3, 30 per cent of all exports (£159,545 gr. Fl.) to the Iberian Peninsula consisted of linen.[72] A third of this linen was from the Oudenaarde area, 15 per cent from Holland and 13 per cent from Rouen.[73] Thus, 56 per cent of total Oudenaarde linen output was exported to the Iberian Peninsula.[74] Interestingly, the customs accounts also show that Iberian and Low Countries merchants re-exported Rouennais linen from Antwerp and Bruges (which was the gateway for large volumes of Flemish linen).[75] Exports to Portugal were much more limited and also displayed clear preference for Oudenaarde linen.[76] These numbers can be compared to linen exports to other European regions. Frequent political conflicts, the resultant trade embargoes and a native linen industry largely explain the low volumes of linen exported to France. In 1544–5 the Hundredth Penny accounts reveal exports of some linen, mostly from Hainaut.[77] Almost ten years later, an anonymous French author valued the total

Low Countries linen importation to France at £48,300 gr. Fl.[78] England proved much more receptive to Low Countries linen, but here too international politics could stymie trade.[79] By 1480–1, 112,637 ells of linen were imported annually, mostly from Holland, 's-Hertogenbosch, Hoogstraten and Hainaut.[80] In the period 1559–66, England imported 27,700 pieces of linen from the Low Countries.[81] In 1544, a mere £8,000 gr. Fl. worth of linen was exported to Italy (4 per cent of total exports to Italy).[82] Very little linen was exported to Germany which boasted its own important linen production sector, especially in Westphalia.[83]

More Holland cloth than that from the southern Low Countries was exported to the Iberian Peninsula; important exceptions were the Armentières outrefins. Foreign, especially English, cloth was less important in this traffic than in the exports to Germany and Italy. South German and Italian fustians were popular re-export articles. The says of Lille and Hondschote were doing particularly well, as were Oudenaarde tapestries. Of the total output of Hondschote says, 18 per cent was exported to Spain and Portugal in these years.[84] At least half of the mercery goods can be considered to have been consumer textiles such as tablecloths, etc. German and Austrian copper found their way to Spain and Portugal, as did large numbers of nails made in the Low Counties, kettles and basins. Other re-export commodities included Baltic wax and leather. The share of exported Low Countries produced goods amounted to 62 per cent of total exports.[85]

Portuguese pepper was the main import article in 1552–3 (one-third of total importation). Spanish wool for the Low Countries textile industry and sugar (half of it from São Tomé) were also important. Next in line were oil, alum (a fixative in the textile industry), salt and southern fruits, such as raisins and figs. In 1552–3 the Low Countries balance of trade showed a substantial export surplus (13 per cent) in trade with the Iberian Peninsula.[86] Brulez concludes his reconstruction of the Low Countries balance of trade by stressing the dependence of the Low Countries on long-distance trade: per capita imports and exports were much higher in the Low Countries than in England or France and a quarter of total industrial production of the region was destined for export.[87]

Commercial Democratization and Geographical Preferences by Merchant Group

Wilfrid Brulez (for the exports to Italy) and Herman Van der Wee have argued that a process of democratization took place in long-distance trade during the sixteenth century, in that smaller players were increasingly able to participate in this trade.[88] The long lists of merchants and their import and export values in 1544 (exports to Italy) and in 1552–3 (imports from and exports to the Iberian Peninsula) allows for statistical evaluation of this argument.

Table 1.4: Distribution of Antwerp exports in 1544–5 by merchant group (in £ gr. Fl.)

	Full sample	French	German	Iberian	Italian	Low Countries
Number of merchants	3,998	453	1,475	252	229	1,499
Share of total export	100.00%	5.24%	28.12%	15.20%	20.83%	29.93%
Mean	254.51	117.16	193.25	614.47	923.71	202.38
St. Dev.	1,186.82	297.39	1,030.13	1,569.76	2287.64	1,166.41
Median	30.00	36.67	25.00	135.00	100.00	25.00
Q1	10.00	15.00	10.00	25.00	28.00	8.33
Q3	101.67	120.00	74.25	503.50	675.50	80.00
HHI	0.006	0.016	0.020	0.030	0.031	0.023
Gini	0.859	0.705	0.862	0.774	0.803	0.861

Source: **Author database Hundredth Penny tax on export.**

Antwerp hosted large groups of German and Low Countries merchants; the much smaller Italian and Iberian mercantile communities, however, held a relatively large share of Antwerp's export. Local traders are less dominant than in London's cloth and wool exports; London denizens exported more than 45 per cent of the total volume of cloth and more than 80 per cent of that of wool in the years 1539–44.[89] In sixteenth-century Antwerp local merchants were an important group but the total group of foreigners was more dominant and the same was true for Lyon; London was the reverse image of this. Because the Hundredth Penny tax registers are such an exceptional source, unfortunately no comparison can be made with the relative shares of different merchant groups in other European commercial cities.

The very low Herfindahl–Hirschman index (0.006) – the sum of the squares of the shares in total exports by firm or exporter size – and the high Gini coefficient of export value per merchant (0.859) prove a striking feature of Antwerp export: next to a few very large enterprises there were many small exporters who were responsible for a large part of Antwerp's export. This analysis now robustly proves the key development of commercial democratization. This distribution is very different from that of the 1569 imports tax in Lyon. The ten largest Lyon importers, almost all Italian merchants, imported 36 per cent of all taxed goods.[90] In Antwerp exports, the ten biggest exporters accounted for 16.87 per cent. The Antwerp export market was a very competitive market environment. In almost all merchant groups (except the French), at least 75 per cent of the merchants had an export value below the average.[91] The average export value of the 25 per cent smallest exporters, £5.6 gr. Fl., amounts to ninety-three times the daily wages of an Antwerp master mason.[92] Put into this perspective, even the low export values of the bottom 25 per cent still represent quite substantial investments which may have been out of reach for many inhabitants of the Low Countries.[93]

Willem van Montfort was the most important Antwerp exporter (£27,270 gr. Fl. or 2.68 per cent of all Antwerp export). Montfort, originally from the German city of Aachen, acted as an agent of several south German merchant houses and mostly shipped English and Low Countries cloth, pepper and English kerseys to Nuremberg.[94] Second in line is Wolf Puschinger,[95] an independent trader and an agent of the Augsburg firms of Hans Herwart and Jacob Herbrot and financial agent to the Low Countries government (£25,468 gr. Fl).[96] Puschinger mainly sent cloth, pepper and spices to Leipzig, Nuremberg, Augsburg and Frankfurt. Erasmus Schetz, also born in Aachen, can be considered to be a Low Countries trader; he was Antwerp's pepper mogul. At a young age, Schetz got into the copper business of his great-uncle Rutger Kranz, was trained as merchant-apprentice in Lisbon and married into the Van Rechtergem spice trader family, also Aachen émigrés.[97] He exported pepper and cloth to Leipzig, Nuremberg and Hamburg (£24,288 gr. Fl.). At the bottom of the exporters list come two Low Countries traders, Pier van Stocken and Willem Plagge who exported salt and wheat worth less than £0.5 gr. Fl., which they probably carried themselves to Hasselt (in the prince-bishopric of Liège) and Aachen. The German Iken Goessens exported brooms for £0.2 gr. Fl. These merchants illustrate the large differences between the opposite ends of the spectrum.

Table 1.5: Distribution of Iberian Peninsula imports to Antwerp in 1552–3 by merchant group (in £ gr. Fl.)

	Full sample	English	French	German	Iberian	Italian	Low Countries
Number of merchants	453	19	1	9	221	19	184
Share of total export	100.0%	0.77%	0.03%	0.29%	72.63%	15.93%	10.35%
Mean	832	161	138	129	1,301	3,317	223
St. Dev.	4,189	218		191	548	9,177	874
Median	92	50	138	48	181	100	45
Q1	17	30	138	8	35	28	8
Q3	360	230	138	87	908	582	21
HHI	0.055	0.097		0.329	0.084	0.434	0.089
Gini	0.869	0.601		0.665	0.828	0.870	0.787

Source: **Author database Hundredth Penny tax on export.**

Table 1.6: Distribution of exports from Antwerp to the Iberian Peninsula in 1552–3 by merchant group (in £ gr. Fl.)

	Full sample	English	French	German	Iberian	Italian	Low Countries
Number of merchants	875	14	7	19	432	33	370
Share of total export	100.00%	3.38%	0.09%	3.03%	69.75%	4.55%	19.19%
Mean	582	1,287	71	852	862	736	277
St. Dev.	1,524	1,446	144	2,171	1,923	1,372	906
Median	55	758	8	123	90	135	35
1st Quartile	12	120	5	9	15	42	12
3rd Quartile	347	2,094	69	265	655	383	118
HHI	0.008	0.155	0.651	0.376	0.014	0.132	0.032
Gini	0.828	0,574	0.751	0.825	0.795	0.759	0.834

Source: **Author database Hundredth Penny tax on export.**

The imports from and exports to the Iberian Peninsula yield a similar finding as the analysis of the export tax of 1544–5. The low HHI index points to a competitive market with many players; the high Gini indicates the presence of a few very large traders. The HHI index is higher for imports than for exports; clearly, importing to the Netherlands was the preserve of a smaller and more unequal group of merchants. The spice monopoly traders immediately come to mind.

Unsurprisingly, merchant groups mostly sent goods from Antwerp to their native regions. Especially German traders did so. Merchants from the Low Countries favoured central Germany and England. Were Antwerp exporters geographically diversified and, if so, did this diversification increase with the scale of their operations? Were some national groups more diversified than others? As an answer, consider a Berry–Herfindahl index constructed for export diversification by region per exporting merchant (scale runs from zero to one, where one is perfectly diversified and zero is not diversified at all).[98] The results indicate that more than three-quarters of all merchants were entirely undiversified; they sent all their goods to one destination. This high degree of regional specialization has also been observed in the case of London merchants in trade with the colonies in 1686.[99] Larger-value exporters were not more geographically diversified than their smaller-scale colleagues.[100]

To judge whether access to Antwerp's export was open – i. e., whether both large and small participants had equal chances – consider the proxy of distance between Antwerp and the most distant destination of each exporter, both by land and by sea (in kilometres and nautical miles). In this case, larger exporters by land sent their goods further but the relationship is not particularly strong: smaller traders could participate as well in long-distance trade.[101]

Commodity Preferences

In Belgian and Dutch historiography Low Countries merchants are credited to have exported the products of Low Countries industry.[102] The sixteenth-century Low Countries profited from the growing European demand for manufactured goods, especially, but not exclusively, textiles. Yet this situation presents rather a chicken-and-egg problem: were the native merchants responsible for the expansion of industry through export? Or was it the other way round, that is, did the growth of the Low Countries industry propel Low Countries merchants into European markets? Coupling merchant groups with particular commodity categories transcends the problem of the commercial ascent of Low Countries traders; access of merchant groups to particular – local and transit – products provides a test for the openness of the market: were foreign traders able to trade in Low Countries products (a sector in which one expects a comparative advantage of the locals) and did Low Countries merchants have access to transit products (such as pepper brought by the Portuguese and often associated with south German traders)? The Hundredth Penny tax records provide further insight in the different specializations of foreign and native traders to corroborate these assertions. All taxed commodities were coded as transit (non–Low Countries products) or as Low Countries products: this analytic operation could thus be conducted for all non-mixed parties of goods for which either the provenance was explicitly specified or could be derived from the literature (pepper for example was clearly a transit good), as well as for a number of categories for which ratios were used to determine the origin of the goods. This second group includes a large amount of cloth besides canvas, iron, copper, frizzed cloth, silk cloth and leather. For example, the findings show that 60 per cent of all cloth, for which a provenance was reported, was a transit commodity (mostly English); this ratio was then used to determine the origins of the cloth for which origin was not explicitly stated in the tax records.[103] The export of Low Countries products by the different merchant groups amounted to between 25 per cent (Italian merchants) and 33 per cent (Low Countries traders) of their exports. While Low Countries merchants indeed did export relatively more native commodities, the difference with the other merchant groups is not as large as one would have expected from the literature asserting Low Countries traders' specialization in native products.[104] Iberian and French traders were as involved in the trade in domestic products.

Moreover, foreign merchants were (almost) as active in the trade in Low Countries products as the locals, despite the insider/local advantage of the latter over the former.[105] Frederik Van der Molen started as an exporter of Low Countries goods: mercery goods and tapestries in 1510.[106] Gradually he moved into the export of transit goods such as English woolfells (1526).[107] His sons exported Low Countries textiles, English kerseys and imported spices from Venice and Italian silks.[108] The Van der Molen are but one example of merchants who started in commerce by trading local goods and gradually branched out to transit goods. As important as the finding that Low Countries traders were not really specialized in local goods, is the observation that they were active in the export of transit goods in which they had to compete against Italians and south Germans. Smaller exporters, too, were not exporting relatively more (or less) transit goods than their larger-scale colleagues; this is also true for the group of Low Countries specifically.[109] Hence, there was no relation between the size of an export enterprise and a preference for either Low Countries or transit goods.

Parallel to the geographical diversification index, a Berry-Herfindahl index for commodity diversification was put together for each exporter.[110] The mean Berry–Herfindahl index for commodity diversification amounted to 0.066; more than 80 per cent of all merchants specialized in only one commodity.[111] Were merchants from the Low Countries more competitive than others due to a larger range of products, i. e., could they offer package deals? Relying on a more fine-grained product classification of seventy-four categories (more than £200 in total exports), calculations were made concerning the average number of product categories exported by merchants from a particular group to a particular destination. Merchants from the Low Countries sent a more heterogeneous mix of goods to Italy compared with the Italians, as well as to central and southern Germany compared with the Germans. The differences are minuscule, even negligible, however.[112] In the export to England Italians respectively outcompeted those from the Low Countries in the extent of the range of products offered.[113] French merchants similarly offered more products on average than their colleagues from the Low Countries in the export to France.[114] Evidently, merchants from the Low Countries were not offering better package deals. The number of product categories exported by a merchant and the diversification index of his enterprise are correlated with the total export value of this merchant; larger-scale merchants had more opportunities to diversify their product mix.[115]

Furthermore, yet another finding results when the indexes for geographical and commodity diversification are combined. In doing so, the different guises of exporters are revealed. Most traders were specializing in a few products and a few destinations. Accordingly, the relation between commodity and geographical diversification is weak, indicating different specialization strategies among exporters.[116]

English kerseys were very popular among Italian traders, while most of the Portuguese pepper export was handled by German merchants; pepper was redistributed by German traders throughout central and eastern Europe, and Italian merchants trans-shipped kerseys to the Levant via Venice and Ancona.[117] The product mix of Low Countries merchants is not very different, though, from that of their foreign counterparts. Again, Low Countries products were not significantly more important in their export package: other traders were equally interested in the success product of the Flemish textile industry, the sayes, and the merchants from the Low Countries exported even more foreign than native cloth. Moreover, merchants from the Low Countries were competing with foreign traders in the products in which these foreigners specialized, such as pepper and kerseys. This was the result of the strategic choice of the English Merchant Adventurers not to venture beyond Antwerp).[118]

Was trade in these strategic commodities the preserve of a few magnates (as in the case of German copper), or were smaller players as active in the export of these products? Mercery goods and Flemish sayes were the most evenly distributed export goods; smaller players were as engaged in the trade in these goods as were their larger-scale colleagues. Commerce in foreign cloth and pepper was dominated by a few large concerns, although many merchants were active in the trade in foreign cloth. Hence, larger and smaller exporters did have different preferences. Considering the minimum value of an exported shipment of key commodities, most of these key commodities still required considerable capital.

In the last decades of the sixteenth century a large-scale Antwerp merchant such as Maarten Della Faille described smaller players as price dumpers who had to sell because their bill was due but argued that they should get their chance at fortune as well.[119] In this way, when financial requirements were met, even a small exporter could send his goods as far as Naples as, for example, Michiel Torlan did by exporting tapestries worth £20 gr. Fl. to the Campanian capital. Smaller exporters had the same options for diversification both geographically and commodity-wise, although they were mostly very specialized, as were many of their larger colleagues. One can conclude that the playing field was rather even for small and large exporters alike, even if exports were unequally distributed and even if the minimum values of shipments of key commodities were beyond the reach of many inhabitants of sixteenth-century Antwerp.

Profits between Antwerp and European Markets

Why did Low Countries merchants enter long-distance trade? A likely incentive would be (potential) profits. Profit can be defined as

> the return for entrepreneurial ability. It is the reward to the entrepreneur for initiating the productive process, for gathering together the factors of production required

and for taking the risks associated with this process [...]. Any entrepreneurial endeavour involves risks. Profits can be seen as a reward for assuming such risks.[120]

Profits in long-distance trade can be obtained from the short- and long-term price differentials between Antwerp and the import/export destinations. Van der Wee indicated the growth of demand for the Low Countries industrial goods in countries with primitive industrial infrastructures (Spain, Portugal and the Baltic) where prices were rising quickly.[121]

Analysis of such price differentials for industrial goods is still lacking.[122] Converting these price differentials into data on potential commercial gross profit is not an easy enterprise: the commodity in question must be clearly identified and must be the same for the exporting and importing city, the quantities must be equal, transaction costs (brokers, storage, etc.), and taxes, tolls and transportation costs must be taken into account. To my knowledge no such systematic research has yet been attempted for the sixteenth century, except for grain prices. In this section I will present two products – linen and sugar – for which such a rudimentary price differential exercise can be done. The reactions of Netherlandish merchants on these price differentials will also be evaluated.

A price series for linen in Old Castile and Leon and in Valencia can be compared with Kempen (the region north of Antwerp) linen prices (acting as a proxy for the entire Low Countries linen industry).[123] Hamilton does not identify where these linens came from, but it is not unreasonable to argue that this Spanish price index could act as a barometer for all types of linen, including those of the Low Countries which (as described earlier) were exported on a large scale to Spain.

Whereas linen prices remained roughly constant in the Low Countries, the prices for linen in Old Castile and Leon increased by a factor of seven in the sixteenth century (even when accounting for inflation). The increase was less pronounced in Valencia but there was still a doubling of the linen price during the second half of the sixteenth century. In the trade with Spain, true profits could be realized. Hence, the massive linen exports are not a surprise. These potential profits must have piqued the interest of many Netherlandish merchants. In any case, it did not escape Roelant van Holland, a linen merchant from Grave, a small town on the banks of the Maas River.[124] On 18 September 1565 he became an Antwerp citizen but had already been in the city before then, co-operating with his uncle Gielis Smissaert, also a merchant. Roelant sent his younger brother Jan Baptiste to Medina del Campo in the fall of 1565. Jan Baptiste's venture account is preserved because he wrote it in Dutch, which was forbidden in Castile; all accounts were required to be recorded in Castilian. His account books were seized but Jan Baptiste escaped with a small fine, having argued that he knew little Castilian when he arrived in Castile and needed to present his accounts to his brother, who did not know any Castilian either.

Jan Baptiste, his brother and their uncle had little experience in the trade with Spain (the uncle only had contacts in Paris, Hamburg and Poland) but they saw opportunities in the linen trade. Jan Baptiste van Holland, or Juan Baptista de Olanda, as he was called in Spain, took with him a large quantity of linen, which he sold at the Medina del Campo fairs and in Bilbao, where his ship arrived. The linen was described as Dutch, from Izegem, Grave and Brabant. He also sold tapestries, carpets, napkins, kerseys says, cloth and pieces of jewellery, all typical products produced in and re-exported from the Low Countries. The proceeds from his sales were transferred by bill of exchange to the Antwerp merchant Jan Vleminck, who paid the bill to Roelant.[125]

Another product for which quantitative data are available is sugar, this time being exported from the Iberian Peninsula and the Atlantic islands to the Low Countries. In the later Middle Ages sugar was produced in the Mediterranean area (Cyprus, Tripoli, Beirut, Damascus and Sicily) and marketed by Italian (mainly Venetian) merchants. But when sugar production started in Madeira, sugar prices at the Antwerp St Bavo fair dropped markedly. Portuguese Madeira flooded the sugar markets in the Atlantic ports of Portugal, France, England and the Low Countries. Much of this sugar was marketed in Antwerp.[126] Antwerp became an important centre for sugar refining; by 1575 at least twenty-eight sugar refineries were active in the Scheldt city.[127]

Several Low Countries families became active as sugar merchants and planters on Madeira, the Canary Islands and the Azores, many of them based in Antwerp, for example the Groenenborch (or Groenenbergh) and Van Dale families.[128] In 1502 Jacob Groenenborch travelled to Lisbon to launch a business for his uncle Johan Byse from Cologne.[129] Groenenborch received grain, silver and Flemish cloth and sent sugar from Madeira back to Antwerp. In 1510 he returned to Antwerp. Three years later, he and his uncle purchased from the south German Welser family a large sugar plantation near Tazacorte on the Canary Island of La Palma. They chose the moment of their purchase wisely (in hindsight): sugar prices were slowly rising at that time. Groenenborch would personally oversee production and his family would become known as the Monteverde. Groenenborch extended his sugar domain with a new plantation in Argual. By 1526, it is estimated that Jacob controlled one-sixth of the island of La Palma (729 km²). Sugar production made the Groenenborch family's fortune. Jacob's eldest son, Melchior, transformed their riches into political power; he held the office of Antwerp alderman several times. Melchior came into financial problems at the end of the 1550s and was forced to sell part of the large family plantation to his father-in-law, Pauwel van Dale.

These sugar prices on Madeira can be compared with those of Antwerp in the period 1494–1531 so as to determine the gross profit rate in this line of trade which had so enriched the Groenenborch family.[130] Sugar merchants could cash substantial gross profits in this line of trade. These profit margins could amount to 46.8 per cent and 112.7 per cent. Willem van Lare, a factor of the Schetz family in Lisbon, calculated in his private merchant manual that around 1530 real profits in sugar importation from Madeira (taking into account storage, transportation costs, taxes and customs, marine insurance and commission fee) ranged between 12.2 per cent and 143.3 per cent.[131]

Unfortunately, no consistent long-term series of real profit rates is available for the sixteenth-century Low Countries. The Della Faille account books give some clue about potential rates but is uncertain whether these are truly representative, given the firm's size. Between 1558 and 1561 Jan Della Faille the elder managed to obtain a gross profit of 100 per cent of the firm's working capital, or a 29.4 per cent annual profit. In 1574–8 this annual profit amounted to 10.1 per cent and 7.6 per cent in the period 1579–82. Between 1583 and 1594 the Della Faille pocketed an annual profit on the company's capital of 12 per cent.[132] Pieter Seghers, a partner and agent of Pieter Aernouts and Robert van Haeften in Seville, managed to multiply his small partnership investment by a factor of six between 1581 and 1586, which put his annual profit rate at 100 per cent.[133] Such rates were definitely worthwhile for many entrepreneurs.[134]

Low Countries Merchants on European Markets in the Sixteenth Century

This book tries to document and explain the ascent of merchants from the Low Countries in the sixteenth century. These traders, operating out of Antwerp, did not only manage to pocket a growing share of Low Countries commerce; they also established themselves abroad to buy and sell in other European trading cities. Determining the numbers of Low Countries merchants active in other European commercial cities is a similarly difficult enterprise as determining the number of native merchants in their commercial capital, Antwerp, let alone determining the chronology and evolution of their presence in these commercial centres. The twenty-first-century historian who wishes to tackle the issue has to rely on the sources from all these cities – for Low Countries merchants were active throughout Europe – which, as in the case of Antwerp, only offer a biased glimpse of Low Countries merchants' presence and on publications on each of these centres. The material is richer for some centres and thinner and fragmentary for others. Most evidence concerns the commercial cities of the Iberian Peninsula and Italy, Paris and the Atlantic ports serving France, the port of London (serving England), the north German cities and those of the eastern Baltic and Frankfurt in southern Germany. Data for other areas and cities are not available. This section also relies on data from the Hundredth Penny tax to identify Low Countries' merchants' preferences for particular cities. In 1544–5, Antwerp's exports key destinations were Ancona, Cologne, Nuremberg,

London, Venice and Leipzig. Combined, they accounted for more than one-third (37 per cent) of exports to specifically defined destinations (place names, not regional names) in the Hundredth Penny tax records.

Portugal

Low Countries merchants were already present in Lisbon, Portugal's capital city, in the first half of the fifteenth century. A 'Flemish' confraternity of Saint Andrew and the Holy Cross, with several merchants among its members, attests this presence in 1411.[135] The Portuguese king granted individual privileges to Low Countries merchants, such as Bruges trader Maarten Lem who received the cork export monopoly in 1456.[136] In the second half of the fifteenth century the Portuguese king also appointed several Flemish expatriates (Jacob van Brugge, Ferdinand van Olmen and Joos de Hurtere) as vassal-governors of parts of the Azores and made them responsible for the island's exploitation and colonization.[137] The Bruges merchant family Despars maintained close commercial relations with Lisbon and the island of Madeira in the late 1470s and 1480s. They sold many of their commodities at the Brabant fairs.[138] In the second half of the fifteenth and the first half of the sixteenth centuries, Low Countries merchants in Lisbon were actively trading textiles and finished products for agricultural products from Portugal, including sugar from Madeira and woad from the Azores. The Aachen merchant Claes van Rechterghem, operating in Antwerp, sent his son-in-law Erasmus Schetz to Lisbon in 1511 to export sugar to the Low Countries and Cologne and to import German copper. Eleven years later, Schetz installed his own agent, Willem van den Lare in Lisbon.[139] At the end of the sixteenth and during the seventeenth centuries the Low Countries community in Lisbon consisted of around 100 merchants.[140]

Spain

Trade with Spain was a motor for the Antwerp market throughout the century and a branch of trade in which Antwerp merchants became ever more important.[141] Merchants from the Low Countries were present, though not always on a permanent basis, in the town of Valladolid, where they enjoyed good connections with Burgos and the Castilian fairs of Medina del Campo and Villalon; they also found a clientele among the courtiers there, because the royal court was often residing in the city.[142] The aforementioned Juan Bautista de Olanda, or Jan Baptist van Holland, noted at least eleven other Netherlandish merchants during his visit to the Medina del Campo fairs in 1565–6.[143] Valladolid did not have native long-distance traders and this opened an opportunity for Netherlandish merchants.[144] Some traders were also active in the Biscayan port town of Bilbao.

In 1475 the Flemish merchant Cornelis Deque, along with fourteen other countrymen and their personnel, was granted a letter of safe conduct by 'los Reyes Católicos' Ferdinand II of Aragon and Isabel I of Castile, for all the roads, towns and villages in their realms.[145]

Sanlúcar de Barrameda, an outport of Seville in the Guadalquivir estuary where the convoys to America departed,[146] counted fifteen Netherlanders between 1514 and 1522 and around seventy in 1537–50.[147] Several Antwerp merchants had factors in this port town.[148] In early sixteenth-century Seville, the Flemish brotherhood of San Andrés had a hospital. Until 1555 only a few Flemish merchants could be found in Seville, but by the end of the sixteenth century, around 200 Flemish traders were present in the city.[149] Pieter Seghers stayed in Seville between 1580 and 1586 as the agent of the rich Antwerp merchant Pieter Arnouts.[150] In 1565 the Flemish nation in Cádiz had a hospital; before 1540 only a few Netherlandish merchants could be found in this port, after which time their number increased and included both Antwerp and Bruges merchants.[151] Intensive research on Low Countries merchants and sugar planters on the Spanish Canary Islands has shown the existence of a large colony that counted 119 individual Low Countries merchants throughout the sixteenth century.[152] This shows that the well-known Groenenborch and Van Dale families were not the only parties involved in this trade.[153] Trade between the Canary Islands and the Low Countries consisted of sugar and wine being shipped to the Low Countries and foodstuffs and textiles shipped the other way.[154]

Italy

The increase of Low Countries merchants in Spain preceded that of their colleagues in Italy, specifically in Venice.[155] In the second third of the sixteenth century, the number of Low Countries merchants and agents in Italy increased rapidly; several of them were trained by pioneer Maarten de Hane, originally from Brussels, who had settled in Venice in the first years of the century. Antwerp merchant families such as the Van der Molen, de Cordes, Van Santvoort, Della Faille and Van Bombergen[156] had agents in the Doge city.[157] Regarding exports to Italy (in 1544–5), the Adriatic ports of Ancona and Venice attracted the largest volumes. Both cities acted as gateways to the Levant.[158] Both Adriatic port cities were gateways to the Levant and profited from the renewed Levantine demand after the peace with the Turks under Suleiman the Magnificent. Especially Ancona attracted large quantities of English and Low Countries cloth (kerseys, *panni di Londra* and Armentières *oltrafini*[159]), brought there by Tuscan merchants for re-export to the Levant.[160] When comparing the preferences of Low Countries traders and other groups, German and Low Countries exporters clearly preferred Venice over Ancona;[161] Italians and Iberians favoured Ancona, however.[162]

Italians chose Ancona because of the low toll tariffs (compared to Venice) and its open market (re-export to the Levant was not limited to Anconitans, while it was the prerogative of Venetian citizens in Venice). Low Countries and German traders selected Venice as an end-station because it offered a guaranteed market (both due to a large home demand in Venice and its Terraferma empire and the re-export to the Levant).[163] One Antwerp merchant family, the Van der Molens, had a branch office in Ancona but closed it down in 1538 because of the destabilizing war with the Ottomans.[164] In Venice, Low Countries traders were able to seize a huge commercial opportunity: Venetian merchants had withdrawn from the Low Countries (leaving trade altogether or focusing on the Levant trade) and now relied on local agents in the Low Countries or bought goods from foreign merchants, Low Countries traders among them, who settled in Venice.[165] Hence, by replacing the Venetians as intermediaries, Low Countries merchants were able to fill a commercial vacuum.

The number of Low Countries traders residing in Venice increased in the last two decades of the sixteenth century, during which time (starting in the 1580s), Antwerp merchants such as the Della Faille family organized direct shipping to Venice and Naples. This so-called Straatvaart required agents in the Italian ports. Some of these agents were Italians, but many were originally from the Low Countries. The shipments, consisting of fish, wool, sheep skins, kerseys and other textiles and the return cargo included rice and spices and pre-dated the grain shipments of 1590, when grain was scarce throughout Italy.[166] The Fall of Antwerp in 1585 caused – and even fuelled – an economic restructuring that gave rise to a diaspora of Antwerp merchants, many of whom emigrated to Venice.[167] Van Gelder counts ten merchants from the Low Countries (southern and northern, but mainly southern)[168] in 1580 in the records of several notaries; in 1590 their number had increased to twenty-one. The year with the largest group of Low Countries merchants in Venice (i. e., 54) was 1610; after that date their numbers oscillated between thirty and forty.[169]

The Medici Grand Dukes tried to attract merchants to Tuscany by installing a free port in Livorno and by proclaiming the 1591 Livornine charters, which bestowed fiscal privileges and a degree of religious tolerance on Jewish merchants and traders from Spain, Portugal, Greece, Italy, the Levant and Germany.[170] In the first half of the seventeenth century, Livorno became an important Mediterranean port. From the 1590s, a community of Low Countries merchants settled there; by 1615–35, at least 100 Netherlanders were active in the city.[171]

England

John Wheeler wrote in his pamphlet 'A Treatise of Commerce' (1601) that around 1520 there were only twelve to sixteen Low Countries merchants in England, of whom only four were of note. By 1560 their number had increased to one hundred.[172] In 1555 fifteen merchants had a Low Countries agent in London, among them Jacob Della Faille (Jan Della Faille's brother) and Willem Marischal, brother of Augustijn Marischal.[173] Low Countries merchants were the most important exporters from Antwerp to London (the Merchant Adventurers being untaxed by the Hundredth Penny (1544–5) and hence not quantified); they exported more than double the amount of the Italians to England. In London, Low Countries merchants had to endure the fierce competition of the English Merchant Adventurers (this is dealt with extensively in the final chapter). The Merchant Adventurers – an association of merchants from various English cities, dominated in the sixteenth century by the London Mercer's Company and backed by the English crown – vied to monopolize the export of English cloth to Antwerp, mostly by raising taxes on foreigners exporting the commodity, by enforcing the use of English ships and by barring imports of foreign commodities.[174] The company in this period enjoyed the strong support of the London city government and of the English monarch.[175]

France

The presence of Antwerp, and more generally Southern Netherlandish, merchants in the French capital Paris was sporadic in the fifteenth century but became more intensive in the sixteenth century, as they were both visitors and agents, as well as permanent residents; this was largely because of the city's rich clientele and the demand this clientele generated for luxuries (for example, Joris Vezeleer and his agents).[176] The Low Countries community in Paris was also involved in the trade of more prosaic commodities. In 1570, Alava, the Spanish ambassador in Paris, reported that more than 400 Antwerp merchants had migrated to Paris.[177] This may have been a serious exaggeration, since Coornaert counted only ten Low Countries merchants in Paris throughout the sixteenth century, which itself is probably an underestimate.[178] Between 1525 and 1585 at least fifty merchants were trading in French Lorraine, twelve very actively.[179] In the sixteenth century many merchants and their agents settled in La Rochelle, Bordeaux and Rouen (and its outports Honfleur and Le Havre).[180] In Lyon, an important city for trade between Italy and northwest Europe, there was only one Flemish trader among the foreign merchants, a group dominated by Italians and south Germans. No colony of South Netherlandish merchants was to be found in the Mediterranean port of Marseille.[181]

Central and South Germany

Low Countries merchants preferred Cologne if they had to choose a German destination from the cities Cologne, Leipzig or Nuremberg. Cologne, strategically situated on the bank of the Rhine, enjoyed an ancient intermediary position in the trade between the Low Countries and Germany.[182] Many small traders also took their goods to Cologne for its large, intermediary market and sold their goods there, after which many were re-exported throughout central Europe.[183] German traders favoured Nuremberg; many were from Nuremberg and goods found their way through Nuremberg to central and eastern Europe.[184] Antwerp's relation with the city of Cologne had an ancient pedigree extending to the thirteenth century.[185] Merchants from Cologne were very actively trading on the Brabant fairs in Bergen-op-Zoom and Antwerp.[186] Their colleagues from the Low Countries were equally numerous in Cologne.[187] During the last decades of the sixteenth century half of all foreign merchants in Cologne came from the Low Countries.[188]

From the 1560s onwards many Flemish and Walloon Reformed and Lutheran merchants emigrated to the central city of Frankfurt.[189] Many of them were frequent visitors of the Frankfurter Messen and had thus become familiar with the city.[190] Frankfurt was centrally located between, on the one hand, south Germany and Italy on the other side of the Alps and, on the other hand, north-western Europe. At least 140 Antwerp merchants settled in Frankfurt, eighty-six of them between 1585 and 1600. Roughly half of the richest taxpayers in Frankfurt were originally from the southern Low Countries.[191] The arrival of 2,800 migrants from the Southern Netherlands accounted for 35 per cent of the city's population growth.[192]

Northern Germany and the Baltic

In the fall of 1563, some 120 Antwerp merchants signed a petition to complain about the frequent harassments by Hanseats they encountered when operating in the eastern Baltic around Danzig, Riga and Reval.[193] These 120 names show that Antwerp merchants were actively involved in the Baltic trade at least from the 1560s onwards. Isolated earlier instances of Antwerp merchants trading in the Baltic evidence that this growing importance was already occurring in the 1540s.[194] This does not imply that all 120 merchants were present in the Baltic themselves; in fact, they made use of both Low Countries and Baltic agents (often Hanseats), especially those from Lübeck, who had intimate knowledge of the Baltic trade and enjoyed extensive Hanseatic rights. Hans Thijs, son of the aforementioned Christoffel Thijs, was able to extend his commercial enterprise extensively through contacts and agents in port cities throughout the Baltic.[195]

While Lübeck city policy tried to avoid the Lübeck merchants becoming mere agents to other merchants, many Netherlandish merchants intensively used the shipping and trading services of Lübeck merchants in the 1560s. Several Netherlandish agents frequently passed through Lübeck to check transhipments or to buy and sell merchandise.[196] Earlier, in the sixteenth century, the Dutch and

Flemish were the most numerous group of foreign merchants; they were admitted to the Danzig Hanseatic Artushof, albeit remaining subject to guest law and the obligation of using Danzig merchants as intermediaries.[197] In absolute numbers these communities of foreign merchants remained rather small when compared to those in Hamburg. The Hamburg Senate actively sought to attract Antwerp merchants after the fall of the Scheldt city in 1585.[198] But Flemish merchants had been operating in the city before that date: Gillis de Greve, for example, who was banished from Antwerp in 1566 set up shop in Hamburg; from there he was able to trade with Italy, England, the Iberian Peninsula and the Baltic area.[199] In 1605 a contract was signed between the Hamburg city council and South Netherlandish migrants, granting the latter freedom of religion and trade in the city for ten years.[200] The contract was signed by 130 Southern Netherlandish heads of household who guaranteed their loyalty to the city of Hamburg. In the event that one of them proved to be disloyal, he would be fined.[201] The Dutch, Flemish, Portuguese and English merchants even outshone Hamburg's native merchants numerically.[202] The Hamburg Exchange Bank counted no less than thirty-two Antwerp expatriates among its forty-two account holders in 1619.[203]

Nicolaes Verjuys and Melker Volger were Netherlandish agents working on behalf of Christoffel Pruynen and the Schetz firm in Stockholm.[204] After 1565, a small community of Netherlandish agents was active in the Muscovite town of Narva, selling luxury products and textiles and buying (mainly) fur and hides; several ships sailed to the Kola Peninsula.[205]

Wilfrid Brulez has argued that Low Countries merchants became especially active in the second half of the sixteenth century; Low Countries merchants manifested themselves in the Baltic, Italy, England, Germany and France, especially after their diaspora from Antwerp in the last two decades of the sixteenth century.[206] In the first half of the century, Low Countries merchants went through a learning phase and acquainted themselves with new business techniques; having mastered those techniques they subsequently according to Brulez, conquered Europe's markets.[207] I believe the evidence, more than fifty years after Brulez, is still too flimsy to either confirm or disprove Brulez's claim. Clearly, Brulez's claim is partially misguided by the massive and highly detailed evidence on Low Countries merchants abroad in Antwerp's certification books of the 1540s to the 1560s (books which are lacking for the period 1512–42). Later research has proven that in Portugal and Spain, Low Countries merchants were already present in the late fifteenth and early sixteenth centuries. The question of chronology and evolution remains open. These observations also call into question the notion of the 'passive' Bruges merchants, as opposed to their active Antwerp counterparts visiting Europe's commercial centres. Several Bruges merchants were involved in trade with Spain, Portugal and their respective island dominions.[208]

Conclusion

Foreign merchants in Antwerp formed a large group in the merchant community of sixteenth-century Antwerp, but immigration and the commercial ascent of Low Countries merchants gradually made the group's numbers expand considerably, culminating in their late sixteenth-century majority. Many of these merchants then branched out to European markets. Trade statistics from the 1540s to the 1560s demonstrate that Low Countries merchants managed to conquer a growing share of long-distance trade. Importantly, these merchants were not specialized in the export of Low Countries products. They were as active in the shipping of transit goods (English kerseys, spices, sugar) as their foreign counterparts. Many Low Countries merchants, and Frederik Van der Molen is a good example here, started in commerce by trading in local products and then gradually branched out into transit goods available on the Antwerp market. The participation of Low Countries merchants did not remain limited to a few large traders; distributions of export and import values show that smaller traders were also active in long-distance trade. Hence commercial democratization took place in sixteenth-century Antwerp. Commercial opportunities differed between regions: Low Countries were able to carve out a niche in the trade with Venice because of the success of Low Countries products in the Levant and the withdrawal of Venetian merchants from the markets of the Low Countries. Linen proved to be a sought-after product in Spain and Portugal which led large profits to be obtained. Further research is needed to verify which opportunities triggered Low Countries merchants' interests in other regions and cities.

As the data bring to light, most merchants specialized in one category of goods, often textiles, and were relatively undiversified geographically (even when they had a larger export enterprise). The scale and scope of the Antwerp market theoretically allowed merchants to broaden their product mix and exports at low cost; large markets made diversification and risk spreading possible.[209] Yet such diversification was not observed in the data presented above; merchants specialized in particular commodities and destinations. They were specialists rather than generalists.[210]

Establishing a chronology of the presence of Low Countries traders with strong links with Antwerp is not an easy task. At least in Spain and Portugal, Low Countries merchants were present in the major commercial cities from the second half of the fifteenth century onwards and they entertained important relations with Bruges, Antwerp's commercial predecessor. In Italy, an embryonic community emerged around Maarten de Hane and the Van Bombergen family in early sixteenth-century Venice. Many of their disciples would become important Italy traders through the century. In England, France and Germany small colonies of Low Countries merchants were growing and by the end of the century would prove very attractive to the diaspora of Antwerp merchants. All numbers and references taken together suggest a chronological process of a growing presence of Low Countries merchants in Antwerp and on European markets.

2 ANTWERP TIES TO THE LOW COUNTRIES HINTERLAND

The Low Countries constituted a vibrant industrial workshop, albeit with important regional differences within its borders.[1] This industry required both importation of inputs and the marketing of domestic produce which created opportunities for merchants. The preceding chapter has established the rise of Low Countries merchants, both in numbers and throughout Europe. Contrary to previous analyses, it was proven that Low Countries merchants were not specialized in local products; they dealt in transit goods as well and to the same extent as their foreign colleagues.[2] Hence, the rise of these merchants cannot be solely attributed to the dynamics of Low Countries industry and the European demand for its commodities. This chapter aims to shed more light on the relationship of Low Countries merchants with local industry and local demand.

Native merchants may not have specialized in local goods but they may have had comparative advantages vis-à-vis their foreign counterparts in commerce – both the export of Low Countries products and the distribution of imports. Jessica Goldberg has recently pointed out the regional embeddedness of merchants. Local knowledge, reputation, connections and personal fiscal privileges allowed eleventh-century Geniza traders – or Maghribi merchants as they are called in the literature – to control the different production phases in Fatimid Egypt and cut out costly middlemen. Yet, fostering and maintaining close relations with the production side required time and local presence. Geniza merchants faced a trade-off: to trade in high-volume, low-value regional products and maintain contacts with local producers, or engage in profitable yet insecure long-distance trade in luxury products throughout the Mediterranean. Of course, merchants' activities ranged within the continuum between localism and 'internationalism', two types of trade with very different investment requirements, geographies of travel, profit expectations and risk. Merchant choices were determined by resources, family ties, training and personal preferences.[3] Merchants in the sixteenth-century Low Countries faced similar choices and constraints.

The previous chapter considered commerce between Antwerp, the Low Countries' main gateway, and Europe. This chapter turns its gaze inward, into the Low Countries which witnessed a profound change in its marketing system during the sixteenth century. Within the Low Countries a complex hierarchical and integrated marketing system, one controlled by merchants, took shape. Antwerp increasingly became the area's commercial capital and its market assumed a permanent character, despite still holding to seasonal patterns. This permanent market pushed forward a process of specialization: in short, producers in the previous fair system could sell their products at fixed times of the year; the permanent market, however, forced them either to set up shop in Antwerp or to leave the marketing to professional intermediaries who collected the goods on regional markets and from there brought them to the gateway and abroad. The transformation of the marketing landscape and the subsequent growth of commercial intermediaries provide another piece of the puzzle in explaining the rise of Low Countries merchants.

The previous chapter has shown that specialization in the export of local products in the 1540s was not as pronounced as one would expect, despite the potential comparative advantages Low Countries merchants may have had over their foreign colleagues: local contacts with producers, speaking the same language as producers, product knowledge... Did foreign traders leave this internal trade to the locals and did they prefer to acquire Low Countries products in Antwerp? Low Countries merchants may have used these advantages as a stepping stone in their commercial ascent but they were not fixated on marketing Low Countries products. The remainder of this chapter firstly analyses how native merchants interacted with different regional industries and producers and, secondly, how they engaged in the distribution of imports, both of raw materials such as alum (hydrated potassium aluminium sulphate, a mordant for dyeing) and woad (a dyestuff) and consumer goods such as wine, grain and spices.

'The Low Countries, the Banlieu of the Marvellous City of Antwerp': Shifts in the Low Countries Commercial System

Henri Pirenne, one of the most famous historians of what is now known as Belgium, in the third volume of his magnum opus *L'histoire de la Belgique*, offers the following observation about Antwerp: 'Durant tout le XVIe siècle, les Pays-Bas ne constituent pour ainsi dire que la banlieu de cette merveilleuse cité [Anvers] qui les soumet à son ascendant'.[4] Yet Pirenne's metaphorical statement obscures the importance of the Netherlands to Antwerp. Without industrial development in other cities and the countryside, the Antwerp market would have had but a thin supply to provide to long-distance merchants. The development of this industrial hinterland is crucial for our understanding of the ascent of Antwerp's merchants. Internal differences in economic activities in the different regions of the Low Countries did not prevent the formation of strongly integrated spatial economy with large commodity flows and exchange between the various regions.[5] The sixteenth century witnessed a profound reorganization of the Low Countries marketing system. Several historians have argued that because of changes in the marketing system of the Low Countries – in particular, the decline of the fairs and the growing permanency of the Antwerp market – producers and merchants were faced with an altered opportunity cost structure.[6]

The Brabant fairs began in the first half of the fourteenth century: those of Antwerp were held at Whitsun and St Bavo (October 1st); those of Bergen-op-Zoom at Easter and All Saints.[7] From the beginning of the fifteenth century onwards, merchants from England, Cologne and south Germany, as well as many merchants active in Bruges, exchanged goods at the Brabant fairs; likewise, many artisans from the Low Countries visited the fairs to sell their produce to local and foreign customers.[8] For artisans from out of town, the fairs provided valuable opportunities to hear about the latest fashions and to buy raw materials at relatively low costs (rent of a stall, lodging costs, etc.) for production at home during specific times of the year (thereby allowing them to spend the rest of the year producing their stocks).[9] Towns and craft guilds invested in purchasing or renting collective halls – often in the Hoogstraat or near the Grand Place – for the sales, storage and taxing of the produce of their citizens/members.[10] Virtually every Brabant drapery centre rented or owned a hall in fifteenth-century Antwerp.[11] Flemish drapery towns were initially more reluctant to procure collective halls in Antwerp in this period, but many Flemish merchants rented or bought commercial buildings.[12] In the first half of the sixteenth century Ypres, Armentières and Nieuwkerke opened halls in Antwerp.[13] The cloth towns of Weert, Armentières, Nieuwkerke, Turnhout and Tongeren also had halls in Bergen-op-Zoom at the end of the fifteenth century and in the early sixteenth century.[14] Antwerp ecclesiastical institutions rented stall spaces in courtyards to merchants and artisans; this led to the creation of the so-called Panden, vending locations which operated only during the fairs and which specialized in certain kinds of goods such as silk, cloth, tapestry, jewellery, silverware and paintings. The Dominican Predikheren-pand was active as early as 1438 (it was situated on the southwest corner of the Dominican friary in the Zwartzustersstraat); the Church of Our Lady decided, in 1460, to build a similar pand for painting sales and Bergen-op-Zoom established its own pand in 1480 for the marketing of luxury products.[15]

The growing scale of the Antwerp market and its increasingly permanent character entailed important shifts in the marketing landscape. In 1524 it was said that 'when there was a market in Ypres, Ghent, Bruges, Brussels, Middelburg, etc., one should better go to Antwerp, where it is always market time, everything is available there and one should not visit these small markets anymore'.[16] The income generated by stalls and shops, owned by the Church of Our Lady, either rented only during the fairs or throughout the whole year, provides substantive evidence for this transition.[17] By the 1520s the church was renting more year-round than fair-only market stalls and shops. Around 1540 the panden, previously open only during the fair periods, opened their doors year-round. New, permanently open and specialized panden were created: these included the Schilderspand, which focused on the paintings trade and was located on the first level of the new Bourse building (built in 1532, but only active from the 1540s onwards)[18] and the Tapissierspand for the tapestry trade (operational in 1554).[19] The older Predikheren and Our Lady's Panden had to close their doors.[20] Yet this growing permanency did not exclude market seasonality or the various attitudes held by particular groups of merchants vis-à-vis Antwerp's permanent market. Monthly statistics are available for Antwerp's export by land and sea in 1544–5.[21] March, August and July were the busiest months.[22] During winter (December and January), when transport was at a lull, fewer exports were noted at the city gates and in the port by tax collectors of the Hundredth Penny tax. No clear peaks around the Whitsuntide and Bamis fairs are observed. English ships mainly visited Antwerp in June, July and August, although after the 1540s shipping activity tended to be continuous throughout the year; notarized shipping contracts (that is, for ships bound for the Iberian Peninsula) show a similar pattern.[23] The Antwerp trading season was not only determined by the exigencies of preindustrial transportation; the presence or absence of particular trading groups was also crucial for trading activity throughout the year. The English Merchant Adventurers, important network makers, only visited Antwerp during the fairs to sell their sought-after kerseys; few English merchants stayed in the city in between fairs.[24] French merchants from Troyes, Metz, Normandy, Bretagne, Paris, Albi and Toulouse also called at Antwerp mainly during the fairs.[25] Even Antwerp's permanent market was determined by seasonal peaks and winter lulls. Trading activity in Antwerp also depended on the peaks in other commercial centres, such as the Frankfurt fairs. Native merchants clearly had an advantage over temporarily visiting foreign traders: they could wait for the right moment to buy and sell.

An important victim of Antwerp's permanent market was its fellow fair town Bergen-op-Zoom. In the 1470s Bergen had tried to outcompete Antwerp – in particular by offering more favourable toll tariffs. But by the first half of the sixteenth century Bergen had experienced Antwerp's commercial power to the fullest extent. Antwerp could offer a larger range of products, had better access to the Brabant and Flemish hinterland and hosted an important cloth finishing industry.[26] Many members of the cloth producers and sellers family Leydecker, which had established itself in Bergen-op-Zoom at the end of the fifteenth century, moved to Antwerp in the first half of the sixteenth century and there they became more active in the marketing of cloth.[27]

Low Countries merchants and artisans were faced with a difficult decision due to growing permanence of the Antwerp market: they either had to move to Antwerp, which they did on a large scale, so as to be permanently present in the city and try to capture the economies of scale (productivity gains through specialization and division of labour) and economies of agglomeration (access to raw materials, trained labour, highly developed services sector, extensive local market, presence of international merchants and information on fashion and taste); or they had to rely on other merchants, increasingly those from Antwerp, for the marketing of their produce in the Scheldt city.[28] Several export industries in smaller towns in Brabant were outcompeted by those of Antwerp.[29] The Flemish export industries seem to have been more adapted to Antwerp as being the new gateway, for they focused more on mass production of textiles which could be finished in Antwerp.[30] These evolutions put merchants residing in Antwerp in a firm position vis-à-vis their colleagues in other towns. Brulez has calculated that one-quarter of all industrial products was destined for export. This means that the other three-quarters were consumed within the Low Countries. These goods had to be moved from producer to consumer as well, again creating opportunities for intermediary merchants.

The next sections will show how Antwerp merchants made use of local agents and intermediary markets for the transfer of commodities from the production centre to the gateway. Intermediary markets like Bruges, Courtrai, Ghent and Lille were highly important for the Low Countries' internal traffic.[31] The expansion of the Low Countries export industry generated job opportunities for many merchants within the Low Countries. The mobilization of rural labour in the fifteenth and sixteenth centuries made nearby towns into markets and finishing centres, which acted to guarantee quality control and served as nerve centres for putting out activity.[32] The fact that many of the successful products of the Low Countries were produced in the countryside by peasants as a part-time activity rendered the presence of intermediaries and markets even more necessary, not least as these peasants could obviously not be present in Antwerp throughout the whole year. When these goods had reached Antwerp, foreign and, increasingly, native merchants exported the products abroad.

Merchant Ties to Low Countries Industries

The dynamics of Low Countries urbanization were fuelled largely by industrial development. In turn this industrial development was dependent on long-distance trade. An anonymous request regarding the currency revaluations of the late 1530s and early 1540s encapsulates the situation perfectly: 'trade feeds mechanical manufacture such as woollen, linen, say and tapestry production and the many labourers who earn their livelihood in this industry'.[33] Domestic demand grew quickly during the later fifteenth and sixteenth centuries due largely to population growth in the Low Countries. Families still spent a major share of their income on foodstuffs, but the growth in the number of families resulted in an increased demand for industrial goods such as building materials, utensils and cheap fabrics. Government demand was also growing, for public works, infrastructure projects and warfare all required industrial goods.[34]

The Low Countries also profited from the growing European demand for industrial goods. Low Countries products managed to outcompete those of the native industries in England, Scandinavia, Germany, Poland and the Iberian Peninsula.[35] During the fourteenth and fifteenth centuries regional European wars harmed long-distance commerce; in this era the restructured industries could rely on domestic demand. When the dust settled on the regional European conflicts, the Low Countries industry was ready to fully reap the rewards of its economic reconversion and to (re-)conquer European markets.[36] The larger cities, now suffering from the contraction of the traditional cloth industry, increasingly focused on luxury segments and high-quality production by skilled artisans and with expensive raw materials. Art and fashion industry became more important and larger cities provided services in the forms of education, entertainment, commercial distribution and banking and finance.[37] Urban industries were closely controlled by craft guilds, which set quality standards.[38] Smaller cities experienced more difficulties; they lacked significant local demand, high levels of human capital and political clout and control over the hinterland. Artistic production and political administration were also less likely to be established in smaller towns.[39] Therefore, small towns had no other option but to invest in mass production of commodities which could compete against low-cost rural products but still yield sufficient added value. Smaller towns also acted as finishing centres and transit markets to siphon off rural production.[40] Such towns specialized in certain new industrial sectors, such as tapestry (in the case of Oudenaarde) and the making of pins and nails (in the case of 's-Hertogenbosch).[41]

A substantial part of the output of the Low Countries manufacturing industries was destined for export: Brulez has estimated the export share of total industrial output at more than a quarter in the middle of the sixteenth century.[42] This means that almost 75 per cent of all manufactured goods was consumed within the Low Countries, which would indicate a huge local demand and relative prosperity in the area. Producing for export markets was risky: conflicts could block trade, prices were volatile and fashion could change quickly. Industry was also very unstable: there were always new competitors in the densely urbanized Low Countries who could provide lower production costs and/or better technology, and better geographical location, causing industry to delocalize quickly, often with disastrous local results.[43]

Several historians have linked the growth of the native merchant community to the flowering of the Low Countries export industry.[44] The restructuring of Low Countries industry had taken place in the fourteenth and fifteenth centuries, when it was mainly foreign merchants who were exporting industrial products, which were collected in the gateway city of Bruges.[45] Only at the end of the fifteenth and the beginning of the sixteenth century do we see Low Countries merchants actively trading on foreign markets and pursuing commercial activities beyond transferring their products to the main commercial gateway in the Netherlands.

Old vs. New Drapery

The now classic history of cloth production in the late middle ages and sixteenth century proceeds as follows: the Flanders and Brabant traditional cloth industries were no match for the English drapery (cheaper quality fabrics such as the kerseys and the broad cloths, products of the rural traditional drapery) and were greatly harmed by English export taxes on the high-quality wool which this industry used.[46] In the fifteenth century many smaller towns and villages shifted to cheaper Spanish merino wools (and also to cheaper English and Scottish wool) but continued imitating the luxury cloths produced by the larger towns. Production costs were also lower, because the spinning wheel was used. Hanseatic merchants especially were eager to buy woollens made from Spanish merino wool and manufactured in Flemish small towns; they even signed contracts with producers to buy their entire outputs.[47] This led to a relation of utter dependency, with cloth producers in the towns of Dendermonde, Poperinge, Menen, Wervik and Tourcoing relying on long-distance merchants. Weavers, so as to feed their families, bought grain with letters of promise from Hanseatic merchants, their factors or brokers. But this so-called *nouvelle draperie* reached its apogee in the 1540s, when it was surpassed by the sayetteries or draperie légère and the unstoppable march of English cloth.[48] At the end of the fifteenth century, 80 per cent of the marketing of Menen cloth was done by a single Bruges broker, Wouter Ameide, who sold the product to foreign merchants who then exported it.[49] The extensive documentation about Ameide shows that such industrial networks linked to the gateway – in this case, Bruges – were not a typically Antwerp or sixteenth-century phenomenon. In fact, Flemish merchants had been active for centuries in producing centre gateway traffic.

Most information about the woollen industry of the Northern Netherlands concerns Holland, especially Leiden. This industry gradually declined in the sixteenth century, being outcompeted by its southern Netherlandish and English counterparts. Some small quantities were still exported abroad.[50] Several Antwerp merchants did establish industrial relations with Dutch cloth production centres. In 1523 a consortium of Spanish merchants residing in Antwerp signed a contract with the city government of Haarlem to purchase a large quantity of cloth at a fixed price.[51] Four years later, a group of Low Countries merchants active in Antwerp signed a similar agreement with Haarlem's magistracy.[52] The

Antwerp entrepreneur Adriaen May (originally from Diksmuide in Flanders) contacted the Haarlem authorities in the same year. He wished to establish a large-scale new drapery in Haarlem, for which he wanted Flemish labourers to relocate to set up production, and market the new drapery's products to German and other European markets. In return May sought the financial support of the city government and exemption from the current drapery rules. The Haarlem magistracy eventually declined May's offer, so as not to harm the interests of the traditional drapery sector.[53] These examples show that Antwerp merchants and entrepreneurs established (or at least tried to establish) industrial relations with Dutch drapery towns. Dutch towns also invested in collective sales in Antwerp. Leiden opened a sales house in the Scheldt port city in 1552 and the Haarlem and Delft drapers collectively sold their cloth through a representative in Antwerp.[54]

Antwerp not only collected and exported goods from the Low Countries, but also attracted much of the massive import flow, which was then redistributed in the Low Countries or re-exported. This concentration of trade flows in the city created opportunities for merchants in the production and finishing of industrial goods. Antwerp did establish industries itself and these were closely tied to trade.[55]

Antwerp's own textile production was already fading in the fourteenth century.[56] The city gradually developed a textile finishing industry (shearing, dyeing) in the fifteenth century; initially, only Low Countries textiles were finished, but soon English cloth was being dyed in Antwerp as well. Mechelen also developed an English cloth dyeing industry in the 1480s; however, it could not really profit from this opportunity, as it was not allowed to actually buy and sell English cloth there.[57] The Antwerp finishing industry had a technological edge on English industry and, being the main European market, was able to respond more quickly to fashion changes. By 1539 around 1,350 Antwerp craftsmen were involved in this line of industry.[58]

Antwerp hosted an important permanent community of cloth merchants who were eager to have their unfinished textiles dyed following the latest fashions and under their own supervision. The presence of a market for dyestuffs and alum made Antwerp a perfect finishing centre.[59] It has been estimated that an Antwerp finishing treatment raised the value of a cloth by 30 per cent.[60] A fine example of an entrepreneur active in the dyeing industry was Frans de Pape.[61] De Pape probably migrated from Ghent to Antwerp, started his career as a cloth cutter and managed to establish himself as a merchant not just of cloth, but also of hops, spices, hides, grain and livestock. He bought English cloth at the Antwerp fairs from the Merchant Adventurers and had the cloth prepared and dyed in Antwerp and in Mechelen.[62] Hence, Mechelen seems to have shifted its industry from the production of traditional luxury cloth to the finishing of non-Mechelen textiles.[63] Most of the English cloth purchased by de Pape was dyed black.[64] In 1540 de Pape owned a cloth finishing workshop, where he employed twelve labourers.[65] Jan Nuyts, an immigrant from Brabant, set up a firm specializing in crimson and violet silk cloth weaving and dyeing and in other, typically Italian silk products, for which he was granted a subsidy by the city government. The government often pursued such policy, so as to selectively attract economically useful migrants.[66] Nuyts purchased raw silk and had it processed by labourers, after which it was dyed. At first, Nuyts sold his output mainly in the Low Countries; when the political and religious disturbances began to emerge in the Low Countries he began traveling to England, Germany, the Baltic and France to sell his merchandise and collect debts from clients.

The family history of the Leydeckers shows how industrial entrepreneurs could become merchants through opportunities offered on the Antwerp market. Bernaert Leydecker was active as a cloth preparer in 1510.[67] He may have come from Bergen-op-Zoom, where several of his family members were active as cloth merchants. Two years later, Leydecker acted as guarantee for the statements of several merchants from Münster.[68] In 1526, Leydecker's daughter married Godevaert van Hout, who died before 1535.[69] Before van Hout died he and his father-in-law had a partnership in cloth preparing and cloth commerce. The two sold cloth produced in their workshop and also had a shop. Bernaert Leydecker died one year later and was succeeded by his son Cornelis.[70] Cornelis continued in his father's steps, combining a cloth preparation enterprise with a commercial operation, which eventually reached up to London, Brunswick, Bremen and the Baltic.[71] By 1561, Cornelis Leydecker had become an important wool merchant.[72] His sisters Maria and Anna married Jan Placquet and Bernaert Lunden, respectively; the former was a grocer, the latter worked as an agent in the Baltic for his brother-in-law.[73] Placquet and Lunden each started a partnership with their brother-in-law, Cornelis Leydecker.[74] The Leydecker case shows how entrepreneurs in Antwerp could make use of the opportunities in cloth production and finishing to establish themselves as long-distance merchants. The sheer scale of Antwerp as a major city, its market and commercial relations surely made this a possible scenario for many other entrepreneurs.

Hondschoote Says: The Success Product of the Sixteenth Century

The most famous example of this type of textile, of course, was the Hondschoote say. The Hondschoote say, the greatest success of the Flemish draperie légère, was a hybrid worsted–woollen fabric with warps made of coarser, straight and local, regional or German wool on a vertical loom. This light fabric was almost finished when it came off the loom and could then be dyed. Its lightness made it a very attractive fabric for southern Europe and the colonies.[75] First produced by rural weavers as a side-line industry in the relatively overpopulated Hondschoote countryside (which was characterized by fragmented landownership), it quickly transformed Hondschoote into a small town. In 1560 the population had reached 15,000 and almost all of the town dwellers were active in say production.[76]

Some of the says were sold in the Low Countries but the largest share was destined for export. In the fifteenth century the export of says and import of wool via Bruges were organized by Hondschoote and Bruges merchants. By that time, however, Antwerp had already managed to attract growing volumes of says for transfer to Cologne and the Frankfurt fairs.[77] Gradually, Hondschoote's commercial focus realigned to Antwerp, which by the sixteenth century had become the dominant gateway for Hondschoote says.[78] Spain, Portugal and Italy were the major customers; from these places says were re-exported to the Atlantic islands, the American Indies, the Levant and India.[79]

Bruges and Antwerp merchants and their local representatives bought the raw fabric from drapers and had it finished (dyed). Several merchants tried to move into the finishing process as well. Nicolas Beydaels, family member and factor of the Antwerp-based De Cordes merchant family, constructed a dyeworks in 1540 for the finishing of says he bought on behalf of his Antwerp principals. His operation was thwarted by the Hondschoote magistracy, which wished to avoid vertical integration and preserve equality among the say producers. The magistracy feared unequal competition, for merchant-owners of dyeworks would have their own says dyed first and would only then accept the says of others.[80] In the second third of the sixteenth century increasing numbers of merchants attempted to establish vertically integrated enterprises.

The merchants and their agents were more successful in monopolizing the supply of raw materials and the marketing of Hondschoote's say output. At first, weavers bought wool and thread on the local markets or from drapers who collected it elsewhere. Gradually, a few merchants managed to control the market for raw materials: drapers sold their says to these merchants in return for new raw materials, credit and loans.[81] Wool could also be traded against finished says and weavers could borrow on the collateral of their future say produce or their loom itself. Merchants were empowered by their ability to procure funds from Antwerp to pay weavers on the spot in cash. For example, the Van der Molen firm sent their agent cash in carts and charged their Italian clients a risk fee (for the bullion transport).[82] Say prices rose when these bullion chariots arrived in Hondschoote.[83]

The say producers gradually became increasingly vulnerable to the fluctuations of long-distance trade. Deyon and Lottin have shown how the ups and downs of American exports in Seville influenced the output of light cloth production in Lille, which rendered the city's labour force highly dependent on the whims of long-distance trade.[84] The Van der Molen firm, in a letter to a Genoese client, described the Hondschoote weavers as follows: 'In Hondschoote it is the poor town-dwellers who make [the says] and as soon as [the says] are ready, the weavers need the money to buy bread to survive'.[85] The poverty of the producers rendered Hondschoote's production of says highly susceptible to capitalized intermediaries.

Export of the Hondschoote says was in theory open to all, yet its concentration in the hands of a few merchants proceeded ever faster.[86] In 1538 sixteen merchants controlled the lion's share of say exports; two of them were responsible for almost half of the total output.[87] Jan Sorbrecht (brother of Gillis Sorbrecht) had married into the De Cordes family and was a major Antwerp merchant; he exported to Spain and Portugal[88] and was responsible for the export of 24 per cent of Hondschoote's total annual say production.[89]

The letters of the Antwerp commission firm Van der Molen reveal many details on agent–principal relations in the Hondschoote say trade. The Van der Molen sold says to court suppliers of the Este in Ferrara and of the Gonzaga in Mantua; they procured their says in Hondschoote from Jacob Van der Tombe, a major say exporter[90] Van der Tombe also worked for other Antwerp principals, including the Milanese merchant and imperial postmaster-general Philippe de Tassis.[91] In May 1543, however, with Van der Tombe having fallen blind, the Van der Molen were looking for a replacement. Anthonis Decker presented himself and was judged by his Antwerp masters to be 'a practical and diligent man ... who has an excellent judgment of colours'.[92] This last quality was especially commendable, since the colour of says was important to the Van der Molen. As the Van der Molen had once written to their former agent Van der Tombe: 'if a say is not beautifully dyed, it is not worth half of its money in Italy. I pray you to always check the colour because it is the colour that sells the say, not the quality of its weave'.[93]

Moreover, Italian clients sometimes sent colour samples (often shades of yellow, but also azure blue and black), which the Van der Molen then forwarded to their Hondschoote agent.[94] At first, the Van der Molen firm was unsure about how they would remunerate Decker: should they pay him a fixed annual wage or a commission fee of 6 d. gr. Fl. per say with a promise of buying at least two thousand pieces annually?[95] If the latter, Decker would earn a substantial £50 gr. Fl., more than four times the annual wage of an Antwerp master mason. In the end, it was decided that Decker would receive a fixed salary.[96]

Whereas the draperie légère was mainly a Flemish affair, the Brabant village of Duffel, between Mechelen and Antwerp, succeeded in creating a successful serge industry.[97] Its vicinity to Antwerp established Duffel as a production centre, one organized by Antwerp merchants. In 1568 the Duffel government signed an exclusivity contract with the Antwerp merchant Jan Andries who would buy the total production of Duffel *vriezen*, a particular kind of cheap textile. Andries supplied Duffel weavers with wool from the Heverlee Park abbey.[98] In this case, the direct intervention of Antwerp merchants in production is easily discernible.

The Linen Industry

The relations between linen producers, intermediaries and Antwerp merchants are even more recognizable in the linen industry. Linen production (in the well-studied region of inland Flanders) took place within the so-called *Kaufsystem*: peasants owned the raw materials and means of production, wage labour was unimportant and most producers worked for their own account.[99] This does not imply that the producers held a powerful position within the economic structure of the sector; merchants did so, however, due to urban market regulations and their strong hold on the finishing phase of the linen, which was often outsourced to other regions. Intermediaries controlled the trade flows between town and countryside.[100]

Linen production offered the countryside an industrial side business to agriculture.[101] The low rural wages in particular – rural weaving was only a part-time activity – made it a sensible strategy to move linen production to the countryside. Small-holding peasants processed flax they grew themselves; sometimes they used imported flax.[102] In the first half of the sixteenth century rural linen production accounted for 20 per cent of the labour input in inland Flanders performed by peasants with small agricultural holdings.[103] Van Bavel estimates the production of inland Flanders at 50,000 pieces of linen per annum and maintains that the industry employed 38,000 half-time workers, or 40 per cent of the rural population of the region.[104] The commercial expansion of the sixteenth century firmly merged the Low Countries linen-producing countryside into European and early colonial trade. From a commercial vantage point, the region's linen trade was highly successful. Between 1560 and 1564 annual linen production for export markets amounted to 4.8 million ells, while almost 8 million ells were produced domestically.[105]

Direct merchant intervention took place in the important finishing of the linen, thereby significantly increasing the added value of the product. Merchants created industrial networks based on regional specialization. Herentals and 's-Hertogenbosch and their hinterlands acted as centres for linen production (Herentals linen was known in Spain as *arrantales*,)[106] linen markets and bleaching locations. 's-Hertogenbosch and its hinterland were also important linen producers.[107] Local bleaching was available in Flanders, but many Flemish linen traders sent their linen, especially the more expensive Courtrai linen, to Herentals and Haarlem to be treated. Ghent and Antwerp merchants had their linen bleached in 's-Hertogenbosch, which was known for its fine water quality.[108] Jeronimus Moeyaerts specialized in buying flax and thread and in linen bleaching in Herentals and surrounding areas between 1567 and 1571. He meticulously recorded the types and amounts of linen and the names of his clients (several of whom were from Antwerp) in his ledger. The linen he dealt in was mainly local but also included Brussels and Paris linen.[109] The 's-Hertogenbosch merchant Jaspar van Bell sold locally bleached linen to Antwerp merchants and sent it to his agent in Spain, Maarten van Elmpt.[110] Holland and especially Haarlem – where cheap buttermilk was readily available – enjoyed a fine reputation for linen bleaching.[111] The bleaching industry is a perfect example of regional specialization resulting from market integration organized by merchants.[112]

Antwerp and to a lesser extent Lille merchants (for export to France) had come to dominate the Flemish linen markets by the middle of the sixteenth century.[113] Antwerp merchants also hired local agents: in 1575 Jaspar Dynghens engaged Geeraerd Coucke from Courtrai as an agent. He was to purchase bleached and unbleached Courtrai damask linen, according to Antwerp orders. For this Coucke would receive a handsome annual fee of £24 gr. Fl. and could continue his own damask-weaving enterprise. However, Coucke could work only for Dynghens and was obliged to deliver an annual report.[114] Coucke himself signed a contract with the Courtrai bleacher Nicasius vander Kindert. The latter would receive 400 pieces of linen in February to be bleached by May, when he would receive a new party (which would need to be ready by August), etc. If the linen was not ready by the deadline, it could be withdrawn and entrusted to another bleacher. The bleaching fee was fixed and set in the contract. Vander Kindert would always sign Coucke's register upon receiving a new batch of linen.[115] The Della Faille company bought most of its linen in Courtrai, Hazebrouck and Ghent, but shifted their purchases and bleaching activities in the late 1580s to Haarlem and Frisian Harlingen. They nonetheless continued to purchase fine linen, such as that of Cambrai, ammelakens and napkins, in Courtrai. The Della Faille had close ties with Courtrai: the firm's founder, Jan the elder, had been born in the Courtrai area, his wife often visited the Roeselare linen market and his son Maarten was actively involved in the organization of the Courtrai linen market. The purchases were executed by independent local linen merchants who received commission fees based on the number of textiles.[116]

The marketing of linen generated much employment, with at least fifty linen traders active in Roeselare alone.[117] These traders not only bought the limited volumes of Roeselare linen but also visited neighbouring markets.[118] Many merchants from other cities such as the important linen exporter Eloy Gouthier from Arras, were very active on the Antwerp market.[119] Four Courtrai *lijnwatiers* (linen merchants) moved to Antwerp between 1570 and 1595 and registered as citizens or *poorters*.[120] Ghent merchants visited the Flemish linen markets and transferred the purchased linen from their hometown to Antwerp for export. Lodewijk Symoens, a Tielt linen trader active on the Roeselare and Deinze markets, moved to Ghent in 1554.[121] Several Ghent merchants worked for and co-operated with Baltic and Cologne firms.[122] Marketing linen could be very profitable as shown by the 1552 's-Hertogenbosch fiscal data: linen merchants sat firmly atop the fiscal pyramid, while the linen weavers found themselves at the bottom.[123]

Tapestry Production

The tapestry industry was highly dependent on capitalized entrepreneurs and merchants. Inequality and dependence on a few large merchants and entrepreneurs cannot but have increased in the sixteenth century:[124] capital had become essential due to expensive raw materials, semi manufactures and means of production (i. e., looms), (Antwerp) market access and the risks involved in the long production period. Tapestry workers became dependent on entrepreneurs for credit (owing to expensive raw materials and the long periods between production and sales), raw materials and the marketing of their output in return for a weekly piece wage.[125] Merchants kept abreast of fashion trends for this luxury product and knew how to market these products.

These tapestries had originally been made in the fifteenth century for the Low Countries market, but production expanded rapidly in the sixteenth century, with large numbers of tapestry products – both high- and low-end – being exported abroad.[126] The towns of Tournai, Arras, Bruges, Ghent and Brussels had already established an important industry in the fourteenth and fifteenth centuries.[127] Smaller towns, such as Leuven, Oudenaarde, Aalst, Diest, Enghien and Sint-Truiden were emerging as centres of tapestry production. For these smaller centres this was quite an achievement, as they had to rely on larger towns for inputs (raw materials, designs) and for marketing of their outputs.[128] Several tapestry masters from Brussels, Leuven, Diest and Tienen were actively selling their products at the Brabant fairs, and the urban government of Oudenaarde procured safe conducts for its merchants for different fairs in the Low Countries, including, of course, the Brabant fairs.[129] While Oudenaarde's success is the most spectacular example in the tapestry industry which boomed from the second third of the sixteenth century onwards, Brussels, Antwerp, Geraardsbergen and Enghien also performed well.[130] Brussels specialized in the high end of the tapestry market.[131] Antwerp, a major gateway for tapestries produced elsewhere, developed its own industry in the 1540s through immigrated tapestry weavers.[132]

Oudenaarde's success in tapestry production in the sixteenth century is largely explained by its close ties with Antwerp and the integration of urban and rural production. Oudenaarde and its countryside specialized in relatively cheaper, mass-produced, standardized 'verdures' (but not exclusively: several complex pieces with hunting scenes or grotesques and even entire figurative series are linked to Oudenaarde); also prevalent were smaller pieces, such as *beeldecussens, fruytcussens* (pillows with figures and fruit motives) and tapestry sold by the ell.[133] Forty-two per cent of Oudenaarde's active urban population was working in the tapestry industry.[134] The city's tapestry craft guild closely controlled rural producers: rural weavers had to be guild members but were strictly regulated and had fewer rights than their urban counterparts. Moreover, the guild was governed by large-scale entrepreneurs and merchants.[135]

Access to the main gateway – first Bruges, later Antwerp – proved to be fundamental to the industrial development of the tapestry business: in these major markets entrepreneurs sold their products in specialized sales venues (Panden), collected information on the latest fashions and bought cartoons, patterns and raw materials (wool and silk yarn, gold and silver thread, etc).[136] Oudenaarde merchants forged strong links with Antwerp: seventy-four *tapissiers* (intermediaries in the tapestry trade), brokers and factors from Oudenaarde became Antwerp citizens during the sixteenth century (1533–1600), forty-eight of them between 1534 and 1568.[137] Linked with their families in Oudenaarde, these intermediaries were vital for Oudenaarde's industrial in- and outputs.[138] The close ties with Antwerp are apparent in the dense web of credit relations between Oudenaarde merchants and their Antwerp suppliers/clients, as evidenced in several inventories of Oudenaarde tapestry workers and dealers.[139] One of these Antwerp merchants, Lanceloot de Robiano, appears in many of these inventories: de Robiano had a partnership with Jan and Willem van Santvoort who were exporting substantial volumes of goods, including tapestries, to Italy.[140] In the Van der Molen correspondence a typical order for tapestries was as follows: in a letter of August 1538 the Van der Molen wrote that they had ordered a tapestry with a surface of 30.9 hand palms, depicting St Martin, for the Venetian merchant Martino di Zerchiari. The Van der Molen had it designed and woven in Brussels. The design cost £1 6s. Fl., the weaving 4s. 6d. Fl. per ell (a total of £6 19s. gr. Fl.). With the commission fee and transport costs added, the St. Martin tapestry carried a price of £8, 18s. and 2d. Fl., to be paid to the partner of the Van der Molen in Venice, Joan Battista di Zanchi.[141] This tapestry must have pleased di Zerchiari because a year later he ordered another. This one, however, was not made to order; instead, it was bought as a readymade on the market.[142] Hence, tapestries could be either produced on order or purchased when finished. Precise measurements were needed and so the Van der Molen repeatedly had to write to their Italian customers to inquire about missing widths or lengths, which might suggest Italian unfamiliarity with the product. The above order shows that the Van der Molen had connections with Brussels and Oudenaarde tapestry masters: in their letters the firm often referred to the *tapezeri* of Brussels and the ordered tapestries from '"el meglior maestro" of Oudenaarde'.[143] Antwerp merchants and dealers such as the Van der Molen were in a powerful position when bargaining with the tapestry makers, for tapestries could be paid for upon delivery or by cash advances before the tapestries were finished. By granting the weavers cash advances, merchants and entrepreneurs could obligate weavers to them.[144] The Van der Molen not only bought from tapestry masters, but also sold them raw materials. Tapestry silk from Venice was sold to (Brussels?) tapezeri, such as Henrick Pipe and Hans Van Brecht, who respectively bought 36 pounds for £7 4s. Fl. and 56 pounds for £16 9 s. Fl.[145] These entrepreneurs, who went back and forth to Antwerp or who had agents in the Scheldt city, were crucial for the success of both the Brussels and Oudenaarde tapestry industries: they had access to an international market for the sale of their produce and purchases of raw materials, patterns and other necessary goods.

Other Industries: Metals, Jewellery and Art

The river basins around Namur, Durbuy, Liège, Huy and Habay, rich in iron ore, water and wood, were important iron production centres and in the sixteenth century underwent major expansion of their production capacity. Global Southern Netherlandish iron production reached an annual output between 1,950 and 5,100 tons around 1562 (in comparison, England produced 9,620 tons of iron in 1580).[146] Commercial capitalists had a firm hand in iron production: three merchants supplied 64 per cent of all iron specified in twenty-nine contracts during the period 1540–1600.[147] The growth in iron output was due largely to technological innovation, particularly due to the introduction of blast furnaces and plate hammering using hydraulic tilt hammers.[148] Some of this iron was exported in raw form, for example to Spain in 1552–3.[149] Large amounts were processed in the Low Countries into nails, pins, keys, locks, knives and other kitchenware and similar items. These objects could be produced both in the countryside (for example, nails were produced in the region between Sambre and Meuse) and in the towns. In the first half of the sixteenth century 's-Hertogenbosch was home to an important pin, nail and knife production, which was organized into guilds to enforce high-quality standards.[150] Much of this produce was sold through the Brabant fairs. The pin makers collectively rented a series of fair stalls in Bergen-op-Zoom; the nail and knife makers operated as individual sellers. In the 1540s the Antwerp merchant Gerard Timback bought large amounts of pins for export to England for which he even obtained a special licence. Jaspar van Bell exported pins and knives to Spain, where 's-Hertogenbosch knifes were known as *belduques*.[151] The Low Countries war machine required large volumes of iron and copper; craftsmen in Mechelen, Brussels, and Liège supplied armies with cannons, guns, ammunition and gunpowder.[152]

Sixteenth-century Antwerp boasted a market for precious stones and jewellery.[153] Foreign and, later, native merchants imported precious stones from Asia, Africa and the Americas (through the Iberian Peninsula and Italy). Initially serving a local noble and middle class clientele, many jewellers subsequently expanded their activities abroad. Local craftsmen and merchants managed to collect sufficient capital to buy large supplies of jewels and sell them abroad, grossing handsome profits, albeit sometimes only after a long wait. They shifted their activities from the industrial to the commercial but still maintained strong ties with producers: they employed journeymen and subcontracted other masters. These merchants vehemently protested against the establishment of a diamond cutters guild in 1577, since they feared that it would obstruct wage labour and subcontracting.[154] They also branched out towards other lines of commerce, such as luxury textiles, and combined wholesale and retail trade. In turn, merchants in these other lines of commerce occasionally bought and sold jewellery. The character of the market also changed: jewellery was initially sold mainly during the fairs in the Panden, but the growing permanency of the market led many goldsmiths and jewellers to set up shops. Antwerp jewellers expanded their operations to other European markets; Guicciardini noted in 1567 that jewellery and precious stones were sent from Antwerp to Venice, Milan, Germany, the Baltic, France and England.[155]

The story of one of these jewellers, Joris Vezeleer, shows how he went through the typical trade trajectory (from the hinterland to Antwerp to European markets) and how he made excellent use of Antwerp's commercial and industrial opportunities. Joris Vezeleer was born in 1493 in the Brabant town of 's-Hertogenbosch.[156] He started his career as a goldsmith, which was also the occupation of his father. In 1515 he became an Antwerp citizen and in 1518 he married Margaretha Boge.[157] His three daughters (Elisabeth, Cecilia and Margareta) were married to fellow merchants. He became dean of the guild of gold and silver smiths in 1524. In the 1520s Vezeleer branched out his enterprise and began including tapestries in his sales. He supplied luxurious tapestries to the king of France, François I, and to a cardinal at the end of the 1520s and the early 1530s. He had established strong connections with top Brussels tapestry producers, including Willem de Kempeneer, to procure the best products available. Jewellery and precious stones remained an important business for Vezeleer: he delivered large pieces of jewellery, precious stones and gold and silver dinnerware to the French king and to Charles V. His intimate knowledge of bullion earned him the appointment as mint-master-general of the Brabant Mint in 1545. Vezeleer was not the only substantial merchant with strong ties to the royal mints. Thomas Gramaye, father of Geerard, Cornelis van Eeckeren and Jacob van Hencxthoven, all wealthy Antwerp merchants and financiers, held important offices in the Antwerp mint.[158] Like Vezeleer, these financiers were well equipped to seize the commercial opportunities of the era. Vezeleer experimented with trade in other products in those years: wine, quicksilver, mercury, leather, wool, beeswax, woad and vermilion. He obtained and marketed those goods through agents (often family members) in Paris, Lyon, Bordeaux and Rouen and organized partnerships with his sons-in-law. Vezeleer also capitalized on Antwerp's growth by investing in real estate in the city and by participating in Gilbert van Schoonbeke's peat digging company in Veenendaal.[159]

In the fifteenth and sixteenth centuries the urban centres of the Low Countries became Europe's fashion capital as the region transitioned to a luxury industry:

the fur, hat, glove and confection industries, as well as artistic production (in such areas as painting, sculpture, wood carving, furniture-making, leather, embroidery, miniatures, music, jewellery, etc.) witnessed a strong growth and became an important export industry as well.[160] Antwerp developed into a major art market in the sixteenth century. At first the marketing of artwork took place within the frame of the Brabant fairs: in the already-mentioned *panden* artists and dealers sold artwork and other luxuries. Later in the sixteenth century specific venues for particular products were created such as the Tapestry Pand or the *Schilders* (Painters') Pand. Merchants such as Joris Vezeleer supplied European courts but they were not the only dealers. From the sixties onwards specialized art dealers became more active and sold large volumes of cheaper pieces of art on spec; many of them were the wives or widows of artists and dealers.[161] Dealers controlled production in other towns and marketed their output: Antwerp dealers ordered and bought large watercolour paintings on thin linen in nearby Mechelen and even intervened in the production process by illegally hiring apprentice labour.[162] Several of these dealers explored foreign markets as well as a result of the growing political instability within the Low Countries.[163] As a result, Antwerp exported art all over Europe, from Seville to Danzig and beyond, to the New World. The Scheldt city owed this its commercial infrastructure, its strategic position within European trade, a strong and old artistic tradition and an orientation toward open market production (as in textile production, for example).[164]

Native merchants operating from Antwerp developed strong relations with Low Countries industry. They provided credit, supplied raw materials and, as we will see, marketed the output. Through middlemen, agents and intermediary markets these products reached the gateway. Merchant intervention in production was evident in the textile production of Hondschoote, Haarlem and Duffel and in the linen-bleaching sector. Only in Haarlem were foreign – in this case Spanish – merchants involved in production. This situation differed from the fourteenth and fifteenth centuries, when foreign merchants did establish more intensive relations with Low Countries industry. At the end of the fourteenth century the well-known (because of the preservation of his account books and correspondence) Tuscan merchant Francesco di Marco Datini from Prato had an agent in Bruges who single handedly acquired most of the cloth output of Wervik – both in Bruges and in Wervik – to be sold in Mediterranean markets.[165] Hanseatic merchants organized monopoly contracts with cloth towns such as Poperinge, Menen and Oudenaarde in the fifteenth century. The city of Bruges even guaranteed those monopoly contracts with cloth towns and the quality standards of the cloth.[166] A century later and with Antwerp as the new gateway, relations between the gateway and the production centres had become the preserve of native merchants, who turned this position into a comparative advantage for themselves, although dealing in local products was not their only strength.

We are largely in the dark about the profits which could be obtained in this production centre–gateway trade. Only the Van der Molen letters provide a glimpse: the Van der Molen bought Hondschote says through a local agent, realizing an average price difference of 1s. gr. Fl. per say. Transport and tolls cost 6d. per say, their agent received 2d. per say and the Van der Molen charged their clients a 2d. per say risk premium to send cash money to Hondschote as payment for the says. This leaves a net profit of 2d. per say for shipment of says from Hondschote to Antwerp.[167] We know that the Van der Molen negotiated with a new Hondschoote agent and promised to buy at least 2,000 says per annum. This means the Van der Molen would earn a total of £16.7 gr. Fl. on the Hondschoote–Antwerp price difference, which is more than what an Antwerp master mason earned from a year's work. One should add that dealing in Hondschoote was just one of the businesses of the Van der Molen. Clearly, this production centre–gateway trade was worthwhile financially. Moreover, it allowed local merchants to provide their foreign clients with goods at lower prices than those which could be obtained at Antwerp.

Control over Imports and their Redistribution

Native merchants did not only tightly control the transit of industrial goods to Antwerp; they also became stronger in the importation of goods to the Low Countries and in the distribution of these goods out of Antwerp and other ports. The previous chapter has already referred to the high (when compared to France and England) per capita imports of the Low Countries.[168] The evidence of their activities in imports and redistribution is sparse. Yet, merchants from the southern Low Countries gradually engaged in the importation of grain, wine, spices and alum, which bears testimony to their increasing importance.

Large cities such as Antwerp and highly urbanized regions, of which there were several in the Low Countries, depended strongly on the importation of foreign grain. From the sixteenth century onwards local foodstuffs were complemented by growing imports of Baltic grain.[169] Up until the late 1550s this trade was largely controlled by Dutch and Hanseatic merchants who supplied Antwerp and the southern Low Countries out of Amsterdam.[170] Amsterdam traders (both Dutch and Hanseatic) relied on the services of Antwerp innkeepers or had their own agents in Antwerp to arrange transportation of the grain to the Scheldt city and its subsequent sales. These agents could be either Antwerp citizens, Low Countries traders or Hanseats.[171] Two processes prompted Antwerp merchants to engage more actively in the Baltic grain trade from the late 1550s. Firstly, Antwerp merchants such as Marten vanden Briele, Adam Schuilenburg, the Schetz family and Gerard Gramaye exported luxury goods (textiles, tapestries, silks and pieces of jewellery) to the Baltic; grain functioned as a return cargo besides wax, iron, copper and hides on these voyages.[172] Secondly, strong rises in the grain prices incited Antwerp-based merchants to import grain and acquire existing stocks in Amsterdam and other places for speculation. Merchants then only had to hoard the grain and bring it on the market at high prices. The bad harvest of 1565 created such a price rise. The Fourmestraux, De Lobel, Mahieu and Van der Leure, all rich merchant families from Lille with branches in Antwerp and Amsterdam, acquired large volumes of grain in the Baltic, Antwerp and Amsterdam at the end of 1565 and tried to corner the market. These families were familiar with the grain trade: they had been buying and selling grain from Artois and Picardy for quite some time. Unfortunately for the cartel, their attempt was discovered by the authorities and they were forced to sell the grain.[173] Pauwels van Dale, a major Antwerp merchant, and his attempt to create an illegal grain monopoly in times of dearth was found out even more spectacularly. On 26 September 1565, when prices were already on the rise, the attic of his granary collapsed, causing the front of the house to break down, upon which the grain flowed out onto the street. Passers-by obviously recognized this as an attempt by van Dale to stock as much grain as possible and sell it off at high prices.[174]

The import of French wine out of the ports of Bordeaux, Rouen, La Rochelle and Nantes and over land in the sixteenth century was subject to a similar tendency of concentration in the hands of a few merchants, although per capita consumption of wine was declining.[175] At the end of the fifteenth century this trade was controlled by many small French traders. The import of French wine in the sixteenth century experienced an important shift: from small French merchants to large Italian and Spanish firms to Low Countries merchants from Lille, Arras and Antwerp.[176] Many tons of wine were re-exported to England and some to the Baltic by Low Countries merchants.[177] The Habsburg–Valois wars of the first half of the sixteenth century tightly regulated the wine trade; only those with a costly licence, which had to be purchased from the Low Countries government, could import French wine. As a result of this, the trade became controlled by an elite of rich Italian and Spanish merchants. Besides these merchants (Guicciardini, Antinori, Nazi, Salviati, Affaitadi, Quintanaduenas), smaller operators from Lille, Arras, Cambrai and Antwerp were importing wine as well, for their own account and as agents for the Italians and Spaniards: from Antwerp, Erasmus Schetz, Jacques Hoefnagel (for the Salviati and Quintanaduenas) and Joris Vezeleer (for the Salviati), Jean De Lobel (from Lille) and Eloy Goutier (from Arras).[178] By 1550 Low Countries merchants had outcompeted French, Italian and Spanish traders. The Lillois merchant Julien Le Febvre alone was responsible for more than 40 per cent of Antwerp's wine imports. Unlike, for example, Schetz, he was fully specialized in French wine.[179] Le Febvre had excellent contacts in Bordeaux and Rouen.[180] Le Febvre was succeeded by Jan Cornelisz and Jean Symonet from Middelburg, the Low Countries wine staple, as major importers.[181] Jean Symonet had worked as the Bordeaux agent of the Antwerp-based Antinori; he also travelled to many wine villages to inspect and purchase the wine himself on good terms. This expertise would have served him well when he became the head of his own firm.[182] The Lillois merchants Fourmestraux and Thieffries also engaged in the wine trade, focusing on La Rochelle.[183] One of Antwerp's most well-known merchants, Pierre de Moucheron, had intensive relations with Rouen, where he acquired wine for import to Middelburg and Antwerp.[184] By 1588, Low Countries merchants bought wine prior to the harvest and held large stocks all over France.[185] Hence, the ties Low Countries merchants had with the production side went beyond the political borders of the Low Countries.

The trade in Portuguese spices, another consumer good, was tightly controlled by the Portuguese king, his agents and monopoly traders at Antwerp who could advance large sums to the king for their spice purchases. Most of the imported spices were re-exported; yet large quantities stayed in the Low Countries. These were then redistributed by local grocers.[186] At the beginning of the sixteenth century Low Countries merchants such as Nicolaes van Rechtergem, Aert Pruynen and Erasmus Schetz acquired large amounts of spices directly from Portugal in return for copper, silver and quicksilver. Yet, from the later years of the first decade of the sixteenth century this trade was monopolized by Italian firms (Affaitadi, Gualterotti, Frescobaldi). From 1515, south German merchants (Fugger, Welser, Hochstetter) took over from the Italians and they themselves were succeeded by Portuguese traders of Marrano origin (Diego Mendez, Antonio and Loys Fernandez). In the 1540s the south German Imhoff and Schetz (based in Antwerp but born in Germany) families were the major exporters of spices (predominantly to Germany). In 1559 the contractors were again Italians, Portuguese and Spaniards. Low Countries merchants still lacked the large capitals and the political and financial clout required to participate in this trade.[187]

Alum was a crucial import for the Low Countries textile industries. High prices and/or insufficient supply meant losses for entrepreneurs and unemployment for textile labourers. Most alum came from Tolfa in the papal state and from Spain (Carthagena, Rodalquilar and especially Mazarron).[188] Spanish alum was of lesser quality than alum from Tolfa. Both in Spain and Italy the exploitation of the mines was farmed out to the highest-bidding merchant. The trade in such faraway markets which required substantial capital and contacts with the mine owners lent itself to monopoly formation in the Low Countries, a monopoly which was often officially granted and approved by the Low Countries government. Antwerp enjoyed the official staple rights for alum from 1491 onwards: all alum shipped to the Low Countries could only be offered for sale the first time on the Antwerp market.[189] Until 1549 all alum distributors in the Low Countries were Italians (Agostino Chigi, Gaspar Musicque, Marco Anthonio, Gaspar Ducci). In 1549 Gaspar Ducci's monopoly contract was declared void by the central government of the Low Countries. The Low Countries merchant Gillis Sorbrecht was charged with the sales of existing alum stocks. New contracts were signed with other Genoese firms (Grimaldi, Sauli).[190] From 1559 to 1568 importation of Spanish alum was the preserve of the Schetz family and their agents, a Low Countries firm.[191] Internal problems within the Schetz group and corruption charges ended the group's control over the alum trade. The Genoese Pallavicino firm took over from the Schetz in 1569 (until 1587). As with spices, the alum trade demanded European political and financial connections and capital, which only very few Low Countries merchants, such as the Schetz, had access to.

The growing presence of Low Countries merchants was more pronounced in the trade of another raw (although perhaps less essential) material for the textile industry: woad. Wine and woad together accounted for two-thirds of imports from France in the middle of the sixteenth century.[192] French woad was mainly produced in the Lauragais, the triangle between Toulouse, Albi and Carcassonne. Prior to 1540 the exportation of French woad was done by merchants from Toulouse (through Bordeaux), who had agents in the Low Countries. Around 1540 this trade was monopolized by Italian merchants (Guicciardini, Ducci and Affaitadi). Gradually, south German (Tucher, Welser) and Low Countries firms (the Lillois Fourmestraux and Thieffries, the Norman Pierre de Moucheron who had established a business in Middelburg and the Antwerp Schetz–Pruynen group through their contacts with the Toulousain Pierre Assezat) started to develop an interest in French woad as well. This trade allowed Low Countries merchants to become agents of important foreign firms; their expertise and contacts could then be used by Low Countries traders to set up their own business. Baudouin Barbier from Antwerp is a good example: in the 1540s he sold woad on behalf of Gaspar Ducci, Tommaso Balbani, the Guicciardini and the Affaitadi to south German firms such as Kaltenhofer and Hans Welser & co. By 1556 Low Countries merchants had become the dominant group in this trade; the Italians moved into financial transactions.[193]

Conclusion

The Low Countries were characterized by a dynamic industrial landscape in which merchants were crucial. The costs of marketing textiles in Antwerp were very low.[194] As a result, industrial production could remain decentralized and spread over different production centres instead of being fixed at the gateway. Consequently, an integrated market took shape in the Low Countries with Antwerp as the top market and gateway. Antwerp itself was linked with many smaller gateways and ports and with smaller intermediary markets which collected commodities from production centres which were then shipped to a market of a higher level and scale. The linen production and trade in the Low Countries provides an excellent example of this market system.

At the regional level, Antwerp merchants and their agents established close ties with producers; they knew what the latest fashions were abroad, extended credit, organized industrial infrastructure and marketed the industrial produce to regional markets and from there to the gateway. Growing specialization as a consequence of changes in the Low Countries marketing system and the fact that many of these industrial goods were produced in the countryside made such intermediation even more necessary. Although a quantitative understanding of this intermediation is problematic, evidence about several of these merchants demonstrates that this line of trade was certainly remunerative. The concentration of trade in Antwerp gradually turned its fair system into a permanent market. This transition confronted many producers with an important choice: continue producing and leave the marketing to professional intermediaries, set up shop in Antwerp on a permanent basis, or become an intermediary themselves. Regional marketing also provided many commercial opportunities for entrepreneurs, for example on the Flemish linen markets. Many merchants, especially from industrialized Flanders, chose to move to Antwerp to seize the commercial opportunities in the Scheldt city. In doing so, they reinforced Antwerp's commercial relations with its hinterland and they brought local product knowledge and contacts with them.

It is tempting to describe the actual and attempted interventions of Low Countries merchants in the production sphere as backward vertical integration, the integration in one company of multiple stages of production. Such vertical integration would have put Low Countries traders in the same sphere of organization as the south German merchants (in the copper and fustian trade).[195] Vertical integration seems to be especially true for the case of Hondschoote where many merchants tried to enter and coordinate the production sphere. A relatively small player such as the Van der Molen acquired says in Hondschoote, shipped them to Antwerp and from there to their branch office and clients in Venice; the Van der Molen combined both backward and forward vertical integration. Yet, not all Low Countries merchants were like the Van der Molen: some preferred to limit their operations to the Low Countries and even to specific productions centres; others purchased products in Antwerp and preferred to sell them internationally. As such, Low Countries merchants faced a similar trade-off as the Maghribi or Geniza traders between localism and 'internationalism', two types of trade with very different investment requirements, geographies of travel, profit expectations and risk. The eventual choices and accents were determined by resources, family ties, training and personal preferences.[196] The actual results of these choices can be read in the activities and histories of merchants who were described in this chapter.

The relationships which Low Countries merchants fostered with the production sphere within the Low Countries will certainly have provided them with a comparative advantage over their foreign colleagues, especially those who only temporarily visited the Scheldt city. Unfortunately, this advantage cannot be calculated. Yet, the virtual absence of foreign merchants at regional markets and in production centres strongly suggests that they acquired most of their commodities in finished form at Antwerp. This is an indication of either the disinterest of foreign traders to interact with the production side or the strong control Low Countries merchants had over local industry. In any case, this provided Low Countries traders with a substantial comparative advantage. Sixteenth-century Antwerp and the Low Countries were not an atypical case of local traders controlling the hinterland (both in place and time). In Lyon in the 1540s and 1550s French merchants reacted vehemently against attempts of Italian traders to penetrate the kingdom of France's internal economy. They considered direct purchases from manufacturers within the country and the redistribution of imported manufactures as their sole privilege. In one case the Luccese Bonvisi firm tried to take complete control over silk production at nearby Tours, which was heavily dependent on the importation of Italian raw silk. After serious protest, the Bonvisi backed down.[197] The Ottoman sultan opened up its ports to foreign traders but forbade foreigners to travel inland to acquire domestic products at the source.[198] In early nineteenth-century Antwerp, when the city had regained access to the Atlantic after the Continental Blockade, local merchants were much more interested in local industry (textiles, especially cotton, and sugar refining) than foreign traders. Foreign traders (Germans, English and French traders) kept to importing raw materials for these industries but did not invest in industrial production in Antwerp. If they wanted their raw materials to be treated, they turned to local entrepreneurs.[199]

Sixteenth-century Low Countries merchants not only controlled relations with industry, they also became a force to be reckoned with in the importation and redistribution of commodities such as grain, wine and woad. In these sectors they were able to outcompete powerful groups such as the Hansa and Italian traders. In the wine and woad trade they even controlled production in France. The question remains whether the strong linkages between Low Countries merchants and local industry were decisive for the commercial ascent of the former. I believe it was not. Local intermediaries had been active in the production centre–gateway trade to Bruges in the fourteenth and fifteenth centuries – for centuries by then. This trade did not propel them onto European markets in that period. Hence, Low Countries merchants' control of the Low Countries' industrial hinterland will certainly have been a necessary condition for their commercial ascent, but not a sufficient one.

3 FINANCING AND ORGANIZING COMMERCE: PARTNERSHIPS

Introduction

On the 29th of November 1565, the secretary of the English Merchant Adventurers at Antwerp wrote to the English Privy Council on the Adventurers' grievances regarding trading in the Low Countries and on the recent disruptions of trade. He singled out the fierce competition of merchants of the Low Countries and more specifically those of Antwerp. He writes: 'the inhabitants [of Antwerp] ... have crept into such credit that almost they rule all trades and moneys'.[1] Clearly these grievances were meant to push the English government to strife for more privileges for its subjects in the Low Countries. The secretary's statement is clearly at odds with current historiography: merchants from the Low Countries are never listed as important players in the money trade in the fifteenth and sixteenth century. The standard narrative of sixteenth-century financial history stresses the succession of Florentine and Luccese financiers by south German bankers (from Augsburg and Nuremberg). In turn, the 'Zeitalter der Fugger' (Ehrenberg) made way for the 'siècle des Génois', the century of the Genoese (1557–1627) (Braudel).[2] Successful merchant groups always engaged in the money trade, often after a relative shift away from commodity trade.[3] South German merchant dynasties such as the Fugger and the Welser stand out as an obvious example: at first, they were active in the textile and metals trade; they engaged in mining and, as a result of their mining activities, they got into contact with the high nobility and princes, prompting them to become the chief creditors of European crowns.[4]

Low Countries merchants definitely played second fiddle to other financial groups on the European market for government credit. Yet, one cannot ignore them altogether: a couple of Low Countries financiers stand out on a European scale and in the Low Countries native merchants did act as important creditors to the central and local governments. During Maximilian of Austria's regency (1506–19) on behalf of his underage grandson, Charles V, large loans were contracted from Genoese, Florentine and Luccese financiers on the Bruges money market. These Italians had to concede ground to south German bankers such as the Imhofs, the Hochstetters, Tuchers, Welsers and especially the Fugger who quenched the Habsburg thirst for short-term government credit payable at the Antwerp Bourse.[5] Agents of the crown and the central government in Brussels, often combining this with the function of treasurer-general, placed such loans on the Antwerp capital market. Several of these agents can be labelled as natives: Pieter van der Straten (1515–23), Gerard Sterck (1528–31) and Gaspar Schetz (from 1552).[6] Sixteenth-century France witnessed a similar shift from foreign to local financiers. The end of Italian financial influence in France was, however, much more violent than in the Low Countries, after hatred had been building against Italian financiers and their involvement in French state finance for years.[7]

Though often ignored in the international literature, the members of the Schetz family played a major role in the financing of the Habsburg empire.[8] The founding father of the Schetz dynasty Erasmus Schetz was the son of Coenrard, a knight and master of the Mint of the prince bishopric of Liège, and Catharina Kranz, the daughter of the Mint-master of Westphalia and owner of several Westphalian copper mines. Schetz migrated to Antwerp to assist his uncle Rutger in his copper business, which Schetz would inherit after the latter's death. Schetz then became the Lisbon agent of Claes van Rechterghem, a rich merchant of Cologne who had settled in Antwerp and who through his marriage owned the Kelmis smithsonite mines of Altenberg (smithsonite was necessary to produce brass from copper). In 1511, Schetz married the daughter of van Rechterghem and after the latter's death gains control of his family-in-law's mines. Erasmus Schetz was in pole position to cash in on the Portuguese demand for copper and became spectacularly wealthy. He subsequently branched out to many different profit opportunities, such as the sugar trade, with which he had become familiarized during his stay in Lisbon.[9] He even founded a sugar mill in São Vicente in Brazil.[10] Erasmus's trading activities focused on his native Germany, Portugal and Brazil. Erasmus started to advance funds to officials of Charles V in 1522; in 1526 the Tucher describe Schetz as an important financier.[11] In 1542 Schetz was the second largest lender in a zero-interest loan to the emperor.[12] His sons Gaspar, Melchior and Balthazar continued the business upon their father's death in 1550. When war with France started again (September 1551), Charles V was able to borrow large sums from the Schetz company.[13] These sums were to be repaid from the Castilian treasury; the Schetz ranked sixth in the list of lenders (after the Fugger, Welser, Grimaldi, Spinola and Gentile) to the Castilian treasury and extended the largest loans on average to the emperor.[14] In 1555 Gaspar Schetz became Philip II's royal factor in Antwerp and in 1564 he was appointed as the Low Countries treasurer-general.[15] The Schetz were seriously affected by the first Habsburg government debt restructuring of 1557 (technically not a bankruptcy).[16] The company vainly sought to recoup its losses in the alum trade.[17] Given the size of their enterprise, their involvement in the metals, alum and spice trade and their contracting of loans for the Brussels government and for the emperor, the Schetz can be called the Fugger of the Low Countries.

Not only the Habsburgs made use of Low Countries financiers. The Antwerp capital market was vital for the English state between 1544 and 1574.[18] English State Papers and especially the correspondence of Thomas Gresham highlight the important and under-researched role of Low Countries financiers in English state finance. The Schetz, again, were among the English crown's creditors. They were able to capitalize on contacts forged in 1546 for the export of emergency wheat and rye from Danzig to English ports.[19] In August 1552 the crown was not able to pay sums due worth £56,000 to the Fugger and Gaspar Schetz. Thomas Gresham, the royal agent at Antwerp, was sent to meet with the bankers and have payment postponed for six months.[20] Other Antwerp merchants acted as English crown financiers besides Schetz. Pauwel Van Dale, whose attic collapsed when he was hoarding grain in 1565, lent more than £4,000 gr. Fl. for one year in 1558 to Queen Mary I through the intermediation of Gresham.[21] Gillis Hooftman received a bond from the Queen for his loan of more than 22,000 florins in 1559; he was owed a larger sum of 42,337 florins contracted on the 4th of August 1566 and due on 20th February 1567.[22] His colleague Christopher Pruynen, a partner of the Schetz, was mentioned in the same list of 1566 lenders (besides the Christoffel Welser and Caspar Rembold from Augsburg) for a loan of 43,322 florins.[23] Low Countries merchants may not have been the leading men in sixteenth-century European state finance but the above bits and pieces do show that they were quite active and at times could play a vital role.[24]

Merchants had three options to finance their businesses: reinvesting profits, debt and equity. Merchants reinvested profits when they felt assured that their business would increase and bring in further profit. Debts could be contracted from family and friends or from strangers, at different interest rates, with different types of collateral and through different instruments. Equity allowed for investment (through labour, fixed assets or capital) by others – family, friends or strangers – in return for a part of the profits.[25] Preferences for certain instruments depended on the purpose of the debt (investment, production, consumption, etc.), the type of collateral, the identity of the lender/borrower and the duration of the debt.[26] The next two chapters will deal with partnerships and bonds as ways to finance mercantile enterprise. Yet, these were not the only financial instruments available on the Antwerp market. Indeed, financial sophistication and the variety of available financial instruments was a function of the size of the financial market.[27] Sixteenth-century Antwerp was one of the major financial centres of the era; consequently, it offered best-practice financial instruments and opportunities.

One of the oldest debt instruments was the annuity.[28] The borrower sold a right on a periodical remuneration or interest to the lender in return for a principal sum. An annuity was structured as a sale, not as a loan. The annuity could be eternal or fixed on the lives of a number of annuity beneficiaries. The annuity seller always had the right to redeem his debt, cancelling the annuity (in Brabant this practice was established by law in 1520). In sixteenth-century Antwerp interest rates on annuities amounted to 6.25 per cent ('penning 16') or lower. Most of these annuities were backed by real estate as collateral. Annuity sales were a well-established practice in sixteenth-century Antwerp and Antwerp merchants were actively buying and selling annuities in 1545, in the midst of a period of strong economic growth.[29] Merchants engaged in annuity transactions for amounts which were higher on average and many of their debtors and creditors were fellow merchants. In 1555 when the market for annuities contracted by the general dip in the economic conjuncture, merchants were feverishly selling annuities in an attempt to obtain capital by which to survive the crisis.[30] Given this intensive use of annuities by merchants, their attention to real estate is understandable. According to real estate magnate Gilbert van Schoonbeke, owning real estate was the only one way to pass as rich and creditworthy, since 'merchants' assets in the form of merchandise were mainly to be found abroad, so losses are hard to identify before one goes bankrupt'.[31] Hence, owning real estate can be considered as having been a signal for creditworthiness. It offered merchants not only valuable collateral, but also a secure and regular income and the possibility to speculate on real estate price rises.[32] Foreign and native merchants alike acquired annuities in Antwerp. Hence, this type of finance did not differentiate the locals from the foreigners.

A second financial instrument was the bill of exchange. Bills of exchange were used to transfer money from one city to another in different currencies.[33] Bills of exchange also had a credit function, as there was a time lapse between the drawing of the bill and its eventual payment abroad. Which function was most important to merchants is matter of debate: Brulez has argued that sixteenth-century Low Countries merchants were using bills mainly to transfer funds, while De Roover has stressed speculation and arbitrage as the major functions of bills of exchange.[34] The risk of such bill transactions lay not only in swift changes in the exchange rate but also in the parties involved in the transactions. This latter risk could be contained to spreading exchange transactions over different bills and by entrusting a bill to solvent merchants.[35] Both city authorities and the central government provided a legislative framework for the use of such bills of exchange.[36] The Antwerp bench of aldermen pronounced a large number of sentences concerning bills of exchange.[37] Moreover, Antwerp notaries registered bills of exchange and protests against such bills.[38] Endorsement (transferring the bill to a third party) and discount (selling bills to a third party at a value lower than the nominal value before the maturity date) of bills of exchange only became common in Antwerp at the end of the sixteenth century.[39]

Low Countries merchants operating out of Antwerp were familiar with bills of exchange from an early date onwards. In 1491 Lottijn van Bomberge from Antwerp declared that around Laetare Sunday (the fourth Sunday of Lent) he had received a letter from Cornelis Henrici in which Henrici (drawee) announced that he had contracted with Jacop van Coudewerve to pay van Coudewerve (drawer and payee) 300 ducats in Venice at an exchange rate of one penny per ducat. Coudewerve would pay the sum to Henrici in Antwerp before Palm Sunday. Van Bomberge (payer) stated that he had prepared the 300 ducats but that Coudewerve, who was about to travel to Venice as a pilgrim, had never arrived there; he goes on to complain that he had thus not been able to invest these 300 ducats in another commercial operation.[40] Antwerp merchants did not only use bills in the trade with the Mediterranean where bills of exchange were common. In 1574 Isidor Dalsz travelled to the eastern Baltic carrying silks, bullion and cash. He sold the silks and then bought Russian leather, flax and wax. In January 1575 he obtained additional funds in Riga through bills of exchange paid out by Antwerp and Lübeck agents in the Baltic port, and used these funds to buy elk skins, tallow and cowhides; the merchandise was then shipped from Riga to Lübeck. All of these bills would be settled in Antwerp or Lübeck.[41] The need among Low Countries merchants to use bills of exchange to transfer funds to other European markets most likely increased along with their growing presence on these markets. Hence, sixteenth-century Low Countries merchants frequently used bills of exchange, but these bills did not provide them with a comparative advantage over other merchants who had been using such bills for a long time by then. Moreover, as the 'Commission Trade' section of this chapter will show, they relied on foreign merchant-bankers as counterparties in bill of exchange transactions.

Merchants could also choose not to draw up a formal debt title but simply record the debt in their account books and offset the debt later.[42] Such book credit has not received much attention in historiography of sixteenth-century Antwerp due to the scarcity of preserved account books. Yet, there are indications of the intensive use of current accounts for such credit.[43] The double entry account books of Gerard Gramaye have several current accounts for his different Baltic companies and included many outstanding debts and credits.[44] This practice was surely reinforced by the gradual acceptance of accounts books as legal evidence.[45] Deposits invested in merchant enterprises were another type of debt; they were mostly invested in companies and partnerships and will be dealt with in this chapter. Marine insurance was another way for merchants to obtain funds: underwriters pocketed the insurance fee in return for promising to pay for the damages in case of calamity or insured risk. Of course, underwriters ran the risk of having to pay out insurance. Sixteenth-century Antwerp became an important insurance market, as we have seen in the first chapter, and Low Countries merchants were active both as underwriters and as insured, yet the major insurers and insurance purchasers were still Italian and Iberian merchants.[46]

This chapter will focus on how Low Countries merchants used partnership structures to set up their business, to attract capital from diverse investors and knowledge and information from partners and agents. Did they obtain funding and knowledge from foreign merchants active in sixteenth-century Antwerp? As in the next chapter, I will take into account both the legal theory and the commercial practice of equity capital organization.

In 1530 or 1531 Jan Della Faille the elder travelled from his native county of Flanders to Venice to serve the successful Brussels expatriate merchant Maarten de Hane with nothing more than a promise from his friends to stand surety for his clothing expenses in the first three years.[47] Della Faille worked three years for de Hane in return for board and lodging, all the while absorbing the skills necessary for a merchant of the time. After 1534 Della Faille continued working for de Hane for a salary and occasional gratuities with which he was allowed to organize his own commercial transactions within the structure of de Hane's firm. Five years later Della Faille acted as de Hane's agent in Antwerp and in 1541 he married Cornelia van der Capelle, a granddaughter of his principal, who had probably organized the match. At that time Della Faille became a salaried partner in the company of Maarten, Maarten's sons and Jacob van Zwijndrecht.

There was substantial discussion about the quality of Della Faille's capacity as an agent between him and Maarten's sons several years later: Jan and Daniel de Hane argued that Della Faille, being a partner, was not allowed to pursue his own commercial enterprise, which Della Faille explicitly denied. Della Faille traded on his own account, first through the de Hane company and agents, but he later by-passed the firm and its agents, trading in the core business of the de Hane firm (textile trade between the Low Countries and Venice) and explored new market opportunities in Spain and England. After Maarten de Hane's death, Della Faille lured away three agents of the de Hane firm to set up his own organization. Jan and Daniel de Hane accused one of these former employees, Gillis van den Brugghe, of having copied company secrets from the de Hane ledgers at night and sending them to Della Faille and, moreover, of stealing the company contract which allegedly stated that Della Faille was a partner of the de Hane company and was not allowed to trade on his own account. The documents of the trial, held at the Antwerp aldermen's bench and the Council of Brabant, show that Della Faille systematically lowered amounts due to the de Hane in his accounts and took out his own capital when it became clear that the bankruptcy of an Italian merchant who owed large sums to the de Hane severely threatened the company. He even forged four account books to that end.[48] When the de

Hane wanted to liquidate the company in 1560, Della Faille continued trading with company capital. Two years later, Della Faille pulled all of his capital out of the partnership. The legal proceedings between the former partners lasted at least until 1576; the de Hane brothers were never able to recoup the full amount of the losses resulting from Della Faille's opportunism. They could only lament that 'they were cheated by a former servant, with a very small capital, who was able to use company credit to amass such riches'.[49]

Much of the capital which Della Faille managed to collect from his licit and less licit enterprises was invested in the company he started with his brother Jacob and his son-in-law Robrecht van Eeckeren in 1558. Several other family members, including Anna de Hane, Jan's mother-in-law (and sister of Jan and Daniel who litigated against Jan Della Faille) invested in the company under the form of deposits on interest. After three years and five months the partnership yielded a profit of 100 per cent, mainly in the trade with Seville. Ninety-two per cent of the total capital plus profit was reinvested in a new company which would last until 1565.[50] Between 1574 and 1578, and 1579 and 1582, Della Faille worked without partners but accepted interest-bearing deposits (most of them at 6.25 per cent, but some at 8 or 9 per cent) from family members, personnel and persons unrelated to his family or firm.[51] The annual profits amounted to 10.1 per cent and 7.6 per cent annually. Jan's eldest son and successor, Maarten, started a new company after his father's death in 1582 under a different form. He took in three partners who also acted as agents in Verona, Venice and London for ten years. One of them, Jan Borne, could not pay his full share, and so Maarten advanced part of Borne's company share at a 6.25 per cent interest. As his father had done, Maarten also accepted deposits from family and outsiders. Moreover, Maarten and his agents took on loans to cope with the slow trade in those difficult years.[52] Despite the slow trade, the company managed to collect an annual profit of 19 per cent.

The subsequent Della Faille partnerships collected at least 74 per cent of their respective partnership's capital from family.[53] The first two partnerships were entirely funded by family capital. When Della Faille undertook the next two companies on his own, but he relied more on outsider deposits.

Brulez argues that such partnerships were anything but new in the sixteenth century. Their numbers, however, were rising rapidly and increasing numbers of smaller merchants were setting up partnerships and not always with partners from their own family or region.[54] Did the partnership constitute a way for Netherlandish merchants to become active in long-distance trade? Were they able to attract outsider finance and to co-operate with foreign traders? Medieval Italy is considered the birthplace of modern capitalism, based on its development of double entry bookkeeping, bills of exchange, limited liability and the holding company.[55] This chapter will evaluate the role of family and outside funding, the partnership connections with foreign merchants and the structure and idiosyncrasies of Netherlandish partnerships as evidenced in partnership contracts, merchant documents, notarial acts, trial files and local urban and central laws.[56] Where possible, comparisons will be made with Italian, Spanish and south German partnership structures.

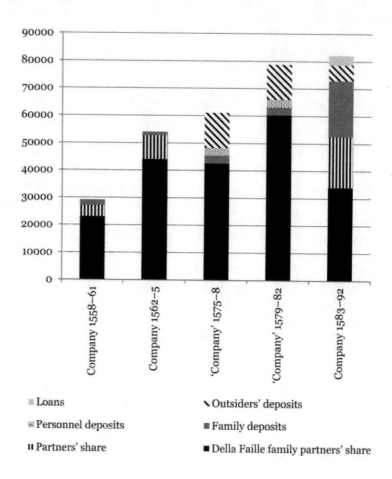

Figure 3.1: **Capital structure of the Della Faille companies, in £ gr. Fl.**
Source: **Own calculations based on Brulez,** *De Firma Della Faille.*

Merchants entered into partnerships to execute commercial operations for which they lacked resources to execute on their own, and to diversify risk. Evidence from medieval Italian companies shows how a division of tasks was established among partners and agents; partners invested capital and/or labour in their partnership. Partnerships formalized relations within families and with outsiders. As such, partnerships combined agency and financing functions.[57] Partners could perform agent duties, at home or abroad, and were less likely be inefficient, since their remuneration was contingent on the partnerships' performance. However, as the Della Faille example shows, partnerships did not eliminate principal agent problems. In a more positive sense, partners could be granted substantial freedom in decision making (by which they could reap market opportunities without having to contact the principal in advance) and they could be entrusted with more complex tasks.[58] Ogilvie and Gelderblom argue that a combination of kinship and friends' networks, contractual instruments, standardized written evidence of transactions and the possibility of formal litigation against agents provided assurance against agent/ partner opportunism.[59] Wijnroks demonstrated that family relations could be important for the continuity of Netherlandish merchant companies in trade with the Baltic and Russia in the 1560s to the 1580s. The typically large age differences between fathers and sons entailed that fathers took care in selecting spouses for their daughters, not least as able sons-in-law could overcome the age gap between father and son and keep the company operational after the pater familias's death until the sons were able to take over.[60]

The relationship between company and family has been a fundamental issue in the literature since Max Weber identified the separation of the household and business as the key to capitalism in its uniquely Occidental form and placed the origins of such depersonalization of market relations firmly in the medieval Italian cities. Yet family partnerships and relations were much more persistent.[61] Even in the era of corporate capitalism, family partnerships retained importance.[62] As Barry Supple has noted:

> In a business world where the unknown was a credit risk and the entrepreneur's success lay so much in the hands of men beyond his immediate control, the ties of the family, of religion and of the social community which went with both, were the cement of commercial confidence and commercial organization.[63]

The prevalence of family firms was due to the generally low need for large-scale organizations in most economic sectors, familial collective responsibility for debts, and the relative advantage of such firms in cost and decision structure (as opposed to public and bureaucratic organizations). In short: 'The business family had to be efficient or it did not survive',[64] Gelderblom turns the argument of collective responsibility around: because of collective responsibility, 'company contracts were often written between entrepreneurs with social ties between them'.[65] Family members could be relied upon because, should they scheme to act opportunistically against family interest, they faced being cut off from much-needed family support.[66] However, children and kin were not always well skilled for a merchant career and did not automatically measure up to expectations.[67] Relying on kin only went so far: merchants often needed information, expertise and finance which their kinship network could not always readily provide.[68]

Our small sample of company contracts and the Netherlandish companies exploring trade with the eastern Baltic and Russia in the 1560s and 1570s allows for quantitative evaluation of the role of kinship in Netherlandish companies in the sixteenth century; this can be compared with the little data that actually provide evidence for the importance of kinship in partnerships.

Sources

This chapter builds on a broad range of sources. The Antwerp notarial acts provided several partnership contracts and documents pertaining to partnerships.[69] Prior the publication of this book, Bram Van Hofstraeten presented a working paper on sixteenth-century partnerships registered in notarial deeds. His sample is larger (144 contracts for the period 1480–1620). His results and findings are consistent with mine.[70] The Collectanea (aldermen's deeds not included in the aldermen's deeds registers) and certificates (various attestations recorded by a city secretary) yield similar information.[71] The judicial archives of the Antwerp bench of aldermen, the Council of Brabant and the Great Council of Mechelen supplied (limited) evidence on partnerships through the sentences and preserved trial files.[72] Not many disputes on partnerships and their liquidation made it into these judicial archives and Antwerp jurists were relatively late in dealing with legal questions about commercial partnerships. Merchants were reluctant to turn to the urban court to solve their partnership conflicts and when they did so, they usually requested appointment of commissioners who would consult the partnership's books and draw up a definitive balance.[73] Moreover, as in England, partnerships were not phrased as such in legal terms but were considered as a creditor preference dispute or a liquidation of accounts.[74]

The Antwerp Costuymen (customary law texts) of 1570 (In Antiquis), 1582 (Impressae) and 1608 (Compilatae) formulated rules for partnerships.[75] While the 1608 Costuymen are more extensive than the edition of 1582, they were less influential because they were not printed and are rather voluminous.[76] Moreover, they were not homologated by the central authorities but were, nonetheless, enforced by the city.[77] Data on the partnerships and companies which became active in the trade with the eastern Baltic area and Russia in the 1560s and 1570s have been coded from Wijnroks's detailed description of that line of trade.[78] Miscellaneous information comes from secondary literature on particular merchants and the original letters, account books and other original documents of these merchants. This is the first systematic analysis of sixteenth-century Antwerp partnerships, albeit coming from rather heterogeneous sources, owing to the scarce and biased survival of partnership data. Throughout the chapter, the Antwerp partnerships will be compared with those of other merchant groups (particularly south German and Medina del Campo traders).

Registration of partnership contracts was not compulsory in sixteenth-century Antwerp.[79] In the later fourteenth century, Luccese merchants in Bruges and in their hometown had their partnerships registered by the nation consuls and the merchant court in Lucca to determine debt liability when necessary.[80] Lübeck merchants relied on their hometown government for registration of equity contracts in the so-called 'societates register'.[81] Gelderblom observes that this practice of public recording had declined by the fifteenth century because merchants were allowed to privately register their partnership contracts. These private documents could be used as legal proof in court.[82] This explains why so few of the Antwerp partnerships were actually recorded. Only in the beginning of the seventeenth century did Antwerp legislation aim at rendering such registration obligatory: the 1608 Costuymen stipulated that all partnership contracts had to be registered by a notary of the Bourse;[83] included in the registration was to be the name of the partnership, the names of all partners and their division of tasks, so that 'anyone knows on what footing the partnership works and be more assured of it'. If the contract was not recorded by a notary, the contract would be invalid and none of the partners could pursue legal action against his companions or outsiders on behalf of the partnership.[84]

Hence, these registered company contracts are not representative for all partnership contracts because, owing to their registration, they are likely to pertain to contracts between strangers who, not knowing each other, felt that registration was prudent. Intra-familial partnerships probably went unrecorded. Sixteenth-century Antwerp private merchant account books, which could be used to document partnership relations, are relatively thin in this respect. Hence, the anomalous registered partnerships are the only way to develop insight into partnership contract design. Twenty-seven commercial partnership contracts could be found in the sample of sources.[85] This lower number is due to the relatively low survival rate of pre-1580 Antwerp notarial deeds. When this result is compared with the late eighteenth-century partnership contracts registered by notaries (for whom many more deeds are preserved), twenty-seven is not a poor result; between 1794 and 1814 Antwerp notaries registered sixty-nine such contracts. [86] The contracts in the sample are dated between 1526 and 1588; most of them between 1530 and 1563.

Contract Design

Like the Florentine and south German company contracts, the Antwerp partnership contracts resembled one another but did not follow a standard model.[87] Several clauses were standard stock in such contracts but registration procedure was sufficiently flexible to add partnership-specific articles. The following table shows the presence of contract particulars and clauses.

Table 3.1: Contract clauses in partnership deeds

Contract clause	Percentage of contracts containing this clause
Partnership identification	
Names of the partners	100.0%
Specific company name	14.8%
Partnership activity specified	74.1%
Duration	77.8%
Partnership capital input and output	
Partner investments	66.7%
Promise of collateral provided by the partners	51.9%
Marriage of one of the partners (dowry)	7.4%
Rules for profit division	74.1%
Division of the partnership's costs	70.3%
Daily operations	
Task division among partners and agents	70.3%
Partner exclusivity	29.6%
Providing accounts	70.3%
Rules about bookkeeping	22.2%
Rules for standing surety and extending loans	22.2%
Partnership termination	
Death of one of the partners (inheritance)	40.7%
Arbitrage in inter-partner conflict	3.7%
Dismissal clause	3.7%
Special liability clause	14.8%
Penalty specified	37.0%

Source: **Database author and supra.**

Two-thirds of the preserved partnerships specified the names of the partners, their capital input, distribution of profits and costs, the duration of the contract and the activity (although mostly in generic terms),[88] and stipulated the rules about partnership accounts. Four of these contracts were recorded in the form of an archaic chirograph: the text was written twice, with specific signs in the middle of the document. The document was then cut through in the middle and could be matched by re-uniting the signs on the edges of the two copies.[89]

Creating Partnerships

Partner Identities

Most of the twenty-seven partnerships involved two partners.[90] The largest of the partnerships united six merchants. The Netherlandish merchant partnerships trading in the Baltic and Russia had, on average, at least one partner more.[91] McLean and Padgett have observed, using the 1427 Catasto and company balances, that Florentine companies of more than three partners were relatively exceptional.[92] The risks inherent to the unlimited liability of these Florentine companies explain this maximum; the more partners, the larger the risk that one of the partner's losses would afflict his partners.[93] South German companies usually had three to four partners and at a maximum eight.[94]

The next step is to identify the ties between these partners: were they mostly family members? Did these Netherlandish merchants establish partnership ties with foreign traders?[95] Nineteen of the twenty-seven partnership contracts united merchants who did not share a family tie. This partner unfamiliarity could well explain why the contract was registered by a notary. This would mean that the sample of partnership contracts is biased towards more unfamiliar partnerships. The family partnerships in the sample included brothers working together and fathers and mothers partnering with their sons. Maarten Della Faille teamed up with his brother-in-law and a nephew.[96] The data for the Baltic and Russia partnerships are less susceptible to this registration bias since these partnerships are reconstructed from a wide range of sources. Of ties between merchants acting together (as recorded) in thirty-five partnerships in the Baltic and Russia trade, 24.8 per cent were (documented) family ties. This is a surprising finding, given the importance attached to kinship in the governance of trade. Although 24.8 per cent is not negligible, the other three-quarters of all partner relations were not structured by family ties. Hence, we can clearly observe that merchant partnerships often looked beyond the family in search for partners performing finance and agency functions. Little comparative quantitative data is available to calibrate this finding. McLean and Padgett have found that 30 per cent of all partner dyads in Florence involved family members.[97] Grassby's collective biography of English businessmen between 1580 and 1740 puts the number of family (immediate family plus kin) relations among partners much higher: 51 per cent.[98] Van Doosselaere has shown how family ties became more important in Genoese debt and equity contracts between 1154 and 1315 (growing from less than 5 per cent of all ties between investors and agents in notarized contracts to slightly over 20 per cent).[99] Likewise, only 20 per cent of notarized partnership contracts from Medina del Campo (1550–75) concerned familial partnerships.[100]

Sometimes family members made sure that the general public knew that, although they had previously co-operated in a partnership, they no longer did so, or had never done so. Pauwels Timmerman had a certificate made up in 1566 concerning the proprietorship of goods sent to Narva which had been confiscated, by the king of Denmark, in the neighbourhood of Reval (now Tallinn) and brought to Stockholm. He testified that he no longer had a partnership with his brothers, Godtschalck in Lübeck and Laureys in Riga. After having closed his account with them in 1551 he did not trade with them anymore.[101]

The fact that the majority of registered partnerships were not contracted between family members is highly significant. It means that native merchants in Antwerp had the opportunity to finance their enterprises with capital from outside the limited family pool, thereby widening the scope of potential merchants with limited family means.[102] Did Netherlandish merchants attract foreign capital and expertise through partnership contracts?[103] According to Brulez, such international partnerships grew in importance in the sixteenth century.[104] Seventeen of the twenty-seven partnership contracts were signed among Netherlandish merchants only, four were between foreigners (all from the same country of origin)[105] and six partnerships can be considered as mixed partnerships (involving Hanseatic and Italian merchants). Of the thirty-two partnerships including Netherlandish merchants in the Baltic and Russian trade, twenty-one were constituted by Netherlandish partners only, eleven recruited foreign partners, almost exclusively Hanseats and a few Italians. The Hanseats, operating on their home market, provided information and agency services, while the few Italians mainly provided capital. Keeping the bias towards partnership contracts between strangers in mind, the degree of partnership internationalization remained fairly limited.[106]

One of these 'international' partnerships is well documented. Frederik Van der Molen, active in trade with Italy, started a partnership with his nephew Pieter Waarloos and the Italian merchant Bernardo di Zanchi from Verona in 1532.[107] Before that date he had co-operated with three Netherlanders: Pieter Waarloos, Adam van Riebeke and Andries Maiol. Maiol was particularly exasperated by his exclusion from the new partnership.[108] How Van der Molen met the Venice-based Zanchi is unclear, but we know that Van der Molen was trained by his cousin Cornelis van Bombergen in Venice and stayed there until at least 1507.[109] The two may have met during Van der Molen's apprenticeship.[110] The first partnership with Zanchi ended in 1536 and was renewed for another four years. The renewal is rather surprising, since Van der Molen was not altogether satisfied with Zanchi's performance as a partner and agent. Zanchi sent the bi-annual partnership account to Antwerp at the end of 1533, reporting that the Venice branch had collected a large gross profit of 20,000 ducats, but in 1534 Van der Molen was informed that much of the reported profits consisted of bad debts in

Turkey.[111] In their 1534 testament Van der Molen and his wife envisioned the foundation of a new £3,000 gr. Fl. family company in which all of their children would be shareholders and which would be governed by the two eldest sons, Pieter and Cornelis. Moreover, Van der Molen and his wife urged their heirs to end the agreement with Zanchi after 1536.[112]

Frederik Van der Molen died in February 1536, but his heirs did not yet suspend the partnership with Zanchi: their letters from March 1538 until March 1540 are still signed as 'eredi di Federicho de Molin e Bernardo di Zanchi'.[113] Complaints about the Zanchi family continued: they were eager in showing off their wealth, a practice frowned upon by the Van der Molen.[114] In the eyes of the Zanchi, this might have been regular behaviour to signal their creditworthiness. In any case, in 1540 the partnership was discontinued and the Van der Molen started their own family company. It was decided that the Van der Molen would receive four-fifths of all receivables and stock and the Zanchi one-fifth.[115] Even with one of the younger brothers, Daniel, in Venice, the settlement between the partners dragged on. Pieter urged the Zanchi to solicit the debtors, divide everything in the presence of Daniel and then turn over their part of the company balance.[116] It is unknown whether the Van der Molen eventually obtained their money or if they had to resort to judicial settlement. The latter is rather unlikely given that Pieter shared his father's opinion about lawyers: 'he who does not turn to lawyers can expect great riches'.[117]

Partnership Goals and Identity

Goals of the partnerships were often recorded in the relevant partnership contract but were almost always phrased in very generic terms, a trait of partnership contracts also observed in the Florentine and south German companies.[118] As such, these contracts were not specific enough to protect partners against fraudulent agents and other risks, since clear guidelines and limitations were not specified in the contract; they were incomplete and relatively open contracts.[119] Willem Borremans and Janne Verheyden would trade 'in the German lands and in Switzerland and in all places on this side of the sea which they seemed fit for trade'.[120] Alaert de Cock from 's-Hertogenbosch and Hans Reynenborch, both merchants in Antwerp, signed an agreement for a partnership which would specialize in linen from 's-Hertogenbosch.[121] Few partnership contracts were explicit about the partnership's name: only the Schetz company stipulated its name: Gaspar Schetz and brothers.[122] The Costuymen were not explicit about company name giving either. The company name was much more an issue in south German and Medina del Campo partnerships: all company documents had to bear the name of the company (the names of the important partners).[123] This does not mean that the company did not have its own identity: in fact, company marks were included in some partnership contracts and all merchandise of the company needed to be identified by these markings.[124]

When merchants signed documents together, they were considered to be partners. Jan Gamel explicitly demanded that neither Pauwels van Houte nor Peter Sobrecht, his co-partners, use his name in the company.[125] Was he trying to stay off the books as a silent investor, so as to avoid liability for the company? Christiaen Zuyderman, who would stay in Antwerp, and Herman Van Reeden, who would travel to London, agreed that they would put only their own name on bills of exchange.[126] Michiel Anthoine was held liable for the debts of his partnership with Anthoine le Dieu and Adam Testart who were trading with the city of Lyon. Among the pieces of evidence advanced by the partnership creditors and preserved in the trial file are two copies of letters which clearly stated that Michiel Anthoine was a member of the partnership, because the letters were signed as: 'Vous serviteurs et amis Michael Anthoine Anthoine le Dieu et compagnons d' Anvers'. But Michiel Anthoine argued that the partnership was not valid, because Testart and Le Dieu had made false promises about sending merchandise from Lyon to Antwerp, they had never transferred their capital input and had already been insolvent at the time of signing the partnership agreement.[127] Christoffel Pruynen would underwrite all insurance policies for his partnership by the following rule: 'Je, Christoffel Pruenen pour et au nom de ma compagnie dasseurance...'[128] Hence, the use of a corporate name, constituted by the names of the partners, was sufficient to demonstrate collective liability, even if it was not explicitly specified in the partnership contract.[129]

Partnership Finance

Let us now consider the capital inputs by the partners in their partnerships. The total capital says less about the scale of the enterprise and more about its initial ambitions and the hierarchy among the partners. Moreover, partnerships obtained much more capital from credit (sales and through financial instruments) than from its equity.[130] Roelant Marijn, Johan Gruter and Paul des Champs set up a partnership to trade in the Baltic area. The three men invested £2,500 gr. Fl. of starting capital. The debt book of the company shows that by the early 1570s this company had a cash account totalling more than £40,000 Fl. gr and had a commodities account worth £30,000 gr. Fl. Their company capital was worth twenty-eight times its equity capital![131] Hence, this one example shows that substantial leverage was possible with limited equity capital.

Sixteen of the twenty-seven partnership contracts specify each partner's share in the company.[132] Equity capital ranged from £36.7 to £52,776 gr. Fl.[133] In eight of these partnerships the equity capital was spread evenly among the partners; in the other sixteen the capital was divided unequally. In two contracts, contractual provisions were made for capital injections through a dowry if one of the partners would marry during the partnership.[134] Robrecht Cools was free to invest (part of) the dowry should he marry in the course of the partnership. If Cools were to subsequently die during the partnership, his father would pay the heirs, when requested to do so, in cash within two months and the rest in merchandise and company credits. If Cools's new spouse died, her dowry would have to remain in the partnership until its termination.[135] The 1608 Costuymen stipulated that should a partner withdraw his equity capital before termination of the partnership, he would have to pay damages and 8 per cent interest on the withdrawn equity capital to the other partners.[136]

The merchant and financier Geeraerd Gramaye was among the first people in the 1560s to set up a large company which would trade directly between Antwerp and the eastern Baltic area, bypassing the Hanseats.[137] He started a partnership ('Sweden Company') in 1562 with Arnoldus Rosenberger, the ambassador of the king of Sweden, Eric XIV, and Herman Boelman, an immigrant from Reval who had settled in Antwerp and had married a niece of Gramaye; the partnership would mainly sell luxuries – tapestries, gold leather, gold and silver silk cloth, jewellery and precious stones – to the court of Eric XIV. But the king proved to be a slow payer and the partnership encountered grave difficulties in retrieving the moneys owed. Moreover, several ships owned by the partnership and/or carrying its commodities were seized during the Northern Seven Years' War (1563–70). Gramaye supplied much of the capital, while Boelman put his commercial knowledge of the Baltic area to use. The second partnership ('Eastland Company'), consisting of the same persons, imported grain and iron from the Baltic. Several parties of wheat and rye imported by the company were sold to another partnership of Gramaye and two of his agents; this wheat and rye were then re-exported to Lisbon, where part of the proceeds was then used to buy and export sugar. The salt partnership consisting of Nicolas Jongelinck, Gramaye and the Italian Nicolas Doria tried to speculate on the price rises of salt but was not very successful and closed with losses of £711 gr. Fl. For his final partnership ('Sweden and Narva Company'), Gramaye had to resort to Italian angel investors (the Genoese Jacomo Cattaneo and Francisco and Pascal Spinola) to finance the loan since his other two partnerships, despite being owed large sums, were not providing him enough capital to front the 60,000 guilders to the Swedish king on his own, should he dare to take that risk. Jacomo Cattaneo paid his share plus half that of Francisco Spinola. Pascal Spinola paid his share of the loan directly to the king. His last company was also active in the commodity trade with Narva. Pascal Spinola advanced the capital necessary to purchase the goods for export and was to be repaid in bonds of Gramaye. But it took several years before Spinola realized his investment in the form of the goods from Narva.

Partnership shares were expressed in monetary values but were not necessarily paid in cash.[138] In 1550 Willem Borremans promised his new partner, Jan Verheyden, to report which goods, some of them still in Paris, he would invest in their new partnership.[139] Gaspar, Melchior and Balthazar Schetz invested all the debts and credits of their former company, their German mines and a house in Leipzig in their new company with Christoffel Pruynen and Adriaen van Hilst; the company would trade with Germany and Adriaen van Hilst would reside in Leipzig.[140] Not all partners were able to invest the full amount of their share in the company. Jan Borne could provide only £4,650 gr. Fl. of his £8,000 gr. Fl. share; Maarten Della Faille, one of the other partners, lent him the rest of his share at a 6.25 per cent interest. Christoffel Pruynen and Adriaen van Hilst, junior partners and managers in the Schetz company, were allowed to recruit other investors to participate in their share of the partnership.[141]

The Antwerp Costuymen (Impressae 1582 and Compilatae 1608) specified that profit and losses of a partnership had to be shared according to each invested share, unless articulated otherwise.[142] A percentage of 74.1 per cent of the partnership contracts mentioned rules for profit division. Profits could be divided pro rata of the invested capital or according to another distribution. In 1540 Jan de Langaigne and his mother, Maria Chatoru, agreed to set up a company dealing in canvas and paper: the widow Chatoru supplied £1,200 gr. Fl. while her son provided only £400 gr. Fl. Despite the fact that Jan would invest all his energies in running the company, he received a profit share equal only to his capital share.[143] Reynairt Muer, a merchant active on Gotland, in the Baltic Sea, fared better: despite his 25 per cent share in the partnership with Govairt Robrechtszone van Huesden from 's-Hertogenbosch, he would receive half of the profits or losses.[144] Very peculiar profit division rules were put into writing for the partnership of Hans Papenbruch and Gerard Paul from Aachen, Ancelme Odeur from 's-Hertogenbosch, Pierre Rousee from Arras and Nicolas de Marretz from Tournai. The five merchants would travel with their merchandise to Spain and some of them could travel to Peru. The five invested unequal sums in the partnership, but profits would be distributed equally. If one of the partners were to find gold in Peru, all profits from his find would go to the company; likewise, if one of them opted to fight the Muslim Infidels, he could keep one-third of the booty for himself, but the other two-thirds would have to be turned over to the company.[145] Hans Bockele and Wouter Pottey invested different amounts but would split the profits equally.[146] The insurance partnerships (1559 and 1563) of the Schetz brothers and Christoffel Pruynen were obliged by the partnership contract, which stipulated that part of the company's capital and profits would remain in the hands of the partnership manager for two years after the partnership's termination as payment of eventual average and costs. After two years, this capital would be returned to the shareholders. [147] Profits were not necessarily paid in cash: Jan Cools and his son Robrecht agreed that profit payments could also be paid in merchandise and debts owed.[148]

Division of the partnership costs was specified in 70 per cent of all partnership contracts. The types of costs described in the contracts were wide ranging: board and lodging, warehouse and commercial building rent, servants, clothing, transport, letters, etc. Some expenses were paid by the partners; others were paid for by the company.[149] In 1561, Melchior Volger started a partnership with Thomas Chamata and Peeter de Zeelander. The company would try to obtain a government privilege for dredging and deepening river bottoms in the king's lands for ten years. It was agreed that Volger would pay all travel and boarding and lodging costs and for half of all the necessary equipment for their enterprise; Chamata and de Zeelander would pay for the other half of the equipment. Volger would be paid back from the first profits the company would collect.[150]

The Schetz company for trade with Germany not only divided profits at the end of the partnership; in the first (1553–8) and second companies (1559–63) annual dividends were also paid out: during the first partnership all partners were allowed to withdraw £200 gr. Fl. per annum from the partnership's earnings; this amount was lowered to £100 gr. Fl. in the second partnership.[151]

Partnership Operation

Most (70.3 per cent) partnership contracts circumscribed a division of tasks between the partners and possibly personnel. Hans Bockele, the junior partner, would move to Nuremberg to manage his partnership's affairs there.[152] While travelling to Spain, those members of the aforementioned Papenbruch–Paul–Odeur–Rousee–de Marretz partnership who contributed smaller shares to the partnership's equity capital were obliged to get up earlier to set the table! All partners in a company were legally considered as each other's factors.[153] None of these tasks were described in detail as much discretionary power was bestowed on the respective partners. Parallel to the south German partnerships, Low Countries partnerships were more about the internal division of tasks and labour than about capital.[154]

Since most partnership contracts did not provide any clauses about the actual organization and activities of the business, these sources do not reveal many details about the corporate governance and decision-making structure of the partnerships.[155] We know that Maarten Della Faille and his partners needed a 75 per cent majority (three of four partners in favour) for important decisions (for example, hiring additional staff in one of the branches).[156] Within the Schetz company, it was not allowed to enter into important contracts without notification and permission of the other partners.[157] Internal differences would be resolved by majority voting. A majority was also needed to continue the partnership after six years.[158] The brothers Schetz also had a share in the company of Gilbert van Schoonbeke, which organized peat-digging operations near Amersfoort from 1550 onwards. In that company the number of shares determined how many votes each partner had in decisions.[159]

Twenty-two per cent of the contracts laid down ground rules for the bookkeeping arrangements of the partnership. Jan Cools and his son Robrecht decided to draw up account books and Christiaen Zuyderman and Herman Van Reeden would record all their costs in a designated 'oncostboeck'.[160] Michiel Anthoine was appointed by his co-partners to keep 'ung livre de raison' which he would present upon request from the other partners and, if necessary, make copies from the original.[161] In 1550, three merchants testified on behalf of the widow of a merchant that 'it is an old custom that all partners should have access to the company books and can copy all those entries pertaining to their own transactions'.[162] The Compilatae Costuymen also declared that partners had to have access to the company books at all times or else could have copies sent to them.[163] The popular bookkeeping manual of Jan Ympyn, *Nieuwe instructive ende bewijs der looffelijcker consten des rekenboecks* (1543), taught two ways of recording partnership transaction in double entry accounts books: in a new and separate partnership book or in the merchant's own account book. If a merchant wished to record the partnership in his own books, he should write down the beginning and end date of the partnership and then enter all the capital inputs of the partners on the credit side and debit the partnership. Ympyn argues that it is better to start a separate account book for the partnership, so as to avoid quarrels and jealousy among the partners.[164] By the late sixteenth century, recording partnership agreements in account books had become accepted practice: a notary even copied the partnership contract of Maarten Della Faille from Maarten's account book.[165] Not only the partners could request extracts from the partnership account books; Thierry de Fourmestraux, a merchant from Lille active in Antwerp, declared in the account book of the company (known as Jan and Nicolas Fourmestreaux, Anthoine de Tieffries and Company) that he was a partner. Robert du Bosquel, an agent of the company, had written that he had sold a party of woad to Henrick Peters Collaert, who had requested Thierry de Fourmestreaux's testimony.[166]

Moreover, 70 per cent of all partnership contracts stipulated regular drawing up of accounts provided by the partners.[167] The partners in the Schetz company presented an annual account. Adriaen Van Hilst, the manager in Leipzig, had to send his account to Antwerp by February, when the company closed the main account of the previous year.[168] In 1566, the year of Iconoclasm and political conflict, the partners deemed the circumstances too turbulent to draw up an annual account and opted to combine the book years of 1566 and 1567.[169] The Van der Molen–Zanchi partnership preferred bi-annual accounts.[170] Partners were not the only ones who were required to deliver accounts; agents working on behalf of the partnership also had to provide such reports.[171] Nicolas Verjuys travelled to Stockholm on behalf of the company of Christoffel Pruynen and the brothers Schetz. He was obliged to register all stock he took with him and all transactions he executed as an agent. At the end of his journey, his double entry journal was checked by his principals.[172]

Partnership Duration: Long-Term or Single Venture?

Most of the partnership contracts (77.8 per cent) mentioned a specific duration for the partnership in question (number of years or an event that would end the partnership, for example when all partners had returned from their journeys). This limited partner liability to the transactions executed during the partnership period.[173] According to the mathematician Gielis van den Hoecke in his *In Arithmetica* published in 1537, there was no difference in rules between partnerships with specified duration ('metter tyt') and those without ('sonder tyt').[174] The terms of partnerships with a specified duration ranged between two and ten years; the average partnership was to last for 5.05 years (median = four years).[175] In Medina del Campo, the average duration of partnerships was four years; south German partnerships lasted 5.2 years.[176] McLean and Padgett found shorter periods (between two and three years) for Florentine companies in the first quarter of the fifteenth century, resembling short-term ventures such as the *commenda*.[177] Although most of these partnership periods were relatively short, they acted as instruments for flexibility and in cases of good performance the partnership was often renewed.[178] The Schetz company contracts described that in the sixth and final year of the partnership, the partners could settle the accounts or start a new partnership if a majority vote was obtained. The Schetz partnership was renewed twice between 1553 and 1569.[179]

The duration of the co-operation could be limited to one journey, as in the Peru trip of Papenbruch & Co.[180] The final accounting and profit dividing would take place when all had returned to Antwerp. In October 1545 Jan Geldolf, a merchant from Aachen operating out of Antwerp, signed an agreement with the Antwerp innkeeper Cornelis. Janss.: Janss. would travel on a ship (which was currently docked at Arnemuiden) to Bordeaux, where he would sell goods and buy new ones with the proceedings.[181] But it is not clear whether Janss. actually travelled to Bordeaux because a month later he and Geldolf jointly appointed Jehan Otte from Antwerp to travel on the same ship to Bordeaux. If Otte could not sell the goods for cash, he was to buy wine or another 'profitable product'. Geldolf and Janss. would send letters of advice on which merchandise Otte should buy.[182]

Such one-time ventures are usually called participations.[183] Merchants participated and let others – staff, family, etc. – participate in a venture in return for a share of the profits. Maarten Della Faille used this technique often, but never in the core business of his firm (textiles) and always in sectors with which he was not familiar, for example the grain ships sent to Majorca, Naples and Genoa in the 1580s and early 1590s.[184] In this line of trade Maarten lacked specialized knowledge and significant capital was necessary to organize such maritime shipments.[185] Herman Janssens was involved in maritime trade to the French ports of Rouen, La Rochelle and Bordeaux, the Portuguese capital of Lisbon and the Canary Islands. His journal lists all his shares in different ventures; in 1564 he, Jan Verhorst, Jan van Ryc and Symon Sohari together had a share in a shipment to Rouen.[186] In Janssens's case such participations ran parallel with his share ownership of ships.[187] Jan van Immerseele would build his entire commercial enterprise on such ventures and commission trading, which allowed him to organize substantial transactions with limited capital of his own.[188] In such participations, the partner was incentivized by making him party to the outcome of the venture. In most participations of this type, one of the partners did the buying while the other sold the goods; likewise, one partner could invest without performing duties on behalf of the partnership. Participations were quite flexible: no formality or official contract was needed and international combinations could be organized through correspondence. As such, the participation closely resembled the commenda, where the travelling partner supplied his labour and one or more passive partners invested capital (money or goods). Profits were divided according to a fixed formula: one-third for the travelling partner and two-thirds for the passive investors.[189] The participation was more flexible: the division of profits was subject to negotiation. In participations both parties performed tasks to bring about the transaction.[190]

The 1608 Costuymen determined that when a group of persons bought commodities together, collectively floated a bill of exchange or jointly lent money to others, in hopes of a collective profit, the group was de jure considered as a partnership, rendering every partner liable for the partnership and for the other partners.[191] Hence, a legal framework for such ventures was well in place. Through such a venture, merchants could quickly seize market opportunities and limit risks.[192] Brulez argues that an increase in participation was one of the causes of the democratization of long-distance trade.[193] But not all merchants were so eager to participate in such ventures: the Van der Molen repeatedly turned down participation offers from their most important client, the Genoese merchant Jeronimo Azeretto, in which he sought to participate in temporary ventures to sell commodities in return for a share of profit. Apparently, they preferred a guaranteed commission fee over an uncertain venture.[194] This shows how different merchants made different decisions concerning the governance of their trade, depending on the risks they were willing to take.Consecutive partnership contracts are difficult to find in the fragmentarily preserved notarial archives, but a few partnership series could be traced. In 1550 Willem Borremans, a jeweller, and Jan Verheyden, a mercer, decided to pool their merchandise in the Low Countries and France so as to trade in Germany and Switzerland; they did not specify the duration or the capital input of each partner.[195] Ten years later, the two partners recorded a new agreement, in which each would invest 1,000 guilders in the new partnership, which would last for four years.[196] Only a year later, the two partners renegotiated the terms; they would raise the partnership's capital significantly. Verheyden would invest £400 gr. Fl.; Borremans supplied the same amount, plus £225 gr. Fl. for which he would receive annual interest of 7.5 per cent.[197]

Partnership Liability

Hansmann, Kraakman and Squire, in their analysis of the history of partnership liability, distinguish entity shielding or asset partitioning from owner shielding.[198] The former protects partnership and firm assets from creditor claims on the constituent partners while the latter shields a partner's personal assets from partnership creditors.[199] Crucial in both types of liability division is the earmarking of particular assets for claims by various creditors. The authors deem the former more important than the (more researched) owner shielding for the development of business ventures. When entity shielding was sufficiently developed it allowed for lower credit monitoring costs for partnerships, quicker bankruptcy proceedings, more stability and potential development of a market for company shares.

The subsequent versions of the Antwerp Costuymen provided little regulation for partnerships. The 1570 version contained one rule on partnerships, the 1582 Impressae nine and the 1608 Compilatae twenty-seven.[200] All three versions established joint and several liability: all partners were accountable for company debts and creditors could recoup (part of) such debt from the other partners.[201] Entity shielding was also provided by the law: partnership assets could be confiscated only for the particular debts of a partner from that partner's share of the partnership's proceedings (after all company debts and costs were paid for).[202] Hansmann et al. would characterize such a legal regime as strong entity shielding: company creditors and the other partners would be paid before the particular creditors of one of the partners.[203] As such, partnerships in the Low Countries entirely resembled south German companies which took the form of joint and several general partnerships.[204]

The 1608 Costuymen provided limited liability for passive investors and deposits (see infra)[205] Partners were not liable for debts from commercial transactions or bills of exchange if they had been executed by one of their partners without their knowledge or being recorded in the company's books. This clause partially protected partners against opportunistic behaviour.[206] Compulsory partnership contract registration, procedures in case a partner died and rules for periodic and final accounting were implemented as well. According to the

1551 *turbe* – a formal declaration by a group of attorneys, jurists, merchants, notaries, and/or brokers on commercial practices which held legal force[207] – and the 1582 Costuymen all partners were regarded as each other's factors.[208] Similarly, south German partners gave each other powers of representation.[209] The 1608 Costuymen explicitly prescribed that all contracts concluded on behalf of the partnership were valid only if the agent was entitled to close them.[210] The partnership was not yet a separate legal entity.[211] It was still identified by the main manager-partner and the other partners were considered as its creditors.[212]

The only turbe relating to partnerships (1551) declared that a letter obligatory signed in the name of a partnership could be paid by every partner only if the signing partner was allowed to write such a bill.[213] The partnership contract of Hans Papenbruch and Co. (1535) prescribed that only Hans Papenbruch and Ancelme Odeur were allowed to sign bills obligatory for the partnership. If the value of such a bill exceeded £50 gr. Fl., they needed permission from the other partners.[214]

External liability, binding partners together for debts concluded with third parties, defines partnerships. Interestingly, sixteenth-century Antwerp (and in general early modern) partnership contracts are much more explicit about internal partnership relations than about external liability.[215] In the case of sixteenth-century Antwerp, the Antwerp Costuymen were sufficient clear on external liability so that partnership contracts could forgo stipulating articles concerning such liability. Specific liability clauses are scarce (four references) in the partnership contract sample, but when they do appear, they show remarkable agreements. The brothers Schetz were only liable for their capital input in the company, 'even if the laws stated the contrary'.[216] The Schetz brothers were also very careful in installing a partitioning clause regarding Christoffel Pruynen's activities as city treasurer. Pruynen's activities as treasurer, which would later bankrupt him, were to be considered as his own and having nothing to do with the Schetz partnership trading in Germany; all profits and, in hindsight, more importantly, losses were his own.[217] Several years later, city lawyers proved that Pruynen had transferred monies from the city treasury to the company on Germany.[218] Michiel Anthoine would have to pay his partners only up to £100 gr. Fl. if they would sustain losses during the partnership.[219] Twenty-two per cent of the contracts contained a clause specifying that all losses resulting from providing surety, granting loans and investing in bills of exchange without notification of the other partners would befall only the partner who had undertaken the action in question; all profits from such operations would go to the partnership. The 1608 Costuymen confirmed this and considered the other partners not liable for debts resulting from such operations if they had not been informed about and/or had not approved them.[220] Sometimes partners' actions were limited: Christoffel Pruynen, the managing partner of a renewed marine insurance company (1559 and 1563) saw his discretionary powers limited to £350 and £400 gr. Fl.[221]

Not many disputes regarding partnerships were handled by the Antwerp civil court. De ruysscher is correct when he argues that this was mainly because partners rarely took their disputes to court, and when they did so, these disputes were framed in terms of arrest and the fulfilment of creditor claims.[222] Such cases disclose little information on the partnerships concerned. I found only two cases (one in the Vonnisboek of 1544 and one trial file) which directly addressed partnerships. Geerd Benghen sued Joose Vielkens for a debt of £14 gr. Fl. resulting from the partnership dealing in Westphalian bacon, which Benghen had undertaken with Vielkens's father. The court ruled that the son could not be held liable for his father's debts, as the son was not involved in the partnership.[223]

In a case before the Council of Brabant, Michiel Anthoine tried to shift liability for debts owed by his partnership with Anthoine le Dieu and Adam Testart onto his two colleagues. Shortly after the signing of the contract, it had become clear that Testart and le Dieu were insolvent and would not be sending Anthoine the goods from Lyon as they promised. Anthoine had signed a bond in the name of the company, payable to an Italian merchant whom he paid on time and from his own purse. Anthoine then sued his former partners to obtain the moneys owed to the company by Jeronimo Salvago.[224]

Proving that merchants were co-operating in a partnership was not always easy for the partnership's creditors. The widow of Jacob vanden Bloke sued Adriane van Delft for the remainder of the proceedings of the money-changing partnership which van Delft had operated with the widow's late husband. Initially, the arbiters decided that van Delft was not liable for anything after 1478 unless the widow could prove that van Delft had still been a partner of her husband after that date. The widow submitted a bill from 1485 which indeed showed that the two were still partners. Hence, van Delft was held liable for the partnership's business until that date.[225] Willem van Spinghele sued Jan Ghoten, another Mechelen cloth merchant, for the debts owed by Ghoten's son. Ghoten denied that he had a partnership with his son but the Mechelen Cloth Hall book proved otherwise.[226] Herman Hoochuys, a woollen cloth merchant residing in Antwerp, sued Philippe vanden Ommeslaghen and Hans Salomon for debts. Salomon was currently in Italy and Hoochuys tried to prove that vanden Ommeslaghen and Salomon were partners. Roelant van Hollant testified that 'he had heard in the Bourse that vanden Ommeslaghen and Salomon had a partnership'. Another witness explained that vanden Ommeslaghen had signed documents in his own name and that of Salomon.[227]

The case of Nicolas Le Fer heard by the Great Council of Mechelen proved to be a landmark case, commented upon many years later by the legal scholar Paulus Christaneus.[228] The Great Council explicitly denied limited liability for active partners in 1549. Ten years earlier in 1539, Nicolas Le Fer and Robert de Neufville who were active as merchants in Lille, Arras and Antwerp, concluded an agreement on paying their partnership's debts to Pierre Hayelle. Moreover, both agreed that they would pay the partnership's debts out of their own pockets when partnership assets were insufficient; Le Fer promised to remunerate de Neufville if the latter should ever be imprisoned for the debts of the former.[229] Ten years later in another sentence of the Great Council, we learn that Le Fer and de Neufville had fled after being sentenced to pay 5,000 carolus guilders to the widow of Pierre Lallart, one of their former partners. The widow in turn was sued by other partnership creditors because she allegedly continued the partnership after the death of her husband.[230] The Great Council ruled that the executors of the partnership would have to hand over all proceedings from the public sale of the partnership's assets and that the widow was to be awarded the requested 5,000 guilders if she provided surety. The partnership's creditors' claim on that sum was not acknowledged by the Great Council. The court clearly denied that Le Fer's liability was limited to his share in the partnership because he was an active partner.[231] In total, the Great Council pronounced just twenty-six sentences concerning partnerships (1465–1580). The Council of Brabant handled only one partnership case in 1544 (of its forty-four sentences that year).

Collateral for a partnership was declared in half of the partnership contracts, although always in generic terms: 'all their [partners'] goods, current and future'.[232] Such general collateral could prove to be problematic: how could one identify a piece of collateral if it always remained implicit?[233] Of course, firms did own assets such as cash, merchandise, annuities, real estate and ships, which could be seized by company creditors.[234] Only the Hureau partnership contract formulated specific collateral, namely the inheritance and hereditary annuities of Nicolas Hureau, which his brother Martin was allowed to use as collateral and sell if necessary.[235]

Non-Partner Investments and Private Equity Transfers

One did not need to be an active partner to invest in a partnership. This type of partnership investment took two forms: that of a deposit with a fixed annual interest rate and that of a share in the profits and losses of the partnership. Both allowed merchants to obtain additional capital for their enterprise.

Jan Verheyden, a partner, invested besides his equity capital another £225 gr. Fl. as a deposit on which he received an annual 7.5 per cent interest.[236] The Schetz company contract stipulated that if the partners wished to invest additional capital as a deposit, they would receive an interest 1 per cent higher than the current Bourse interest.[237] Between 1559 and 1569 a 9 to 10 per cent interest was paid to the partners with deposits. When the company was renewed in 1563, it was decided that new deposit inputs would only be accepted upon agreement by all partners and that deposits could be withdrawn only after notification six months prior to the withdrawal. Eighty-three per cent to 100 per cent of the partnership's deposit capital was provided by the partners.[238]

In the first six years the Schetz partnership relied on equity capital and rein-vested profits. After the first renewal, in 1558, the partners' equity capital was lowered and converted into interest-bearing deposits. The share of deposits drasti-cally increased after the second renewal, amounting to half of the total partnership capital. After Iconoclasm, the firm sustained large losses and saw its equity capital vanishing. Jan Della Faille the elder and his partnerships were much more reluc-tant in accepting deposits.[239] But when Della Faille the elder started on his own he did accept deposits, especially from outsiders (people who were not his fam-ily or personnel).[240] His son Maarten obtained a large amount of deposits from family members (24 per cent of total partnership capital). Goldthwaite notes that outsider deposits in Florentine merchant banks could be quite substantial and even outstrip the partnership's equity capital.[241] South German companies also accepted deposits.[242] The Schetz and Della Faille companies show that merchants combined equity with debt contracts to fund their operations. The Schetz broth-ers were hoping that annual profits would be higher than the interests they were paying on deposits. As we will see, the Schetz brothers invested part of their capital in the company because deposits were subject to limited liability rules.

Silent partners received a share of the profits and refrained from participat-ing actively in the daily business of the partnership.[243] Pieter Waarloos invested £1,000 gr. Fl. as a silent partner in the Van der Molen–Zanchi partnership: he would return seven shillings for every pound of profit he would receive to Fred-erik Van der Molen for the latter's efforts. Waarloos would not do anything for the partnership which Frederik Van der Molen would manage.[244] Both Antwerp and central law tried to regulate the practice of silent investment. In 1540 a royal ordinance was proclaimed which forbade non-merchants to give their money to merchants to have 'sure gain' without entering a partnership.[245] This likely indi-cates that many non-merchants were already doing so.[246]

The 1608 Costuymen prescribed that non-partners participating in a part-nership in return for part of the profits or losses could be sued only for company debts less than the amount of their investment and that none of their personal assets could be claimed for company debts.[247] The Great Council of Mechelen was of the same opinion by that time.[248] These rules effectively established limited liability for silent investors.[249] The Costuymen even supplied a model contract for such investments.[250] Silent investments could be withdrawn on a three-month notice. Such an investment contract closely resembled the Italian *accomandita*, a contract that allowed outsiders to invest in a partnership and share profits on the same terms as the other partners, without risking anything beyond their investment. Unlike the Florentine *accomandita*, registration of such investments was not required in the partnership books in Antwerp.[251] The rules for limited liability passive investments were only in place by 1608, yet this does not mean that people had already been investing in this way. The Della

Faille partners collected important deposits from outsiders and these depositors must have felt assured about the liability issues underpinning their investment ex ante.[252] In the firm of Jan Della Faille the elder, rich bureaucrats invested as passive investors, including the chancellor of Brabant Jan Scheyff, who invested large sums.[253] Low Countries merchants could also rely on rich foreign merchants residing in Antwerp to fund their businesses through limited liability investments. However, I could not find any traces of such investments.[254]

The available bits of evidence of private equity transfers show that partnership shares were mostly transferred to family members, not to strangers.[255] Gaspar Schetz granted his equity capital (£22,923 gr. Fl.) and deposits (£8,939.75 gr. Fl.) in the Schetz–Pruynen-Vleminck partnership to his son-in-law Jehan Vleminck. These shares were described as *perceros*.[256] Shares of the Van Schoonbeke peat digging company (near Amersfoort), in which the Schetz were a partner, could be transferred to others, but only after three months, during which time only the current partners had the right to buy the shares.[257] The only more anonymous private equity transfer concerned transfer of a lease by Erasmus Schetz. In 1525 Erasmus Schetz and his partners Jan Vleminck and Aerd Pruynen transferred a one-sixth part of their smithsonite lease to Jan Cock, a merchant from 's-Hertogenbosch, and to Gherijt Parijs from Limburg. The two would receive an annual account of the expenses of the mining enterprise and would contribute in the costs. Profits or losses would be calculated and shared at the end of the lease. Cock and Parijs were not allowed to extract additional smithsonite or to buy and sell ore from other mines.[258] Of course, the peculiarity of the enterprises (insurance and mining) renders this evidence somewhat unrepresentative for commercial partnerships. But the people involved in these private equity transfers were merchants. This shows that, already quite early in the sixteenth century, subdividing companies into shares and transferring such company shares had become established practice. However, these shares were generally transferred to family and acquaintances. Public quotations of equity shares were not available in sixteenth-century Antwerp. This innovation would have to wait until the VOC and the Amsterdam market in shares.[259]

Commission Trade

Partnerships (and equity contracts in general) were not the only way for Low Countries traders to establish commercial relationships with foreign merchants. Wilfrid Brulez and Herman Van der Wee have valued commission trading – buying and/or selling or providing financial services on behalf of a third party in return for a fixed percentage share of the volume of the transaction – as having been particularly important in the emancipation of the Low Countries traders and the democratization of long-distance trade.[260] This flexible commercial technique allowed small-scale merchants to engage in transactions in far-away commercial cities: via payment of small fee and correspondence merchants had access to well-informed agents in every market.[261] Of course, commission trade was not particular to the Low Countries merchants. Bruges merchants and inn-keepers performed commission business on behalf of third parties and Hanseatic trade was based on *Sendeve* (reciprocal commission without charge).[262]

Jacques Savary, in his merchant manual *Le parfait négociant* (1675), noted 'qui fait ses affaires par commission va à l'Hôpital en personne', yet at the same time he realized that in his day and age commerce could no longer do without commission trading.[263] He sought to warn his readers about the risks of com-mission trade. Such risks lay in the fact that commission trading concerned open-ended, hard-to-specify and incomplete contracts.[264] In a commission transaction, one merchant asked another through a letter to act on his behalf to the best of the latter's abilities. As such, commission trading is marked by a strong resemblance to Avner Greif's Maghribi coalition – a private order solu-tion in Greif's analysis – which relied only on reputation, social sanctions and the prospect of future transactions.[265] However, commission transactions were firmly embedded in public order institutions to which a principal could turn if his agent did not behave satisfactorily. These transactions could be enforced through the gradual acceptance of the documents underlying such commission transactions – letters and account books – as legal evidence in the court of law, as Oscar Gelderblom has shown.[266] If necessary, testimonies could be written up and formalized: for example, Nicolas Fourmestraux asked Jehan Dansque, an Antwerp merchant and commission agent of Michiel de Seville, to testify that Dansque had bought goods from Fourmestraux for a certain amount of money and had sent them to Seville.[267] Hence, commission letters were considered as legally binding and enforceable agency contracts.[268] Agents were thus motivated by various incentives, including economic (prospect of future transactions), social (effects on reputation) and legal (they could be sued). However, suing would not have been an easy matter since the letters were open ended and the instructions therein often vague.[269] The risk of the principal was limited to the value of the goods bought or sold.[270]

Various letters of the Van Bombergen and Van der Molen families, two merchant dynasties operating from Antwerp, to their Italian clients have been preserved.[271] Both merchant houses were active in Italy on their own account in the first half of the sixteenth century and executed commission transactions for Italian traders. The Van der Molen company increasingly focused on commission trading after the death of the pater familias. The letters are written in a direct and vivid style, interspersed with a Venetian dialect (both families had intimate ties with the Lagoon City and many of their clients were residing there). They start with an overview of the dates of the letters sent and received and sometimes include a copy of the previous letter in case it had gone lost.[272] The letters proceed with the latest commercial and political news and report on transactions executed, potentially profitable bargains and transportation of the goods. The letters typically end with commodity prices and exchange rates. These letters were both a monitoring device for the principals and an instrument for the agents to report on their performance. Gunnar Dahl defines this monitoring as the remote control function through instrumental writing: 'catch a person's attention, make him understand what you want, and make him do it. It requires a psychologically convincing communication that creates a team spirit working towards a common goal'.[273] The Van der Molen, as commission agents, in turn relied on a discourse of civility and obligingness; they always signed their letters as 'a servitio de vostri sempre siamo' ('we are always at your service') or in short 'vostri siamo' ('we are yours').[274] Responding in a regular and frequent fashion was another way for a commission agent to show his diligence and reciprocal esteem.[275]

The Van der Molen wrote to their customers that they would do their utmost to obtain profits for their clients, as they would for themselves.[276] However, this documents a potential conflict of interests inherent to commission trading: commission agents could have several clients and often combined this with trading on their own account. But who would get the best goods and receive the most diligence?[277] The commission agent's own activities also exposed his principal to the risks that the principal's goods would be seized if the agent got into trouble.[278] A good commission agent therefore had to carefully balance his own interests with those of his principals.

Attracting a commission agent in another city proceeded via the social network of a merchant by inquiring about a good agent among family, friends and colleagues.[279] Francesco Formento, a Rome client of the Van der Molen, advised Battista, Clemente and Tommaso di Viviani from Brescia to use the firm's services.[280] Pieter Van der Molen asked Bernardo Morando to recommend his younger brother Cornelis Van der Molen to his friends.[281] The first transaction was always a test of the performance of the commission agent.[282] Although theoretically the agent could act opportunistically, in that he could favour short-term gain over the prospects of future transactions (for example by selling the principal's goods for his own account), such behaviour could result in social sanctions and potentially even a lawsuit.[283] Cheating would also besmirch the reputation of the merchant who had recommended the agent in the first place; thus, the recommending merchant could exert pressure on the agent not engage in underhanded business practices.[284]

The Van der Molen charged their customers a commission fee of 3 per cent, but sometimes granted their good clients a discount.[285] Due to the popularity of commission trading and the growing group of commission services suppliers, this percentage dropped to a standard 2 per cent in the second half of the sixteenth century.[286] In the companies of Jan Della Faille (1574–82) and his son Maarten (1583–94) half of the proceeds from commission transactions for third parties went to the company, the other half to the partner who had executed the transaction.[287] Agents supplied their clients with invoices of the transactions, several of which were copied into the preserved Van Bombergen and Van der Molen letters. Agents and principals held mutual accounts.[288] Payments were made through bills of exchange.[289] These exchange operations were handled by Italian bankers with branches in Antwerp: such bankers included the Affaitadi from Cremona; the Guicciardini and Strozzi from Florence; the Balbani, Bonvisi, Burlamacchi, Cenami and Guinigi from Lucca; and the Cattaneo, Grimaldi, Doria, Imperiale and Pallavicini from Genoa. The Fugger and Welser also provided the Van der Molen with money transfers. In several cases the Van der Molen in Antwerp drew bills on Daniel Van der Molen, the youngest brother and agent in Venice, or on Maarten de Hane, a Flemish trader in the *Serenissima*.

The operation of commission trading not only depended on social and economic incentives of agent–principal relationships; it was also determined by the general commercial environment. When traffic between two commercial centres or regions was particularly intense, information circulation was dense. Dean Williamson has demonstrated the existence of monitoring by proxy for the medieval Venetian trade with Crete; information circulation was so dense that principals could ask others for information on the business environment and compare this with information they received from their agents.[290] Such monitoring by proxy was certainly possible in trade between Italy and the Low Countries. Not only was such trade very intense, Low Countries traders were present in Italian cities and Italian merchants were active in Antwerp. Hence, both groups of merchants could always monitor the behaviour of their agents through one of their countrymen, or to phrase it differently, through a multilateral reputation management and monitoring mechanism. Moreover, quality information on commodities was becoming increasingly standardized through samples: in 1540 the Van der Molen ordered cloth in London according to a colour sample they had received from Italy.[291] The Van der Molen also routinely enclosed price currents in their letters.[292] In August 1540 the Van der Molen informed their clients that they would no longer provide hand-written commodity prices in their letters; this would be done through enclosed printed price lists.[293] These lists enabled the Italian clients to verify whether the Van der Molen had obtained a good price for their transaction and were reporting honestly.[294] Given the pivotal importance of correspondence for the commission trade, fast and efficient postal connections were absolutely necessary. The Van der Molen letters show that every three weeks couriers of the imperial postal services departed for Italy. It took two weeks for letters from Genoa, Rome and Venice to reach Antwerp and three for those from Ancona.[295] The Van der Molen also made use of the services of couriers working for individual Italian firms, such as the Affaitadi.[296]

The Van der Molen letters also provide details about how commission relations could turn sour. In the fall of 1539 Niccolò Dolze, a merchant from Venice, sent a large shipment of turquoises to his Antwerp commission agent, the Van der Molen.[297] The Van der Molen reported in every subsequent letter to Dolze that there was no demand for these gems and that they were unable to sell them at a reasonable price.[298] After two and half years, Dolze lost patience and ordered the Van der Molen to return the stones to Venice; the Van der Molen charged Dolze a one per cent commission fee, which was customary for unsold goods.[299] In case of dissatisfactory performance, however, a principal could ask to transfer his goods to another agent. This happened between the Venetian Martino di Zerchiari and the Van der Molen when the two parties could not agree on a good price to sell di Zerchiari's English cloth; di Zerchiari eventually asked the Van der Molen to transfer the cloth to the Antwerp branch of the Luccese merchant family Di Poggio.[300] The Ancona merchant Bernardo Morando had also previously worked with Frederik Van der Molen; at one point, in the spring of 1540, he became dissatisfied with how the Van der Molen were handling his business and had his account transferred to the Antwerp agent of the Fagnani family and a certain Bertolini. But Bertolini died in 1538 and the Fagnani no longer had an agent in the Scheldt town. Hence, Morando was likewise without a valuable representative in Antwerp. The sons of Frederik Van der Molen recognized the opportunity and sought to reconnect with Morando. In a letter to him, they offered their services, apologized for the mistakes made by their father and underscored the long friendship the family and Morando shared. They assured Morando that they would do their utmost to serve him better in the future. With a circumstantial report of business in Antwerp and the Low Countries, including prices of Flemish cloth, kerseys and camlets, they endeavoured to persuade Morando to re-establish business ties. In the end their efforts were successful: they kept corresponding with Morando until the end of the letter-book but Morando was still hard to satisfy.[301] Hence, if principals were not satisfied, they could demand the return of their goods or could switch to other commission providers.

Commission trade allowed Low Countries traders to carve out a commercial niche in European trade. As I have shown in a previous article, Venetian merchants left the markets of the Low Countries but used Netherlandish commission agents such as the Van Bombergen and Van der Molen.[302] The Venetians saw the advantages of relying on local merchants: such merchants had intimate knowledge of the Low Countries market, had connections with the production side, were citizens and knew the language. Moreover, in Antwerp the Venetian principals had no overhead costs, such as rent, living allowance, etc. which they would have to pay if they had their own agent or partner in the Scheldt port. Hence, the following process can be observed in the trade between the Low Countries and Italy in the later middle ages and the sixteenth century: Italian merchants sent

Italian agents to the Low Countries to do business; the Italian merchants then made use of the services of local Low Countries agents, who were sending their own agents to Italian cities (Venice in particular). This strongly resembles the transformation witnessed by Price and Clemens in the tobacco trade between England and its North American colonies between 1660 and 1740.[303]

It is no coincidence that the two documented merchant families involved in commission trade were established merchant houses whose members were trained in Italy and who maintained branches there. Each family could rely on longstanding contacts and could substitute its own trade with commissions on behalf of others. Commission trading afforded more security than did trading on one's own account but was far less remunerative.[304] The Van der Molen brothers were the second generation of their family's merchant house and may have preferred the sure gains from commission trade over risky but potentially more lucrative personal trading.[305] Both Brulez and Kohn have argued that commission trade was the ideal solution for small traders with limited capital to reap the gains from commerce.[306] I would add that this would have been possible only if these merchants were already tied into a commercial network and if they were content with the small commission fees. Of course, through their principals commission agents could get in touch with other markets, if their performance was well received. Commission trading was often practiced by older apprentices or merchants at the start of their careers.[307] These youngsters could build upon the contacts of their (former) masters. An example of this would be Marten van Elmpt, a trainee of Sir Jan Bernarts in Cadiz, who was a commission agent for several Antwerp traders. Bernarts and the 's-Hertogenbosch merchant Jaspar van Bell (van Bell's brother-in-law) made an agreement that van Elmpt, would sell van Bell's goods in commission in Cadiz and receive the commission fees.[308]

The commission system was both flexible and limited at the same time: it could work only in trades with dense information flows and third-party information to allow agent monitoring, and these flows were not always available. Moreover, the incentives for commission agents strongly differed from those of a partner who had a share in the profits of the transactions. Partners could be trusted with more complex transactions than commission traders.[309]

Conclusion

This initial exploration of sixteenth-century Antwerp partnerships has yielded important results. Since registration of equity contracts was not compulsory, the evidence of these contracts is sketchy. Because the preserved contracts were registered, they are in a sense atypical: they bound merchants who were not family and who felt the need to register their contract because of mutual unfamiliarity. Indeed, the number of family partnerships is rather low. This shows that through equity contracts, which were supported and enforced by Antwerp law, Low Countries merchants were able to attract equity capital from outside their family circles. Moreover, the preserved equity contracts provide details on contract design and contract clauses which demonstrate the relative flexibility of such contracts. In the Russia trade, a new line of trade for Antwerp merchants, equity contracts were used to collect capital and knowledge. Geeraerd Gramaye could rely on the financial support of Italian merchants residing in Antwerp. Many Russia partnerships made use of Hanseatic partners and agents who had intimate knowledge of the Baltic trade and substantial trade privileges which they could invest in the partnership.

Contract flexibility was evident in the registered contracts. According to Antwerp law, profits had to be divided pro rata of the partners' investments or otherwise; several contracts used different keys to divide the profits. The contracts were also open and incomplete, thereby allowing the partners sufficient discretionary decision powers. The law considered all partners jointly and severally liable for company debts; however, although partner creditors had claims on company assets, they had to wait until the company creditors and other partners were paid (strong entity shielding). Little by little, limited liability was installed for passive investors whether they were owed part of the profits or fixed interest on their deposits. Through this investor protection, merchants could collect additional capital from family and strangers; yet, the available evidence on the well-known Della Faille and Schetz cases and the more unknown examples cited in this chapter show that most equity capital came from the partners or from their respective family members. However, in the new Baltic trade, partnerships with outsider capital were formed. Hence, the ascent of Antwerp's merchants was likely to have been influenced by the relative ease of obtaining sufficient working capital, as firmly grounded in Antwerp law, and experimentation with flexible contracts. Furthermore, equity contracts also prescribed agency duties and liabilities within the partnership – albeit in relatively generic terms – which could be used to make partners obey senior partners and refrain from cheating and risky transactions. These regulations were not always effective as evidenced in the early career of Jan Della Faille the elder.

As such, partnerships provided Low Countries merchants a one-fits-all solution to issues of capitalization, liability, opportunism, representation, internal task division and the collection of information and expertise.[310] A standard menu of partnership modalities took shape but remained flexible: Merchants could design their partnerships à la carte. When one compares these partnerships to those of Italian, Spanish and south German merchants, as this chapter has done, the many similarities are striking. Surely, Low Countries merchants will have learned from the legal traditions, customs and practices of their competitors. These traditions, customs and practices became embedded in Antwerp commercial law (albeit often after being adapted to local needs and sensibilities), together with older, local traditions, customs and practices of the Low Countries. Exactly because partnership structures were so similar among the different merchant groups in the sixteenth century, and although they seem modern and efficient and Antwerp may have initiated new or at least fuelled ongoing legal changes and adaptations, commercial partnerships did not propel Low Countries merchants onto European markets and allow them to outcompete other traders.[311] One could easily turn this potential causality on its head: because Low Countries merchants were operating internationally, they needed partnerships and, as a consequence of this need, changes in partnership structures took place. What is clear is that Low Countries partnership structures were instrumental in the organization of mercantile business; they allowed Low Countries merchants to gather the means to enter foreign trade but they did not constitute a comparative advantage. The same is true for commission trade: it allowed Low Countries merchants to co-operate all over Europe but since other merchant groups were doing the exact same thing, commission agency did not prove to be a comparative advantage either.

4 DEBT FINANCE THROUGH BILLS OBLIGATORY

The Conundrum of Flexibility vs. Uncertainty: Introduction

Jan Gamel, an Antwerp textile merchant and financier, passed away in 1572. His probate inventory shows the crucial importance of bonds and bills obligatory in his investment portfolio: half of his property consisted of such financial titles.[1] This chapter considers the use of obligations among merchants in late fifteenth- and sixteenth-century Antwerp, focusing especially on the frequent usage by native merchants and the different attitudes towards these private credit instruments among merchants from other regions active in the Scheldt city. Did IOUs fuel the ascent of Low Countries merchants and small-scale traders? Were bonds instrumental in the democratization and emancipation of Low Countries traders? The evidence does indeed point in that direction. Small-scale merchants used the credit modality of the bond to buy merchandise and to pay for the bond with the sales proceeds. In doing so, these traders of course ran the risk of having to sell at an undesirable price, so as obtain ready money to pay their bonds on time. On the other hand, they could make substantial profits on these transactions. Larger merchants, such as Jan Della Faille and his agents, complained about what they regarded as under-cutters, who were selling at whatever price they could to obtain the money to repay their bonds. Tellingly, Jan Della Faille also stated that 'the road must be open for everybody'.[2]

Obligations were not a sixteenth-century innovation; they had been circulating at the thirteenth-century Champagne and Flanders fairs and had been registered by the city authorities of Ypres.[3] The IOUs used in sixteenth-century Antwerp originated in the fair cycle that had laid the foundations for Antwerp's spectacular economic growth: these traditional IOUs were written by buyers and sellers for payment at the next fair in Antwerp or Bergen-op-Zoom (roughly every three months).[4] Increasingly, these debt contracts were passed on by the creditor to others. The commercial growth was stimulated by this transferability of IOUs yet also endangered by it: the growing scale of the market, the permanent character it had assumed and the rising merchant population created a growing and potentially undermining anonymity. Did a new creditor still know the original debtor mentioned in the contract? Or did evolving laws and commercial custom render this familiarity obsolete?

To what extent did the authorities recognize the pressure between flexibility and uncertainty in using IOUs? How did they regulate this practice and enforcement? Did they provide registration opportunities? Was registration of an IOU by a state institution a condition siné qua non for its enforcement or was there also a legal framework which could enforce private and informal bonds? How did the growing market, the resultant anonymity and the increasingly longer chains of interdependence affect the daily practices of bills obligatory and their transferability?[5] Was the circulation of IOUs indeed more limited and more uncertain than for a bill of exchange which had four signatures and four parties to turn to should a problem arise, compared to the single debtor signature on the bill obligatory?[6]

Previous scholarship on these informal instruments and their use has been framed around modernity, a perspective which has regarded the evolution of the IOU as being an evolutionary process of innovation. Scholars thus sought for the first instances of the bearer clause, assignment of IOUs and the first *disconto*.[7] It was implicitly assumed that, upon such a practice becoming established, the practice would then have automatically gained importance and become used by ever more merchants. Little attention has been paid to the actual use of the instruments and these new techniques, and to the repercussions on the daily operations of merchants. A quantitative appreciation of IOU use is lacking as well. Reconstructing a total number of obligations traded on the Antwerp market is an illusionary enterprise, but we can develop an idea of how many obligations were registered by various authorities and how many were disputed in the courts of the Low Countries. Moreover, no serious attempt has been made to assess bond values. Were they used only for low amounts because of their informal nature and the absence of clear collateral? This lack of interest is all the more striking, since Van der Wee has argued that throughout the entire sixteenth century the financial instrument of the obligation continued to predominate in payments of commercial debts on the Antwerp market.[8]

The frequent use of bonds in the Low Countries (and in England) has often been explained as having been due to the lack of the Southern-style deposit banks which could transfer money through accounts.[9] Economic historians are fascinated by banks' role in the creation of credit. But as Price argues for England:

> the key institutions of pre-corporate credit were at work in Britain before anything called a 'bank' appeared on the scene: mortgage, bond, note, bill of exchange, discount, and ordinary commercial credit, short and long-term. When banks appeared they made more efficient a system whose key elements were already in place and working.[10]

Van der Wee has argued that the outlawing and subsequent disappearance of money changers, who were also active in deposit and giro-banking at the end of the fifteenth century, put a premium on the development of bond negotiability.[11] Recently, Erik Aerts has nuanced this point of view, arguing that money changers and cashiers partially substituted public banks.[12] While Aerts demonstrates the presence of cashiers, it is impossible to state how important they were, how important the deposit banking services they provided were, and how they impacted on the circulation of IOUs.

Obligation: What's in a Name?

A clear definition of what we understand as a so-called IOU (I owe you) is needed before we proceed, given the more specific terminology used in English for different forms of such contracts. The Antwerp sources use the terms *obligatie, obligasi, obligacie, obligation, schuldbekentenisse, schuldbrief* and *hantschrift* to denote what we today understand to have been a contract between a debtor and a creditor, in which the debtor promised to pay the creditor a specified sum of money on a specified date. The sum had to be paid in local currency, in which a bill obligatory differed from a bill of exchange. Failure to provide this basic information nullified the contract, as the creditors of the Merchant Adventurer Robert Silvesters found out after their debtor had fled, leaving the creditors a worthless piece of paper which did not even specify the amount of the debt.[13] The reason for the debt in question (sold commodities for example) could be mentioned in the contract, but often was not. It could be registered by an authority, such as the city's aldermen or a notary, or it could be a private instrument, signed only by the debtor. In England, only higher-value bonds were registered. In the English context of the fourteenth to the sixteenth centuries a debt contract not registered by an authority was a bond (bill obligatory was a synonym), such that a registered IOU obtained the status of a legal recognisance.[14] In the Low Countries, and in Antwerp in particular, there was no linguistic difference between an IOU, whether it was registered or not. Legal historians distinguish IOUs and obligations from bills obligatory and bonds. The latter were automatically transferable (through a bearer clause and legal changes, as we will see); the former were not.[15] However, in sixteenth-century Antwerp no separate terminology was used to denominate the two types of debt. Therefore, in this chapter I will treat IOUs, bonds, promissory notes, obligations and bills obligatory as synonyms and distinguish between the two types of debt where necessary.

Besides the basic information of the document (debtor's name, creditor's name, amount, date of the document, final repayment date), the payment terms, place of payment and contingency clauses upon the fulfilment of certain specific conditions could also be specified. Pledges could be recorded, a bearer clause (payable to creditor or the bearer of the document) could be included and partial payments and/or the names of creditors who have the document could be listed on the back, or *dos*, of the document. IOUs could carry a merchant's seal.[16] The obligation was a credit instrument granting deferred payment and, when transferable, a means of payment, thus obtaining the status of currency. I will deal with private IOUs only in this chapter; governments could also issue obligations.[17] The trial proceedings concerning a bond between Coenraerd Schetz and Jan Spierinck in 1567 provide a full-text copy of a typical bond:

> I Jan Spierinck confess and declare by my own handwriting to owe the honourable lord Coenraerdt Schetz the sum of four hundred pounds Flemish groat and this on the account of the equal sum I have received from him to my satisfaction. I promise to fully pay the aforementioned lord Coenraerdt Schetz or the bearer of this on the fourth day of the forthcoming month of August without any delay, committing my person and all my possessions now and in the future. In the year 1565 June 11.[18]

Sources

The sources documenting these bonds form three clusters. First, the IOUs or their registered versions provide information on the possibility of transferring the IOU to another merchant (for example through a bearer clause), the sums involved, the duration of the credit and payment terms, and the institutions registering these documents and whether registration was necessary. Second, other merchant documents, such as merchant inventories, account books and letters, demonstrate how merchants handled their obligations: could these private instruments act as collateral, could they be discounted (bought/sold before the closure date, at a price lower than its nominal value), how many times were these bills passed on, and could they be rolled over, i.e., extended after each expiry date and effectively become a long-term financial instrument? Third, the legislative framework for these private credit instruments is considered together with cases of litigation. I will show how the pluriformity of laws and legislation turned the IOU into an efficient credit instrument. The sixteenth-century judicial cases and their resultant sentences offer unique insight into the problems and risks a merchant could encounter in using a bill obligatory; likewise, because of their attention to detail and context these cases enable us to reconstruct the various uses of bills obligatory and the different intermediaries involved, such as brokers and cashiers. Taken together, these three clusters of sources provide a comprehensive view on the development of Antwerp's IOU market and its development throughout the sixteenth century.

Five different types of sources have been scrutinized in search of bills obligatory: the Antwerp certification books and aldermen's registers (1490–1514), and civil sentences pronounced by the Antwerp aldermen in cases of litigation

(1504–5 and 1544); notarial acts by Zeger Adriaan 's Hertoghen and Willem Stryt (1540); post-mortem inventories (Jan Gamel) and a bankrupt individual's inventory (Jan Spierinck); account books (Daniel de Bruyne, Frans de Pape, Herman Janssens, Christophe Plantin, Jaspar Van Bell and the Moriel brothers); and the proclaimed lost obligations (1546–87).[19] In total, I identified values and information on the identities of the debtors and creditors for 1,276 bonds, which were collected from this rather heterogeneous collection of sources.[20]

The signalled lost bonds are the most peculiar source in the sample and point to the need to install mechanisms to deal with the decentralized circulation of bonds. This procedure, something akin to an early modern Card Stop, was mentioned for the first time in September 1546, when IOUs had already long been common practice on the Antwerp market. The adjunct-sheriff, mayors and aldermen announced for the first time a lost bond. In this bill two English partners, Philips Coqueran and Janne Aboro, promised to pay the Italian company of Bonaventura Michaeli or the bearer of the letter £251.95 gr. Fl. However, the bill in question could not be found and was thus considered null and void; the city ordered the bill to be returned to the city authorities. All these descriptions were registered in the *Gebodboeken*, together with all the other public announcements and city orders.[21]

Signalling lost IOUs had also been performed earlier by notaries: for example, the notary 's Hertoghen cancelled an obligation lost by the courier in 1540.[22] The notarial act could prove the loss of an obligation in case somebody should find it and attempt to cash it, but this information was not made public (notarial acts are private),[23] whereas publication by city authorities reached a much wider audience. Some announcements described the circumstances of the loss of the bill. The Gebodboeken include both registered and unregistered bills.[24] The obligations announced as lost were often declared missing by debtors who feared that they would be addressed by an unknown bearer, especially when the bill had already been paid. Other reasons for loss were: theft, the Spanish Fury of 1576, loss through negligence, loss during the sending of the bond, shipwreck and fire. The spread of the bearer clause and its legal framework made bills obligatory worthwhile for thieves.[25] In 1552 the Italian Francesco Martignoni was alleged to have stolen a £100 gr. Fl. bill payable in six terms over three years owed by Willem Borremans from his master Benedicto Capriani. Martignoni tried to collect the money from the debtor Borremans and even took this matter to court when the latter refused to pay.[26] Much commercial paper was stolen during the Spanish Fury between 4 and 8 November in 1576 during which more than 5,000 mutinous Spanish and German soldiers plundered the city, a coldly planned, methodical and brutal operation.[27] Trade was at a lull since many merchants had departed the city a few months earlier when their security was no longer guaranteed. Yet there were still ample riches up for looting and destroying. Cash, jewellery and precious objects were of course the first items on their wish list but the mutineers also searched for bills obligatory, or IOUs. When extorting Antwerp's civilians, the unpaid soldiers accepted either existing bills or forced burghers to write up new ones, as happened to the governor of the English Merchant Adventurers Heton.[28] After the pillagers had left, a series of announcements of the city government signalled and cancelled IOUs stolen during the pillage of the city in the years 1576–7. Spanish mutineers and other highwaymen also stole several other bonds when they were mailed.[29] Because bonds were highly liquid assets, they were an easy target for thieves and mutineers. This underlines the fragile nature of these instruments. In total 304 IOUs were registered as lost between 1546 and 1587.

Measuring the Values of Bills Obligatory

Table 4.1: Selected bills obligatory by source category (mean, median and standard deviation in grams of silver)

Source	Period	Number of bonds	Mean	Median	Std. Dev.
Aldermen's register acts	1479–1514	339	6,335	2,551	12,547
Certificates	1479–1514	44	12,517	6,133	15,653
Civil court sentences	1495–1544	87	13,168	4,195	27,864
Lost bonds	1546–87	304	18,462	9,491	863,835
Merchant account books					
Frans De Pape	1539–47	120	6,225	5,645	3,474
Herman Janssens	1551–1570	54	5,618	3,070	7,995
Christophe Plantin	1559–89	26	13,108	1,649	23,204
Daniel De Bruyne	1561–68	55	18,254	7,776	31,490
Jaspar Van Bell	1563–6	29	8,562	4,050	12,001
Moriel	1567	16	3,017	3,270	2,030
Merchant inventories					
Jan Spierinck	1565	35	12,858	2,502	39,608
Jan Gamel	1572	59	32,551	10,109	65,017
Notarial acts	1540	108	13,603	6,067	25,193
Total		1,276	12,615	5,184	36,018

Source: **See data appendix.**

The table shows the distribution of the bills obligatory over the different source types. Relatively low numbers of bonds were found, given that more than 1,000 merchants were active in Antwerp around the middle of the sixteenth century. And we can expect that such merchants would have handled several IOUs per year. Yet, this is the first time that a significant amount of bonds has been collected. Moreover, the sample contains both informal and formal(ized) bills obligatory. I recognize that these bonds are only the so-called tip of the iceberg; however, they do provide important information about the value and identities of the debtors and creditors involved. This is especially true of the one-year sample of notarial acts, which presents an impressive number of deeds on merchant's bonds.[30] Unfortunately, it is impossible to reconstruct the total number of commercial bonds, as there is no way to calculate which share of all IOUs was registered in any of the source series.[31] Nonetheless, the sample of obligations from different source series can be used to gain a quantitative understanding of the value of IOUs. To account for currency differences and for sixteenth-century inflation, which account for IOUs having higher nominal values as the century proceeded, I have recalculated and deflated the nominal values to their value in the weight (grams) of silver.[32]

IOU values in grams of silver (1,188 observations) ranged between 7.934 grams and 863.835 kilograms (or between £0.058 and 8,887.2 gr. Fl.).[33] For comparison, 50 per cent of all obligations were worth less than 4.57 times an annual mason's wage, which was a sizeable sum.[34] Between 1598 and 1602 the Southern Netherlandish expatriate Hans Thijs operated in Amsterdam and used IOUs to fund his jewellery trade. Thijs's bonds had values of up to 4,200 guilders.[35] Thijs did not want to take the risk of having IOUs of higher denominations, as could be found earlier in Antwerp.

The above table demonstrates that there was remarkable variety in bond values which points to a diversified market for such instruments; while these bills obligatory may seem similar in their wording, they clearly served different needs. The values of bills obligatory registered in different sources could differ significantly.[36] Bills registered by the aldermen had substantially lower values. Hence, formal registration of a bill could even be done for low denominations, which indicates a relatively efficient urban bureaucratic apparatus. Bills signalled as lost mostly – and unexpectedly – had a relatively high value. Bills in merchant inventories too had a higher value on average, especially the valuable bonds of Jan Gamel which were mainly financial assets. The bills obligatory mentioned in the account books of Frans De Pape and Herman Janssens emanated from commodity transactions; Christophe Plantin was owed small amounts of money by his workers and was indebted, through bills obligatory, for substantial sums to his financiers. Clearly, different bills obligatory served different needs and were subject to different degrees of contractual security.[37]

If a reason for the obligation was provided in the source, it often concerned the purchase of merchandise. A 1559 turbe decided that the cause of the bond was unimportant, as the bond was always legally valid even if the reason was not provided or false.[38] A bond could also be drawn up to clear a book debt: Nuremberg merchant Philips Massenhamer had partnered with the Antwerp trader Janne Fourmestraux in 1540. When the two closed the books, Massenhamer owed £181.5 gr. Fl. to Fourmestraux for which he drew up a bond payable in six months.[39] Most bonds were drawn up in Dutch, but examples were found in French, English, Low German and High German, Italian, Spanish and Portuguese – in short, the various languages spoken and written on the Antwerp market. The contents of the bills obligatory sheds light on the gradually growing importance of native merchants throughout the sixteenth century. I have coded the identities of the debtor and creditor of the IOUs, based on their names and geographic information, found in bonds registered in the aldermen's act, the certification books, notarial deeds, civil sentences and lost bonds.[40] Native merchants used bills obligatory much more frequently than their foreign colleagues. Foreign creditors favoured native creditors and native creditors preferred to deal with other natives and both groups slightly preferred a party from the same group as a debtor or creditor.[41] Foreign merchants were extending larger credit amounts through bonds to other foreigners and less to native debtors. There is no significant difference between the average credit granted by native creditors to foreign and native debtors. This shows that while native merchants were handling increasing numbers of bonds, foreigners were still outperforming them in terms of the bond values.

Transferring Obligations

Modes of Transferring Bonds

Sixteenth-century Antwerp witnessed extensive experimentation with bills obligatory: the original debt of a debtor to a creditor and its record could be transferred to a new party, who would be paid by the original debtor when the bill was due. The crux of the problem lay in the liability of the creditor who passed on the IOU.

Already in the fifteenth century a third party could collect the proceeds of bill on behalf of the original creditor. A formal *power of attorney* was still needed for the authorized agent.[42] The situation was similar in fourteenth- and fifteenth-century England.[43] Powers of attorney were often used to collect money from bonds in other regions and jurisdictions. Members of the Leydecker cloth merchant family extended powers of attorney to merchants in England and France to collect dues from bills obligatory.[44]

The practice of informing a debtor that an agent would collect the debt gave rise to the *bearer clause*, which entailed full legal rights of the document bearer. This usually concerned a mixed bearer clause: 'payable to X (name of the creditor) or to bearer'.[45] The bearer clause already existed in thirteenth-century Flanders; in these early documents the bearer clause merely indicates that an agent of the creditor would collect the debt.[46] IOUs with bearer clauses were already circulating during the Antwerp fairs in the 1510s; the certification books and aldermen's registers show that the bearer clause had already become an established practice by the 1490s: in fact, by this time there were more bonds with a bearer clause than without.[47] (105 bonds with a bearer clause vs. eighty-two without (1479–1514)).[48] Such a clause converted the bond into a fully negotiable instrument. Interestingly, bonds with a bearer clause had a higher average and median value than bills without such a clause.[49] The higher nominal value may have increased the need to make the bond transferable. Merchants needed to be able to transfer the larger sums in case of liquidity problems, but transferring bonds also entailed sizeable risks for the new creditor.

The legal rights of the bond bearer were acknowledged by jurists such as Willem van der Tannerijen (in writings dating from 1474–6), a former Antwerp city secretary, and Philip Wielant (in the early 1500s), who wrote that debt certificate holders could sue a debtor, were not obliged to submit a formal proof of a power of attorney and were allowed to transfer such instruments to others.[50] Van der Tannerijen's and Wielant's opinions were completely at odds with those of some of their colleagues working for the Grand Council of Mechelen: the latter argued that unless the bearer could prove that the bond had been legally transferred unto him, he would not have any legal rights pertaining to the bill obligatory.[51] In March 1508 the Grand Council of Mechelen denied Jacop Casseleere, bearer of a bond of a debt owed by Aert Cloet to the Sicilian merchant Jehan Panthaleon, the right to sue the debtor Cloet.[52] Yet, less than one year before this sentence, the Antwerp city government ruled by a turbe that a bearer had full legal powers without having to prove his ownership of the bond.[53] Antwerp followed the precedents created in England (Davey vs. Burton in 1436)[54] and in Lübeck (1499 and 1502).[55] The influence of English bond practice on Antwerp remained powerful due to the widespread and extensive commercial flows between the two regions and the presence of the Merchant Adventurers in the Scheldt port.[56] Antwerp merchants did not wait to use bonds to bearer until the discussion between jurists and legislators had been settled. Bruges, Dordrecht and Utrecht followed after 1527.[57] The central government would issue an ordinance in 1537 establishing what had already been accepted in Antwerp much earlier.[58] This clearly indicates institutions moving at different speeds, such that the local government starkly outpaced the central authorities. The ordinances of the central government allowed for bearer rights in the entire territory of the Low Countries.[59]

The transfer of a bond by a creditor to a new creditor could be executed through the legal concepts of *transport*, or '*cession*', and through *assignment*, or '*bewysinghe*'. The older concept of transport definitively transferred all legal rights from the old creditor to the new one; the transfer dismissed the former from all claims by the latter. The transport was needed for the new creditor to obtain all legal rights to pursue a debtor and was usually accompanied by a power of attorney.[60] Transports were often registered by notaries or by the aldermen; oral testimony on the transport was also considered as legal evidence.[61] When the transfer of a bill was not registered by a notary, it was not unusual for the assignee to ask the debtor whether he recognized the debt and whether he would pay on the bond's maturity date.[62] In England bonds were transferred without transport; this lowered transaction costs, but also left the bond legally unprotected, causing a high potential risk of default.[63] In sixteenth-century Lyon transport was the only way to transfer a bond.[64]

In case of an assignment, the ceding creditor retained liability in case the debtor did not pay.[65] For example: Daniel de Bruyne had ceded a bill obligatory owed to him by Jaspar Nijs to the Spanish merchant Francisco Rodrigues; Nijs did not pay the bill and de Bruyne had to pay the legal costs for arresting Nijs.[66] The ceding creditor was relieved from this liability only when the debtor had fully satisfied the new creditor. This assignment originated in the medieval practice of a payment order.[67] The debtor was only acquitted from the new creditor's claim when he could prove that he had already paid his due.[68] However, there was a difference between a payment order (ordering A to pay to B) and the transferral of an existing claim (through transport or a bearer clause).[69]

The name of the debtor and his creditworthiness could enhance the circulation of the bill: the bonds of the Fugger, the so-called *Fuggerbriefe*, circulated most freely.[70] Already in 1504 we find an example of an IOU assignment: Ambrosius de Groote was indebted to Godevaert Gheerdss. De Groote had assigned his debt to his own debtor Jan Kiel, and had given the IOU on Kiel to his own creditor, Gheerdss., and considered himself thereby exempted from the debt. Gheerdss. had Kiel arrested in Bergen-op-Zoom for his debt, but this arrest was repudiated, on grounds that Kiel was an Antwerp citizen and thus had to be sued in Antwerp. The Antwerp court ruled that De Groote would have to pay his debt to Gheerdss. and would receive again his IOU on Kiel. This example shows how an assignment could work in the other direction as well: a debtor assigning his debt to his own debtor.[71]

The practice of transferring bonds through assignment became quickly popular in the first half of the sixteenth century: in 1532 the Van Bombergen were awaiting reply from their Venetian client Vendramin about whether to trade his IOU; the Englishman Thomas Washington testified in a 1537 lawsuit about the circulation of bonds and assignment had expanded.[72] In 1539 Frans de Pape bought English kerseys from an English merchant and gave him a bond, but eventually paid to Thomas Balbani, who was perhaps a creditor of the English merchant.[73] In the same year the financier Erasmus Schetz wrote to the Antwerp pensionary in Brussels, Herbouts, insisting that 'the central government would receive God's blessing when it would legalize and regulate the practice of assignment and would equate paying by assignment with paying in cash'.[74] The central government did so, convinced by Schetz's request, in an ordinance in October 1541.[75] The 1548 Antwerp Antiquissimae Costuymen also regulated assignment: a debtor who fled or disappeared lost the right to perform assignments.[76] In the 1570 Costuymen the city government went a step further: even if the name of the original creditor was fictitious, the IOU remained a legally valid document.[77] The Antwerp civil sentences (1544 sample) show the popularity of assignment and circulation of bills obligatory. The civil court always considered a transfer as an assignment unless one could prove that the transfer was final and definitive.[78]

Transfer Risk

Assigning bonds was a flexible technique, but one that could imply risks as well. The consequence of the popularity of assignment was such that a merchant often had to contact various people in order to obtain his money.[79] It has already been mentioned how the Spanish mutineers organized a focused search for commercial paper during the Spanish Fury; the looters, because of the bearer clause, could try and cash the obligations. Transferable bonds were also an easy target for confidencemen and swindlers: in 1568 Hans Roodecrans cajoled his sister-in-law Anna Dul, the wife of his bond creditor, out of a bill obligatory. Hans assured Anna that he would arrange swift payment of the bond but never gave her the money or the bill. The bond was then blocked, as noted in the Gebodboeken.[80] The legal proceedings concerning a transferred bond could also become quite complex. In 1544 the Spanish merchant Diego de Rotondo was indebted for £40 gr. Fl. to the Luccese merchant Simon Turchi and had given Turchi a bill obligatory; Turchi had then passed on the bill to his compatriot Thomas Maglio, who had paid his debt with the IOU to the Spanish trader Diego de la Lantadilia.[81]

Even with the clear turbe of 1507, the status of the bearer clause could be used strategically by litigants, as the 1526 case of Augustin di Prato vs. Steven van der Capelle demonstrates.[82] The Italian di Prato sued the Antwerp jeweller van der Capelle over a £13.8 gr. Fl. bond owed by van der Capelle's son Gerard. Van der Capelle had sent his son to the *Frankfurter Messe* to sell merceries and jewellery. It was during this fair that Gerard took up the debt. The creditor of the bond was Anthoine Vento, a Genoese merchant in Nuremberg. Gerard provided a £16.17 gr. Fl. bill obligatory with debtor Andries Heyden, a Nuremberg merchant, as surety for his debt towards Vento. It is not clear how di Prato was able to obtain

Vento's obligation; it could be that di Prato obtained the Vento bill from Gerard as a surety for a small debt owed to him by Gerard. Gerard's father wanted the Heyden IOU and sued di Prato at the Antwerp aldermen's court. Augustin di Prato, for his part, took legal action against Steven van der Capelle over the obligation owed by his son; di Prato was able to do so, as he held the IOU as bearer. The elder van der Capelle refuted di Prato's claim via the following arguments. He first sought to raise doubts as to the authenticity of the Vento obligation: why would his son have contracted such a debt when he had silver worth more than £66 gr. Fl. and could have used the silver as collateral instead of the IOUs? His son, as an agent, was also not allowed to contract debts without his father's permission. Van der Capelle employed this argument to prove that he was not an involved party; the debt was to be arranged between his son, Vento, and di Prato as the bearer. Van der Capelle was willing to pay only the small debt owed directly by his son to di Prato but argued that di Prato could not prove this debt. Moreover, he suspected that his prodigal son had colluded with di Prato to con him. Van der Capelle also refused to acknowledge the rights of di Prato as bearer of the document since di Prato could not supply a transport or power of attorney.[83]

Foreign Merchants' Attitudes towards Bonds

Foreign merchants had different attitudes towards assignment and transport of IOUs. Italian and Spanish traders were often suspicious of IOU assignments.[84] In looking at the notarized transports in 1540, it becomes clear that they almost exclusively concern French and Spanish merchants.[85] Native merchants were using notaries as intensively as these merchant groups but registered fewer transports. Hence, French and Spanish merchants seem to have preferred the definitive transport over the assignment. Pietre de Villasana, a Spanish merchant, transported twenty IOUs to his countrymen Arnoul de Planco and Pietre de Suaso and supplied them with powers of attorney; the names and whereabouts of the debtors, the amounts involved and the payment terms were meticulously recorded in the notarial deed.[86] In 1565, when the Antwerp magistracy, in an attempt to benefit its own secretaries, tried to curtail the practices of notaries in the city, the nation of Lucca argued in favour of the notaries, whose services they used to record powers of attorney and transports.[87] The nation explicitly condemned assignment, or, as they called it 'transportz privez de main a main': they claimed it caused collusion and fraud involving substantial sums and had ruined several merchants.[88] But native merchants also continued to make use of a formal cession: Jan Spierinck had executed a formal transport of a bill owed to him by Jacques Comperez to his creditor Wouter Seroye; this transport was registered by the Antwerp aldermen.[89] Powers of attorney were still deemed necessary in specific cases. Henricus Dryes, an Antwerp cloth merchant, granted powers of attorney to his brother Jaspar to collect £120 gr. Fl. from Joachim Gruysman, even though the obligation specifically contained a bearer clause.[90]

The English practice of assigning bills within the community of Merchant Adventurers differed from Antwerp customs: when a member of the Merchant Adventurers transferred a bond to a colleague, he was acquitted fully and could not be held liable anymore.[91] The 1555 legal case of Thomas Nichols vs. Gianbattista Gondi in which this custom became clear offers insight into the risks involved in transferring bonds. Both parties were influential figures: Nichols was then secretary of the Fellowship of Merchant Adventurers in London; Gondi had been a *consigliere* of the Florentine nation in Antwerp. A few years earlier Nichols had sold Gondi a number of woollens. Gondi had paid for the merchandise with an IOU of another Merchant Adventurer, Hamlet Bracy. Afterwards, it came to light that Bracy was bankrupt. Gondi, however, refused to provide Nichols with a new and valid IOU because, according to English practice, Nichols had accepted the IOU as full and definitive payment in case the debtor was a member of the Merchant Adventurers. Gondi also argued that Nichols should have known about Bracy's reputation and claimed that Bracy was not bankrupt when he had transferred the bill to him. Nichols, on the other hand, told the court that Gondi knew about Bracy's compromised situation and wanted to dispose of this toxic asset. Nichols also claimed that some of Gondi's other countrymen had used Bracy's bills obligatory to swindle other Merchant Adventurers, that the Florentines had colluded upon learning of Bracy's financial travail and that they had foisted his toxic assets onto others. The Antwerp court ruled that Nichols had taken the obligation in assignment and not as 'fynalycken ende absoluut'; Gondi had to provide a new bond or pay Nichols in cash.[92] This practice of dumping toxic assets before the problems became public was widespread. In 1556 the Antwerp merchant Augustijn Mariscal encountered financial problems, but one of his creditors, Herman Janssens managed to offload his obligations onto the unsuspecting Augustijn Bene.[93]

The original debtor had little say in the transferring of the bill. If he had allowed a bearer clause to be attached to the bond, he had no say in the subsequent matter and had acknowledged beforehand that his bond could be passed on.[94] This could entail potential problems: if the new creditor was unknown to the debtor, it would be more difficult to achieve an amicable settlement in case of debtor payment problems.[95] However, a 1528 Antwerp turbe confirmed that a bearer had all legal rights to execute an amicable settlement with the original debtor and could even acquit the debtor of his debt.[96] This problem was also raised by the 1565 aforementioned remonstrance of the nation of Lucca.[97] The Merchant Adventurers decreed that a fellow could only accept an obligation owed by a colleague if he gave notice thereof to the debtor or, in his absence, to his representative. This rule did not concern bonds with a bearer clause, which could be transferred automatically without further notice.[98]

The bills could change hands several times before their maturity. The sources abound with evidence of this high degree of circulation. Yet it is hard to measure exactly how many times a bond was passed on, since only the original creditor and debtor are named. Daniel de Bruyne paid the goldsmith Matheus Valck with an IOU by a certain Sneuwater, but it is unclear whether de Bruyne was the original creditor and how many times the bill was forwarded after Valck had received it.[99] The Cologne merchant Guel Tack, then residing in the town of Duisburg in the duchy of Guelders, was the debtor of a £66 gr. Fl. IOU in 1540. This IOU ended up in the hands of Jan Blondel, an English merchant, who used it to pay Philips Le Seur for says. Le Seur eventually appointed Janne Trant, a messenger, to collect the due from the bond from Tack.[100] The 1608 Costuymen explicitly regulated these assignment chains and documented that a bond could be passed on to 'four or five persons and more'; all ceding persons remained liable and linked to the original debtor of the bond.[101] This cascade of liability, enforced by city law, turned the obligation into legal tender. Unfortunately, it is impossible to calculate the potential differences in circulation and speed among foreign and native merchants, differences which we might expect given the preference for formal transfers and the aversion of assignment among foreign merchants.

In a climate where assignment was automatically assumed, it would seem that there was little need to prove an assignment unless one wanted to prove the contrary that the passing on of the bill constituted a final payment. Merchant account books could be used as evidence, but not all merchants kept books or were eager to show them. Moreover, to ascertain an assignment chain, the judges had to check all account books of all ceding creditors, which was surely a cumbersome and time-consuming task. In 1622 Gerard de Malynes mentions in his *Lex Mercatoria* the existence of an official IOU transfer registry system in Rouen and Lisbon.[102] No such system existed in Antwerp. On the one hand, registering a transfer would have increased transaction costs, thereby hindering the flexibility offered by trading bonds. On the other hand, this registration would have increased the security of the final creditor who, in the Antwerp scenario, could only either hope that the debtor would pay or appeal to the person from whom he had received the bond. The English Merchant Adventurers were obliged to produce a document which proved that they were assigning the bond and not transferring it as a final payment.[103] In 1567 Daniel de Bruyne issued a similar 'billet van assignatie' concerning a partially assigned bond owed by Anthoni Raedt.[104]

Endossment

The small step from a bill of assignment to writing the assignment on the obligation itself was only taken relatively late in sixteenth-century Antwerp, in 1571.[105] The late arrival of *endossement* ('en dos'), or endorsement, can be explained by three reasons. First, in a system where obligations were circulating freely through the bearer clause and assignment and where the bearer was sufficiently protected legally, the extra guarantee of being able to identify the entire chain of assignees may well have been deemed superfluous. Second, merchants were already writing other information on the backs of the bills, such as the partial payments already executed on the bill (this was also called endorsement). In 1555 the Antwerp aldermen publicized a lost IOU owed by two Spanish merchants to two citizens from Oudenaarde. The bill was worth £261.99 gr. Fl. and it was written on the back that 71 pounds had already been paid.[106] A similar description was dispersed but in this case it was explicitly stated that the partial payment was not written on the back of the bond.[107] Third, the advent of endorsement was probably delayed by the practice of *borge principael*.

A borge principael, or principal surety, was a third party who stood surety for the payment of the bond; the guarantors wrote their names on the back of the bill. The 1570 In Antiquis Costuymen bolstered this custom.[108] The guarantors were often family members and compatriots: in 1540 a French merchant transported a £787.5 gr. Fl. IOU to a merchant from Navarra. The original debtor, Jehan Koenen, a citizen of Maastricht, was backed by two family members and two other Maastricht citizens. Interestingly, while the transport formally acquitted the French merchant of all responsibility for the bill, he did put his signature on it.[109] Two bonds, lost on a sunken ship, were signed as surety by the Antwerp agent of the debtor.[110] The surety was not always written on the bond itself; a separate act could attest it and could be made up after the original IOU.[111] Daniel de Bruyne recorded in his account books bonds for which he himself or others acted as guarantors; Jan Gamel's inventory also mentions several guarantors on bonds.[112] The database of lost bonds shows that the nineteen bonds with a borge principael were worth relatively more (as expressed in silver) than the lost bonds without a guarantor.[113] The identity of the debtor and/or creditor did not have an effect on whether a surety was needed or not.[114] The relationships between the guarantors and the debtors were strong: foreigners preferred foreigners and natives used other natives as guarantors.[115]

Discounting Bonds

Brokers, cashiers and other intermediaries were also involved in the *disconto* of bonds, i. e., buying a bond before maturity at a price (premium) lower than the bond's nominal value. Such discounting of debts originated in the medieval practice of creditors who, when in need of cash, requested an earlier payment from their debtor in exchange for a rebate.[116] The earliest instance (1536) of discounting a bill obligatory in Antwerp is in the papers of the English merchant Thomas Kitson. Kitson had sold a bill owed by a Lübeck merchant for cloth, payable at the Bamis fair, during the earlier Pentecost fair to the Antwerp merchant Aert van Dale. The premium was £5 gr. Fl. in every hundred pounds minus 5s., or a 4.9 per cent premium.[117] Disconto remained a peculiar phenomenon in sixteenth-century Antwerp; most merchants kept their bonds until maturity, unless they needed cash quickly.[118] Valentin Mennher's merchant manual *Practique brifve pour cyffrer et tenir livres de comptes*, printed in 1550, discusses several examples of discounting. Mennher provides fictitious premiums of 1 and 1.5 per cent.[119] In 1560 the Antwerp city secretary Alexander Grapheus reported to the Council of Brabant how several cashiers and brokers were buying up bills obligatory during the Easter fair at a 1 or 1.5 per cent premium instead of assigning a bill. Grapheus suggested that the council forbid such practice.[120] Unfortunately, it is unclear how the council reacted to this request. In 1563 Daniel de Bruyne bought two bonds owed by Geeraerd Gramaye from Nicolaes Jongelinck and Jan Wobbecom, probably Gramaye's creditors, before their maturity dates (for one of the bonds we know that the bill was due six months later).[121] Two years later, De Bruyne sold a £424 gr. Fl. bond he had obtained from Hans Glaeser for £295.475 gr. Fl. and took a 30.3 per cent loss on this bill.[122] Why De Bruyne opted to take such a loss is unclear, but he must have needed cash. Jan Spierinck was in similar circumstances when he was sued over a bond by Coenraed Schetz. Spierinck's inventory describes how Spierinck had given a £110 gr. Fl. bill obligatory to his broker Jan van Zevenhoven to sell at a maximum 10 per cent loss. Van Zevenhoven managed to do so and obtained £24 gr. Fl. in cash and a batch of merchandise from Marcus Maes.[123] Jan Gamel even organized the purchasing of commercial paper: Caspar Crop put in one-third of the capital with which Gamel bought bonds from Jacob van Valckenborch owed by Valerius Rutz.[124]

Van der Wee points to the increasing need to discount bonds in a climate of faster circulation and assignments of bonds.[125] Yet it remains impossible to evaluate, based on the presented source material, how common the practice of discounting bills obligatory was. Most of the references concern the 1560s and only a few examples of discounting could be found in the account books of De Bruyne and Janssens. Brulez and Van der Wee agree that it was only desirable to discount longer-term obligations (to avoid the risk of the death or insolvency of the debtor in the long run); short-term bonds could be assigned.[126] Most merchants retained their bonds in a portfolio. Yet they always had the option, when in need of cash, to discount the bond.

Payment Procedures

Terms

Can IOUs be considered to have been long-term instruments? Not all creditors and debtors were punctual in payment of their bonds: in 1585 a widow discovered a small silk bag containing an IOU owed to her late husband which was six weeks in arrears.[127] There were several variations on bond maturity dates: a fixed calendar date (such as 3 March or fixed holy days such as St Jansmis (Nativity of St John the Baptist)); a period of time after the date when the bill was recorded (for example, eight weeks later); a note that it was payable when produced or a period of time after being shown; and finally payment during one of the next four fairs in Antwerp and Bergen-op-Zoom. The exact fair could be specified. Payment could also be spread over several fairs. In some cases there was no deadline: Jacob van Valckenborch was to repay the money he had received whenever he could;[128] Jan Gamel could ask Jan van Hilst to repay the £25.2 Fl gr. any time.[129] Explicit terms were more advantageous than deposits because a merchant was always aware of upcoming bond payments; however, deposits, often extended by family members, could be withdrawn on quick notice.[130]

The exact periodization of the fair payments became a matter of contention several times throughout the sixteenth century. In the 1521 ordinance the emperor declared that the presentation days of bills obligatory with a fair as maturity date would commence on the twenty-seventh day of the freedom of the fair and would last through the thirtieth. Payments had to take place from the thirty-first day to the thirty-seventh.[131] Sixteen years later, Erasmus Schetz consulted the most important Antwerp merchants and asked the Antwerp pensionary to address the Council of Brabant on the issue of the payment periods. Schetz and the other Antwerp merchants agreed that payments should commence after the six weeks of fair freedom and end within fourteen days; debtors should pay with assignments or in cash.[132] This policy was confirmed in the 1539 ordinance. During this two-week payment period debtors were still protected from their creditors; only after the expiration of the payment period could they be sued. Because several of the fairs (Easter and Pentecost) were structured around shifting holy days, the exact dates of the fairs and their payment periods differed from year to year. This was remedied in October 1541: the four payment periods were to last ten days and started on 31 October, 31 January, 1 May and 1 August.[133] This brought an end to the shifting fair periods linked to changing holy days. From then on, payment periods were at three-month intervals. The development of fixed payment periods mirrors the growing permanence of the Antwerp market throughout the year.[134] While the fairs of Bergen-op-Zoom were still mentioned as payment dates, it was implied that the debts would be paid in Antwerp. The central government was forced several times to extend the payment periods so as to be able to pay its own debts.[135]

This increasing precision of the payment periods was also requested by the English Merchant Adventurers in 1537.[136] The Adventurers complained about the procrastination of merchants from Antwerp, Bergen-op-Zoom, Brussels and other cities in Flanders who told their creditors that they would pay during the next fair in Antwerp or Bergen. Agents of the Adventurers had to stay longer in the Low Countries just to collect their debts owed. Often more than 300 creditors could not collect a single penny because their debtors had shifted their payments to the next fair. While previously a merchant could collect money three or four times a year, this was now reduced to one time. The Adventurers even threatened to leave the Low Countries, which would have significantly harmed the 'Common Good of the Realm'. They suggested that the emperor urge all debtors to pay their debts on time, adapt the court procedure and force recalcitrant debtors to at least a *namptisatie* – transferring the moneys involved to the court who would keep it in custody for the duration of the trial – of the debt owed.[137] I was able to extract the total durations for 334 bonds.[138]

Most bonds were to be paid within three, four or six months, often coinciding with the fair periods. Of all bills, 88.6 per cent had to be satisfied within a year. Three hundred and sixty-two bonds mentioned the number of payments terms; 71.8 per cent were to be paid at one time; an additional 17.1 per cent at two times. Van der Wee has argued that sixteenth-century merchants agreed to much longer terms of payment, especially for letters obligatory.[139] My analysis cannot support this unproven statement.[140] Interestingly, there was no connection between the value of the bond (expressed in grams of silver) and the length of the payment period; IOUs with a higher value did not require longer payment terms.[141] No difference in term length based on the identity of either creditor nor debtor (native or foreign) was observed. It has been shown for late sixteenth- and early seventeenth-century Amsterdam that merchants allowed for bills to roll over on expiry for a period of up to two years.[142] Such practice could not be found in the account books of any Antwerp merchant.[143] This does not mean that IOU conditions could not be renegotiated. Herman Janssens. allowed his debtor Henric van Paessen to pay his bill in March 1559, even though it should have been paid in July 1558.[144] Anthoine de Ruede had bought linen, but was not yet successful in selling it; in the meantime, the Spanish merchant Gregoire de Astudillo, the bearer of de Ruede's IOU, approached him after the payment deadline. Both merchants co-operated to sell the linen, mobilizing brokers and other intermediaries to hasten the sales.[145] Renegotiation could also be an excuse for late payers: Jeronimus de Cock argued that he had been granted an extension by his creditor, but the latter formally denied that and de Cock was sentenced to pay forthwith.[146]

Collateral

Gelderblom considers the collateral of IOUs to have been a general collateral (pledging of person and goods). This could raise potential problems, since liquidation of a bad debt could be problematic with such general collateral.[147] Even this general collateral disappeared from the bonds: in 1569 the city lawyers of Antwerp declared that the clause of obligation of person and goods was no longer needed, since it was always implied by law.[148] The Antwerp Costuymen and several ordinances regulated that in cases of disputed bonds the debtor always had to pay the full value of the bond to the court, which would hold the money in custody (namptisatie). Merchants sometimes supplied additional and specific security measures. Deeds to real estate and annuities could be offered;[149] Herman Janssens lent money to shipmasters through an IOU with their *waterbrief* (ship ownership deed)[150] as surety; and Daniel de Bruyne accepted five fine silver dishes as bond collateral.[151] Moreover, bonds could act as security for new letters obligatory. Segher Peeters, a linen weaver from Oudenaarde, owed money to the Antwerp merchant Joos van den Steene; the notary wrote an IOU and van den Steene received two other obligations as surety, which exactly equalled the value of the new bond.[152] The Italian merchant Jan Michaeli had written an IOU to the credit of the Englishman Robrecht Boucher, worth £75.75 gr. Fl. Michaeli had given this IOU to his broker, Janne Baptista Saliti, until Boucher would supply the goods; however, the broker had loaned the IOU to Baptista Bardi for £22 gr. Fl. and Bardi then tried to collect the money from Michaeli.[153] The aforementioned case of di Prato versus van der Cappelle also demonstrates how bonds were used as surety and how one could borrow money on another bond.

In most cases, the IOU was based on a commodity transaction and the underlying goods could be returned or arrested when the bond was not paid. In the first half of the sixteenth century, IOUs were still intimately connected with the commodities trade. This is evidenced by the implicit contingency clause that the IOU was valid only when the goods were delivered to the buyer. In 1540 Augustijn Baroir from Lübeck had drawn up a notarial deed that he would not pay a £102.9 gr. Fl. obligation to Willem de Buys, an Antwerp merchant, since the goods in question (Mediterranean sweet wine and capers from the Barbary Coast) were not delivered.[154] If the quality of the goods fell short of expectations, this could invalidate the underlying bond. In 1544 Jan Baron, an Antwerp grocer, had bought English cloth from the Englishman Abraham Cordewaen and had provided Cordewaen with an IOU. When Cordewaen demanded payment of the bond, Baron argued that, because the cloth was substandard, he should not have to pay.[155]

Gradually, the letter obligatory developed into a means to finance enterprise and became detached from actual commercial transactions in commodities. Hence, it evolved into a full financial instrument. This process was most pronounced in late sixteenth-century Amsterdam but was also evident in Antwerp as well.[156] In 1559 Valerius Rutz wrote two fictive obligations of £1,261 and 1,350 gr. Fl. respectively, neither of which pertained to commodity transactions. He gave these to a broker, Jacob van Valckenborch, who was to try to raise money with the obligations as collateral. Jacob van Valckenborch promised to return the bonds but fell into financial difficulties and gave the bonds to one of his creditors, who in turn sued Rutz for payment.[157]

Payment and Interest Rates

Bond payment could be settled in a wide variety of ways. Cash payment was always valued more than assigned commercial paper: the Van der Molen[158] regularly quoted the cash premium (compared to assignments), which rose from 0.66 per cent to 2 per cent between 14 December 1538 and 21 June 1539.[159] The imperial ordinance of the 31 October 1541 caused much controversy among Antwerp merchants: it stipulated that all bills of exchange and obligations were to be paid in cash, two-thirds in gold and one-third in silver. The central government had devalued gold coins in 1539, causing a tightening money market and rising transaction costs for cash payments.[160]

The always-looming shortage of cash forced creditors to accept as payments whatever they could: merchandise, book credit[161] or bills of exchange. Juan Henriquez and Willem Jaspar Centurione had to pay a substantial bond to Laureys Bernardi; Henriquez and Centurione suggested that Bernardi take up the equivalent of the IOU as a bill of exchange on the August fair in Lyon which Henriquez and Centurione would repay on that same fair.[162] Some bills also contained a re-change clause: when a debtor defaulted on his bill, the creditor was allowed to draw a bill of exchange on him to obtain the money, with all costs would to be paid by the debtor.[163]

Recently, Lars Boerner has pointed to the practice of *rescontre*, a periodical meeting where all merchants cleared mutual debts and organized clearing chains so that only the net amounts of money needed to be settled.[164] However, no signs of organized rescontre sessions involving large groups of merchants could be found for sixteenth-century Antwerp. The evidence Van der Wee adduces proves the mutual clearing of merchant-to-merchant debts but does not demonstrate that rescontre was a large-scale organized phenomenon, a shape it assumed in the seventeenth and eighteenth centuries.[165] The practice of mutual debt clearing was very common: Andries Bricx had supplied building materials for Daniel de Bruyne's house; the value of these materials (£50 gr. Fl.) was deducted from Bricx's larger outstanding debt to de Bruyne.[166]

Interest rates on bonds were mostly hidden in the value of the bond or covered up as a fee for not paying immediately in cash. The central government set the legal maximum interest at 12 per cent; all interests above this ceiling were considered usurious.[167] In a few cases I was able to find implicit interest rates on bonds. For example, Franchois van Lare had borrowed £100 gr. Fl. from Daniel de Bruyne in January 1561 and had to pay £106 gr. Fl. back six months later (12 per cent per annum). The inventory of Melchior Schetz and his wife shows interest rates on bills obligatory owed by Schetz between 5.5 and 8 per cent.[168] Herman Van der Wee has stressed the psychological effect on investments caused by the falling interest rates throughout the sixteenth century: smaller merchants used short-term bonds to finance their enterprise.[169] In Amsterdam interest rates on IOUs dropped from 8 per cent to 6.75 per cent between 1596 and 1612 and to less than 5.5 per cent in 1620.[170]

A Micro-Study of IOU Use by an Antwerp Merchant

The best and most substantive information on how and when bills obligatory were used come from the primitive account book of Frans de Pape, a small trader in English and Flemish textiles (1539–47). The book records all de Pape's purchases (N=274) at the Brabant fairs and how he would pay for them (in cash, with an IOU or in goods).[171] De Pape mostly paid his larger debts (starting at £30 gr. Fl.) through an IOU. De Pape's foreign creditors, mostly English Merchant Adventurers, preferred to receive a bond from de Pape rather than an unregistered debt; his native creditors were less discriminatory.[172] This preference for bonds by the foreign creditors was not due to a higher value of the debts owed to them.[173] Because de Pape meticulously noted the payment dates (both the ones written in the bond and the actual payment dates), we can investigate the relation between the timing of the debt, whether it was embedded in a bond or not, and its value. The average expected duration of debts paid for with a bond was twenty-seven days longer on average than non-bond debts.[174] No relation could be observed between both the expected and the real duration of the payment and the value of the debt and between the duration of delays and the value of the debt.[175] The number of payments executed was positively correlated to the value of the debt.[176] De Pape did not need more time for larger debts but he did adopt different payment policies (more individual payments) for them. According to De Pape's account book, sixty-nine of his bonds were paid out to de Pape's original creditor; in fifty-two cases the beneficiary was not the original creditor and hence de Pape's bond was transferred or assigned.[177] In one case, de Pape explicitly noted that he paid the bond to the bearer.[178] Hence, assignment was very common in de Pape's business. Unregistered debts (for which De Pape did not write out an IOU) were much less likely to be paid out to a third party.[179] De Pape also paid his own debts with bonds owed to him.[180] The case of de Pape clearly demonstrates how a Low Countries merchant relied on the IOU system to finance his purchases from English merchants and how his preferences shaped the payment modalities.

Disputing a Bond

The preceding discussion has included several quotes about merchants disputing their responsibility towards a certain bond. In 1504 12 per cent of all Antwerp civil sentences concerned bills obligatory, 5.4 per cent in 1505 and 9 per cent in 1544.[181] Of the sentences pronounced in 1544 by the Council of Brabant, 8.5 per cent were for obligation disputes (in a total of 47). The Great Council of Mechelen (which had only limited jurisdiction in Antwerp) addressed five IOU cases in 1504 (6 per cent), two in 1505 (3 per cent) and eight in 1544 (5.2 per cent). These numbers may seem low at first sight. But given the wide variety of cases dealt with by these courts, bond disputes constituted an important aspect of the courts' jurisdiction.

The legal rights of a debtor were increasingly curtailed throughout the sixteenth century. The legal specialist Van der Tannerijen argued in the 1470s that a debtor of a bearer clause bond could only defend himself in case of fraud.[182] According to the 1507 turbe a debtor had rights of defence but had to testify immediately when the trial started, regardless of whether or not he had signed the IOU. The 1537 ordinance ordered that any debtor, when sued, had to produce the money in question which would be held by the court for the remainder of the trial. The creditor could have the money at his disposal if he provided surety. If the debtor denied that he had signed the bond and it was proven otherwise, he lost all rights of defence. The Costuymen of 1570 stipulated that a debtor had no rights of plea against a creditor, even a bearer, unless he had already paid the bill to the ceding creditor.[183] De Ruysscher has shown that debtors were more likely to sue a bond bearer than the original creditor, since there was more reason to doubt the new creditor's rights.[184]

Only in case of fraud did a debtor have substantial rights of defence, and fraud and forgery could always be just around the corner. Several decades later Maarten Della Faille experienced such a story. He had received three bonds owed by an English merchant, Aldersey, from his London agent, Nicolas Jones, as payment. Della Faille contacted Aldersey, who told him that the IOUs were forged. Della Faille had Jones secretly arrested in London; Jones confessed that he had forged the bonds to obtain credit and had wanted to provide Della Faille with the money when the bills fell due. Jones found some friends to vouch for him and to repay Della Faille. Della Faille demanded that Jones contact all the other merchants he had cheated and keep quiet about the affair.[185] Bonds could be manipulated by adding words or characters; an unscrupulous Calais Stapler, Richard Whitecroft, paid several Leiden merchants with two bonds, to which he had added a 'C' to the amount, thereby rendering the bonds a hundred times more valuable.[186] The signature and the seal were deemed especially crucial for the validity of the document. Conrard Hombrechts sued Peter Sandelin in absentia and his father,

Adriaen Sandelin. The son had given an IOU to Hombrecht, but the bill was not 'getekent oft besegelt' and 'bounced' when Hombrechts tried to collect it. Meanwhile, Peter had taken to his heels.[187] Hence, it does not come as a surprise that notaries often registered testimonies on the authenticity of signatures.[188]

The most spectacular case of IOU fraud was that of Jeronimus de Moye. On the 13th of June 1540 friends and family members of Jeronimus de Moye, a former Bruges merchant and alderman, begged emperor Charles V's representatives in the Council of Brabant for mercy.[189] De Moye was being held prisoner in the Steen, the municipal prison of city of Antwerp, and had tried to hang himself with a floor cloth; this attempt on his own life was thwarted by the prison guards at the last second. In 1532 de Moye gone mad after several blows of bad luck; henceforth, his family had to keep close watch on him. One night, he managed to escape the vigilant eyes of his kin and followed his brother-in-law Cornelis and threw several stones at him.

De Moye was charged by the Antwerp sheriff with counterfeiting bills obligatory owed by the Antwerp trader Guillaume Caluwaert. Caluwaert owed money to de Moye and wrote him an IOU in 1535; De Moye changed the date into 1536 and passed the bill onto the French merchant Claude Chasteau, alias Bourgogne, a man with powerful connections at the highest political echelons. De Moye also tampered with two other IOUs owed by Caluwaert: he had bought one of those from a creditor of Caluwaert and written a higher amount due on the bill. Both de Moye and Chasteau summoned Caluwaert to the Bruges bench of aldermen for the payment for defaulting on the payment of his bills. Caluwaert did not appear, because as an Antwerp citizen he was to be tried by the aldermen of his native Antwerp.

It seems that the insane de Moye had planned a fully-fledged vendetta against Caluwaert, who may have been a former business partner. De Moye had written several anonymous letters (his handwriting was later recognized by several witnesses) to Caluwaert's father-in-law, detailing how Caluwaert had lost all his credit because of an unpaid bill to the influential Claude Chasteau. Many people were gossiping about Caluwaert's affairs: he was said to be on the verge of bankruptcy and had handed over a large part of his assets to his main creditor, Jan Mannaert. De Moye advised the father-in-law to tell Caluwaert not to sue his creditors, since these creditors had influential friends and he would lose much-needed money.[190] These influential creditors cannot but have been Chasteau and de Moye himself, trying to avoid litigation. De Moye had also intercepted and opened letters addressed to Caluwaert.

The Council of Brabant sentenced de Moye to 3,000 Carolus guilders to be relieved of all claims, but it is not clear whether the fine was paid by de Moye or by his family and friends. The unhinged de Moye's plot seems to have been generally effective: in 1544 Caluwaert was officially declared bankrupt and ceded all his assets to his creditors. Caluwaert argued that the cause of his bankruptcy were the false IOUs and other of his 'treacheries and improper practices' of the now deceased Jeronimus de Moye. Even then, however, Caluwaert owed money to de Moye's estate.[191] A few months after de Moye's family and friends had pleaded for mercy on his behalf, an Antwerp notary registered a witness account, requested by Caluwaert, stating that Chasteau had declared that he had had nothing to do with the disputed letters obligatory between de Moye and Caluwaert but that others, unknown to him, were doing so.[192] Clearly, Chasteau wished to avoid becoming implicated in this complex case.

Conclusion

The De Moye case reveals the dangers inherent in the flexibility of private obligations. How could one trust a handwritten note that could easily be forged or altered and passed on to an unsuspecting third party? The essential answer was because lawmakers at the city and the central government stepped in, often on the request of the mercantile community, to provide registration of, if necessary, legislation on and contract enforcement of these privately circulating pieces of paper, as witnessed in the case of de Moye. Legal guarantees were installed which created a responsibility cascade: the assigner remained liable for the bond if the assignee could not obtain payment from the original debtor. The urban authorities – and the central government lagging behind – and the merchant community alike sought to balance the flexibility of private obligations with legal guarantees. It is striking that they did not take the step of establishing central registration, such as the compulsory registration of annuity sales concerning Antwerp real estate. In other cities, such as Rouen and Lisbon, registration of bonds did take place in special registers. Antwerp merchants could choose to register their bonds, for example through a notary, but were not obliged to do so; they were able to decide where they preferred flexibility over the peace of mind offered by legal registration. These episodes in the commercial history of Antwerp demonstrate that private order solutions always relied on public order institutions.[193] As Stephen Quinn has noted, 'Unlike bank transfer, payments using these methods [written notes] were limited to circles of personal familiarity and were not final until the promises were settled'.[194]

This chapter, using both quantitative and qualitative analysis of a quite heterogeneous dataset, has shown that in the early years of Antwerp's commercial growth an archaic debt instrument evolved into a highly flexible contract to underpin the transfer of big and small sums. The Antwerp urban government stepped in, at the request of the mercantile community, to secure a flexible system which allowed merchants to transfer monies and extend credit in the city. As such, an alternative was created for deposit banking, money-changers executing transfers and public exchange banksl; in short a payment system embodied in financial intermediaries and public institutions. Antwerp hosted a decentralized, flexible, yet effective payment system through IOU circulation, legalized and enforced when necessary by the urban government. The micro-analysis of the de Pape's and other traders' accounts has shown how merchants used these bonds in day-to-day transactions. Native and foreign traders had different views on these bonds, with the latter showing a more reluctant attitude towards the instrument. Native traders preferred the flexibility of assignment and used IOUs more intensively than their foreign counterparts. Bonds could be used to start up a commercial enterprise. Jan Della Faille's testimony about small merchants buying goods on credit using bonds and then having to sell their goods at depressed prices (because they had to pay their bonds) proves that the credit function of bills obligatory was indeed used to fund small and starting businesses. A good reputation was of course necessary to be granted credit. Acquiring a reputation and familiarity may have been a burden for starting merchants but the legal certainty of the bills obligatory ensured that creditors were willing to grant credit to borrowers with whom they were not (yet) familiar. Low Countries merchants could only rely on the IOU system when in Antwerp. In other European cities they had to make use of other, local payment methods; they could transfer funds through bills of exchange just like all other traders. It cannot be denied that their use of IOUs distinguished Low Countries merchants from other merchant groups. Hence, the IOU system is one of the factors which explain the ascent of Low Countries merchants. The system worked because it was backed by urban courts and by a government willing to change the rules to make the system work. Low Countries merchants profited from the institutional changes which took place in sixteenth-century Antwerp. These institutions are the subject of the last chapter.

Data Appendix

Five different types of Antwerp sources have been scrutinized in search of bills obligatory.

Antwerp certification books and aldermen's registers (1490–1514): the Antwerp magistracy produced certificates (written declarations) on behalf of private persons, often local and foreign merchants, concerning various commercial and/or juridical issues. I used Renée Doehaerd's publication of the certification books (1488–1513). She summarized all certificates with references to 'international trade' and I have selected all 'lettres obligatoires', which provided 189 cases between 1479 and 1514.[195] Doehaerd's selection criteria are: (1) all certificates with references to foreigners doing business in Antwerp (from abroad); (2) all certificates with references to Low Countries merchants active abroad; (3) documents with references to distribution and consumption of foreign goods in the

Netherlands; and (4) documents with references to distribution and consumption of Low Countries products abroad. Some 'mandats et procurations' contain quantitative information on debts but Doehaerd's abbreviated notes specify whether the debt is in fact a bill obligatory. The Antwerp aldermen's registers are integrally preserved from 1394 to 1797. All transactions concerning immovable goods had to be registered in these ledgers. A large variety of other contracts could also be registered by the aldermen's clerks. The sheer size of these ledgers (roughly between 2,000 and 4,000 deeds per year) renders this source problematic for an individual historian.[196] Fortunately, Doehaerd also recorded all aldermen's deeds concerning international trade. Moreover, I have used a database constructed by Tim Bisschops and his students, in which they digitalized written summaries of the aldermen's registered for several years in the period 1490–3. I would like to express my gratitude to Tim Bisschops for letting me use his data. All bonds have been extracted from the Doehaerd and Bisschops records; these have been double checked to eliminate double entries.

Civil sentences pronounced by the Antwerp aldermen in cases of litigation (1504–5 and 1544): in 1488 the bench of aldermen adopted a written procedure for registering its sentences in civil cases.[197] Litigants could request a copy of the sentence, which was then reproduced in a *vonnisboek*. Not all of these ledgers have been preserved. Hence, I have chosen three sample years: 1504 (ninety-four sentences), 1505 (ninety-two sentences) and 1544 (583 sentences). In 1504, 12 per cent of all pronounced sentences concerned bills obligatory; 5.4 per cent did so in 1505 and 9 per cent in 1544.[198]

Notarial acts by Zeger Adriaan 's Hertoghen and Willem Stryt (1540): merchants frequently used the services of notaries to register their obligations and operations concerning these obligations (transports, procurations, receipts).[199] I have selected 1540 as a sample year; the deeds of two notaries have been preserved for that year. Seventy-four acts (9.8 per cent) of all the notarial acts recorded by Adriaen Zeger 's Hertoghen and Willem Stryt in 1540 mentioned a bond.[200]

Post-mortem inventory Jan Gamel 1572: according to the inventory of a textile trader and financier, his estate was owed more than £20,000 gr. Fl. in bonds and half of his wealth consisted of obligations. Registered on 11 August 1572 by notary Henrick van Uffele.[201]

Bankrupt merchant's inventory Jan Spierinck 1565: in 1565 the merchant Jan Spierinck was sued by his creditor Coenraerd Schetz over a £400 gr. Fl. obligation and imprisoned. Spierinck wished to prove that he was not insolvent and thus could not be detained as a bankrupt. He argued that he was 'not so godless that he wanted to deny his debt' and had an inventory made up to prove that he was still creditworthy.[202]

Account books Frans de Pape 1539–47: cloth trader Frans de Pape bought most of his merchandise from English or Antwerp merchants. He organized his account book around the four fairs, noting from whom he had bought the textiles, providing specific details (description and price) and the credit terms (usually payable at the next fair or the following). He also noted the bonds he had drawn up ('hantscrift').[203]

Account books Herman Janssens 1551–70: Herman Janssens co-operated with his sister Anna and several of his brothers in the trade with England, Portugal, Spain and the Canary Islands. His daybook in which he recorded costs and yields of his enterprises documents his operations between 1551 and 1570.[204]

Notes and accounts of printer and bookseller Christophe Plantin (1559–89): Christophe Plantin migrated to Antwerp in 1549 and started his own printing company in 1555.[205] In two bundles of Plantin's accounts, several bonds can be found.[206]

Account books Daniel de Bruyne 1561–8: Daniel de Bruyne was a jeweller and was also active in real estate speculation, maritime insurance and organizing lotteries. His double entry journal has been preserved because it was confiscated when de Bruyne and his patron, Christoffel Pruynen were implicated in a large-scale government fraud case. De Bruyne noted fifty-five bonds in this journal.[207]

Account books Jaspar Van Bell 1563–1566: the 's-Hertogenbosch merchant Jaspar van Bell sold locally bleached linen, pins and knives to Antwerp merchants and in Spain.[208]

Account books of Jehan and Mathieu Moriel 1567: the two nephews traded in textiles and grain and had agents in Lyon and Danzig.[209]

Proclaimed lost obligations 1546–87: see chapter four.[210]

5 INSTITUTIONS AND THE POLITICAL ECONOMY OF SIXTEENTH-CENTURY ANTWERP COMMERCE

Introduction

So far, the story told about the ascent of Low Countries merchants operating out of Antwerp in the sixteenth century may not strike the reader as unique or revolutionary. Other groups such as the Florentines in the thirteenth century, the south Germans in the fifteenth century, the English Merchant Adventurers in the sixteenth century and Dutch merchants in the sixteenth and seventeenth centuries have similarly relied on specialization in the export of local products, on advanced commercial and financial techniques and on the provision of market infrastructure. Yet there is something odd about sixteenth-century Antwerp when one considers the historiography and compares the city's political economy with that of other commercial cities.

Recent analyses of commercial institutions have portrayed Antwerp as a place where open-access institutions – defined as 'those whose rules apply uniformly to everyone in a society, regardless of their identity or their membership in particular groups, e.g. a state in which a rule of law is established to some degree, or a competitive market with free entry'[1] – allowed merchants outside local or foreign merchant guilds to participate in the city's trade.[2] Municipal authorities provided secure property rights and important market infrastructure to all players; they opened up the city's administration and courts to all traders, as well as integrated commercial customs of different commercial groups into the city's laws. The city government and the market provided alternative solutions for merchants to organize their trade, which led to the subsequent decline of merchant guilds in Antwerp.[3] This chapter has three aims: to point out the peculiarity of sixteenth-century Antwerp's urban government; to demonstrate that the city did manage to set up an efficient and neutral court system which serves as an example of an open-access institution; and to nuance the decline of merchant guilds in Antwerp by providing evidence of several failed attempts by Low Countries merchants to set up a merchant guild. Indeed a close reading of the histories of these attempts and those of foreign merchant guilds in sixteenth-century Antwerp reveals the urban government's preference for attracting foreign traders over furthering the commercial interests of its own citizens and countrymen.

Antwerp's Urban Government

Prosopographical research for 1520–55 and 1550–66 shows that noblemen and university-trained professionals dominated the Antwerp magistracy (mayor, aldermen and treasurer-general); only a small minority of them were merchants.[4] The low number of merchants (16 per cent of the aldermen and 13 per cent of all magistracy positions in 1550–66) is striking. Half of those merchants were elected only once.[5] In Antwerp during the period 1568–75, more university-trained lawyers managed to secure seats on the bench of aldermen, but the number of aldermen-merchants remained low.[6] After the Iconoclasm of 1566 the city magistracy came under pressure from the central government and found it increasingly difficult to guarantee the Antwerp privileges. The Spanish Fury of 1576 drastically accentuated this evolution. During the Calvinist Republic (1577–85) merchants exercised real political power in the city together with the deans of the craft guilds. To defend the city, Antwerp organized compulsory military service (applicable to all able male citizens) into the *schuttersgilden*. The command of this civil militia lay in the hands of eight colonels: twenty-one of the twenty-seven colonels were merchants. The colonels controlled security within the city and took care of the military preparations. Explanations for this radical stance of merchant-colonels can be adduced to their Calvinist beliefs and their attempt to secure the commercial faith of the city and their own commercial interests.[7]

Why were merchants not interested in holding a political position? Three options come to mind. First, merchants had no business in the magistracy since their interests were already being taken care of by a government which did everything within its power to appease them. While this is true to a certain extent, one could imagine that the Antwerp–England traders might have lamented not having an inside man within the magistracy, especially when they asked for a merchant guild in 1565. Magistrates also proved to be rather receptive in other instances: Gilbert van Schoonbeke's political connections paid off handsomely for his real estate and brewery conglomerate.[8] Hence, one need not have been an alderman to have things go his way. Second, merchants did not want to withdraw from the lucrative activities of commerce. Third, the social status of a political career may have been superfluous, since these merchants already had high status because of their wealth and the noble titles they were able to purchase.[9]

The relative absence of direct political power is at odds with evidence from other sixteenth-century commercial cities. In Lyon, also a commercial centre that developed from a fair town into a permanent market, the mercantile elite seized power in the first half of the sixteenth century to the detriment of the old 'republique des clercs'.[10] Sixteenth-century Seville was ruled by an oligarchy of noblemen with firm roots in commerce and the London aldermen and mayors were often members of the Merchant Adventurers' Company.[11] Italian city-states such as Venice and Genoa were similarly controlled by mercantile and financial elites, although their elites were acquiring more landed wealth in the sixteenth century.[12] Antwerp also had to share power and negotiate with the central government in Brussels.[13] Hence, sixteenth-century Antwerp was not a true merchant republic.[14]

Antwerp Courts of Law as Open-Access Institutions

The previous chapters have drawn heavily upon court cases registered in civil sentences and case files produced by the Antwerp aldermen's court and the royal courts, the Council of Brabant (highest court in Brabant) and the Great Council of Mechelen (the highest court in the Low Countries). This section looks at these institutions themselves: how efficient were they and could every merchant turn to them?

Going to court was of course not the only option available to mitigate relationships that had turned sour. In line with research on criminal history, historians have demonstrated the wide range of available modes of conflict settlement, which ranged from verbal and physical threats and violence and informal mediation by family, friends and neighbours to the formal services of notaries and other urban public officials.[15] Merchants preferred amicable settlement over formal adjudication; not least as such a settlement was much more discrete than a public court case.[16] If two parties could not reach an understanding, they could turn to arbiters.[17] Two options existed: the disputing parties could choose the arbiters themselves or the court could appoint them.[18] The first arbiters could apply various rules, including those of their home-town in the case of foreign merchants, while the court-appointed arbiters had to obey local laws. Arbitrage was also quick and cheap.[19] Moreover, arbitrators were better able to come to an equitable solution than adhere to the strict letter of the law. In many cases the Antwerp aldermen first sent the litigants to the *goede mannen* who had to listen to both the litigants, inspect the evidence and then try to reconcile the litigants. If no reconciliation could be reached, the arbiters had to write a report which could then be used by the aldermen to formulate a verdict. Some contracts, such as partnership agreements, already included clauses on arbitrage (as discusses earlier). Mediation allowed the courts to lower their case load and deal with those cases where arbitrage had not led to agreement between the parties. The integration of informal arbitrage in the formal court system is a perfect example of the embeddedness of private solutions in the framework of public institutions.[20]

In 1505 and 1544 respectively 14 per cent and 20 per cent of the sentences concerning mercantile cases mentioned arbitrage. Fellow merchants could act as arbiters, men of honour, *goede mannen, cooplieden neutrael, marchands neutraux, bonos viros*; city officials (like the Orphan Chamber masters, the treasurer or the *commissarissen*)[21] and representatives from the craft guilds could mediate as well.[22] It is highly likely that the litigants were acquainted with the arbiters. In many cases the aldermen first sent the litigants to the *goede mannen*. If no reconciliation could be reached, the arbiters had to write a report, which could then be used by the aldermen to formulate a verdict. Notaries often registered and formalized arbitrage proceedings.

Most of the civil cases started on a voluntary basis, after a formal complaint by one of the litigants.[23] Going to court was of course not the only option available to mitigate relationships that had turned sour. Martin Dinges and Craig Muldrew have shown that many court cases in early modern England and France never ended in a decisive verdict, since the litigants had come to an agreement during the trial.[24] Formal litigation could end the dispute and court officials could intervene in the final settlement process. The early modern litigant has been portrayed as a critical consumer in the legal and extra-legal marketplace of conflict settlement.[25] This early modern consumer of justice relied both on informal solutions and the public judicial services offered by the urban government and the central state.[26] This consumer however was constrained by the rules and procedures of the court system. It is these consumers of justice and the services of the Antwerp court system which will be scrutinized in this section.

Structure of the Local Antwerp Court

Already in the twelfth-century sources, the Antwerp aldermen are documented as performing judicial functions, even before they had obtained governmental power.[27] In the sixteenth century increasing numbers of aldermen had received formal university training in law and some had experience in commerce.[28] The growing scale and scope of commerce in Antwerp cannot but have caused growing pains for the judicial apparatus. No separate merchant courts were formed, thus mercantile cases were treated alongside with other civil cases.[29] The *extraordinarisse rol*, a division of the aldermen's college, slowly assumed particular authority over mercantile matters. It consisted of the amman, the ducal officer in civil matters, who summoned two or three aldermen and a registrar. In this extraordinary roll the civil cases were registered and dealt with in sequence. This court could act faster for cases requiring speedy resolution[30] The development of a separate fair court did not occur in Antwerp. The bench of aldermen dealt with all contractual disputes, also those occurring at the fairs. Privileges granted by the duke of Brabant, dating from the thirteenth and fourteenth century, determined the legal framework of the fairs and the judicial role of the bench of aldermen. In 1488 Maximilian of Austria granted the bench of aldermen full and sovereign jurisdiction over the Antwerp fairs. No appeal or *reformatie* could be had against sentences by the aldermen concerning fair transactions.[31]

Already at the end of the thirteenth century, the duke of Brabant had granted consular jurisdiction to English merchants, but the English started to use this prerogative only from the middle of the fifteenth century onwards. The German Hanse received similar privileges of consular jurisdiction in the fourteenth and fifteenth centuries. The Portuguese, Genoese, Florentines and Luccese followed in the sixteenth century. Several groups of merchants, the south Germans and the French most conspicuously, did not enjoy these privileges but nonetheless were very active on the Antwerp market.[32] Like in Bruges, Antwerp's commercial predecessor, the local court and the consular courts were complementary and co-operating institutions.[33] Their respective tasks were clearly divided: consular courts dealt with intra-community affairs. When litigation concerned merchants from a different country, the aldermen handled the case. Besides, the city's aldermen and the consular courts, the Cloth Hall court (1308) also dealt with cases involving the production and commerce of textiles. The aldermen's court acted as an appellate court for the Cloth Hall.[34] The aldermen's court and its subdivisions (the various *rollen*) handled all civil cases, including the mercantile ones. The Cloth Hall, the craft guilds, the Orphan Chamber, the Peacemakers and the Erfscheyders (arbiters involved in real estate boundary disputes) acted as courts *ratione materiae*.[35] This construction of merchant nations, ancillary courts, the bench of aldermen and its subdivisions handled all civil and mercantile cases. At least one attempt was made in sixteenth-century Antwerp to install a specialized mercantile court in the fashion of the French and Italian merchant courts, or *mercanzias*.[36] In the middle of the sixteenth century, the aldermen proposed establishment of a mercantile court ruling that adjudicated disputes between merchants from different regions according to commercial customs, royal legislation and equity. The prince would annually elect four consuls from a list of ten Antwerp, ten German, ten Italian and ten Iberian merchants (six Spanish and four Portuguese). These consuls, together with an alderman, would sit three times per week; appeal to sentences pronounced by this court could be obtained at the bench of aldermen. The project was never executed after its submission to the Privy Council.[37]

Having detailed the structures of the Antwerp courts, I will turn to how these courts were used by merchants. In 1488 the bench of aldermen adopted a written procedure to register its sentences in civil cases.[38] Litigants could request a copy of the sentence, which was then reproduced in a *vonnisboek*.[39] Not all of these ledgers have been preserved. I have chosen two sample years: 1504–5 (186 sentences) and 1544 (583 sentences).[40] Because the mercantile cases were mixed among other civil disputes, the commerce-related cases can be compared to the other civil cases, which serve as a control group. In 1505, 25.8 per cent (forty-eight) of the sentences referred to cases involving merchants and/or mercantile affairs, in 1544 this amounted to 30 per cent (177). Hence, the Antwerp bench of aldermen had become increasingly important for merchant affairs.

Like the sentences, the arguments and evidence were increasingly recorded on paper.[41] This resulted in a growing series of preserved case files. I examined more than 180 files of cases which were taken to court between 1482 and 1559: twenty-two of those were cases between merchants or commerce-related disputes.[42] The number of sentences per capita increased during the first half of the sixteenth century.[43] Presumably, this increase was not spread evenly over the urban population: the growing number of entrepreneurs and merchants caused by the economic growth of the city are likely to have been responsible for most of this increased number of sentences.[44] The late fifteenth- and sixteenth-century Antwerp curve roughly corresponds with the general European pattern: a dramatic rise of the levels of civil litigation in the sixteenth century.[45] Wollschläger's time series of litigation rates for the German city of Bremen and its countryside offers the most consistent observation of this distinctive pattern. Others just count the number of survived case files, which biases the time series, because of the higher likelihood of survival for historically more recent files. Wollschläger's litigation rates are the number of civil sentences pronounced by the urban government per 1,000 inhabitants of Bremen. [46] In the case of Antwerp, this growing number of sentences can be largely explained by growing population size; this is corroborated by fact that the number of sentences declines after the 1568 population peak.[47]

The growing load of court cases on a European level stands in stark contrast with contemporary accounts and historians' descriptions of the early modern justice system as being expensive, time intensive, inaccessible and infested by corruption and nepotism – in short, as inefficient.[48] However, recent histories of the early modern English judiciary have qualified this alleged inefficiency.[49] The urban courts of seventeenth-century Nantes and Lyon were relatively accessible in terms of the social profile of the litigants and the costs and duration of the trial.[50] The civil sentences provide two proxies by which to measure the efficiency of the local court and the access to local justice in sixteenth-century Antwerp. The first is the value of the stake. If disputes with low stakes were taken to court, this would suggest that people could rely on the court to enforce small claims quickly and at reasonable costs. Of the 769 sentences, 392 mention the amounts of money at stake.[51]

The large difference between mean and median values of both the stake values and the stake values deflated in yearly wages and the large standard deviations demonstrate the presence of several high-stakes court cases. The drop of the median stake and the 25 and 50 percentile values between 1505 and 1544 reveal that over time more cases of lesser values were taken to court. Nonetheless, the stakes still represented substantial parts of a master mason's annual wage.[52] Hence, the court was used mostly for disputing transactions which were quite large in monetary and social terms. Other divisions of the city court were available for cases involving lower stakes, for example the Maandagse and the Woensdagse rol (Monday and Wednesday Rolls).[53]

For 1544 it is also possible to look at the difference in stakes between mercantile cases and other civil cases. As expected, the mercantile cases had much higher stakes in both sample years.[54] A second proxy to assess the efficiency of the local court is the duration of the cases. For this measure I selected cases with a clear and (presumably) final sentence, ruled in favour of the plaintiff or the defendant and containing a starting date of the legal case between the litigants.[55] More than half of the cases in 1544 were settled within a year. In dividing the 1544 trial duration data between the mercantile and non-mercantile cases, it appears that mercantile cases took slightly longer than other civil cases (median).[56]

Another proxy would be the legal costs of a civil case. Unfortunately, neither the selected case files nor the sentences provide adequate data to make such calculations. Three trial files do show that most of the costs concerned administrative expenses, which could become quite sizeable in cases requiring large amounts of registered evidence, testimonies, etc.[57] Van Dijck has pointed to the high costs for cases of the Great Council of Mechelen.[58] The Antwerp sentences show that in most cases the losing litigant had to pay the incurred costs.[59]

For litigants to make use of the services offered by the court system, the courts not only had to be efficient in handling cases but also offer litigants fair and impartial judgment. This impartiality is not always assured in courts. For example, in seventeenth-century Istanbul Christians shunned the courts because their cases against Muslim subjects were likely to result in biased judgment.[60] In 1544, foreign merchants in sixteenth-century Antwerp were (somewhat) more inclined to have a legal dispute with another foreigner than with a local; mercantile conflicts between locals were recorded less frequently in the civil sentences.

Table 5.1: Numbers of mercantile civil cases, by plaintiff and defendant identities

| | 1504–5 | | | 1544 | | |
	Foreign defendant	Local defendant	Total	Foreign defendant	Local defendant	Total
Foreign plaintiff	25	10	35	104	38	142
Local plaintiff	15	48	63	59	81	140
Total	35	58	98	163	119	282

Source: CAA, sentence books, V # 1233 & V # 1238–1240.

Did the Antwerp court favour foreign or local traders or was it neutral? A favourable treatment of foreign merchants would have attracted them to the Antwerp market. A pro-local bias would strengthen local traders but it would deter the foreigners. The Antwerp court had strong incentives not to favour either group since it competed with other cities for commerce; a judicial bias would likely divert this commerce to another commercial centre. [61] From the richer data for 1544 it appears that local plaintiffs had a better chance of winning against a foreign defendant than vice versa. To truly gauge potential bias between locals and foreigners, it is necessary to compare those cases in which such parties met each other as litigants. No significant statistical bias could be found in the chances of winning a case by foreigners and natives.[62] Foreign merchants did not hesitate to make use of the urban court. However, there were large differences in the frequency of their use of the local courts, depending on the merchant's origin and allegiance to particular nations.[63] We can compare the numbers of merchants involved in civil cases in 1544 and the estimated numbers of different merchant groups in the middle of the sixteenth century.

Not coincidentally, the Portuguese and English merchants who had been granted extensive privileges and separate jurisdictions did not often appear in the aldermen's court, just like the Venetians and the German Hansa in Bruges.[64] Genoese merchants, who did have a nation, frequently resorted to the aldermen's court.[65] As in Bruges, attitudes towards the bench of aldermen differed from nation to nation. Moreover, the local court was not often used as a court of appeal for consular judgments. For 1544 I found only two such cases, one involving, unsurprisingly, Portuguese merchants. Symoen Fernandes wanted Cristoffelen de la Haye to honour his debt of £5 gr. Fl. to which de la Haye had already been sentenced by the consuls of the Portuguese nation.[66]

How were foreign merchants perceived and described in the court sentences? One would expect that much attention was given to the identification of these merchants because of the legal privileges some of them enjoyed by being member of a nation. Interestingly, the practice of identification of a merchant as a foreigner was subject to change in sixteenth-century Antwerp. In 1505 around half of the merchants who could be identified as foreigners (based on their names) were explicitly described as foreigners in the Antwerp civil sentences of that year.[67] In 1544 only 17 per cent of the foreign plaintiffs and 13 per cent of the foreign defendants were explicitly identified as foreigners.[68] Thus, at least the registrars of the sentences did not deem it necessary to record that a litigant was a foreigner; perhaps this was not recorded because origin and nation allegiance were considered irrelevant, since all were equal before the law. This might show the breakdown of merchants' corporate identities and the growing irrelevance of the privileges of their merchant nation.[69]

The Royal Courts of Law in the Low Countries

Douglass North has argued that the development of the European economy went hand in hand with the process of state formation. North assumed that merchants and other economic actors would have benefited from the ability of stronger states to act as third party contract enforcers. According to North, the creation of a central court system from the fifteenth century onwards led to the decline of corporate jurisdictions.[70] However, the local level of government seems to have maintained its importance for contract enforcement and protection more than the central government, since Europe remained a patchwork of local and regional privileged jurisdictions.[71] Moreover, the central state saw the court system as means of revenue, prioritizing courts and types of cases which were likely to bring in money and disregarding less financially interesting courts and cases.[72] In the case of bankruptcies, intervention of the prince through his 'justice and grace' affirmed his royal power.[73]

In 1512 the Council of Brabant (formally created in 1430) obtained independence from the Great Council of Mechelen and became the sovereign court for the duchy of Brabant.[74] Since 1488 the Council of Brabant had acted as a limited and final court of appeal for the Antwerp local court. This appeal was limited to *reformaties*: litigants could lodge an objection to a local court judgement within a year of the ruling. The execution of the sentence pronounced by the local court was not suspended and the councillors used the case file produced by the local court.[75] Six sentences in 1505 and seventeen sentences in 1544 indicate the involvement of the Council of Brabant in an Antwerp case. In 1544 the Council of Brabant handled thirty-one cases regarding Antwerp merchants (or 12.75 per cent of all its caseload of that year).[76] This was less than the 134 sentences pronounced by the Antwerp aldermen in mercantile cases but the number of Council of Brabant is not negligible. The assistance of the Council of Brabant was frequently called in to obtain the necessary permissions for confiscation and sales and to start specific legal procedures, such as in the case of bankruptcies. Furthermore, the Council of Brabant served as a repository for the evidence of 'international' cases: in 1544 textile trader Joose Geerts sued his agent, Jaspar Lissens, in the Spanish city of Sanlúcar de Barrameda for various debts. The case started in the Antwerp aldermen's court but was subsequently taken to the Council of Brabant. The Council requested the defendant Lissens to send his original accounts to Brussels. This order was executed and the Council received and kept the original agent accounts.[77] The Council of Brabant also acted as the court of law for the case between the Antwerp agent Jan Della Faille and his Venetian principals, the de Hane brothers. The de Hane brothers accused their agent of withholding credits in Antwerp and London which were due to them. In 1566 the Council ruled that Della Faille had to deliver his account books to the court so that the de Hane or their representatives could inspect them. The Council also sent an agent to Venice to examine the de Hane books.[78] These two examples show that the Council of Brabant could collect evidence beyond its jurisdictional boundaries. But the local court also had considerable scope to act on its own and negotiate with other courts, not only with nearby Middelburg but also with the French admiralty and the *Casa de Contratación* in Seville in 1544.[79]

We can compare the stake values and duration of trials handled in 1544 with those of the urban court of Antwerp. The few stake values we have for mercantile cases at the Council of Brabant are significantly higher than those of the urban court (both median and average).[80] Hence, merchants brought their cases to the Council of Brabant, but generally only those with high stake value which justified the trouble.[81] In nineteen cases we could determine the beginning and end dates of Council of Brabant trials. The cases lasted much longer than those handled by the aldermen (938 days on average vs. 489 days at the Antwerp bench of aldermen).[82] This proves the assertion of several authors that merchants were careful in going to such provincial and central courts.[83]

The involvement of the Council of Brabant in Antwerp mercantile cases remained small, but was larger than that of the highest central court, the Great Council or Parlement of Mechelen. The Great Council originated in the course of 1435–45 as a separate itinerant court of law from the Sovereign's Council. It settled in 1473 in Mechelen but became itinerant again, after abolishment of the Parlement, in 1477. In 1504 the Great Council was re-established in Mechelen.[84] The Great Council had the ambition to act as a court of first instance for foreign merchants.[85] Gelderblom has proven that merchants were unlikely to take their case to the Great Council of Mechelen, the highest court in the Netherlands.[86] This average duration is comparable to that of the Council of Brabant but was much slower than that of the Antwerp bench of aldermen. Moreover, the appeal procedure offered the option of postponing judgement, a shortcoming which was remedied only after instalment of new rules for the Great Council in 1459 and 1488.[87] But even after that, many procedural delays were possible.[88] The Great Council of Mechelen was mentioned twice in each of the three sample years I selected in the civil sentences of the aldermen's court (1504–5 and 1544). In 1540–50 the Great Council handled fifty-four cases involving foreign merchants.[89] These sparse references to the Great Council indicate that it rarely intervened in the local aldermen's court, which handled many more cases on an annual basis than the Great Council. Yet, the Council was still an authority in jurisprudence and its rulings acted as points of reference.[90] In 1505, 13 per cent of the cases handled by the Great Council concerned merchants and mercantile matters; in 1544 these cases amounted to only 7 per cent.[91] All of the cases were appeals from courts from Flanders, Holland, Zeeland and Artois, none of them from Brabant.

This reluctance of merchants in the Low Countries to use the central courts is at odds with North's hypothesis about the role of state formation; in fact, the local level remained pivotal for contract enforcement issues.[92] Merchants enjoyed shorter communication lines with the local court and government. Supplications and requests could be submitted to the aldermen by both individuals and groups of merchants. Moreover, the mercantile community was often consulted on legal matters. These consultations resulted in turben, formal declarations by a group of merchants, notaries, brokers and/or attorneys on commercial practices, and held legal force.[93]

Merchant Guilds in Sixteenth-Century Antwerp

To assess the Antwerp position in the current debate on merchant guilds a short sketch of this debate is required.[94] Merchant guilds can be defined as associations of merchants active in long-distance trade; they are to be distinguished from craft guilds and guilds of local retailers.[95] The debate is mainly structured around the functions which these merchant guilds are said to have performed: the guilds are seen mainly from an instrumental perspective as having been a solution to problems experienced by merchants operating in long-distance trade. However, merchant guilds were not the only service providers: central states and local authorities also offered services to merchants.[96]

Greif, Milgrom and Weingast have argued that merchant guilds ensured that princes and governments provided security for foreign merchants within their jurisdictions and thus contributed to commercial growth. Merchants would not call at trading cities unless they were assured about the security of their persons and goods, since otherwise they were vulnerable to arbitrary expropriation and violence. Merchants who joined forces and organized themselves into a guild could choose to boycott governments reluctant to provide visiting merchants with sufficient guarantees of security. When merchants avoided such cities, their governments missed out on trade, a potentially lucrative source of government income. Hence, through the threat of boycott, rulers and governments could credibly commit to the security of foreign merchants.[97] With keen attention to detail, historians have reconstructed the workings of these merchant guilds and the local context in which they were active.[98] Unfortunately, this impeded pan-European comparison and understanding of merchant guilds and of the determining factors within local contexts for development of these guilds.[99]

Sheilagh Ogilvie presents a critical synthesis of European merchant guilds from 1000 to 1800 (but mostly up to the sixteenth century); she is particularly interested in the relations between merchant guilds, social capital and economic development.[100] Ogilvie distinguishes local from alien merchant guilds and merchant hanses (a federation of the merchant guilds of a group of towns; the most impressive example being the German Hansa).[101] Both local merchant guilds and alien merchant guilds sought to obtain legal monopolies from local rulers which they vigorously tried to enforce.[102] Moreover, alien merchant guilds faced competition from other alien guilds and local merchant guilds in the cities where they traded. According to Ogilvie, merchant guilds acted as a deadweight loss on the pre-industrial economy and society. They did not enable commercial growth, or – as Ogilvie puts it – they did not seek to produce a larger aggregate economic pie; rather, they sought to maximize their part of the pie to the advantage of their guild members. The relations between guilds and the local rulers explain merchant guild persistence through the centuries: rulers and cities granted privileges to merchant guilds in return for fees, loans, tax assistance and political and military support from these guilds. Because of their sizeable political influence and power, merchant guilds managed to survive for centuries. Ogilvie adduces evidence denying merchant guild efficiency in solving merchants' problems such as commercial security, contract enforcement, principal agent problems, information and price volatility. Merchant guilds could even exacerbate these problems. Moreover, there were other, often more efficient, solutions provided by public institutions and the market. These open-access institutions started to emerge at the same time (in the twelfth century) as merchant guilds. The presence and significance of open-access, public institutions determined a region's commercial potential. Sixteenth-century Antwerp plays an important role in Ogilvie's analysis. The city government and the market provided alternative solutions for merchants to organize their trade, which led to the subsequent decline of merchant guilds.[103]

Gelderblom and Grafe have argued, based on analysis of merchant guilds that were active in the commercial cities of the Low Countries (Bruges, Antwerp and Amsterdam) and the Spanish port of Bilbao, that merchant guilds lost their original purpose from the fifteenth and sixteenth centuries onwards.[104] This decline, they argue, was caused by the process of state formation: a more powerful state could provide merchants with neutral courts of law and could protect trade through diplomacy, convoying and even warfare. This process of state formation did not pass without incidents; military competition between states may even have increased hostilities and insecurities, and merchants continued to organize themselves to shield their persons and merchandise from violence.

The commercial heartlands of Europe, such as the commercial gateways of Italy and the Low Countries, are said to have witnessed an early shift from merchant associations to individually operating merchants, because these cities supplied security and contract enforcement to all parties, not just to certain merchant guild members.[105] Cities in the densely urbanized Low Countries were bound by political and economic inter-city competition.[106] Many merchant associations survived after their economic functions became obsolete, thanks to their social and cultural functions; merchant guilds often held meetings and feasts, patronized chapels in particular churches and monasteries and formed religious confraternities. According to Gelderblom and Grafe, this process was dependent on the level of trade and the power of local governments and explains the regional differences in the decline of merchant guilds. Larger markets lowered the potential benefits of organization.[107]

Foreign Merchant Guilds in Sixteenth-Century Antwerp

The Antwerp market hosted both native and foreign traders.[108] The granting of the first privileges to groups of foreign merchants took place within the context of the establishment of the Antwerp fairs. The end of the thirteenth and the beginning of the fourteenth century witnessed the organization of the Brabant fairs.[109] Merchants from nearby Aachen, Cologne and Hamburg already enjoyed privileges in the thirteenth century. John III, duke of Brabant, actively tried to attract German merchants to his territories, probably at the behest of the politically powerful Brabant cities (Brussels, Leuven and Antwerp), and granted them extensive privileges on 28 October 1315. The German privilege confirmed mercantile property rights, set the Bergen-op-Zoom and Antwerp tolls for a long series of commodities,[110] distinguished wholesale trade from retail and arranged reasonable price setting for real estate. Moreover, the privilege arranged the judicial division of tasks between the Antwerp sheriff, the aldermen and the German mercantile community. German merchants were allowed to appoint a consul or captain and host meetings among themselves. Breaches of contracts and trade conflicts could be judged within their community; capital offences and inter-community conflicts would always be decided by the aldermen. German merchants were also explicitly allowed to change currencies and execute payments in cash or with promissory letters. Moreover, the duke of Brabant promised the merchants to compensate for loss, arrest or theft of goods within his territories. In case of war between the duke and parts of Germany, the merchants would receive a forty days' notice to leave the territory without harm to them or their goods. Finally, the merchants were exempt from the excises on beer and wine they consumed.[111] A little earlier, English merchants had obtained their first privileges in 1296.[112] Later, the English merchants were incorporated within the Merchant Adventurers which established strong control over English traders in Antwerp.[113] In 1315, in the same year when the duke of Brabant granted privileges to the German merchants, the duke tried to entice Genoese and Florentine merchants into visiting the fairs of Bergen-op-Zoom and Antwerp with a consular jurisdiction.

After these early privileges the documentation remains mute on the subject until the late fifteenth century, when Antwerp's commercial prospects improved substantially. In 1488, Maximilian of Austria ordered all foreign merchants to leave the city of Bruges; this was intended as punishment to the city for its rebellion against him.[114] Maximilian and the city of Antwerp were quick to grant the Hanseats, Portuguese, Venetians, Florentines, Genoese and Luccese the same privileges and security guarantees for their goods, persons and families as they had previously enjoyed in Bruges.[115] The Genoese negotiated for new privileges, similar to the ones they enjoyed in Bruges, with Philip the Fair in 1501 and transferred their consulate to Antwerp in 1515, as did the Florentines. The Genoese were granted a consular jurisdiction in 1564. In 1498 the factor of the king of Portugal established himself in Antwerp and in 1511 the entire community of Portuguese merchants obtained a privilege. Aragonese and Catalan traders had a consulate in 1527 and the Luccese received privileges in 1549.[116] Scottish traders had a wool staple in Antwerp in 1539–41, but had no formal organization before or after this period. The German Hansa moved ploddingly in transferring their Kontor from Bruges to Antwerp. The Antwerp city government granted a house to the Hansa in 1468 and reached an agreement on civil jurisdiction with the Germans in 1546 but it was only in 1533 that the Hansa Kontor was transferred to Antwerp.[117] Their Castilian colleagues repeatedly tried to establish a consulate independent from the Bruges Castilians (in 1560 and 1589) but their efforts did not succeed.[118] The Antwerp government desperately sought to counter the loss of several merchant groups during the political and religious disturbances in the 1570s and 1580s: the city reconfirmed the privileges of the Portuguese and granted rights to a new group of merchants from Armenia and Greece in 1582.[119]

Merchant attitudes towards incorporation and the intensity of incorporation differed from group to group. The Portuguese and English, two of the three important suppliers of the major products traded at Antwerp in the first half of the sixteenth century, seem to have had the most elaborate merchant guilds. The English already enjoyed substantial privileges in the fourteenth century and when the Bruges market started to decline, Antwerp was quick to attract the Portuguese. All subjects of the Portuguese king arriving in Antwerp had to register with the Portuguese nation's consuls; the nation organized weekly meetings and had its own jurisdiction.[120] The Merchant Adventurers went one step further: they could exclude non-compliant guild members from the lucrative cloth trade.[121]

Merchants from Venice, Milan, south Germany, Scandinavia and France did not receive any specific privileges in the sixteenth century.[122] These groups of merchants must have felt comfortable relying on Antwerp's open access institutions without creating nation-like structures. Gelderblom argues that the commitment of the city of Antwerp to the protection and efficient transfer of property rights obviated the incorporation in merchant guilds.[123] Sixteenth-century Antwerp's foreign merchant guilds were mainly the result of pre-existing and ancient privileges and of the active strategy of urban and central authorities to attract particular groups of traders and their commerce, especially in the commercial vacuum left by Bruges during the Flemish Revolt.[124]

Native Merchant Guilds in Antwerp

Foreign merchant guilds were not the only form of merchant incorporation. Foreign merchant guilds were in fact exceptional; local merchant guilds were much more common. These local merchant guilds, defined as 'an association of men who claimed exclusive rights over trade in a particular locality', are considered to have declined after about 1500 in the Low Countries and England.[125]

However, there were several important instances of Antwerp merchants – coming from the Low Countries and Antwerp itself – organizing themselves into a formal merchant guild – or least attempting to do so. The attempts at incorporation in Antwerp have been overlooked in accounts of merchant guilds in the later middle ages and the first century of the early modern era.[126] The decline of merchant guilds was not an absolute process; even in a large market (such as Antwerp) with open-access institutions, merchant incorporation could persist.[127] All these merchant guild projects took place during insecure and violent times; Antwerp merchants closed ranks to obtain privileges which could protect them from violence and expropriation.[128] The presence of these incorporation projects sheds light on the eventual benefits of merchant guild privileges for indigenous merchants. Moreover, if these merchant guilds were powerful, they could have excluded potential new merchants from trade, which could have hindered commercial democratization. Incorporation may also have been a logical result of the growing group identity of Antwerp merchants, as shown by Soly: this shared group identity of Antwerp merchants is evidenced in their epitaphs circumscribing them as 'mercatores' and by their high numbers among the Antwerp colonels during the period of the Calvinist republic, when Calvinist merchants militarized the city to fend off the Habsburg armies.[129]

The 1485 'Common College or Society and Common Bourse'

On the fifth of May, 1485, the sheriff and the aldermen of Antwerp acknowledged that they had been contacted by the 'common merchants living in this city of Antwerp who traded abroad'.[130] These merchants had elaborated on how they and their personnel had been importing and exporting goods from and to Antwerp by land and by sea for years, much to the benefit of the commonwealth. However, they increasingly were falling victim to random tolls and taxes in the Baltic area, Norway, England, Scotland, France and Germany, with the aim to shield those markets from Antwerp merchants. Robbery and theft also threatened Antwerp merchants. To remedy this arbitrary taxation and insecurity, they requested the right to organize a 'common college or society and a common moneybox' to protect them from harassment. Security was an argument often invoked by merchants when negotiating with urban and central authorities, as can be seen in the early privileges bestowed to foreign merchants trading at Antwerp.[131] The merchants explicitly argued that the privilege would lead to an increase in trade, to the advantage of the commonwealth. The city government subsequently granted them this privilege.

The remainder of the text tells us more about the structure of the guild. Only merchants trading abroad and living on a permanent basis in Antwerp could become members of this 'society or brotherly assembly'. No one who was in conflict with the city government was allowed to join. The guild was to be ruled by four elected officers, who had to respect and enforce guild ordinances.[132] Every year the longest-sitting official was replaced by a new one; the members chose two candidates, from whom the sheriff and aldermen selected the new official. The four officials controlled the guild's fund used to compensate members for arbitrary taxation and theft abroad. This fund was financed by reasonable contributions from its members 'according to each one's state'; the fund thus functioned as a mutual insurance. Every member who did not pay his contribution was fined an extra contribution, to be divided among the duke of Brabant, the city and the wardens of the church of Our Lady. The officials had to draw up an annual account of the fund and a list of the current members. The guild could always be contacted for advice on trade by the duke and the city. The guild was also granted jurisdiction over its members: if two members had a conflict, the guild officials were allowed to summon them and to resolve the difficulties. If this attempt at reconciliation failed, the litigators were to go the aldermen. The guild's jurisdiction remained limited to arbitrage in civil cases; all criminal cases were dealt with by the aldermen. The guild was not allowed to accept privileges granted by foreign rulers or cities if such privileges contradicted the laws of Brabant or Antwerp. The aldermen would always check foreign privileges awarded to the guild. Guild membership would not result in preferential treatment in craft guilds: merchant guild members had to pay the same fees as non-members. Finally, the aldermen were always allowed to change the rules of the guild and withdraw its privilege. This new merchant guild left no traces other than this deed of foundation, which may be an indication that the project failed. However, it did create a powerful precedent for a similar project almost a century later.

The foundation of this merchant guild must be seen within the context of general political uncertainty and economic shifts within the Low Countries.[133] The growing particularism of the Flemish cities after the death of Charles the Bold and the marriage of his daughter Mary of Burgundy to Maximilian of Austria gradually resulted in open revolt.[134] Hostility between the Flemish cities and Antwerp were also detrimental to trade.[135] The Genoese and Hanseats left Bruges for Antwerp in April 1485; two months later Bruges was defeated, leading to the Peace of Bruges. This precarious peace treaty was broken in January 1488, when Bruges imprisoned Maximilian. Almost immediately upon his release,

Maximilian ordered all foreign merchants to leave Bruges; most of them went to Antwerp.[136] The county of Flanders remained insecure until October 1492. During the 1480s the Atlantic coast was similarly unsafe, with privateers from various nationalities and shifting allegiances operating in the area.[137] Why Antwerp merchants were harassed abroad is unclear. It might have been an excuse to install a corporation that would allow its members to compete with the growing numbers of foreign merchants coming from Bruges whose presence in the Scheldt town was on the rise.

All this raises the question of what exactly the function of this merchant guild was. If insecurity abroad was indeed the issue, the guild's privilege would have included measures against threats and insecurity, but it did not. At first glance, exclusion of other entrepreneurs and merchants does not seem to have been at stake: any inhabitants of the city could become member and formal citizenship was not required. However, one needed to be resident in the city on a permanent basis; this clause may have been inserted to exclude non-local merchants and entrepreneurs who were present only during the fairs or who had only temporarily settled in the city while awaiting the course of political events in Bruges. Each member's contribution went into a mutual insurance fund and it was promised that this contribution would not exceed the member's financial capability. Therefore, it is not unwarranted to assume that member contribution was not installed to prevent others from becoming member of the guild. I believe the guild was created to address economic goals: mutual insurance against insecurity, attempting to obtain privileges abroad, standing strong against the growing competition of foreign merchants entering the Scheldt port through exclusion (permanent residency requirement) and to establish communication lines with the city government. The timing of the request for the privilege attests to the fact that Antwerp's merchants may have feared future foreign competition coming from merchants leaving Bruges for Antwerp.

The Failed Attempt at Establishing an Antwerp Merchant Guild in England, Anno 1565

A second episode of attempted incorporation of Antwerp merchants took place around 1565 during the negotiations for a new Intercursus Treaty between England and the Low Countries, while the Anglo-Dutch trade war still continued.[138] The English Merchant Adventurers, backed by the English crown, vied to monopolize the export of English cloth to Antwerp, mostly by raising taxes on foreigners exporting the commodity, enforcing the use of English ships and barring imports of foreign commodities in the second half of the 1550s.[139] The Merchant Adventurers had a strong control over exports, mainly of English cloth, through export quota, collective shipping and marketing, and officials apprehending smugglers and transgressors of guild rules. The company in this period enjoyed the strong support of the London city government and of the English prince.[140]

Merchants from the Low Countries, and from Antwerp in particular, were suffering in England at this time. In 1555, several Antwerp merchants trading in England addressed the Antwerp city magistracy to complain about the random implementation of new rules governing exchange.[141] The Antwerp merchants wondered why they were being discriminated against in England even as their English colleagues were enjoying a positive discrimination in their hometown of Antwerp. This stark contrast between the warm welcome the Merchant Adventurers enjoyed in Antwerp and the maltreatment of Antwerp merchants in England was often noted.[142]

With the Anglo-French war exacerbating the general state of affairs even further, the trade climate had become so hostile that both the English and Low Countries governments declared a general embargo on each other in 1563. The Merchant Adventurers left Antwerp for Emden.[143] Antwerp's city magistracy instantly panicked, for both its trade and industry were dependent on the import of semi-finished English cloth. The city even bypassed the Brussels government and sent their own representatives to the English king to reconcile.[144] In the winter of 1564 England and the Low Countries reached a settlement to restore the Intercursus during negotiations for a new trade treaty between the two realms and the fellowship returned to Antwerp.[145] When trade with England resumed in January 1565, Antwerp merchants trading in England were afflicted by piracy and differential tax tariffs and had to purchase export licenses from their competitors, the Merchant Adventurers. Their number had fallen to about twenty merchants.[146]

A small group of England traders coalesced around Gillis Hooftman, born in Trier and an important Antwerp merchant active in trade with England and as a creditor of the English crown. The Hooftman faction wished to obtain equal privileges in London as those enjoyed by the Merchant Adventurers in Antwerp. To that end, they wanted to organize a company of their own, in the style of the Fellowship of Merchant Adventurers, with an office in London. The city council, eager to avoid offending the Merchant Adventurers, did not wish to support a plan which would empower the Fellowship's Antwerp competitors. The council tried to defuse this volatile situation which risked spurring the departure of the fellowship out of Antwerp; such a break would fundamentally undermine the city's commercial position. The magistracy argued that the city's wealth and the prosperity of the Low Countries were dependent on the 'connexiteyt', or connectivity, forged by foreign merchant nations; if the link of the Merchant Adventurers were to be disconnected, this entire economic chain would collapse.[147]

The group of England merchants also tried their luck on the other side of the Channel. In London the group presented a request to the English Privy Council to relieve them from the aforementioned export licenses and other fees. Councillor William Cecil dismissed them as agitators and as 'worthy not only to be banished out of England but also out of their own countries for their doings'.[148] Hooftman and his crew had thus bypassed the Antwerp government, which feared a renewed Merchant Adventurers's boycott; the company had just started trading with the city again. The Antwerp magistracy reacted by trying to dismiss the faction as 'particular men, which seek but their particular commodity'.[149] The city government was also backed in its support for the Merchant Adventurers by a consortium of several Italian, German and Netherlandish merchants who deemed the presence of the fellowship in Antwerp as indispensable for the commonwealth and demanded enforcement of the fellowship's organization and monopoly.[150]

The fact that there were Merchant Adventurers supporters and adversaries among Antwerp's merchants indicates that not all of them were interested in a guild which might try to outcompete the Merchant Adventurers. Or did the adversaries believe that the guild would not stand a chance in obtaining protection and privileges in England, where the Crown favoured the Merchant Adventurers? The Intercursus negotiations ended in complete victory for the English and the Merchant Adventurers in June 1566 because of Antwerp's dependence on the Merchant Adventurers. Differential taxation on exports in England imposed by the English Crown continued and the attempted incorporation failed to materialize. Arbitrary confiscations also continued.[151] Despite this rather unwelcoming attitude the Low Countries merchants' community continued to grow quickly in the English capital.[152]

The College of Antwerp England Traders, 1580s

Fifteen years later, in the spring of 1580, a new attempt was made at incorporating Antwerp merchants trading in England; another guild was set up by traders in the west Atlantic coast of France, Spain, Portugal and the Mediterranean.[153] In the period 1577–85 Antwerp was governed by a Calvinist regime which had close ties with native merchants. The government no longer needed to be so careful not to step on the toes of the English Merchant Adventurers, for they had moved their staple from Antwerp to Hamburg in 1567.[154] A request was sent to the Estates-General to complain of several merchants who were trading in England but posing as traders from the Low Countries to evade taxes. This request in itself is puzzling: why would merchants try to pass themselves off as merchants from the Low Countries when such status did not entail any clear privileges and may even have worked to their detriment? The request proposed a new organization, of which only inhabitants of the Low Countries could become members. This organization would have an elected governor and a number of councillors, both in Antwerp and in London. Any merchant who traded in England without being registered as a guild member would be fined. To fund the society, members would pay a contribution consisting of an ad valorem tax on their merchandise and on bills of exchange.[155] The collectors of the Brabant and Zeeland tolls had to provide the college data on the imports and exports to England, so that the college could collect the ad valorem dues from its members.[156] Low Countries merchants trading in England would need to declare all their imports and exports to the guild authorities. The city appointed two commissioners to consult several (unfortunately unknown) Antwerp England traders who all gave a favourable judgment on the proposal. In June of the same year the unofficial governor Mathias of Austria[157] granted the patent to establish such a nation according to the rules set forward in the earlier proposal.[158] However, the nation was not allowed to fine defaulters on the contribution. The first elections took place in the house of Jacob Della Faille: Jan Celos, who had been one of the proponents of the attempt to incorporate Antwerp's England traders fifteen years earlier, was to be the headman in Antwerp and Pieter Bosquel his London colleague. In December 1580 Della Faille replaced Celos as Antwerp headman and granted a room in his house in the Vekestraat which would become the college's meeting room.

In May 1582 the new prince of the Low Countries, the duke of Anjou, promulgated a renewed patent.[159] This new patent granted the guild the right to issue its own rules, in accordance with the laws of the realm, regulating the behaviour of their guild comrades, and its own jurisdiction. All Netherlanders, trading and/or living in England, were subject to the rules of the college. The England branch had jurisdiction over all conflicts involving Netherlanders and between Netherlanders and others (it is unclear whether this was accepted in England, since this constituted an infringement on English jurisdiction). The guild administrators were allowed to fine and imprison transgressors.[160]

However, the college was not to be entirely independent. The Antwerp magistracy, still careful not to offend the English government, wanted to keep a check on the college. A second act was issued at the same time as the 1582 patent; this second act granted the Antwerp city government close control over the College: new guild statutes had to be approved by the aldermen (as would arrests of guild ordinance offenders), sentences would have to executed by city officials and the college was bound to keep residence in Antwerp.[161]

The incorporation of the England traders must be contextualized within the financial dealings between the Estates-General and the English crown. In October 1577 the Estates-General borrowed £100,000 sterling from the English Queen Elizabeth I; however, the Estates had difficulties in paying just the annual interests, let alone the principal. Several merchant-bankers had left the Netherlands after the Spanish Fury, making it difficult for the Estates to obtain more credit; moreover, not all provinces could or wanted to pay their contribution. Pestered by her own creditors, Elizabeth I threatened to arrest the goods of Low Countries citizens. Collective action culminating in the establishment of the college does not come as a surprise in these circumstances.

Paul Anraet, secretary of the Antwerp office of the college, urged both the English government and the authorities of the Low Countries to reach an agreement on repayment of the loan. More importantly, the college and its members agreed to repay a share of the loan in 1582. In 1583, the college was asked by a senior English government official to stand surety for the interest payments of the Estates-General loan. The queen would in return recognize establishment of the college in London and would grant privileges.[162] This sort of bartering of cash transfers by a guild to a ruler and guild assistance in state loans in return for privileges is what kept merchant guilds in control of the preindustrial economy.[163] It is highly unlikely that the English Crown would have granted privileges to the college in London: Thomas Longston, pensionary of the Merchant Adventurers, warned Sir Francis Walsingham, secretary of state, about the college's plan to stand surety in return for privileges. All concessions to merchants from the Low Countries could endanger the English merchants because '[merchants from the Low Countries] are too cunning for us, notwithstanding our long experience, and would eat us out if they get but a little further or more of us'![164]

The military operations around Antwerp around 1585 and the exodus of the city's merchants after its reconquest by the Spanish armies proved lethal to the organization of Antwerp's England traders.[165] Moreover, the statute of the college did not go uncontested. Several England traders resisted the forced incorporation and refused to pay their contribution. In 1582 a group of England traders from Flanders asked the aldermen of Middelburg for assistance in their efforts to cancel the college patent. They maintained that the patent was completely at odds with the old privileges and rights of the county of Flanders and free trade treatises such as the Magnus Intercursus. They accused the college of seeking to control the England trade not only from Antwerp and London but from all Low Countries ports. The opponents also wrote that they did not agree to the patent, countering the college's claim that all merchants had agreed upon its contents.[166] The opponents eventually took their matter to the Privy Council, which officially dissolved the college in 1589, probably because the open war between England and the Spanish monarch now rendered the trade organization obsolete. The guild was never re-established again.[167]

Why did all these attempts to establish of a native merchant guild eventually fail? The uncertainties caused by political disturbances and powerful, privileged foreign merchants, such as the Merchant Adventurers, were hindrances that these projects of incorporation sought to resist but which precluded the development of such projects. The political momentum and the dependence on foreign merchants hindered the native merchants' efforts towards incorporation of the native merchants – subsequently they had to make do without a merchant guild and the privileges abroad it would have enabled. Moreover, both the central and urban government were not neutral in trying to benefit the entire merchant community, since they were not eager to support native merchants in their efforts to incorporate. Even within the native merchant community there was no unanimous backing for these projects: the 1565 proposal and the two 1580s organizations did not go unopposed and each experienced difficulties in rooting out free-riders. This shows that these guilds did not enjoy the unconditional support of every native merchant. This was very different elsewhere, for example in London, where the Merchant Adventurers were firmly in power through their close contacts with the urban government and the Crown, and in Hanseatic cities which deliberately discriminated against foreigners.[168] In the end, power relations and the extent of power of the different stakeholders in Antwerp long-distance commerce proved to be decisive. Both the urban and the central governments chose not to further the interests of Antwerp's native merchants.

Historians who claim to observe the demise of merchant guilds in sixteenth-century Antwerp would see these episodes as unequivocal evidence for the correctness of their thesis: the attempts by native merchants towards incorporation were ineffectual because the merchants could rely on alternative institutions, mainly the state, for such matters. But if the state was indeed providing the services native merchants required, why did the merchants still request a guild four times in the long sixteenth century? I believe that native merchants truly did desire a guild of their own which would protect them from the various adversities which they faced but that they were effectively blocked from establishing such an organization; this blockage was carried out by the state, which put a premium on the presence of well-organized foreign nations. The government assumed that such groups would bring merchandise to Antwerp and boost trade to and from the city, the Low Countries' principal gateway; however, the state also feared that these merchant nations which could swiftly leave the city and the region if trade conditions were altered unfavourably for them (such as by the establishment of a local, native merchants' guild). On the other hand, the absence of merchant guilds meant that long-distance trade was open for new players, but only if they were able to contend with the competition from foreign traders and their merchant guilds. To compete with these merchants, new Antwerp merchants could not rely on the protection offered by having their own merchant guild; thus, they had to rely on business techniques, strong products, the flexibility of the payment system and the courts' intervention in contract enforcement.

Guilds and Privileges of Low Countries Merchants Abroad

Alien merchant guilds depended on their local equivalents in their home-town and their home-town authorities. Rulers abroad were more willing to recognize an alien merchant guild when it was recognized by its home authorities. Moreover, when the local merchant guild was able to influence home-town policies, it could induce the home government into negotiations with the foreign ruler to recognize its branch abroad. The home government could also be actively involved in the daily operations of the alien branch, such as by appointing officials and through close supervision.[169] Consequently, given the relative weakness of the guilds of native merchants in sixteenth-century Antwerp and their indirect influence on city policy over trade, Low Countries merchants abroad likely received a poor deal. Indeed very few formal guilds of Low Countries merchants were found in the European commercial cities where they were actively trading (Portugal, Spain, Italy, France, Germany and the Baltic).[170] When merchant guilds and consulates were established, this often happened in the last decades of the sixteenth century and the early seventeenth century, when Low Countries merchants were already present for a longer period. Moreover, the merchants who constituted these associations often came from Antwerp but their interests were shifting to other commercial cities in the Low Countries, such as Amsterdam, and no longer centred on Antwerp.[171]

In 1644, Edouard Sonnemans, a merchant originating from Delft and residing in the town of Funchal, on the island of Madeira, petitioned the king of Portugal to grant him the privileges granted to Flemish and German merchants.[172] Sonnemans listed all privileges extended to these merchant groups: sixty stipulations in total.[173] In 1452 king Afonso V bestowed a series of rights on citizens from the Low Countries, Germany, France and England who wished to settle in Portugal:[174] they would be exempt from tributes, impositions and voluntary gifts to the prince; they were to be fined only in well-described circumstances; they were relieved from military service and from supplying horses to the military; their houses were not to be searched in order to claim provisions; they would enjoy freedom of movement throughout the kingdom; and they were not to be subjected to guest law (i.e., foreign merchants needed a local host who would stand surety for his local liabilities and who would intermediate on his behalf).[175] Moreover, the privileged community disposed of its own judge and even received precedence of service in travellers' inns.[176] In 1457 and 1478 the subjects of the duke of Burgundy who were trading with Portugal received additional rights concerning trade in copper, precious metals and cloth: they were for example exempt from the royal tithe.[177] It is highly likely that these privileges were granted in return for a similar favour granted by the duke of Burgundy to Portuguese merchants in 1411. The 1509 privilege which was extended to the South Germans also mentions the free trade that the 'Flemish' (i.e., Low Countries subjects) had already enjoyed for a while.[178] These privileges were of course theoretical in the sense that they could be mitigated by other royal decrees, as often happened.[179] In two cases it was deemed necessary to explicitly confirm the privileges of Low Countries merchants.[180] In the second half of the fifteenth century the Portuguese king also appointed several Flemish expatriates (Jacob van

Brugge, Ferdinand van Olmen and Joos de Hurtere) as vassal-governors of parts of the Azores and made them responsible for the island's exploitation and colonization. C. Verlinden, 'De Vlaamse Kolonisten Op De Azoren', in J. Everaert and E. Stols (eds), *Vlaanderen En Portugal: Op De Golfslag Van Twee Culturen* (Antwerp: Mercatorfonds, 1991), pp. 81–97, on pp. 81–92.

Low Countries merchants were already present in Lisbon, Portugal's capital city, in the first half of the fifteenth century. A 'Flemish' confraternity of Saint Andrew and the Holy Cross with several merchants among its members attests this presence in 1411; the goal of the confraternity was mainly religious and charitable in nature, but the group also had its own judge to deal with internal conflicts.[181] At the end of the sixteenth and in the seventeenth centuries the Low Countries community in Lisbon consisted of around 100 merchants and had its own judge, always a Portuguese, who passed rulings in low-level trade and testamentary conflicts; civil and criminal cases of substance were decided upon by the Portuguese authorities.[182] In 1571 the community had a consul at its disposal, the Flemish Herman Thielmansz. The consul mainly dealt with shipping matters and with defending the community's privileges; in return he received a percentage fee on the value of all shipped merchandise.[183] Around 1580 the Antwerp magistracy sent a letter to the Portuguese royal council to recommend Jan Cassiopin for the office of consul of the Flemish in Lisbon; this position became vacant after Thielmansz's death. A few weeks later, the Antwerp magistracy ratified the decision of the Portuguese king who had appointed Hans Cleynaerts Mathyssone.

Several Low Countries merchant colonies took shape in sixteenth-century Spain. Trade with Spain was one of the motors of the Antwerp market throughout the century and a branch of trade where Antwerp merchants became ever more important.[184] La Coruña had a consulado in 1475 for foreign merchants; it is unclear if this included Low Countries traders and what happened to the institution after 1475. The only formally organized *nacion* of Flemish merchants in Spain was in Sanlúcar de Barrameda, an outport of Seville in the Guadalquivir estuary. In this town the convoys departed to and arrived from the Americas.[185] Sanlúcar counted fifteen Netherlanders between 1514 and 1522 and around seventy in 1537–50. In the first half of the sixteenth century, the Netherlanders, clustered around the 'calle de los Flamencos', disposed of their own consulado and their consuls were appointed by the duke of Medina Sidonia, the ruler of the town. As a privileged group they were entitled to carry arms. The consulado was not specifically organized around merchants; it also included many craftsmen and mariners. Several Antwerp merchants had factors in this port town.[186]

In early sixteenth-century Seville, the Flemish brotherhood of San Andrés de los Flamencos had a hospital. [187] Pieter Seghers stayed in Seville between 1580 and 1586 as the agent of the wealthy Antwerp merchant Pieter Arnouts. Arnouts was elected as treasurer of the Flemish San Andrés brotherhood; he had to collect the percentage fees on trade volume which were to be paid by the brotherhood's members and to manage the relations with the Seville authorities as spokesman, or *deputado*, of the community.[188] As Fagel notes, Netherlandish merchants, while present before that time, only started to establish organizations in the important cities of Cádiz, Seville, Puerto de Santa Maria, Gibraltar, Valencia and Alicante at the end of the sixteenth century.[189]

The increase in the numbers of Low Countries merchants in Spain preceded that of their colleagues in Italy, and more specifically in Venice.[190] The results were similar: an informally organized group of Low Countries merchants without specific group privileges. In the second third of the sixteenth century, the numbers of Low Countries merchants and agents increased rapidly, but no formal organization took place.[191] This group increased in the last two decades of the sixteenth century. The fall of Antwerp in 1585 caused – or in fact, stimulated – an economic restructuring giving rise to a diaspora of Antwerp merchants, many of whom emigrated to Venice.[192] In 1596 the Venetian senate consulted several groups of foreign merchants on the erection of a *banco di scritta*, or clearing bank. Twenty-one merchants from the Low Countries signed the report and were described as the *nazione fiamenga*.[193] This nazione was not an official organization since it was not recognized by the Venetian state, but the collective did co-operate to petition different echelons of the Venetian state apparatus, most often the *Cinque Savi alla Mercanzia*, the council responsible for the city's commerce. The nazione requested certain preferential treatments, exemption from taxes and security measures, and complained about certain practices. Between 1589 and 1651 thirty-three collective and eighty-three individual petitions were submitted.[194] A community of Low Countries merchants settled in the port town of Livorno, beginning in the early 1590s, and by 1597 they were electing, together with mariners and shipmasters, their own consul to protect and assist Dutch trade in return for small fees. Many of these merchants had been born in Antwerp and all of them had strong relationships with the northern Low Countries.[195] Netherlandish merchants in Ancona, Rome and Genoa did not have a formal representative or organization.[196]

Merchants of Brabant, Flanders, Holland and Zeeland complained in 1462 about burdensome customs and rules, frequent wars, the *droit d'aubaine*[197] and the *droit de naufrage* prevailing in France.[198] The French king Louis XI granted them extensive privileges: the right to levy a tax on Flemish merchant to pay for maintenance of their chapel in La Rochelle; in cases of litigation the aldermen of the town would be assisted by one or two Low Countries merchants and the *droits d'aubaine et de naufrage* were abolished, so the merchants and their goods could no longer be arrested for reprisal. Low Countries merchants were also allowed to buy and sell among each other in the region and to sell merchandise on their ship before it was unloaded in the ports of La Rochelle and the Aunis region.[199] Despite these privileges, Low Countries merchants did not immediately settle in the region, because of the wars between the duke of Burgundy Charles the Bold and Louis XI. Only in the sixteenth century did many merchants and their agents settle in La Rochelle and other ports of western France such as Bordeaux.[200] Low Countries merchants were also numerous in the Atlantic ports of Rouen (and its outports Honfleur and Le Havre) but as in La Rochelle this larger number did not give rise to any formal organization of Low Countries traders.[201] The presence of Antwerp merchants in the French capital of Paris materialized despite the lack of any privileges bestowed to them.

Antwerp merchants frequented the Frankfurt fairs and later on established permanent operations in that city. These Antwerp expatriates were at the forefront of the 1613 organization of a *Kaufmannsgesellschaft*.[202] Several Flemish merchants were also members of the newly created Frankfurt grocers and spices dealers' guild.[203] Nuremberg awarded privileges to Antwerp citizens at an unknown date. Peter van Leyen, an Antwerp émigré, reported on these privileges to his Antwerp-based brother-in-law Jan Van Immerseel in a letter of August 1589.[204] In return for exemption of tolls, Antwerp citizens trading in Frankfurt now had to go to the Nuremberg city council in procession each year and offer a symbolic gift of a pound of pepper, a pair of gloves and two gold guilders.[205] Van Leyen added that the toll amounted to 1 per cent of the value of the merchandise, which would cut deeply into his profits if the exemption would be withdrawn.[206]

Van Leyen explained in his letter that he feared discontinuation of the toll exemption. The day before, the Nuremberg magistracy had not been as welcoming during the ritual as in previous years. To enjoy the toll exemption, one had to provide a certificate with an Antwerp seal confirming one's Antwerp citizenship. Van Leyen noted that this measure to withdraw the privileged status of Antwerp merchants who had immigrated to Nuremberg was probably taken at the behest of Nuremberg merchants, of whom many sat on the Nuremberg city council.[207] Public opinion turned against Antwerp merchants: Van Leyen stated he would rather have lived in a religiously tolerant Antwerp than abroad, where foreign merchants were regarded as 'the dog in the hodgepodge'.[208] For Protestant Antwerp merchants who had left the Scheldt city, the required certificate could be difficult to obtain from the Antwerp government, which was once more profoundly Catholic. The Nuremberg government was well aware of this. This anecdote shows that even when Low Countries merchants enjoyed privileges, city governments could and did exploit the political climate against them to cancel previously granted privileges.[209]

Danzig pursued an outright xenophobic policy towards foreign merchants. Flemish and Dutch traders (and others) were not allowed to live and work in Danzig without official permission in the seventeenth century; they were only allowed to do so after a probation period, during which they were meticulously monitored.[210] Earlier, in the sixteenth century, the Dutch and Flemish were the most numerous group of foreign merchants in Danzig and were admitted to the local Hanseatic Artushof, but remained subject to guest laws and the obligation of using Danzig merchants as intermediaries.[211]

That other important port of the Baltic, Hamburg, preferred a very different policy: the city admitted the Merchant Adventurers in 1567 and opened to other foreign merchants as well, while allowing trade to be less regulated, unlike other Hanseatic cities, where foreign merchants were not allowed to trade with each other.[212] This policy did not proceed without protest from the other Hansa towns, especially Lübeck.[213] The city of Hamburg was attractive because of its access to the sea, the Baltic and other German Regions and its neutral trade with the Iberian Peninsula. In 1605 a contract was signed between the city council and South Netherlandish migrants granting the latter freedom of religion and trade in the city for ten years.[214] The contract was signed by 130 Southern Netherlandish heads of household who guaranteed their loyalty to the city of Hamburg. In case one of them proved to be disloyal, he would be fined.[215] The particular privileges granted by the 1605 contract did not lead to any formal organization of the Low Countries merchants in Hamburg.

The previous overview of Low Countries merchant colonies in various European commercial cities shows that most of these communities, some of them rather numerous, retained an informal character. This does not preclude the reception of certain privileges which occurred in several cities. What is most remarkable is the very limited support from the Antwerp merchants in Antwerp, the Antwerp government and the central government. Even when the Antwerp or central government tried to have a say in the appointment of an official of the Antwerp merchants abroad, they were often overruled by the local ruler. If privileges were granted abroad, Low Countries merchants had themselves to thank for their success. Institutionalization of these colonies only took place at the end of the sixteenth century, after the fall of Antwerp and the subsequent merchant diaspora, while the presence of Low Countries merchants was substantial in several cities well before that date. This was partially caused by the reluctance of foreign governments to provide privileges to merchants who could outcompete their own subjects and perhaps also by the growing importance of alternative state institutions that offered services to merchants in these foreign cities. Cities such as Venice, which was an important node in the commercial network of the Low Countries merchants, provided all services necessary to foreign merchants but also closely monitored their dealings and preserved the valuable Levant trade for its citizens.[216] But the evidence presented above does show that Low Countries merchants valued privileges and feared their abolishment, especially since their persons and goods were not always safe abroad. It is certain that these merchants could have benefited from a more formal organization, especially when it would have enjoyed support at home. Yet Low Countries merchants managed to become an important player in European trade even despite the conspicuous absence of their own merchant guilds, both in Antwerp and abroad.

Conclusion

The ascent of merchants from the Low Countries differs from the dynamics of other commercially successful groups in pre-industrial Europe. The Italians, the Hanseats and the Merchant Adventurers relied on strong support from their home governments. Because these merchants had a strong hold on their respective governments they were able to obtain privileges and set up merchant organizations abroad. Some, such as the Venetians, even set up their own state-organized transportation.[217] Low Countries traders found themselves in a very different situation. Sixteenth-century Antwerp offered open-access institutions such as a court which was efficient, neutral and open for all. The IOU system discussed in the previous chapter is another example of such an open-access institution since all merchants could participate in it and knew that their bond was embedded in the law and could be enforced when necessary. Clearly, Low Countries merchants did well out of these open access institutions. The city's benevolent attitude towards commerce and traders might well have been the result of the relative absence of merchants in the town council (a feature in which Antwerp again differed from many other commercial cities). As such, native merchants were not able to engage in rent-seeking activities excluding foreign merchants from the Antwerp market, if they wanted to do so. Perhaps the politicization of Antwerp's merchants and the resultant control of the Antwerp market was stopped short by the fall of 1585; prior to that date Antwerp merchants had become more active as town rulers during the Calvinist regime and had intervened in commerce and foreign relations (the College of England traders for example).

From the beginning of Antwerp's Golden Age, the city's rulers had preferred to attract foreign traders and keep them within in the city walls, even if this hurt the interests of its growing – both in numbers and influence – community of native merchants. Gelderblom, Grafe and Ogilvie have used sixteenth-century Antwerp as an example of one of the places where merchant guilds went into decline. Indeed, there were several important foreign merchant groups who did not rely on a nation structure, even as others still did so. The strongest example is the Merchant Adventurers whom the city government deemed indispensable. The Antwerp city government was convinced that its wealth first and foremost relied on the presence of foreign traders. It had invested in the commercial infrastructure and institutions of the city and did not want to risk it all by antagonizing groups of foreign merchants. As a result of that, merchants such as Adventurers found themselves in a comfortable bargaining position and were able to harass Low Countries merchants, their direct competitors in the Low Countries–England trade and a force to be reckoned with according to Thomas Longston, pensionary of the Merchant Adventurers. It is one of history's ironies: sixteenth-century Antwerp set up open-access institutions but still favoured one group over another, and not the group one would expect when comparing Antwerp to other commercial cities.

The overview of attempts to set up a native merchant guild has made clear that some Antwerp merchants still valued having a merchant guild, especially in times of commercial insecurity and in the face of the adversities caused by their competitors. They worried about competition from foreign merchants coming from Bruges in 1485 and complained about the Merchant Adventurers colluding with English authorities and about the Antwerp government's fear of harming the interests of the Adventurers, which were to the detriment of Antwerp traders in 1565. Clearly, Antwerp merchants were well aware of the distributive effects of foreign merchant guilds in their city and wanted a slice of the economic pie for themselves, which they hoped to secure through incorporation and support of the city. The lack of support Low Countries received from the Antwerp urban government also explains the relative absence of formal organization of Low Countries merchants in other commercial centres. Low Countries merchants were very present in the important commercial gateways but these presences retained an informal character during most of the sixteenth century. Only after the diaspora of Antwerp merchants did such Low Countries merchants nations begin to emerge. Hence, the creation of open-access institutions in sixteenth-century Antwerp did not necessarily result in a lack of interest in guilds. Yet, Low Countries merchants prospered without having a strong merchant guild... they requested merchant organization only in hard times. At other times they could rely on the city's inclusive commercial regime and were able to cope with European markets.

CONCLUSION

John Wheeler's 1601 *Treatise of Commerce*, with which this book started, ascribed the ascent of the Low Countries traders to their 'eating out' of other merchant groups and their firm control of important commodities in European trade.[1] Taxes on trade and other sources indicate the growing market share of Low Countries merchants in imports to and exports from the Low Countries from the middle of the sixteenth century onwards. Low Countries merchants popped up in the commercial cities of Italy, the Iberian Peninsula, France, England, the Baltic and Russia; in some of these cities a sizeable community of Low Countries traders developed throughout the sixteenth century. Were merchants from the Low Countries operating out of Antwerp just like all other successful merchant groups such as the Italians, the Hanseats, the south Germans, the English Merchant Adventurers and the Dutch who relied on the combination of a set of factors: the export of local products; the adoption of advanced commercial techniques such as partnerships to incorporate capital, know-how and relations; the accumulation of capital; and the establishment of open-access institutions? Or did they enjoy comparative advantages which set them apart from their competitors, can explain their commercial rise and rendered them unique?

Traditional historiography on Low Countries merchants assumed a tight relation between the restructuring and sixteenth-century success of Low Countries industry and the ascent of merchants from the Low Countries. Detailed analysis of 1540s tax registers has proven this assumption wrong. Low Countries merchants did not specialize more in home-grown products such as Hondschoote says, tapestries and linen, relative to their foreign colleagues. Moreover, Low Countries traders were equally as active in the transit goods – English cloth, sugar and spices – which were re-exported from Antwerp as foreign merchants, which indicates their commercial strength from the 1540s onwards. Hence, Low Countries merchants did not turn the success of their industry into a comparative advantage by specializing in the marketing of its products. The scarce price indices on sugar imports and linen exports demonstrate the profitability of Low Countries merchants trade; the price difference will definitely have attracted many traders. Contrary to their seventeenth-century Dutch successors (many

Amsterdam traders of the early seventeenth century had roots in the southern Low Countries) and to Venetian merchants who could rely on state-organized convoys, sixteenth-century Low Countries traders could not boast a strong commercial navy; for marine transportation they relied on the shipping services of others, especially skippers from the northern parts of the Low Countries, whose cost efficiency was becoming clear throughout the sixteenth century. For land-based transport they turned to professional carriers and transport firms which transported goods owned by Low Countries merchants on their behalf, for example, to Italy. Outsourcing transportation was convenient but also made Low Countries traders dependent on others.

Gradually, Low Countries merchants were also able to engage in the internal redistribution of imports: they imported grain from Amsterdam when grain prices were soaring, merchants from Lille and Arras with agents in Antwerp increased their market share in the trade in French wine and woad and a few wealthy merchants such as the Schetz even managed to engage in the spices and alum monopoly trade. All these products were then distributed in the Low Countries by native traders; very few foreigners were active in the internal redistribution, except perhaps the Hanseats in the grain trade. Parallel to the commercial ascent of Low Countries merchants, another crucial development took place in sixteenth-century Antwerp: commercial democratization. Analysis of the export tax registers of 1544–5 provides definitive evidence for the presence of a multitude of smaller and middle-sized merchants (type Van der Molen), besides a few large concerns (type Schetz). These smaller traders traded in similar products to their large-scale colleagues, albeit in smaller volumes, they ventured as far and exhibited similar degrees of specialization in commodities and destinations.

The assumed connection between Low Countries traders and Low Countries industry did work in the other direction: Low Countries traders had close ties to the production process, although they did not specialize in the marketing of these native commodities. The booming production centres of the Low Countries afforded employment to many intermediaries who collected industrial produce on regional markets and shipped it to the gateway Antwerp. Such intermediaries were necessary because several successful Low Countries export products were produced in the countryside by peasants. Due to growing permanency (albeit with seasonal peaks and lows) of the Antwerp market many producers and intermediaries were faced with the choice of whether to settle in Antwerp or not. Antwerp merchants and their agents established close ties with producers; they knew what the latest fashions were abroad, extended credit, organized industrial infrastructure and marketed the industrial produce to regional markets and from there to the gateway. Importantly, they often spoke the same language as local producers. Merchants not only sought to skim off industrial produce; they also intervened in the production process; some tried to set up a vertically integrated enterprise. Massive merchant migration, especially from the Flanders production centres, evidences that the lure of Antwerp was highly seductive. By migrating to Antwerp, these merchants created relations between Antwerp and the production centres and contributed know-how and the necessary connections. Not all merchants controlled the entire commodity chain from producer to foreign consumer. Many faced the essential trade-off between localism and internationalism.

Foreign traders did not entertain such lively relations with the industrial hinterland of the Low Countries. The sparse evidence on profits to be made in trafficking between production centre and gateway indicates that Low Countries merchants with ties to the production side could and did enjoy a cost advantage over those who bought their goods in Antwerp (which virtually every foreigner did). This situation of native merchants controlling the hinterland differed to some extent from the fourteenth and fifteenth centuries when Italian and Hanseat merchants residing in Bruges, Antwerp's commercial predecessor, were active in industrial centres. Lyon traders and Antwerp merchants of the nineteenth century equally protected the local hinterland. Hence, close relations with Low Countries industry did provide Low Countries merchants with a comparative advantage but this did not translate into a larger preference for local goods. In this sense they mirrored medieval Italian merchants who sold eastern spices and silks and Italian textiles across Europe.

Although several contemporary testimonies stressed the creditworthiness of Low Countries traders, this fact has largely been ignored in the history of sixteenth-century finance. Several Low Countries merchants did extend credit to the Habsburg empire and to the princes of England and France. Two financial instruments have been considered as a potential comparative financial advantage: partnerships and bonds. Through the partnership structure Low Countries merchants could pool resources and skills. Some historians have argued that partnerships enabled smaller merchants to become active in long-distance trade and allowed them to co-operate with foreign merchants. My analysis of partnership contracts has shown that through partnership contracts merchant were able to obtain information, expertise and financing beyond their family networks. In the case of the growing group of Low Countries merchants, such outside inputs must have been inevitable. 'Internationalization' through partnerships was less common, although the notarized partnership contracts I have scrutinized were the ideal structure by which to shape such international partnerships. Partnership contracts were constructed through standard clauses on partnership characteristics such as duration, capital in- and output, daily operations and eventual termination, yet the format was flexible enough so that the partners could forge optimal contractual co-operation.

Urban legislation slowly developed standard rules for contracts, but merchants could choose to deviate from standard rules, as did the Schetz in their partnership for trade with Germany. Gradually, legal protection for partners was installed: partnership assets were shielded from particular creditors of individual partners and partnership creditors could only appropriate a partner's assets when partnership assets proved insufficient. Limited liability – i. e., liability limited to the value of the investment – was developed for passive investors and depositors; the 1608 Costuymen even included a standard contract for passive investments in partnerships. Hence, financing from outside one's pool of family and friends became possible. However, it is unclear how these legal developments specifically affected investments in merchant enterprises; the Della Faille, in particular, were able to capitalize their partnerships through outside finance but it is unclear if this firm was representative of the entire community of Low Countries traders. Partnership capital could be quite small as compared to total amount of purchase and sales credit partnerships obtained and the deposits and investments they received from non-partners. Careful comparison with south German and Spanish partnerships has revealed the many similarities with Low Countries merchants partnerships. Surely, Low Countries merchants will have learned from the legal traditions, customs and practices of their competitors and have improved theirs. These traditions, customs and practices became embedded in Antwerp commercial law (albeit often after being adapted to local needs and sensibilities), together with older, local traditions, customs and practices of the Low Countries. Because Low Countries partnerships did not differ from those of other merchant groups, partnerships were not a factor of distinction and did not (solely) fuel the ascent of Low Countries traders. One could also reverse the direction of causality: because Low Countries merchants were operating internationally, they needed partnerships for finance, business management and know-how and, as a consequence of this need, changes in partnership structures took place. Low Countries partnership structures were instrumental in the organization of mercantile business; they allowed Low Countries merchants to gather the means to enter foreign trade but they did not constitute a comparative advantage.

Low Countries merchants could alternatively finance their operations through bonds. The Della Faille described how small merchants bought their goods on credit and often had to sell these goods at a commercially unappealing price because they had to pay for the goods. This would explain why small merchants could be active in long-distance trade, as became clear in the analysis of the trade tax registers. This type of credit was often recorded in an IOU, a financial instrument with roots in the fair system. The instrument was characterized by its flexibility and consequent uncertainty. Throughout the sixteenth century, it became a common practice to assign IOUs, i. e., give them to a third party as payment. IOUs began circulating at increasing rates and risks arose that the final creditor would have difficulties in identifying the original debtor and the previous holders of the IOU and to estimate the debtor's default risk. Bearer clauses also became popular and allowed the passing on of IOUs; bonds with such a clause were subject to the same risks. Two solutions were developed to deal with these risks of uncertainty. First, urban legislation acknowledged the circulation of IOUs; central legislation followed a few decades later. Creditors who passed on an IOU remained liable until payment of the debt, enlarging in effect the pool of people whom the final creditor could address for payment. Second, IOUs could be formalized by notaries and town administrations. Informal pieces of paper given by the debtor to his creditor could be registered, for example as a piece of evidence in case of a lawsuit. Moreover, when the IOUs were recorded in letters or account books, these documents could serve as evidence if necessary. The urban courts also stepped in to enforce payment in bond disputes. Precise payment periods were installed by the urban and central government to make the payment process more transparent. Antwerp did not turn to compulsory registration of IOU transactions. This is highly significant: it left merchants the choice to make costs by registering the bond to ensure its payment. This choice of course depended on the trust and reputation the creditor and debtor enjoyed in the mercantile community.

Attitudes towards the flexibility of IOUs differed between merchant groups. The Luccese merchants, who, as international bankers, were definitely not unfamiliar with complex financial contracts, were not comfortable with the flexibility of IOUs. The English Merchant Adventurers in Antwerp considered the transfer of a bond to be definitive; creditors who passed on the bond were no longer liable for its payment. Moreover, foreign merchants had much more transports of IOUs recorded by notaries than native merchants which indicates that foreign merchant more often wanted concrete, written proof of a bond's circulation; they were more reluctant to rely strongly on the IOU payment system. Hence, foreign and native merchants displayed different attitudes towards bonds. The ease and flexibility with which Low Countries merchants used this low-cost payment system, framed by laws and enforceable by courts, amounts to a comparative advantage in business finance. Both large and small relied on flexible IOUs to finance their trade. One of the imperfections of the historiography – including this book – is our inadequate understanding of financial preferences in pre-industrial Europe: why did merchants and other entrepreneurs utilize particular financial instruments and in which circumstances?[2] Only a sufficient corpus of explicit inventories, account books and correspondences can improve our knowledge of pre-industrial financial behaviour: sixteenth-century Antwerp is unfortunately poorly endowed in this regard. I can only hope that the selection and use of available sources has allowed some deeper insight.

Although bonds did circulate across state boundaries (from Antwerp to London for example), the payment system was geographically limited to the Low Countries and to Antwerp in particular. Low Countries did use bills of exchange to transfer monies to other commercial cities. The need among Low Countries merchants to use bills of exchange to transfer funds to other European markets most likely increased with their growing presence on these markets. Low Countries merchants did not enjoy a dominant position in the financial network (yet): foreign, especially, Italian bankers functioned as the counterparties in these transactions. Sixteenth-century Antwerp served as a training ground and test site for commercial techniques and know-how as a result of the concentration of representatives of all European traders in one city. Low Countries merchants showed themselves eager students: they were trained by foreign merchants in Antwerp and abroad (either Low Countries expats or citizens of particular cities) and Antwerp's printing presses – Antwerp was one of the most important book production centres in sixteenth-century Europe – produced so-called *Ars Mercatoria guides* or 'Doing business for dummies'.[3] Hence, Low Countries merchants could easily pick up information on Italian-style accounting, letter writing, mathematics, business techniques such as the bill of exchange and languages.[4] This training allowed them to catch up with the most recent techniques but it did not give them an advantage over their competitors who were familiar with the same techniques.

Besides working through partnerships (although partnerships with foreigners were quite rare), paying with bills of exchange and knowing and using the business techniques of other groups to set up international co-operation, Low Countries merchants particularly engaged in commission trade with merchants, both other Low Countries traders and foreigners, in other cities. Another means of international co-operation for Low Countries merchants was commission trade. Because of their extensive contacts with Low Countries industry, permanent presence on the Antwerp market – many foreign traders were only in the Scheldt town for a couple of weeks during which they had to buy and sell – and the fact that they were locals, Low Countries merchants became sought-after commission agents for foreign firms. Low Countries merchants executed simple commercial transactions for foreign third parties in return for commission fees which allowed them to establish their own contacts with these foreign markets themselves. These agency relations relied on flexible contracts structured by reputation mechanisms, the legal value of letters and accounts which circulated between principals and agents, the information density of the Antwerp market (through price currents and commodity samples), and the intensive commercial ties between Antwerp and other European commercial cities. Commission trade has been put forward as having been a flexible mechanism for merchants to become active in international trade, i. e., it promoted commercial democratization. However, access to commission trade networks was often the result of being trained by or serving a master merchant who was already firmly embedded in the commercial web. Commission trade was also an important consequence of a merchant's own businesses and contacts; established companies such as the Van der Molen and Van Bombergen could capitalize on their acquired contacts for such commission businesses, especially the second generations of these firms. Though commission trade allowed Low Countries merchants to establish contacts with foreign principals and offer their relatively low-cost services (because of their permanent residence, reputation, citizenship rights and contacts with local industry), it did not constitute a comparative advantage. While foreign principals will definitely have realized the cost advantages of having a local representative, many foreign traders still preferred to have an Antwerp representative from their own home-town.

Several historians have put forward sixteenth-century Antwerp as an exemplary case of transition from a trade governed by particular and privileged groups to an open market accessible to all market participants and fuelled by open-access institutions provided by the city government. Sixteenth-century Antwerp was committed to the protection and security of all merchants and their private property rights and to that end it held the local monopoly of violence; permanent trading venues – with the Antwerp Bourse as the most impressive example – were built and opened up to all traders; postal facilities and contract registration services were available (for a fee); and there were institutions for conflict resolution. Urban competition induced sixteenth-century Antwerp to set up these open-access institutions and adapt other institutions to the needs of the mercantile community. The final chapter has singled out one such open-access institution: courts of law. The Antwerp city court dealt with many mercantile cases quite efficiently: half of all mercantile civil cases received a final sentence within a year. The city court was not biased against either native or foreign traders, it can be considered as neutral. Moreover, its services were accessible to all merchants, not only those with merchant guild membership and even protestants. The central courts – the Council of Brabant and the Great Council of Mechelen – were willing to adjudicate mercantile cases but as a result of the much longer procedures they handled far fewer cases than the Antwerp aldermen. Merchants only appealed to the Council of Brabant for cases involving high stakes. However, the influence of these central courts should not be ignored, for they adjudicated complex cases involving parties residing in different jurisdictions, had a larger geographical influence and saw their important cases used as reference in other courts. The chapters on partnerships and IOUs have made clear that the urban government supported such contracts by implementing efficient legislation, by leaving merchants the choice of whether or not to register their contracts and by offering contract registration services and contract enforcement by its court of aldermen when necessary. In partnerships, default rules were available, yet merchants could compose their individual partnership by selecting from a flexible menu of contract clauses. Legislation was conceived through communication with the mercantile community and adapted to and embedded in local legal traditions. This clearly shows the commitment of the urban government to streamlining transactions and to the creation and maintenance of open-access institutions. One could ascribe the ascent of Low Countries merchants to the availability of and the reliance of this merchants on such best-practice open-access institutions.

However, the path of institutional change had more bumps and holes than the straight route assumed by several economic historians. Sixteenth-century Antwerp was the odd man out when compared to other commercial cities. Contrary to trade emporia such as Venice, Genoa, Seville, Lisbon, Rouen, Lyon, Augsburg, Nuremberg, London, Amsterdam, Danzig and Lübeck, the Antwerp urban government did not grant its merchant-citizens a preferential treatment. Indeed, the institutional climate was less favourable than expected for Low Countries merchants. The last chapter has nuanced the decline of merchant guilds in Antwerp. Foreign merchants who had been the market makers in Bruges had been attracted to the city by the renewal of ancient privileges and the granting of new ones. When the foreigners had settled in the Scheldt town, the city government was eager to retain them. The city government could turn directly to these foreign nations for loans and taxes, although they were careful not to ask for too much (as can be seen in the loans and taxes discussed in the first chapter). Much larger was the indirect effect of the presence of foreign traders through the taxes on trade and markets and through the employment secured by trade on which so many inhabitants relied. Many merchants trading at Antwerp were indeed unincorporated but a few foreign merchant guilds – especially the English Merchant Adventurers – still held, used and enforced ancient privileges.

Native merchants too displayed a corporate reflex at times in the face of strong competition from incorporated traders and adversities abroad. All submitted proposals for the incorporation of Antwerp merchants presented a relatively open institution: members would have to pay fees but these were used to pursue group interests. All attempts at organizing were motivated by the (potential) competition from foreign merchants and their nations. The 1485 guild coincided with the increased presence of foreign merchant on the Antwerp market and that of the mid-1560s targeted the powerful Merchant Adventurers. The Merchant Adventurers enjoyed strong political ties with the Crown and made trade for Low Countries merchants in England increasingly difficult. Both that attempt and the actual guild of the 1580s sought to establish an office in London by which to acquire political bargaining power and privileges so as to compete with the Merchant Adventurers and to collectively act against discrimination in London. However, the Antwerp magistracy did not dare to offend the Merchant Adventurers, who had boycotted Antwerp and only recently returned to the city. As a result, the city government would not (and perhaps could not) approve a native merchant guild which might openly defy the Merchant Adventurers. An anonymous critic penned a libel in 1565 in which he castigated the Antwerp government for its policy of favouring foreign merchants which he thought threatened the wealth of the city. This attitude had already destroyed Bruges; the author advised Antwerp to be more like Venice or Florence.[5]

Perhaps the city government was not yet convinced of the commercial prowess of its native merchants. Even in the few cases where a merchant guild was actually allowed by the city government, the government closely monitored and controlled the guild. Support for the native merchant guilds was not unanimous, as witnessed by the many free-riders and opponents. Hence, the native merchant guilds were either never approved, remained a dead letter or were otherwise stymied, with non-existent to weak merchant guilds as a result. In this regard, the Antwerp city government, with few active merchants in its ranks for most part of the city's Golden Age, definitely assumed an ambiguous position: on the one hand, it sought to organize open-access institutions; on the other hand, it carried the burden of its past decisions epitomized in the strong merchant guilds of, for example, the Merchant Adventurers who could even extort a preferential treatment from Antwerp by threatening to leave the city. By denying requests of native merchants to set up their guild or keeping a close eye on merchant associations which were permitted, the city government discriminated against its own merchant-citizens. Antwerp's ambiguous position was unparalleled among sixteenth-century trade centres; these reserved important roles for its own merchants while exerting strong control on foreign traders. Only in the 1580s was this Antwerp attitude changed slightly, but by then it was perhaps too late to turn the tide.

Because of the absence of a strong native merchant guild in Antwerp, it was unlikely that Low Countries merchants abroad would set up merchant nations without home support. The colonies of Low Countries merchants throughout Europe were numerous but informally organized. This was also a result of the attitude of the particular host ruler: for example in Portugal the king appointed the Flemish nation representative; Antwerp had little say in this process. Only after the fall of Antwerp and the subsequent merchant diaspora did formal nations of Low Countries merchants arise, probably as a result of the growing colonies in various European commercial centres. Yet, this lack of merchant guild support abroad did not especially hinder the ascent of Low Countries merchants, whereas merchants' collective pressure on host rulers to secure their property rights and offer them protection could have been an advantage for the Low Countries traders. The Antwerp merchant guild could have been an important interlocutor to negotiate for privileges with host rulers. In cases when they did have privileges, they were eager to defend them when the privileges were threatened by the host ruler. The lack of strong state support – either from the Antwerp city government or from the central government in Brussels – in the organization of trade – collective action, representation abroad, organization of shipping – renders the experience and ascent of Low Countries unique. Eventually, however, Low Countries traders managed to do well without merchant guilds.

To summarize, four comparative advantages of Low Countries traders were identified: they maintained strong relations with Low Countries industry which produced fashionable products which were in demand throughout Europe; they were able to acquire credit through flexible IOUs; they had best-practice open-access institutions at their fingertips; and through their permanent presence or representation in Antwerp – the major and well-connected commercial entrepôt at that time – these merchants had a finger on the pulse regarding the latest news and commercial knowhow. Antwerp did propel these traders onto European markets. The fall of Antwerp in 1585 was in fact the biggest contribution of Low Countries traders to European commerce: through their diaspora Low Countries traders exported their relations, know-how, commercial practices and techniques. Besides comparative advantages, important exogenous factors played into the game of Low Countries merchants as well. Or to put it differently: Low Countries traders had the right items at the right time at the right place.

Low Countries merchants seized commercial opportunities created by the opening up of new markets and the choices of other merchant groups. Fifteenth-century Flemish merchants were among the first to exploit Madeira, the Canary Islands and the Azores by setting up sugar plantations. Sugar provided these Flemish merchants (Despars) with a much-coveted and thus strategic product; when the centre of gravity moved from Bruges to Antwerp, Low Countries merchants with strong ties to Antwerp (the Groenenborch and Van Dale families for example) took over the trade in sugar and its exploitation on the Atlantic Islands. Atlantic sugar was shipped from the Iberian Peninsula to Antwerp where it was re-exported to the German hinterland and England. The money trade offered a second opportunity for Low Countries traders. The growing demand for credit as a function of state formation and European wars was largely met by Italian merchant-bankers who had been in this business for centuries and by the capital-rich south Germans, but parallel to their commercial ascent, a few Low Countries merchants entered the market for government finance. The Habsburgs were of course their biggest clients but several Antwerp traders also acted as lenders to the French and English Crown, through the intermediation of royal agents such as Thomas Gresham. A second category of opportunities was the consequence of the decisions by other merchant groups. The withdrawal of Venetian merchants from the Low Countries markets at the beginning of the sixteenth century left a commercial vacuum which Low Countries traders filled in; they exported English and Low Countries textiles and even some spices to the city of the Doges and acted as the agents of Venetian principals and Low Countries merchants who had set up shop in Venice. The re-export of these textiles to the Levant remained the exclusive privilege of Venetian traders. Second, though the English Merchant Adventurers may have been a formidable competitor in the Antwerp–England trade, up to the 1550s they did not actively explore European markets; for them, Antwerp itself offered enough sales opportunities. Low Countries merchants stepped in to market English textiles on European markets out of Antwerp. The sixteenth-century decline of the dominance of the Hanseatic League and the gradual penetration of the Dutch in the Baltic attracted Antwerp merchants as well. Dutch shipmasters and Antwerp merchants and their agents explored Russian markets, which they even tried to reach via the northern route.

This book has tried to describe and explain the commercial ascent of Low Countries merchants. It has done so through the perspective of sixteenth-century Antwerp, its market, its commercial techniques and practices and its institutions. More research in European archives can provide more details on the communities of Low Countries in European commercial cities; London and several Iberian cities are especially promising in this regard. Throughout the book I have compared experiences of Low Countries traders with those of other merchant groups. Comparative research on merchant groups and commercial cities is fundamental to increase our knowledge of the mechanisms and dynamics of pre-industrial trade. Hence, I sincerely hope that this book will serve as a point of reference and a source to compare Low Countries merchants and their hub, sixteenth-century Antwerp, for new comparisons.

WORKS CITED

Primary Sources

City Archive Antwerp (CAA)

Certificatieboeken (certification books): CERT # 5, 6, 13, 16, 18, 20, & 25 (1542–66).

Collectanea: Coll # 5, 14 (1520–49, 1560–73).

Gebodboeken (city ordinances): Pk # 914–17 (1489–1589).

Gilden & ambachten (craft guilds), schoolmasters guild: GA # 4537 (1468–1700).

Insolvente Boedelkamer (Chamber of Insolvency): IB # 258 (Jan Van Immerseel, 1576–1598), 776 (jaarmarktboek Frans de Pape, 1538–50), 788 (journal Daniel de Bruyne, 1561–5), 2898 (correspondence Van der Molen, 1538–44).

Notariaat (notarial archives): N # 544 (Stephanus Claeys), 863 (Jacob de Kimpe), 1177 (Adriaan de Witte), 1329, 1330 (Jan Dries), 2071, 2072, 2074, 2077 (Adriaan Zeger 's-Hertoghen), 2078 (Zeger 's-Hertoghen), 2875 (Jan Rogge), 3132, 3133 (Willem Stryt), 3568 (Gielis Vanden Bossche), 3635 (Dierick Van den Bossche), 4456 (Lieven Van Rokeghem) 9024 (Cornelis Reedgeelt).

Processen, 7 # 240, 1818, 3916, 11282, 11292, 12144.

Processen Supplement: 288 # 692, 696, 1266, 1490, 1503, 1577, 1640, 1641, 1657, 1679, 1680, 1685, 3881, 6152, 6157, 8926, 8933, 9479, 9846.

Privilegiekamer (Privilege Chamber), Gebodboeken (ordinance books): Pk # 914, 915, 916, 917 (1489–1589).

Privilegiekamer, Raeckt den handel: Pk # 1012 (rekwesten schippersambacht, 1464–1610), 1018 (wissels, 1502–1788), 1022 (register of the West traders 1581–8).

Privilegiekamer, Vreemde natiën, Duitse natie: Pk # 1065 (1562–1680).

Privilegiekamer, Vreemde natiën, Engelse natie: Pk # 1052 (1501–48), 1053 (1549–57), 1059 (complaints, sixteenth century).

Privilegiekamer, Vreemde natiën, Natie van Lucca: Pk # 1076 (1501–1605).

Rekwestboeken (request books): Pk # 657 (1579–80).

Schepenregisters (Aldermen's registers): SR # 137, 162, 187, 252, 268, 281, 288, 297, 316, 392 (1510–88).

Tresorij (Treasury): T # 737 (1575).

Vierschaar, Schetz–Pruynen trial: V # 327 a.

Vierschaar, Turbeboeken ('Turbe books): V # 68, 69.

Vierschaar, Vonnisboeken (sentence books): V # 1233 (1504–5), 1238, 1239, 1240 (1544), 1249 (1566–7).

Weesmeesterkamer (Orphan Chamber): WK # 91 (1588).

Algemeen Rijksarchief Brussel (General State Archives Brussels, ARB)

Rekenkamer (Account Chamber): Hundredth Penny export tax, 23358–9, 23361 (1543–5).

Rekenkamer (Account Chamber): 2 per cent import and export tax, 23469–74 (1552–3).

Rekenkamer (Account Chamber), dozen: doos nr. 326.

Rijksarchief Antwerpen (State Archive Antwerp, RAA)

Chartarium Sint-Bernards: 800.

Notariaat (notarial archives): 522, 523, 524, 525 (Jacobus de Platea 1524–43).

Rijksarchief Brussel (State Archive Brussels, RAB)

Council of Brabant sentence books: 504 (1504), 505 (1505), 589–90 (1544).

Council of Brabant, lawsuit files of private individuals: 99, 165, 198, 263, 295.

Museum Plantin-Moretus (MPM)

Manuscripts: Arch. 681, Journal Herman Janssens (1550–70).

Manuscripts: MS. 318, account book Willem Van den Lare (1522–30).

Zeeuw Archief Middelburg (ZAM)

70 Familie De Jonge van Ellemeet, Pieces concerning the parents or ancestors of Maria Oyens: 40, 41, 45 (documents pertaining to the Van der Molen family).

Secondary Sources

Abatino, B., G. Dari-Mattiacci and E. C. Perotti, 'Depersonalization of Business in Ancient Rome', *Oxford Journal of Legal Studies*, 31:2 (20 June 2011), pp. 365–89.

Abraham-Thisse, S., 'De lakenhandel in Brugge', in A. Vandewalle (ed.), *Hanzekooplui en Medicibankiers: Brugge, wisselmarkt van Europese culturen* (Oostkamp: Stichting Kunstboek, 2002), pp. 65–70.

Acemoglu, D., S. Johnson and J. Robinson, 'The Rise of Europe: Atlantic Trade, Institutional Change, and Economic Growth', *American Economic Review*, 95 (2005), pp. 546–79.

Aerts, E., 'The Absence of Public Exchange Banks in Medieval and Early Modern Flanders and Brabant (1400–1800): A Historical Anomaly to Be Explained', *Financial History Review*, 18:1 (2011), pp. 91–117.

—, 'Geld, krediet en financiën in de Zuidelijke Nederlanden Ca. 1500–50', in M. Danneel (ed.), *Keizer Karels geldbeurs: geld en financiën in de 16de eeuw* (Brussels: Nationale Bank van België, 2000), pp. 32–79.

Al-Hussein, A., 'Trade and Business Community in Old Castile: Medina Del Campo 1500–1575' (PhD dissertation, University of East Anglia, 1982).

Archer, I. W., *The Pursuit of Stability: Social Relations in Elizabethan London* (Cambridge: Cambridge University Press, 1991).

Arnade, P., *Beggars, Iconoclasts, and Civic Patriots: The Political Culture of the Dutch Revolt* (Ithaca, NY: Cornell University Press, 2008).

Asaert, G., 'De oudste Certificatiën van de Stad Antwerpen (1468–1482)', *Handelingen van de Koninklijke Commissie voor Geschiedenis*, 132 (1966), pp. 261–96.

—, 'Documenten voor de geschiedenis van de Antwerpse scheepvaart voornamelijk de Engelandvaart (1404–1485)', in *Collectanea Maritima* (Brussels: Koninklijke Academie voor Wetenschappen, Letteren en Schone Kunsten van België. Wetenschappelijk Comité voor Maritieme Geschiedenis, 1985).

—, 'Gasten uit Brugge: nieuwe gegevens over Bruggelingen op de Antwerpse markt in de vijftiende eeuw', in H. Coppejans and G. Hansotte (eds), *Album Carlos Wijffels: aangeboden door zijn wetenschappelijke medewerkers* (Brussels: Algemeen Rijksarchief, 1987), pp. 23–41.

Aslanian, S., 'The Circulation of Men and Credit: The Role of the Commenda and the Family Firm in Julfan Society', *Journal of the Economic and Social History of the Orient*, 50 (2007), pp. 124–70.

—, *From the Indian Ocean to the Mediterranean: The Global Trade Networks of Armenian Merchants from New Julfa*, The California World History Library (Berkeley, CA: University of California Press, 2011).

—, 'Social Capital, "Trust" and the Role of Networks in Julfan Trade: Informal and Semi-Formal Institutions at Work', *Journal of Global History*, 1:3 (2006), pp. 383–402.

Asser, W. D. H, *In solidum of pro parte: een onderzoek naar de ontwikkelingsgeschiedenis van de hoofdelijke en gedeelde aansprakelijkheid van vennoten tegenover derden* (Leiden: Brill, 1983).

Astorri, A., and D. Friedman, 'The Florentine Mercanzia and its Palace', *I Tatti Studies: Essays in the Renaissance*, 10 (2005), pp. 11–68.

Avonds, P., *Brabant tijdens de regering van hertog Jan III (1312–1356): de grote politieke krisissen* (Brussels: Paleis der Academien, 1984).

Baetens, R., *De nazomer van Antwerpens welvaart: de diaspora en het handelshuis De Groote tijdens de eerste helft der 17de eeuw*, 2 vols (Brussels: Gemeentekrediet, 1976).

Bateman, Victoria N., 'The Evolution of Markets in Early Modern Europe, 1350–1800: A Study of Wheat Price', *Economic History Review*, 64:2 (2011), pp. 447–71.

Benedict, P., 'Rouen's Foreign Trade during the Era of the Religious Wars (1560–1600)', *Journal of European Economic History*, 13:1 (1984), pp. 29–74.

—, *Rouen during the Wars of Religion* (Cambridge: Cambridge University Press, 2003).

Bennassar, B., 'Marchands flamands et italiens à Valladolid au XVIe siècle', in H. Kellenbenz (ed.), *Fremde Kaufleute auf der Iberischen Halbinsel* (Köln: Böhlau, 1970), pp. 48–55.

Berthe, J.-P., 'Les Flamands à Seville au 16e siècle', in H. Kellenbenz (ed.), *Fremde Kaufleute Auf Der Iberischen Halbinsel* (Köln: Böhlau, 1970), pp. 239–51.

Black, P., T. Hartzenberg and B. Standish, *Economics: Principles & Practice. A Southern African Perspective*, 2 edn (Cape Town: Pearson Education, 2000).

Blanchard, I., 'English Royal Borrowing at Antwerp, 1544–1574', in M. Boone and W. Prevenier (eds), *Finances publiques et finances privées au bas Moyen Âge: actes du colloque, Gand, les 5 et 6 mai 1995 = Public and Private Finances in the Late Middle Ages* (Leuven: Garant, 1996), pp. 57–73.

—, *The International Economy in the Age of Discoveries, 1470–1570: Antwerp and the English Merchants' World* (Stuttgart: Franz Steiner Verlag, 2009).

Blockmans, F. 'Van wanneer dateren de Antwerpse jaarmarkten?', *Handelingen van het Vlaamse filologencongres* (1947), pp. 58–9.

Blockmans, F., J. Van Roey, R. de Roo and D. Defourny, *Inventaris der Schepenregisters, 'Collectanen', 'Certificatieboeken' en 'Coopers en Comparanten'* (Antwerp: Stadsarchief Antwerpen, 1948).

Blockmans, W., 'The Creative Environment: Incentives to and Functions of Bruges Art Production', in M. W. Ainsworth (ed.), *Petrus Christus in Renaissance Bruges: An Interdisciplinary Approach* (New York/Turnhout: The Metropolitan Museum of Art/Brepols, 1995), pp. 11–20.

—, *Metropolen aan de Noordzee: de geschiedenis van Nederland, 1100–1560* (Amsterdam: Bakker, 2010).

—, 'Transactions at the Fairs of Champagne and Flanders. 1249–1291', in S. Cavaciocchi (ed.), *Fiere e mercati nella integrazione delle economie europee, secc. 13–18: atti della 'Trentaduesima Settimana di Studi', 9–12 maggio 2000* (Florence: Monnier, 2001), pp. 993–1000.

Blockmans, W., and W. Prevenier, *The Promised Lands: The Low Countries under Burgundian Rule, 1369–1530* (Philadelphia, PA: Penn, 1999).

Blomme, J., and H. Van der Wee, 'The Belgian Economy in a Long-Term Perspective: Economic Development in Flanders and Brabant, 1500–1812', in *Economic Growth and Structural Change: Comparative Approaches over the Long Run on the Basis of Reconstructed National Accounts: International Colloquium, Leuven, 8–11 September 1993* (Leuven: KUL, 1993), pp. 1–15.

Blondé, B., *De sociale structuren en economische dynamiek van 's-Hertogenbosch, 1500–1550* (Tilburg: Stichting Zuidelijk Historisch Contact, 1987).

—, 'The "Reconquista" and the Structural Transformations in the Economy of the Southern Netherlands', Paper presented at the Las Sociedades Ibéricas y el mar a finales del siglo 16: congreso internacional, Lisbon, 1998.

Blondé, B., O. Gelderblom and P. Stabel, 'Foreign Merchant Communities in Bruges, Antwerp and Amsterdam', in D. Calabi and S. T. Christensen (eds), *Cities and Cultural Exchange in Europe, 1400–1700*, Cultural Exchange in Early Modern Europe (Cambridge: Cambridge University Press, 2007), pp. 154–74.

Blondé, B., and J. Hanus, 'Beyond Building Craftsmen. Economic Growth and Living Standards in the Sixteenth-Century Low Countries: The Case of 'S-Hertogenbosch (1500–1560)', *European Review of Economic History*, 14:2 (2009), pp. 179–207.

Blondé, B., and M. Limberger, 'De gebroken welvaart', in R. Van Uytven (ed.), *Geschiedenis van Brabant van het hertogdom tot heden* (Zwolle: Waanders, 2011), pp. 307–30.

Blondé, B., and R. Van Uytven, 'De smalle steden en het Brabantse stedelijke netwerk in de late Middeleeuwen en de Nieuwe Tijd', *Lira Elegans*, 6 (1999), pp. 129–82.

Bochaca, M., 'Le règlement des litiges commerciaux entre bourgeois et étrangers: les juridictions pour "fait de marchandises" à Bordeaux au milieu du XVe au milieu du XVIe siècle', *Annales de Bretagne et des pays de l'Ouest*, 117:1 (2010), pp. 133–47.

Boerner, L., and J. W. Hatfield, *The Economics of Debt Clearing Mechanisms* (Berlin: Free University Berlin, School of Business & Economics, 2010).

Boerner, L., and D. Quint, 'Medieval Matching Markets' (Berlin: Free University Berlin, School of Business & Economics, 2010).

Boerner, L., and A. Ritschl, 'The Economic History of Sovereignty: Communal Responsibility, the Extended Family, and the Firm', *Journal of Institutional and Theoretical Economics JITE*, 165 (2009), pp. 99–112.

—, 'Individual Enforcement of Collective Liability in Premodern Europe', *Journal of Institutional and Theoretical Economics*, 158 (2002), pp. 205–13.

Bolton, J. L., and F. G. Bruscoli, 'When Did Antwerp Replace Bruges as the Commercial and Financial Centre of North-Western Europe? The Evidence of the Borromei Ledger for 1438', *Economic History Review*, 61:2 (2008), pp. 360–79.

Bonazzoli, V., 'Mercanti lucchesi ad Ancona nel Cinquecento', in T. Fanfani and R. Mazzei (eds), *Lucca e l'Europa degli affari, secoli XV-XVII* (Lucca: Maria Pacini Fazzi Editore, 1990), pp. 75–107.

Boockmann, H., *Die Stadt im Späten Mittelalter* (München: Beck, 1986).

Boone, M., 'Les toiles de lin des Pays-Bas bourguignons sur le marché anglais (fin XIVe–XVIe siècles)', in J.-M. Cauchies (ed.), *L'Angleterre et les Pays bourguignons: relations et comparaisons (XVe–XVIe s.): rencontres d'Oxford (22 au 25 septembre 1994)* (Neuchâtel: Centre européen d'études bourguignonnes (XIVe–XVIe s.), 1995), pp. 61–81.

Bossy, J., *Disputes and Settlements: Law and Human Relations in the West* (Cambridge: Cambridge University Press, 2003).

Botticini, M., 'A Loveless Economy? Intergenerational Altruism and the Marriage Market in a Tuscan Town, 1415–1436', *Journal of Economic History*, 59:1 (1999), pp. 104–21.

Botticini, M., and A. Siow, 'Why Dowries?', *American Economic Review*, 93:4 (2003), pp. 1385–98.

Bottin, J., 'Commerce, finances et pouvoir: la redistribution des aluns méditerranéens dans l'Europe du Nord-Ouest et en France au XVIe Siècle', *Mélanges de l'École française de Rome*, 126:1 (2014), available online.

Boumans, R., *Het Antwerps stadsbestuur voor en tijdens de Franse overheersing: bijdrage tot de ontwikkelingsgeschiedenis van de stedelijke bestuursinstellingen in de Zuidelijke Nederlanden* (Bruges: De Tempel, 1965).

Boyer-Xambeu, M.-T., G. Deleplace and L. Gillard, *Private Money and Public Currencies: The 16th Century Challenge*, trans. A. Azodi (New York: M. E. Sharpe, 1994).

Braudel, F., *La Méditerranée et le monde méditerranéen à l'époque de Philippe II* (Paris: Colin, 1949).

—, *Le temps du monde. Civilisation matérielle, économie et capitalisme, 15e–18e siècle*, 3 vols (Paris: Colin, 1967), vol. 3.

—, *The Mediterranean in the Age of Philip II*, 2 vols (New York: Harper & Row, 1972).

—, *The Perspective of the World. Civilization and Capitalism, 15th–18th Century*, 3 vols (London: Collins, 1982), vol. 3.

Brenner, R., *Merchants and Revolution: Commercial Change, Political Conflict, and London's Overseas Traders, 1550–1653* (Princeton, NJ: Princeton University Press, 1993).

Bril, L., *De handel tussen de Nederlanden en het Iberisch Schiereiland (midden XVIe eeuw)* (Ghent: University of Ghent, 1962).

Brulez, W., 'Anvers de 1585 à 1650', *Vierteljahresschrift für Sozial- und Wirtschaftsgeschichte*, 54:1 (1967), pp. 75–99.

—, 'The Balance of Trade of the Netherlands in the Middle of the 16th Century', *Acta historiae Neerlandica*, 4 (1970), pp. 20–48.

—, 'Bruges and Antwerp in the 15th and 16th Centuries: An Antithesis?', *Acta historiae Neerlandica*, 6 (1973), pp. 1–26.

—, 'De diaspora der Antwerpse kooplui op het einde van de 16e eeuw', *Bijdragen tot de geschiedenis*, 15 (1960), pp. 279–306.

—, *De firma Della Faille en de internationale handel van Vlaamse firma's in de 16de eeuw* (Brussels: Paleis der Academiën, 1959).

—, 'De Handel', in W. Couvreur (ed.), *Antwerpen in de XVIde Eeuw* (Antwerp: Mercurius, 1975), pp. 109–42.

—, 'De handelsbalans in het midden van de 16de eeuw', *Bijdragen voor de geschiedenis der Nederlanden*, 21 (1967), pp. 278–310.

—, 'De scheepvaartwinst in de Nieuwe Tijden', *Tijdschrift voor geschiedenis*, 92:1 (1979), pp. 1–19.

—, 'L'exportation des Pays-Bas vers l'Italie par voie de terre au milieu du XVIe siècle', *Annales. Economies, Sociétés, Civilisations*, 14:3 (1959), pp. 461–91.

—, 'La navigation flamande vers la Méditerranée à la fin du XVIe siècle', *Revue belge de philologie et d'histoire*, 36 (1958), pp. 1210–42.

—, 'Les routes commerciales d'Angleterre en Italie au XVIe siècle', in *Studi in Onore di Amintore Fanfani* (Milan: A. Giuffrè, 1962), pp. 123–84.

—, 'Lettres commerciales de Daniel et Antoine De Bombergen à Antonio Grimani (1532–43)', *Bulletin de l' Institut Historique belge de Rome*, 31 (1958), pp. 169–205.

—, 'Maarten De Hane', *Nationaal Biografisch Woordenboek*, 1 (1964), pp. 593–6.

—, 'Scheepvaart in de Zuidelijke Nederlanden', in D. P. Blok (ed.), *Algemene Geschiedenis der Nederlanden* (Haarlem: Fibula-Van Dishoeck, 1979), k, pp. 123–8.

Brulez, W., and G. Devos, *Marchands flamands à Vénise* (Brussels: Institut historique belge de Rome, 1965).

Brunelle, G. K., 'Migration and Religious Identity: The Portuguese of Seventeenth-Century Rouen', *Journal of Early Modern History*, 7:3–4 (2003), pp. 283–311.

Bulut, M., *Ottoman–Dutch Economic Relations in the Early Modern Period, 1571–1699* (Hilversum: Verloren, 2001).

Burgon, J. W., *The Life and Times of Sir Thomas Gresham* (London: Jennings, 1839).

Campbell, T. P. (ed.), *Tapestry in the Renaissance: Art and Magnificence* (New York: Metropolitan Museum of Art, 2006).

Carande, R., *Carlos V y sus banqueros* (Madrid: Soeciedag de estudios y publicaciones, 1949).

Carus-Wilson, E. M., and O. Coleman, *England's Export Trade, 1275–1547* (Oxford: Clarendon, 1963).

Casson, M., 'Entrepreneurship', in J. Mokyr, M. Botticini and M. Berg (eds), *The Oxford Encyclopedia of Economic History* (Oxford: Oxford University Press, 2003), pp. 211–15.

Clark, G., *A Farewell to Alms: A Brief Economic History of the World* (Princeton, NJ: Princeton University Press, 2007).

Cobb, H. S., *The Overseas Trade of London. Exchequer Customs Accounts 1480–81*, 71 vols (London: London Record Society Publications, 1990), vol. 27.

Colli, A., *The History of Family Business, 1850–2000* (New York: Cambridge University Press, 2003).

Coopmans, J. P. A., 'De jaarmarkten van Antwerpen en Bergen op Zoom als centra van rechtsverkeer en rechtsvorming', in M. J. G. C. Raaijmakers, H. C. F. Schoordijk and B. Wachter (eds), *Handelsrecht tussen koophandel en Nieuw BW: opstellen van de vakgroep privaatrecht van de Katholieke Universiteit Brabant bij het 150-jarig bestaan van het WVK* (Deventer: Kluwer, 1988), pp. 1–22.

Coornaert, E., *Anvers et le commerce parisien au 16ième siècle* (Brussels: Paleis der Academiën, 1950).

—, *La draperie-sayetterie d'Hondschoote, 14–18ième siècle. Un centre industriel d'autrefois* (Paris: PUF, 1930).

—, 'Le commerce de la Lorraine vu d'Anvers à la fin du XVe et au début du XVIe siècle', *Annales de l'Est*, 1 (1950), pp. 105–30.

—, *Les Français et le commerce international à Anvers, fin du 15e-16e siècle* (Paris: Rivière, 1961).

Coornaert, K., 'De Vlaamse natie op de Canarische eilanden in de 16de eeuw' (Ghent: University of Ghent, 2000).

Cooter, R., and J. T. Landa, 'Personal Versus Impersonal Trade: The Size of Trading Groups and Contract Law', *International Review of Law and Economics*, 4:1 (1984), pp. 15–22.

Cordes, A., 'Nord- und Süddeutsche Handelsgesellschaften Vor 1800', in S. Kalss and F.-S. Meissel (eds), *Zur Geschichte des Gesellschaftsrechts in Europa*, Veröffentlichungen des Ludwig-Boltzmann-Institutes für Rechtsvorsorge und Urkundenwesen (Vienna: Wiener Rechtsgeschichtliche Gesellschaft, 2003), pp. 27–41.

Cordes, A., K. Friedland and R. Sprandel, *Societates. Das Verzeichnis der Handelsgesellschaften im Lübecker Niederstadtbuch 1311–1361* (Köln: Böhlau Verlag, 2003).

Craeybeckx, J., 'De organisatie en de konvooiering van de koopvaardijvloot op het einde van de regering van Karel V: bijdrage tot de geschiedenis van de scheepvaart en de Admiraliteit', *Bijdragen voor de geschiedenis der Nederlanden*, 3:3–4 (1949), pp. 179–208.

—, 'Handelaars en neringdoenden: de 16de eeuw', in J. L. Broeckx, C. de Clercq and J. Dhondt (eds), *Flandria nostra: ons land en ons volk, zijn standen en beroepen door de tijden heen* (Antwerp: Standaard, 1957), pp. 409–64.

—, *Un grand commerce d'importation: les vins de France aux Anciens Pays-Bas (13e–16e siècle)* (Paris: SEVPEN, 1958).

Crailsheim, E., 'Behind the Atlantic Expansion: Flemish Trade Connections of Seville in 1620', *Research in Maritime History*, 43:2 (2010), pp. 21–46.

Curtin, P. D., *Cross-Cultural Trade in World History* (Cambridge: Cambridge University Press, 1984).

Cuypers, J., 'Geeraard Gramaye: sociaal-ekonomische studie van een Antwerpse persoonlijkheid uit de tweede helft der XVIde eeuw' (Ghent: Ghent University, 1948).

d'Ursel, B., *Les Schetz* (Brussels: Office généalogique et héraldique de Belgique, 2004).

Dahl, G., *Trade, Trust and Networks: Commercial Culture in Late Medieval Italy* (Lund: Nordic Academic Press, 1998).

Dambruyne, J., *Mensen en centen: het 16de-eeuwse Gent in demografisch en economisch perpectief* (Ghent: Maatschappij voor Geschiedenis en Oudheidkunde, 2001).

De Cock, S., *Gaspar Ducci, bankier van Keizer Karel, heer van Schoonsel en Kruibeke* (Borgerhout: Drukkerij Cools, 1979).

De Goey, F. M. M. 'Ondernemersgeschiedenis in Amerika, Nederland en België (1940–1995)', *NEHA-Jaarboek*, 59 (1996), pp. 21–65.

De Groote, H. L. V., 'De vermogensbalans van Melchior Schetz en zijn vrouw Anna Van Stralen met hun testament van 1 juli 1569', *Bijdragen tot de geschiedenis*, 55 (1972), pp. 226–63.

—, *De zeeassurantie te Antwerpen en te Brugge in de zestiende eeuw* (Antwerp: Marine Academie, 1975).

—, 'Zeeverzekering', in G. Asaert (ed.), *Maritieme Geschiedenis der Nederlanden* (Bussum: De Boer Maritiem, 1976), pp. 206–19.

De Longé, G., *Coutumes du pays et duché de Brabant: quartier d'Anvers* (Brussels: Gobbaerts, 1870).

De Marchi, N., and H. J. Van Miegroet, 'The Antwerpen-Mechelen Production and Export Complex', in A. Golahny, M. M. Mochizuki and L. Vergara (eds), *In his Milieu: Essays on Netherlandish Art in Memory of John Michael Montias* (Amsterdam: Amsterdam University Press, 2006), pp. 133–48.

De Meester, J., 'De gebruiks- en meerwaarde van poortersboeken voor historici: Antwerpen in de zestiende eeuw', *Vlaamse Stam: tijdschrift voor familiegeschiedenis* 43:3–4 (2007), pp. 276–88, 317–31.

—, *Gastvrij Antwerpen? Arbeidsmigratie naar het zestiende-eeuwse Antwerpen* (Antwerp: PhD dissertation University of Antwerp, 2011).

De Moor, T., 'The Silent Revolution: A New Perspective on the Emergence of Commons, Guilds, and Other Forms of Corporate Collective Action in Western Europe', *International Review of Social History*, 53, supplement 16 (2008), pp. 179–212.

De Munck, B., *Technologies of Learning: Apprenticeship in Antwerp from the 15th Century to the End of the Ancien Régime*, Studies in European Urban History (1100–1800) (Turnhout: Brepols, 2007).

De Peuter, R., 'Mooie kleren voor hoge heren. Beschouwingen over de textielhandel te Brussel in het midden van de zestiende eeuw', *Textielhistorische bijdragen*, 34 (1994), pp. 30–49.

De Ridder-Symoens, H., 'De universitaire vorming van de Brabantse stadsmagistraten en stadsfunktionarissen – Leuven en Antwerpen, 1430–1580', *Varia historica Brabantica*, 6–7 (1978), pp. 21–126.

De Roover, R., *L'évolution de la lettre de change, 14e–18e siècles* (Paris: Colin, 1953).

—, 'La communauté des marchands lucquois à Bruges de 1377 à 1404', *Handelingen van het Genootschap voor Geschiedenis te Brugge*, 86 (1949), pp. 23–89.

—, *The Rise and Decline of the Medici Bank, 1397–1494* (Cambridge, MA: Harvard University Press, 1963).

De Ruysscher, D., 'Bankruptcy, Insolvency and Debt Collection among Merchants in Antwerp (*c.*1490–*c.*1540)', in T. M. Safley (ed.), *The History of Bankruptcy: Economic, Social and Cultural Implications in Early Modern Europe* (New York: Routledge, 2013), pp. 185-199.

—, 'A Business Trust for Partnerships? Early Conceptions of Company-Related Assets in Legal Literature and Antwerp Forensic and Commercial Practice (Later Sixteenth–Early Seventeenth Century)', in W. Decock, F. Stevens and B. Van Hofstraeten (eds), *Company Law in Late Medieval and Early Modern Europe* (Brussels: Paleis der Academiën, 2015).

—, 'From Usages of Merchants to Default Rules: Practices of Trade, Ius Commune and Urban Law in Early Modern Antwerp', *Journal of Legal History*, 33:1 (1 April 2012), pp. 3–29.

—, *Handel En Recht in De Antwerpse Rechtbank (1585–1713)* (Leuven: UGA, 2009).

—, 'Innovating Financial Law in Early Modern Europe: Transfers of Commercial Paper and Recourse Liability in Legislation and Ius Commune (Sixteenth to Eighteenth Centuries)', *European Review of Private Law*, 19:5 (2011), pp. 505–18.

—, 'Law Merchant in the Mould. The Transfer and Transformation of Commercial Practices into Antwerp Customary Law (16th–17th Centuries)', in V. Duss et al. (eds), *Rechtstransfer in der Geschichte. Legal Transfer in History* (Munich: Meidenbauer, 2006), pp. 433–45.

—, 'Over Themis en Mercurius: handelsgebruiken en -recht in Antwerpen (vijftiende–zeventiende eeuw)', *Revue belge de philologie et d'histoire*, 88:4 (2010), pp. 1105–35.

De ruysscher, D., and J. Puttevils, 'The Art of Compromise. Legislative Talks for Marine Insurance Institutions in Antwerp (*c.*1550–*c.*1570)', *Low Countries Historical Review* (forthcoming).

De Smedt, H., 'Antwerpen en de opbloei van de Vlaamse verhandel tijdens de 16e eeuw. Rijkdom en inkomen van de Antwerpse koopman Jan Gamel volgens zijn staat van goed, 1572', 2 vols (Leuven: Katholieke Universiteit Leuven, 1970).

—, 'De Antwerpse koopman Jan Gamel', *Bijdragen tot de geschiedenis van de Nederlanden*, 56 (1971), pp. 211–24.

De Smedt, O., *De Engelse Natie te Antwerpen in de 16e eeuw (1496–1582)*, 2 vols (Antwerp: Sikkel, 1954).

—, 'De keizerlijke verordeningen van 1537 en 1539 op de obligaties en wisselbrieven: eenige kantteekeningen', *Nederlandsche Historiebladen: driemaandelijks tijdschrift voor de geschiedenis en de kunstgeschiedenis van de Nederlanden*, 3 (1940-1), pp. 15–35.

—, 'Een Antwerpsch plan tot organisatie van den Nederlandschen zeehandel op het Westen', *Antwerpsch Archievenblad*, 2:2 (1927), pp. 14–30.

—, 'Het College der Nederlandsche kooplieden op Engeland', *Antwerpsch Archievenblad*, 1:2–3 (1926), pp. 113–20, 321–48.

De Smidt, J. T., et al., *Chronologische lijsten van de geëxtendeerde sententiën berustende in het archief van de Grote Raad van Mechelen, 1465 [–1580]* (Brussels: Koninklijke commissie voor de uitgave der oude wetten en verordeningen van België, 1966).

De Vries, J., and A. van der Woude, *Nederland, 1500–1815: De Eerste Ronde Van Moderne Economische Groei* (Amsterdam: Balans, 1995).

Deceulaer, H., 'Guilds and Litigation: Conflict Settlement in Antwerp (1585–1796)', in M. Boone and M. Prak (eds), *Statuts Iindividuels, statuts corporatiefs et status judiciaires dans les villes européennes (Moyen Âge et Temps Modernes): actes du colloque tenu à Gand les 12–14 octobre 1995* (Leuven: Garant, 1996), pp. 171–208.

Degryse, K., *De Antwerpse fortuinen: kapitaalaccumulatie, -investering en -rendement te Antwerpen in de 18de eeuw* (Antwerp: Genootschap voor Antwerpse Geschiedenis, 2005).

—, *Pieter Seghers: een koopmansleven in troebele tijden* (Antwerp: Hadewijch, 1989).

Delumeau, J., *L'alun de Rome, 15e–19e Siècle* (Paris: SEVPEN, 1962).

Deneweth, H., 'A Fine Balance: Household Finance and Financial Strategies of Antwerp Households, 17th–18th Century', *Tijdschrift voor sociale en economische geschiedenis*, 8:4 (2011), pp. 15–43.

Denucé, J., *Afrika in de 16de eeuw en de handel van Antwerpen* (Antwerp: Sikkel, 1937).

—, 'De Beurs van Antwerpen: oorsprong en eerste ontwikkeling 15e en 16e eeuwen', *Antwerpsch Archievenblad*, 6 (1931), pp. 81–145.

—, *De Hanze en de Antwerpsche handelscompagnieën op de Oostzeelanden* (Antwerp: De Sikkel, 1938).

—, 'Familie De Pape met stamtafel', *Antwerpsch Archievenblad*, 33 (1928), pp. 98–104.

—, 'Geeraerd Gramaye', *Antwerpsch Archievenblad*, 33 (1928), pp. 81–98.

—, *Inventaire des Affaitadi, banquiers italiens à Anvers de l'année 1568* (Antwerp: De Sikkel, 1934).

—, *Italiaansche koopmansgeslachten te Antwerpen in de 16e-18e eeuwen* (Mechelen: Het Kompas, 1934).

—, 'Privilèges commerciaux accordés par les rois de Portugal aux Flamands et aux Allemands', *Archivo Historico Portuguez*, 7 (1909), pp. 310–19, 377–92.

Dessi, R., and S. Ogilvie, 'Social Capital and Collusion: The Case of Merchant Guilds', in *Cambridge Working Papers in Economics* (Cambridge: Cambridge University, 2004).

Deyon, P., and A. Lottin, 'Evolution de la production textile à Lille aux XVIe et XVIIe siècles', *Revue du Nord*, 49 (1967), pp. 23–34.

Dietz, A., *Frankfurter Handelsgeschichte*, 5 vols (Glashütten im Taunus: Auvermann, 1970).

Dietz, B., 'Antwerp and London: The Structure and Balance of Trade in the 1560s', in E. W. Ives, R. J. Knecht and J. J. Scarisbrick (eds), *Wealth and Power in Tudor England: Essays Presented to S. T. Bindoff* (London: The Athlone Press, 1978), pp. 186–203.

—, *The Port and Trade of Early Elizabethan London Documents* (London: London Record Society, 1972).

Dilis, E., *Les courtiers anversois sous l'Ancien Régime* (Antwerpen: Van Hille-De Backer, 1910).

Dinges, M., 'The Uses of Justice as a Form of Social Control in Early Modern Europe', in H. Roodenburg and P. Spierenburg (eds), *Social Control in Europe, 1500–1800* (Columbus, OH: Ohio State University Press, 2004), ch. 9, pp. 159–74.

Dixit, A. K., *Lawlessness and Economics: Alternative Modes of Governance* (Princeton, NJ: Princeton University Press, 2004).

Doehaerd, R., *Etudes anversoises: documents sur le commerce international à Anvers, 1488–1514*, 3 vols (Paris: SEVPEN, 1962–3).

Dollinger, P., *The German Hansa* (London: Macmillan, 1970).

Donnet, F., *Coup d'oeil sur l'histoire financière d'Anvers au cours des siècles* (Antwerp: Buschmann, 1927).

—, 'Les Anversois aux Canaries, un voyage mouvementé au XVIe siècle', *Bulletin de la Société de Géographie d'Anvers*, 18–19 (1895–6), pp. 276–311, 202–365.

—, 'Les exilés anversois à Cologne (1582–1585)', *Bulletin de l'Académie Royale d'archéologie de Belgique (1899)*, pp. 288–355.

—, 'Les origines d'une entreprise commerciale anversoise aux Canaries au XVIe siècle', *Bulletin de la Société de Géographie d'Anvers (1919)*, pp. 103–10.

Drelichman, M., and H.-J. Voth, *Lending to the Borrower from Hell: Debt, Taxes, and Default in the Age of Philip II* (Princeton, NJ: Princeton University Press, 2014).

Drost, M. A., *Documents pour servir à l'histoire du commerce des Pays-Bas avec la France jusqu'à 1585 (Bordeaux & La Rochelle)* ('s-Gravenhage: Instituut voor Nederlandse Geschiedenis, 1984).

Duplessis, R. S., *Lille and the Dutch Revolt: Urban Stability in an Era of Revolution, 1500–1582* (Cambridge: Cambridge University Press, 1991).

Duverger, E., 'De Antwerpse poortersboeken van 1533 tot 1609. Een bron voor de geschiedenis van de tapijtkunst en van de textiele kunsten', *Artes Textiles: bijdragen tot de geschiedenis van de tapijt-, borduur- en textielkunst*, 9 (1978), pp. 137–44.

—, 'De Steurbouts, een Oudenaards-Antwerps tapissiersgeslacht', *Artes Textiles*, 6 (1965), pp. 31–74.

—, *Jan, Jacques en Frans De Moor, tapijtwevers en tapijthandelaars te Oudenaarde, Antwerpen en Gent (1560 tot ca. 1680)* (Ghent: Interuniversitair Centrum voor de geschiedenis van de Vlaamse tapijtkunst, 1960).

Earle, P., 'The Commercial Development of Ancona, 1479–1551', *Economic History Review*, 22:1 (1969), pp. 28–44.

Edler, F., 'The Effects of the Financial Measures of Charles V on the Commerce of Antwerp, 1539–1542', *Belgisch tijdschrift voor filologie en geschiedenis*, 16: 3–4 (1937), pp. 665–73.

—, 'Le commerce d'exportation des sayes d'Hondschoote vers Italie d'après la correspondance d'une firme anversoise, Entre 1538 Et 1544', *Revue du Nord*, 22 (1936), pp. 249–66.

—, 'The Market for Spices in Antwerp, 1538–1544', *Revue belge de philologie et d'histoire*, 17 (1938), pp. 212–21.

—, 'The Van Der Molen, Commission Merchants of Antwerp: Trade with Italy, 1538–44', in J. L. Cate and E. N. Anderson (eds), *Medieval and Historiographical Essays in Honour of James Westfall Thompson* (Chicago, IL: University of Chicago Press, 1938), pp. 78–145.

Edwards, J., and S. Ogilvie. 'Contract Enforcement, Institutions, and Social Capital: The Maghribi Traders Reappraised', *Economic History Review*, 65:2 (2012), pp. 421–44.

Ehrenberg, R., *Das Zeitalter der Fugger: Geldkapital und Creditverkehr im 16* (Jahrhundert Jena: Fischer, 1912).

—, *Capital & Finance in the Age of the Renaissance: A Study of the Fuggers and their Connections* (Fairfield, NJ: Kelley, 1985).

Engels, M.-C., *Merchants, Interlopers, Seamen and Corsairs: The 'Flemish' Community in Livorno and Genoa (1615–1635)* (Hilversum: Verloren, 1997).

Enthoven, V., 'The Closure of the Scheldt: Closure, What Closure? Trade and Shipping in the Scheldt Estuary, 1559–1609', in P. Holm and J. Edwards (eds), *North Sea Ports and Harbours: Adaptations to Change: Second North Sea History Conference, Esbjerg* (Esbjerg: Fiskeri- og Søfartsmuseet, 1992), pp. 11–37.

Epstein, S. R., 'Fairs, Towns, and States in Renaissance Europe', in S. Cavaciocchi and F. Datini (eds), *Fiere e mercati nella integrazione delle economie europee, secc. 13–18: atti della 'Trentaduesima Settimana di Studi', 8–12 maggio 2000*, Settimani di studi Istituto internazionale di storia economica (Florence: Monnier, 2001), pp. 71–90.

—, *Freedom and Growth: The Rise of States and Markets in Europe, 1300–1750* (London: Routledge, 2001).

—, 'Regional Fairs, Institutional Innovation, and Economic Growth in Late Medieval Europe', *Economic History Review*, 47:3 (1994), pp. 459–82.

Epstein, S. A., 'Secrecy and Genoese Commercial Practices', *Journal of Medieval History*, 20:4 (1994), pp. 313–25.

Everaert, J., 'The Flemish Sugar Connection: Vlamingen in de Atlantische suikereconomie (1480–1648)', *Bijdragen tot de geschiedenis*, 84 (2001), pp. 257–65.

—, 'Marchands flamands à Lisbonne et l'exportation du sucre de Madère (1480–1530)', Paper presented at the Actas do I Coloquio de Historia da Madeira, Funchal, 1986.

—, 'Vlaamse suikerbaronnen op Madeira (Omstreeks 1480–1620)', in J. Everaert and E. Stols (eds), *Vlaanderen en Portugal: op de golfslag van twee culturen* (Antwerp: Mercatorfonds, 1991), pp. 99–117.

Everaert, J., and E. Stols, *Vlaanderen en Portugal: op de golfslag van twee culturen* (Antwerp: Mercatorfonds, 1991).

Ewert, U. C., and S. Selzer, 'Verhandeln und Verkaufen, Vernetzen und Vertrauen. Über die Netzwerkstruktur des Hansischen Handels', *Hansische Geschichtsblätter*, 119 (2001), pp. 135–62.

Ewing, D., 'Marketing Art in Antwerp, 1460–1560: Our Lady's Pand', *Art Bulletin*, 72:4 (1990), pp. 558–84.

Fagel, R., *De Hispano-Vlaamse wereld: de contacten tussen Spanjaarden en Nederlanders, 1496–1555* (Brussels: Archief- en Bibliotheekwezen in België, 1996).

—, 'De Koopmansboeken van Juan Bautista de Olanda: een Nederlandse koopman in Medina del Campo 1565–1566', *Archief- en bibliotheekwezen in België*, 1–4 (1997), pp. 265–311.

Fernández, J. L., and E. O. Montes, 'De aprendiz a mercader: el factor en el comercio internacional inglés del siglo XVI', *Pecvnia*, 5 (2007), pp. 145–80.

Filippini, J. P., 'Les nations à Livourne (XVII–XVIIIe siècles)', in S. Cavaciocchi (ed.), *I porti come impresa economica: atti Della 'Diciannovesima Settimana di Studi', 2–6 maggio 1987* (Prato: Le Monnier, 1988), pp. 581–94.

Forestier, A., 'Risk, Kinship and Personal Relationships in Late Eighteenth-Century West Indian Trade: The Commercial Network of Tobin & Pinney', *Business History*, 52:6 (2010), pp. 912–31.

Formsma, W. J., and L. P. L. Pirenne, *Koopmansgeest te 's-Hertogenbosch in de vijftiende en zestiende eeuw: het kasboek van Jaspar Van Bell, 1564–1568* (Nijmegen: Centrale Drukkerij, 1962).

Friedrichs, C. R., *Urban Society in an Age of War: Nördlingen, 1580–1720* (Princeton, NJ: Princeton University Press, 1979).

Gairdner, J., and R. H. Brodie (eds), *Letters and Papers, Foreign and Domestic, Henry VIII*, 21 vols (London: Longman, 1908), vol. 21:1.

Gamberini, A., and I. Lazzarini, *The Italian Renaissance State* (Cambridge: Cambridge University Press, 2012).

Gascon, R., *Grand commerce et vie urbaine au 16e siècle: Lyon et ses marchands (environs de 1520–environs de 1580)* (Paris: Mouton, 1971).

Gelderblom, O., 'Antwerp Merchants in Amsterdam after the Revolt, 1578–1630', in B. Blondé, A. Greve and P. Stabel (eds), *International Trade in the Low Countries (14th–16th Centuries): Merchants, Organization, Infrastructure: Proceedings of the International Conference Ghent-Antwerp, 12th–13th January 1997* (Leuven: Garant, 2000), pp. 223–41.

—, *Cities of Commerce: The Institutional Foundations of International Trade in the Low Countries, 1250–1650* (Princeton, NJ: Princeton University Press, 2013).

—, 'The Decline of Fairs and Merchant Guilds in the Low Countries, 1250–1650', *Jaarboek voor middeleeuwse geschiedenis* (2004), pp. 199–238.

—, 'Entrepreneurs in the Golden Age of the Dutch Republic', in W. J. Baumol, D. S. Landes and J. Mokyr (eds), *The Invention of Enterprise: Entrepreneurship from Ancient Mesopotamia to Modern Times* (Princeton, NJ: Princeton University Press, 2010), ch. 6, pp. 156–82.

—, 'From Antwerp to Amsterdam: The Contribution of Merchants from the Southern Netherlands to the Rise of the Amsterdam Market', *Review. A Journal of the Fernand Braudel Center for the Study of Economies, Historical Systems, and Civilizations*, 26:3 (2003), pp. 247–82.

—, 'The Governance of Early Modern Trade: The Case of Hans Thijs, 1556–1611', *Enterprise & Society*, 4:4 (2003), pp. 606–39.

—, 'Het juweliersbedrijf in de Lage Landen, 1450–1650', unpublished working paper.

—, 'The Organization of Long-Distance Trade in England and the Dutch Republic, 1550–1650', in O. Gelderblom (ed.), *The Political Economy of the Dutch Republic* (Farnham: Ashgate, 2009), ch. 9, pp. 223–54.

—, 'Uitdagingen voor de vroegmoderne ondernemersgeschiedenis', *NEHA-Bulletin*, 16:2 (2002), pp. 69–81.

—, *Zuid-Nederlandse kooplieden en de opkomst van de Amsterdamse stapelmarkt (1578–1630)* (Hilversum: Verloren, 2000).

Gelderblom, O., A. De Jong and J. Jonker, 'An Admiralty for Asia: Isaac Le Maire and Conflicting Conceptions about the Corporate Governance of the VOC', in J. G. S. Koppell (ed.), *The Origins of Shareholder Advocacy* (New York: Palgrave Macmillan 2011), pp. 29–60.

Gelderblom, O., and R. Grafe. 'The Rise, Persistence and Decline of Merchant Guilds. Re-Thinking the Comparative Study of Commercial Institutions in Pre-Modern Europe', *Journal of Interdisciplinary History*, 40:4 (2010), pp. 477–511.

Gelderblom, O., and J. Jonker, 'Completing a Financial Revolution: The Finance of the Dutch East India Trade and the Rise of the Amsterdam Capital Market, 1595–1612', *Journal of Economic History*, 64:3 (2004), pp. 641–72.

Gelderblom, O., and J. Luiten van Zanden, 'Vroegmodern ondernemerschap in Nederland', *NEHA-Bulletin*, 11:2 (1997), pp. 3–15.

Génard, P., *Jean-Baptiste Ferrufini et les assurances maritimes à Anvers au 16e siècle* (Antwerp: Impr. De Backer, 1882).

—, 'L'Hotel des Monnaies d'Anvers', *Annales de l'Académie d'Archéologie de Belgique*, 30 (1874), pp. 5–170.

—, 'La Furie Espagnole', *Annales de Académie Royale d'Archéologie de Belgique*, 32 (1876), pp. 5–728.

—, 'Un acte de société commerciale au XVIième siècle (La maison Schetz frères d'Anvers)', *Bulletin de la Société de Géographie d'Anvers*, 7 (1882), pp. 475–99.

Geudens, E., *Het hoofdambacht der meerseniers* (Antwerp: Dela Montagne, 1891).

Girard, A., *Le commerce français à Seville et Cadix au temps des Habsbourg: contribution à l'étude du commerce étranger en Espagne aux XVIe et XVIIIe siècles* (Paris: de Boccard, 1932).

—, 'Note sur les consuls étrangers en Espagne avant le Traité des Pyrénées', *Revue d'histoire moderne*, 9 (1934), pp. 120–38.

Godding, P., 'Le Conseil de Brabant sous Philippe le Bon. L'institution et les hommes', in R. Stein (ed.), *Powerbrokers in the Late Middle Ages. The Burgundian Low Countries in a European Context* (Turnhout: Brepols, 2001), pp. 101–14.

—, *Le droit privé dans les Pays-Bas méridionaux du 12e au 18e siècle* (Brussels: Palais des Académies, 1987).

—, 'Les lettres de justice, instrument du pouvoir central en Brabant (1430–1477)', *Archief- en bibliotheekwezen in België*, 61 (1990), pp. 385–402.

—, 'Une justice parallèle? L'arbitrage au Conseil de Brabant', in J. M. I. Koster-van Dijk and A. Wijffels (eds), *Miscellanea Forensia Historica: ter gelegenheid van het afscheid van Prof. Mr. J. Th. De Smidt* (Amsterdam: Werkgroep Grote Raad van Mechelen, 1988), pp. 123–41.

Godfrey, M. 'Arbitration and Dispute Resolution in Sixteenth Century Scotland', *Legal History Review*, 70:1–2 (2002), pp. 109–35.

Goldberg, J., *Trade and Institutions in the Medieval Mediterranean: The Geniza Merchants and their Business World* (Cambridge: Cambridge University Press, 2012).

Goldthwaite, R. A., *The Economy of Renaissance Florence* (Baltimore, MD: Johns Hopkins University Press, 2009).

—, 'The Medici Bank and the World of Florentine Capitalism', *Past and Present*, 114 (1987), pp. 3–31.

Gonzalez de Lara, Y., 'Enforceability and Risk-Sharing in Financial Contracts: From the Sea Loan to the Commenda in Late Medieval Venice', *Journal of Economic History*, 61:2 (2001), pp. 500–4.

Goris, J.-M. 'Herentals: van welvarend Industrieel centrum tot arme garnizoensstad (1560– 1650)', *Bijdragen tot de geschiedenis*, 73:3–4 (1990), pp. 211–35.

Goris, J.-A., 'Eene Antwerpsche handelsexpeditie in de Oostzeelanden (1562–1569)', *Bijdragen tot de geschiedenis*, 16 (1924–5), pp. 133–44.

—, *Etude sur les colonies marchandes méridionales (Portugais, Espagnols, Italiens) à Anvers de 1488 à 1587* (Leuven: Uytspruyt, 1925).

—, 'Turksche kooplieden te Antwerpen in de XVIe eeuw', *Bijdragen tot de geschiedenis*, 14:1 (1922), pp. 30–8.

Gotzen, M., 'Het oud-Antwerps burgerlijk procesrecht volgens de costumiere redacties van de 16e-17e eeuw', *Rechtskundig tijdschrift voor België*, 41 (1951), pp. 291–315, 424–68.

Graeber, D., *Debt: The First 5,000 Years* (New York: Melville House, 2011).

Grassby, R. *Kinship and Capitalism: Marriage, Family, and Business in the English-Speaking World, 1580–1740* (Washington, DC: Woodrow Wilson Center Press, 2001).

Gravesteijn, C., and J. J. McCusker, *The Beginnings of Commercial and Financial Journalism: The Commodity Price Currents, Exchange Currents, and Money Currents of Early Modern Europe* (Amsterdam: NEHA, 1991).

Greefs, H., 'Zakenlieden in Antwerpen tijdens de eerste helft van de negentiende eeuw' (PhD dissertation, University of Antwerp, 2004).

Greif, A., 'Contract Enforceability and Economic Institutions in Early Trade: The Maghribi Traders' Coalition', *American Economic Review*, 83:3 (1993), pp. 525–48.

—, 'The Fundamental Problem of Exchange: A Research Agenda in Historical Institutional Analysis', *European Review of Economic History*, 4:3 (2000), pp. 251–84.

—, 'Impersonal Exchange and the Origin of Markets: From the Community Responsibility System to Individual Legal Responsibility in Pre-Modern Europe', in M. Aoki and Y. Hayami (eds), *Communities and Markets in Economic Development* (Oxford: Oxford University Press, 2001), pp. 3–41.

—, 'Institutions and International Trade: Lessons from the Commercial Revolution', *American Economic Review*, 82:2 (1992), pp. 128–33.

—, *Institutions and the Path to the Modern Economy: Lessons from Medieval Trade* (Cambridge: Cambridge University Press, 2006).

—, 'The Maghribi Traders: A Reappraisal?', *Economic History Review*, 65:2 (2012), pp. 445–69.

—, 'Reputation and Coalitions in Medieval Trade: Evidence on the Maghribi Traders', *Journal of Economic History*, 49:4 (1989), pp. 857–82.

—, 'Trading Institutions and the Commercial Revolution in Medieval Europe', in A. Aganb-egyan, O. Bogomolov and M. Kaser (eds), *System Transformation: Eastern and Western Assessments*; Economics in a Changing World: Proceedings of the Tenth World Congress of the International Economic Association, Moscow (Basingstoke: Macmillan, 1994), ch. 8, pp. 115–25 .

Greif, A., P. Milgrom, and B. R. Weingast, 'Coordination, Commitment, and Enforcement: The Case of the Merchant Guild', *Journal of Political Economy*, 102:4 (1994), pp. 745–76.

Greve, A., 'Brokerage and Trade in Medieval Bruges: Regulation and Reality', in B. Blondé, A. Greve and P. Stabel (eds), *International Trade in the Low Countries (14th–16th Centuries): Merchants, Organisation, Infrastructure: Proceedings of the International Conference Ghent-Antwerp, 12th–13th January 1997* (Leuven: Garant, 2000), pp. 37–44.

—, 'Die Bedeutung der Brügger Hosteliers für Hansische Kaufleute im 14. und 15. Jahrhundert', *Jaarboek voor middeleeuwse geschiedenis*, 4 (2001), pp. 259–96.

—, *Hansische Kaufleute, Hosteliers und Herbergen im Brügge des 14. und 15 Jahrhunderts* (Frankfurt am Main: Lang, 2011).

—, 'Jacob Sconebergh and his Short Career as a Hosteller in Fourteenth-Century Bruges', in W. Blockmans, M. Boone and T. de Hemptinne (eds), *Secretum Scriptorum: Liber Alumnorum Walter Prevenier* (Leuven: Garant, 1999), pp. 213–24.

Guicciardini, L., *Beschryvinghe van alle de Nederlanden, anderssins ghenoemt Neder-Duytslandt* (Amsterdam: Facsimile Uitgaven Nederland, 1968).

—, *Descrittione di tutti i Paesi Bassi, altrimenti detti Germania Inferiore* (Antwerp: Guglielmo Silvio, 1567).

Guicciardini, L., and B. Aristodemo, *Descrittione di tutti i Paesi Bassi: edizione critica* (Amsterdam: Universiteit van Amsterdam, 1994).

Häberlein, M., *Brüder, Freunde und Betrüger: Soziale Beziehungen, Normen und Konflikte in der Augsburger Kaufmanschaft im die Mitte des 16 Jahrhunderts* (Berlin: Akademie Verlag, 1998).

—, *The Fuggers of Augsburg: Pursuing Wealth and Honor in Renaissance Germany. Studies in Early Modern German History* (Charlottesville, VA: University of Virginia Press, 2012).

Haemers, J., '"Ende Hevet tvolc goede cause jeghens hemlieden te rysene" Stedelijke opstanden en staatsvorming in het graafschap Vlaanderen (1477–1492)' (PhD dissertation, Ghent University, 2006).

—, *For the Common Good: State Power and Urban Revolts in the Reign of Mary of Burgundy (1477–1482)* (Turnhout: Brepols, 2009).

Haemers, J., and P. Stabel, 'From Bruges to Antwerp. International Commercial Firms and Government's Credit in the Late 15th and Early 16th Century', in *Banca, crédito y capital. La monarquía hispánica y los antiguos Países Bajos (1505–1700)* (Madrid: Fundación Carlos de Amberes, 2006), pp. 21–37.

Hamilton, E. J., *American Treasure and the Price Revolution in Spain, 1501–1650* (New York: Octagon Books, 1965).

Hansmann, H., R. Kraakman, and R. Squire, 'Law and the Rise of the Firm', *Harvard Law Review*, 119:5 (2006), pp. 1335–403.

Hanus, J., 'Affluence and Inequality in the Low Countries. The City of 'S-Hertogenbosch in the Long Sixteenth Century, 1500–1650' (PhD dissertation, Universiteit Antwerpen, 2010).

—, 'Een efficiënte pre-industriële kapitaalmarkt? Het vroeg zestiende-eeuwse 's-Hertogenbosch als voorbeeld', *Tijdschrift voor sociale en economische geschiedenis*, 6:3 (2009), pp. 82–113.

—, 'Real Inequality in the Early Modern Low Countries: The City of 'S-Hertogenbosch, 1500–1660', *Economic History Review*, 66:3 (2012), pp. 733–56.

—, *Tussen stad en eigen gewin: stadsfinanciën, renteniers en kredietmarkten in 's-Hertogenbosch (begin zestiende eeuw)* (Amsterdam: Aksant, 2007).

Hardwick, J., *Family Business: Litigation and the Political Economies of Daily Life in Early Modern France* (Oxford: Oxford University Press, 2009).

Harreld, D. J., 'Atlantic Sugar and Antwerp's Trade with Germany in the Sixteenth Century', *Journal of Early Modern History*, 7:2 (2003), pp. 148–63.

—, 'German Merchants and their Trade in Sixteenth-Century Antwerp', in B. Blondé, A. Greve and P. Stabel (eds), *International Trade in the Low Countries (14th–16th Centuries): Merchants, Organisation, Infrastructure: Proceedings of the International Conference Ghent-Antwerp, 12th–13th January 1997* (Leuven: Garant, 2000), pp. 169–91.

—, *High Germans in the Low Countries: German Merchants and Commerce in Golden Age Antwerp* (Leiden: Brill, 2004).

—, 'The Individual Merchant and the Trading Nation in Sixteenth-Century Antwerp', in C. H. Parker and J. H. Bentley (eds), *Between the Middle Ages and Modernity: Individual and Community in the Early Modern World* (Lanham: Rowman & Littlefield, 2007), pp. 271–84.

—, 'Trading Places: The Public and Private Spaces of Merchants in Sixteenth-Century Antwerp', *Journal of Urban History*, 29:6 (2003), pp. 657–69.

Harris, R., 'The Institutional Dynamics of Early Modern Eurasian Trade: The Commenda and the Corporation', *Journal of Economic Behavior & Organization*, 71:3 (2009), pp. 606–22.

Heller, H., *Anti-Italianism in Sixteenth-Century France* (Toronto, ON: University of Toronto Press, 2003).

Hindle, S., *The State and Social Change in Early Modern England* (Basingstoke: Palgrave Mac-Millan, 2001).

Höhlbaum, K., *Hansisches Urkundenbuch*, 8 ed., 6 vols (Halle: Buchhandlung des Waisenhauses, 1876–99), vol. 2.

Hoock, J., and Pierre J. (eds), *Ars Mercatoria: Handbücher und Traktate für den Gebrauch des Kaufmanns, 1470–1820: eine Analytische Bibliographie = Ars Mercatoria: manuels et traités à l'usage des marchands, 1470–1820*, 3 vols (Paderborn: Schöningh, 1991).

Howell, M. C., *The Marriage Exchange: Property, Social Place, and Gender in Cities of the Low Countries, 1300–1550* (Chicago, IL: University of Chicago Press, 1998).

Hunt, E. S., *The Medieval Super-Companies: A Study of the Peruzzi Company of Florence* (Cambridge: Cambridge University Press, 1994).

Hunt, E. S., and J. M. Murray, *A History of Business in Medieval Europe, 1200–1550* (Cambridge: Cambridge University Press, 1999).

Huys Janssen, P., *Werken aan kunst: economische en bedrijfskundige aspecten van de kunst-produktie, 1400–1800* (Hilversum: Verloren, 1995).

Irsigler, F., 'Köln, Die Frankfurter Messen und die Handelsbeziehungen mit Oberdeutschland im 15. Jahrhundert', *Mitteilungen aus dem Stadtarchiv von Köln*, 60 (1971), pp. 341–430.

Israel, J. I., *Diasporas within a Diaspora: Jews, Crypto-Jews and the World Maritime Empires (1540–1740)* (Leiden: Brill, 2002).

—, 'The Dutch Merchant Colonies in the Mediterranean During the Seventeenth Century', *Renaissance and Modern Studies*, 30:1 (1 January 1986), pp. 87–108.

—, *European Jewry in the Age of Mercantilism, 1550–1750* (Oxford: Clarendon Press, 1985).

Jeannin, P., 'Anvers et la Baltique au XVIe siècle', *Revue du Nord*, 37 (1955), pp. 93–113.

—, 'Distinction des compétences et niveaux de qualification: les savoirs négociants dans l'Europe moderne', in F. Angiolini and D. Roche (eds), *Cultures et formations négociantes dans l'Europe moderne* (Paris: Ecole des hautes études en sciences sociales, 1995), pp. 363–97.

—, *Les marchands au 16e siècle* (Paris: Seuil, 1957).

—, 'Les relations économiques des villes de la Baltique avec Anvers au XVIe siècles', *Viertel-jahresschrift für Sozial- und Wirtschaftsgeschichte*, 43:3–4 (1956), pp. 193–217, 323–55.

Jonker, J., and K. Sluyterman, *Thuis op de wereldmarkt: Nederlandse handelshuizen door de eeuwen heen* (Den Haag: Sdu, 2000).

Kagan, R. L. *Lawsuits and Litigants in Castile, 1500–1700* (Chapel Hill, NC: University of North Carolina Press, 1981).

Kagan, R. L., and P. D. Morgan, *Atlantic Diasporas: Jews, Conversos, and Crypto-Jews in the Age of Mercantilism, 1500–1800* (Baltimore, MD: Johns Hopkins University Press, 2009).

Kaptein, H., *De Hollandse textielnijverheid, 1350–1600: conjunctuur en continuïteit* (Hilversum: Verloren, 1998).

Kellenbenz, H., 'Antwerpener Nordeuropahandel um 1580', in *Album aangeboden aan Charles Verlinden ter gelegenheid van zijn dertig jaar professoraat = Album offert à Charles Verlinden à l'occasion de ses trente ans de professorat* (Ghent: Universa, 1975), pp. 211–22.

—, 'The Economic Significance of the Archangel Route (from the Late 16th to the Late 18th Century)', *Journal of European Economic History*, 2:3 (1973), pp. 541–81.

—, *Unternehmerkräfte im Hamburger, Portugal- und Spanienhandel, 1590–1625* (Hamburg: Verlag der Hamburgischen Bücherei, 1954).

Kessler, A. D., *A Revolution in Commerce: The Parisian Merchant Court and the Rise of Commercial Society in Eighteenth-Century France* (New Haven, CT: Yale University Press, 2007).

Kieckens, R. P. F., 'Une sucrerie anversoise au Brésil à la fin du XVIe siècle', *Bulletin de la Société de Géographie d'Anvers*, 7 (1882), pp. 467–74.

Kingdon, R. M. 'Christopher Plantin and his Backers, 1575–90. A Study in the Problem of Financing Business During War', in *Mélanges d'histoire économique et sociale en hommage au Professeur Antony Babel* (Geneva: Imprimerie de la Tribune, 1963), pp. 303–16.

Klep, P., 'Het Brabantse stedensysteem en de scheiding der Nederlanden, 1565–1650', *Bijdragen tot de geschiedenis*, 73:3–4 (1990), pp. 101–29.

Kohn, M., 'Bills of Exchange and the Money Market to 1600', 1999, unpublished working paper, available at http://www.dartmouth.edu/~mkohn/ [accessed 28 February 2015].

—, 'Business Management in Pre-Industrial Europe', 2003, unpublished working paper, available at http://www.dartmouth.edu/~mkohn/ [accessed 28 February 2015].

—, 'Business Organization in Pre-Industrial Europe', 2003, unpublished working paper, available at http://www.dartmouth.edu/~mkohn/ [accessed 28 February 2015].

—, 'Merchant Associations in Pre-Industrial Europe', 2003, unpublished working paper, available at http://www.dartmouth.edu/~mkohn/ [accessed 28 February 2015].

Kole, H., and C. Van Bochove, 'The Private Credit Market of Eighteenth-Century Amsterdam: Big Money in a Small World', in *Research Group Social Economic History* (Utrecht: Utrecht University, 2011).

Kooijmans, L., *Vriendschap en de kunst van het overleven in de zeventiende en achttiende Eeuw* (Amsterdam: Bakker, 1997).

Koppe, W., 'Antwerpener Handelsunternehmungen "Auf Ostland"', *Hansische Geschichtsblätter*, 63 (1938), pp. 226–36.

Kortlever, Y. E., 'The Easter and Cold Fairs of Bergen-Op-Zoom (14th–16th Centuries)', in S. Cavaciocchi (ed.), *Fiere e mercati nella integrazione delle economie europee, secc. 13–18: atti della 'Trentaduesima Settimana di Studi', 8–12 maggio 2000* (Florence: Le Monnier, 2001), pp. 625–43.

Kuehn, T., *Heirs, Kin, and Creditors in Renaissance Florence* (Cambridge: Cambridge University Press, 2008).

Kuran, T., 'Judicial Biases in Ottoman Istanbul: Islamic Justice and its Compatibility with Modern Economic Life', *Journal of Law and Economics*, 55 (2012), pp. 631–66.

Laenens, C., and L. Leemans, *De geschiedenis van het Antwerps gerecht* (Antwerp: Van de Velde, 1953).

Laga, C., 'O engenho dos Erasmos Schetz en Sao Vicente: resultado de perquisas in arquivos belgas', *Estudos Historicos*, 1 (1963), pp. 13–43.

Lambert, B., '"Considéré que lesquels marchans ont souvent question les ungs contre les autres": commerciële conflictbeheersing in het laat-middeleeuwse Brugge', paper presented at the Sixth European Social Science History Conference, Amsterdam, 2006, pp. 1–16.

—, 'De Genuese aanwezigheid in laatmiddeleeuws Brugge (1435–1495): een laboratorium voor de studie van instellingen en hun rol in de economische geschiedenis' (PhD dissertation, Ghent University, 2011).

Lamoreaux, N. R., and J.-L. Rosenthal, 'Entity Shielding and the Development of Business Forms: A Comparative Perspective', *Harvard Law Review*, 119 (2006), pp. 238–45.

Lanaro, P., 'Reinterpreting Venetian Economic History', in P. Lanaro (ed.), *At the Centre of the Old World: Trade and Manufacturing in Venice and the Venetian Mainland 1400–1800* (Toronto, ON: Toronto University Press, 2006), pp. 16–69.

Landa, J. T., 'Doing the Economics of Trust and Informal Institutions', in S. G. Medema and W. J. Samuels (eds), *Foundations of Research in Economics: How Do Economists Do Economics* (Cheltenham: Elgar, 1996), ch. 13, pp. 142–62.

—, 'A Theory of the Ethnically Homogeneous Middleman Group: An Institutional Alternative to Contract Law', *Journal of Legal Studies*, 10:2 (1981), pp. 349–62.

—, *Trust, Ethnicity, and Identity: Beyond the New Institutional Economics of Ethnic Trading Networks, Contract Law, and Gift-Exchange* (Ann Arbor, MI: University of Michigan Press, 1994).

Landes, D. S., *Dynasties: Fortunes and Misfortunes of the World's Great Family Businesses* (New York: Penguin, 2006).

Larivière, C. J. de, 'Entre gestion privée et contrôle public: les transports maritimes à Venise à la fin du Moyen Age', *Histoire urbaine*, 12 (2005), pp. 57–68.

—, *Naviguer, commercer, gouverner. Economie maritime et pouvoirs à Venise* (Leiden: Brill, 2008).

Laurent, C., J.-P.-A. Lameere and H. Simont, *Recueil des ordonnances des Pays-Bas: 2e série, 1506–1700*, 6 vols (Brussels: Goemaere, 1893–1922), vol. 4.

Le Bailly, M.-C., *Recht voor de Raad: Rechtspraak voor het Hof van Holland, Zeeland en West-Friesland in het midden van de vijftiende eeuw* (Hilversum: Verloren, 2001).

Lejeune, J., *La formation du capitalisme moderne dans la principauté de Liège au 16e siècle* (Liège: Faculté de Philosophie et Lettres, 1939).

Lesger, C., 'Migrantenstromen en economische ontwikkeling in vroegmoderne steden: nieuwe burgers in Antwerpen en Amsterdam, 1541–1655', *Stadsgeschiedenis*, 2 (2006), pp. 97–121.

—, 'Over het nut van huwelijk, opportunisme en bedrog. Ondernemers en ondernemerschap tijdens de vroegmoderne tijd in theoretisch perspectief', in C. A. Davids et al. (eds), *Kapitaal, ondernemerschap en beleid: studies over economie en politiek in Nederland, Europa en Azië, van 1500 tot heden: afscheidsbundel voor Prof. Dr. P. W. Klein*, NEHA-Series (Amsterdam: NEHA, 1996), pp. 55–75.

—, *The Rise of the Amsterdam Market and Information Exchange: Merchants, Commercial Expansion and Change in the Spatial Economy of the Low Countries, c.1550–1630* (Aldershot: Ashgate, 2006).

Lesger, C., and E. Wijnroks, 'The Spatial Organization of Trade: Antwerp Merchants and the Gateway Systems in the Baltic and the Low Countries c.1550', in H. Brand (ed.), *Trade, Diplomacy and Cultural Exchange: Continuity and Change in the North Sea Area and the Baltic, c.1350–1750* (Hilversum: Verloren, 2005), ch. 1, pp. 15–35.

Lijten, M. J. H. A., *Het burgerlijk proces in stad en meijerij van 's-Hertogenbosch, 1530–1811* (Assen: Van Gorcum, 1987).

Limberger, M., 'No Town in the World Provides More Advantages: Economies of Agglomeration and the Golden Age of Antwerp', in P. O'Brien, D. Keene and M. 't Hart (eds), *Urban Achievement in Early Modern Europe: Golden Ages in Antwerp, Amsterdam and London* (Cambridge: Cambridge University Press, 2001), pp. 39–62.

—, *Sixteenth-Century Antwerp and its Rural Surroundings: Social and Economic Changes in the Hinterland of a Commercial Metropolis (ca. 1450–ca. 1570)* (Turnhout: Brepols, 2008).

Lindberg, E., 'Club Goods and Inefficient Institutions: Why Danzig and Lübeck Failed in the Early Modern Period', *Economic History Review*, 62:3 (2009), pp. 604–28.

—, 'The Rise of Hamburg as a Global Marketplace in the Seventeenth Century: A Comparative Political Economy Perspective', *Comparative Studies in Society and History*, 50:3 (2008), pp. 641–62.

Lindemann, M., *The Merchant Republics: Amsterdam, Antwerp, and Hamburg, 1648–1790* (New York: Cambridge University Press, 2015).

Lingelbach, W. E., 'The Merchant Adventurers at Hamburg', *American Historical Review*, 9:2 (1904), pp. 265–87.

Louant, A., 'Gaspard Schetz, seigneur de Grobbendonck, facteur du roi d'Espagne à Anvers (1555–1561)', *Annales de l'Académie royale d'archéologie de Belgique*, 77 (1930), pp. 315–28.

Lucassen, L., and W. Willems (eds), *Waarom mensen in de stad willen wonen, 1200–2010* (Amsterdam: Bakker, 2010).

Lutz, E., *Die Rechtliche Struktur Süddeutscher Handelsgesellschaften in der Zeit der Fugger. Studien zur Fuggergeschichte* (Tübingen: Mohr, 1976).

Maes, L. T, M. Kocken et al., *Het Parlement en de Grote Raad van Mechelen, 1473–1797* (Antwerp: De Vries-Brouwers, 2009).

Malines, G., *Consuetudo, Vel, Lex Mercatoria or the Ancient Law-Merchant* (London: Redmayne, 1685).

Marechal, J., *Geschiedenis van de Brugse Beurs* (Bruges: Anjelier, 1949).

—, 'Le départ de Bruges des marchands étrangers (XVe et XVIe siècles)', *Handelingen van het Genootschap voor Geschiedenis: driemaandelijks tijdschrift voor de studie van geschiedenis en oudheden van Vlaanderen*, 88 (1951), pp. 26–74.

Marnef, G., *Antwerp in the Age of Reformation: Underground Protestantism in a Commercial Metropolis, 1550–1577* (Baltimore, MD: Johns Hopkins University Press, 1996).

—, *Antwerpen in De Tijd Van De Reformatie: Ondergronds Protestantisme in Een Handelsmetropool, 1550–1577* (Antwerp: Kritak, 1996).

Materné, J., 'Antwerpen als verdeel- en veredelingscentrum van specerijen en suiker van de late 15de eeuw tot de 17de eeuw', in F. De Nave (ed.), *Europa aan tafel. Een verkenning van onze eet- en tafelcultuur* (Antwerp: MIM, 1993), pp. 48–61.

—, 'Haven en hinterland: de Antwerpse specerijenmarkt in de 16de eeuw', in *Specerijkelijk: de specerijenroutes: 27 maart–14 juni 1992, ASLK-galerij* (Brussels: ASLK, 1992), pp. 169–81.

—, 'Schoon ende bequaem tot versamelinghe der cooplieden: Antwerpens beurswereld tijdens de Gouden zestiende eeuw', in G. De Clercq (ed.), *Ter Beurze: geschiedenis van de aandelenhandel in België, 1300–1990* (Bruges: Van de Wiele, 1992), pp. 50–85.

Materné, J., and H. Van der Wee, 'Antwerp as a World Market in the Sixteenth and Seventeenth Centuries', in J. Van der Stock (ed.), *Antwerp, Story of a Metropolis, 16th–17th Century* (Ghent: Snoeck-Ducaju, 1993), pp. 19–31.

McCusker, J. J., 'The Demise of Distance: The Business Press and the Origins of the Information Revolution in the Early Modern Atlantic World', *American Historical Review*, 110:2 (2005), pp. 295–321.

McLean, P. D., and J. F. Padgett, 'Obligation, Risk, and Opportunity in the Renaissance Economy: Beyond Social Embeddedness to Network Co-Constitution', in F. Dobbin (ed.), *The Sociology of the Economy* (New York: Russell Sage Foundation, 2004), ch. 8, pp. 193–227.

Mees, K., 'Koopman in troebele tijden: Jan van Immerseele (1550–1612)', *Spiegel Historiael*, 19 (1984), pp. 545–51.

Melis, F., 'La diffusione nel Mediterraneo occidentale dei panni di Wervicq e delle altre città della Lys attorno al 1400', in *Studi in onore di Amintore Fanfani* (Milan: Giuffré, 1962), pp. 219–43.

Mertens, F. H., and K. L. Torfs, *Geschiedenis van Antwerpen sedert de stichting der stad tot onze tyden* (Antwerp: Van Dieren, 1845).

Meulleners, J. L., *De Antwerpsche bankier Erasmus Schetz en zijne geassocieërden Jan Vleminck en Arnold Proenen in hunne betrekking tot Maastricht en Aken* (Maastricht: Le Courrier de la Meuse, 1890).

Mokyr, J., 'Entrepreneurship and the Industrial Revolution in Britain', in W. J. Baumol, D. S. Landes and J. Mokyr (eds), *The Invention of Enterprise: Entrepreneurship from Ancient Mesopotamia to Modern Times* (Princeton, NJ: Princeton University Press, 2010), ch. 7, pp. 183–210.

Muldrew, C., 'Credit and the Courts: Debt Litigation in a Seventeenth-Century Urban Community', *Economic History Review*, 46:1 (1993), pp. 23–38.

—, *The Economy of Obligation: The Culture of Credit and Social Relations in Early Modern England* (New York: Palgrave, 1998).

Mummenhoff, E. and H. Wallraff, *Das Rathaus in Nürnberg* (Nürnberg: J. L. Schrag, 1891).

Munro, J. H., 'Bruges and the Abortive Staple in English Cloth: An Incident in the Shift of Commerce from Bruges to Antwerp in the Late Fifteenth Century', *Revue belge de philologie et d'histoire*, 44:4 (1966), pp. 1137–59.

—, 'English "Backwardness" and Financial Innovations in Commerce with the Low Countries, 14th to 16th Centuries', in B. Blondé, A. Greve and P. Stabel (eds), *International Trade in the Low Countries (14th–16th Centuries): Merchants, Organisation, Infrastructure: Proceedings of the International Conference Ghent-Antwerp, 12th–13th January 1997* (Leuven: Garant, 2000), pp. 105–69.

—, 'The Low Countries' Export Trade in Textiles with the Mediterranean Basin: A Cost–Benefit Analysis of Comparative Advantages in Overland and Maritime Trade Routes', *International Journal of Maritime History*, 11:2 (1999), pp. 1–30.

—, 'The "New Institutional Economics" and the Changing Fortunes of Fairs in Medieval and Early Modern Europe: The Textile Trades, Warfare and Transaction Costs', *Vierteljahresschrift für Sozial- und Wirtschaftsgeschichte*, 88 (2001), pp. 1–47.

—, 'Spanish Merino Wools and the Nouvelles Draperies: An Industrial Transformation in the Late Medieval Low Countries', *Economic History Review*, 58:3 (2005), pp. 431–84.

Murray, J. M., *Bruges: Cradle of Capitalism 1280–1390* (Cambridge: Cambridge University Press, 2006).

Mus, O., 'De Brugse Compagnie Despars op het einde van de 15de eeuw', *Handelingen van het Genootschap voor Geschiedenis: driemaandelijks tijdschrift voor de studie van geschiedenis en oudheden van Vlaanderen*, 101:1 (1964), pp. 5–118.

—, 'Wouter Ameyde, Een Brugs waard-makelaar op het einde van de 15de eeuw', in *Album Albert Schouteet* (Bruges: Westvlaams Verbond van Kringen voor Heemkunde, 1973), pp. 117–32.

Neal, L., 'The Finance of Business during the Industrial Revolution', in R. Floud and D. McCloskey (eds), *The Economic History of Britain since 1700* (Cambridge: Cambridge University Press, 1994), ch. 7, pp. 151–81.

Neelen, P., 'Het Antwerpse meerseniersambacht in de zestiende eeuw' (Ghent: Universiteit Gent, 1997).

Nicholas, D., 'Commercial Credit and Central Place Function in Thirteenth-Century Ypres', in L. Armstrong, I. Elbl, M. M. Elbl and J. H. A. Munro (eds), *Money, Markets and Trade in Late Medieval Europe: Essays in Honour of John H. Munro* (Leiden: Brill, 2007), pp. 310–48.

Nightingale, P., 'The Rise and Decline of Medieval York: A Reassessment', *Past & Present*, 206:1 (1 February 2010), pp. 3–42.

North, D. C., *Institutions, Institutional Change and Economic Performance* (Cambridge: Cambridge University Press, 1990).

—, 'Institutions, Transaction Costs and the Rise of the Merchant Empires', in J. D. Tracy (ed.), *The Political Economy of Merchant Empires* (Cambridge: Cambridge University Press, 1991), pp. 22–41.

—, *Structure and Change in Economic History* (New York: Norton, 1981).

North, M., 'Banking and Credit in Northern Germany in the Fifteenth and Sixteenth Centuries', in D. Puncuh and G. Felloni (eds), *Banchi pubblici, banchi privati e Monti di Pietà nell'Europa preindustriale: amministrazione, tecniche operative e ruoli economici*, Atti della Società Ligure di Storia Patria (Geneva: Società Ligure di Storia Patria, 1991), pp. 809–206.

O'Rourke, K. H., and J. G. Williamson. 'Did Vasco Da Gama Matter for European Markets?', *Economic History Review*, 62:3 (2009), pp. 655–84.

Oden, B., 'A Netherlandish Merchant in Stockholm in the Reign of Erik XIV', *Scandinavian Economic History Review*, 10:1 (1962), pp. 3–37.

Ogilvie, S., *Institutions and European Trade: Merchant Guilds, 1000–1800* (Cambridge: Cambridge University Press, 2011).

Ogilvie, S., and A. W. Carus, 'Institutions and Economic Growth in Historical Perspective', in A. Philippe and N. Durlauf Steven (eds), *Handbook of Economic Growth* (Amsterdam: Elsevier, 2014), ch. 8, pp. 403–513.

Ogilvie, S., and M. Cerman, 'Proto-Industrialization, Economic Development and Social Change in Early Modern Europe', in S. Ogilvie and M. Cerman (eds), *European Proto-Industrialization* (Cambridge: Cambridge University Press, 1996), pp. 227–40.

—, 'The Theories of Proto-Industrialization', in S. Ogilvie and M. Cerman (eds), *European Proto-Industrialization* (Cambridge: Cambridge University Press, 1996), pp. 1–11.

Ogilvie, S., M. Küpker and J. Maegraith, 'Household Debt in Early Modern Germany: Evidence from Personal Inventories', *Journal of Economic History*, 72:1 (2012), pp. 134–67.

Oosterbosch, M., 'Het openbare notariaat in Antwerpen tijdens de late Middeleeuwen (1314–1531): een institutionele en prosopografische studie in Europees perspectief' (Leuven: KUL, 1992).

—, '"Van groote abuysen ende ongeregeltheden" Overheidsbemoeiingen met het Antwerpse notariaat tijdens de XVIde eeuw', *Legal History Review*, 63 (1995), pp. 83–101.

Outhwaite, R. B., 'The Trials of Foreign Borrowing: The English Crown and the Antwerp Money Market in the Mid-Sixteenth Century', *Economic History Review*, 19:2 (1966), pp. 289–305.

Pádron, F. M., 'The Commercial World of Seville in Early Modern Times', *Journal of European Economic History*, 2:2 (1973), pp. 294–319.

Pamuk, S., 'Changes in Factor Markets in the Ottoman Empire, 1500–1800', *Continuity and Change*, 24:1, special issue 1 (2009), pp. 107–36.

Peeters, J.-P., 'De Mechelse ververs en lakenscheerders en het verval van de stedelijke draperie in de 16de eeuw (1520–1601)', *Handelingen van de Koninklijke Kring voor Oudheidkunde, Letteren en Kunst van Mechelen*, 93 (1989), pp. 153–97.

Peeters, T., and H. Van der Wee, 'Een dynamisch model voor de seculaire ontwikkeling van de wereldhandel en de welvaart', *Tijdschrift voor geschiedenis*, 82 (1969), pp. 233–49.

—, 'Un modèle économique de croissance interséculaire du commerce mondial (XIIe–XVIIe siècles)', *Annales. Economies, Sociétés, Civilisations*, 25:1 (1970), pp. 100–26.

Persson, K. G., *Grain Markets in Europe, 1500–1900: Integration and Deregulation* (Cambridge: University Press, 1999).

Petram, L., *De bakermat van de Beurs: hoe in zeventiende-eeuws Amsterdam de moderne aandelenhandel Ontstond* (Amsterdam: Atlas, 2011).

—, 'The World's First Stock Exchange: How the Amsterdam Market for Dutch East India Company Shares Became a Modern Securities Market, 1602–1700' (PhD dissertation, University of Amsterdam, 2011).

Pettegree, A., *Foreign Protestant Communities in Sixteenth-Century London* (Oxford: Clarendon, 1986).

Pike, R., *Aristocrats and Traders: Sevillian Society in the Sixteenth Century* (Ithaca, NY: Cornell University Press, 1972).

Pirenne, H., *Histoire de Belgique: de la mort de Charles le Téméraire à l'arrivée du duc d'Albe dans les Pays-Bas (1567). Histoire de Belgique*, 3 edn, 7 vols (Brussels: Maurice Lamertin, 1923), vol. 3.

Poelwijk, A., *In dienste vant suyckerbacken: de Amsterdamse suikernijverheid en haar ondernemers, 1580–1630* (Hilversum: Verloren, 2003).

Pohl, H., 'Köln und Antwerpen um 1500', *Mitteilungen aus dem Stadtarchiv von Köln*, 60 (1971), pp. 469–552.

Postan, M. M., *Medieval Trade and Finance* (Cambridge: Cambridge University Press, 1974).

Posthumus, N. W., *De uitvoer van Amsterdam, 1543–1545* (Leiden: Brill, 1971).

Poussou, J.-P., 'Les étrangers à Bordeaux à l'époque moderne', *Annales de Bretagne et des pays de l'Ouest*, 117:1 (2010), pp. 149–64.

Prak, M. and J. Luiten Van Zanden, 'Towards an Economic Interpretation of Citizenship: The Dutch Republic between Medieval Communes and Modern Nation-States', *European Review of Economic History*, 10:2 (2006), pp. 111–45.

Price, J. M., 'What Did Merchants Do? Reflections on British Overseas Trade, 1660–1790', *Journal of Economic History*, 49:2 (1989), pp. 267–84.

Price, J. M., and P. G. E. Clemens. 'A Revolution of Scale in Overseas Trade: British Firms in the Chesapeake Trade, 1675–1775', *Journal of Economic History*, 47:1 (1987), pp. 1–43.

Prims, F., 'De Antwerpse jaarmarkten', *Antwerpiensia*, 18 (1948), pp. 38–41.

—, *De kolonellen van de 'Burgersche Wacht' te Antwerpen* (December 1577–August 1585) (Antwerp: Standaard, 1942).

—, 'De taxatie van 300 Personen (24 oktober 1579)', *Antwerpiensia*, 15 (1941), pp. 179–91.

—, 'Erasmus Schetz in 1525–1532', *Antwerpiensia*, 13 (1939), pp. 63–9.

—, *Geschiedenis van Antwerpen*, 28 vols (Antwerp: Standaard, 1939), vol. 17.

—, 'Jacob Gramaye, ontvanger der Staten van Brabant te Antwerpen aan gouverneur Requesens, ter verzekering der hem verschuldigde kapitalen (rond 1574)', *Bijdragen tot de geschiedenis*, 30 (1939), pp. 143–5.

—, *Rechterlijk Antwerpen in de Middeleeuwen: de rechterlijke instellingen* (Mechelen: Confraternitas Sancti Yvonis, 1936).

Prims, F., and J. van Roey, *Geschiedenis van Antwerpen* (Brussels: Kultuur en Beschaving, 1977).

Priotti, J.-P., *Bilbao et ses marchands au XVIe siècle: genèse d'une croissance* (Villeneuve d'Ascq: Presses universitaires du Septentrion, 2004).

Pryor, J. H. 'Commenda: The Operation of the Contract in Long Distance Commerce at Marseilles During the Thirteenth Century', *Journal of European Economic History*, 13:2 (1984), pp. 397–440.

Put, E., *Inventaris van het archief van de Raad van Brabant*, 2 vols (Brussels: Algemeen Rijksarchief, 1999).

Puttevils, J., 'The Ascent of Merchants from the Southern Low Countries: From Antwerp to Europe, 1480–1585' (PhD dissertation, University of Antwerp, 2012).

—, '"Eating the Bread out of their Mouth": Antwerp's Export Trade and Generalized Institutions, 1544–1545', *Economic History Review* (forthcoming 2015).

—, 'I mercanti fiamminghi: Nederlandse kooplieden in Venetië', in M. Boone and P. Stabel (eds), *Fiamminghi a Venezia: sporen van de Lage Landen in Venetië* (Brussels: Unibook, 2010), pp. 56–76.

—, 'Klein gewin brengt rijkdom in: de Zuid-Nederlandse handelaars in de export naar Italië in de jaren 1540', *Tijdschrift voor sociale en economische geschiedenis*, 6:1 (2009), pp. 26–52.

—, 'Midden in het web van de internationale politiek: Nederlandse diplomaten in Venetië', in M. Boone and P. Stabel (eds), *Fiamminghi a Venezia: sporen van de Lage Landen in Venetië* (Brussels: Unibook, 2010), pp. 115–33.

—, 'A servitio de vostri sempre siamo. De effecten van de handel tussen Antwerpen en Italië op de koopmansfamilie Van Der Molen' (MA thesis, University of Antwerp, 2007).

—, 'Sixteenth-Century Antwerp, a Hyper-Market for All? The Case of Low Countries Merchants', in B. Blondé, B. De Munck, G. Marnef, J. Puttevils and M. F. Van Dijck (eds), *Antwerp and the Renaissance* (Turnhout: Brepols, forthcoming).

—, 'Voor macht en winst. Koopmansgilden en collectieve actie in pre-industrieel Europa, een overzicht', *Leidschrift*, 25:2 (2010), pp. 97–114.

Puttevils, J., P. Stabel, and B. Verbist, 'Een eenduidig pad van modernisering van het handels-verkeer: van het liberale Brugge naar het gereguleerde Antwerpen?', in B. Blondé et al. (eds), *Overheid en economie: geschiedenissen van een spanningsveld* (Antwerp: University Press Antwerp, 2014), pp. 39–54.

Quinn, S., 'Money, Finance and Capital Markets', in R. Floud and P. Johnson (eds), *Industrialisation, 1700–1860, The Cambridge Economic History of Modern Britain* (Cambridge: Cambridge University Press, 2004), pp. 147–74.

Rambert, G., *Histoire du commerce de Marseille* (Paris: Plon, 1949).

Ramsay, G. D., *The City of London in International Politics at the Accession of Elizabeth Tudor* (Manchester: Manchester University Press, 1975).

—, *The Queen's Merchants and the Revolt of the Netherlands: The End of the Antwerp Mart*, 2 vols (Manchester: Manchester University Press, 1986), vol. 2.

Rappaport, S., *Worlds within Worlds: Structures of Life in Sixteenth-Century London* (Cambridge: Cambridge University Press, 1989).

Regtdoorzee Greup-Rolandus, S. C., *Geschiedenis der Haarlemmer bleekerijen* ('s-Gravenhage: Nijhoff, 1936).

Richman, B. D., 'How Community Institutions Create Economic Advantage: Jewish Diamond Merchants in New York', *Law & Social Inquiry*, 31:2 (2006), pp. 383–420.

Roche Dasent, J., *Acts of the Privy Council of England, 1558–1570*, 46 vols (London: Eyre and Spottiswoode, 1890), vol. 7.

Rooms, E., 'Een nieuwe visie op de gebeurtenissen die geleid hebben tot de Spaanse Furie te Antwerpen op 4 november 1576', *Bijdragen tot de geschiedenis*, 54 (1971), pp. 31–55.

Rosenthal, J.-L., and R. Bin Wong, *Before and beyond Divergence: The Politics of Economic Change in China and Europe* (Cambridge, MA: Harvard University Press, 2011).

Rößner, R., *Hansische Memoria in Flandern: Alltagsleben und Totengedenken der Osterlingen in Brügge und Antwerpen (13. bis 16. Jahrhundert)* (Frankfurt am Main: Lang, 2001).

Sabbatini, R., *Cercar esca: mercanti lucchesi ad Anversa nel Cinquecento* (Florence: Salimbeni, 1985).

Sabbe, E., *Anvers: métropole de l'Occident (1492–1566)* (Brussels: Renaissance du livre, 1952).

—, *De Belgische vlasnijverheid. Deel 1: de Zuid-Nederlandse vlasnijverheid tot het Verdrag van Utrecht (1713)* (Kortrijk: Nationaal Vlasmuseum, 1975).

Sachs, S. E., 'Burying Burton: Burton v. Davy and the Law of Negotiable Instruments', 2002, unpublished working paper, available at http://www.stevesachs.com/papers/paper_burton.html [accessed 28 February 2015].

Safley, T. M., 'Institutions and their Discontents', *Tijdschrift voor sociale en economische geschiedenis*, 11:4 (2014), pp. 61–73.

Savary, J., *Le Parfait Négociant, ou: Instruction générale pour ... le commerce des marchandises de France, et des pais étrangers*, 8th edn (Amsterdam: Roger, 1717).

Schlugleit, D., 'De Predikheerenpand en St.-Niklaasgilde te Antwerpen (1445–1553)', *Bijdragen voor de geschiedenis*, 29 (1938–9), pp. 99–119.

—, 'De zilverhandel van de Meerse en de ordonnantiën van de goudsmeden te Antwerpen in de zestiende Eeuw', *Bijdragen tot de geschiedenis*, 30 (1939), pp. 39–61.

Schlugleit, D., and F. Prims, *Geschiedenis van het Antwerpsche diamantslijpersambacht, 1582–1797* (Antwerp: Gullaume, 1935).

Schulz, C. M., *De invloed van het oude Brabant op de zakencultuur van Hamburg en Frankfurt (1554–1600)* (Oosterhout: SteppingForward Uitgeverij, 2011).

Shaw, J., *The Justice of Venice: Authorities and Liberties in the Urban Economy, 1550–1700* (Oxford: Oxford University Press, 2006).

—, 'Liquidation or Certification? Small Claims Disputes and Retail Credit in Seventeenth-Century Venice', in B. Blondé, P. Stabel, J. Stobart and I. Van Damme (eds), *Buyers and Sellers. Retails Circuits and Practies in Medieval and Early Modern Europe* (Turnhout: Brepols, 2006).

Sicking, L., *Neptune and the Netherlands: State, Economy and War at Sea in the Renaissance* (Leiden: Brill, 2004).

Slootmans, C. J. F., 'Huiden en Ppelzen op de jaarmarkten van Bergen-Op-Zoom', in L. G. Verberne and A. Weijnen (eds), *Land van mijn hart: Brabantse feestbundel voor Mgr Prof. Dr Th.J.A. Goossens op zijn zeventigste verjaardag (8 febr. 1952)* (Tilburg: Henri Bergmans, 1952).

—, *Paas- en Koudemarkten te Bergen-op-Zoom, 1365–1565*, 3 vols (Tilburg: Stichting Zuidelijk Historisch Contact, 1985).

Smail, D., Lord, *The Consumption of Justice: Emotions, Publicity, and Legal Culture in Marseille, 1264–1423* (Ithaca, NY: Cornell University Press, 2003).

Smekens, F., 'Braakliggend terrein betreffende onze nationale zeevaartgeschiedenis in de moderne tijden', *Marine academie van België. Mededelingen*, 10 (1956), pp. 45–67.

Smit, H. J., *Bronnen tot de geschiedenis van den handel met Engeland, Schotland en Ierland* ('s-Gravenhage: Nijhoff, 1928).

Smith, S. H., 'A Question of Quality: The Commercial Contest between Portuguese Atlantic Spices and Their Venetian Levantine Equivalents During the Sixteenth Century', *Itinerario*, 26:2 (2002), pp. 45–63.

Sneller, Z. W., and W. S. Unger, *Bronnen tot de geschiedenis van den handel met Frankrijk* ('s-Gravenhage: Nijhoff, 1930).

J. Ángel, S. Telechea and B. A. Bolumburu, 'Protéger et contrôler la présence et les activités des étrangers dans les villes portuaires du Nord de la couronne de Castille au Moyen Âge', *Annales de Bretagne et des pays de l'Ouest*, 117:1 (2010), pp. 209–22.

Soly, H., 'The "Betrayal" of the Sixteenth-Century Bourgeoisie: A Myth? Some Considerations of the Behaviour Pattern of Merchants of Antwerp in the Sixteenth Century', *Acta historiae Neerlandica*, 8 (1975), pp. 31–49.

—, 'De aluinhandel in de Nederlanden in de 16e eeuw', *Belgisch tijdschrift voor filologie en geschiedenis*, 52 (1974), pp. 800–57.

—, 'De Antwerpse onderneemster Anna Janssens en de economische boom na de Vrede van Cateau-Cambrésis (1559)', *Bijdragen tot de geschiedenis*, 52 (1969), pp. 139–64.

—, 'De bouw van de Antwerpse citadel (1567–1571): sociaal-economische aspecten', *Belgisch tijdschrift voor militaire geschiedenis*, 21:6 (1976), pp. 549–78.

—, 'De economische betekenis van de Zuidnederlandse brouwindustrie in de 16de eeuw. Problematiek', in *Histoire économique de la Belgique: traitement des sources et état des questions: actes du colloque de Bruxelles, 17–19 nov. 1971 = Economische geschiedenis van België: behandeling van de bronnen en problematiek: handelingen van het colloquium te Brussel, 17–19 november 1971* (Brussels: Algemeen Rijksarchief en Rijksarchief in de Provinciën, 1970), pp. 97–117.

—, 'De schepenregisters als bron voor de conjunctuurgeschiedenis van Zuid- en Noordnederlandse steden in het Ancien Régime. Een concreet voorbeeld: de Antwerpse immobiliënmarkt in de 16de eeuw', *Tijdschrift voor geschiedenis*, 87 (1974), pp. 521–44.

—, 'Economische vernieuwing en sociale weerstand. De betekenis en aspiraties der Antwerpse middenklasse in de 16de eeuw', *Tijdschrift voor geschiedenis*, 83 (1970), pp. 520–35.

—, 'Een Antwerpse compagnie voor de levensmiddelenbevoorrading van het leger in de zestiende eeuw', *Bijdragen en mededelingen betreffende de geschiedenis der Nederlanden*, 186 (1971), pp. 350–62.

—, 'Fortificaties, belastingen en corruptie te Antwerpen in het midden der 16e eeuw', *Bijdragen tot de geschiedenis*, 53 (1970), pp. 191–210.

—, 'Het "Verraad" der 16de-eeuwse burgerij: een mythe? Enkele beschouwingen betreffende het gedragspatroon der 16de-eeuwse Antwerpse ondernemers', *Tijdschrift voor geschiedenis*, 83 (1973), pp. 262–80.

—, 'Nijverheid en kapitalisme te Antwerpen in de 16e eeuw', in *Album aangeboden aan Charles Verlinden ter gelegenheid van zijn dertig jaar professoraat = album offert à Charles Verlinden à l'occasion de ses trente ans de professorat* (Ghent: Universa, 1975), pp. 331–52.

—, *Urbanisme en kapitalisme te Antwerpen in de 16de eeuw: de stedebouwkundige en industriële ondernemingen van Gilbert van Schoonbeke* (Brussels: Gemeentekrediet, 1977).

Soly, H., and A. K. L. Thijs, 'Nijverheid in de Zuidelijke Nederlanden 1490–1580', in D. P. Blok (ed.), *Algemene Geschiedenis der Nederlanden* (Haarlem: Fibula-Van Dishoeck, 1979), pp. 27–57.

Spufford, P., 'From Antwerp and Amsterdam to London: The Decline of Financial Centres in Europe', *De Economist*, 154:2 (2006), pp. 143–75.

Stabel, P., 'Ambachten en textielondernemers in kleine Vlaamse steden tijdens de overgang van Middeleeuwen naar Nieuwe Tijd', in C. Lis and H. Soly (eds), *Werelden van verschil: ambachtsgilden in de Lage Landen* (Brussels: VUB Press, 1997), pp. 79–98.

—, 'De gewenste vreemdeling: Italiaanse kooplieden en stedelijke maatschappij in het laat-Middeleeuwse Brugge', *Jaarboek voor middeleeuwse geschiedenis*, 4 (2001), pp. 189–221.

—, *De kleine stad in Vlaanderen: bevolkingsdynamiek en economische functies van de kleine en secundaire stedelijke centra in het Gentse Kwartier (14de-16de eeuw)* (Brussels: Paleis der Academiën, 1995).

—, '"Dmeeste, oirboirlixste ende proffitelixste let ende neringhe": een kwantitatieve benadering van de lakenproductie in het laatmiddeleeuwse en vroegmoderne Vlaanderen', *Handelingen van de Maatschappij voor Geschiedenis en Oudheidkunde te Gent*, 51 (1997), pp. 113–53.

—, *Dwarfs among Giants: The Flemish Urban Network in the Late Middle Ages* (Leuven: Garant, 1997).

—, 'Entre commerce international et entrepreneurs locaux: le monde financier de Wouter Ameide (Bruges, fin 15e–début 16e siècle)', in M. Boone (ed.), *Finances privées et finances publiques* (Leuven: Garant, 1995), pp. 75–99.

—, 'Guilds in Late Medieval Flanders: Myths and Realities of Guild Life in an Export-Oriented Environment', *Journal of Medieval History*, 30:2 (2004), pp. 187–212.

—, 'Italian Merchants and the Fairs in the Low Countries (12th–16th Centuries)', in P. Lanaro (ed.), *La pratica dello scambio. Sistemi di fiere, mercanti e città in Europa (1400–1700)* (Venice: Marsilio, 2003), pp. 131–160.

—, 'Kooplieden in de stad', in A. Vandewalle (ed.), *Hanzekooplui en Medicibankiers: Brugge, wisselmarkt van Europese culturen* (Oostkamp: Stichting Kunstboek, 2002), pp. 85–96.

—, 'Marketing Cloth in the Low Countries: Foreign Merchants, Local Businessmen and Urban Entrepreneurs: Markets, Transport and Transaction Costs (14th–16th Century)', in B. Blondé, A. Greve and P. Stabel (eds), *International Trade in the Low Countries (14th–16th Centuries): Merchants, Organisation, Infrastructure: Proceedings of the International Conference Ghent-Antwerp, 12th–13th January 1997* (Leuven: Garant, 2000), pp. 15–36.

—, 'Organisation corporative et production d'oeuvres d'art à Bruges à la fin du Moyen Age et au début des Temps Modernes', *Le Moyen Âge: revue d'histoire et de philologie*, 113 (2007), pp. 91–134.

—, 'Public or Private, Collective or Individual? The Spaces of Late Medieval Trade in the Low Countries', in D. Calabi and S. Beltramo (eds), *Il mercante patrizio: palazzi e botteghe nell'Europa del Rinascimento* (Milan: Mondadori, 2008), pp. 37–54.

—, 'Schippers, wagenvoerders en kruiers: de organisatie van de stedelijke vervoersector in het laat-middeleeuwse Vlaanderen', *Bijdragen tot de geschiedenis*, 82 (1999), pp. 159–85.

—, 'Venice and the Low Countries: Commercial Contacts and Intellectual Inspirations', in B. Aikema and B. L. Brown (eds), *Renaissance Venice and the North. Crosscurrents in the Time of Bellini, Dürer and Titian* (Milan: Bompiani, 1999), pp. 30–42.

Stabel, P., and B. Lambert. 'Squaring the Circle: Merchant Guilds in Bruges', 2006, unpublished paper presented at the Workshop on Mercantile Organization in Pre-Industrial Europe, Antwerp, 18–19 November 2005.

Stasavage, D., *States of Credit: Size, Power, and the Development of European Polities* (Princeton, NJ: Princeton University Press, 2011).

—, 'Was Weber Right? The Role of Urban Autonomy in Europe's Rise', *American Political Science Review*, 108:2 (2014), pp. 337–54.

Stevens, F., *Revolutie en notariaat: Antwerpen, 1794–1814* (Assen: Van Gorcum, 1994).

Stols, E., 'De Iberische en koloniale horizonten van de handel der Nederlanden in de 16de eeuw', in F. de Nave, D. Imhof and C. Depauw (eds), *Christoffel Plantijn en de Iberische wereld = Christophe Plantin et le monde ibérique* (Antwerp: Museum Plantin-Moretus, 1992), pp. 21–42.

—, *De Spaanse Brabanders of de handelsbetrekkingen der Zuidelijke Nederlanden met de Iberische wereld, 1598–1648*, 2 vols (Brussels: Paleis der Academiën, 1971).

—, 'De Vlaamse Natie te Lissabon (15de–17de eeuw)', in J. Everaert and E. Stols (eds), *Vlaanderen en Portugal: op de golfslag van twee culturen* (Antwerp: Mercatorfonds, 1991), pp. 119–41.

—, 'Gens des Pays-Bas en Amérique espagnole aux première siècles de la Colonisation', *Bulletin de l'Institute Historique Belge de Rome*, 44 (1974), pp. 565–99.

—, 'Um dos primeiros documentos sobre o engenho dos Schetz em Sao Vicente', *Revista de Historia*, 76 (1968), pp. 407–19.

Stols, E., and W. Thomas, 'Flanders and the Canary Islands in the First Widening of the World 1450–1550', in F. J. G. Gómez, E. Stols, W. Thomas and H. Nieuwdorp (eds), *Lumen Canariense: El Cristo de la Laguna y su tiempo* (San Cristóbal de La Laguna: Excmo. Ayuntamiento de San Cristóbal de La Laguna, 2003), pp. 27–50.

Stone, L., 'Elizabethan Overseas Trade', *Economic History Review*, 2:1 (1949), pp. 30–58.

Strieder, J., *Aus Antwerpener Notariatsarchiven: Quellen zur Deutschen Wirtschaftsgeschichte des 16 Jahrhunderts* (Berlin: Deutsche Verlags-Anstalt, 1930).

Supple, B.. 'The Nature of Enterprise', in E. E. Rich and C. H. Wilson (eds), *The Economic Organization of Early Modern Europe, The Cambridge Economic History of Europe* (Cambridge: Cambridge University Press, 1977), ch. 6, pp. 393–461.

Sutton, A. F., 'The Merchant Adventurers of England: Their Origins and the Mercers' Company of London', *Historical Research*, 75:187 (2002), pp. 25–46.

't Hart, M., and M. Van der Heijden, 'Het geld van de stad. Recente historiografische trends in het onderzoek naar stedelijke financiën in de Nederlanden', *Tijdschrift voor sociale en economische geschiedenis*, 3:3 (2006), pp. 3–35.

—, 'Stadslucht maakt vrij: autonomie en rivaliteit in de vroegmoderne Noordelijke Nederlanden', in L. Lucassen and W. Willems (eds), *Waarom mensen in de stad willen wonen, 1200–2010* (Amsterdam: Bert Bakker, 2009).

't Hart, M., J. Jonker and J. Luiten van Zanden, *A Financial History of the Netherlands* (Cambridge: University Press, 1998).

Thielemans, M.-R., *Bourgogne et Angleterre: relations politiques et économiques entre les Pays-Bas bourguignons et L'Angleterre, 1435–1467* (Brussels: Presses universitaires de Bruxelles, 1966).

Thijs, A. K. L., 'De geschiedenis van de suikernijverheid te Antwerpen (16de–19de eeuw), een terreinverkenning', *Bijdragen tot de geschiedenis*, 62:1–2 (1979), pp. 23–50.

—, *De zijdenijverheid te Antwerpen in de zeventiende eeuw* (Brussel: Pro Civitate, 1969).

—, 'Een ondernemer uit de Antwerpse textielindustrie, Jan Nuyts (ca. 1512–1582)', *Bijdragen tot de geschiedenis*, 51 (1968), pp. 53–68.

—, 'Minderheden te Antwerpen (16de / 20ste eeuw)', in H. Soly and A. K. L. Thijs (eds), *Minderheden in Westeuropese steden (16de–20ste eeuw). Minorities in Western European Cities (Sixteenth–Twentieth Century)* (Rome: Belgisch Historisch Instituut te Rome, 1995), pp. 17–42.

—, 'Structural Changes in the Antwerp Industry from the Fifteenth to the Eighteenth Century', in H. Van der Wee (ed.), *The Rise and Decline of Urban Industries in Italy and in the Low Countries (Late Middle Ages-Early Modern Times)* (Leuven: Leuven University Press, 1988), pp. 207–12.

—, *Van 'werkwinkel' tot 'fabriek': de textielnijverheid te Antwerpen, einde 15de–begin 19de eeuw* (Brussels: Gemeentekrediet, 1987).

—, 'Van "werkwinkel" tot "fabriek": de textielnijverheid te Antwerpen van het einde der vijftiende tot het begin der negentiende eeuw' (Ghent, PhD dissertation, Rijksuniversiteit Gent, 1978).

Thimme, H., 'Der Handel Kölns am Ende des 16. Jahrhunderts und die Internationale Zusammensetzung der Kölner Kaufmannschaft', *West-deutsche Zeitschrift*, 31 (1912), pp. 389 sqq.

Thoen, E., *Landbouwekonomie en bevolking in Vlaanderen gedurende de late Middeleeuwen en het begin van de Moderne Tijden: testregio: de kasselrijen van Oudenaarde en Aalst (eind 13de–eerste helft 16de eeuw)* (Ghent: Belgisch Centrum voor Landelijke Geschiedenis, 1988).

Thomas, F., *Die Persönliche Haftung von Gesellschaftern von Personengesellschaften in der Historischen Entwicklung der Neuzeit* (Berlin: Duncker und Humblot, 2003).

Tihon, C., 'Un consulat belge à Palerme au début du XVIIe siècle', *Bulletin de l'Institut Historique Belge de Rome*, 19 (1938), pp. 77–82.

Tracy, J. D., *Emperor Charles V, Impresario of War: Campaign Strategy, International Finance, and Domestic Politics* (Cambridge: Cambridge University Press, 2002).

Tranchant, M., 'Au risque de l'étranger: un sujet majeur de gouvernance à La Rochelle à la fin du Moyen Âge', *Annales de Bretagne et des pays de l'Ouest*, 117:1 (2010), pp. 91–108.

Trivellato, F., *The Familiarity of Strangers: The Sephardic Diaspora, Livorno, and Cross-Cultural Trade in the Early Modern Period* (New Haven, CT: Yale University Press, 2009).

Trocmé, E., and M. Delafosse, *Le commerce Rochelais de la fin du 15e siècle au début du 17e siècle* (Paris: SEVPEN, 1952).

Unger, W. S., *Bronnen tot de geschiedenis van Middelburg in den Landsheerlijken Tijd*, 3 vols ('s-Gravenhage: Nijhoff, 1931), vol. 3.

Van Aert, L. 'Van appelen tot zeemleer: koopvrouwen in Antwerpen in de 16de eeuw' (MA thesis, Free University of Brussel, 2002).

Van Bavel, B., 'Early Proto-Industrialization in the Low Countries? The Importance and Nature of Market-Oriented Non-Agricultural Activities on the Countryside in Flanders and Holland, c. 1250–1570', *Revue belge de philologie et d'histoire* (2003), pp. 1109–65.

—, *Manors and Markets: Economy and Society in the Low Countries, 500–1600* (Oxford: Oxford University Press, 2010).

Van den Branden, F. J., 'De Spaansche muiterij ten jare 1574', *Antwerpsch Archievenblad*, 22, pp. 133–480.

Van Den Brulle, N., 'De commerciële praktijk in het zestiende-eeuwse Antwerpen aan de hand van registers uit de Insolvente Boedelskamer' (MA thesis, Universiteit Gent, 2010).

Van den Heuvel, D., *Women and Entrepreneurship: Female Traders in the Northern Netherlands, c. 1580–1815* (Amsterdam: Aksant, 2007).

Van den Kerkhove, A., 'Joris Vezeleer, een Antwerps koopman van de XVIde eeuw', paper presented at the 43e Congres Federatie van Kringen voor Oudheidkunde en Geschiedenis van België vzw, Sint-Niklaas-Waas, 1974.

Van den Nieuwenhuizen, J., 'Antwerpse maatregelen voor het notariaat in het Ancien Régime', in G. Maréchal (ed.), *Een kompas met vele streken: studies over Antwerpen, scheepvaart en archivistiek, aangeboden aan Dr. Gustaaf Asaert ter gelegenheid van zijn 65ste verjaardag*, Archiefkunde: Verhandelingen aansluitend bij Bibliotheek- en Archiefgids (Antwerp: Vlaamse Vereniging voor Bibliotheek-, Archief- en Documentatiewezen, 1994), pp. 177–183.

—, *Beknopte inventaris van de Insolvente Boedelskamer in het stadsarchief van Antwerpen* (Brussels: Algemeen Rijksarchief, 1998).

—, 'Bestuursinstellingen van de stad Antwerpen (12de eeuw–1795)', in R. van Uytven, C. Bruneel, H. Coppens and B. Augustyn (eds), *De gewestelijke en lokale overheidsin-stellingen in Brabant en Mechelen tot 1795* (Brussels: Algemeen Rijksarchief, 2000), pp. 462–510.

Van der Essen, L, 'Contribution à l'histoire du port d'Anvers 1553–1554', *Bulletin de l'Académie Royale de la Belgique*, 3 (1920), pp. 39–58.

Van der Heijden, M., *Geldschieters van de Stad: financiële relaties tussen stad, burgers en over-heden 1550–1650* (Amsterdam: Bert Bakker, 2006).

—, E. van Nederveen Meerkerk, G. Vermeersch et al., *Serving the Urban Community: The Rise of Public Facilities in the Low Countries* (Amsterdam: Aksant, 2009).

Van der Wee, H., G. Kurgan-van Hentenryk, R. Bogaert et al., *A History of European Banking* (Antwerp: Mercatorfonds, 2000).

Van der Wee, H., 'Antwerp and the New Financial Methods of the 16th and 17th Centuries', trans. L. Fackelman, in H. Van der Wee (ed.), *The Low Countries in the Early Modern World* (Aldershot: Ashgate, 1993), ch. 8, pp. 145–66.

—, 'Antwerpens bijdrage tot de ontwikkeling van de moderne geld- en banktechniek', *Tijd-schrift voor economie*, 4 (1965), pp. 488–500.

—, 'Anvers et les innovations de la technique financière aux XVIe et XVIIe siècles', *Annales: Economies, Sociétés, Civilisations*, 22:5 (1977), pp. 1067–89.

—, 'Das Phänomen des Wachstums und der Stagnation im Lichte der Antwerpener und Südniederlandischen Wirtschaft des 16. Jahrhunderts', *Vierteljahrschrift für Sozial- und Wirtschaftsgeschichte*, 54:2 (1967), pp. 203–49.

—, 'Doehaerd (Renée). Etudes anversoises. Documents sur le commerce international à Anvers, 1488–1514', *Revue belge de philologie et d'histoire*, 43:2 (1965), pp. 671–4.

—, 'Geld- krediet- en bankwezen in de Zuidelijke Nederlanden 1490–1580', in D. P. Blok (ed.), *Algemene Geschiedenis der Nederlanden* (Haarlem: Fibula-Van Dishoeck, 1979), pp. 98–108.

—, *The Growth of the Antwerp Market and the European Economy (Fourteenth–Sixteenth Cen-turies)*, 3 vols (Den Haag: Nijhoff, 1963).

—, 'Handel in de Zuidelijke Nederlanden', in *Nieuwe Algemene Geschiedenis der Nederlanden* (Haarlem: Fibula-Van Dishoeck, 1978), pp. 75–95.

—, 'Industrial Dynamics and the Process of Urbanization and De-Urbanization in the Low Countries from the Late Middle Ages to the Eighteenth Century. A Synthesis', in H. Van der Wee (ed.), *The Rise and Decline of Urban Industries in Italy and in the Low Coun-tries (Late Middle Ages-Early Modern Times)* (Leuven: Leuven University Press, 1988), pp. 307–88.

—, 'Les innovations de la technique financière à Bruges, Anvers et Amsterdam (XIIIe-XVIIIe Siècle)', *Belgisch tijdschrift voor filologie en geschiedenis*, 89:2 (2011), pp. 861–73.

—, 'Monetary, Credit and Banking Systems', in E. E. Rich and C. H. Wilson (eds), *The Eco-nomic Organization of Early Modern Europe, The Cambridge Economic History of Europe* (Cambridge: Cambridge University Press, 1977), ch. 5, pp. 290–392.

—, 'Sporen van disconto te Antwerpen tijdens de XVIe eeuw', *Bijdragen voor de geschiedenis der Nederlanden*, 10 (1955), pp. 68–70.

—, 'Structural Changes and Specialization in the Industry of the Southern Netherlands, 1100–1600', *Economic History Review*, 28:2 (1975), pp. 203–21.

—, 'Structural Changes in European Long-Distance Trade and Particularly in the Re-Export Trade from South to North, 1350–1750', in J. D. Tracy (ed.), *The Rise of Merchant Empires: Long-Distance Trade in the Early Modern World, 1350–1750* (Cambridge: Cambridge University Press, 1990), ch. 1, pp. 14–33.

—, 'Trade in the Southern Netherlands, 1493–1587', trans. L. Fackelman, in H. Van der Wee (ed.), *The Low Countries in the Early Modern World* (Aldershot: Ashgate, 1993), ch. 5, pp. 87–114.

—, 'The Western European Woollen Industries, 1500–1750', in D. Jenkins (ed), *The Cambridge History of Western Textiles* (Cambridge: Cambridge University Press, 2003), ch. 8, pp. 397–472.

Van der Wee, H., and J. Materné, 'Het kredietsysteem in Brabant tijdens de late Middeleeuwen en in het begin van de Nieuwe Tijd', in H. F. J. M. van den Eerenbeemt (ed.), *Bankieren in Brabant in de loop der eeuwen* (Tilburg: Stichting Zuidelijk Historisch Contact, 1987), ch. 4, pp. 59–78.

Van Dijck, M. F., 'Towards an Economic Interpretation of Justice? Conflict Settlement, Social Control and Civil Society in Urban Brabant and Mechelen During the Late Middle Ages and the Early Modern Period', in M. Van der Heijden, E. Van Nederveen Meerkerk, G. Vermeesch and M. Van der Burg (eds), *Serving the Urban Community: The Rise of Public Facilities in the Low Countries* (Amsterdam: Aksant, 2009), pp. 62–88.

Van Dixhoorn, A., 'The Grain Issue of 1565–1566: Policymaking, Public Opinion, and Common Good in the Habsburg Netherlands', in E. Lecuppre-Desjardin and A.-L. Van Bruaene (eds), *De Bono Communi: The Discourse and Practice of the Common Good in the European City (13th–16th C.): Discours et pratique du Bien Commun dans les villes d'Europe (XIIIe au XVIe siècle)* (Turnhout: Brepols, 2009), pp. 171–204.

Van Doosselaere, Q., *Commercial Agreements and Social Dynamics in Medieval Genoa* (Cambridge: Cambridge University Press, 2009).

Van Gelder, H. A. E., *De Nederlandse munten* (Antwerp: Spectrum, 1966).

Van Gelder, M., 'How to Influence Venetian Economic Policy: Collective Petitions of the Netherlandish Merchant Community in the Early Seventeenth Century', *Mediterranean Historical Review*, 24 (2009), pp. 29–47.

—, *Trading Places: The Netherlandish Merchants in Early Modern Venice* (Leiden: Brill, 2009).

Van Gerven, J., 'Antwerpen in de veertiende eeuw. Kleine stad zonder toekomst of opkomend handelscentrum?', *Belgisch tijdschrift voor filologie en geschiedenis*, 76:4 (1998), pp. 907–38.

Van Hofstraeten, B., 'Small-Scale Business Enterprises in Sixteenth-Century Antwerp (1480–1620)', paper presented at the European Business History Association Conference, Utrecht, 2014.

Van Houtte, J. A., 'Bruges et Anvers, marchés "nationaux" ou "internationaux" du XIVe au XVIe Siècle', *Revue du Nord*, 34 (1952), pp. 89–108.

—, *Die Beziehungen zwischen Köln und den Niederlanden vom Hochmittelalter bis sum Beginn des Industriezeitalters* (Köln: Universität zu Köln, 1969).

—, 'Les foires dans la Belgique ancienne', in *La Foire. Receuils de la Société Jean Bodin* (Brussels: Librairie encyclopédique, 1953), pp. 175–207.

—, 'Makelaars en waarden te Brugge van de 13e tot de 16e eeuw', *Bijdragen voor de geschiedenis der Nederlanden*, 5 (1950–1), pp. 1–30, pp. 177–97.

—, 'Quantitative Quellen zur Geschichte des Antwerpener Handels', *Beiträge zur Wirtschafts- und Stadtgeschichte. Festschrift für Hektor Amman* (1965), pp. 193–204.

—, 'The Rise and Decline of the Market of Bruges', *Economic History Review*, 19:1 (1966), pp. 29–47.

Van Laar, A., 'De handelsvloot van Antwerpen in het bloeitijdvak', *Bijdragen tot de geschiedenis*, 16 (1923), pp. 25–40.

Van Meeteren, A., *Op hoop van akkoord: instrumenteel forumgebruik bij geschilbeslechting in Leiden in de zeventiende eeuw* (Hilversum: Verloren, 2006).

Van Papenbroeck, D., *Annales antverpienses ab urbe condita ad annum 1700 Collecti ex ipsius civitatis monumentis*, 5 vols (Antwerp: Buschmann, 1845).

Van Rhee, C. H., *Litigation and Legislation: Civil Procedure at First Instance in the Great Council for the Netherlands in Malines (1522–1559)* (Brussels: Algemeen Rijksarchief, 1997).

Van Roey, J., *Antwerpse poortersboeken*, 6 vols (Antwerp: Stadsarchief, 1978).

—, 'De bevolking', in W. Couvreur (ed.), *Antwerpen in de XVIde eeuw* (Antwerp: Mercurius, 1975), pp. 95–108.

—, 'De correlatie tussen het sociale-beroepsmilieu en de godsdienstkeuze op het einde der XVIe eeuw', in *Bronnen voor de religieuze geschiedenis van België: Middeleeuwen en Moderne Tijden. Bibliothèque de la Revue d'Histoire ecclésiastique* (Leuven: Publications universitaires, 1968), pp. 239–58.

—, 'De sociale structuur en de godsdienstige gezindheid van de Antwerpse bevolking op de vooravond van de reconciliatie met Farnèse (17 augustus 1585)' (PhD dissertation, Universiteit Gent, 1963).

—, 'Handelsvaart van de Zuidnederlanders', in G. Asaert (ed.), *Maritieme Geschiedenis der Nederlanden* (Bussum: De Boer Maritiem, 1976), pp. 249–60.

—, 'Notarissen en schepenen te Antwerpen in de 16de eeuw', *Kroniek. Orgaan van Stabuco. Vereniging stadspersoneel Antwerpen*, 1:12 (1950), pp. 49–51.

Van Rompaey, J., 'De Bourgondische staatsinstellingen', in D. P. Blok (ed.), *Algemene Geschiedenis der Nederlanden* (Haarlem: Fibula-Van Dischoeck, 1977–83), pp. 136–55.

—, *De Grote Raad van de hertogen van Boergondië en het Parlement van Mechelen* (Brussels: Paleis der Academiën, 1973).

—, 'Het ontstaan van de Grote Raad onder Filips de Goede', in H. De Schepper (ed.), *Miscellanea Consilii Magni* (Amsterdam: Universiteit van Amsterdam, 1980), pp. 63–76.

Van Setter, P. 'Index der Gebodboeken', *Antwerpsch Archievenblad*, 1:1 (1864), pp. 120–464.

Van Tielhof, M., *De Hollandse graanhandel, 1470–1570: koren op de Amsterdamse molen* (The Hague: Stichting Hollandse Historische Reeks, 1995).

—, *The 'Mother of All Trades': The Baltic Grain Trade in Amsterdam from the Late 16th to the Early 19th Century* (Leiden: Brill, 2002).

Van Uytven, R., 'Brabantse en Antwerpse centrale plaatsen (14de–19de eeuw)', in *Le réseau urbain en Belgique dans une perspective historique (1350–1850): une approche statistique et dynamique = Het stedelijk netwerk in België in historisch perspectief (1350–1850): een statistische en dynamische benadering* (Brussels: Gemeentekrediet, 1992), pp. 29–79.

—, *De geschiedenis van Mechelen: van heerlijkheid tot stadsgewest* (Tielt: Lannoo, 1991).

—, 'De triomf van Antwerpen en de grote Steden', in R. Van Uytven (ed.), *Geschiedenis van Brabant van het hertogdom tot heden* (Zwolle: Waanders, 2011), pp. 241–52.

—, 'Een rekening betreffende Edmond Claysson, handelaar te Antwerpen (ca. 1518–1520)', *Bijdragen tot de geschiedenis, inzonderheid van het oud hertogdom Brabant*, 42 (1959), pp. 27–42.

—, 'In de schaduwen van de Antwerpse groei: het Hageland in de zestiende eeuw', *Bijdragen tot de geschiedenis*, 57 (1974), pp. 171–88.

—, 'Landtransport durch Brabant im Mittelalter und im 16. Jahrhundert', in F. Burgard and A. Haverkamp (ed.), *Auf den Römerstrassen ins Mittelalter: Beiträge zur Verkehrsgeschichte zwischen Maas und Rhein von der Spätantike bis ins 19. Jahrhundert* (Mainz: Von Zabern, 1997), pp. 471–99.

—, 'Wijnhandel en -verbruik in het Antwerpen van de 16de eeuw', in F. De Nave and C. Depauw (eds), *Europa aan Tafel: een verkenning van onze eet- en tafelcultuur* (Antwerp: MIM, 1993), pp. 41–7.

Van Uytven, R., C. Bruneel, and A. M. Koldeweij. *Geschiedenis van Brabant van het hertogdom tot heden* (Zwolle: Waanders, 2004).

Van Werveke, H., *Brugge en Antwerpen: acht eeuwen Vlaamsche handel* (Ghent: Rombaut-Fecheyr, 1941).

—, 'Die Stellung des Hansischen Kaufmanns dem Flandrischen Tuchproduzenten gegenüber', in *Beiträge zur Wirtschafts- und Stadtgeschichte. Festschrift für Hektor Ammann* (Wiesbaden: Steiner, 1965), pp. 296–304.

Van Zanden, J. L., 'Holland en de Zuidelijke Nederlanden in de periode 1500–1570: divergerende ontwikkelingen of voortgaande economische integratie', in E. Aerts, B. Henau, P. Janssens and R. Van Uytven (eds), *Studia Historica Oeconomica. Liber Amicorum Herman Van der Wee* (Leuven: Leuven University Press, 1993), pp. 357–67.

—, *The Long Road to the Industrial Revolution: The European Economy in a Global Perspective, 1000–1800. Global Economic History Series*, ed. M. Prak and J. L. Van Zanden, (Leiden: Brill, 2009).

Van Zanden, J. L., and M. van Tielhof, 'Roots of Growth and Productivity Change in Dutch Shipping Industry, 1500–1800', *Explorations in Economic History*, 46:4 (2009), pp. 389–403.

Vanden Hoecke, G., *Arithmetica: een sonderlinge excellent boeck, leerende veel schoone ende perfecte regulen der selver conste thantwerpen: by my Symon Cock* (Antwerp: Symon Cock, 1545).

Vanneste, T., *Global Trade and Commercial Networks: Eighteenth-Century Diamond Merchants* (London: Pickering & Chatto, 2011).

Vanwelden, M., *Productie van wandtapijten in de regio Oudenaarde: een symbiose tussen stad en platteland (15de tot 17de eeuw)* (Leuven: Universitaire Pers, 2006).

Verbist, B., *Traditie of innovatie? Wouter Ameyde, een Makelaar in het laatmiddeleeuwse Brugge, 1498–1507: proefschrift* (PhD dissertation, University of Antwerp, 2014).

Verellen, J. R., 'Linnennijverheid te Herentals vooral in de 16e eeuw', *Taxandria. Tijdschrift van de Koninklijke geschied- en oudheidkundige kring van de Antwerpse Kempen*, 29:2 (1957), pp. 3–19.

Verlinden, C., 'De Vlaamse kolonisten op de Azoren', in J. Everaert and E. Stols (eds), *Vlaanderen en Portugal: op de golfslag van twee culturen* (Antwerp: Mercatorfonds, 1991), pp. 81–97.

—, 'De zeeverzekeringen der Spaanse kooplui in de Nederlanden gedurende de XVIe Eeuw', *Bijdragen voor de geschiedenis der Nederlanden* (1948), pp. 191–216.

—, *Dokumenten voor de geschiedenis van prijzen en lonen in Vlaanderen en Brabant = Documents pour l'histoire des prix et des salaires en Flandre et en Brabant* (Bruges: Tempel, 1959).

Vermaut, J., 'Nieuwe gegevens over het industrieel verleden van Roeselare en omgeving 1350–1800', *Rollariensia*, 6 (1974), pp. 134–82.

Vermeylen, F., 'De export vanuit de Zuidelijke Nederlanden naar Duitsland omstreeks het midden van de 16de eeuw' (MA thesis, Catholic University of Louvain, 1989).

—, 'In de ban van Antwerpen: de Kempen tijdens de zestiende eeuw', *Taxandria*, 63 (1991), pp. 229–43.

—, *Painting for the Market: Commercialization of Art in Antwerp's Golden Age* (Turnhout: Brepols, 2003).

Vermoesen, R., 'Gescheiden door de wallen? Commerciële circuits in de stad en op het platteland, 1650–1800', *Stadsgeschiedenis*, 3:2 (2008), pp. 105–21.

Vieira, A., 'Sugar Islands: The Sugar Economy of Madeira and the Canaries, 1450–1650', in S. B. Schwartz (ed.), *Tropical Babylons: Sugar and the Making of the Atlantic World, 1450–1680* (Chapel Hill, NC: University of North Carolina Press, 2004), pp. 237–88.

Voet, L.. 'De Typografische Bedrijvigheid Te Antwerpen in De 16e Eeuw', in W. Couvreur (ed.), *Antwerpen in De Xvide Eeuw* (Antwerp: Mercurius, 1975), pp. 233–55.

—, *The Golden Compasses: A History and Evaluation of the Printing and Publishing Activities of the Officina Plantiniana at Antwerp* (Amsterdam: Vangendt, 1969).

Volckart, O., and A. Mangels, 'Are the Roots of the Modern Lex Mercatoria Really Medieval?', *Southern Economic Journal*, 65:3 (1999), pp. 427–50.

Von Ciriachy-Wantrup, K., *Familien- und Erbrechtliche Gestaltungen von Unternehmen der Renaissance: eine Untersuchung der Augsburger Handelsgesellschaften zur Frühen Neuzeit. Augsburger Schriften zur Rechtsgeschichte* (Berlin: LIT, 2007).

Wastiels, A., 'Juan Henriquez, makelaar in zeeverzekeringen te Antwerpen (1562–1563)' (Ghent: Licentiaat, Rijksuniversiteit Gent, 1967).

Wells, G. E., *Antwerp and the Government of Philip II, 1555–1567 S.l.* (Ithaca, NY: Cornell University, 1982).

—, 'Emergence and Evanescence: Republicanism and the Res Publica at Antwerp before the Revolt of the Netherlands', in H. G. Koenigsberger and E. Müller-Luckner (eds), *Republiken und Republikanismus im Europa der Frühen Neuzeit* (Munich: Oldenbourg, 1988), pp. 155–68.

Wheeler, J., *A Treatise of Commerce* (New York: Columbia University Press, 1931).

Wijffels, A., 'Business Relations between Merchants in Sixteenth-Century Belgian Practice-Orientated Civil Law Literature', in V. Piergiovanni (ed.), *From Lex Mercatoria to Commercial Law, Comparative Studies in Continental and Anglo-American Legal History* (Berlin: Duncker & Humblot, 2005), pp. 255–90.

Wijnroks, E. H., *Handel tussen Rusland en de Nederlanden, 1560–1640: een netwerkanalyse van de Antwerpse en Amsterdamse kooplieden, handelend op Rusland* (Hilversum: Verloren, 2003).

—, '"Nationale" en religieuze tegenstellingen in de Nederlandse Ruslandhandel, 1600–1630', in C. Lesger and L. Noordegraaf (eds), *Ondernemers & bestuurders: economie en politiek in de Noordelijke Nederlanden in de late Middeleeuwen en vroegmoderne tijd* (Amsterdam: NEHA, 1999), pp. 621–32.

Willems, B., *Leven op de pof: krediet bij de Antwerpse middenstand in de achttiende eeuw* (Amsterdam: Aksant, 2009).

Williamson, D. V., 'Transparency, Contract Selection and the Maritime Trade of Venetian Crete, 1303–1351', 2002, unpublished working paper, available at http://www.researchgate.net/publication/245549729_Transparency_Contract_Selection_and_the_Maritime_Trade_of_Venetian_Crete_1303-1351 [accessed 28 February 2015].

Wollschläger, C., 'Civil Litigation and Modernization: The Work of the Municipal Courts of Bremen, Germany, in Five Centuries, 1549–1984', *Law & Society Review*, 24:2 (1990), pp. 261–81.

Wouters, K., 'Tussen verwantschap en vermogen: de politieke elite van Antwerpen (1520–1555): een elite-onderzoek door middel van de prosopografische methode' (Brussels: Free University of Brussels, 2001).

Wyffels, C., and G. des Marez. *Analyses de reconnaissances de dettes passées devant les échevins d'Ypres (1249–1291)* (Brussels: Palais des académies, 1991).

Ympyn, J., *Nieuwe Instructie ende Bewijs der Looffelijcker Consten des Rekenboecks* (London: Scholar, 1979).

Zahedieh, N., *The Capital and the Colonies: London and the Atlantic Economy, 1660–1700* (Cambridge: Cambridge University Press, 2010).

Zuijderduijn, C. J., 'Conjunctuur in laatmiddeleeuws Haarlem: schepenregisters als bron voor de economische ontwikkeling van een Hollandse stad', *Holland. Historisch Tijdschrift*, 40:1 (2008), pp. 3–17.

—, 'The Emergence of Provincial Debt in the County of Holland (Thirteenth-Sixteenth Centuries)', *European Review of Economic History*, 14:3 (2010), pp. 335–59.

—, *Medieval Capital Markets: Markets for Renten, State Formation and Private Investment in Holland (1300–1550)* (Leiden: Brill, 2009).

NOTES

Introduction

1. J. Wheeler, *A Treatise of Commerce* (New York: Columbia University Press, 1931), pp. 36–8.

2. S. Ogilvie, *Institutions and European Trade: Merchant Guilds, 1000–1800* (Cambridge: Cambridge University Press, 2011); O. Gelderblom, *Cities of Commerce: The Institutional Foundations of International Trade in the Low Countries, 1250–1650* (Princeton, NJ: Princeton University Press, 2013); S. Ogilvie and A. W. Carus, 'Institutions and Economic Growth in Historical Perspective', in A. Philippe and N. Durlauf Steven (eds), *Handbook of Economic Growth* (Amsterdam: Elsevier, 2014), ch. 8, pp. 403–513.

3. See the historiographical and theoretical overviews on the history of entrepreneurship in: C. Lesger, 'Over het nut van huwelijk, opportunisme en bedrog. Ondernemers en ondernemerschap tijdens de vroegmoderne tijd in theoretisch perspectief', in C. A. Davids et al. (ed.), *Kapitaal, ondernemerschap en beleid: studies over economie en politiek in Nederland, Europa en Azië, van 1500 tot heden: afscheidsbundel voor Prof. Dr. P. W. Klein*, NEHA-Series (Amsterdam: NEHA, 1996), pp. 55–75; F. M. M. De Goey, 'Ondernemersgeschiedenis in Amerika, Nederland en België (1940–1995)', *NEHA-Jaarboek*, 59 (1996), pp. 21–75; O. Gelderblom and J. L. van Zanden, 'Vroegmodern ondernemerschap in Nederland', *NEHA-Bulletin*, 11:2 (1997), pp. 69–81; O. Gelderblom, 'Uitdagingen voor de vroegmoderne ondernemersgeschiedenis', *NEHA-Bulletin*, 16 (2002), pp. 69–81; O. Gelderblom, 'Entrepreneurs in the Golden Age of the Dutch Republic', in W. J. Baumol, D. S. Landes and J. Mokyr (eds), *The Invention of Enterprise: Entrepreneurship from Ancient Mesopotamia to Modern Times* (Princeton, NJ: Princeton University Press, 2010), ch. 6, pp. 156–82; J. Mokyr, 'Entrepreneurship and the Industrial Revolution in Britain', in Baumol, Landes and Mokyr (eds), *The Invention of Enterprise*, ch. 7, pp. 183–210.

4. C. Lesger, *The Rise of the Amsterdam Market and Information Exchange: Merchants, Commercial Expansion and Change in the Spatial Economy of the Low Countries, c. 1550–1630* (Aldershot: Ashgate, 2006).

5. Lesger, *The Rise of the Amsterdam Market and Information Exchange*, pp. 10–12.

6. This definition of entrepreneurs comes from M. Casson, 'Entrepreneurship', in J. Mokyr, M. Botticini and M. Berg (eds), *The Oxford Encyclopedia of Economic History* (Oxford: Oxford University Press, 2003), pp. 211–15, and is also used in Gelderblom, 'Entrepreneurs', p. 156. On female merchants: L. Van Aert, 'Van appelen tot zeemleer: koopvrouwen in Antwerpen in de 16de eeuw' (MA dissertation, Free University of Brussel, 2002); D. Van den Heuvel, *Women and Entrepreneurship: Female Traders in the Northern Netherlands, c. 1580–1815* (Amsterdam: Aksant, 2007).

7. R. Ehrenberg, *Das Zeitalter der Fugger: Geldkapital und Creditverkehr im 16. Jahrhundert* (Jena: Fischer, 1912), p. 363; H. Pirenne, *Histoire de Belgique: de la mort de Charles Le Téméraire à* l'arrivée du duc d'Albe dans les Pays-Bas (1567), Histoire de Belgique, 3rd edn, 7 vols. (Brussels: Maurice Lamertin, 1923), vol. 3, pp. 267–82.

8. H. van Werveke, *Brugge en Antwerpen: acht eeuwen Vlaamsche handel* (Ghent: Rombaut-Fecheyr, 1941).

9. L. Van der Essen, 'Contribution à l'histoire du port d'Anvers 1553–1554', *Bulletin de l'Académie Royale de la Belgique*, 3 (1920), pp. 39–58; J.-A. Goris, 'Eene Antwerpsche handelsexpeditie in de Oostzeelanden (1562–1569)', *Bijdragen tot de geschiedenis*, 16 (1924–5), pp. 133–44; J.-A. Goris, *Etude sur les colonies marchandes méridionales (Portugais, Espagnols, Italiens) à Anvers de 1488 à 1587* (Leuven: Uytspruyt, 1925); O. de Smedt, 'Het College der Nederlandsche kooplieden op Engeland', *Antwerpsch Archievenblad*, 1:2–3 (1926), pp. 113–20, 321–48; O. de Smedt, 'Een Antwerpsch plan tot organisatie van den Nederlandschen zeehandel op het Westen', *Antwerpsch Archievenblad* 2:2 (1927); O. de Smedt, *De Engelse natie te Antwerpen in de 16e eeuw (1496–1582)*, 2 vols (Antwerp: Sikkel, 1950), vol. 1; *De Engelse Natie te Antwerpen in de 16e eeuw (1496–1582)*, 2 vols (Antwerp: Sikkel, 1954), vol. 2; J. Denucé, *Afrika in de 16de eeuw en de handel van Antwerpen* (Antwerp: Sikkel, 1937); J. Denucé, *De Hanze en de Antwerpsche handelscompagnieën op de Oostzeelanden* (Antwerp: De Sikkel, 1938); F. Prims, *Geschiedenis van Antwerpen*, 10 vols (Antwerp: Standaard, 1939), vol. 17, 194–202, 257–64.

10. J. Craeybeckx, 'Handelaars en neringdoenden: de 16de eeuw', in J. L. Broeckx, C. de Clercq and J. Dhondt (eds), *Flandria Nostra: ons land en ons volk, zijn standen en beroepen door de tijden Heen* (Antwerp: Standaard, 1957).

11. W. Brulez, *De firma Della Faille en de internationale handel van Vlaamse firma's in de 16de eeuw* (Brussels: Paleis der Academiën, 1959).

12. Brulez, *De firma Della Faille*; W. Brulez, 'De handel', in W. Couvreur (ed.), *Antwerpen in de XVIde eeuw* (Antwerp: Mercurius, 1975).

13. H. Van der Wee, *The Growth of the Antwerp Market and the European Economy (Fourteenth–Sixteenth Centuries)*, 3 vols (The Hague: Nijhoff, 1963), vol. 2, pp. 321–3; H. Van der Wee, 'Structural Changes and Specialization in the Industry of the Southern Netherlands, 1100–1600', *Economic History Review*, 28:2 (1975), pp. 203–21; H. Van der Wee, 'Industrial Dynamics and the Process of Urbanization and De-Urbanization in the Low Countries from the Late Middle Ages to the Eighteenth Century. A Synthesis', in Van der Wee (ed.), *The Rise and Decline of Urban Industries in Italy and in the Low Countries (Late Middle Ages-Early Modern Times)* (Leuven: Leuven University Press, 1988), pp. 336–44.

14. Many of these case studies are based on the fragments of sixteenth-century Antwerp merchant documents preserved in the Insolvente Boedelkamer Archive of the Felix Archive (City Archive Antwerp). Detailed overviews of these documents can be found in Antwerpsch Archievenblad 1927–32, vols 32–7, and J. Van den Nieuwenhuizen, *Beknopte inventaris van de Insolvente Boedelkamer in het Stadsarchief van Antwerpen* (Brussels: Algemeen Rijksarchief, 1998). The following list is not entirely exhaustive; new information on several native merchants is found in other, often more general, publications on the Antwerp market, and these will be quoted in this dissertation when I refer to these merchants.

15. On Gillis Hooftman: P. Jeannin, *Les marchands au 16e siècle* (Paris: Seuil, 1957). On Edmond Claysson: R. Van Uytven, 'Een rekening betreffende Edmond Claysson,

handelaar te Antwerpen (ca. 1518–1520)', *Bijdragen tot de geschiedenis, inzonderheid van het oud hertogdom Brabant*, 42 (1959), pp. 27–42; on the silk entrepreneur Jan Nuyts: A. K. L. Thijs, 'Een ondernemer uit de Antwerpse textielindustrie, Jan Nuyts (ca. 1512–1582)', *Bijdragen tot de geschiedenis*, 51 (1968), pp. 53–68; on Jan Gamel: H. De Smedt, '*Antwerpen en de Opbloei van de Vlaamse verhandel tijdens de 16e eeuw. Rijkdom en inkomen van de Antwerpse koopman Jan Gamel volgens zijn staat van goed, 1572*' (Leuven: Katholieke Universiteit Leuven, 1970); H. De Smedt, 'De Antwerpse koopman Jan Gamel', *Bijdragen tot de geschiedenis van de Nederlanden*, 56 (1971), pp. 221–4; on Joris Vezeleer: A. Van den Kerkhove, 'Joris Vezeleer, een Antwerps koopman Van de XVIde Eeuw', paper presented at the 43e Congres Federatie van Kringen voor Oudheidkunde en Geschiedenis van België vzw, Sint-Niklaas-Waas, 1974; on the real estate entrepreneur and sometimes-merchant Gilbert van Schoonbeke: H. Soly, *Urbanisme en kapitalisme te Antwerpen in de 16de eeuw: de stedebouwkundige en industriële ondernemingen van Gilbert van Schoonbeke* (Brussels: Gemeentekrediet, 1977); on Jan van Immerseel: K. Mees, 'Koopman in troebele tijden: Jan van Immer-seele (1550–1612)', *Spiegel Historiael*, 19 (1984), pp. 545–51; on Pieter Seghers: K. Degryse, *Pieter Seghers: een koopmansleven in troebele tijden* (Antwerp: Hadewijch, 1989); on an anonymous silk merchant: R. De Peuter, 'Mooie kleren voor hoge heren. Beschouwingen over de textielhandel te Brussel in het midden van de zestiende eeuw', *Textielhistorische bijdragen* 34 (1994), pp. 30–49; on the Moriel, Goyart Janssen, Cattelyne van Hontsum and Peter Janssen-Houbraken (mainly on their accounts): N. Van Den Brulle, 'De commerciële praktijk in het zestiende-eeuwse Antwerpen aan de hand van registers uit de Insolvente Boedelskamer' (Master, Universiteit Gent, 2010).

16. On the Schetz: P. Génard, 'Un acte de société commerciale au XVIième siècle (la maison Schetz frères d'Anvers)', *Bulletin de la Société de Géographie d'Anvers*, 7 (1882), pp. 475–99; J. L. Meulleners, *De Antwerpsche bankier Erasmus Schetz en zijne geas-socieërden Jan Vleminck en Arnold Proenen in hunne betrekking tot Maastricht en Aken* (Maastricht: Le Courrier de la Meuse, 1890); Armand Louant, 'Gaspard Schetz, seigneur de Grobbendonck, facteur du roi d'Espagne à Anvers (1555–1561)', *Annales de l'Académie royale d'archéologie de Belgique*, 77 (1930), pp. 315–28; F. Prims, 'Erasmus Schetz in 1525–1532', *Antwerpiensia*, 13 (1939), pp. 63–9; Jeannin, *Les marchands au 16e siècle*; H. L. V. De Groote, 'De vermogensbalans van Melchior Schetz en zijn vrouw Anna Van Stralen met hun testament van 1 juli 1569', *Bijdragen tot de geschiedenis*, 55 (1972), pp. 226–63; H. Soly, 'De aluinhandel in de Nederlanden in de 16e eeuw', *Belgisch tijdschrift voor filologie en geschiedenis*, 52 (1974), pp. 800–57; B. d'Ursel, *Les Schetz* (Brussels: Office généalogique et héraldique de Belgique, 2004); on the Van Dale: F. Donnet, 'Les Anversois aux Canaries, un voyave mouvementé au XVIe Siècle', *Bulletin de la Société de Géographie d'Anvers* 18–19 (1895–6), pp. 276–311, 202–365; F. Donnet, 'Les origines d'une entreprise commerciale anversoise aux Canaries Au XVIe Siècle', *Bulletin de la Société de Géographie d'Anvers* (1919), pp. 103–10; K. Coornaert, 'De Vlaamse natie op de Canarische eilanden in de 16de eeuw' (Ghent: University of Ghent, 2000); on the Van der Molen Florence: F. Edler, 'The Van Der Molen, Commission Merchants of Antwerp: Trade with Italy, 1538–44', in J. L. Cate and E. N. Anderson (eds), *Medieval and Historiographical Essays in Honour of James Westfall Thompson* (Chicago, IL: University of Chicago Press, 1938), pp. 78–145; Brulez, *De Firma Della Faille*; J. Puttevils, 'A servitio de vostri sempre siamo. De effecten van de handel tussen Antwerpen en Italië op de koopmansfamilie Van der Molen' (MA thesis, University of Antwerp, 2007); on the Gramaye family: J. Denucé, 'Geeraerd Gramaye',

Antwerpsch Archievenblad, 33 (1928), pp. 81–98; F. Prims, 'Jacob Gramaye, ontvanger der Staten van Brabant te Antwerpen aan gouverneur Requesens, ter verzekering der hem verschuldigde kapitalen (Rond 1574)', *Bijdragen tot de geschiedenis*, 30 (1939), pp. 143–5; J. Cuypers, 'Geeraard Gramaye: sociaal-ekonomische studie van een Antwerpse persoonlijkheid uit de tweede helft der XVIde Eeuw' (Ghent: Ghent University, 1948); on the Van Bombergen: W. Brulez, 'Lettres commerciales de Daniel et Antoine de Bombergen à Antonio Grimani (1532–43)', *Bulletin de l'Institute Historique Belge de Rome*, 31 (1958), pp. 169–205; on the Janssens family: H. Soly, 'De Antwerpse onderneemster Anna Janssens en de economische boom na de Vrede van Cateau-Cambrésis (1559)', *Bijdragen tot de geschiedenis*, 52 (1969), pp. 139–64; on the Thijs family: O. Gelderblom, *Zuid-Nederlandse kooplieden en de opkomst van de Amsterdamse stapelmarkt (1578–1630)* (Hilversum: Verloren, 2000); O. Gelderblom, 'The Governance of Early Modern Trade: The Case of Hans Thijs, 1556–1611', *Enterprise & Society* 4:4 (2003), pp. 606–39.

17. On Oudenaarde tapestry enterpreneurs with close ties to Antwerp: E. Duverger, *Jan, Jacques en Frans De Moor, Tapijtwevers en tapijthandelaars te Oudenaarde, Antwerpen en Gent (1560 tot ca. 1680)* (Ghent: Interuniversitair Centrum voor de geschiedenis van de Vlaamse tapijtkunst, 1960); E. Duverger, 'De Steurbouts, een Oudenaards-Antwerps tapissiersgeslacht', *Artes Textiles* 6 (1965), pp. 31–74; M. Vanwelden, *Productie van wandtapijten in de regio Oudenaarde: een symbiose tussen stad en platteland (15de tot 17de eeuw)* (Leuven: Universitaire Pers, 2006); on Antwerp merchants active in Sweden: B. Oden, 'A Netherlandish Merchant in Stockholm in the Reign of Erik XIV', *Scandinavian Economic History Review*, 10:1 (1962), pp. 3–37; on Antwerp merchants supplying the imperial army: H. Soly, 'Een Antwerpse compagnie voor de levensmiddelenbevoorrading van het leger in de zestiende eeuw', *Bijdragen en mededelingen betreffende de geschiedenis der Nederlanden*, 186 (1971), pp. 350–62; on merchants active in the trade with Russia: H. Kellenbenz, 'The Economic Significance of the Archangel Route (from the Late 16th to the Late 18th Century)', *Journal of European Economic History*, 2:3 (1973), pp. 541–81; H. Soly, 'Antwerpener Nordeuropahandel um 1580', in *Album Aangeboden Aan Charles Verlinden Ter Gelegenheid Van Zijn Dertig Jaar Professoraat = Album Offert À Charles Verlinden À L'occasion De Ses Trente Ans De Professorat* (Ghent: Universa, 1975); E. H. Wijnroks, *Handel tussen Rusland en de Nederlanden, 1560–1640: een netwerkanalyse van de Antwerpse en Amsterdamse kooplieden, handelend op Rusland* (Hilversum: Verloren, 2003); on merchants from Lille with close ties to Antwerp: R. S. Duplessis, *Lille and the Dutch Revolt: Urban Stability in an Era of Revolution, 1500–1582* (Cambridge: Cambridge University Press, 1991); on female merchants: L. Van Aert, 'Van appelen tot zeemleer'; on jewelers: Gelderblom, 'Het juweliersbedrijf in de Lage Landen, 1450–1650'. For the late sixteenth and seventeenth centuries: E. Stols, *De Spaanse Brabanders of de handelsbetrekkingen der Zuidelijke Nederlanden met de Iberische wereld, 1598–1648*, 2 vols (Brussels: Paleis der Academiën, 1971); R. Baetens, *De nazomer van Antwerpens welvaart: de diaspora en het handelshuis De Groote tijdens de eerste helft der 17de eeuw*, 2 vols (Brussels: Gemeentekrediet, 1976).

18. Wijnroks, *Handel tussen Rusland en de Nederlanden*.

19. Gelderblom, *Zuid-Nederlandse kooplieden*; O. Gelderblom, 'Antwerp Merchants in Amsterdam after the Revolt, 1578–1630', in B. Blondé, A. Greve and P. Stabel (eds), *International Trade in the Low Countries (14th–16th Centuries): Merchants, Organization, Infrastructure: Proceedings of the International Conference Ghent-Antwerp, 12th-13th January 1997* (Leuven: Garant, 2000); O. Gelderblom, 'From Antwerp to

Amsterdam: The Contribution of Merchants from the Southern Netherlands to the
Rise of the Amsterdam Market', *Review. A Journal of the Fernand Braudel Center for the
Study of Economies, Historical Systems, and Civilizations*, 26:3 (2003), pp. 247–82.
20. J. Puttevils, 'Klein gewin brengt rijkdom in: de Zuid-Nederlandse handelaars in de
export naar Italië in de jaren 1540', *Tijdschrift voor sociale en economische geschiedenis*
6:1 (2009), pp. 26–52.
21. H. Van der Wee, *The Growth of the Antwerp Market and the European Economy (Four-
teenth–Sixteenth Centuries)*, 3 vols (Den Haag: Nijhoff, 1963), vol. 2, pp. 331–2; H.
Van der Wee, 'Handel in de zuidelijke Nederlanden', in *Nieuwe Algemene Geschiedenis
Der Nederlanden* (Haarlem: Fibula-Van Dishoeck, 1978), pp. 75–95; H. Van der Wee,
'Industrial Dynamics and the Process of Urbanization and De-Urbanization in the
Low Countries from the Late Middle Ages to the Eighteenth Century. A Synthesis', in
H. Van der Wee (ed.), *The Rise and Decline of Urban Industries in Italy and in the Low
Countries (Late Middle Ages-Early Modern Times)* (Leuven: Leuven University Press,
1988), pp. 307–88; H. Van der Wee, 'Trade in the Southern Netherlands, 1493–1587',
in H. Van der Wee (ed.), The Low Countries in the Early Modern World (Aldershot:
Ashgate, 1993).
22. T. Peeters and H. Van der Wee, 'Een dynamisch model voor de seculaire ontwikkeling van de wereldhandel en de welvaart', *Tijdschrift voor geschiedenis*, 82 (1969), pp.
233–49; T. Peeters and H. Van der Wee, 'Un modèle économique de croissance interséculaire du commerce mondial (XIIe-XVIIIe siècles)', *Annales. Economies, Sociétés,
Civilisations*, 25:1 (1970), pp. 100–26.
23. This model was partially reiterated in H. Van der Wee, 'Structural Changes in European
Long-Distance Trade and Particularly in the Re-Export Trade from South to North,
1350–1750', in J. D. Tracy (ed.), *The Rise of Merchant Empires: Long-Distance Trade in
the Early Modern World, 1350–1750* (Cambridge: Cambridge University Press, 1990),
ch. 1, pp. 14–33.
24. J. H. Munro, 'The Low Countries' Export Trade in Textiles with the Mediterranean
Basin: A Cost–Benefit Analysis of Comparative Advantages in Overland and Maritime
Trade Routes', *International Journal of Maritime History*, 11:2 (1999), pp. 1–30; J.
H. Munro, 'The "New Institutional Economics" and the Changing Fortunes of Fairs
in Medieval and Early Modern Europe: The Textile Trades, Warfare and Transaction
Costs', *Vierteljahresschrift für Sozial- und Wirtschaftsgeschichte*, 88 (2001), pp. 1–47.
25. S. R. Epstein, 'Regional Fairs, Institutional Innovation, and Economic Growth in Late
Medieval Europe', *Economic History Review*, 47:3 (1994), pp. 459–82; S. R. Epstein,
'Fairs, Towns, and States in Renaissance Europe', in S. Cavaciocchi and F. Datini (eds),
*Fiere e mercati nella integrazione delle economie europee, secc. 13–18: atti della 'trenta-
duesima settimana di studi', 8–12 maggio 2000*, Settimani di studi Istituto internazionale di storia economica (Florence: Monnier, 2001), pp. 71–90.
26. Van der Wee, *The Growth of the Antwerp Market and the European Economy*, vol. 1, pp.
510–17; R. Van Uytven, 'Landtransport durch Brabant im Mittelalter und im 16. Jahrhundert', in F. Burgard and A. Haverkamp (eds), *Auf den Römerstrassen ins Mittelalter:
Beiträge zur Verkehrsgeschichte zwischen Maas und Rhein von der Spätantike bis ins 19.
Jahrhundert* (Mainz: Von Zabern, 1997), p. 497.
27. W. Brulez, 'La navigation flamande vers la Méditerranée à la fin du XVIe siècle', *Revue
belge de philologie et d'histoire*, 36 (1958), pp. 1210–42; W. Brulez, *De firma Della
Faille en de internationale handel van Vlaamse firma's in de 16de eeuw* (Brussels: Paleis
der Academiën, 1959), pp. 124–84; W. Brulez, 'De scheepvaartwinst in de Nieuwe

Tijden', *Tijdschrift voor geschiedenis*, 92:1 (1979), pp. 1–19; W. Brulez, 'Scheepvaart in de Zuidelijke Nederlanden', in D. P. Blok (ed.), *Algemene Geschiedenis der Nederlanden* (Haarlem: Fibula-Van Dishoeck, 1979), k, pp. 123–8.; M. van Tielhof, *De Hollandse graanhandel, 1470–1570: koren op de Amsterdamse molen* (Den Haag: Stichting Hollandse Historische Reeks, 1995); M. Van Tielhof, *The 'Mother of All Trades': The Baltic Grain Trade in Amsterdam from the Late 16th to the Early 19th Century* (Leiden: Brill, 2002); J. Luiten van Zanden and M. van Tielhof, 'Roots of Growth and Productivity Change in Dutch Shipping Industry, 1500–1800', *Explorations in Economic History*, 46:4 (2009), pp. 389–403. There has been discussion on the existence of an Antwerp and Southern Low Countries trading fleet: A. Van Laar, 'De handelsvloot van Antwerpen in het bloeitijdvak', *Bijdragen tot de geschiedenis*, 16 (1923), pp. 25–40; F. Smekens, 'Braakliggend terrein betreffende onze nationale zeevaartgeschiedenis in de moderne tijden', *Marine academie van België. Mededelingen*, 10 (1956), pp. 45–67; J. Van Roey, 'Handelsvaart van de Zuidnederlanders', in G. Asaert (ed.), *Maritieme geschiedenis der Nederlanden* (Bussum: De Boer Maritiem, 1976), pp. 249–60.

28. Brulez, *De firma Della Faille*, pp. 408–31; 'L'exportation des Pays-Bas vers l'Italie par voie de terre au milieu du XVIe siècle', *Annales. Economies, Sociétés, Civilisations*, 14:3 (1959), pp. 461–91; 'Les routes commerciales d'Angleterre en Italie Au XVIe siècle', in *Studi in Onore Di Amintore Fanfani* (Milaan: A. Giuffrè, 1962), pp. 123–84; J. Puttevils, 'Klein gewin brengt rijkdom in: de Zuid-Nederlandse handelaars in de export naar Italië in de jaren 1540', *Tijdschrift voor sociale en economische geschiedenis*, 6:1 (2009), pp. 26–52, on pp. 40–1.

29. J. Goldberg, *Trade and Institutions in the Medieval Mediterranean: The Geniza Merchants and their Business World* (Cambridge: Cambridge University Press, 2012), pp. 242–3, 275–6, 286–8

30. Goldberg, *Trade and Institutions in the Medieval Mediterranean*, pp. 238–9.

31. M. 't Hart, J. Jonker, and J. Luiten van Zanden, *A Financial History of the Netherlands* (Cambridge: University Press, 1998); M. 't Hart and M. Van der Heijden, 'Het geld van de Stad. Recente historiografische trends in het onderzoek naar stedelijke financiën in de Nederlanden', *Tijdschrift voor sociale en economische geschiedenis*, 3:3 (2006), pp. 3–35; M. van der Heijden, *Geldschieters van de stad: financiële relaties tussen stad, burgers en overheden 1550–1650* (Amsterdam: Bert Bakker, 2006); J. Hanus, *Tussen stad en eigen gewin: stadsfinanciën, renteniers en kredietmarkten in 's-Hertogenbosch (begin zestiende eeuw)* (Amsterdam: Aksant, 2007); J. Hanus, 'Een efficiënte pre-industriële kapitaalmarkt? Het vroeg zestiende-eeuwse 's-Hertogenbosch als voorbeeld', *Tijdschrift voor sociale en economische geschiedenis*, 6:3 (2009), pp. 82–113; C. J. Zuijderduijn, *Medieval Capital Markets: Markets for Renten, State Formation and Private Investment in Holland (1300–1550)* (Leiden: Brill, 2009); O. Gelderblom, 'Entrepreneurs in the Golden Age of the Dutch Republic', in W. J. Baumol, D. S. Landes and J. Mokyr (eds), *The Invention of Enterprise: Entrepreneurship from Ancient Mesopotamia to Modern Times*, (Princeton, NJ: Princeton University Press, 2010), ch. 6, pp. 156–82.

32. R. Ehrenberg, *Capital & Finance in the Age of the Renaissance: A Study of the Fuggers and their Connections* (Fairfield, NJ: Kelley, 1985); M. Drelichman and H.-J. Voth, *Lending to the Borrower from Hell: Debt, Taxes, and Default in the Age of Philip II* (Princeton, NJ: Princeton University Press, 2014).

33. Especially: H. Van der Wee, 'Sporen van disconto te Antwerpen tijdens de XVIe Eeuw', *Bijdragen voor de geschiedenis der Nederlanden*, 10 (1955), pp. 68–70; Van der Wee, *The Growth of the Antwerp Market*, vol. 2, pp. 333–68; H. Van der Wee, 'Antwerpens

bijdrage tot de ontwikkeling van de moderne geld- en banktechniek', *Tijdschrift voor economie*, 4 (1965), pp. 488–500; H. Van der Wee, 'Anvers et les innovations de la technique financière aux XVIe et XVIIe siècles', *Annales: Economies, Sociétés, Civilisations*, 22:5 (1977), pp. 1067–89; H. Van der Wee, 'Monetary, Credit and Banking Systems', in E. E. Rich and C. H. Wilson (eds), *The Economic Organization of Early Modern Europe, The Cambridge Economic History of Europe* (Cambridge: Cambridge University Press, 1977), ch. 5, pp. 290–392; H. Van der Wee, 'Geld- krediet- en bankwezen in de Zuidelijke Nederlanden 1490–1580', in D. P. Blok (ed.), *Algemene Geschiedenis der Nederlanden* (Haarlem: Fibula-Van Dishoeck, 1979), pp. 98–108; H. Van der Wee, 'Les innovations de la technique financière à Bruges, Anvers et Amsterdam (XIIIe-XVIIe Siècle)', *Belgisch tijdschrift voor filologie en geschiedenis*, 89:2 (2011), pp. 861–73.

34. D. C. North, *Institutions, Institutional Change and Economic Performance* (Cambridge: Cambridge University Press, 1990), pp. 3–5.

35. A. Greif, *Institutions and the Path to the Modern Economy: Lessons from Medieval Trade* (Cambridge: Cambridge University Press, 2006), p. 30.

36. W. Brulez, 'De diaspora der Antwerpse kooplui op het einde van de 16e eeuw', *Bijdragen tot de geschiedenis*, 15 (1960), pp. 279–306.

37. T. Vanneste, *Global Trade and Commercial Networks: Eighteenth-Century Diamond Merchants* (London: Pickering & Chatto, 2011), p. 3. On diasporas: P. D. Curtin, *Cross-Cultural Trade in World History* (Cambridge: Cambridge University Press, 1984); J. I. Israel, *European Jewry in the Age of Mercantilism, 1550–1750* (Oxford: Clarendon Press, 1985); J. I. Israel, *Diasporas within a Diaspora: Jews, Crypto-Jews and the World Maritime Empires (1540–1740)* (Leiden: Brill, 2002); R. L. Kagan and P. D. Morgan, *Atlantic Diasporas: Jews, Conversos, and Crypto-Jews in the Age of Mercantilism, 1500–1800* (Baltimore, MD: Johns Hopkins University Press, 2009).

38. Greif, *Institutions*. This book combines Greif's previous contributions: 'Reputation and Coalitions in Medieval Trade: Evidence on the Maghribi Traders', *Journal of Economic History*, 49:4 (1989), pp. 857–82; 'Institutions and International Trade: Lessons from the Commercial Revolution', *American Economic Review*, 82:2 (1992), pp. 128–33; 'Contract Enforceability and Economic Institutions in Early Trade: The Maghribi Traders' Coalition', *American Economic Review*, 83:3 (1993), pp. 525–48; 'Trading Institutions and the Commercial Revolution in Medieval Europe', in A. Aganbegyan, O. Bogomolov and M. Kaser (eds), *System Transformation: Eastern and Western Assessments, Economics in a Changing World: Proceedings of the Tenth World Congress of the International Economic Association, Moscow* (Basingstoke: Macmillan, 1994), ch. 8, pp. 115–25; 'The Fundamental Problem of Exchange: A Research Agenda in Historical Institutional Analysis', *European Review of Economic History*, 4:3 (2000), pp. 251–84; on private order institutions in economics: A. K. Dixit, *Lawlessness and Economics: Alternative Modes of Governance* (Princeton, NJ: Princeton University Press, 2004); a case study on private order mechanisms among Jewish New York City diamond dealers: B. D. Richman, 'How Community Institutions Create Economic Advantage: Jewish Diamond Merchants in New York', *Law & Social Inquiry*, 31:2 (2006), pp. 383–420.

39. On cross-cultural diasporas: Curtin, *Cross-Cultural Trade*; on the Sephardim merchants: F. Trivellato, *The Familiarity of Strangers: The Sephardic Diaspora, Livorno, and Cross-Cultural Trade in the Early Modern Period* (New Haven, CT: Yale University Press, 2009), pp. 102–31; on the Armenians: S. Aslanian, 'Social Capital, "Trust" and the Role of Networks in Julfan Trade: Informal and Semi-Formal Institutions at Work', *Journal of Global History*, 1:3 (2006), pp. 124–70; S. Aslanian, *From the Indian Ocean*

to the Mediterranean: The Global Trade Networks of Armenian Merchants from New Julfa, The California World History Library (Berkeley, CA: University of California Press, 2011).

40. R. Grassby, *Kinship and Capitalism: Marriage, Family, and Business in the English-Speaking World, 1580–1740* (Washington, DC: Woodrow Wilson Center Press, 2001); O. Gelderblom, 'The Governance of Early Modern Trade: The Case of Hans Thijs, 1556–1611', *Enterprise & Society*, 4:4 (2003), pp. 606–39; A. Forestier, 'Risk, Kinship and Personal Relationships in Late Eighteenth-Century West Indian Trade: The Commercial Network of Tobin & Pinney', *Business History*, 52:6 (2010), pp. 919–31; U. C. Ewert and S. Selzer, 'Verhandeln Und Verkaufen, Vernetzen Und Vertrauen. Über Die Netzwerkstruktur Des Hansischen Handels', *Hansische Geschichtsblätter*, 119 (2001), pp. 135–62; M. Häberlein, *Brüder, Freunde und Betrüger: soziale Beziehungen, Normen und Konflikte in der Augsburger Kaufmanschaft um die Mitte des 16. Jahrhunderts* (Berlin: Akademie Verlag, 1998); on early modern friendship: L. Kooijmans, *Vriendschap en de kunst van het overleven in de zeventiende en achttiende eeuw* (Amsterdam: Bakker, 1997).

41. On medieval Italian merchants, see: G. Dahl, *Trade, Trust and Networks: Commercial Culture in Late Medieval Italy* (Lund: Nordic Academic Press, 1998).

42. Gunnar Dahl, *Trade, Trust and Networks*, p. 20.

43. On Maghribi relying on courts and other public institutions: J. Edwards and S. Ogilvie, 'Contract Enforcement, Institutions, and Social Capital: The Maghribi Traders Reappraised', *Economic History Review*, 65:2 (2012), pp. 421–44; and a response by Greif: A. Greif, 'The Maghribi Traders: A Reappraisal?', *Economic History Review*, 65:2 (2012), pp. 445–69; Trivellato, *The Familiarity of Strangers*, p. 14. The complete revision can be found in: Goldberg, *Trade and Institutions in the Medieval Mediterranean*; on the shared interests of rulers and merchant guilds: S. Ogilvie, *Institutions and European Trade: Merchant Guilds, 1000–1800* (Cambridge: Cambridge University Press, 2011); on the community responsibility system: A. Greif, 'Impersonal Exchange and the Origin of Markets: From the Community Responsibility System to Individual Legal Responsibility in Pre-Modern Europe', in M. Aoki and Y. Hayami (eds), *Communities and Markets in Economic Development* (Oxford: Oxford University Press, 2001), pp. 3–41; L. Boerner and A. Ritschl, 'Individual Enforcement of Collective Liability in Premodern Europe', *Journal of Institutional and Theoretical Economics*, 158 (2002), pp. 205–13; L. Boerner and A. Ritschl, 'The Economic History of Sovereignty: Communal Responsibility, the Extended Family, and the Firm', *Journal of Institutional and Theoretical Economics JITE*, 165 (2009), pp. 99–112.

44. O. Gelderblom, *Cities of Commerce: The Institutional Foundations of International Trade in the Low Countries, 1250–1650* (Princeton, NJ: Princeton University Press, 2013), p. 9.

45. J.-L. Rosenthal and R. Bin Wong, *Before and Beyond Divergence: The Politics of Economic Change in China and Europe* (Cambridge, MA: Harvard University Press, 2011), pp. 72–85.

46. Ogilvie, *Institutions and European Trade*, pp. 414–26.

47. Ogilvie, *Institutions and European Trade*, pp. 427–34.

48. Gelderblom, *Cities of Commerce*.

49. O. Gelderblom and R. Grafe, 'The Rise, Persistence and Decline of Merchant Guilds. Re-Thinking the Comparative Study of Commercial Institutions in Pre-Modern Europe', *Journal of Interdisciplinary History*, 40:4 (2010), pp. 477–511, on p. 485.

50. S. R. Epstein, *Freedom and Growth: The Rise of States and Markets in Europe, 1300–1750* (Londen: Routledge, 2001), pp. 147–55.

51. On commercial infrastructure, see: M. Limberger, 'No Town in the World Provides More Advantages: Economies of Agglomeration and the Golden Age of Antwerp', in P. O'Brien, D. Keene and M. 't Hart (eds), *Urban Achievement in Early Modern Europe: Golden Ages in Antwerp, Amsterdam and London* (Cambridge: Cambridge University Press, 2001), pp. 39–62; D. J. Harreld, 'Trading Places: The Public and Private Spaces of Merchants in Sixteenth-Century Antwerp', *Journal of Urban History*, 29:6 (2003), pp. 657–69; P. Stabel, 'Public or Private, Collective or Individual? The Spaces of Late Medieval Trade in the Low Countries', in D. Calabi and S. Beltramo (eds), *Il mercante patrizio: palazzi e botteghe nell'Europa del Rinascimento* (Milan: Mondadori, 2008), pp. 37–54. The literature on Antwerp brokers and hostellers is limited, not very detailed and superannuated compared to the available work on Bruges. For Antwerp: E. Dilis, *Les courtiers anversois sous l'Ancien Régime* (Antwerp: Van Hille-De Backer, 1910); J. Puttevils, P. Stabel and B. Verbist, 'Een eenduidig pad van modernisering van het handelsverkeer: van het liberale Brugge naar het gereguleerde Antwerpen?', in B. Blondé et al. (eds), *Overheid en economie: geschiedenissen van een spanningsveld* (Antwerp: University Press Antwerp, 2014), pp. 39–54; on Bruges brokers and hostellers: J. A. Van Houtte, 'Makelaars en waarden te Brugge van de 13e tot de 16e eeuw', *Bijdragen voor de geschiedenis der Nederlanden*, 5 (1950–1), pp. 1–30, pp. 177–97; O. Mus, 'Wouter Ameyde, Een Brugs waard-makelaar op het einde van de 15de eeuw', in *Album Albert Schouteet* (Bruges: Westvlaams Verbond van Kringen voor Heemkunde, 1973); Peter Stabel, 'Entre commerce international et entrepreneurs locaux: le monde financier de Wouter Ameide (Bruges, Fin 15e–Début 16e Siècle)', in M. Boone (ed.), *Finances Privées, Finances Publiques* (Leuven: Garant, 1995); A. Greve, 'Jacob Sconebergh and his Short Career as a Hosteller in Fourteenth-Century Bruges', in W. Blockmans, M. Boone and T. de Hemptinne (eds), *Secretum Scriptorum: Liber alumnorum Walter Prevenier* (Leuven: Garant, 1999), pp. 213–24; A. Greve, 'Brokerage and Trade in Medieval Bruges: Regulation and Reality', in B. Blondé, A. Greve and P. Stabel (eds), *International Trade in the Low Countries (14th–16th Centuries): Merchants, Organisation, Infrastructure: Proceedings of the International Conference Ghent-Antwerp, 12th–13th January 1997* (Leuven: Garant, 2000), pp. 37–44; A Greve, 'Die Bedeutung der Brügger Hosteliers für Hansische Kaufleute im 14. und 15. Jahrhundert', *Jaarboek voor middeleeuwse geschiedenis*, 4 (2001), pp. 259–96; J. M. Murray, *Bruges: Cradle of Capitalism 1280–1390* (Cambridge: Cambridge University Press, 2006); A. Greve, *Hansische Kaufleute, Hosteliers und Herbergen im Brügge des 14. und 15. Jahrhunderts* (Frankfurt am Main: Lang, 2011); B. Verbist, *Traditie of innovatie? Wouter Ameyde, een makelaar in het laatmiddeleeuwse Brugge, 1498–1507: Proefschrift* (University of Antwerp, PhD dissertation, 2014). Gelderblom has calculated brokerage costs in Bruges and Antwerp and found them very low: Gelderblom, *Cities of Commerce*, pp. 47–54. On medieval brokers in general: L. Boerner and D. Quint, 'Medieval Matching Markets' (Berlin: Free University Berlin, School of Business & Economics, 2010).

52. J. Denucé, 'De beurs van Antwerpen: oorsprong en eerste ontwikkeling in de 15e en 16e eeuwen', *Antwerpsch Archievenblad*, 6 (1931), pp. 81–145; J. Marechal, *Geschiedenis van de Brugse Beurs* (Bruges: Anjelier, 1949); J. Materné, 'Schoon ende bequaem tot versamelinghe der cooplieden: Antwerpens beurswereld tijdens de Gouden zestiende eeuw', in G. De Clercq (ed.), *Ter Beurze: Geschiedenis van de aandelenhandel in België, 1300–1990* (Bruges: Van de Wiele, 1992), pp. 50–85.

53. D. De ruysscher, *Handel en recht in de Antwerpse rechtbank (1585–1713)* (Leuven: UGA, 2009); and his other publications (partially) based on this book: 'Law Merchant in the Mould. The Transfer and Transformation of Commercial Practices into Antwerp Customary Law (16th–17th Centuries)', in V. Duss et al., *Rechtstransfer in der Geschichte. Legal Transfer in History* (Munich: Meidenbauer, 2006); 'Over Themis en Mercurius: handelsgebruiken en -recht in Antwerpen (vijftiende-zeventiende Eeuw)', *Revue belge de philologie et d'histoire*, 88:4 (2010), pp. 1105–35; 'Innovating Financial Law in Early Modern Europe: Transfers of Commercial Paper and Recourse Liability in Legislation and Ius Commune (Sixteenth to Eighteenth Centuries)', *European Review of Private Law*, 19:5 (2011), pp. 505–18; 'From Usages of Merchants to Default Rules: Practices of Trade, Ius Commune and Urban Law in Early Modern Antwerp', *Journal of Legal History*, 33:1 (2012), pp. 3–29.

54. T. M. Safley, 'Institutions and their Discontents', *Tijdschrift voor sociale en economische geschiedenis*, 11:4 (2014), pp. 61–73.

55. On the political effects of commercial interest groups: D. Acemoglu, S. Johnson and J. Robinson, 'The Rise of Europe: Atlantic Trade, Institutional Change, and Economic Growth', *American Economic Review*, 95 (2005), pp. 546–79, on p. 550; D. Stasavage, *States of Credit: Size, Power, and the Development of European Polities* (Princeton, NJ: Princeton University Press, 2011); D. Stasavage, 'Was Weber Right? The Role of Urban Autonomy in Europe's Rise', *American Political Science Review*, 108:2 (2014), pp. 337–54.

56. J. Van Roey, 'De bevolking', in W. Couvreur (ed.), *Antwerpen in de XVIde eeuw* (Antwerp: Mercurius, 1975).

57. R. Cooter and J. T. Landa, 'Personal Versus Impersonal Trade: The Size of Trading Groups and Contract Law', *International Review of Law and Economics*, 4:1 (1984), pp. 15–22, on pp. 15–16; J. T. Landa, 'Doing the Economics of Trust and Informal Institutions', in S. G. Medema and W. J. Samuels (eds), *Foundations of Research in Economics: How Do Economists Do Economics* (Cheltenham: Elgar, 1996), ch. 13, pp. 142–62, on p. 149; J. T. Landa, 'A Theory of the Ethnically Homogeneous Middleman Group: An Institutional Alternative to Contract Law', *Journal of Legal Studies*, 10:2 (1981), pp. 349–62; J. T. Landa, *Trust, Ethnicity, and Identity: Beyond the New Institutional Economics of Ethnic Trading Networks, Contract Law, and Gift-Exchange* (Ann Arbor, MI: University of Michigan Press, 1994).

58. F. Braudel, *Le temps du monde. Civilisation matérielle, économie et capitalisme, 15e–18e siècle*, 3 vols (Paris: Colin, 1967), vol. 3, pp. 17–24.

59. This brief introduction of Antwerp's economic history is based on Herman Van der Wee's classic analysis of the Antwerp market: H. Van der Wee, *The Growth of the Antwerp Market and the European Economy (Fourteenth–Sixteenth Centuries)*, 3 vols (Den Haag: Nijhoff, 1963), vol. 2, and the more recent J. Materné and H. Van der Wee, 'Antwerp as a World Market in the Sixteenth and Seventeenth Centuries', in J. Van der Stock (ed.), *Antwerp, Story of a Metropolis, 16th–17th Century* (Ghent: Snoeck-Ducaju, 1993), pp. 19–31; H. Van der Wee, 'Handel in de Zuidelijke Nederlanden', in *Nieuwe Algemene Geschiedenis der Nederlanden* (Haarlem: Fibula-Van Dishoeck, 1978), pp. 75–95; W. Brulez, 'De handel', in W. Couvreur (ed.), *Antwerpen in de XVIde eeuw* (Antwerp: Mercurius, 1975), pp. 109–42; M. Limberger, 'No Town in the World Provides More Advantages: Economies of Agglomeration and the Golden Age of Antwerp', in P. O'Brien, D. Keene and M. 't Hart (eds), *Urban Achievement in Early Modern Europe: Golden Ages in Antwerp, Amsterdam and London* (Cambridge: Cambridge University Press, 2001), pp. 39–62. See also C. Lesger, *The Rise of the*

Amsterdam Market and Information Exchange: Merchants, Commercial Expansion and Change in the Spatial Economy of the Low Countries, c.1550–1630 (Aldershot: Ashgate, 2006). For Antwerp's fair twin Bergen-op-Zoom: C. J. F. Slootmans, *Paas- en Koudemarkten te Bergen-Op-Zoom, 1365–1565*, 3 vols (Tilburg: Stichting Zuidelijk Historisch Contact, 1985) and Y. E. Kortlever, 'The Easter and Cold Fairs of Bergen-Op-Zoom (14th–16th Centuries)', in S. Cavaciocchi (ed.), *Fiere e mercati nella integrazione delle economie europee, secc. 13–18: atti della 'trentaduesima settimana di studi', 8–12 Maggio 2000* (Florence: Le Monnier, 2001). O. Gelderblom, *Cities of Commerce: The Institutional Foundations of International Trade in the Low Countries, 1250–1650* (Princeton, NJ: Princeton University Press, 2013), pp. 25–33 provides the most up-to-date overview with references to the older literature as well.

60. J. A. Van Houtte, 'Les foires dans la Belgique ancienne', in *La Foire, receuils de la Société Jean Bodin* (Brussels: Librairie encyclopédique, 1953), pp. 175–207, on p. 189; Slootmans, *Paas- en Koudemarkten*, vol. 1, pp. 6–8; Kortlever, 'The Easter and Cold Fairs', pp. 626–7, cited in Gelderblom, *Cities of Commerce*, p. 26.

61. O. de Smedt, *De Engelse Natie te Antwerpen in de 16e eeuw (1496–1582)*, 2 vols (Antwerp: Sikkel, 1954), vol. 1, I, pp. 63, 77–8, 86; M. Gotzen, 'Het oud-Antwerps burgerlijk procesrecht volgens de costumiere redacties van de 16e–17e eeuw', *Rechtskundig tijdschrift voor België*, 41 (1951), pp. 291–315, 424–68, on p. 466; R. Rößner, *Hansische Memoria in Flandern: Alltagsleben und Totengedenken der Osterlingen in Brügge und Antwerpen (13. Bis 16. Jahrhundert)* (Frankfurt am Main: Lang, 2001), p. 50, cited in Gelderblom, *Cities of Commerce*, p. 26.

62. W. Blockmans and W. Prevenier, *The Promised Lands: The Low Countries under Burgundian Rule, 1369–1530* (Philadelphia, PA: Penn, 1999), pp. 54–6; Slootmans, *Paas-En Koudemarkten*, vol. 1, I, pp. 8–10, 121–3; Van der Wee, *The Growth of the Antwerp Market*, vol. 2, pp. 20–8, 37–41, cited in Gelderblom, *Cities of Commerce*, p. 26.

63. Gelderblom, *Cities of Commerce*, pp. 26–7.

64. J. L. Bolton and Francesco Guidi Bruscoli, 'When Did Antwerp Replace Bruges as the Commercial and Financial Centre of North-Western Europe? The Evidence of the Borromei Ledger for 1438', *Economic History Review*, 61:2 (2008), pp. 360–79; G. Asaert, 'Gasten uit Brugge: nieuwe gegevens over Bruggelingen op de Antwerpse markt in de vijftiende eeuw', in H. Coppejans and G. Hansotte (eds), *Album Carlos Wijffels: aangeboden door zijn wetenschappelijke medewerkers* (Brussels: Algemeen Rijksarchief, 1987). Only during the Flemish Revolt in the 1480s against Maximilian of Austria did Antwerp take over from Bruges. J. Haemers, '"Ende hevet tvolc goede cause jeghens hemlieden te rysene" Stedelijke opstanden en staatsvorming in het graafschap Vlaanderen (1477–1492)' (PhD dissertation, Ghent University, 2006); J. Hamers, *For the Common Good: State Power and Urban Revolts in the Reign of Mary of Burgundy (1477–1482)* (Turnhout: Brepols, 2009); W. Blockmans, *Metropolen aan de Noordzee: de geschiedenis van Nederland, 1100–1560* (Amsterdam: Bakker, 2010), pp. 520–31 All foreign merchants were ordered to leave Bruges for Antwerp in 1485 and 1488 and many remained in Antwerp after the Revolt ended. J. Marechal, 'Le départ de Bruges des marchands étrangers (XVe et XVIe siècles)', *Handelingen van het Genootschap voor Geschiedenis: driemaandelijks tijdschrift voor de studie van geschiedenis en oudheden van Vlaanderen*, 88 (1951), pp. 26–74; J. H. Munro, 'Bruges and the Abortive Staple in English Cloth: An Incident in the Shift of Commerce from Bruges to Antwerp in the Late Fifteenth Century', *Revue belge de philologie et d'histoire*, 44:4 (1966), pp. 1137–59, on pp. 1150–1. Antwerp's ancient privileges for foreign merchants were

reaffirmed and the city was granted the alum staple. Munro, 'Bruges and the Abortive Staple in English Cloth', p. 1149; H. Soly, 'De aluinhandel in de Nederlanden in de 16e eeuw', *Belgisch tijdschrift voor filologie en geschiedenis*, 52 (1974), pp. 800–57, on p. 803.

65.   W. Brulez, 'Bruges and Antwerp in the 15th and 16th Centuries: An Antithesis?', *Acta historiae Neerlandica*, 6 (1973), pp. 1–26; P. Spufford, 'From Antwerp and Amsterdam to London: The Decline of Financial Centres in Europe', *De Economist*, 154:2 (2006), pp. 143–75.

66.   H. Van der Wee, 'Trade in the Southern Netherlands, 1493–1587', trans. L. Fackelman, in H. Van der Wee (ed.), *In The Low Countries in the Early Modern World* (Aldershot: Ashgate, 1993), ch. 5, pp. 87–114.

67.   F. Edler, 'The Market for Spices in Antwerp, 1538–1544', *Revue belge de philologie et d'histoire*, 17 (1938), pp. 212–21.

68.   J. A. Goris, *Etude sur les colonies marchandes méridionales (Portugais, Espagnols, Italiens) à Anvers De 1488 À 1587* (Leuven: Uytspruyt, 1925), pp. 317–37. My own calculations in: J. Puttevils, 'A Servitio De Vostri Sempre Siamo. De Effecten Van De Handel Tussen Antwerpen En Italië Op De Koopmansfamilie Van Der Molen' (MA thesis, University of Antwerp, 2007).

69.   W. Brulez, 'The Balance of Trade of the Netherlands in the Middle of the 16th Century', *Acta historiae Neerlandica*, 4 (1970), pp. 20–48.

70.   Slootmans, *Paas- en Koudemarkten*, vol. 1, pp. 1556–70; Kortlever, 'The Easter and Cold Fairs'; Van Houtte, 'Les Foires', pp. 194–6.

71.   V. Enthoven, 'The Closure of the Scheldt: Closure, What Closure? Trade and Shipping in the Scheldt Estuary, 1559–1609', in P. Holm and J. Edwards (ed.), *North Sea Ports and Harbours: Adaptations to Change: Second North Sea History Conference, Esbjerg* (Esbjerg: Fiskeri- og Søfartsmuseet, 1992) and the thematic issue of *Tijdschrift voor geschiedenis*, 4 (2010). 'Stad en stroom: Antwerpse identiteit(en) en vijf eeuwen discours rond de sluiting van de Schelde'.

72.   W. Brulez, 'De diaspora der Antwerpse kooplui op het einde van de 16e eeuw', *Bijdragen tot de geschiedenis*, 15 (1960), pp. 279–306; O. Gelderblom, *Zuid-Nederlandse kooplieden en de opkomst van de Amsterdamse stapelmarkt (1578–1630)* (Hilversum: Verloren, 2000).

73.   W. Brulez, 'Anvers de 1585 à 1650', *Vierteljahresschrift für Sozial- und Wirtschaftsgeschichte*, 54:1 (1967), pp. 75–95; R. Baetens, *De nazomer van Antwerpens welvaart: de diaspora en het handelshuis De Groote tijdens de eerste helft der 17de eeuw*, 2 vols (Brussels: Gemeentekrediet, 1976).

1 Antwerp, its Merchants and their Trade

1.   This chapter is partially based on: J. Puttevils, '"Eating the Bread out of their Mouth": Antwerp's Export Trade and Generalized Institutions, 1544–1545', *Economic History Review* (forthcoming 2015).

2.   H. Van der Wee, *The Growth of the Antwerp Market and the European Economy (Fourteenth–Sixteenth Centuries)*, 3 vols (Den Haag: Nijhoff, 1963), vol. 2, pp. 191–2, 317–32 ; O. Gelderblom, *Zuid-Nederlandse kooplieden en de opkomst van de Amsterdamse stapelmarkt (1578–1630)* (Hilversum: Verloren, 2000), pp. 46–7.

3.   S. Ogilvie, *Institutions and European Trade: Merchant Guilds, 1000–1800* (Cambridge: Cambridge University Press, 2011); O. Gelderblom, *Cities of Commerce: The Institutional Foundations of International Trade in the Low Countries, 1250–1650* (Princeton,

NJ: Princeton University Press, 2013); S. Ogilvie and A. W. Carus, 'Institutions and Economic Growth in Historical Perspective', in A. Philippe and N. Durlauf Steven (eds), *Handbook of Economic Growth* (Amsterdam: Elsevier, 2014), ch. 8, pp. 403–513; Puttevils, '"Eating the Bread out of Their Mouth"'.

4. L. Guicciardini, *Descrittione di tutti i Paesi Bassi, altrimenti detti Germania Inferiore* (Anversa: apresso Guglielmo Silvio, 1567), pp. 155–6; L. Guicciardini and B. Aristodemo, *Descrittione di tutti i Paesi Bassi: edizione critica* (Amsterdam: Universiteit van Amsterdam, 1994), pp. 277–8.

5. R. Doehaerd, *Etudes anversoises: documents sur le commerce international à Anvers, 1488–1514*, 3 vols (Paris: SEVPEN, 1962–63); G. Asaert, 'De oudste certificatiën van de stad Antwerpen (1468–1482)', *Handelingen van de Koninklijke Commissie voor Geschiedenis*, 132 (1966), pp. 261–96. There are separate ledgers of certificates for the years: 1488–94, 1505–9, 1512, 1542, 1544–7, 1550–60, 1552–73 and 1575–1614. Felixarchief, CERT # 1–74. Series of certificates can also be found in other cities: Bergen-op-Zoom, Ghent, Bruges and even rural Deurne. A certificate cost eight stivers in 1558. H. Soly, 'Een Antwerpse compagnie voor de levensmiddelenbevoorrading van het leger in de zestiende eeuw', *Bijdragen en mededelingen betreffende de geschiedenis der Nederlanden*, 186 (1971), pp. 350–62, on p. 353, n. 318. For translations into French, Latin or Spanish (catering to the needs of foreigners), this fee was doubled. 'Ordonnantie ende Verhael vanden Stijl ende Maniere van Procederen 1532' (vanden secretarisse ende heure clercken). This text is published in F. H. Mertens, K. L. Torfs and O. Rederykkamer de, *Geschiedenis van Antwerpen sedert de stichting der stad tot onze tyden* (Antwerp: Van Dieren, 1845), II, pp. 600–84, available online at http://www.kuleuven-kortrijk.be/facult/rechten/Monballyu/Rechtlagelanden/Brabantsrecht/antwerpen/style.html [accessed 28 February 2015]. We are referring to the article 'vanden secretarisse ende heure clercken' on pp. 657–61. Another edition can be found in: G. de Longé, *Coutumes du Pays et Duché de Brabant: quartier d'Anvers* (Brussels: Gobbaerts, 1870); D. De ruysscher, *Handel en recht in de Antwerpse rechtbank (1585–1713)* (Leuven: UGA, 2009), pp. 101–2; F. Blockmans et al., *Inventaris der schepenregisters, 'Collectanen', 'Certificatieboeken' en 'Coopers en Comparanten'* (Antwerp: Stadsarchief Antwerpen, 1948).

6. O. Gelderblom, *Cities of Commerce: The Institutional Foundations of International Trade in the Low Countries, 1250–1650* (Princeton, NJ: Princeton University Press, 2013), pp. 90–1.

7. Renée Doehaerd summarized all certificates and aldermen's acts with references to 'international trade' between 1488 and 1513. Doehaerd, *Etudes anversoises*, pp. 17–18. Doehaerd's selection criteria are: (1) all certificates with references to foreigners doing business in Antwerp (from abroad); (2) all certificates with references to Low Countries merchants active abroad; (3) documents with references to distribution and consumption of foreign goods in the Netherlands; and (4) documents with references to distribution and consumption of Low Countries products abroad. See also H. Van der Wee, 'Doehaerd (Renée). Etudes anversoises. Documents sur le commerce international à Anvers, 1488–1514', *Revue belge de philologie et d'histoire*, 43:2 (1965), pp. 671–4.

8. Doehaerd, *Etudes anversoises*.

9. For these years the highest amount of certifications and aldermen's deeds could be found in Doehaerd, *Etudes anversoises*.

10. Brokers, inn-keepers, agents, etc. Shipmasters and waggoners are excluded.

11. 1492: foreign merchants: Italy: 13; Portugal: 3; France: 2; Spain: 18; Germany: 26; Eng-

land: 7; 1512: foreign merchants: Italy: 17; France: 12; Spain: 4; Germany: 37; England: 7.

12. CAA, Notarial archives, notary Zeger Adriaan 's-Hertoghen, N # 2071. N=100 deeds. Foreign merchants: Italy: 15; Portugal: 3; France: 30; Spain: 35; Germany: 43; England and Scotland: 23; total foreign merchants: 147; Low Countries: 88. Those of Willem Stryt are not representative since he mainly catered a Spanish merchant clientele in 1540. R. Fagel, *De Hispano-Vlaamse wereld: de contacten tussen Spanjaarden en Nederlanders, 1496–1555* (Brussels: Archief- en Bibliotheekwezen in België, 1996), pp. 71–3.

13. The accounts of these taxes are preserved. ARB, Rekenkamer, Hundredth Penny export tax, 1543–5, 23357–64. The registers have been used by several historians. J.-A. Goris, *Etude sur les colonies marchandes méridionales (Portugais, Espagnols, Italiens) à Anvers de 1488 à 1587* (Leuven: Uytspruyt, 1925); W. Brulez, *De firma Della Faille en de internationale handel van Vlaamse firma's in de 16de eeuw* (Brussels: Paleis der Academiën, 1959); D. J. Harreld, *High Germans in the Low Countries: German Merchants and Commerce in Golden Age Antwerp* (Leiden: Brill, 2004); J. Puttevils, 'A servitio de vostri sempre siamo. De effecten van de handel tussen Antwerpen en Italië op de koopmansfamilie Van der Molen' (MA thesis, University of Antwerp, 2007); J. Puttevils, 'Klein gewin brengt rijkdom in: de Zuid-Nederlandse handelaars in de export naar Italië in de jaren 1540', *Tijdschrift voor sociale en economische geschiedenis*, 6:1 (2009), pp. 26–52.; W. Brulez, 'L'exportation des Pays-Bas vers l'Italie par voie de terre au milieu du XVIe siècle', *Annales. Economies, Sociétés, Civilisations*, 14:3 (1959), pp. 461–91; F. Vermeylen, 'De export vanuit de Zuidelijke Nederlanden naar Duitsland omstreeks het midden van de 16de eeuw' (MA thesis, Catholic University of Louvain, 1989); C. Lesger, *The Rise of the Amsterdam Market and Information Exchange: Merchants, Commercial Expansion and Change in the Spatial Economy of the Low Countries, c.1550–1630* (Aldershot: Ashgate, 2006); L. Bril, 'De handel tussen de Nederlanden en het Iberisch schiereiland (midden XVIe eeuw)' (Ghent: Universiteit Gent, 1962); N. W. Posthumus, *De uitvoer van Amsterdam, 1543–1545* (Leiden: Brill, 1971).

14. H. Van der Wee, 'Handel in de Zuidelijke Nederlanden', in *Nieuwe Algemene Geschiedenis der Nederlanden* (Haarlem: Fibula-Van Dishoeck, 1978), pp. 75–95; Van der Wee, *The Growth of the Antwerp Market*, vol. 2, pp. 177–83.

15. See table I.8.

16. ARB, Rekenkamer, 23469–74. The original Antwerp tax ledger for the years 1553–4 can be found in ARB, Rekenkamer, Cartons, carton n° 326, see L. Van der Essen, 'Contribution à l'histoire du port d'Anvers 1553–1554', *Bulletin de l'Académie Royale de la Belgique*, 3 (1920), pp. 39–58. Van der Essen counts 284 Iberian, 187 Low Countries and seventeen Italian traders.

17. J. Craeybeckx, 'De organisatie en de konvooiering van de koopvaardijvloot op het einde van de regering van Karel V: bijdrage tot de geschiedenis van de scheepvaart en de Admiraliteit', *Bijdragen voor de geschiedenis der Nederlanden*, 3:3–4 (1949), pp. 179–208; Bril, 'De handel', p. 9. Our numbers are based on Bril.

18. See table I.8.

19. Published in: D. van Papenbroeck, *Annales antverpienses ab urbe condita ad annum 1700 collecti ex ipsius civitatis monumentis*, 5 vols (Antwerp: Buschmann, 1845), vol. 3, pp. 384–94. See also H. Soly, *Urbanisme en kapitalisme te Antwerpen in de 16de eeuw: de stedebouwkundige en industriële ondernemingen van Gilbert van Schoonbeke* (Brussels: Gemeentekrediet, 1977), p. 430; H. De Smedt, 'Antwerpen en de opbloei van de Vlaamse verhandel tijdens de 16e Eeuw. Rijkdom en inkomen van de Antwerpse koopman Jan Gamel volgens zijn staat van goed, 1572' (Leuven, Katholieke Universiteit

Leuven, 1970), pp. 54–5.

20. We selected sixty-eight lenders who could be clearly identified as Low Countries merchants drawing on our own archival research and the overview of the available literature.

21. Published as F. J. Van den Branden, 'De Spaansche Muiterij ten jare 1574', *Antwerpsch Archievenblad*, 22, pp. 133–480; G. Marnef, *Antwerp in the Age of Reformation: Underground Protestantism in a Commercial Metropolis, 1550–1577* (Baltimore, MD: Johns Hopkins University Press, 1996), pp. 29–31; O. Gelderblom, *Zuid-Nederlandse kooplieden en de opkomst van de Amsterdamse stapelmarkt (1578–1630)* (Hilversum: Verloren, 2000), p. 45.

22. Gelderblom, *Zuid-Nederlandse Kooplieden*, p. 45. The English merchants cannot have been that important anymore since the Merchant Adventurers had already moved their headquarters out of Antwerp. Van der Wee, *The Growth of the Antwerp Market*, vol. 2, pp. 237–8; W. E. Lingelbach, 'The Merchant Adventurers at Hamburg', *American Historical Review*, 9:2 (1904), pp. 265–87.

23. Published in F. Prims, 'De taxatie van 300 personen (24 Oktober 1579)', *Antwerpiensia*, 15 (1941), pp. 179–91.

24. The monthly loan was structured in the following way: fifteen people paid 1,000 guilders per month, twenty-five paid 400 guilders, sixty paid 200 guilders, 100 paid 100 guilders and another 100 paid fifty guilders. This would raise 52,000 guilders.

25. J. Van Roey, 'De sociale structuur en de godsdienstige gezindheid van de Antwerpse bevolking op de vooravond van de reconciliatie met Farnèse (17 Augustus 1585)' (PhD dissertation, Universiteit Gent, 1963), 83–120; 'De correlatie tussen het sociale-beroepsmilieu en de godsdienstkeuze op het einde der XVIe eeuw', in *Bronnen voor de religieuze geschiedenis van België: Middeleeuwen en Moderne Tijden, Bibliothèque de la Revue d'Histoire écclésiastique* (Leuven: Publications universitaires, 1968); Marnef, *Antwerp in the Age of Reformation*, pp. 31–4; Gelderblom, *Zuid-Nederlandse kooplieden*, pp. 45–6.

26. Included are: merchants without specification, textile merchants, grain merchants, wine merchants, traders in Spanish wares, dyestuff traders, metal merchants, jewellers, leather traders and merchants of various sorts of goods. (Gelderblom for his estimation probably excluded grain, wine and Spanish wares merchants, *Zuid-Nederlandse Kooplieden*, pp. 45–6.) Excluded are dairy merchants, fruit sellers, fish merchants, livestock sellers and salt traders since it is likely that they were retail merchants, not internationally active traders. The number of native merchants increases to 1,500 native merchants if one includes the grocers and chemists who often were trading on a wholesale level besides their retail activities.

27. Gelderblom, *Zuid-Nederlandse kooplieden*, pp. 45–6; Van Roey, 'De sociale structuur', pp. 115–18.

28. Own calculations based on Van Roey, 'De sociale structuur', Median values: 15.00 vs. 7.50 guilders.

29. W. Brulez, 'De diaspora der Antwerpse kooplui op het einde van de 16e Eeuw', *Bijdragen tot de geschiedenis*, 15 (1960), pp. 279–306.

30. J. Van Roey, *Antwerpse poortersboeken*, 6 vols (Antwerp: Stadsarchief, 1978), Database Dr Jan De Meester. J. De Meester, *Gastvrij Antwerpen? Arbeidsmigratie naar het zestiende-eeuwse Antwerpen: Proefschrift* (Antwerp: PhD dissertation University of Antwerp, 2011).

31. For an extensive overview of the usefulness of poortersboeken: 'De gebruiks- en meer-

waarde van poortersboeken voor historici: Antwerpen in de zestiende eeuw', *Vlaamse Stam: tijdschrift voor familiegeschiedenis*, 43:3–4 (2007), pp. 276–88, 317–31.

32. A. K. L. Thijs, 'Minderheden te Antwerpen (16de / 20ste eeuw)', in H. Soly and A. K. L. Thijs (eds), *Minderheden in Westeuropese steden (16de-20ste eeuw). Minorities in Western European Cities (Sixteenth-Twentieth Century)* (Rome: Belgisch Historisch Instituut te Rome, 1995), pp. 19–20.

33. C. Lesger, 'Migrantenstromen en economische ontwikkeling in vroegmoderne steden: nieuwe burgers in Antwerpen en Amsterdam, 1541–1655', *Stadsgeschiedenis*, 2 (2006), pp. 97–121; De Meester, *Gastvrij Antwerpen?*, pp. 117–22.

34. De Meester, *Gastvrij Antwerpen?*, pp. 124–5.

35. Included are those persons who were registered as exercising the following occupations: merchants, buyers of certain products and jewellers. Grocers and chemists are also selected because they often were active in wholesale international operations as well. Gelderblom, *Zuid-Nederlandse kooplieden*, p. 40, n. 15.

36. Van der Wee, *The Growth of the Antwerp Market*, vol. 2, pp. 222–32.

37. Van der Wee, *The Growth of the Antwerp Market*, vol. 2, pp. 177–86.

38. Gelderblom, *Zuid-Nederlandse kooplieden*, pp. 40–1.

39. De Meester, *Gastvrij Antwerpen?*, p. 126. Gelderblom arrives at the same findings in: Gelderblom, *Zuid-Nederlandse kooplieden*, pp. 40–4.

40. J. A. Van Houtte, 'Quantitative Quellen zur Geschichte des Antwerpener Handels', *Beiträge zur Wirtschafts- und Stadtgeschichte. Festschrift für Hektor Amman* (1965), pp. 193–204.

41. H. Van der Wee, *The Growth of the Antwerp Market and the European Economy (Fourteenth–Sixteenth Centuries)*, 3 vols (Den Haag: Nijhoff, 1963), vol. 2, pp. 132, 225–7, 323–4; H. Van der Wee, 'Structural Changes and Specialization in the Industry of the Southern Netherlands, 1100–1600', *Economic History Review*, 28:2 (1975), pp. 203–21; Van der Wee, *The Growth of the Antwerp Market and the European Economy*, vol. 2, pp. 336–44.

42. The next sections are partially based on J. Puttevils, '"Eating the Bread out of their Mouth": Antwerp's Export Trade and Generalized Institutions, 1544–1545', *Economic History Review* (forthcoming 2015).

43. See also: V. Enthoven, 'The Closure of the Scheldt: Closure, What Closure? Trade and Shipping in the Scheldt Estuary, 1559–1609', in P. Holm and J. Edwards (eds), *North Sea Ports and Harbours: Adaptations to Change: Second North Sea History Conference, Esbjerg* (Esbjerg: Fiskeri- og Søfartsmuseet, 1992), pp. 11–37.

44. The original tax accounts for Arnemuiden, Middelburg and Veere are published in W. S. Unger, *Bronnen tot de geschiedenis van Middelburg in den landsheerlijken tijd*, 3 vols ('s-Gravenhage: Nijhoff, 1931), vol. 3. We used the destination data for Amsterdam and Dordrecht from C. Lesger, *The Rise of the Amsterdam Market and Information Exchange: Merchants, Commercial Expansion and Change in the Spatial Economy of the Low Countries, c.1550–1630* (Aldershot: Ashgate, 2006), p. 29.

45. Lesger, *The Rise of the Amsterdam Market*, p. 42.

46. Counted together the share of the North Sea harbours of Gravelines, Duinkerke, Oostende and Nieuwpoort (0.56 per cent) is small but notable.

47. J. A. Goris, *Etude sur les colonies marchandes méridionales (Portugais, Espagnols, Italiens) à Anvers de 1488 à 1587* (Leuven: Uytspruyt, 1925), pp. 325–8.

48. O. de Smedt, *De Engelse Natie te Antwerpen in de 16e eeuw (1496–1582)*, 2 vols (Antwerp: Sikkel, 1954), vol. 1, pp. 441.

49. D. J. Harreld, *High Germans in the Low Countries: German Merchants and Commerce in Golden Age Antwerp* (Leiden: Brill, 2004), pp. 129, 136.

50. On Nördlingen: C. R. Friedrichs, *Urban Society in an Age of War: Nördlingen, 1580–1720* (Princeton, NJ: Princeton University Press, 1979).

51. Harreld, *High Germans*, pp. 135–9, 156–68.

52. Lesger, *The Rise of the Amsterdam Market*, p. 29.

53. First, we used the precise valuations in monetary value of the commodities (67.83 per cent of the dataset); one pack of kerseys worth £100 Fl. gr. for example. Second, we used instances of commodity categories (full dataset); the abovementioned party of mixed goods is split up in references to English kerseys, sugar and Hondschote sayes.

54. Lesger, *The Rise of the Amsterdam Market*, p. 33.

55. A very light twilled woollen fabric. W. Brulez, *De firma Della Faille en de internationale handel van Vlaamse firma's in de 16de eeuw* (Brussels: Paleis der Academiën, 1959), pp. 588–91.

56. Thin, cheap English cloth. Brulez, *De firma Della Faille*.

57. Twilled woollen fabric. Brulez, *De firma Della Faille*.

58. Mixed fabric with a silk warp and a woollen weft. Brulez, *De firma Della Faille*.

59. Mixed fabric with a linen warp and a cotton weft. Brulez, *De firma Della Faille*.

60. D. J. Harreld, 'Atlantic Sugar and Antwerp's Trade with Germany in the Sixteenth Century', *Journal of Early Modern History*, 7:2 (2003), pp. 148–63.

61. L. Guicciardini, *Beschryvinghe van alle de Nederlanden, anderssins ghenoemt Neder-Duytslandt* (Amsterdam: Facsimile Uitgaven Nederland, 1968), pp. 8, 92, 95–9.

62. On average, a ton of mercery goods was more expensive than a ton of herring, a ton of sugar, a bale of kerseys (around the same weight), a bale of sayes or a bale of cloth; only a bale of pepper was more expensive. Mean value of a ton of mercery goods: £22.43 Fl. gr. (N=245); a ton of herring: £3.10 Fl. gr. (N=106); a ton of sugar: £13.77 Fl. gr. (N=140); a bale of English kerseys: £16.84 Fl. gr. (N=478); a bale of Flemish sayes: £20.49 Fl. gr. (N=139); a bale of cloth: £17.58 Fl. gr. (N=546); a bale of pepper: £23.40 Fl. gr. (N=176). One bale equals one barrel: Brulez, *De firma Della Faille*, p. 475.

63. A. K. L. Thijs, *Van 'werkwinkel' tot 'fabriek': de textielnijverheid te Antwerpen, einde 15de-begin 19de eeuw* (Brussels: Gemeentekrediet, 1987), pp. 62–6, 86; A. K. L. Thijs, 'Structural Changes in the Antwerp Industry from the Fifteenth to the Eighteenth Century', in H. Van der Wee (ed.), *The Rise and Decline of Urban Industries in Italy and in the Low Countries (Late Middle Ages-Early Modern Times)* (Leuven: Leuven University Press, 1988), pp. 207–12, on p. 207; F. Vermeylen, 'De export vanuit de Zuidelijke Nederlanden naar Duitsland omstreeks het midden van de 16de eeuw' (MA thesis, Catholic University of Louvain, 1989), p. 52.

64. K. H. O'Rourke and J. G. Williamson, 'Did Vasco Da Gama Matter for European Markets?', *Economic History Review*, 62:3 (2009), pp. 655–84; F. Edler, 'The Market for Spices in Antwerp, 1538–1544', *Revue belge de philologie et d'histoire*, 17 (1938), pp. 212–21; S. H. Smith, 'A Question of Quality: The Commercial Contest between Portuguese Atlantic Spices and their Venetian Levantine Equivalents During the Sixteenth Century', *Itinerario*, 26:2 (2002), pp. 45–63.

65. Edler, 'The Market for Spices', p. 213; Smith, 'A Question of Quality'.

66. Brulez, *De firma Della Faille*, p. 417–18.

67. J. A. Van Houtte, 'Bruges et Anvers, marchés "nationaux" ou "internationaux" du XIVe au XVIe siècle', *Revue du Nord*, 34 (1952), pp. 89–108; J. A. Van Houtte, 'The Rise and

Decline of the Market of Bruges', *Economic History Review*, 19:1 (1966), pp. 89–108; W. Brulez, 'The Balance of Trade of the Netherlands in the Middle of the 16th Century', *Acta historiae Neerlandica*, 4 (1970), pp. 20–48; E. S. Hunt and J. M. Murray, *A History of Business in Medieval Europe, 1200–1550* (Cambridge: Cambridge University Press, 1999), p. 146; P. Stabel, 'Kooplieden in de stad', in A. Vandewalle (ed.), *Hanze-kooplui en Medicibankiers: Brugge, wisselmarkt van Europese culturen* (Oostkamp: Stichting Kunstboek, 2002), p. 85.

68. ARB, Rekenkamer (Account chamber): 2 per cent import and export tax, 23469–74 (1552–3). The original Antwerp tax ledger for the years 1553–4 can be found in Rekenkamer, Cartons, carton n° 326, see L. Van der Essen, 'Contribution à l'histoire du port d'Anvers 1553–1554', *Bulletin de l'Académie Royale de la Belgique*, 3 (1920), pp. 39–58. Van der Essen counts 284 Iberian, 187 Low Countries and seventeen Italian traders. This tax is analysed in L. Bril, *De handel tussen de Nederlanden en het Iberisch schiereiland (midden XVIe eeuw)* (Ghent: University of Ghent, 1962).

69. J. Craeybeckx, 'De organisatie en de konvooiering van de koopvaardijvloot op het einde van de regering van Karel V: bijdrage tot de geschiedenis van de scheepvaart en de Admiraliteit', *Bijdragen voor de geschiedenis der Nederlanden*, 3:3–4 (1949), pp. 179–208; Bril, 'De Handel', p. 9.

70. Bril, 'De handel', pp. 146–7.

71. E. Sabbe, *De Belgische vlasnijverheid. Deel 1: De Zuid-Nederlandse vlasnijverheid tot het Verdrag van Utrecht (1713)* (Kortrijk: Nationaal Vlasmuseum, 1975), pp. 171–5.

72. Bril, 'De handel', pp. 146–7.

73. Other types of linen that are mentioned in the 2 per cent tax registers are in declining order of magnitude: Brabant, Hainaut, canvas, Herentals, grey or white, Flemish, grey linen from Bruges, bokraal, Bruges, 's Hertogenbosch, Ghent, grey linen from Ghent, grey linen from Rouen, toilettes, damask linen, gold linen, Augsburg, Ghent canvas, Cambrai linen, and Rouen bokralen. Bril, 'De handel'.

74. Based on own calculations deduced from Sabbe, *De Belgische vlasnijverheid*, p. 263.

75. Sabbe, *De Belgische vlasnijverheid*, pp. 261–6.

76. Sabbe, *De Belgische vlasnijverheid*, p. 267.

77. Total value of £27,901 Fl. gr. Sabbe, *De Belgische vlasnijverheid*, pp. 249–54.

78. W. Brulez, 'De handelsbalans in het midden van de 16de eeuw', *Bijdragen voor de geschiedenis der Nederlanden*, 21 (1967), pp. 278–310, on p. 300.

79. Sabbe, *De Belgische vlasnijverheid*, pp. 254–61. In April 1543 five Low Countries (and Antwerp-based) merchants were exporting linen to England: Lodewijk Ferraryn, Ghijsbrecht van Oudenhove, Jan van Immerzele, Jacob van Zwijndrecht and Daen van Clermont.

80. M. Boone, 'Les toiles de lin des Pays-Bas bourguignons sur le marché anglais (fin XIVe -XVIe siècles)', in J.-M. Cauchies (ed.), *L'Angleterre et les Pays bourguignons: relations et comparaisons (XVe-XVIe s.)': rencontres d'Oxford (22 au 25 septembre 1994). Publication du Centre européen d'études bourguignonnes (XIVe-XVIe s.)* (Neuchâtel: Centre européen d'études bourguignonnes (XIVe-XVIe s.), 1995), pp. 61–81, on p. 76 citing G. Asaert, *Documenten voor de geschiedenis van de Antwerpse scheepvaart voornamelijk de Engelandvaart (1404–1485)*, Collectanea Maritima (Brussels: Koninklijke Academie voor Wetenschappen, Letteren en Schone Kunsten van België. Wetenschappelijk Comité voor Maritieme Geschiedenis, 1985); H. S. Cobb, *The Overseas Trade of London. Exchequer Customs Accounts 1480–81*, (London: London Record Society Publications, 1990).

81. L. Stone, 'Elizabethan Overseas Trade', *Economic History Review*, 2:1 (1949), pp. 30–58, on p. 38 cited in E. Thoen, *Landbouwekonomie en bevolking in Vlaanderen gedurende de late Middeleeuwen en het begin van de Moderne Tijden: Testregio: De kasselrijen van Oudenaarde en Aalst (eind 13de-eerste helft 16de eeuw)* (Ghent: Belgisch Centrum voor Landelijke Geschiedenis, 1988), p. 982. In 1551–2 Ghent linen proved especially important in the English import trade. De Smedt, *De Engelse Natie*, vol. 2, pp. 416–17.

82. Database Hundredth Penny 1544 by author.

83. Sabbe, *De Belgische vlasnijverheid*, p. 268; Harreld, *High Germans*.

84. Based on Bril, 'De handel', p. 165; E. Coornaert, *La draperie-sayetterie d'Hondschoote, 14–18ième siècle. Un centre industriel d'autrefois* (Paris: PUF, 1930), p. 493.

85. Bril, 'De handel', p. 58.

86. Exports amounted to 3,168,938 guilders, imports to 2,395,870 guilders.

87. Brulez, 'The Balance of Trade', p. 48.

88. W. Brulez, *De firma Della Faille en de internationale handel van Vlaamse firma's in de 16de eeuw* (Brussels: Paleis der Academiën, 1959), p. 369; H. Van der Wee, *The Growth of the Antwerp Market and the European Economy (Fourteenth–Sixteenth Centuries)*, 3 vols (Den Haag: Nijhoff, 1963), vol. 2, pp. 191–2, 317–32. See also: D. J. Harreld, 'German Merchants and their Trade in Sixteenth-Century Antwerp', in B. Blondé, A. Greve and P. Stabel (eds), *International Trade in the Low Countries (14th–16th Centuries): Merchants, Organisation, Infrastructure: Proceedings of the International Conference Ghent-Antwerp, 12th–13th January 1997* (Leuven: Garant, 2000), pp. 169–91, on pp. 182–3; B. Blondé, O. Gelderblom and P. Stabel, 'Foreign Merchant Communities in Bruges, Antwerp and Amsterdam', in D. Calabi and S. T. Christensen (eds), *Cities and Cultural Exchange in Europe, 1400–1700*, Cultural Exchange in Early Modern Europe (Cambridge: Cambridge University Press, 2007), pp. 154–74, on pp. 165–6.

89. E. M. Carus-Wilson and O. Coleman, *England's Export Trade, 1275–1547* (Oxford: Clarendon, 1963), pp. 74, 118–19.

90. R. Gascon, *Grand commerce et vie urbaine au 16e siècle: Lyon et ses marchands (environs de 1520–environs de 1580)* (Paris: Mouton, 1971), pp. 203–4.

91. A one-way ANOVA analysis of variance test results in a 18.80 F-ratio and a p-value significant at the 99 per cent level, indicating that the means of the export value per merchant per merchant group are different.

92. Data from John Munro: http://www.economics.utoronto.ca/munro5/AntwerpWage. xls. Blondé and Hanus point out the unrepresentativeness of builders' wage. 's-Hertogenbosch masons were spread over the entire social spectrum and in the sixteenth century they descended in the fiscal hierarchy. B. Blondé and J. Hanus, 'Beyond Building Craftsmen. Economic Growth and Living Standards in the Sixteenth-Century Low Countries: The Case of 'S-Hertogenbosch (1500–1560)', *European Review of Economic History*, 14:2 (2009), pp. 179–207.

93. J. Hanus, 'Real Inequality in the Early Modern Low Countries: The City of 'S-Hertogenbosch, 1500–1660', *Economic History Review*, 66:3 (2012), pp. 733–56; J. Hanus, 'Affluence and Inequality in the Low Countries. The City of 'S-Hertogenbosch in the Long Sixteenth Century, 1500–1650' (PhD dissertation, Universiteit Antwerpen, 2010).

94. D. J. Harreld, *High Germans in the Low Countries: German Merchants and Commerce in Golden Age Antwerp* (Leiden: Brill, 2004), pp. 140, 152–3, 160–141.

95. In the 1 per cent tax registers he is always referred to as Putchinger while in other sources

and the work of Donald Harreld his name is spelled slightly differently (Puschinger).

96. Harreld, *High Germans*, pp. 73–4, 85.

97. B. d' Ursel, *Les Schetz* (Brussels: Office généalogique et héraldique de Belgique, 2004);
P. Génard, 'Un acte de société commerciale au XVIième siècle (La maison Schetz
frères d'Anvers)', *Bulletin de la Société de Géographie d'Anvers*, 7 (1882), pp. 475–99;
J. L. Meulleners, *De Antwerpsche bankier Erasmus Schetz en zijne geassocieërden Jan
Vleminck en Arnold Proenen in hunne betrekking tot Maastricht en Aken* (Maastricht: Le
Courrier de la Meuse, 1890); F. Prims, 'Erasmus Schetz in 1525–1532', *Antwerpiensia*,
13 (1939), pp. 63–9.

98. Regions are: England; France; Italy; the Liège region; North, Central and South
Germany; and the Iberian Peninsula. Export values per region are used as segment sizes.
The results are similar when references to commodity categories, not taxed values, are
used: 72 per cent of all exporters are entirely undiversified.

99. N. Zahedieh, *The Capital and the Colonies: London and the Atlantic Economy,
1660–1700* (Cambridge: Cambridge University Press, 2010), pp. 103, 286.

100. Linear regression between log total export value and each's merchant's Berry–Herfindahl–geographical diversification index is statistically significant at the 99 per cent level,
yet reports a low R^2 (0.0721). The results remain the same when references to commodity categories, not taxed values, are used: $R^2 = 0.0372$.

101. A linear regression between the log total export value and the log maximum distance
between Antwerp and commodity destination gives an R^2 of 0.2634 and a statistically
significant (at 99 per cent) coefficient. For export by sea, there was no relationship
between a merchant's total export value and the maximum maritime distance from
Antwerp; a linear regression between the log total export value and the log maximum
distance between Antwerp and commodity destination gives an R^3 of 0.0148. This may
have been caused by the fewer possible values for distance from Antwerp by sea (thirty
possible values vs. seventy for transport over land).

102. H. Van der Wee, 'Industrial Dynamics and the Process of Urbanization and De-Urbanization in the Low Countries from the Late Middle Ages to the Eighteenth Century.
A Synthesis', in H. Van der Wee (ed.), *The Rise and Decline of Urban Industries in Italy
and in the Low Countries (Late Middle Ages-Early Modern Times)* (Leuven: Leuven
University Press, 1988), pp. 307–88, on pp. 337–8; O. Gelderblom, *Zuid-Nederlandse
kooplieden en de opkomst van de Amsterdamse stapelmarkt (1578–1630)* (Hilversum:
Verloren, 2000), pp. 46–8; H. Van der Wee, 'From Antwerp to Amsterdam: The Con-
tribution of Merchants from the Southern Netherlands to the Rise of the Amsterdam
Market', *Review. A Journal of the Fernand Braudel Center for the Study of Economies,
Historical Systems, and Civilizations*, 26:3 (2003), pp. 247–82.

103. Ratios for the other goods are: canvas 50 per cent transit, copper 80 per cent transit,
frisé cloth 60 per cent, silk cloth 90 per cent and leather 20 per cent.

104. German traders: 28.12 per cent; French merchants: 32.70 per cent; Iberian merchants:
31.47 per cent of their exports are Low Countries products. A one-way ANOVA test
on the percentage of Low Countries products exported by each merchant of commercial groups (German, Italian, Low Countries, Iberian) provides no significant evidence
for different preferences.

105. This issue will be dealt with in more detail in the next chapter.

106. CAA, Certification Books, 3, 1509, 155v; CAA, Certification Books, 3, 1510, 70v.

107. State Archive Antwerp (SAA), Notaries, Notarial acts of Jacobus de Platea, 521,
1518–41, 167–167v; State Archive Antwerp (SAA), Notaries, Notarial acts of Jacobus
de Platea, 521, 1518–41, 185–185v.

108. F. Edler, 'The Van Der Molen, Commission Merchants of Antwerp: Trade with Italy, 1538–44', in J. L. Cate and E. N. Anderson (eds), *Medieval and Historiographical Essays in Honour of James Westfall Thompson* (Chicago, IL: University of Chicago Press, 1938), pp. 78–145; J. Puttevils, 'A servitio de vostri sempre siamo. De effecten van de handel tussen Antwerpen en Italië op de koopmansfamilie Van der Molen' (MA thesis, University of Antwerp, 2007).

109. Linear regressions of log total export value and the percentage of transit/Low Countries products exported by a merchant yield a very low (0.0208) R^2. Within the subsample of Low Countries traders an even lower R^2 is reported (0.0076).

110. Export values per product category are used as segment sizes. There are twenty-six product categories. See table 1.2.

111. The results are similar when references to commodity categories, not taxed values, are used: the mean Berry–Herfindahl index is higher, 0.2739. Fifty-three per cent of all exporters only exports one category of commodities.

112. Not more than 0.2 product categories. Difference of means of two samples with unequal variances tests on the number of product categories exported by Low Countries traders and Italians to Italy report a -0.08 t-test statistic and a 0.93 p-value; Low Countries and German exporters to south Germany: -0.16 t-test statistic, 0.87 p-value; Low Countries and German exporters to central Germany: -0.46 t-test statistic, 0.65 p-value. The results remain the same when references to commodity categories, not taxed values, are used: Low Countries and Italian exporters to Italy: 0.04 t-test statistic, 0.97 p-value; Low Countries and German exporters to south Germany: 0.07 t-test statistic, 0.94 p-value; Low Countries and German exporters to central Germany: -0.94 t-test statistic, 0.36 p-value.

113. Difference of means of two samples with unequal variances tests on the number of product categories exported by Low Countries traders and Italians to England report a 2.25 t-test statistic and a 0.03 p-value. The results are similar when references to commodity categories, not taxed values, are used: 2.12 t-test statistic and a 0.04 p-value.

114. French traders (N=159) mean = 2.327 product categories vs. Low Countries traders (N=49) mean = 1.286, t-test statistic 3.51, p-value 0.00. The results remain the same when references to commodity categories, not taxed values, are used: French traders (N=261) mean = 3.261 product categories vs. Low Countries traders (N=82) mean = 2.927; t-test statistic 0.83, p-value 0.41.

115. Linear regression between number of product categories (Lesger classification) and the log total export value gives an R^2 of 0.2612; a second linear regression between the diversification index and the log total export value provides an R^2 of 0.1318. Similar results are obtained when references to commodity categories, not taxed values, are used: linear regression between number of product categories (Lesger classification) and the log total number of shipments per exporter gives an R^2 of 0.7085; a second linear regression between the diversification index and the log total number of shipments provides an R^2 of 0.5117.

116. $R^2 = 0.0782$. W. Brulez, *De firma Della Faille en de internationale handel van Vlaamse firma's in de 16de eeuw* (Brussels: Paleis der Academiën, 1959), pp. 479–85.

117. Brulez, *De firma Della Faille*, p. 477; D. J. Harreld, *High Germans in the Low Countries: German Merchants and Commerce in Golden Age Antwerp* (Leiden: Brill, 2004), p. 169.

118. G. D. Ramsay, *The City of London in International Politics at the Accession of Elizabeth Tudor* (Manchester: Manchester University Press, 1975); R. Brenner, *Merchants and Revolution: Commercial Change, Political Conflict, and London's Overseas Traders, 1550–1653* (Princeton, NJ: Princeton University Press, 1993), pp. 8–11

119. Brulez, *De firma Della Faille*, pp. 391–3.
120. P. Black, T. Hartzenberg and B. Standish, *Economics: Principles & Practice. A Southern African Perspective*, 2 edn (Cape Town: Pearson Education, 2000), pp. 163–4, cited in J. Hanus, 'Affluence and Inequality in the Low Countries. The City of 'S-Hertogenbosch in the Long Sixteenth Century, 1500–1650' (PhD dissertation, Universiteit Antwerpen, 2010), p. 191; O. Gelderblom, 'Entrepreneurs in the Golden Age of the Dutch Republic', in W. J. Baumol, D. S. Landes and J. Mokyr (eds), *The Invention of Enterprise: Entrepreneurship from Ancient Mesopotamia to Modern Times*, (Princeton, NJ: Princeton University Press, 2010), ch. 6, pp. 156–82, on pp. 156–7.
121. H. Van der Wee, 'Industrial Dynamics and the Process of Urbanization and De-Urbanization in the Low Countries from the Late Middle Ages to the Eighteenth Century. A Synthesis', in H. Van der Wee (ed.), *The Rise and Decline of Urban Industries in Italy and in the Low Countries (Late Middle Ages-Early Modern Times)* (Leuven: Leuven University Press, 1988), pp. 307–88, on pp. 337–8.
122. Some very fragmentary data can be found in W. Brulez, *De firma Della Faille en de internationale handel van Vlaamse firma's in de 16de eeuw* (Brussels: Paleis der Academiën, 1959), passim. Consistent series of price differential data are only available for grain. See the recent V. N. Bateman, 'The Evolution of Markets in Early Modern Europe, 1350–1800: A Study of Wheat Prices', *Economic History Review*, 64:2 (2011), pp. 447–71. The classic study is of grain price market integration is K. G. Persson, *Grain Markets in Europe, 1500–1900: Integration and Deregulation* (Cambridge: Cambridge University Press, 1999).
123. E. J. Hamilton, *American Treasure and the Price Revolution in Spain, 1501–1650* (New York: Octagon Books, 1965), available at http://www.iisg.nl/hpw/data.php#spain [accessed 28 February 2015]. H. Van der Wee, *The Growth of the Antwerp Market and the European Economy (Fourteenth–Sixteenth Centuries)*, 3 vols (Den Haag: Nijhoff, 1963), vol. 1, pp. 275–6.
124. R. Fagel, 'De koopmansboeken van Juan Bautista de Olanda: een Nederlandse koopman in Medina del Campo 1565–1566', *Archief- en bibliotheekwezen in België*, 1–4 (1997), pp. 265–311.
125. Jan Vleminck from Maastricht was a family member and partner of the Schetz family. J. L. Meulleners, *De Antwerpsche bankier Erasmus Schetz en zijne geassocieërden Jan Vleminck en Arnold Proenen in hunne betrekking tot Maastricht en Aken* (Maastricht: Le Courrier de la Meuse, 1890).
126. J. Materné, 'Antwerpen als verdeel- en veredelingscentrum van specerijen en suiker dan de late 15de eeuw tot de 17de eeuw', in F. De Nave (ed.), *Europa aan tafel. Een verkenning van onze eet- en tafelcultuur* (Antwerpen: MIM, 1993), p. 52; A. Poelwijk, *In dienste vant suyckerbacken: de Amsterdamse suikernijverheid en haar ondernemers, 1580–1630* (Hilversum: Verloren, 2003), pp. 37–8.
127. A. K. L. Thijs, 'De geschiedenis van de suikernijverheid te Antwerpen (16de–19de eeuw), een terreinverkenning', *Bijdragen tot de geschiedenis* 62:1–2 (1979), pp. 23–50; Poelwijk, *In dienste vant suyckerbacken*, p. 38.
128. There is a large literature on these planters: F. Donnet, 'Les anversois aux Canaries, un voyage mouvementé au XVIe siècle', *Bulletin de la Société de Géographie d'Anvers 18–19 (1895–1896)*, pp. 276–311, 202–365; F. Donnet, 'Les origines d'une entreprise commerciale anversoise aux Canaries au XVIe siècle', *Bulletin de la Société de Géographie d'Anvers (1919)*, pp. 103–10; J. Everaert, 'Vlaamse suikerbaronnen op Madeira (omstreeks 1480–1620)', in J. Everaert and E. Stols (eds), *Vlaanderen en Portugal: op de*

golfslag van twee culturen (Antwerp: Mercatorfonds, 1991), pp. 99–117; C. Verlinden, 'De Vlaamse kolonisten op de Azoren', in J. Everaert and E. Stols (eds), *Vlaanderen en Portugal: op de golfslag van twee culturen* (Antwerp: Mercatorfonds, 1991), pp. 81–97; K. Coornaert, 'De Vlaamse natie op de Canarische eilanden in de 16de eeuw' (Ghent: University of Ghent, 2000); E. Stols and W. Thomas, 'Flanders and the Canary Islands in the First Widening of the World 1450–1550', in F. J. G. Gómez, E. Stols, W. Thomas and H. Nieuwdorp (eds), *Lumen Canariense: El Cristo De La Laguna Y Su Tiempo* (San Cristóbal de La Laguna: Excmo. Ayuntamiento de San Cristóbal de La Laguna, 2003), pp. 27–50; A. Vieira, 'Sugar Islands: The Sugar Economy of Madeira and the Canaries, 1450–1650', in S. B. Schwartz (ed.), *Tropical Babylons: Sugar and the Making of the Atlantic World, 1450–1680* (Chapel Hill, NC: University of North Carolina Press, 2004), pp. 237–88.

129. On the Groenenborch family: J. Everaert, 'Marchands flamands à Lisbonne et l'exportation du sucre de Madère (1480–1530)', paper presented at the Actas do I Coloquio de Historia da Madeira, Funchal, 1986, p. 448; Donnet, 'Les Origines D'une Entreprise Commerciale'; Donnet, 'Les anversois aux Canaries'; F. Donnet, *Coup d'oeil sur l'histoire financière d'Anvers au cours des siècles* (Antwerp: Buschmann, 1927), pp. 85–6; Everaert, 'Vlaamse suikerbaronnen', p. 259.

130. Van der Wee, *The Growth of the Antwerp Market*, vol. 1, pp. 318–24; Everaert, 'Marchands flamands à Lisbonne', pp. 465–8.

131. Everaert, 'Marchands flamands à Lisbonne', p. 468.

132. Brulez, *De firma Della Faille*, pp. 24, 41, 79, 24, 41, 79. Annual merchant profit rates in Lyon ranged between 4.2 and 28.6 per cent. R. Gascon, *Grand commerce et vie urbaine au 16e siècle: Lyon et ses marchands (environs de 1520–environs de 1580)* (Paris: Mouton, 1971), II, p. 659, cited in H. Soly, *Urbanisme en kapitalisme te Antwerpen in de 16de eeuw: De stedebouwkundige en industriële ondernemingen van Gilbert van Schoonbeke* (Brussels: Gemeentekrediet, 1977), p. 314.

133. K. Degryse, *Pieter Seghers: een koopmansleven in troebele tijden* (Antwerp: Hadewijch, 1989), p. 28.

134. Compare these profit margins with Soly, *Urbanisme en kapitalisme*, pp. 313–15.

135. E. Stols, *De Spaanse Brabanders of de handelsbetrekkingen der Zuidelijke Nederlanden met de Iberische wereld, 1598–1648*, 2 vols (Brussels: Paleis der Academiën, 1971), vol. 1, pp. 81–4.

136. E. Stols, 'De Vlaamse natie te Lissabon (15de–17de eeuw)', in J. Everaert and E. Stols (eds), *Vlaanderen en Portugal: op De golfslag van twee culturen* (Antwerp: Mercatorfonds, 1991), pp. 119–41, on p. 122.

137. C. Verlinden, 'De Vlaamse kolonisten op de Azoren', in *Vlaanderen en Portugal: op de golfslag van twee culturen*, pp. 81–92.

138. O. Mus, 'De Brugse compagnie Despars op het einde van de 15de eeuw', *Handelingen van het Genootschap voor Geschiedenis: driemaandelijks tijdschrift voor de studie van geschiedenis en oudheden van Vlaanderen*, 101:1 (1964), pp. 23–89. Also J. Everaert, 'Marchands flamands à Lisbonne et l'exportation du sucre de Madère (1480–1530)', Paper presented at the Actas do I Coloquio de Historia da Madeira, Funchal, 1986.

139. Everaert, 'Marchands flamands à Lisbonne', pp. 447, 451.

140. Stols, *De Spaanse Brabanders*, vol. 1, p. 86.

141. H. Van der Wee, *The Growth of the Antwerp Market and the European Economy (Fourteenth–Sixteenth Centuries)*, 3 vols (Den Haag: Nijhoff, 1963), vol. 2, pp. 177–83; L. Bril, *De handel tussen de Nederlanden en het Iberisch schiereiland (midden XVIe Eeuw)* (Ghent: University of Ghent, 1962).

142. R. Fagel, *De Hispano-Vlaamse wereld: de contacten tussen Spanjaarden en Nederlanders, 1496–1555* (Brussels: Archief- en Bibliotheekwezen in België, 1996), pp. 212–45.

143. R. Fagel, 'De koopmansboeken van Juan Bautista de Olanda: een Nederlandse koopman in Medina del Campo 1565–1566', *Archief- en bibliotheekwezen in België*, 1–4 (1997), pp. 265–311.

144. B. Bennassar, 'Marchands flamands et Italiens à Valladolid au XVIe siècle', in H. Kellenbenz (ed.), *Fremde Kaufleute auf der Iberischen Halbinsel* (Köln: Böhlau, 1970), pp. 48–9.

145. Fagel, *De Hispano-Vlaamse wereld*, pp. 220–1; J. Ángel, S. Telechea and B. A. Bolumburu, 'Protéger et contrôler la présence et les activités des étrangers dans les villes portuaires du nord de la couronne de Castille au Moyen Âge', *Annales de Bretagne et des pays de l'Ouest*, 117:1 (2010), pp. 209–22, on p. 216.

146. F. M. Pádron, 'The Commercial World of Seville in Early Modern Times', *Journal of European Economic History*, 2:2 (1973), pp. 294–319, on p. 308.

147. A. Girard, 'Note sur les consuls étrangers en Espagne avant le Traité des Pyrénées', *Revue d'histoire moderne*, 9 (1934), pp. 120–38, on pp. 120–1; Fagel, *De Hispano-Vlaamse wereld*, pp. 263–4.

148. *De Hispano-Vlaamse wereld*, pp. 263–4.

149. E. Stols, 'Gens des Pays-Bas en Amérique espagnole aux premières siècles de la colonisation', *Bulletin de l'Institute Historique Belge de Rome*, 44 (1974), pp. 565–99, on pp. 569–70, 572; Fagel, *De Hispano-Vlaamse wereld*, pp. 267–9; E. Stols, 'De Iberische en koloniale horizonten van de handel der Nederlanden in de 16de eeuw', in F. de Nave, D. Imhof and C. Depauw (eds), *Christoffel Plantijn en de Iberische wereld = Christophe Plantin et le monde ibérique* (Antwerp: Museum Plantin-Moretus, 1992), pp. 21–42, on p. 25; J.-P. Priotti, *Bilbao et ses marchands au XVIe siècle: genèse d'une croissance* (Villeneuve d'Ascq: Presses universitaires du Septentrion, 2004), pp. 30–1.

150. K. Degryse, *Pieter Seghers: een koopmansleven in troebele tijden* (Antwerp: Hadewijch, 1989), pp. 30–1.

151. Fagel, *De Hispano-Vlaamse wereld*, p. 266–7; A. Girard, *Le commerce français à Seville et Cadix au temps des Habsbourg: contribution à L'étude du commerce étranger en Espagne aux XVIe Et XVIIIe siècles* (Paris: de Boccard, 1932), pp. 36–8, 94–6

152. Coornaert, 'De Vlaamse natie'.

153. F. Donnet, 'Les Anversois aux Canaries, un voyage mouvementé au XVIe siècle', *Bulletin de la Société de Géographie d'   Anvers 18–19 (1895–1896)*, pp. 276–311, 202–365; F. Donnet, 'Les origines d'une entreprise commerciale anversoise aux Canaries au XVIe Siècle', *Bulletin de la Société de Géographie d'Anvers (1919)*, pp. 103–10.

154. Coornaert, 'De Vlaamse natie'.

155. Stols, *De Spaanse Brabanders*, vol. 1, p. 56.

156. W. Brulez and G. Devos, *Marchands flamands à Vénise* (Brussels: Institut historique belge de Rome, 1965); J. Puttevils, 'A servitio de vostri sempre Siamo. De effecten van de handel tussen Antwerpen en Italië o p de koopmansfamilie Van der Molen' (MA thesis, University of Antwerp, 2007), pp. 187–94.

157. P. Stabel, 'Venice and the Low Countries: Commercial Contacts and Intellectual Inspirations', in B. Aikema and B. L. Brown (eds), *Renaissance Venice and the North. Crosscurrents in the Time of Bellini, Dürer and Titian* (Milan: Bompiani, 1999), pp. 30–42, on pp. 39–40, 43; P. Stabel, 'Italian Merchants and the Fairs in the Low Countries (12th–16th Centuries)', in P. Lanaro (ed.), *La pratica dello scambio. Sistemi di fiere, mercanti e città in Europa (1400–1700)* (Venice: Marsilio, 2003), pp. 131–160, on pp.

158–60. On de Hane specifically: W. Brulez, 'Maarten De Hane', *Nationaal Biografisch Woordenboek*, 1 (1964), pp. 593–6.

158. J. Puttevils, 'Klein gewin brengt rijkdom in: de Zuid-Nederlandse handelaars in de export naar Italië in de Jaren 1540', *Tijdschrift voor sociale en economische geschiedenis*, 6:1 (2009), pp. 26–52, on pp. 41–8; W. Brulez, *De firma Della Faille en de internationale handel van Vlaamse firma's in de 16de eeuw* (Brussels: Paleis der Academiën, 1959), pp. 472; Van der Wee, *The Growth of the Antwerp Market*, vol. 2, pp. 180–1; P. Earle, 'The Commercial Development of Ancona, 1479–1551', *Economic History Review*, 22:1 (1969), pp. 28–44; H. Van der Wee, 'Structural Changes in European Long-Distance Trade and Particularly in the Re-Export Trade from South to North, 1350–1750', in J. D. Tracy (ed.), *The Rise of Merchant Empires: Long-Distance Trade in the Early Modern World, 1350–1750* (Cambridge: Cambridge University Press, 1990), ch. 1, pp. 14–33, on pp. 31–2.

159. Fine woollen cloth.

160. Earle, 'Ancona'; V. Bonazzoli, 'Mercanti Lucchesi ad Ancona nel Cinquecento', in T. Fanfani and R. Mazzei (eds), *Lucca e l'Europa degli affari, secoli XV-XVII* (Lucca: Maria Pacini Fazzi Editore, 1990), pp. 75–107.

161. Germans and Low Countries traders sent respectively 90 per cent and 55 per cent of their goods to Venice (total of Venice and Ancona combined). A frequency table of merchant origins (Italians & Low Countries traders) x destination (Ancona & Venice) reports a Cramer's V of 0.304 (p-value is < 0,0001).

162. Italian and Iberian traders sent respectively 75 per cent and 92 per cent of their goods to Ancona (total of Venice and Ancona combined).

163. Puttevils, 'Klein gewin'; Stabel, 'Venice and the Low Countries'; Stabel, 'Italian Merchants'.

164. F. Edler, 'The Van Der Molen, Commission Merchants of Antwerp: Trade with Italy, 1538–44', in J. L. Cate and E. N. Anderson (eds), *Medieval and Historiographical Essays in Honour of James Westfall Thompson* (Chicago, IL: University of Chicago Press, 1938), pp. 78–145.

165. P. Lanaro, 'Reinterpreting Venetian Economic History', in P. Lanaro (ed.), *At the Centre of the Old World: Trade and Manufacturing in Venice and the Venetian Mainland 1400–1800* (Toronto, ON: Toronto University Press, 2006), pp. 16–69, on pp. 49–50; Puttevils, 'Klein Gewin'.

166. W. Brulez, 'La navigation flamande vers la Méditerranée à la fin du XVIe Siècle', *Revue belge de philologie et d'histoire*, 36 (1958), pp. 1210–42; Brulez, *De firma Della Faille*, pp. 124–84. Also: F. Braudel, *La Méditerranée et le monde méditerranéen à L'époque de Philippe II* (Paris: Colin, 1949), pp. 635–40; J. I. Israel, 'The Dutch Merchant Colonies in the Mediterranean During the Seventeenth Century', *Renaissance and Modern Studies*, 30:1 (1986), pp. 87–108; M. Van Gelder, *Trading Places: The Netherlandish Merchants in Early Modern Venice* (Leiden: Brill, 2009), pp. 9–11 and ch. 2.

167. W. Brulez, 'De diaspora der Antwerpse kooplui op het einde van de 16e eeuw', *Bijdragen tot de geschiedenis*, 15 (1960), pp. 279–306, on pp. 279–81, 300–5; Brulez and Devos, *Marchands flamands*, I, pp. xix–xxvi.

168. Van Gelder, *Trading Places*, pp. 106–10.

169. Van Gelder, *Trading Places*, p. 100.

170. F. Trivellato, *The Familiarity of Strangers: The Sephardic Diaspora, Livorno, and Cross-Cultural Trade in the Early Modern Period* (New Haven, CT: Yale University Press, 2009), pp. 70–93; R. A. Goldthwaite, *The Economy of Renaissance Florence* (Baltimore, MD: Johns Hopkins University Press, 2009), 167 sqq; J. P. Filippini, 'Les nations

à Livourne (XVIIe–XVIIIe Siècles)', in S. Cavaciocchi (ed.), *I porti come impresa economica: atti della 'Diciannovesima Settimana di Studi', 2–6 Maggio 1987* (Prato: Le Monnier, 1988).

171. M.-C. Engels, *Merchants, Interlopers, Seamen and Corsairs: The 'Flemish' Community in Livorno and Genoa (1615–1635)* (Hilversum: Verloren, 1997), passim.

172. J. Wheeler, *A Treatise of Commerce* (New York: Columbia University Press, 1931), p. 38.

173. CAA, Privilegiekamer, Engelse natie, IV, taxation list Low Countries traders in England. Cited in Brulez, *De firma Della Faille*, p. 16.

174. O. de Smedt, *De Engelse Natie te Antwerpen in de 16e eeuw (1496–1582)*, 2 vols (Antwerp: Sikkel, 1954), vol. 1, pp. 206–7; Van der Wee, *The Growth of the Antwerp Market*, vol. 2, p. 214; O. Gelderblom, 'The Organization of Long-Distance Trade in England and the Dutch Republic, 1550–1650', in O. Gelderblom (ed.) *The Political Economy of the Dutch Republic* (Farnham: Ashgate, 2009), pp. 229.

175. A. F. Sutton, 'The Merchant Adventurers of England: Their Origins and the Mercers' Company of London', *Historical Research*, 75:187 (2002), pp. 25–46; S. Ogilvie, *Institutions and European Trade: Merchant Guilds, 1000–1800* (Cambridge: Cambridge University Press, 2011).

176. See chapter two for more on Vezeleer.

177. E. Coornaert, *Anvers et le commerce parisien au 16ième siècle* (Brussel: Paleis der Academiën, 1950), pp. 6–9

178. Coornaert, *Anvers et le commerce parisien au 16ième siècle*, pp. 10–11, 22.

179. E. Coornaert, 'Le commerce de la Lorraine vu d'Anvers à la fin du XVe et au début du XVIe siècle', *Annales de l'Est*, 1 (1950), pp. 105–30.

180. J. Craeybeckx, *Un grand commerce d'importation: les vins de France aux anciens Pays-Bas (13e-16e siècle)* (Paris: SEVPEN, 1958), pp. 123–6; M. Tranchant, 'Au risque de l'étranger: un sujet majeur de gouvernance à la Rochelle à la fin du Moyen Âge', *Annales de Bretagne et des pays de l'Ouest*, 117:1 (2010), pp. 91–108; on p. 98; Brulez, 'De diaspora', pp. 285–7; J.-P. Poussou, 'Les étrangers à Bordeaux à l'époque moderne', *Annales de Bretagne et des pays de l'Ouest*, 117:1 (2010), pp. 149–64; M. Bochaca, 'Le règlement des litiges commerciaux entre bourgeois et étrangers: les juridictions pour "fait de marchandises" à Bordeaux au milieu du XVe au milieu du XVIe siècle', *Annales de Bretagne et des pays de l'Ouest*, 117:1 (2010), pp. 133–47; E. Trocmé and M. Delafosse, *Le commerce rochelais de la fin du 15e siècle au début du 17e siècle* (Paris: SEVPEN, 1952); M. A. Drost, *Documents pour servir à l'histoire du commerce des Pays-Bas avec la France jusqu'à 1585 (Bordeaux & La Rochelle)* ('s-Gravenhage: Instituut voor Nederlandse Geschiedenis, 1984); P. Benedict, 'Rouen's Foreign Trade during the Era of the Religious Wars (1560–1600)', *Journal of European Economic History*, 13:1 (1984), pp. 29–74; P. Benedict, *Rouen during the Wars of Religion* (Cambridge: Cambridge University Press, 2003).

181. Several nations present in this Mediterranean port were organized, such as the Genoese who had a consul. G. Rambert, *Histoire du commerce de Marseille* (Paris: Plon, 1949), II, p. 224 and passim.

182. J. A. van Houtte, *Die Beziehungen zwischen Köln und den Niederlanden vom Hochmittelalter bis zum Beginn des Industriezeitalters* (Köln: Universität zu Köln, 1969); H. Pohl, 'Köln und Antwerpen um 1500', *Mitteilungen aus dem Stadtarchiv von Köln*, 60 (1971), pp. 462–552; F. Irsigler, 'Köln, Die Frankfurter Messen und die Handelsbeziehungen mit Oberdeutschland Im 15. Jahrhundert', *Mitteilungen aus dem Stadtarchiv von Köln*, 60 (1971), pp. 341–430; D. J. Harreld, *High Germans in the Low Countries: German Merchants and Commerce in Golden Age Antwerp* (Leiden: Brill, 2004), pp. 29–32.

183. Harreld, *High Germans*, pp. 31–2, 129.
184. Harreld, *High Germans*, p. 135–6. A frequency table merchant origins (German & Low Countries traders) x destination (Cologne & Nuremberg) reports a Cramer's V of 0.050 (p-value is 0.014).
185. van Houtte, *Die Beziehungen zwischen Köln und den Niederlanden*.
186. C. P. F, *Paas- en Koudemarkten te Bergen-op-Zoom, 1365-1565*, 3 vols (Tilburg: Stichting Zuidelijk Historisch Contact, 1985), vol. 1, pp. 525–31, 534–6, 548–52, 594–6, 620–30.
187. F. Donnet, 'Les exilés anversois à Cologne (1582–1585)', *Bulletin de l'Académie Royale d'archéologie de Belgique* (1899), pp. 288–355; H. Thimme, 'Der Handel Kölns am Ende des 16. Jahrhunderts und die Internationale Zusammensetzung der Kölner Kaufmannschaft', *West-deutsche Zeitschrift*, 31 (1912), pp. 389 sqq.
188. Brulez, 'De diaspora', pp. 291–2. Dollinger even argues that many Low Countries merchants left Cologne again because of the cities 'conservative' commercial traditions and xenophobic mentality, but he does not substantiate this claim. P. Dollinger, *The German Hansa* (London: Macmillan, 1970), p. 355.
189. A. Dietz, *Frankfurter Handelsgeschichte*, 5 vols (Glashütten im Taunus: Auvermann, 1970), vol. 2, pp. 11–41.
190. Dietz, *Frankfurter Handelsgeschichte*, vol. 2, p. 25.
191. Brulez, 'De diaspora'. Based on: Dietz, *Frankfurter Handelsgeschichte*, vol. 2.
192. C. M. Schulz, *De invloed van het ioude Brabant op de zakencultuur van Hamburg en Frankfurt (1554–1600)* (Oosterhout: SteppingForward Uitgeverij, 2011), p. 66.
193. CAA, Privilegiekamer, Oosterlingen, Pk 1065/14 & 15. Partially reproduced in E. H. Wijnroks, *Handel tussen Rusland en de Nederlanden: een netwerkanalyse van de Antwerpse en Amsterdamse kooplieden, handelend op Rusland* (Hilversum: Verloren, 2003), p. 417.
194. Wijnroks, *Handel tussen Rusland en de Nederlanden*, pp. 21–3 and passim.
195. O. Gelderblom, *Zuid-Nederlandse kooplieden en de opkomst van de Amsterdamse stapelmarkt (1578–1630)* (Hilversum: Verloren, 2000), pp. 164–8; O. Gelderblom, 'The Governance of Early Modern Trade: The Case of Hans Thijs, 1556–1611', *Enterprise & Society*, 4:4 (2003), pp. 606–39.
196. E. Lindberg, 'Club Goods and Inefficient Institutions: Why Danzig and Lübeck Failed in the Early Modern Period', *Economic History Review*, 62:3 (2009), pp. 604–28, on p. 109; Dollinger, *The German Hansa*, pp. 360–2; Wijnroks, *Handel tussen Rusland en de Nederlanden*, p. 131.
197. Lindberg, 'Club Goods and Inefficient Institutions', p. 622.
198. E. Lindberg, 'The Rise of Hamburg as a Global Marketplace in the Seventeenth Century: A Comparative Political Economy Perspective', *Comparative Studies in Society and History*, 50:3 (2008), pp. 641–62, on p. 656.
199. On de Greve: H. Kellenbenz, *Unternehmerkräfte im Hamburger, Portugal- und Spanienhandel, 1590–1625* (Hamburg: Verlag der Hamburgischen Bücherei, 1954), pp. 179–240; Brulez, *De firma Della Faille*, pp. 182, 492.
200. The contract was renewed in 1615 and 1639. Schulz, *De invloed van het oude Brabant*, pp. 39–41.
201. Schulz, *De invloed van het oude Brabant*, pp. 48–9.
202. Dollinger, *The German Hansa*, p. 357.
203. Brulez, 'De diaspora', p. 290.
204. J.-A. Goris, 'Eene Antwerpsche handelsexpeditie in de Oostzeelanden (1562–1569)',

16 (1924/1925); B. Oden, 'A Netherlandish Merchant in Stockholm in the Reign of Erik XIV', *Scandinavian Economic History Review*, 10:1 (1962), pp. 3–37; Wijnroks, *Handel tussen Rusland en de Nederlanden*; J. Denucé, *De Hanze en de Antwerpsche handelscompagnieën op de Oostzeelanden* (Antwerp: De Sikkel, 1938).

205. Wijnroks, *Handel tussen Rusland en de Nederlanden*.
206. Brulez, 'De diaspora'.
207. Brulez, *De firma Della Faille*, p. 458–9.
208. Brulez also had his doubts about this passivity put forward by Van Houtte in J. A. Van Houtte, 'Bruges et Anvers, marchés "nationaux" ou "internationaux" du XIVe Au XVIe siècle', *Revue du Nord*, 34 (1952), pp. 89–108; Brulez, *De firma Della Faille*, pp. 445–9. For these Bruges firms see: Mus, 'De Brugse compagnie Despars'; O. Mus, 'Wouter Ameyde, een Brugs waard-makelaar op het einde van de 15de eeuw', in *Album Albert Schouteet* (Bruges: Westvlaams Verbond van Kringen voor Heemkunde, 1973), pp. 117–32; Everaert, 'Marchands flamands à Lisbonne et l'exportation du sucre de Madère (1480–1530)'; J. Everaert, 'Vlaamse suikerbaronnen op Madeira (omstreeks 1480–1620)', in J. Everaert and E. Stols (eds), *Vlaanderen en Portugal: op de golfslag van twee culturen* (Antwerp: Mercatorfonds, 1991), pp. 99–117; J. Everaert and E. Stols, *Vlaanderen en Portugal: op de golfslag van twee culturen* (Antwerpe: Mercatorfonds, 1991); Stols, 'De Vlaamse natie te Lissabon (15de–17de eeuw)'; Verlinden, 'De Vlaamse kolonisten op de Azoren', *Vlaanderen en Portugal: op de golfslag van twee culturen*; Stabel, 'Entre commerce international'; J. Everaert, 'The Flemish sugar connection: Vlamingen in de Atlantische suikereconomie (1480–1648)', *Bijdragen tot de geschiedenis*, 84 (2001), pp. 257–65'; E. Stols and W. Thomas, 'Flanders and the Canary Islands in the First Widening of the World 1450–1550', in F. J. G. Gómez, E. Stols, W. Thomas and H. Nieuwdorp (eds), *Lumen Canariense: El Cristo De La Laguna Y Su Tiempo* (San Cristóbal de La Laguna: Excmo. Ayuntamiento de San Cristóbal de La Laguna, 2003), pp. 27–50.
209. O. Gelderblom, *Cities of Commerce: The Institutional Foundations of International Trade in the Low Countries, 1250–1650* (Princeton, NJ: Princeton University Press, 2013), p. 207.
210. Or as Pierre Jeannin has it: 'Selon des conceptions assez répandues chez les historiens, le marchand et le négociant, chacun à son échelle, préféraient en général une certaine diversification à une spécialisation trop poussée; ils saisissaient volontiers toute occasion d'entreprendre... Le "marchand universel" s'intéressait aux marchandises les plus diverses, mais pas toutes sur le même plan: des notes dominantes, certaines durables et d'autres à pondération changeante, coloraient toujours cette universalité'. P. Jeannin, 'Distinction des compétences et niveaux de qualification: les savoirs négociants dans l'Europe Moderne', in F. Angiolini and D. Roche (eds), *Cultures et formations négociantes dans l'Europe Moderne* (Paris: Ecole des hautes études en sciences sociales, 1995), pp. 363–97, on p. 313; W. Brulez, *De firma Della Faille*, p. 485.

2 Antwerp Ties to the Low Countries Hinterland

1. For this regional comparison see B. van Bavel, *Manors and Markets: Economy and Society in the Low Countries, 500–1600* (Oxford: Oxford University Press, 2010) and the debate contributions in *Tijdschrift voor sociale en economische geschiedenis*, 2 (2011), pp. 61–138. For a synthesis on Low Countries industry: H. Van der Wee, 'Industrial Dynamics and the Process of Urbanization and De-Urbanization in the Low Countries from the Late

Middle Ages to the Eighteenth Century. A Synthesis', in H. Van der Wee (ed.), *The Rise and Decline of Urban Industries in Italy and in the Low Countries (Late Middle Ages–Early Modern Times)* (Leuven: Leuven University Press, 1988), pp. 307–88.

2. H. Van der Wee, *The Growth of the Antwerp Market and the European Economy (Fourteenth–Sixteenth Centuries)*, 3 vols (Den Haag: Nijhoff, 1963), vol. 2, pp. 132, 225–7, 323–4; Van der Wee, 'Industrial Dynamics and the Process of Urbanization and De-Urbanization in the Low Countries from the Late Middle Ages to the Eighteenth Century'.

3. J. Goldberg, *Trade and Institutions in the Medieval Mediterranean: The Geniza Merchants and their Business World* (Cambridge: Cambridge University Press, 2012), pp. 242–3, 275–6, 286–8.

4. 'During the whole sixteenth century the Low Countries were but the suburbs of the marvellous city of Antwerp who subjected the Low Countries to its ascendancy'. H. Pirenne, *Histoire de Belgique: de la mort de Charles le Téméraire à l'arrivée du duc d'Albe dans les Pays-Bas (1567). Histoire de Belgique*, 3 edn, 7 vols (Brussels: Maurice Lamertin, 1923), vol. 3, p. 267.

5. Indications of this internal trade are hard to find. P. Stabel, 'Schippers, wagenvoerders en kruiers: de organisatie van de stedelijke vervoersector in het laat-middeleeuwse Vlaanderen', *Bijdragen tot de geschiedenis*, 82 (1999), pp. 159–85; C. Lesger, *The Rise of the Amsterdam Market and Information Exchange: Merchants, Commercial Expansion and Change in the Spatial Economy of the Low Countries, c.1550–1630* (Aldershot: Ashgate, 2006), pp. 42–3.

6. H. Van der Wee, *The Growth of the Antwerp Market and the European Economy (Fourteenth–Sixteenth Centuries)*, 3 vols (Den Haag: Nijhoff, 1963), vol. 2, pp. 328–30; B. Blondé and R. Van Uytven, 'De smalle steden en het Brabantse stedelijke netwerk in de late Middeleeuwen en de Nieuwe Tijd', *Lira Elegans*, 6 (1999), pp. 129–82; P. Stabel, 'Marketing Cloth in the Low Countries: Foreign Merchants, Local Businessmen and Urban Entrepreneurs: Markets, Transport and Transaction Costs (14th–16th Century)', in B. Blondé, A. Greve and P. Stabel (eds), *International Trade in the Low Countries (14th–16th Centuries): Merchants, Organisation, Infrastructure: Proceedings of the International Conference Ghent-Antwerp, 12th–13th January 1997* (Leuven: Garant, 2000), pp. 15–36, on pp. 34–5.

7. The Antwerp fairs were installed between 1317 and 1324 and those of Bergen-op-Zoom between 1337 and 1359. F. Blockmans, 'Van wanneer dateren de Antwerpse jaarmarkten?', *Handelingen van het Vlaamse filologencongres* (1947), pp. 58–9; F. Prims, 'De Antwerpse jaarmarkten', *Antwerpiensia*, 18 (1948), pp. 38–41; J. A. Van Houtte, 'Les foires dans la Belgique ancienne', in *La Foire. Receuils de la Société Jean Bodin* (Brussels: Librairie encyclopédique, 1953), pp. 175–207; C. J. F. Slootmans, *Paas- en Koudemarkten te Bergen-Op-Zoom, 1365–1565*, 3 vols (Tilburg: Stichting Zuidelijk Historisch Contact, 1985); Y. E. Kortlever, 'The Easter and Cold Fairs of Bergen-Op-Zoom (14th–16th Centuries)', in S. Cavaciocchi (ed.), *Fiere e Mmercati nella integrazione delle economie europee, secc. 13–18: atti della 'Trentaduesima Settimana di Studi', 8–12 Maggio 2000* (Florence: Le Monnier, 2001), pp. 625–43, on pp. 626–7.

8. G. Asaert, 'Gasten uit Brugge: nieuwe gegevens over Bruggelingen op de Antwerpse markt in de vijftiende eeuw', in H. Coppejans and G. Hansotte (eds), *Album Carlos Wyffels: Aangeboden door zijn wetenschappelijke medewerkers* (Brussels: Algemeen Rijksarchief, 1987), pp. 23–41; J. L. Bolton and F. G. Bruscoli, 'When Did Antwerp Replace Bruges as the Commercial and Financial Centre of North-Western Europe?

'The Evidence of the Borromei Ledger for 1438', *Economic History Review*, 61:2 (2008), pp. 360–79.

9.   P. Stabel, *De kleine stad in Vlaanderen: bevolkingsdynamiek en economische functies van de kleine en secundaire stedelijke centra in het Gentse Kwartier (14de-16de Eeuw)* (Brussels: Paleis der Academiën, 1995), p. 109; B. Blondé, 'The "Reconquista" and the Structural Transformations in the Economy of the Southern Netherlands', paper presented at the Las Sociedades Ibéricas y el mar a finales del siglo 16: congreso internacional, Lisbon, 1998, p. 195; B. Blondé and M. Limberger, 'De gebroken welvaart', in R. Van Uytven (ed.), *Geschiedenis van Brabant van het hertogdom tot heden* (Zwolle: Waanders, 2011), pp. 307–30, on p. 308; R. Van Uytven, 'De triomf van Antwerpen en de grote steden', in R. Van Uytven (ed.), *Geschiedenis van Brabant van het hertogdom tot heden* (Zwolle: Waanders, 2011), pp. 241–52, on p. 249. Many furriers and leather workers bought hides and furs at the Brabant fairs. Dendermonde drapers were visiting the Brabant fairs by the middle of the fifteenth century.

10. Armentières's hall in Antwerp: Stabel, 'Marketing Cloth in the Low Countries', p. 25. Arendonk and Turnhout had buildings in Bergen-op-Zoom and Antwerp from 1460 to at least 1531: F. Vermeylen, 'In de ban van Antwerpen: de Kempen tijdens de zestiende eeuw', *Taxandria*, 63 (1991), pp. 229–43, on p. 230; Van Uytven, 'De triomf van Antwerpen', p. 248. 's-Hertogenbosch and Diest: Blondé and Limberger, 'De gebroken welvaart', *Taxandria*, p. 312; A. K. L. Thijs, 'Van "werkwinkel" tot "fabriek": de textielnijverheid te Antwerpen, einde 15de–begin 19de eeuw' (Brussels: Gemeentekrediet, 1987), pp. 39–49.

11. Diest, Lier, Herentals, Zichem, Hasselt, Hoogstraten, Leiden. Thijs, 'Van "werkwinkel" tot "fabriek"', p. 39–41.

12. Thijs, 'Van "werkwinkel" tot "fabriek"', p. 42.

13. Thijs, 'Van "werkwinkel" tot "fabriek"', pp. 47–9. Weert and Maastricht opened a hall in 1540 and 1564: Thijs, 'Van "werkwinkel" tot "fabriek"', pp. 42, 54.

14. Slootmans, *Paas- En Koudemarkten*, vol. 1, pp. 345–52.

15. O. Gelderblom, 'Het juweliersbedrijf in de Lage Landen, 1450–1650', unpublished working paper, pp. 11–12; D. Ewing, 'Marketing Art in Antwerp, 1460–1560: Our Lady's Pand', *Art Bulletin*, 72:4 (1990), pp. 558–84; F. Vermeylen, *Painting for the Market: Commercialization of Art in Antwerp's Golden Age* (Turnhout: Brepols, 2003), pp. 19–28; D. Schlugleit, 'De Predikheerenpand en St.-Niklaasgilde te Antwerpen (1445–1553)', *Bijdragen voor de geschiedenis*, 29 (1938–9), pp. 99–119.

16. D. Schlugeit, 'De zilverhandel van de Meerse en de ordonnantiën van de goudsmeden te Antwerpen in de zestiende eeuw', *Bijdragen tot de geschiedenis*, 30 (1939), pp. 39–61, on p. 42, cited in Thijs, 'Van "werkwinkel" tot "fabriek"', p. 53.

17. Van der Wee, *The Growth of the Antwerp Market*, vol. 1, pp. 503–6.

18. Vermeylen, *Painting for the Market*, pp. 50–61.

19. H. Soly, *Urbanisme en kapitalisme te Antwerpen in de 16de eeuw: de stedebouwkundige en industriële ondernemingen van Gilbert Van Schoonbeke* (Brussels: Gemeentekrediet, 1977), pp. 221–3, 234–8; Vermeylen, *Painting for the Market*, pp. 47–8.

20. Vermeylen, *Painting for the Market*, pp. 46–50.

21. The same test was done with the Antwerp certificates registered in 1492 and 1512 but no clear patterns could be deduced from this evidence mainly because these certificates do not represent exact times of transactions. The certificates could be requested long after the transaction had taken place.

22. ARB (Algemeen Rijksarchief Brussels), Rekenkamer, Hundredth Penny export tax,

23358–9 & 23361. See also: J. Puttevils, 'A servitio de vostri sempre siamo. De effecten van de handel tussen Antwerpen en Italië op de koopmansfamilie Van der Molen' (MA thesis, University of Antwerp, 2007); D. J. Harreld, *High Germans in the Low Countries: German Merchants and Commerce in Golden Age Antwerp* (Leiden: Brill, 2004).

23. O. de Smedt, *De Engelse Natie te Antwerpen in de 16e eeuw (1496–1582)*, 2 vols (Antwerp: Sikkel, 1954), vol. 1, II, pp. 276–7; J.-A. Goris, *Etude sur les colonies marchandes méridionales (Portugais, Espagnols, Italiens) à Anvers de 1488 à 1587* (Leuven: Uytspruyt, 1925), pp. 162–7, cited in O. Gelderblom, *Cities of Commerce: The Institutional Foundations of International Trade in the Low Countries, 1250–1650* (Princeton, NJ: Princeton University Press, 2013), p. 43.

24. F. Edler, 'The Van Der Molen, Commission Merchants of Antwerp: Trade with Italy, 1538–44', in J. L. Cate and E. N. Anderson (eds), *Medieval and Historiographical Essays in Honour of James Westfall Thompson* (Chicago, IL: University of Chicago Press, 1938), pp. 78–145, on p. 115; de Smedt, *De Engelse Natie*, vol. 2, pp. 123–8.

25. E. Coornaert, *Les Français et le commerce international à Anvers, fin du 15e-16e siècle* (Paris: Rivière, 1961), II, pp. 145–6, 186–7.

26. Van Houtte, 'Les foires', pp. 185, 194, cited in Gelderblom, *Cities of Commerce*, p. 44. Blondé and Van Uytven, 'De smalle steden', p. 139; Kortlever, 'The Easter and Cold Fairs'; Van Uytven, 'De triomf van Antwerpen', p. 145; Blondé and Limberger, 'De gebroken welvaart'.

27. Courtesy of Irène Leydecker-Brackx. She and her husband perused the aldermen's deeds, notarial archives and certification books of Bergen-op-Zoom and Antwerp to reconstitute their family history back to the late fifteenth century.

28. Blondé, 'The "Reconquista" and the Structural Transformations in the Economy of the Southern Netherlands', p. 195; Blondé and Van Uytven, 'De smalle steden', p. 140; Stabel, *De kleine stad*, p. 109.

29. Blondé and Van Uytven, 'De smalle steden'; Blondé, 'The "Reconquista" and the Structural Transformations in the Economy of the Southern Netherlands'; R. Van Uytven, 'In de Schaduwen van de Antwerpse groei: Het Hageland in de zestiende eeuw', *Bijdragen tot de geschiedenis*, 57 (1974), pp. 171–88; Vermeylen, 'In de ban van Antwerpen'.

30. P. Stabel, *Dwarfs among Giants: The Flemish Urban Network in the Late Middle Ages* (Leuven: Garant, 1997), pp. 149–50; Stabel, 'Marketing Cloth in the Low Countries', p. 35.

31. P. Stabel, 'Ambachten en textielondernemers in kleine Vlaamse steden tijdens de overgang van Middeleeuwen naar Nieuwe Tijd', in C. Lis and H. Soly (eds), *Werelden van verschil: ambachtsgilden in de Lage Landen* (Brussels: VUB Press, 1997), pp. 79–98, on p. 81. Lille would even usurp Antwerp's role as an export center for Flemish textiles in the last decades of the sixteenth century. Thijs, 'Van "werkwinkel" tot "fabriek"', p. 72.

32. Stabel, *De kleine stad*, pp. 175–204.

33. 'Item que la merchandise nourrist aussy en ces pays beaucoup de mainfactures mechaniques comme lanefices linguefices sayetteries tapiceries mesmement aussy beaucoup de peuple travailleurs par ce gaignans leur vie', CAA, Privilegiekamer, Raeckt den handel, Pk 1018, piece 9.

34. H. Soly and A. K. L. Thijs, 'Nijverheid in de Zuidelijke Nederlanden 1490–1580', in D. P. Blok (ed.), *Algemene Geschiedenis der Nederlanden* (Haarlem: Fibula-Van Dishoeck, 1979), pp. 27–57, on pp. 30–1.

35. H. Van der Wee, 'Industrial Dynamics and the Process of Urbanization and De-Urbanization in the Low Countries from the Late Middle Ages to the Eighteenth Century.

A Synthesis', in H. Van der Wee (ed.), *The Rise and Decline of Urban Industries in Italy and in the Low Countries (Late Middle Ages-Early Modern Times)* (Leuven: Leuven University Press, 1988), pp. 307–88, on pp. 337–8.

36. Van der Wee, 'Industrial Dynamics and the Process of Urbanization and De-Urbanization in the Low Countries from the Late Middle Ages to the Eighteenth Century', pp. 334–5; J. H. Munro, 'The Low Countries' Export Trade in Textiles with the Mediterranean Basin: A Cost–Benefit Analysis of Comparative Advantages in Overland and Maritime Trade Routes', *International Journal of Maritime History*, 11:2 (1999), pp. 1–30; J. H. Munro, 'The "New Institutional Economics" and the Changing Fortunes of Fairs in Medieval and Early Modern Europe: The Textile Trades, Warfare and Transaction Costs', *Vierteljahresschrift für Sozial- und Wirtschaftsgeschichte*, 88 (2001), pp. 1–47.

37. The best synthesis is Van der Wee, 'Industrial Dynamics and the Process of Urbanization', pp. 330–2. Also H. Van der Wee, 'Structural Changes and Specialization in the Industry of the Southern Netherlands, 1100–1600', *Economic History Review*, 28:2 (1975), pp. 203–21.

38. Van der Wee, 'Structural Changes', p. 213; P. Stabel, *De kleine stad in Vlaanderen: bevolkingsdynamiek en economische functies van de kleine en secundaire stedelijke centra in het Gentse Kwartier (14de-16de Eeuw)* (Brussels: Paleis der Academiën, 1995), p. 203; P Stabel, 'Guilds in Late Medieval Flanders: Myths and Realities of Guild Life in an Export-Oriented Environment', *Journal of Medieval History*, 30:2 (2004), pp. 187–212.

39. Stabel, *De kleine stad*, pp. 200–1.

40. Stabel, *De kleine stad*, pp. 201–2.

41. Other Flemish textile examples include cloth from Menen, Courtrai table linen, Dendermonde baaien and fustians, tapestries and linen from Alost, linen from Tielt, Harelbeke or Hulst, and bag-cloth from Ronse. Van der Wee, 'Industrial Dynamics and the Process of Urbanization', pp. 332–3; Stabel, *De kleine stad*, pp. 201–2.

42. W. Brulez, 'The Balance of Trade of the Netherlands in the Middle of the 16th Century', *Acta historiae Neerlandica*, 4 (1970), pp. 20–48, on p. 48.

43. Soly and Thijs, 'Nijverheid in de Zuidelijke Nederlanden', p. 33; P. Klep, 'Het Brabantse stedensysteem en de scheiding der Nederlanden, 1565–1650', *Bijdragen tot de geschiedenis*, 73:3–4 (1990), pp. 101–29, on pp. 113–14; P. Stabel, '"Dmeeste, oirboirlixste ende proffitelixste let Ende neringhe": een kwantitatieve benadering van de lakenproductie in het laatmiddeleeuwse en vroegmoderne Vlaanderen', *Handelingen van de Maatschappij voor Geschiedenis en Oudheidkunde te Gent*, 51 (1997), pp. 113–53, on p. 114; P. Stabel, *Dwarfs among giants: the Flemish urban network in the late Middle Ages* (Leuven: Garant, 1997), p. 143; P. Stabel, 'Marketing Cloth in the Low Countries: Foreign Merchants, Local Businessmen and Urban Entrepreneurs: Markets, Transport and Transaction Costs (14th–16th Century)', in B. Blondé, A. Greve and P. Stabel (eds), *International Trade in the Low Countries (14th–16th Centuries): Merchants, Organisation, Infrastructure: Proceedings of the International Conference Ghent-Antwerp, 12th–13th January 1997* (Leuven: Garant, 2000), pp. 15–36, on p. 32.

44. H. Van der Wee, *The Growth of the Antwerp Market and the European Economy (Fourteenth–Sixteenth Centuries)*, 3 vols (Den Haag: Nijhoff, 1963), vol. 2, pp. 191–2, 317–32 ; O. Gelderblom, *Zuid-Nederlandse kooplieden en de opkomst van de Amsterdamse stapelmarkt (1578–1630)* (Hilversum: Verloren, 2000), pp. 46–7. For a short overview of the Low Countries export industry see: H. Van der Wee, 'Handel in de Zuidelijke Nederlanden', in *Nieuwe Algemene Geschiedenis der Nederlanden* (Haarlem: Fibula-Van Dishoeck, 1978), pp. 75–95, on pp. 86–93.

45. For the fourteenth century: J. M. Murray, *Bruges: Cradle of Capitalism 1280–1390* (Cambridge: Cambridge University Press, 2006). For the fifteenth century: P. Stabel, 'Entre commerce international et entrepreneurs locaux: le monde financier de Wouter Ameide (Bruges, fin 15e–début 16e siècle)', in M. Boone (ed.), *Finances privées et finances publiques* (Leuven: Garant, 1995), pp. 75–99; Stabel, 'Marketing Cloth in the Low Countries'; Stabel, 'Guilds in Late Medieval Flanders: Myths and Realities of Guild Life in an Export-Oriented Environment'; P. Stabel, 'Public or Private, Collective or Individual? The Spaces of Late Medieval Trade in the Low Countries', in D. Calabi and S. Beltramo (eds), *Il mercante patrizio: palazzi e botteghe nell'Europa del Rinascimento* (Milan: Mondadori, 2008), pp. 37–54.

46. Soly and Thijs, 'Nijverheid in de Zuidelijke Nederlanden', pp. 38–9; R. Van Uytven, 'De triomf van Antwerpen en de grote steden', in R. Van Uytven (ed.), *Geschiedenis van Brabant van het hertogdom tot Heden* (Zwolle: Waanders, 2011), pp. 241–52, on p. 246.

47. Stabel, 'Marketing Cloth in the Low Countries', pp. 15–16; J. H. Munro, 'Spanish Merino Wools and the Nouvelles Draperies: An Industrial Transformation in the Late Medieval Low Countries', *Economic History Review*, 58:3 (2005), pp. 431–84, on pp. 459–60.

48. Munro, 'Spanish Merino Wools and the Nouvelles Draperies', pp. 474–5; H. Van der Wee, 'The Western European Woollen Industries, 1500–1750', in D. Jenkins (ed), *The Cambridge History of Western Textiles* (Cambridge: Cambridge University Press, 2003), ch. 8, pp. 397–472, on p. 399.

49. P. Stabel, 'Ambachten en textielondernemers in kleine Vlaamse steden tijdens de overgang van Middeleeuwen naar Nieuwe Tijd', in C. Lis and H. Soly (eds), *Werelden van verschil: ambachtsgilden in de Lage Landen* (Brussels: VUB Press, 1997), pp. 79–98, on pp. 88–90; Stabel, 'Entre commerce international'. See also: O. Mus, 'Wouter Ameyde, een Brugs waard-makelaar op het einde van de 15de eeuw', in *Album Albert Schouteet* (Bruges: Westvlaams Verbond van Kringen voor Heemkunde, 1973), pp. 117–32.

50. J.de Vries and A. van der Woude, *The First Modern Economy : Success, Failure, and Perseverance of the Dutch Economy, 1500-1815* (Cambridge: Cambridge University Press, 1997), pp. 330–1; H. Kaptein, *De Hollandse textielnijverheid, 1350–1600: conjunctuur en continuïteit* (Hilversum: Verloren, 1998).

51. Kaptein, *De Hollandse textielnijverheid*, pp. 154–5.

52. Kaptein, *De Hollandse textielnijverheid*, pp. 156.

53. Kaptein, *De Hollandse textielnijverheid*, pp. 163–5.

54. Kaptein, *De Hollandse textielnijverheid*, pp. 140, 156, 158.

55. There is a large literature on sixteenth-century Antwerp industry. For a recent overview: B. De Munck, *Technologies of Learning: Apprenticeship in Antwerp from the 15th Century to the End of the Ancien Régime*, Studies in European Urban History (1100–1800) (Turnhout: Brepols, 2007). On textile production: A. K. L. Thijs, *Van 'werkwinkel' Tot 'fabriek': de textielnijverheid te Antwerpen, einde 15de–begin 19de eeuw* (Brussels: Gemeentekrediet, 1987). Specifically on silk production: A. K. L. Thijs, 'Een ondernemer uit de Antwerpse textielindustrie, Jan Nuyts (ca. 1512–1582)', *Bijdragen tot de geschiedenis*, 51 (1968), pp. 53–68; A. K. L. Thijs, *De zijdenijverheid te Antwerpen in de zeventiende eeuw* (Brussels: Pro Civitate, 1969). On the construction industry: H. Soly, 'De bouw van de Antwerpse citadel (1567–1571): sociaal-economische aspecten', *Belgisch tijdschrift voor militaire geschiedenis*, 21:6 (1976), pp. 549–78; H. Soly, *Urbanisme en kapitalisme te Antwerpen in de 16de eeuw: de stedebouwkundige en industriële ondernemingen van Gilbert Van Schoonbeke* (Brussels: Gemeentekrediet, 1977). On

Antwerp breweries: H. Soly, 'De economische betekenis van de Zuidnederlandse brouwindustrie in de 16de eeuw. problematiek', in *Histoire économique de la Belgique: traitement des sources et état des questions: actes du colloque de Bruxelles, 17–19 Nov. 1971
= Economische geschiedenis van België: behandeling van de bronnen en problematiek:
Handelingen van het colloquium te Brussel, 17–19 November 1971* (Brussels: Algemeen
Rijksarchief en Rijksarchief in de Provinciën, 1972), pp. 97–117; Soly, *Urbanisme en
kapitalisme*. On printing: L. Voet, *The Golden Compasses: A History and Evaluation of
the Printing and Publishing Activities of the Officina Plantiniana at Antwerp* (Amsterdam: Vangendt, 1969); L. Voet, 'De typografische bedrijvigheid te Antwerpen in de
16e eeuw', in W. Couvreur (ed.), *Antwerpen in de XVIde Eeuw* (Antwerp: Mercurius,
1975), pp. 233–55. On sugar refining: A. K. L. Thijs, 'De geschiedenis van de suikernijverheid te Antwerpen (16de–19de eeuw), een terreinverkenning', *Bijdragen tot de
geschiedenis*, 62:1–2 (1979), pp. 23-50.

56. Thijs, 'Van "werkwinkel" tot "fabriek"', p. 80 and passim.
57. Thijs, 'Van "werkwinkel" tot "fabriek"', pp. 81–4; J.-P. Peeters, 'De Mechelse ververs en
     lakenscheerders en het verval van de stedelijke draperie in de 16de eeuw (1520–1601)',
     *Handelingen van de Koninklijke Kring voor Oudheidkunde, Letteren en Kunst van
     Mechelen*, 93 (1989), pp. 153–87.
58. O. de Smedt, *De Engelse Natie te Antwerpen in de 16e eeuw (1496–1582)*, 2 vols
     (Antwerp: Sikkel, 1954), vol. 1, pp. 353–66; Thijs, 'Structural Changes in the Antwerp
     Industry', p. 207; Thijs, *De textielnijverheid te Antwerpen*, pp. 62–6, 88.
59. Thijs, 'Van "werkwinkel" tot "fabriek"', pp. 120–33.
60. W. Brulez, 'De handelsbalans in het midden van de 16de eeuw', *Bijdragen voor de
     geschiedenis der Nederlanden*, 21 (1967), pp. 278–310, on p. 302; R. Van Uytven, *De
     geschiedenis van Mechelen: van heerlijkheid tot stadsgewest* (Tielt: Lannoo, 1991).
61. J. Denucé, 'Familie De Pape met stamtafel', *Antwerpsch Archievenblad*, 33 (1928), pp.
     98–104. Large parts of his archive have been preserved in the Insolvente Boedelskamer.
     CAA, Insolvente Boedelskamer, Archive De Pape, IB # 770–87.
62. Thijs, *De textielnijverheid te Antwerpen*, p. 140. His purchases of English cloth on the
     Antwerp fairs are documented in his Jaarmarktboek. CAA, Insolvente Boedelskamer,
     Archive De Pape, Jaarmarktboek, IB # IB 776.
63. Peeters, 'De Mechelse ververs en lakenscheerders en het verval van de stedelijke draperie
     in De 16de eeuw (1520–1601)'.
64. De Smedt, *De Engelse Natie*, vol. 2, pp. 361–2.
65. H. Soly, 'Nijverheid en kapitalisme te Antwerpen in de 16e eeuw', in *Album aangeboden
     aan Charles Verlinden ter gelegenheid van zijn dertig jaar professoraat = Album offert à
     Charles Verlinden à l'occasion de ses trente ans de professorat* (Ghent: Universa, 1975), p. 337.
66. Thijs, 'Jan Nuyts'.
67. References and data by courtesy of Irène Leydecker-Brackx. CAA, Aldermen's registers,
     SR # 137, 24/1/1510.
68. R. Doehaerd, *Etudes anversoises: documents sur le commerce international à Anvers,
     1488–1514*, 3 vols (Paris: SEVPEN, 1962–3), vol. 2, nr. 2238, 2246, 2247 and 2248.
69. CAA, Notarial archives, notary Cornelis Reedgeelt, N # 9024, 10/7/1526.
70. CAA, Aldermen's registers, SR 187, 20/10/1535; CAA, Weesmeesterkamer, WK 91,
     25/8/1588.
71. CAA, Certification books, CERT # 6; 20/4/1545, Notarial archives, notary Adriaen
     Zeger 's-Hertoghen, N # 2074, 57v, 3/5/1549; CAA, Aldermen's registers, SR # 288,
     15/4/1562; Aldermen's registers, SR # 297, 19/12/1564.

72. CAA, Aldermen's registers, SR # 281, 21/3/1561.
73. On Placquet: CAA, Aldermen's registers, SR # 268, 11/2/1559. On Lunden: Stadsarchief Antwerpen, CAA, Certification books, CERT # 6, 20/4/1545.
74. CAA, Aldermen's registers, SR # 316, 31/7/1568.
75. The town's name became a synonym for its says throughout Europe: hansecotte in Liège, hundskutt in Germany, escot in France, anacosta in Spain, scotto in Italy. E. Coornaert, *La draperie-sayetterie d'Hondschoote, 14–18ième siècle. Un centre industriel d'autrefois* (Paris: PUF, 1930), p. 30.
76. Van der Wee, 'The Western European Woollen Industries', pp. 428–30; Thijs, 'Structural Changes in the Antwerp Industry', pp. 346–7; the major study on Hondschoote is still: Coornaert, *La draperie-sayetterie d'Hondschoote.*
77. The Hondschoote merchants rented their own hall in Bruges, A la Halle de Paris, to that end. Coonaert, *La draperie-sayetterie d'Hondschoote*, pp. 237–8.
78. Coonaert, *La draperie-sayetterie d'Hondschoote*, pp. 238–40.
79. Coonaert, *La draperie-sayetterie d'Hondschoote*, pp. 244–54.
80. Coonaert, *La draperie-sayetterie d'Hondschoote*, pp. 287–8.
81. Coonaert, *La draperie-sayetterie d'Hondschoote*, pp. 281, 315–18.
82. F. Edler, 'Le commerce d'exportation des sayes d'Hondschoote vers Italie d'après la correspondance d'une firme anversoise, entre 1538 et 1544', *Revue du Nord*, 22 (1936), pp. 249–66, on pp. 255–6; Coornaert, *La draperie-sayetterie d'Hondschoote*, p. 327. The Della Faille also sent hard currency to Courtrai in the last quarter of the sixteenth century: W. Brulez, *De firma Della Faille en de internationale handel van Vlaamse firma's in de 16de eeuw* (Brussels: Paleis der Academiën, 1959), pp. 311–13.
83. E. Coornaert, *Les Français et le commerce international à Anvers, Fin du 15e-16e siècle* (Paris: Rivière, 1961), II, p. 158, II, pp. 202–3.
84. P. Deyon and A. Lottin, 'Evolution de la production textile à Lille aux XVIe et XVIIe siècles', *Revue du Nord*, 49 (1967), pp. 23–34, on pp. 26–7, cited in R. S. Duplessis, *Lille and the Dutch Revolt: Urban Stability in an Era of Revolution, 1500–1582* (Cambridge: Cambridge University Press, 1991, p. 89.
85. 'A Honschott sono poveri vilani che le fano et subitto fatti bisogna abino li danari per comprar del pane per vivere' CAA, Insolvente Boedelkamer, IB # 2898, Letterbook Van der Molen, letter to Jeronimo Azeretto, 30 March 1538, 6r.
86. See tables in Coornaert, *La draperie-sayetterie d'Hondschoote*, pp. 366–7.
87. 'Li sono hora sul locho xvj conpratori che li stano di fermo, delli quali 2 hano incircha la metà dele saije se li fano. Et chadaun di loro vol monstrar d'esser el maestro. Li altri xiiij fano al melgio che possino' CAA, Insolvente Boedelkamer, IB # 2898, Letterbook Van der Molen, letter to Julio del Moro, 16 November 1538, 47r.
88. L. Bril, *De handel tussen de Nederlanden en het Iberisch schiereiland (midden XVIe eeuw)* (Ghent: University of Ghent, 1962), pp. 88, 126.
89. Throughout his career as a Hondschoote agent (1537–72) Jan Sorbrecht had an average export output of 12.58 per cent. Calculations based on: Coornaert, *La draperie-sayetterie d'Hondschoote*, p. 361.
90. Coonaert, *La draperie-sayetterie d'Hondschoote*, p. 362.
91. CAA, Insolvente Boedelkamer, IB # 2898, Letterbook Van der Molen, letter to Jacob Van der Tombe, 13 November 1538, 41v–42r.
92. CAA, Insolvente Boedelkamer, IB # 2898, Letterbook Van der Molen, letter to Daniel Van der Molen, 6 May 1543, 262v. Letter to Jeronimo Piperario, 22 June 1543, 265.
93. 'Als een saye niet schoon van verve is, in Italien ten is gheen halff ghelt weert. Ick bidde

u wilt boven al altijts naer die scoon coluere sien want de coluer doet tsay vercope ende niet de duecht' CAA, Insolvente Boedelkamer, IB # 2898, Letterbook Van der Molen, letter to Jacob Van der Tombe, 13 November 1538, 41v–42.

94. Edler, 'Le commerce d'exportation', p. 255.

95. CAA, Insolvente Boedelkamer, IB # 2898, Letterbook Van der Molen, letter to Daniel Van der Molen, 6 May 1543, 262v.

96. 'Quanto de far comprar saye donschott sul locho noj li habiamo un homo che compra giornalmente per noi et li diamo un salario fermo al anno' CAA, Insolvente Boedelkamer, IB # 2898, Letterbook Van der Molen, letter to Jeronimo Piperario, 22 June 1543, 265r.

97. Thijs, *De textielnijverheid te Antwerpen*, pp. 54, 58; R. Van Uytven, 'Brabantse en Antwerpse centrale plaatsen (14de–19de eeuw)', in *Le réseau urbain en Belgique dans une perspective historique (1350–1850): une approche statistique et dynamique = Het stedelijk netwerk in België in historisch perspectief (1350–1850): een statistische en dynamische benadering* (Brussel: Gemeentekrediet, 1992), p. 42; B. Blondé and M. Limberger, 'De gebroken welvaart', in R. Van Uytven (ed.), *Geschiedenis van Brabant van het hertogdom tot heden* (Zwolle: Waanders, 2011), pp. 307–30, on p. 317.

98. Thijs, 'Van "werkwinkel" tot "fabriek"', pp. 56–7; M. Limberger, *Sixteenth-Century Antwerp and its Rural Surroundings: Social and Economic Changes in the Hinterland of a Commercial Metropolis (Ca. 1450–Ca. 1570)* (Turnhout: Brepols, 2008), pp. 124–8.

99. For an overview see: R. Vermoesen, 'Gescheiden door de wallen? Commerciële Circuits in de stad en op het platteland, 1650–1800', *Stadsgeschiedenis*, 3:2 (2008), pp. 105–21, on p. 106; S. Ogilvie and M. Cerman, 'The Theories of Proto-Industrialization', in S. Ogilvie and M. Cerman (eds), *European Proto-Industrialization* (Cambridge: Cambridge University Press, 1996), pp. 1–11; S. Ogilvie and M. Cerman, 'Proto-Industrialization, Economic Development and Social Change in Early Modern Europe', in S. Ogilvie and M. Cerman (eds), *European Proto-Industrialization* (Cambridge: Cambridge University Press, 1996), pp. 227–40.

100. B. Van Bavel, 'Early Proto-Industrialization in the Low Countries? The Importance and Nature of Market-Oriented Non-Agricultural Activities on the Countryside in Flanders and Holland, C. 1250–1570', *Revue belge de philologie et d'histoire* (2003), pp. 1109–65, on pp. 1145–7.

101. Stabel, *De kleine stad*, p. 177, citing E. Thoen, *Landbouwekonomie en bevolking in Vlaanderen gedurende de late Middeleeuwen en het begin van de moderne tijden: testregio: de Kasselrijen van Oudenaarde en Aalst (eind 13de–eerste helft 16de eeuw)* (Ghent: Belgisch Centrum voor Landelijke Geschiedenis, 1988), pp. 986–7.

102. Van Bavel, 'Early Proto-Industrialization in the Low Countries?', p. 1145.

103. B. Van Bavel, *Manors and Markets: Economy and Society in the Low Countries, 500–1600* (Oxford: Oxford University Press, 2010), p. 361. See also Van Bavel, 'Early Proto-Industrialization in the Low Countries?'.

104. Van Bavel, 'Early Proto-Industrialization in the Low Countries?', pp. 1121–2. For comparison, by the year 1500 rural woollen production in the same region accounted for 3,000 full-time workers. Van Bavel, 'Early Proto-Industrialization in the Low Countries?', pp. 1122–3.

105. J. Blomme and H. Van der Wee, 'The Belgian Economy in a Long-Term Perspective: Economic Development in Flanders and Brabant, 1500–1812', in *Economic Growth and Structural Change: Comparative Approaches over the Long Run on the Basis of Reconstructed National Accounts: International Colloquium, Leuven, 8–11 September*

1993 (Leuven: KUL, 1993), p. 9. Detailed numbers for the different export regions will be dealt with in the Conclusion of this chapter.

106. F. Vermeylen, 'In de ban van Antwerpen: de Kempen tijdens de zestiende eeuw', *Taxandria*, 63 (1991), pp. 229–43, on p. 230; J.-M. Goris, 'Herentals: van welvarend industrieel centrum tot arme garnizoensstad (1560–1650)', *Bijdragen tot de geschiedenis*, 73:3–4 (1990), pp. 211–35.

107. B. Blondé, *De sociale structuren en economische dynamiek van 's-Hertogenbosch, 1500–1550* (Tilburg: Stichting Zuidelijk Historisch Contact, 1987), p. 111.

108. E. Sabbe, *De Belgische vlasnijverheid. Deel 1: De Zuid-Nederlandse vlasnijverheid tot het Verdrag van Utrecht (1713)* (Kortrijk: Nationaal Vlasmuseum, 1975), pp. 210–11; J. R. Verellen, 'Linnennijverheid te Herentals vooral in de 16e eeuw', *Taxandria. Tijdschrift van de Koninklijke geschied- en oudheidkundige kring van de Antwerpse Kempen*, 29:2 (1957), pp. 3–19; Blondé, *De sociale structuren en economische dynamiek*, pp. 108–14; Stabel, *De kleine stad*, pp. 182–4.

109. Verellen, 'Linnennijverheid te Herentals vooral in de 16e eeuw', pp. 11–12.

110. W. J. Formsma and L. P. L. Pirenne, *Koopmansgeest te 's-Hertogenbosch in de vijftiende en zestiende eeuw: het kasboek van Jaspar Van Bell, 1564–1568* (Nijmegen: Centrale Drukkerij, 1962), pp. 77, 100, cited in Blondé, *De sociale structuren en economische dynamiek*, p. 110.

111. S. C. Regtdoorzee Greup-Rolandus, *Geschiedenis der Haarlemmer bleekerijen* ('s-Gravenhage: Nijhoff, 1936) Kaptein doubts this importance of Haarlem bleaching before 1575. Kaptein, *De Hollandse textielnijverheid*, pp. 202–5; Stabel, *De kleine stad*, p. 182. The Della Faille shifted both their linen purchases and bleaching activities to Haarlem in the late 1580s and early 1590s. Brulez, *De firma Della Faille*, pp. 248–9.

112. Stabel, *De kleine stad*, p. 182; Van Bavel, *Manors and Markets*, p. 362.

113. Sabbe, *De Belgische vlasnijverheid*, pp. 273–6; Stabel, *De kleine stad*, p. 184.

114. He also had to lodge Dynghens's family and personnel in his house when they would visit Courtrai. Sabbe, *De Belgische vlasnijverheid*, p. 276.

115. Sabbe, *De Belgische vlasnijverheid*, p. 280.

116. Brulez, *De firma Della Faille*, pp. 248–55, 310–14; Sabbe, *De Belgische vlasnijverheid*, p. 275.

117. Sabbe, *De Belgische vlasnijverheid*, p. 277.

118. J. Vermaut, 'Nieuwe gegevens over het industrieel verleden van Roeselare en omgeving 1350–1800', *Rollariensia*, 6 (1974), pp. 134–82, on p. 142.

119. Sabbe, *De Belgische vlasnijverheid*, pp. 270, 274.

120. The poortersboeken for the period 1533 to 1608 are published in: J. Van Roey, *Antwerpse poortersboeken*, 6 vols (Antwerp: Stadsarchief, 1978). Dr Jan De Meester has put this published source into an MS Excel which he kindly granted to me. He used the database for his own research which can be consulted in: J. De Meester, *Gastvrij Antwerpen? Arbeidsmigratie Naar Het Zestiende-Eeuwse Antwerpen* (Antwerp: PhD dissertation University of Anwerp, 2011), p. 27. Linen workers also moved to the Scheldt city.

121. Sabbe, *De Belgische vlasnijverheid*, pp. 214–20.

122. Sabbe, *De Belgische vlasnijverheid*, pp. 276–7.

123. Blondé, *De sociale structuren en economische dynamiek*, pp. 113–14; Blondé and Limberger, 'De gebroken welvaart', pp. 326–7.

124. Detailed data on firm sizes and types in Oudenaarde, a major tapestry production centre, in: M. Vanwelden, *Productie van wandtapijten in de regio Oudenaarde: een symbiose*

tussen stad en platteland (15de tot 17de eeuw) (Leuven: Universitaire Pers, 2006), pp. 160–70. The inequality was even visible in the town's space: the merchants and entrepreneurs all lived around the town square while the weavers lived in the suburbs. Stabel, *De kleine stad*, p. 192.

125. Stabel, *De kleine stad*, pp. 192–3; Van Bavel, 'Early Proto-Industrialization in the Low Countries?', pp. 1148–50; Vanwelden, *Productie van wandtapijten*, p. 50.

126. On demand in the fifteenth century: Vanwelden, *Productie van wandtapijten*, pp. 82–90. There are some indications to be found on tapestry exports: Vanwelden, *Productie van wandtapijten*, pp. 88–90.

127. Stabel, *De kleine stad*, 190.

128. Vanwelden, *Productie van wandtapijten*, pp. 48–50, 67–72, 81.

129. Vanwelden, *Productie van wandtapijten*, pp. 73, 87; Van Uytven, 'De triomf van Antwerpen', p. 248.

130. Vanwelden, *Productie van wandtapijten*, pp. 101–4.

131. Soly and Thijs, 'Nijverheid in de Zuidelijke Nederlanden', p. 43. Aalst, which had close ties to Brussels, also did well but produced mainly for the Low Countries and not for export. Stabel, *De kleine stad*, pp. 195–6.

132. Soly and Thijs, 'Nijverheid in de Zuidelijke Nederlanden', pp. 42–3.

133. Vanwelden, *Productie van wandtapijten*, pp. 92, 190, 193; Stabel, *De kleine stad*, p. 190.

134. Stabel, *De kleine stad*, p. 191; Vanwelden, *Productie van wandtapijten*, pp. 98–101.

135. Stabel, *De kleine stad*, pp. 192–3.

136. Vanwelden, *Productie van wandtapijten*, pp. 93, 185.

137. E. Duverger, 'De Antwerpse poortersboeken van 1533 tot 1609. Een bron voor de geschiedenis van de tapijtkunst en van de textiele kunsten', *Artes Textiles: bijdragen tot de geschiedenis van de tapijt-, borduur- en textielkunst*, 9 (1978), pp. 137–44, cited in Vanwelden, *Productie van wandtapijten*, pp. 105, 238.

138. For the many examples see: Vanwelden, *Productie van wandtapijten*, pp. 204–7.

139. Vanwelden, *Productie van wandtapijten*, pp. 165, 168–9.

140. Vanwelden, *Productie van wandtapijten*, p. 172; J. Puttevils, 'A servitio de vostri sempre siamo. De effecten van de handel tussen Antwerpen en Italië op de koopmansfamilie Van der Molen' (MA thesis, University of Antwerp, 2007), p. 56; W. Brulez, *De firma Della Faille*, p. 470.

141. CAA, Insolvente Boedelkamer, IB # 2898, Letterbook Van der Molen, letter to Martino di Zerchari, 14 December, 1538, 45r.

142. CAA, Insolvente Boedelkamer, IB # 2898, Letterbook Van der Molen, letters to Martino di Zerchari, 9 March 1539, 61r; 29 March 1539, 68v; 21 June 1539 92r.

143. CAA, Insolvente Boedelkamer, IB # 2898, Letterbook Van der Molen, letter to Julio Moro, 9 March 1538, 3v; letter to Julio Moro and Bastiano del Baylo, 9 January 1541, 190r.

144. Edler, 'The Van Der Molen', p. 100; E. Duverger, *Jan, Jacques en Frans De Moor, tapijtwevers en tapijthandelaars te Oudenaarde, Antwerpen en Gent (1560 tot ca. 1680)* (Ghent: Interuniversitair Centrum voor de geschiedenis van de Vlaamse tapijtkunst, 1960), p. 50; P. H. Janssen, *Werken aan kunst: economische en bedrijfskundige aspecten van de kunstproduktie, 1400–1800* (Hilversum: Verloren, 1995), p. 76.

145. CAA, Insolvente Boedelkamer, IB # 2898, Letterbook Van der Molen, letter to Jeronimo Cibo Donato, 7 March 1539, 63v.

146. Soly and Thijs, 'Nijverheid in de Zuidelijke Nederlanden', p. 45–6.

147. Soly and Thijs, 'Nijverheid in de Zuidelijke Nederlanden', p. 56.

148. Soly and Thijs, 'Nijverheid in de Zuidelijke Nederlanden'; van Bavel, *Manors and Markets*, pp. 353–5.

149. Bril, 'De handel', p. 152.

150. Blondé, *De sociale structuren en economische dynamiek*, pp. 115, 118, 119–20, 123.

151. Blondé, *De sociale structuren en economische dynamiek*, pp. 114–26. Also: Blondé, 'The "Reconquista" and the Structural Transformations in the Economy of the Southern Netherlands', pp. 194–5.

152. Soly and Thijs, 'Nijverheid in de Zuidelijke Nederlanden', p. 45; van Bavel, *Manors and Markets*, pp. 353–5.

153. This is based on Gelderblom, 'Het juweliersbedrijf in de Lage Landen, 1450–1650', unpublished working paper and *Zuid-Nederlandse kooplieden*, p. 48. In 1552–3 diamonds, pearls and rubies were imported from Spain and Portugal for a value of 7717 guilders. Bril, 'De handel', p. 160. Most of these precious stones were imported by the Antwerp merchant Lancelot de Robiano. Goris, *Etude sur les colonies marchandes*, pp. 268–9, cited in Gelderblom, *Zuid-Nederlandse kooplieden*, p. 50.

154. On this craft guild: D. Schlugleit and F. Prims, *Geschiedenis van het Antwerpsche diamantslijpersambacht, 1582–1797* (Antwerp: Gullaume, 1935), pp. 13–18

155. L. Guicciardini, *Descrittione di tutti i Paesi Bassi, altrimenti detti Germania Inferiore* (Antwerp: Guglielmo Silvio, 1567), pp. 95–8, quoted in Gelderblom, *Zuid-Nederlandse kooplieden*, p. 53.

156. A. Van den Kerkhove, 'Joris Vezeleer, een Antwerps koopman van de XVIde Eeuw', paper presented at the 43e Congres Federatie van Kringen voor Oudheidkunde en Geschiedenis van België vzw, Sint-Niklaas-Waas, 1974; Vermeylen, *Painting for the Market*, pp. 63–6; Gelderblom, 'Het juweliersbedrijf in de Lage Landen, 1450–1650', unpublished working paper, p. 19; T. P. Campbell (ed.), *Tapestry in the Renaissance: Art and Magnificence* (New York: Metropolitan Museum of Art, 2006), pp. 280–1.

157. It is probably for this occasion that their double-portrait was made by Joos van Cleve.

158. P. Génard, 'L'Hotel des Monnaies d'Anvers', *Annales de l'Académie d'archéologie de Belgique*, 30 (1874), pp. 5–170. On Thomas Gramaye: J. Cuypers, 'Geeraard Gramaye: sociaal-ekonomische studie van een Antwerpse persoonlijkheid uit de tweede helft der XVIde eeuw' (Ghent: Ghent University, 1948), pp. 1–14. On Cornelis van Eeckeren and Jacob van Hencxthoven: Soly, 'De bouw van de Antwerpse citadel'; H. Soly, 'Economische vernieuwing en sociale weerstand. De betekenis en aspiraties der Antwerpse middenklasse in de 16de eeuw', *Tijdschrift voor geschiedenis*, 83 (1970), pp. 520–35; H. Soly, 'Een Antwerpse compagnie voor de levensmiddelenbevoorrading van het leger in de zestiende eeuw', *Bijdragen en mededelingen betreffende de geschiedenis der Nederlanden*, 186 (1971), pp. 350–62; H. Soly, 'Het "verraad" der 16de-eeuwse Burgerij: een mythe? Enkele beschouwingen betreffende het gedragspatroon der 16de-eeuwse Antwerpse ondernemers', *Tijdschrift voor geschiedenis*, 83 (1973), pp. 262–80; Soly, *Urbanisme en kapitalisme*.

159. Peat was used as fuel in many Antwerp households and in industry. Soly, *Urbanisme en kapitalisme*, pp. 251–62.

160. Van der Wee, 'Structural Changes', pp. 213, 216; Van der Wee, 'Industrial Dynamics and the Process of Urbanization', pp. 340–1. For example: P. Stabel, 'Organisation corporative et production d'oeuvres d'art à Bruges à la fin du Moyen Age et au début des Temps Modernes', *Le Moyen Âge: revue d'histoire et de philologie*, 113 (2007), pp. 91–134; W. Blockmans, 'The Creative Environment: Incentives to and Functions of Bruges Art Production', in M. W. Ainsworth (ed.), *Petrus Christus in Renaissance*

Bruges: An Interdisciplinary Approach (New York/Turnhout: The Metropolitan Museum of Art/Brepols, 1995), pp. 11–20; Vermeylen, *Painting for the Market*. On furs: Cornelis J. F. Slootmans, 'Huiden en pelzen op de jaarmarkten van Bergen-Op-Zoom', in L. G. Verberne and A. Weijnen (eds), *Land Van mijn hart: Brabantse feestbundel voor Mgr Prof. Dr Th.J.A. Goossens op zijn zeventigste verjaardag (8 febr. 1952)* (Tilburg: Henri Bergmans, 1952).

161. Vermeylen, *Painting for the Market*, pp. 62–78.
162. N. De Marchi and H. J. Van Miegroet, 'The Antwerpen-Mechelen Production and Export Complex', in A. Golahny, M. M. Mochizuki and L. Vergara (eds), *In his Milieu: Essays on Netherlandish Art in Memory of John Michael Montias* (Amsterdam: Amsterdam University Press, 2006), pp. 133–48.
163. Vermeylen, *Painting for the Market*, pp. 170–1.
164. Vermeylen, *Painting for the Market*, p. 99.
165. F. Melis, 'La diffusione nel Mediterraneo occidentale dei panni di Wervicq e delle altre città della Lys attorno al 1400', in *Studi in onore di Amintore Fanfani* (Milan: Giuffré, 1962).
166. H. Van Werveke, 'Die Stellung des Hansischen Kaufmanns dem Flandrischen Tuchproduzenten gegenüber', in *Beiträge zur Wirtschafts- und Stadtgeschichte. Festschrift für Hektor Ammann* (Wiesbaden: Steiner, 1965), p. 67; Dollinger, *The German Hansa*; Stabel, 'Marketing Cloth in the Low Countries', p. 19; S. Abraham-Thisse, 'De lakenhandel in Brugge', in A. Vandewalle (ed.), *Hanzekooplui en Medicibankiers: Brugge, wisselmarkt van Europese culturen* (Oostkamp: Stichting Kunstboek, 2002), pp. 65–70.
167. Calculations based on Puttevils, 'A servitio de vostri'; Edler, 'Le commerce d'exportation'.
168. W. Brulez, 'The Balance of Trade of the Netherlands in the Middle of the 16th Century', *Acta historiae Neerlandica*, 4 (1970), pp. 20–48, on p. 48.
169. M. van Tielhof, *De Hollandse graanhandel, 1470–1570: koren op de Amsterdamse molen* (The Hague: Stichting Hollandse Historische Reeks, 1995).
170. The sixteenth-century Holland economy was firmly oriented towards Antwerp. J. Luiten Van Zanden, 'Holland en de Zuidelijke Nederlanden in de periode 1500–1570: divergerende ontwikkelingen of voortgaande economische integratie', in E. Aerts, B. Henau, P. Janssens and R. Van Uytven (eds), *Studia historica oeconomica. Liber amicorum Herman Van Der Wee* (Leuven: Leuven University Press, 1993), pp. 357–67.
171. Van Tielhof, *De Hollandse graanhandel, 1470–1570: koren op de Amsterdamse molen*, pp. 209–12.
172. Van Tielhof, *De Hollandse graanhandel*, p. 213; E. H. Wijnroks, *Handel tussen Rusland en de Nederlanden, 1560–1640: een netwerkanalyse van de Antwerpse en Amsterdamse kooplieden, handelend op Rusland* (Hilversum: Verloren, 2003).
173. van Tielhof, *De Hollandse Graanhandel*, pp. 223–5; A. van Dixhoorn, 'The Grain Issue of 1565–1566: Policymaking, Public Opinion, and Common Good in the Habsburg Netherlands', in E. Lecuppre-Desjardin and A.-L. Van Bruaene (eds), *De Bono Communi: The Discourse and Practice of the Common Good in the European City (13th–16th C.): Discours et pratique du bien commun dans les villes d'Europe (XIIIe au XVIe siècle)* (Turnhout: Brepols, 2009), pp. 171–204. On these Lille families: R. S. Duplessis, *Lille and the Dutch Revolt: Urban Stability in an Era of Revolution, 1500–1582* (Cambridge: Cambridge University Press, 1991), pp. 68–73.
174. van Dixhoorn, 'The Grain Issue of 1565–1566', p. 176.
175. On wine consumption in the sixteenth-century Low Countries: Craeybeckx, *Un grand*

commerce d'importation: les vins de France aux anciens Pays-Bas (13e–16e siècle) (Paris: SEVPEN, 1958); R. Van Uytven, 'Wijnhandel en -verbruik in het Antwerpen van de 16de eeuw', in F. De Nave and C. Depauw (eds), *Europa aan tafel: een verkenning van onze eet- en tafelcultuur* (Antwerp: MIM, 1993), pp. 41–7. On concentration in the wine trade: Craeybeckx, *Un grand commerce d'importation*, pp. 199, 207.

176. Craeybeckx, *Un grand commerce d'importation*, pp. 242–3. The dominance of Low Countries traders in the French wine imports in the second half of the sixteenth century is also confirmed by notarial acts from Bordeaux. Craeybeckx, *Un grand commerce d'importation*, pp. 228–9; M. A. Drost, *Documents pour servir à l'histoire du commerce des Pays-Bas avec la France jusqu'à 1585 (Bordeaux & La Rochelle)* ('s-Gravenhage: Instituut voor Nederlandse Geschiedenis, 1984).

177. Craeybeckx, *Un grand commerce d'importation*, pp. 250–6.

178. Craeybeckx, *Un grand commerce d'importation*, pp. 213–16.

179. Craeybeckx, *Un grand commerce d'importation*, p. 225.

180. Craeybeckx, *Un grand commerce d'importation*, p. 246.

181. Craeybeckx, *Un grand commerce d'importation*, pp. 228–9.

182. Craeybeckx, *Un grand commerce d'importation*, p. 239.

183. Craeybeckx, *Un grand commerce d'importation*, p. 244.

184. Craeybeckx, *Un grand commerce d'importation*, p. 248.

185. Craeybeckx, *Un grand commerce d'importation*, pp. 232–3.

186. E. Geudens, *Het hoofdambacht der meerseniers* (Antwerp: Dela Montagne, 1891); P. Neelen, 'Het Antwerpse meerseniersambacht in de zestiende eeuw' (Ghent: Universiteit Gent, 1997).

187. J.-A. Goris, *Etude sur les colonies marchandes méridionales (Portugais, Espagnols, Italiens) à Anvers de 1488 à 1587* (Leuven: Uytspruyt, 1925), pp. 194–205; J. Materné, 'Haven en hinterland: de Antwerpse specerijenmarkt in de 16de eeuw', in *Specerijkelijk: de specerijenroutes: 27 maart–14 juni 1992, ASLK-Galerij* (Brussels: ASLK, 1992); J. Materné, 'Antwerpen als verdeel- en veredelingscentrum van specerijen en suiker van de late 15de eeuw tot de 17de eeuw', in F. De Nave (ed.), *Europa aan tafel: een verkenning van onze eet- en tafelcultuur* (Antwerp: MIM, 1993), pp. 48–61.

188. Sometimes Turkish alum still reached the Low Countries in the sixteenth century. H. Soly, 'De aluinhandel in de Nederlanden in de 16e eeuw', *Belgisch tijdschrift voor filologie en geschiedenis*, 52 (1974), pp. 800–57, on p. 802. On Italian alum: J. Delumeau, *L'alun de Rome, 15e-19e siècle* (Paris: SEVPEN, 1962). For France: J. Bottin, 'Commerce, finances et pouvoir: la redistribution des aluns méditerranéens dans l'Europe du Nord-Ouest et en France au XVIe siècle', *Mélanges de l'École française de Rome*, 126:1 (2014).

189. J. H. Munro, 'Bruges and the Abortive Staple in English Cloth: An Incident in the Shift of Commerce from Bruges to Antwerp in the Late Fifteenth Century', *Revue belge de philologie et d'histoire*, 44:4 (1966), pp. 1137–59, on p. 1149; Soly, 'De aluinhandel', p. 803.

190. Soly, 'De aluinhandel', pp. 804–22.

191. Soly, 'De aluinhandel', pp. 822–35.

192. Craeybeckx, *Un grand commerce d'importation*, p. 38.

193. Craeybeckx, *Un grand commerce d'importation*, pp. 234–9.

194. This calculation was based on Sint-Winoksbergen says in Antwerp in 1538. The account provides information on transport, wrapping, sales and storage costs and excludes taxation and brokerage fees that can be derived from other sources. These transaction costs amounted to 4.4 per cent of the sales value of the say. P. Stabel, 'Mar-

keting Cloth in the Low Countries: Foreign Merchants, Local Businessmen and Urban Entrepreneurs: Markets, Transport and Transaction Costs (14th–16th Century)', in B. Blondé, A. Greve and P. Stabel (eds), *International Trade in the Low Countries (14th–16th Centuries): Merchants, Organisation, Infrastructure: Proceedings of the International Conference Ghent-Antwerp, 12th–13th January 1997* (Leuven: Garant, 2000), pp. 15–36, on pp. 33–5.

195. R. Ehrenberg, *Das Zeitalter der Fugger: Geldkapital und Creditverkehr im 16* (Jahrhundert Jena: Fischer, 1912); R. Ehrenberg, *Capital & Finance in the Age of the Renaissance: A Study of the Fuggers and their Connections* (Fairfield, NJ: Kelley, 1985).

196. J. Goldberg, *Trade and Institutions in the Medieval Mediterranean: The Geniza Merchants and their Business World* (Cambridge: Cambridge University Press, 2012).

197. R. Gascon, *Grand commerce et vie urbaine au 16e siècle: Lyon et ses marchands (environs de 1520–environs de 1580)* (Paris: Mouton, 1971), I, pp. 329–33, II, pp. 653–324, 695, 698; H. Heller, *Anti-Italianism in Sixteenth-Century France* (Toronto, ON: University of Toronto Press, 2003), pp. 43–4.

198. M. Bulut, *Ottoman–Dutch Economic Relations in the Early Modern Period, 1571–1699* (Hilversum: Verloren, 2001), pp. 107–28, 203–8; S. Pamuk, 'Changes in Factor Markets in the Ottoman Empire, 1500–1800', *Continuity and Change*, 24, special issue 1 (2009), pp. 107–36, on p. 12.

199. H. Greefs, 'Zakenlieden in Antwerpen tijdens de eerste helft van de negentiende eeuw' (PhD dissertation, University of Antwerp, 2004), pp. 173–80.

3 Financing and Organizing Commerce: Partnerships

1.   Calendar of State Papers Foreign, Elizabeth, 1558–9, vol. 7: 1564–5, 70/81 f.62, Nov. 29 1565.

2.   R. Ehrenberg, *Das Zeitalter der Fugger: Geldkapital und Creditverkehr im 16* (Jahrhundert Jena: Fischer, 1912); F. Braudel, *The Mediterranean in the Age of Philip II*, 2 vols (New York: Harper & Row, 1972), vol. 2, pp. 500–4; F. Braudel, *The Perspective of the World*, 3 vols, vol. 3: *Civilization and Capitalism, 15th–18th Century* (London: Collins, 1982), pp. 157–73

3.   M.-T. Boyer-Xambeu, G. Deleplace, and L. Gillard, *Private Money and Public Currencies: The 16th Century Challenge*, trans. Azizeh Azodi (New York: M. E. Sharpe, 1994); E. S. Hunt, *The Medieval Super-Companies: A Study of the Peruzzi Company of Florence* (Cambridge: Cambridge University Press, 1994); E. S. Hunt and J. M. Murray, *A History of Business in Medieval Europe, 1200–1550* (Cambridge: Cambridge University Press, 1999), pp. 195–8; M. Drelichman and H.-J. Voth, Voth, *Lending to the Borrower from Hell: Debt, Taxes, and Default in the Age of Philip II* (Princeton, NJ: Princeton University Press, 2014).

4.   Ehrenberg, *Das Zeitalter Der Fugger*; M. Häberlein, *The Fuggers of Augsburg: Pursuing Wealth and Honor in Renaissance Germany*, Studies in Early Modern German History (Charlottesville, VI: University of Virginia Press, 2012).

5.   J.-A. Goris, *Etude sur les colonies marchandes méridionales (Portugais, Espagnols, Italiens) à Anvers de 1488 à 1587* (Leuven: Uytspruyt, 1925), pp. 393–7; R. Ehrenberg, *Capital & Finance in the Age of the Renaissance: A Study of the Fuggers and their Connections* (Fairfield, NJ: Kelley, 1985), II, pp. 248–80; E. Aerts, 'Geld, krediet en financiën in de Zuidelijke Nederlanden ca. 1500–1550', in M. Daneel (ed.), *Keizer Karels geldbeurs: geld en financiën in de 16de eeuw* (Brussels: Nationale Bank van België,

2000), pp. 69–70; Haemers, Jelle, and Peter Stabel. "From Bruges to Antwerp. International Commercial Firms and Government's Credit in the Late 15th and Early 16th Century." in *Banca, crédito y capital. La monarquía hispánica y los antiguos Países Bajos (1505-1700)*, (Madrid: Fundación Carlos de Amberes, 2006), pp. 21-37.

6. Foreigners holding this position were the south German Lazarus Tucher (1529–41) and the Italian Gaspar Ducci (1542–50). On Tucher: Ehrenberg, *Capital & Finance in the Age of the Renaissance*, pp. 177–83. On Ducci: J. Denucé, *Italiaansche koopmansgeslachten te Antwerpen in de 16e-18e eeuwen* (Mechelen: Het Kompas, 1934); S. de Cock, *Gaspar Ducci, bankier van keizer Karel, heer van Schoonsel en Kruibeke* (Borgerhout: Drukkerij Cools, 1979); Ehrenberg, *Capital & Finance in the Age of the Renaissance*, pp. 222–6.

7. H. Heller, *Anti-Italianism in Sixteenth-Century France* (Toronto, ON: University of Toronto Press, 2003).

8. P. Génard, 'Un acte de société commerciale au XVIième siècle (La maison Schetz frères d'Anvers)', *Bulletin de la Société de Géographie d' Anvers*, 7 (1882), pp. 475–99; J. L. Meulleners, *De Antwerpsche bankier Erasmus Schetz en zijne geassocieërden Jan Vleminck en Arnold Proenen in hunne betrekking tot Maastricht en Aken* (Maastricht: Le Courrier de la Meuse, 1890); A. Louant, 'Gaspard Schetz, seigneur de Grobbendonck, facteur du roi d'Espagne à Anvers (1555–1561)', *Annales de l'Académie royale d'archéologie de Belgique*, 77 (1930), pp. 315–28; F. Prims, 'Erasmus Schetz in 1525–1532', *Antwerpiensia*, 13 (1939), pp. 63–9; H. L. V. De Groote, 'De vermogensbalans van Melchior Schetz en zijn vrouw Anna Van Stralen met hun testament van 1 juli 1569', *Bijdragen tot de geschiedenis*, 55 (1972), pp. 226–63; H. Soly, 'De aluinhandel in de Nederlanden in de 16e eeuw', *Belgisch tijdschrift voor filologie en geschiedenis*, 52 (1974), pp. 800–57, on pp. 822–35; B. d' Ursel, *Les Schetz* (Brussels: Office généalogique et héraldique de Belgique, 2004).

9. R. P. F. Kieckens, 'Une sucrerie anversoise au Brésil à la fin du XVIe siècle', *Bulletin de la Société de Géographie d'Anvers*, 7 (1882), pp. 467–74; Meulleners, *De Antwerpsche bankier*; F. Donnet, *Coup d'oeil sur l'histoire financière d'Anvers au cours des siècles* (Antwerp: Buschmann, 1927); J. Denucé, *Afrika in de 16de eeuw en de handel van Antwerpen* (Antwerp: Sikkel, 1937), pp. 40–1; Soly, 'De aluinhandel', pp. 822–3; J. Everaert, 'Marchands flamands à Lisbonne et l'exportation du sucre de Madère (1480–1530)', Paper presented at the Actas do I Coloquio de Historia da Madeira, Funchal, 1986; J. Materné, 'Antwerpen als verdeel- en veredelingscentrum van specerijen en suiker van de late 15de eeuw tot de 17de eeuw', in F. De Nave (ed.), *Europa aan tafel. Een verkenning van onze eet- en tafelcultuur* (Antwerp: MIM, 1993), pp. 48–61.

10. Kieckens, 'Une Sucrerie Anversoise Au Brésil À La Fin Du Xvie Siècle'; C. Laga, 'O Engenho Dos Erasmos En Sao Vicente: Resultado De Perquisas in Arquivos Belgas', *Estudos Historicos*, 1 (1963), pp. 13–43; E. Stols, 'Um Dos Primeiros Documentos Sobre O Engenho Dos Schetz Em Sao Vicente', *Revista de Historia*, 76 (1968), pp. 407–19.

11. Ehrenberg, *Das Zeitalter der Fugger*, I, pp. 366–7.

12. Ehrenberg, *Das Zeitalter der Fugger*, I, p. 368.

13. Ehrenberg, *Das Zeitalter Der Fugger*, II, pp. 152–3.

14. J. D. Tracy, *Emperor Charles V, Impresario of War: Campaign Strategy, International Finance, and Domestic Politics* (Cambridge: Cambridge University Press, 2002), p. 101. Based on the tables in R. Carande, *Carlos V y sus banqueros* (Madrid: Soeciedag de estudios y publicaciones, 1949).

15. Ehrenberg, *Das Zeitalter der Fugger*, I, pp. 370–1; Louant, 'Gaspard Schetz', pp. 315–19.

16. Ehrenberg, *Das Zeitalter der Fugger*, II, pp. 154–5; Soly, 'De Aluinhandel', pp. 826–7. On Habsburg payment difficulties: Drelichman and Voth, *Lending to the Borrower from Hell: Debt, Taxes, and Default in the Age of Philip II*, pp. 18, 53, 95 (on the 1557 default).

17. Soly, 'De Aluinhandel', p. 827.

18. R. B. Outhwaite, 'The Trials of Foreign Borrowing: The English Crown and the Antwerp Money Market in the Mid-Sixteenth Century', *Economic History Review*, 19:2 (1966), pp. 289–305; I. Blanchard, 'English Royal Borrowing at Antwerp, 1544–1574', in M. Boone and W. Prevenier (eds), *Finances publiques et finances privées au bas Moyen Âge: actes du colloque, Gand, les 5 et 6 mai 1995 = Public and Private Finances in the Late Middle Ages* (Leuven: Garant, 1996), pp. 57–73.

19. J. Gairdner and R. H. Brodie (eds), Gairdner, J., and R. H. Brodie (eds), *Letters and Papers, Foreign and Domestic, Henry VIII*, 21 vols (London: Longman, 1908), vol. 21:1, p. 119.

20. J. W. Burgon, *The Life and Times of Sir Thomas Gresham* (London: Jennings, 1839), p. 86.

21. Calendar of State Papers Foreign, Mary, 1553–1558, SP 69/12 f.155, letter from Thomas Gresham to Queen Mary (May 23 1558).

22. Calendar of State Papers Foreign, Elizabeth, Volume 2, 1559–1560, The Queen's debts in Flanders (November 2 1559). J. R. Dasent, *Acts of the Privy Council of England, 1558–1570*, 46 vols (London: Eyre and Spottiswoode, 1890), vol. 7, pp. 340–1.

23. Dasent, *Acts of the Privy Council of England, 1558–1570*.

24. Additional research is necessary to determine their quantitative role.

25. L. Neal, 'The Finance of Business during the Industrial Revolution', in R. Floud and D. McCloskey (eds), *The Economic History of Britain since 1700* (Cambridge: Cambridge University Press, 1994), ch. 7, pp. 151–81; O. Gelderblom, 'Entrepreneurs in the Golden Age of the Dutch Republic', in W. J. Baumol, D. S. Landes and J. Mokyr (eds), *The Invention of Enterprise: Entrepreneurship from Ancient Mesopotamia to Modern Times*, (Princeton, NJ: Princeton University Press, 2010), ch. 6, pp. 156–82; M. Kohn, 'Business Management in Pre-Industrial Europe', 2003, unpublished working paper, available at http://www.dartmouth.edu/~mkohn/Papers/15.%20Management.pdf [accessed 28 February 2015); M. Kohn, 'Business Organization in Pre-Industrial Europe', 2003, unpublished working paper, available at http://www.dartmouth.edu/~mkohn/Papers/14.%20Business%20organization.pdf [accessed 28 February 2015].

26. B. Willems, *Leven op de pof: krediet bij de Antwerpse middenstand in de achttiende eeuw* (Amsterdam: Aksant, 2009), p. 91; H. Deneweth, 'A Fine Balance: Household Finance and Financial Strategies of Antwerp Households, 17th–18th Century', *Tijdschrift voor sociale en economische geschiedenis*, 8:4 (2011), pp. 15–43; S. Ogilvie, M. Küpker and J. Maegraith, 'Household Debt in Early Modern Germany: Evidence from Personal Inventories', *Journal of Economic History*, 72:1 (2012), pp. 134–67.

27. O. Gelderblom, 'The Governance of Early Modern Trade: The Case of Hans Thijs, 1556–1611', *Enterprise & Society*, 4:4 (2003), pp. 606–39.

28. H. Soly, 'De schepenregisters als bron voor de conjunctuurgeschiedenis van Zuid- en Noordnederlandse steden in het Ancien Régime. Een concreet voorbeeld: de Antwerpse immobiliënmarkt in de 16de eeuw', *Tijdschrift voor geschiedenis*, 87 (1974), pp. 521–44; H. Soly, *Urbanisme en kapitalisme te Antwerpen in de 16de eeuw: de stedebouwkundige en industriële ondernemingen van Gilbert van Schoonbeke* (Brussels: Gemeentekrediet, 1977), pp. 51–107; J. Dambruyne, *Mensen en centen: het 16de-eeuwse Gent in demografisch en*

economisch perpectief (Ghent: Maatschappij voor Geschiedenis en Oudheidkunde, 2001); M. 't Hart and M. Van der Heijden, 'Het geld van de Stad. Recente historiografische trends in het onderzoek naar stedelijke financiën in de Nederlanden', *Tijdschrift voor sociale en economische geschiedenis*, 3:3 (2006), pp. 3–35; M. Van der Heijden, *Geldschieters van de stad: financiële relaties tussen stad, burgers en overheden 1550–1650* (Amsterdam: Bert Bakker, 2006); J. Hanus, *Tussen stad en eigen gewin: stadsfinanciën, renteniers en kredietmarkten in 's-Hertogenbosch (begin zestiende eeuw)* (Amsterdam: Aksant, 2007); C. J. Zuijderduijn, 'Conjunctuur in laatmiddeleeuws Haarlem: schepenregisters als bron voor de economische ontwikkeling van een Hollandse stad', *Holland. Historisch Tijdschrift*, 40:1 (2008), pp. 3–17; C. J. Zuijderduijn, *Medieval Capital Markets: Markets for Renten, State Formation and Private Investment in Holland (1300–1550)* (Leiden: Brill, 2009); J. Hanus, 'Een efficiënte pre-industriële kapitaalmarkt? Het vroeg zestiende-eeuwse 's-Hertogenbosch als voorbeeld', *Tijdschrift voor sociale en economische geschiedenis*, 6:3 (2009), pp. 82–113; Gelderblom, 'Entrepreneurs', p. 166.

29. Compare the high per capita sums of new annuity sales in Antwerp compared to 's-Hertogenbosch, Ghent and Paris. Hanus, 'Een efficiënte pre-Industriële kapitaalmarkt?', p. 98.
30. Soly, *Urbanisme en kapitalisme*, pp. 81–4, 95–8.
31. Soly, *Urbanisme en kapitalisme*, pp. 71–2.
32. Soly, *Urbanisme en kapitalisme*, p. 66.
33. The most extensive work on bills of exchange is R. de Roover, *L'évolution de la lettre de change, 14e-18e siècles* (Paris: Colin, 1953). Also, W. Brulez, *De firma Della Faille en de internationale handel van Vlaamse firma's in de 16de eeuw* (Brussels: Paleis der Academiën, 1959), pp. 394–407.
34. De Roover paid a lot of attention to change and re-change bill transactions which were not very common. *L'évolution de la lettre de change*, pp. 130–1, cited in Brulez, *De firma Della Faille*, pp. 394–5. Van der Wee confirms the opinion of Brulez, by saying that Low Countries merchants mainly used the bill of exchange to transfer funds. H. Van der Wee, 'Antwerp and the New Financial Methods of the 16th and 17th Centuries', trans. L. Fackelman, in H. Van der Wee (ed.), *The Low Countries in the Early Modern World* (Aldershot: Ashgate, 1993), ch. 8, pp. 145–66, on pp. 149–50.
35. Brulez, *De firma Della Faille*, pp. 399–400.
36. O. de Smedt, 'De keizerlijke verordeningen van 1537 en 1539 op de obligaties en wisselbrieven: eenige kantteekeningen', *Nederlandsche Historiebladen: driemaandelijks tijdschrift voor de geschiedenis en de kunstgeschiedenis van de Nederlanden*, 3 (1940–1), pp. 15–35; F. Edler, 'The Effects of the Financial Measures of Charles V on the Commerce of Antwerp, 1539–1542', *Belgisch tijdschrift voor filologie en geschiedenis*, 16:3–4 (1937), pp. 665–73; D. De Ruysscher, *Handel en recht in de Antwerpse rechtbank (1585–1713)* (Leuven: UGA, 2009), pp. 249–78.
37. De Ruysscher, *Handel en recht*, pp. 247–65.
38. 2.3 per cent of all notarial acts registered by 's-Hertogen in 1540 concerned bills of exchange, CAA, Notarial archives, notary Adriaen Zeger 's-Hertoghen, N # 2071; 5.2 per cent of all acts of Stryt in that year, CAA, Notarial archives, notary Willem Stryt, N # 3133.
39. Van der Wee, 'Antwerp and the New Financial Methods', pp. 161, 164–6. Brulez maintains that discounting (selling bills to a third party at a value lower than the nominal value before the maturity date) and endossement (transferring the bill to a third party) developed relatively late since there was little need to trade this short-term form of

credit (three months at most). Brulez, *De firma Della Faille*, pp. 401–5.

40. R. Doehaerd, *Etudes anversoises: documents sur le commerce International à Anvers, 1488–1514*, 3 vols (Paris: SEVPEN, 1962–3), vol. 2, nr. 384 & 397.

41. C. Lesger and E. Wijnroks, 'The Spatial Organization of Trade: Antwerp Merchants and the Gateway Systems in the Baltic and the Low Countries *c*.1550', in H. Brand (ed.),*Trade, Diplomacy and Cultural Exchange: Continuity and Change in the North Sea Area and the Baltic, c.1350–1750* (Hilversum: Verloren, 2005), ch. 1, pp. 15–35, on pp. 22–6, with further examples on pp. 24–6.

42. This was a frequent practice in Florence. Correspondence with Richard Goldthwaite.

43. H. Van der Wee, 'Anvers et les innovations de la technique financière aux XVIe et XVIIe siècles', *Annales: Economies, Sociétés, Civilisations*, 22:5 (1977), pp. 1067–89, on pp. 1069, 1073; H. Vand der Wee, 'Geld- krediet- en bankwezen in de Zuidelijke Nederlanden 1490–1580', in D. P. Blok (ed.), *Algemene Geschiedenis der Nederlanden* (Haarlem: Fibula-Van Dishoeck, 1979), pp. 98–108, on p. 101.

44. J. Cuypers, 'Geeraard Gramaye: sociaal-ekonomische studie van een Antwerpse persoonlijkheid uit de tweede helft der XVIde eeuw' (Ghent: Ghent University, 1948), p. 79.

45. O. Gelderblom, *Cities of Commerce: The Institutional Foundations of International Trade in the Low Countries, 1250–1650* (Princeton, NJ: Princeton University Press, 2013), p. 97. More evidence on non-formalized debts can be found in the next chapter.

46. P. Génard, *Jean-Baptiste Ferrufini et les assurances maritimes à Anvers au 16e siècle* (Antwerp: Impr. De Backer, 1882); Goris, *Etude sur les colonies marchandes*, pp. 178–94; C. Verlinden, 'De zeeverzekeringen der Spaanse kooplui in de Nederlanden gedurende de XVIe Eeuw', *Bijdragen voor de geschiedenis der Nederlanden* (1948), pp. 191–216; A. Wastiels, 'Juan Henriquez, makelaar in zeeverzekeringen te Antwerpen (1562–1563)' (Licentiaat, Rijksuniversiteit Gent, 1967); H. L. V. De Groote, *De zeeassurantie te Antwerpen en te Brugge in de zestiende eeuw* (Antwerp: Marine Academie, 1975); H. L. V. De Groote, 'Zeeverzekering', in G. Asaert (ed.), *Maritieme Geschiedenis Der Nederlanden* (Bussum: De Boer Maritiem, 1976), pp. 206–19; De Ruysscher, *Handel en Recht*, pp. 283–303; D. De Ruysscher and J. Puttevils, 'The Art of Compromise. Legislative Talks for Marine Insurance Institutions in Antwerp (*c*.1550–*c*.1570)', *Low Countries Historical Review* (forthcoming).

47. Brulez, *De firma Della Faille*, pp. 3–21. RAB, Council of Brabant, Lawsuit files of private individuals, 198, Redenen voer Daniel de Hane cum suis originael supplianten tegen Jan de la Faille originael gedaegde, 1r.

48. Brulez, *De firma Della Faille*, pp. 17–21. RAB, Council of Brabant, Lawsuit files of private individuals, 198, Redenen voer Daniel de Hane, 9v. 'Verclerende voerts dat die gedaagde zoude schuldich wesen exhibitie te doen van alle zyne boecken die hy vanden voers handele gehouden hadde. Welcken nyettegenstaende is die voers gedaagde gebleven even gebrekelyck ende heeft blyven continueren zyne voers quade trouwe hebbende in handen vande voers commissarissen geexhibeert zekere imperfecte rekeninge zonder pertinente declaratie ende specificatie gemaeckt ende tot dyen contrarie der innehouden van zyne eygen boecken missiven ende balancen den supplianten naer venegien overgesonden ende om het selve bedroch betere te bedecken heeft gefabriceert vier yeuwe rekenboecken nyet corresponderende opde balance in rechte geexhibeert maer alleenlyck op zyne voerscreven nyeuwe gefabriceerde rekeninge'.

49. 'Dwelck in respecte vers voers gedaagde nyet cleyn en is geweest als die gene die by middele vande voers compaignie is geworden tgene hy is zynde van eenen huysknecht

gewordden compagnon ende met een cleyn capitael inde selve compaignie ontfangen ende deur het credit vande selve compaignie alzoe gebeneficieert dat zyne 2270 ducaten 2 grooten die hy ten aengaende vande voers compaignie alleenlyck heeft gehadt zyn in 19 jaeren boven alle oncosten gewassen tot 12426 ducaten 14 grooten zuyver capitaels gelyck dat vuyte voergaende deductien is blyckende'; RAB, Council of Brabant, Lawsuit files of private individuals, 198, Redenen voer Daniel de Hane, 18v-19r.

50. Calculations based on Brulez, *De firma Della Faille*, pp. 23–4.
51. Brulez, *De firma Della Faille*, pp. 35–8, 41.
52. Brulez, *De firma Della Faille*, pp. 63–72.
53. Della Faille partners, partners who were family members and family deposits.
54. Brulez, *De firma Della Faille*, pp. 363–5.
55. R. de Roover, *The Rise and Decline of the Medici Bank, 1397–1494* (Cambridge, MA: Harvard University Press, 1963); R. A. Goldthwaite, 'The Medici Bank and the World of Florentine Capitalism', *Past and Present*, 114 (1987), pp. 3–31; P. D. McLean and J. F. Padgett, 'Obligation, Risk, and Opportunity in the Renaissance Economy: Beyond Social Embeddedness to Network Co-Constitution', in F. Dobbin (ed.), *The Sociology of the Economy* (New York: Russell Sage Foundation, 2004), ch. 8, pp. 193–227, on p. 196; R. A. Goldthwaite, *The Economy of Renaissance Florence* (Baltimore, MD: Johns Hopkins University Press, 2009).
56. According to Thijs, sixteenth-century Antwerp artisans, unlike merchants, generally did not set up partnerships. Most industrial businesses were one-person enterprises, although this does not preclude that some of these businesses disposed of a sizeable capital. In the Antwerp cloth finishing industry all partnerships had to be registered and all profits and losses had to be divided equally. A. K. L. Thijs, 'Van "werkwinkel" tot "fabriek": de textielnijverheid te Antwerpen van het einde der vijftiende tot het begin der negentiende eeuw' (Ghent: Rijksuniversiteit Gent, 1978), III, 2, pp. 1131–6.
57. On the division between agency and finance: M. M. Postan, *Medieval Trade and Finance* (Cambridge: University Press, 1974), pp. 66–7; Kohn, 'Business Organization in Pre-Industrial Europe', p. 32.
58. F. Trivellato, *The Familiarity of Strangers: The Sephardic Diaspora, Livorno, and Cross-Cultural Trade in the Early Modern Period* (New Haven, CT: Yale University Press, 2009), p. 142.
59. S. Ogilvie, *Institutions and European Trade: Merchant Guilds, 1000–1800* (Cambridge: Cambridge University Press, 2011), p. 330; Gelderblom, *Cities of Commerce*, pp. 76–8.
60. E. H. Wijnroks, *Handel tussen Rusland en de Nederlanden, 1560–1640: een netwerkanalyse van de Antwerpse en Amsterdamse kooplieden, handelend op Rusland* (Hilversum: Verloren, 2003), pp. 181–5.
61. Trivellato, *The Familiarity of Strangers*, pp. 140, 146–7; Goldthwaite, *The Economy of Renaissance Florence*, pp. 69–76; Ogilvie, *Institutions and European Trade*, pp. 331–2.
62. A. Colli, *The History of Family Business, 1850–2000* (New York: Cambridge University Press, 2003); D. S. Landes, *Dynasties: Fortunes and Misfortunes of the World's Great Family Businesses* (New York, NY: Penguin, 2006). Cited in: Trivellato, *The Familiarity of Strangers*, pp. 146–7.
63. B. Supple, 'The Nature of Enterprise', 'The Nature of Enterprise', in E. E. Rich and C. H. Wilson (eds), *The Economic Organization of Early Modern Europe, The Cambridge Economic History of Europe* (Cambridge: Cambridge University Press, 1977), ch. 6, pp. 393–461, on p. 410. Or as Grassby put it: 'in the early modern economy it was inevitable that most business activity would be in the hands of small family firms'. R. Grassby,

Kinship and Capitalism: Marriage, Family, and Business in the English-Speaking World, 1580–1740 (Washington, DC: Woodrow Wilson Center Press, 2001), pp. 415–16.

64. Supple, *Kinship and Capitalism: Marriage, Family, and Business in the English-Speaking World, 1580–1740*, pp. 415–16.

65. Gelderblom, 'Entrepreneurs', p. 164.

66. Kohn, 'Business Organization in Pre-Industrial Europe', p. 36.

67. Kohn, 'Business Organization in Pre-Industrial Europe', p. 38; Wijnroks, *Handel Tussen Rusland En De Nederlanden*, pp. 180–1.

68. Ogilvie, *Institutions and European Trade*, p. 332.

69. RAA, Notarial archives, notary Jacobus de Platea, 522 and 523, 1524–6 & 1531–40 (and his drafts (524 & 525) for 1535–9 and 1539–43). For 1535: CAA, Notarial archives, notary Willem Stryt, N # 3132. For the later years, sample years were selected. For 1540: CAA, Notarial archives, notary Adriaan Zeger 's Hertoghen, N # 2071; CAA, Notarial archives, notary Willem Stryt, N # 3133. For 1550–1: CAA, Notarial archives, notary Adriaan Zeger 's Hertoghen, N # 2074; CAA, Notarial archives, notary Zeger 's Hertoghen, N # 2078. For 1560–1561: CAA, Notarial archives, notary Adriaan Zeger 's Hertoghen, N # 2077, CAA, Notarial archives, notary Stephanus Claeys, N # 544. For 1570: CAA, Notarial archives, notary Jan Dries, N # 1329; CAA, Notarial archives, notary Jacob De Kimpe, N # 863; CAA, Notarial archives, notary Jan Rogge, N # 2875; and CAA, Notarial archives, notary Dierick van den Bossche, N # 3635. All partnership contracts involving Netherlandish merchants published in J. Strieder, *Aus Antwerpener Notariatsarchiven: Quellen zur Deutschen Wirtschaftsgeschichte des 16* (Jahrhunderts Berlin: Deutsche Verlags-Anstalt, 1930) are also included in our sample.

70. B. Van Hofstraeten, 'Small-Scale Business Enterprises in Sixteenth-Century Antwerp (1480–1620)', paper presented at the European Business History Association Conference, Utrecht, 2014.

71. Accessed through index available in the Stadsarchief Antwerpen. For certificates, see G. Asaert, 'De oudste Certificatiën van de stad Antwerpen (1468–1482)', *Handelingen van de Koninklijke Commissie voor Geschiedenis*, 132 (1966), pp. 261–96.

72. For the Antwerp bench of aldermen: CAA, Vierschaar, Sentence books, V 1233, 1504–5; CAA, Vierschaar, Sentence books, V 1239–40, 1544. CAA, Processen & Processen supplement (until 1570). For the Council of Brabant: RAB, Council of Brabant, Sentence books, 504 (1504), 505 (1505), 589–90 (1544). RAB, Council of Brabant, Lawsuit files of private individuals, 1–343 (until 1590). For the Great Council: J. T. de Smidt et al., *Chronologische lijsten van de geëxtendeerde sententiën berustende in het archief van de Grote Raad van Mechelen, 1465 [–1580]* (Brussels: Koninklijke commissie voor de uitgave der oude wetten en verordeningen van België, 1966).

73. D. De Ruysscher, 'A Business Trust for Partnerships? Early Conceptions of Company-Related Assets in Legal Literature and Antwerp Forensic and Commercial Practice (Later Sixteenth–Early Seventeenth Century)', in W. Decock, F. Stevens and B. Van Hofstraeten (eds), *Company Law in Late Medieval and Early Modern Europe* (Brussels: Paleis der Academiën, 2015), p. 3.

74. Postan has observed this for late medieval England and pointed out that partnership disputes were translated into conflicts about account and debt. M. M. Postan, *Medieval Trade and Finance* (Cambridge: Cambridge University Press, 1974), p. 4.

75. A recent discussion of these texts can be found in: D. De Ruysscher, *Handel en recht in de Antwerpse rechtbank (1585–1713)* (Leuven: UGA, 2009), pp. 46–98. The Costuy-

men texts can be consulted at: https://www.kuleuven-kulak.be/facult/rechten/Mon-ballyu/Rechtlagelanden/Brabantsrecht/brabantsrechtindex.htm [accessed 28 February 2015].

76. De Ruysscher, 'A Business Trust for Partnerships?', p. 8.
77. De Ruysscher, *Handel en Recht*, pp. 59–68.
78. E. H. Wijnroks, *Handel tussen Rusland en de Nederlanden*, pp. 65–124, 179–210.
79. There was no registration of partnerships in south German cities either, despite interest in the constitution of partnerships for reasons of liability. E. Lutz, *Die Rechtliche Struktur Süddeutscher Handelsgesellschaften in der Zeit der Fugger. Studien zur Fuggergeschichte* (Tübingen: Mohr, 1976), pp. 197–8.
80. R. De Roover, 'La communauté des marchands lucquois à Bruges de 1377 à 1404', *Handelingen van het Genootschap voor Geschiedenis te Brugge*, 86 (1949), pp. 23–89, on pp. 61–5, cited in: O. Gelderblom, *Cities of Commerce*, p. 85.
81. A. Cordes, K. Friedland and R. Sprandel, *Societates. Das Verzeichnis der Handelsgesellschaften im Lübecker Niederstadtbuch 1311–1361* (Köln: Böhlau Verlag, 2003), p. 89.
82. O. Gelderblom, 'Entrepreneurs in the Golden Age of the Dutch Republic', p. 164; Gelderblom, *Cities of Commerce*, p. 89.
83. Living in the Bourse neighbourhood.
84. Costuymen 1608, IX, articles 2, 3.
85. Twenty-one of them in the notarial acts. One of these was even recorded twice with exact the same wording. CAA, Notarial archives, notary Zeger Adriaan 's-Hertoghen, N # 2071, 208r and 258r.
86. F. Stevens, *Revolutie en notariaat: Antwerpen, 1794–1814* (Assen: Van Gorcum, 1994). p. 281.
87. E. Lutz, *Die Rechtliche Struktur*, p. 65.
88. This is also rare in Florentine and south German contracts. Lutz, *Die Rechtliche Struktur*, pp. 206–9; R. A. Goldthwaite, *The Economy of Renaissance Florence*, p. 65.
89. CAA, Notarial archives, notary Adriaan Zeger 's Hertoghen, N # 2077, 45r, 115r and 45r (1560–1). CAA, Certification books, CERT # 18, 100r.
90. Median = 2, average = 2.77. Van Hofstraeten's 144 contract sample yields similar results: an average of 2.7 and a median of two partners per partnership. B. Van Hofstraeten, 'Small-Scale Business Enterprises in Sixteenth-Century Antwerp (1480–1620)'.
91. Median = 3, average = 3.74 Based on E. H. Wijnroks, *Handel tussen Rusland en de Nederlanden*, part 1.
92. P. D. McLean and J. F. Padgett, 'Obligation, Risk, and Opportunity in the Renaissance Economy: Beyond Social Embeddedness to Network Co-Constitution', in F. Dobbin (ed.), *The Sociology of the Economy* (New York: Russell Sage Foundation, 2004), ch. 8, pp. 192–227, on. p. 200.
93. R. A. Goldthwaite, *The Economy of Renaissance Florence*, p. 467.
94. E. Lutz, *Die Rechtliche Struktur*, p. 243.
95. This is based on surnames, the entire range of primary sources used in this book and the secondary literature on Antwerp merchants.
96. W. Brulez, *De firma Della Faille*, pp. 63–72.
97. 25 per cent of all dyads were father-son relations or partnerships between brothers. McLean and Padgett, 'Obligation, Risk, and Opportunity', pp. 203–4.
98. R. Grassby, *Kinship and Capitalism: Marriage, Family, and Business in the English-Speaking World, 1580–1740* (Washington, DC: Woodrow Wilson Center Press,

2001), p. 291.

99. Q. Van Doosselaere, *Commercial Agreements and Social Dynamics in Medieval Genoa* (Cambridge: Cambridge University Press, 2009), pp. 177–80

100. A. Al-Hussein, 'Trade and Business Community in Old Castile: Medina Del Campo 1500–1575' (PhD dissertation, University of East Anglia, 1982), p. 216.

101. CAA, Certification books, CERT # 25, 257v. Jan and Merten Weverseyn had long worked together but after mutually cancelling each other's debts, they agreed to no longer co-operate. CAA, Notariaat, Adriaan Zeger 's Hertoghen, 2074, 187r; Sebastiaan and Francois de Fevre explicitly stated that after ending their partnership they were no longer liable for each other. CAA, Collectanea, COLL # 5, 160r.

102. Gelderblom, 'Entrepreneurs', p. 164.

103. We define foreign here as 'not originating from the Low Countries'. This means that some foreigners who were naturalized as poorters are still considered as foreigners.

104. Brulez, *De firma Della Faille*, p. 364.

105. Three Italians, two Spanish merchants and two pairs of Hanseatic traders.

106. Unfortunately, both datasets are too small to provide a chronological view on the importance of foreign partners. I split up the heterogeneous dataset of partnership observations (mainly from notarial deeds) into the first half and the second half of the sixteenth century. In the first half of the century twelve of the fifty-two partners were foreigners (28 per cent) (twenty observations), in the second half nine of seventy-five partners were foreigners (12 per cent) (twenty-six observations). Given the heterogeneous nature of the dataset I have opted to avoid drawing conclusions from this observation.

107. RAA, Notarial archives, notary Jacobus de Platea, 523, 185r-v.

108. ZAM, 70 Familie De Jonge van Ellemeet, Pieces concerning the parents or ancestors of Maria Oyens, 45, Family history of the Van der Molen by Pieter van der Molen, 1545. RAA, Notarial archives, notary Jacobus de Platea, 523, 30v.

109. ZAM, 70 Familie De Jonge van Ellemeet, Pieces concerning the parents or ancestors of Maria Oyens, 45, Family history of the Van der Molen by Pieter van der Molen, 1545.

110. In 1535 both Bernardo and his son Giovanni Battista di Zanchi were in Venice. Elias Ghysbrechts testified that in the Venice house of Giovanni Battista di Zanchi, Bernardo's son, Macus Maza, another merchant from Verona, gave a bond to Bernardo di Zanchi. This testimony was done on behalf of Pieter Van der Molen in 1538. CAA, Collectanea, COLL # 5, 193r-v.

111. ZAM, 70 Familie De Jonge van Ellemeet, Pieces concerning the parents or ancestors of Maria Oyens, 45, Family history of the Van der Molen by Pieter van der Molen, 1545.

112. ZAM, 70 Familie De Jonge van Ellemeet, Pieces concerning the parents or ancestors of Maria Oyens, 40, Testament Frederik van der Molen and Alijt Ballincx.

113. For example: CAA, Insolvente Boedelkamer, IB # 2898, Letterbook Van der Molen, letter to Juliano Cibo Donato, 18 April 1538, 12r.

114. 'Li Zanchi sono molto magnanemi avendo apiacere a monstrar la lor richeza et noj siamo dj contraria opinione ... habiamo determinato che qui solo se dira Piero di Molin e fratelli et a Venezia Daniel de Molin a fine daquistar fama de ben fare et non de gran pompa ne richeza', CAA, Insolvente Boedelkamer, IB # 2898, Letterbook Van der Molen, letter to Bastiano del Baylo, 7 December 1540, 127v.

115. 'Le robe e debitori della compagnia de nostri Zanchi che loro tengino di tutto 1/5 e dia a noj li 4/5', CAA, Insolvente Boedelkamer, IB # 2898, Letterbook Van der Molen, letter to Bastiano del Baylo, 4 April 1540, 145v.

116. 'Speramo per le prime vostre aver el saldo et fine del vostro chonto et harete tuttj lj debi-

torj cattivj et longi in una partite per poter saldar et cadaun la sua rata. Et non essendo [fatto] vj pregamo se narete voglia chome ditto che non manchate di farlo che hormai saria tenpo Et ne vien in fastidio replicarvj tante volte una cossa che in un hora podete inscontrar el tutto con Daniel nostro, siche non ne diremo altro per hora, per esser ditto et replicato assai. Attendiamo solvere li effetti… Altro non diremo vj recommandamo dj solicitar li debitori', CAA, Insolvente Boedelkamer, IB # 2898, Letterbook Van der Molen, letter to Giovanni-Battista Zanchi, 18 September 1541, 215r.

117. ZAM, 70 Familie De Jonge van Ellemeet, Pieces concerning the parents or ancestors of Maria Oyens, 45, Family history of the Van der Molen by Pieter van der Molen, 1545.

118. Lutz, *Die Rechtliche Struktur*, pp. 206–9; Goldthwaite, *The Economy of Renaissance Florence*, p. 65.

119. Similarly, south German companies tried to limit opportunism through forbidding sureties and the extension of credit without the approval of the other partners. Lutz, *Die Rechtliche Struktur*, pp. 324–6. Contrary to Gelderblom, 'Entrepreneurs', p. 164.

120. Stadsarchief Antwerpen, Notariaat Adriaan Zeger 's Hertoghen, N 2074, 119v.

121. Stadsarchief Antwerpen, Notariaat Adriaan Zeger 's Hertoghen, N 2076, 19r.

122. P. Génard, 'Un acte de société', p. 483.

123. Lutz, *Die Rechtliche Struktur*, pp. 337, 449–454; Al-Hussein, 'Medina Del Campo', pp. 220–1; Katharina von Ciriachy-Wantrup, *Familien- und Erbrechtliche Gestaltungen von Unternehmen der Renaissance: eine Untersuchung der Augsburger Handelsgesellschaften zur Frühen Neuzeit. Augsburger Schriften zur Rechtsgeschichte* (Berlin: LIT, 2007), p. 237.

124. Génard, 'Un acte de société', p. 484. CAA, Notarial archives, notary Zeger Adriaan 's-Hertoghen, N # 2074, 212v. Such signs abound in the Antwerp certification books. See for example: Doehaerd, *Etudes anversoises*.

125. 'Ende mit conditie dat Pauwels van Houte den naem van Jan Gamell in gheender manieren en sal moegen gebruycken' CAA, Notarial archives, notary Zeger Adriaan 's-Hertoghen, N # 2077, 45r. See also: H. De Smedt, 'Antwerpen en de opbloei van de Vlaamse verhandel tijdens de 16e eeuw. rijkdom en inkomen van de Antwerpse koopman Jan Gamel volgens zijn staat van goed, 1572' (Leuven: Katholieke Universiteit Leuven, 1970), p. 52.

126. CAA, Notarial archives, notary Zeger Adriaan 's-Hertoghen, N # 2074, 212v.

127. CAA, Processen, 7 # 240.

128. De Groote, *De zeeassurantie*, p. 165.

129. See for the eighteenth century: Trivellato, *The Familiarity of Strangers*, p. 140.

130. Goldthwaite, *The Economy of Renaissance Florence*, p. 66.

131. Unfortunately the author does not note the current location of this debt book. Wijnroks, *Handel tussen Rusland en de Nederlanden*, pp. 142–3.

132. We also include data from the Schetz company trading on Germany, the Della Faille companies and on the equity capital values on a few of the Baltic and Russia partnerships. Génard, 'Un acte de société'; Brulez, *De firma Della Faille*; Wijnroks, *Handel tussen Rusland en de Nederlanden*. We also found equity capital data for two additional partnerships (not in partnership contracts) in the notarial archives and in the sentences of the Council of Brabant. Total of twenty-four observations.

133. Or between 1.86 and more than 2,000 equivalents of a master builder's annual wage. Mean equity capital in £ gr. Fl. = £8604.21 gr. Fl. (Median = £ 1,900 gr. Fl.) Available at http://www.economics.utoronto.ca/munro5/AntwerpWage.xls [accessed 28 February 2015].

134. A theoretical consideration of the history of dowries can be found in: M. Botticini, and

A. Siow, 'Why Dowries?', *American Economic Review*, 93:4 (2003), pp. 1385–98. On dowries in fifteenth-century Florence: M. Botticini, 'A Loveless Economy? Intergenerational Altruism and the Marriage Market in a Tuscan Town, 1415–1436', *Journal of Economic History*, 59:1 (1999), pp 104–21. On dowries among the seventeenth- and eighteenth-century Western Sephardim: F. Trivellato, *The Familiarity of Strangers*, pp. 133–9. For the Low Countries: M. C. Howell, *The Marriage Exchange: Property, Social Place, and Gender in Cities of the Low Countries, 1300–1550* (Chicago, IL: University of Chicago Press, 1998).

135. Stadsarchief Antwerpen, Notariaat Willem Stryt, N 3133, 368v.
136. Compilatae, IX, article 16, 22.
137. J. Van den Nieuwenhuizen, *Beknopte inventaris van de Insolvente Boedelskamer in het stadsarchief van Antwerpen* (Brussels: Algemeen Rijksarchief, 1998), pp. 766–9. Parts of these accounts are published in: J. Denucé, *De Hanze*, pp. 139–57. On his partnerships: J. Cuypers, 'Geeraerd Gramaye', pp. 63–91; P. Jeannin, 'Anvers et la Baltique au XVIe siècle', *Revue du Nord*, 37 (1955), pp. 93–113, on pp. 96–7; P. Jeannin, 'Les relations économiques des villes de la Baltique avec Anvers au XVIe siècles', *Vierteljahresschrift für Sozial- und Wirtschaftsgeschichte*, 43:3–4 (1956), pp. 193–217, 323–55, on pp. 213–15; Wijnroks, *Handel tussen Rusland en de Nederlanden*.
138. This is also true in south German partnerships: Lutz, *Die Rechtliche Struktur*, p. 248; Von Ciriachy-Wantrup, *Augsburger Handelsgesellschaften*, p. 225.
139. CAA, Notarial archives, notary Adriaan Zeger 's Hertoghen, N # 2074, 150r.
140. Génard, 'Un acte de société', pp. 485–6. See also: Soly, 'De aluinhandel', pp. 823–4.
141. Génard, 'Un acte de société', articles 4, 26.
142. Impressae, LII, article 8; Compilatae, IX, articles 23–4.
143. CAA, Notarial archives, notary Adriaan Zeger 's Hertoghen, N # 2071, 208r.
144. RAA, Notarial archives, notary Jacobus de Platea, 522, 204r.
145. CAA, Notarial archives, notary Adriaan Zeger 's Hertoghen, N 2070, 62r. See also: Fagel, *De Hispano-Vlaamse wereld*, pp. 261–2.
146. CAA, Collectanea, COLL # 3, 149r-v.
147. De Groote, *De zeeassurantie*, p. 165.
148. CAA, Notarial archives, notary Willem Stryt, N # 3133, 368v. This is similar in south German companies. Von Ciriachy-Wantrup, *Augsburger Handelsgesellschaften*, p. 236.
149. Italian, south German and Medina del Campo companies also stipulated articles on company costs.
150. CAA, Notarial archives, notary Adriaan Zeger 's Hertoghen, N # 2077, 115r.
151. Génard, 'Un acte de société', articles 23, 36.
152. CAA, Collectanea, COLL # 3, 149r-v.
153. De Ruysscher, 'A Business Trust for Partnerships?', p. 8.
154. Lutz, *Die Rechtliche Struktur*, pp. 59, 245, 276, 480; Von Ciriachy-Wantrup, *Augsburger Handelsgesellschaften*, pp. 230, 254.
155. In south German companies unanimity was often required in decision making. Lutz, *Die Rechtliche Struktur*, p. 365.
156. Brulez, *De firma Della Faille*, p. 66.
157. Génard, 'Un acte de société', article 19. Such a clause can also be found in: CAA, Notarial archives, notary Adriaan Zeger 's Hertogen, N # 2074, 25r.
158. Génard, 'Un acte de société', articles 3, 20.
159. Soly, *Urbanisme en kapitalisme*, p. 257.
160. CAA, Notarial archives, notary Willem Stryt, N # 3133, 368v; CAA, Notarial ar-

chives, notary Adriaan Zeger 's Hertoghen, N # 2074, 212v.

161. 'Et de touttes lesdits commissions tant de vente que dachapt et argent prins et trouve a interes comme de touttes aultres affairs de ce dependant se fera ung livre de raison lequel ledit Michiel Anthoine tiendra et sera tenu le monstrer ausdit Anthoine le Dieu et Adam Testart toutes et quantes fois que requis en sera et mesme leur ballier copie de ce que se sera negotie en estant requis', CAA, Processen Processen 7 # 240, document 9.

162. CAA, Notarial archives, notary Zeger Adriaan 's Hertoghen, N # 2074, 216v.

163. Compilatae, IX, articles 17, 18.

164. J. Ympyn, *Nieuwe Instructie ende Bewijs der Looffelijcker Consten des Rekenboecks* (London: Scholar, 1979), ch. 18. See also: O. Gelderblom, *Cities of Commerce*, p. 96. I would like to thank Botho Verbist (University of Antwerp) for this reference.

165. CAA, Notarial archives, notary Lieven van Rokeghem, N#4456, 94r. Geeraerd Gramaye likewise copied his Lisbon trade partnership into his main ledger. Cuypers, 'Geeraard Gramaye', pp. 66–8.

166. CAA, Certification books, CERT # 20, 99v.

167. South German companies: Lutz, *Die Rechtliche Struktur*, pp. 297–300, 388–94.

168. Génard, 'Un acte de société', article 12 and yearly account closures.

169. Génard, 'Un acte de société', article 12 and yearly account closures.

170. RAA, Notarial archives, notary Jacobus de Platea, 523, 185r-v.

171. The trial between Hendrik vander Beke and Franchois Schot – the former had served as an agent to supply army garrisons on behalf of the latter – provides a final account by vander Beke, listing all revenues and expenses. Vander Beke demanded payment of 4,709 guilders from Schot. CAA, Processen Supplement, 288 # 997, piece 3. Also cited in: Soly, 'Een Antwerpse compagnie voor de levensmiddelenbevoorrading', p. 357.

172. Stadsarchief Antwerpen, Vierschaar, V 322/9. The journal is published in Denucé, *De Hanze*, pp. 35–133. Reviewed by W. Koppe, 'Antwerpener Handelsunternehmungen "Auf Ostland"', *Hansische Geschichtsblätter*, 63 (1938), pp. 226–36. See also: J. A. Goris, 'Eene Antwerpsche handelsexpeditie in de Oostzeelanden (1562–1569)', *Bijdragen tot de geschiedenis*, 16 (1924–5), pp. 133–44; B. Oden, 'A Netherlandish Merchant in Stockholm in the Reign of Erik XIV', *Scandinavian Economic History Review*, 10:1 (1962), pp. 3–37; Wijnroks, *Handel tussen Rusland en de Nederlanden*, pp. 85–89. A similar example of such an agent account is that by Isidor Dalsz, who travelled to Russia on behalf of Aert Fabri. Published in Denucé, *De Hanze*, pp. 12–34; Wijnroks, *Handel tussen Rusland en de Nederlanden*, p. 104.

173. Gelderblom, 'Entrepreneurs', p. 164.

174. G. Vanden Hoecke, *In Arithmetica: een sonderlinge excellent boeck, leerende veel schoone ende perfecte regulen der selver conste* (Thantwerpen: by my Symon Cock, 1545), p. 143 sqq., quoted in Goris, *Etude sur les colonies marchandes*, p. 105, n. 103, cited by O. Gelderblom, A. De Jong and J. Jonker, 'An Admiralty for Asia: Isaac Le Maire and Conflicting Conceptions about the Corporate Governance of the VOC', in J. G. S. Koppell (ed.), *The Origins of Shareholder Advocacy* (New York: Palgrave Macmillan 2011) p. 35

175. Van Hofstraeten's 144 contract sample yields similar results: an average of 5.5 years and a median of six years. B. Van Hofstraeten, 'Small-Scale Business Enterprises in Sixteenth-Century Antwerp (1480–1620)'.

176. Lutz, *Die Rechtliche Struktur*, p. 211 (229 contracts); A. Al-Hussein, 'Trade and Business Community in Old Castile: Medina Del Campo 1500–1575' (PhD dissertation, University of East Anglia, 1982), p. 225.

177. McLean and Padgett, 'Obligation, Risk, and Opportunity in the Renaissance Economy', p.196. On the commenda: J. H. Pryor, 'Commenda: The Operation of the Contract in Long Distance Commerce at Marseilles During the Thirteenth Century', *The Journal of European Economic History*, 13:2 (1984), pp. 397–440, on pp. 397; Y. Gonzalez de Lara, 'Enforceability and Risk-Sharing in Financial Contracts: From the Sea Loan to the Commenda in Late Medieval Venice', *Journal of Economic History*, 61:2 (2001), pp 500–4; S. Aslanian, 'The Circulation of Men and Credit: The Role of the Commenda and the Family Firm in Julfan Society', *Journal of the Economic and Social History of the Orient*, 50 (2007), pp. 124–70; R. Harris, 'The Institutional Dynamics of Early Modern Eurasian Trade: The Commenda and the Corporation', *Journal of Economic Behavior & Organization*, 71:3 (2009), pp. 606–22.

178. Lutz, *Die Rechtliche Struktur*, pp. 212–28; M. Kohn, 'Business Organization in Pre-Industrial Europe', 2003, unpublished working paper, available at http://www. dartmouth.edu/~mkohn/Papers/14.%20Business%20organization.pdf (accessed 28 February 2015), p. 39.

179. Génard, 'Un acte de société'.

180. See the section, 'Partnership Finance'.

181. CAA, Notarial archives, notary Adriaan Zeger 's-Hertoghen, N # 2072, 178r. Published in Strieder, *Aus Antwerpener Notariatsarchiven*, nr 297. Jan Geldolf was active in the copper and brass trade between Antwerp, Rouen and Bordeaux. He also had contacts with English and Italian merchants and with Hanseatic shipmasters. See also: Craeybeckx, *Un grand commerce d'importation;* J. Craeybeckx, 'Handelaars en neringdoenden: de 16de eeuw', in J. L. Broeckx, C. de Clercq and J. Dhondt (eds), *Flandria Nostra: ons land en ons volk, zijn standen en beroepen door de tijden heen* (Antwerp: Standaard, 1957), p. 434.

182. CAA, Notarial archives, notary Adriaan Zeger 's-Hertoghen, N # 2072, 204r. Published in Strieder, *Aus Antwerpener Notariatsarchiven*, nr 302.

183. J. Jonker and K. Sluyterman, *Thuis op de Wereldmarkt: Nederlandse handelshuizen door de eeuwen heen* (Den Haag: Sdu, 2000), p. 30.

184. On the Straatvaart of Antwerp merchants carrying grain to Spain and Italy: W. Brulez, 'La navigation flamande vers la Méditerranée à la fin du XVIe siècle', *Revue belge de philologie et d'histoire*, 36 (1958), pp. 1220–42, on especially pp. 1225–1227; M. Van Gelder, *Trading Places: The Netherlandish Merchants in Early Modern Venice* (Leiden: Brill, 2009).

185. Brulez, *De firma Della Faille*, pp. 50–2, 102–6, 139–41, 146–8.

186. MPM, Manuscripts, Arch. 681, Journal Herman Janssens, 102r. Other shares on: 33v, 81r, 77r, 79r, and 88r; on Herman Janssens and his family: see H. Soly, 'De Antwerpse Onderneemster Anna Janssens en de economische boom na de Vrede van Cateau-Cambrésis (1559)', *Bijdragen tot de geschiedenis*, 52 (1969), pp. 139–64. Herman Janssens is listed in the 1562–3 tax on import from and export to the Iberian Peninsula; he was ranked 426th of all importers (total of 486) (he imported for a value of twenty-seven guilders) and as nr. 212 of all exporters (total of 947) (for a value of 2526 guilders). Bril, *De handel*, pp. 96, 142.

187. Van der Wee, *The Growth of the Antwerp Market*, vol. 2, p. 323.

188. Brulez, *De firma Della Faille*, pp. 356–7, 366–7; K. Mees, 'Koopman in troebele tijden: Jan Van Immerseele (1550–1612)', *Spiegel Historiael*, 19 (1984), pp. 545–51.

189. Gelderblom, *Cities of Commerce*, pp. 76–9 and the literature cited there.

190. Brulez, *De firma Della Faille*, pp. 356–7, 366–7.

191. Compilatae, IX, article 10.
192. Brulez, *De Firma Della Faille*, pp. 366–7.
193. Brulez, *De firma Della Faille*, p. 502.
194. CAA, Insolvente Boedelkamer, IB # 2898, Letterbook Van der Molen, letters to Jeronimo Azeretto, 30 March 1538, 6r; 14 December 1538, 49r; 29 February 1540, 141v; 30 May 1540, 156r; 17 October, 1540, 181r.
195. CAA, Notarial archives, notary Adriaan Zeger 's Hertogen, N # 2074, 119v.
196. CAA, Notarial archives, notary Adriaan Zeger 's Hertogen, N # 2077, 45r.
197. CAA, Notarial archives, notary Adriaan Zeger 's Hertogen, N # 2077, 45r (1561).
198. H. Hansmann, R. Kraakman and R. Squire, 'Law and the Rise of the Firm', *Harvard Law Review*, 119:5 (2006), pp. 1335–403. And the response: N. R. Lamoreaux and J.-L. Rosenthal, 'Entity Shielding and the Development of Business Forms: A Comparative Perspective', *Harvard Law Review*, 119 (2006), pp. 238–45. See De ruysscher's remarks on the embedment of this contribution in the 'law and economics' and 'law and finance' approaches, both of which are very focused on the American corporation. De ruysscher, 'A Business Trust for Partnerships?', p. 11. Also: B. Abatino, G. Dari-Mattiacci, and E. C. Perotti, 'Depersonalization of Business in Ancient Rome', *Oxford Journal of Legal Studies*, 31:2 (20 June 2011), pp. 365–89.
199. Kohn describes owner shielding as forward asset partitioning and entity shielding as backward portioning or limited liability. M. Kohn, 'Business Organization in Pre-Industrial Europe', 2003, unpublished working paper, available at http://www.dartmouth.edu/~mkohn/Papers/14.%20Business%20organization.pdf [accessed 28 February 2015], p. 11.
200. De ruysscher finds eleven sections in 1582 and thirty-nine in 1608 on partnerships. But several of those concerned shared house ownership and the group payment of food and drink. De ruysscher, 'A Business Trust for Partnerships?', p. 3.
201. In Antiquis, XXVI; Impressae, LII, article 1; Compilatae, IX, article 4.
202. Impressae, LII, article 5; Compilatae, IX, article 25
203. Hansmann, Kraakman and Squire, 'Law and the Rise of the Firm', pp. 1337–8. Different partnerships related through the same partners were not liable for each other's debts. Impressae LII, articles 3–4; Compilatae, IX, article 26. Inter-partnership credit transactions were not unusual: revenues of the Gramaye Sweden company were transferred to the Eastland company and the former paid certain expenses of the latter. Cuypers, 'Geeraard Gramaye', pp. 81, 86.
204. Lutz, *Die Rechtliche Struktur*, pp. 332–4, 464, 480; F. Thomas, *Die Persönliche Haftung von Gesellschaftern von Personengesellschaften in der Historischen Entwicklung der Neuzeit* (Berlin: Duncker und Humblot, 2003), pp. 62–79; A. Cordes, 'Nord- und Süddeutsche Handelsgesellschaften vor 1800', in S. Kalss and F.-S. Meissel (eds), *Zur Geschichte des Gesellschaftsrechts in Europa*, Veröffentlichungen Des Ludwig-Boltzmann-Institutes Für Rechtsvorsorge und Urkundenwesen (Vienna: Wiener Rechtsgeschichtliche Gesellschaft, 2003), pp. 27–41; Von Ciriachy-Wantrup, *Augsburger Handelsgesellschaften*, p. 242.
205. Compilatae, IX, articles 8, 9.
206. Compilatae, IX, article 7. In south Germany every partner remains liable for the other, even if one of the partners does something without prior approval. Lutz, *Die Rechtliche Struktur*, p. 330.
207. After 1480, the Antwerp magistracy used the French technique of 'enquête par turbe' to register the opinions and testimonies of experts on a certain rule of law. While these

turben, which were registered in separate turbeboeken, were not considered as a source of law, they could reflect city law when the opinions within them were shared by the aldermen. Through the registration of turben, the urban government tried to register private law rules which could not be found in fifteenth-century law texts. Between 1500–30 fourteen enquêtes par turbe were held and registered; no merchant participated in these turben. The participants were university-trained jurists or juridical practitioners. After 1560 merchants were invited for their opinion as well. De ruysscher, *Handel en recht,* sections 2.2.2, 2.6; D. De ruysscher, 'Over Themis en Mercurius: handelsgebruiken en -recht in Antwerpen (vijftiende–zeventiende Eeuw)', *Revue belge de philologie et d'histoire,* 88:4 (2010), pp. 1105–35.

208. CAA, Vierschaar, V 69, Turbe 1551, 159r. Cited by De ruysscher, 'A Business Trust for Partnerships?', p. 8. On the rights and duties of factors: D. De ruysscher, *Handel en Recht,* pp. 201–14.

209. Lutz, *Die Rechtliche Struktur,* pp. 333–4; von Ciriachy-Wantrup, *Augsburger Handelsgesellschaften,* p. 240.

210. Compilatae, IX, article 6.

211. This is also true for south German companies. Lutz, *Die Rechtliche Struktur,* p. 237; von Ciriachy-Wantrup, *Augsburger Handelsgesellschaften,* p. 319.

212. De ruysscher, 'A Business Trust for Partnerships?', pp. 3–4.

213. CAA, Vierschaar, V 69, Turbe 1551, 159r. Cited in De ruysscher, 'A Business Trust for Partnerships?', p. 6.

214. CAA, Notarial archives, notary Adriaan Zeger 's Hertoghen, N 2070, 62r.

215. This is also true in other contexts: Lutz, *Die Rechtliche Struktur,* p. 443; A. D. Kessler, *A Revolution in Commerce: The Parisian Merchant Court and the Rise of Commercial Society in Eighteenth-Century France* (New Haven, CT: Yale University Press, 2007), p. 172; Goldthwaite, *The Economy of Renaissance Florence,* p. 65.

216. Génard, 'Un acte de société', article 6.

217. Gerard, 'Un acte de Société', article 35, on pp. 495–7.

218. 'Het comptoir van de voirs. Compagnie, gehouden ten huyse van Christoffel Pruyenen, was oyck het comptoir van der stadt', cited in Soly, 'De aluinhandel', p. 832.

219. CAA, Processen, 7 # 240.

220. Compilatae, IX, article 7. This was different in south German partnerships: partners remained liable for every action of the other partners. Lutz, *Die Rechtliche Struktur,* pp. 324–30.

221. De Groote, *De zeeassurantie,* pp. 166–7.

222. De ruysscher, 'A Business Trust for Partnerships?', pp. 3–4.

223. CAA, Vierschaar, Sentence books, V 1239, 36r-v.

224. CAA, Processen, 7 # 240.

225. CAA, Vierschaar, Sentence books, V 1233, 1504–5, 90r.

226. De Smidt et al., *Chronologische lijsten,* p. 175.

227. CAA, Certification books, CERT # 28, 1568, 47r.

228. W. D. H. Asser, *In solidum of pro parte: een onderzoek naar de ontwikkelingsgeschedenis van de hoofdelijke en gedeelde aansprakelijkheid van vennoten tegenover derden* (Leiden: Brill, 1983), p. 255.

229. De Smidt et al., *Chronologische Lijsten,* III, nr 417, 418.

230. De Smidt et al., *Chronologische Lijsten,* IV, nr 1232.

231. Asser, *In solidum of pro parte,* p. 257.

232. For example in the Jan Gamel, Pauwels van Houte and Peter Sobrecht partnership:

'onder tverbant van hueren goeden tegenwoirdighe ende toecomende'. CAA, Notarial archives, notary Adriaan Zeger 's Hertoghen, N # 2077, 45r. This is called a 'generale verbindtenis' in the Antwerp Costuymen of 1582, LVII, article 49. 'Item generale verbindtenissen van hem selven ende alle sijne goeden, ruerende ende onruerende, tegenwoordelijck ende toecomende, en induceren geen realiteyt oft affectatie van goeden binnen deser stadt oft vrijheydtder selver geleghen, al waren alsulcke generale hypoteken oft verbintenissen voor Schepenen deser stadt, oft oock inden Rade van Brabant ghepasseert'.

233. Gelderblom, 'Entrepreneurs', pp. 165–7.

234. The Gramaye, Lescluse, Winterkoning companies owned ships. Cuypers, 'Geeraard Gramaye', p. 80; Wijnroks, *Handel tussen Rusland en de Nederlanden*, pp. 80, 101, 109. The Della Faille also purchased ships. Brulez, 'La navigation flamande'.

235. CAA, Notarial archives, notary Adriaan Zeger 's Hertoghen, N # 2072, 47r

236. CAA, Notarial archives, notary Adriaan Zeger 's Hertoghen, N # 2077, 45r.

237. Génard, 'Un acte de société', article 22.

238. Génard, 'Un acte de société', article 22.

239. See Figure 3.1.

240. Total share of deposits in Jan's two companies: 30 per cent and 23 per cent.

241. Goldthwaite, *The Economy of Renaissance Florence*, p. 66.

242. Lutz, *Die Rechtliche Struktur*, p. 59.

243. Non-activity was also the criterion in south German cities to qualify as a passive investor. Lutz, *Die Rechtliche Struktur*, pp. 224, 254, 461; Thomas, *Die Persönliche Haftung*, pp. 125–30; Von Ciriachy-Wantrup, *Augsburger Handelsgesellschaften*, pp. 242, 245.

244. RAA, Notarial archives, notary Jacobus de Platea, 523, 185v. Another example is Michiel Wachmans who was a silent partner in many of Herman Boelman's trading activities in the Baltic. Wijnroks, *Handel tussen Rusland en de Nederlanden*, p. 76.

245. 'Verbiedende oock allen onsen ondersaten van wat conditie oft state sy syn, hun niet onderwindende mitte coopmanschap ende niet hebbende geselschap mit coopluyden op gewin oft verlies, te gevene hun gelt den voirschreven coopluyden om seker gewin te hebbene alle jaere, opte pene van confiscatie van t voirschreven gelt ende boven dien gehouden ende geacht te wordene openbaere woekers ende over sulck gestraft ende gecorrigeert', C. Laurent, J.-P.-A. Lameere and H. Simont, *Recueil des ordonnances des Pays-Bas: 2e série, 1506–1700*, 6 vols (Brussels: Goemaere, 1893–1922), vol. 4, p. 235

246. De ruysscher considers this ordinance to have been a restriction on partnership investment: all investors who desired to speculate on the partnership's profits now had to be partners. De ruysscher, 'A Business Trust for Partnerships?', p. 6. Although the passage is rather cryptic, I believe that the ordinance was aimed more against usury (interests above 12 per cent), since these rules were preceded by usury regulations. Moreover, the ordinance stipulated that such investors should not automatically expect any positive results (this may be an inference to results that exceeded a 12 per cent interest level and which were thus usurious), since they were investing in risk.

247. Compilatae, IX, article 8.

248. W. D. H. Asser, *In solidum of pro parte*, p. 258.

249. Nuremberg already had such a limited liability in 1464. In sixteenth-century Augsburg some investors enjoyed limited liability as well. Lutz, *Die Rechtliche Struktur*, pp. 224, 254, 461; von Ciriachy-Wantrup, *Augsburger Handelsgesellschaften*, pp. 242, 245.

250. 'Ick, onderschreven, kenne mits desen onfangen te hebben van N. de somme van ..., om die voor hem te bekeeren in geoorloffden handel oft coopmanschappe; welcke somme

mette proffijten van dijen tegens den pen-ninck sesthiene, ick hem in den selven handel oft coopmanschappeversekere, behoudelijck dat hij mij laet het meerder gewin dat daerop sal commen te vallen, gelove [gelovende]den voorschreven N. de selve proffijten jaerlijcx goet te doen, naer advenant van den tijde dat ick dese voorschreve somme in den voorschreven handel hebben ende houden sal, ende hem de selve somme oock weder te geven tot sijnder geliefte, naer dijen bij hem den voorschreven handel drije maenden te voorens sal hebben [sal sijn] opgeseght', Compilatae, I, articles 9, 10.

251. Legalized in Florence in 1408 but only used extensively in the sixteenth century. Goldthwaite, *The Economy of Renaissance Florence*, pp. 67–8, 438; Trivellato, *The Familiarity of Strangers*, p. 142.

252. See 'Introduction'.

253. Brulez, *De firma Della Faille*, pp. 35–7.

254. The Italian angel investors of Geeraerd Gramaye (see supra) were active partners who were jointly and severally liable.

255. This was the case in south Germany too where shares were personal and could only be transferred to one's heirs when explicitly stipulated. Lutz, *Die Rechtliche Struktur*, pp. 355, 438.

256. Génard, 'Un acte de société', articles 42, 43. Other examples: Jehan Dounrin bequeathed his son-in-law Jehan de Bourgoigne his shares in a partnership with Jehan de Thumbes from Brussels and Jehan Baptista Jani from Florence; the partners were silk cloth merchants who were following the imperial court. CAA, Notarial archives, notary Willem Stryt, N 3133, 91v-92r & 109v-110v. Barbele Warniers, widow of Cornelis Pels, demanded payment from Jacob Stuer, her husband's former partner in a Venetian crystal enterprise, who had bought out her share after Pels's death. De Smidt et al., *Chronologische lijsten*, V, September 15 1551.

257. Soly, *Urbanisme en kapitalisme*, p. 257.

258. RAA, Notarial archives, notary Jacobus de Platea, 522, 84v–86v.

259. L. Petram, *De bakermat van de Beurs: hoe in zeventiende-eeuws Amsterdam de moderne aandelenhandel ontstond* (Amsterdam: Atlas, 2011); L. Petram, 'The World's First Stock Exchange: How the Amsterdam Market for Dutch East India Company Shares Became a Modern Securities Market, 1602–1700' (PhD dissertation, University of Amsterdam, 2011).

260. Brulez, *De firma Della Faille*, pp. 354, 367–74; Van der Wee, *The Growth of the Antwerp Market*, vol. 2, p. 323.

261. W. Brulez, 'Lettres commerciales de Daniel et Antoine de Bombergen à Antonio Grimani (1532–43)', *Bulletin de l'Institute Historique Belge de Rome*, 31 (1958), pp. 169–205, on p.180.

262. U. C. Ewert and S. Selzer, 'Verhandeln und Verkaufen, Vernetzen und Vertrauen. Über die Netzwerkstruktur des Hansischen Handels', *Hansische Geschichtsblätter*, 119 (2001), pp. 135–62; M. Kohn, 'Business Organization in Pre-Industrial Europe', 2003, unpublished working paper, available at http://www.dartmouth.edu/~mkohn/Papers/14.%20Business%20organization.pdf [accessed 28 February 2015]; Gelderblom, *Cities of Commerce*, p. 79 and literature on Bruges cited there. The Florentine Medici bank made use of commission agents prior to the establishment of a branch in Bruges. R. De Roover, *The Rise and Decline of the Medici Bank, 1397–1494* (New York: Norton, 1966), pp. 317 sqq.

263. J. Savary, *Le Parfait Négociant, ou: instruction générale pour ... le commerce des marchandises de France, et des pais étrangers*, 8th edn (Amsterdam: Roger, 1717), II, chs 47, 33, 55, p. 143

264. Trivellato, *The Familiarity of Strangers*, pp. 154, 168–9.

265. A. Greif, 'Reputation and Coalitions in Medieval Trade: Evidence on the Maghribi Traders', *Journal of Economic History*, 49:4 (1989), pp. 857–82; A. Greif, 'Contract Enforceability and Economic Institutions in Early Trade: The Maghribi Traders' Coalition', *American Economic Review*, 83:3 (1993), pp. 525–48; A. Greif, *Institutions and the Path to the Modern Economy: Lessons from Medieval Trade* (Cambridge: Cambridge University Press, 2006).

266. Trivellato, *The Familiarity of Strangers*, pp. 168–9; Gelderblom, *Cities of Commerce*, pp. 79–80, 82–3, 87–94.

267. CAA, Notarial archives, notary Willem Stryt, N # 3133, 240v.

268. The legal responsibility of commission agents is quite unclear since various types of agency are dealt with in a mixed fashion in Antwerp customary law: De ruysscher, *Handel en Recht,* pp. 201–14.

269. Trivellato, *The Familiarity of Strangers*, p. 169.

270. De facto limited liability. Kohn, 'Business Organization in Pre-Industrial Europe'.

271. Brulez, 'Lettres commerciales' pp. 169–205; Edler, 'The Van der Molen'; Brulez, *De firma Della Faille*, p. 489; Puttevils, 'A servitio de vostri sempre siamo', part 2.

272. Brulez, 'Lettres commerciales', pp. 181–2. CAA, Insolvente Boedelkamer, IB # 2898, Letterbook Van der Molen, passim.

273. G. Dahl, *Trade, Trust and Networks: Commercial Culture in Late Medieval Italy* (Lund: Nordic Academic Press, 1998), pp. 295–6.

274. On the discourse of trust in eighteenth-century merchant letters: Trivellato, *The Familiarity of Strangers*, pp. 153, 167–70, 177 sqq.

275. Trivellato, *The Familiarity of Strangers*, pp. 174.

276. 'Vederete che cerchamo tanto el profito e vantagio vostro quanto per noj medexi' CAA, Insolvente Boedelkamer, IB # 2898, Letterbook Van der Molen, letter to Martino di Zerchiari, 17 October 1540, 176v.

277. Brulez, *De firma Della Faille*, p. 371.

278. Kohn, 'Business Organization in Pre-Industrial Europe', pp. 50–1.

279. Brulez, *De firma Della Faille*, pp. 370–1.

280. Edler, 'The Van der Molen', pp. 97–8.

281. 'El nostro Cornelio se rechomanda assai a voj et dj quel vj potra far piacere sara sempre vostro/ pregandovj dj recomandarlo a tuttj li amici', CAA, Insolvente Boedelkamer, IB # 2898, Letterbook Van der Molen, letter to Bernardo Morando, 14 September 1538, 35r-v.

282. Trivellato, *The Familiarity of Strangers*, p. 182.

283. Gelderblom, *Cities of Commerce*, pp. 76–8.

284. Trivellato, *The Familiarity of Strangers*, pp. 182–3.

285. Edler, 'The Van der Molen', pp. 109–10.

286. Brulez, *De firma Della Faille*, pp. 373–4.

287. Brulez, *De firma Della Faille*, pp. 53–5, 66.

288. Edler, 'The Van der Molen', pp. 110–13; Brulez, 'Lettres commerciales', pp. 195, 199; Gelderblom, *Cities of Commerce*, pp. 81–2.

289. Edler, 'The Van der Molen', p. 100; Puttevils, 'A servitio de vostri', p. 268.

290. D. V. Williamson, 'Transparency, Contract Selection and the Maritime Trade of Venetian Crete, 1303–1351', 2002, unpublished working paper, available at http://www.researchgate.net/publication/245549729_Transparency_Contract_Selection_and_the_Maritime_Trade_of_Venetian_Crete_1303-1351 [accessed 28 February 2015].

291. CAA, Insolvente Boedelkamer, IB # 2898, Letterbook Van der Molen, letter to Bernardo Morando, 14 November 1540, 184r. Brulez, *De firma Della Faille*, p. 373, 388.

292. CAA, Insolvente Boedelkamer, IB # 2898, Letterbook Van der Molen, letter to Francesco Da Fin, 17 August 1539, 104v. C. Gravesteijn and J. J. McCusker, *The Beginnings of Commercial and Financial Journalism: The Commodity Price Currents, Exchange Currents, and Money Currents of Early Modern Europe* (Amsterdam: NEHA, 1991), pp. 85–6; John J. McCusker, 'The Demise of Distance: The Business Press and the Origins of the Information Revolution in the Early Modern Atlantic World', *American Historical Review*, 110:2 (2005), pp. 295–321.

293. CAA, Insolvente Boedelkamer, IB # 2898, Letterbook Van der Molen, letter to Jeronimo Azeretto, 22 August 1540 and 19 September 1540, 171v.

294. The Low Countries trader Pauwel Van Dale also published exchange rates. E. Sabbe, *Anvers: métropole de l'Occident (1492–1566)* (Brussels: Renaissance du livre, 1952), p. 61.

295. Edler, 'The Van der Molen', pp. 130–1.

296. On the Affaitadi: J. Denucé, *Inventaire des Affaitadi, banquiers italiens à Anvers de l'année 1568* (Antwerp: De Sikkel, 1934)

297. CAA, Insolvente Boedelkamer, IB # 2898, Letterbook Van der Molen, letter to Niccolò Dolze, 2 October 1539, 110v.

298. CAA, Insolvente Boedelkamer, IB # 2898, Letterbook Van der Molen, letters to Niccolò Dolze, 4 January 1540, 129v; 1 February 1540, 134r; 29 February 1540, 140v; 30 May 1540, 153v; 18 September 1540, 174v.

299. CAA, Insolvente Boedelkamer, IB # 2898, Letterbook Van der Molen, letter to Niccolò Dolze, 1 May 1541, 203v.

300. CAA, Insolvente Boedelkamer, IB # 2898, Letterbook Van der Molen, letters to Martino di Zerchiari, 18 September 1540, 174r; 17 October 1540, 175v.

301. CAA, Insolvente Boedelkamer, IB # 2898, Letterbook Van der Molen, letter to Bernardo Morando, 14 September 1538, 35r-v.

302. Puttevils, 'Klein gewin brengt rijkdom in'.

303. First, English merchants sent agents with the ships to buy tobacco and sell European products. Then, they appointed commission agents who bought tobacco and sold European commodities. After that, the planters were sending tobacco to England themselves to be sold there by commission agents and later sent their own agents to England. J. M. Price and P. G. E. Clemens, 'A Revolution of Scale in Overseas Trade: British Firms in the Chesapeake Trade, 1675–1775', *Journal of Economic History*, 47:01 (1987), pp. 1–43, on pp. 5–8, cited in: Jonker and Sluyterman, *Thuis op de wereldmarkt*, pp. 84–5.

304. For example Jan Van Immerseele, who was very active as a commission trader but combined this with partnerships and shares in ventures. Brulez, *De firma Della Faille*, pp. 356–7. On profit rates see section 'Profits between Antwerp and European Markets & Merchant Ties to Low Countries Industries'.

305. Brulez, *De firma Della Faille*, p. 490.

306. Brulez, *De firma Della Faille*, p. 368; Kohn, 'Business Organization in Pre-Industrial Europe', p. 48.

307. Brulez, *De firma Della Faille*, p. 368; Kohn, 'Business Organization in Pre-Industrial Europe', p. 48; J. L. Fernández and E. O. Montes, 'De aprendiz a mercader: el factor en el comercio internacional inglés del siglo XVI', *Pecvnia*, 5 (2007), pp. 145–80.

308. Formsma and Pirenne, *Koopmansgeest te 's-Hertogenbosch*, pp. 85–6. See also the section 'Merchant Ties to Low Countries Industries' of this book.

309. Gelderblom, *Cities of Commerce*, p. 83.

310. See also Kessler, *A Revolution in Commerce*, p. 148.

311. Van Hofstraeten comes to the same finding on the similarities of Antwerp partnership contracts. Van Hofstraeten, 'Small-Scale Business Enterprises in Sixteenth-Century Antwerp (1480–1620)'.

4 Debt Finance through Bills Obligatory

1. De Smedt, 'Antwerpen en de opbloei', p. 84.

2. Brulez, *De firma Della Faille*, pp. 391–3.

3. C. Wyffels and G. Des Marez, *Analyses de reconnaissances de dettes passées devant les échevins d'Ypres (1249–1291)* (Brussels: Palais des académies, 1991); W. Blockmans, 'Transactions at the Fairs of Champagne and Flanders. 1249–1291', in S. Cavaciocchi (ed.), *Fiere e mercati nella integrazione delle economie europee, secc. 13–18: atti della 'Trentaduesima Settimana di Studi', 9–12 maggio 2000* (Florence: Monnier, 2001), pp. 993–1000; D. Nicholas, 'Commercial Credit and Central Place Function in Thirteenth-Century Ypres', in L. Armstrong, I. Elbl, M. M. Elbl and J. H. A. Munro (eds), *Money, Markets and Trade in Late Medieval Europe: Essays in Honour of John H. Munro* (Leiden: Brill, 2007), pp. 310–48.

4. Van der Wee, *The Growth of the Antwerp Market*, vol. 2, p. 338.

5. Issues also raised by H. Van der Wee, 'Antwerp and the New Financial Methods of the 16th and 17th Centuries', trans. L. Fackelman, in H. Van der Wee (ed.), *The Low Countries in the Early Modern World* (Aldershot: Ashgate, 1993), ch. 8, pp. 145–66, on pp. 23, 25.

6. O. Gelderblom and J. Jonker, 'Completing a Financial Revolution: The Finance of the Dutch East India Trade and the Rise of the Amsterdam Capital Market, 1595–1612', *Journal of Economic History*, 64:3 (2004), pp. 641–72, on p. 646.

7. Van der Wee, *The Growth of the Antwerp Market*, vol. 2; H. Van der Wee, 'Antwerpens bijdrage tot de ontwikkeling van de moderne geld- en banktechniek', *Tijdschrift voor economie*, 4 (1965), pp. 488–500; H. Van der Wee, 'Monetary, Credit and Banking Systems', in E. E. Rich and C. H. Wilson (eds), *The Economic Organization of Early Modern Europe, The Cambridge Economic History of Europe* (Cambridge: Cambridge University Press, 1977), ch. 5, pp. 290–392; H. Van der Wee, 'Anvers et les innovations de la technique financière aux XVIe et XVIIe siècles', *Annales: Economies, Sociétés, Civilisations*, 22:5 (1977), pp. 1067–89; H. Van der Wee, 'Geld- krediet- en bankwezen in de Zuidelijke Nederlanden 1490–1580', in D. P. Blok (ed.), *Algemene Geschiedenis der Nederlanden* (Haarlem: Fibula-Van Dishoeck, 1979), pp. 98–108; H. Van der Wee and J. Materné, 'Het kredietsysteem in Brabant tijdens de Late Middeleeuwen en in het begin van de Nieuwe Tijd', in H. F. J. M. van den Eerenbeemt (ed.), *Bankieren in Brabant in de loop der eeuwen* (Tilburg: Stichting Zuidelijk Historisch Contact, 1987), ch. 4, pp. 59–78; Van der Wee, 'Antwerp and the New Financial Methods'. A good summary of Van der Wee's position on Antwerp's financial revolution can be found in H. van der Wee, G. Kurgan-van Hentenryk, R. Bogaert et al., *A History of European Banking* (Antwerp: Mercatorfonds, 2000), pp. 180–98. More recently: M. Kohn, 'Bills of Exchange and the Money Market to 1600', 1999, unpublished working paper, available at http://www.dartmouth.edu/~mkohn/Papers/99-04.pdf [accessed on 28 February 2015]

8. Van der Wee, 'Antwerp and the New Financial Methods', p. 150. This article is a translation of Van der Wee, 'Anvers et les Innovations'. We will refer to the English transla-

tion in the remainder of this text. For obligations in eighteenth-century Antwerp: K. Degryse, *De Antwerpse fortuinen: kapitaalsaccumulatie, -investering en -rendement te Antwerpen in de 18de eeuw* (Antwerp: Genootschap voor Antwerpse Geschiedenis, 2005); Willems, *Leven op de pof*, pp. 108–12.

9.   Van der Wee, 'Antwerp and the New Financial Methods', p. 150; Kohn, 'Bills of Exchange', p. 142; J. H. Munro, 'English "Backwardness" and Financial Innovations in Commerce with the Low Countries, 14th to 16th Centuries', in B. Blondé, A. Greve and P. Stabel (eds), *International Trade in the Low Countries (14th–16th Centuries): Merchants, Organisation, Infrastructure: Proceedings of the International Conference Ghent-Antwerp, 12th–13th January 1997* (Leuven: Garant, 2000), pp. 105–69, on pp. 142–4. On the deposit and giro services of fourteenth-century Bruges money changers: J. M. Murray, *Bruges: Cradle of Capitalism 1280–1390* (Cambridge: Cambridge University Press, 2006), pp. 168–70.

10. J. M. Price, 'What Did Merchants Do? Reflections on British Overseas Trade, 1660–1790', *Journal of Economic History*, 49:2 (1989), pp. 267–84, on p. 278.

11. Van der Wee and Materné, 'Het kredietsysteem in Brabant', p. 72.

12. E. Aerts, 'The Absence of Public Exchange Banks in Medieval and Early Modern Flanders and Brabant (1400–1800): A Historical Anomaly to Be Explained', *Financial History Review*, 18:1 (2011), pp. 91–117. Aerts acknowledges the declining numbers of money-changer-bankers in the late fifteenth and early sixteenth centuries; however, he indicates that the group of money-changers who combined their activities with cashier services was growing and had survived decades of mistrust and central and urban government regulation. There is still discussion about the independence of these cashiers who handled income and expenses, did bookkeeping and kept money in a coffer. Were they self-employed, working for different clients, or were they merchant employees? These intermediaries performed several of the tasks which public banks were doing in southern Europe and which money changers had been doing in Bruges and on the Brabant fairs.

13. CAA, Vierschaar, Sentence books, V 1233, 1504, 67v.

14. M. M. Postan, *Medieval Trade and Finance* (Cambridge: Cambridge University Press, 1974), pp. 28–40. On bonds in sixteenth-century Lyon: Gascon, *Grand commerce et vie urbaine*, I, pp. 273–9.

15. De ruysscher, *Handel en recht*, pp. 236–47.

16. We were unable to find an original IOU with a seal in the different source series we have used for this chapter. The Belgian archival practice to remove the seals from archival documents because of their sigillographic value might be responsible for this conspicuous absence. de Smedt, *De Engelse Natie*, vol. 2, p. 562.

17. Van der Wee, *The Growth of the Antwerp Market*, vol. 2, pp. 354–5; C. J. Zuijderduijn, 'The Emergence of Provincial Debt in the County of Holland (Thirteenth–Sixteenth Centuries)', *European Review of Economic History*, 14:3 (2010), pp. 335–59.

18. 'Ick Jan Spierinck bekenne ende vercleere midts desen mynder eyghen hantscrift schuldich te zyne de eersame heer coenraerdt schetz de somme van vier hondert ponden grooten vlems ende dat ter causen van gelycke somme die ick van hem tot mynen contentemente ontfanghen hebbe welcke voorscreven somme van vier hondert ponden vlems gelove ick den voorscreven heeren Coenraerdt Schetz oft den brenger van desen wel ende duechdelyck te betalen den vierden dach vander maent van augustus naestcomende sonder eenich langer vertreck dilay oft vuytstellinghe daer voore verobligerende mynen persoon ende alle myn goeden van wat qualiteyt die syn mochten/ present ende

toecomende ... in den jaere 1565 Junio 11', CAA, Processen, 7 # 12144, Copye obligacie.

19. The dates refer to the dates of the documents themselves: some bills obligatory were drawn up before the registration in one of the sources.

20. For more details on the different sources, see data appendix.

21. CAA, Gebodboeken, Pk # 913–29 (1439–1794). Published in: P. Van Setter, 'Index der Gebodboeken', *Antwerpsch Archievenblad*, 1:1 (1864), pp. 120–464. Materné has also used these references and quantified the number of lost bonds, but nothing more. J. Materné, 'Schoon ende bequaem tot versamelinghe der cooplieden: Antwerpens beurswereld tijdens de Gouden zestiende eeuw', in G. De Clercq (ed.), *Ter Beurze: geschiedenis van de aandelenhandel in België, 1300–1990* (Bruges: Van de Wiele, 1992), pp. 50–8, on p. 62.

22. CAA, Notarial archives, notary Adriaan Zeger 's-Hertoghen, N # 2071, 51r-v.

23. On the secrecy of notarial acts: S. A. Epstein, 'Secrecy and Genoese Commercial Practices', *Journal of Medieval History*, 20:4 (1994), pp. 313–25.

24. CAA, Gebodboeken, Pk # 915–17.

25. Bearer clause bonds will be dealt with later in this chapter.

26. CAA, Processen Supplement, 288 # 1657.

27. On the Spanish Fury: P. Génard, 'La Furie espagnole', *Annales de Académie Royale d'Archéologie de Belgique*, 32 (1876), pp. 5–728; E. Rooms, 'Een nieuwe visie op de gebeurtenissen die geleid hebben tot de Spaanse Furie te Antwerpen op 4 november 1576', *Bijdragen tot de geschiedenis*, 54 (1971) pp. 33–51; P Arnade, *Beggars, Iconoclasts, and Civic Patriots: The Political Culture of the Dutch Revolt* (Ithaca, NY: Cornell University Press, 2008), pp. 212–59.

28. G. D. Ramsay, *The Queen's Merchants and the Revolt of the Netherlands: The End of the Antwerp Mart*, 2 vols (Manchester: Manchester University Press, 1986), vol. 2, p. 184.

29. Seven bills between 1577 and 1585.

30. Registering all bonds in notarial acts for the sixteenth century is an impossible task for one researcher. In 1540 the acts of two notaries were preserved. The number of notaries leaving documents rose to five or more in 1565 and to more than ten in 1580. CAA, Notarial archives.

31. Given the fact that the source origin of these bills is heterogeneous, the above graph is not a time series.

32. Using the silver values of a d. gr. Fl. from C. Verlinden, *Dokumenten voor de geschiedenis van prijzen en lonen in Vlaanderen en Brabant = Documents pour l'histoire des prix et des salaires en Flandre et en Brabant* (Bruges: Tempel, 1959), II, pp. xxxvi–xxxix.

33. Mean = 12,667.37 grams, Median = 5,225.85 grams.

34. Available at http://www.economics.utoronto.ca/munro5/AntwerpWage.xls [accessed 28 February 2015].

35. Gelderblom, 'The Governance of Early Modern Trade', pp. 627–8; Gelderblom and Jonker, 'Completing a Financial Revolution', p. 648.

36. A one-way ANOVA difference of variance test is significant at the 1 per cent level (p < 0,0001). The non-parametric independent Kruskall–Wallis test similarly rejects the null hypothesis.

37. Postan, *Medieval Trade and Finance*, p. 37; Rosenthal and Bin Wong, *Before and beyond Divergence*, p. 7.

38. De ruysscher, *Handel en recht*, p. 239.

39. CAA, Notarial archives, notary Willem Stryt, N # 3133, 166v–167r.

40. Native = all merchants from the Low Countries, including Liège; and Foreign = all

merchants from other regions. We always use relative numbers given the unequal distribution of the obligations over time. Merchant inventories and account books are left out of this analysis since they were all produced by native merchants. As such, these sources may be biased towards native debtors and creditors. Foreign merchants had a more equal chance to show up in the sources which were used for this exercise.

41. A cross table with the identities of creditors and debtors counts the number of bonds (N=864). Pearson Chi-Square p-value < 0.001 Cramers's V 0.580.

42. De Smedt, *De Engelse Natie*, vol. 2, p. 568.

43. Postan, *Medieval Trade and Finance*, pp. 43, 46–7, 52.

44. CAA, Aldermen's registers, SR # 288, 15 April 1562. Courtesy of Irène Leydecker-Brackx.

45. D. De ruysscher, 'Innovating Financial Law in Early Modern Europe: Transfers of Commercial Paper and Recourse Liability in Legislation and Ius Commune (Sixteenth to Eighteenth Centuries)', *European Review of Private Law*, 19:5 (2011), pp. 505–18, on p. 505, n. 501.

46. H. Van der Wee, 'Antwerp and the New Financial Methods of the 16th and 17th Centuries', p. 151; Munro, 'English "Backwardness"', p. 133.

47. Van der Wee, *The Growth of the Antwerp Market*, vol. 2, p. 141.

48. Doehaerd, *Etudes anversoises*.

49. Bond with bearer clause: mean £80.441 gr. Fl., median £53 gr. Fl. (N=95), bonds without clause: mean £59.079 gr. Fl., median £24.625 gr. Fl. (N=74).

50. De ruysscher, 'Innovating Financial Law', on p. 505, para. 1.

51. De Smedt, 'De keizerlijke verordeningen', pp. 32–3; A Wijffels, 'Business Relations between Merchants in Sixteenth-Century Belgian Practice-Orientated Civil Law Literature', in V. Piergiovanni (ed.), *From Lex Mercatoria to Commercial Law, Comparative Studies in Continental and Anglo-American Legal History* (Berlin: Duncker & Humblot, 2005), pp. 255–90, on pp. 267–8.

52. De Smidt et al., *Chronologische lijsten*, p. 58.

53. CAA, Vierschaar, V # 68, 13r, 7 June 1507. After 1480, the Antwerp magistracy used the French technique of 'enquête par turbe' to register the opinions and testimonies of experts on a certain rule of law. While these turben, which were registered in separate turbeboeken, were not considered as a source of law, they could reflect city law when the opinions within them were shared by the aldermen. Through the registration of turben, the urban government tried to register private law rules which could not be found in fifteenth-century law texts. Between 1500 and 1530 fourteen enquêtes par turbe were held and registered; no merchant participated in these turben. The participants were university-trained jurists or juridical practitioners. After 1560 merchants were invited for their opinion as well. De ruysscher, *Handel en recht* ; De ruysscher, 'Over Themis en Mercurius'.

54. Munro, 'English "Backwardness"', pp. 105–65, on pp. 144–51. Although this is not undisputed: S. E. Sachs, 'Burying Burton: Burton v. Davy and the Law of Negotiable Instruments', 2002, unpublished working paper, available at http://www.stevesachs.com/papers/paper_burton.html [accessed 28 February 2015].

55. M. North, 'Banking and Credit in Northern Germany in the Fifteenth and Sixteenth Centuries', in D. Puncuh and G. Felloni (eds), *Banchi pubblici, banchi privati e Monti di Pietà nell'Europa preindustriale: amministrazione, tecniche operative e ruoli economici*, Atti Della Società Ligure Di Storia Patria (Geneva: Società Ligure di Storia Patria, 1991), pp. 809–206, on pp. 821–2; Munro, 'English "Backwardness"', p. 151;

De ruysscher, *Handel en recht*, p. 237.

56. Munro, 'English "Backwardness"', p. 105. On the Merchant Adventurers in Antwerp: De Smedt, *De Engelse Natie*, p. 1.

57. Van der Wee, 'Antwerp and the New Financial Methods', p. 152; Munro, 'English "Backwardness"', p. 152.

58. C. Laurent, J.-P.-A. Lameere and H. Simont, *Recueil des ordonnances des Pays-Bas: 2e série, 1506–1700*, 6 vols (Brussels: Goemaere, 1893–1922), vol. 4, pp. 1515–17, 1537.

59. However, the bearer clause in bonds did not become standard practice outside the commercial gateways of the Netherlands: in Liège the bearer clause was almost non-existent and the circulation of bonds remained limited. J. Lejeune, *La formation du capitalisme moderne dans la principauté de Liège au 16e siècle* (Liège: Faculté de Philosophie et Lettres, 1939), p. 65

60. Van der Wee, 'Antwerp and the New Financial Methods', pp. 151–2.

61. Van der Wee, 'Antwerp and the New Financial Methods', pp. 155–6.

62. Brulez, *De firma Della Faille*, p. 403.

63. Munro, 'English "Backwardness"', pp. 134, 142.

64. Gascon, *Grand commerce et vie urbaine*, pp. 277–9.

65. P. Godding, *Le droit privé dans les Pays-Bas méridionaux du 12e au 18e siècle* (Brussels: Palais des Académies, 1987), pp. 420 sqq., 489–90; De ruysscher, *Handel en recht*, pp. 242–4.

66. CAA, Insolvente Boedelkamer, IB # 788, Journal Daniel de Bruyne, 66r.

67. Van der Wee, 'Antwerp and the New Financial Methods', pp. 152–3; De ruysscher, *Handel En Recht*, pp. 233, 236, 242–4.

68. In 1544 Peter Reyniers was sued by Lauwereys Martyn for the payment of £10.3 gr. Fl. Reyniers was asked if he could prove having paid the bill, within eight days. CAA, Vierschaar, Sentence books, V # 1239, 1544, 21v.

69. Email correspondence with Dr D. De ruysscher.

70. M. Kohn, 'Bills of Exchange and the Money Market to 1600', 1999 unpublished working paper, available at http://www.dartmouth.edu/~mkohn/Papers/99-04.pdf [accessed 28 February 2015], p. 26.

71. CAA, Vierschaar, Sentence books, V # 1233, 1504, 41v.

72. Brulez, 'Lettres commerciales', pp. 183–4, 189; Van der Wee, 'Antwerp and the New Financial Methods', p. 153.

73. CAA, Insolvente Boedelskamer, IB # IB 776, Jaarmarktboek Frans De Pape, 1v–2r; and several other instances.

74. De Smedt, 'De keizerlijke verordeningen', pp. 25–6; Van der Wee, *The Growth of the Antwerp Market*, vol. 2, p. 345; Van der Wee, 'Antwerp and the New Financial Methods', p. 153. The original can be found in: CAA, Privilegiekamer, Engelse natie, Pk # 1052, 1 July 1537.

75. Laurent, Lameere and Simont, *Recueil des Ordonnances*, vol. 4, IV, pp. 329–31.

76. Antiquissimae, title IV, arrestementen art 28; http://www.kuleuven-kulak.be/facult/rechten/Monballyu/Rechtlagelanden/Brabantsrecht/antwerpen/antiquissimae.html [accessed 28 February 2015].

77. De Smedt, 'De Keizerlijke Verordeningen', p. 35; De ruysscher, *Handel en recht*, pp. 239–40.

78. CAA, Vierschaar, Sentence books, V 1239, 1544, 14r, 29r, 97r, 6v and 192r; RAB, Council of Brabant, Sentence books, 589, 1544223r. Van der Wee, 'Antwerp and the New Financial Methods', p. 155.

79. Aerts, 'The Absence of Public Exchange Banks', p. 103.
80. CAA, Gebodboeken, Pk # 916, 101v.
81. CAA, Vierschaar, Sentence books, V 1240, 1544, 14r.
82. CAA, Processen Supplement, 288 # 1679.
83. CAA, Processen Supplement, 288 # 1679, dupliek Steven van der Capellen, 21v-23r.
84. Van der Wee, *The Growth of the Antwerp Market*, vol. 2, p. 343.
85. Fourteen in total.
86. CAA, Notarial archives, notary Adriaan Zeger 's-Hertoghen, N # 2071, 74v.
87. Stadsarchief Antwerpen Pk 1079 4 July 1565. Goris, *Etude sur les colonies marchandes*, pp. 111, 309. See also: M. Oosterbosch, '"Van groote abuysen ende ongeregeltheden" Overheidsbemoeiingen met het Antwerpse notariaat tijdens de XVIde eeuw', *Legal History Review*, 63 (1995), pp. 83–101.
88. 'Laquelle est pretext notoirement de infinies simulations et collusion voires aussy de tant importantes sommes que soubz ombre d'icelle clause plusieurs deviennent à ruyne', Goris, *Etude sur les colonies marchandes*, p. 111.
89. CAA, Processen, 7 # 12144, inventory of Jan Spierinck.
90. CAA, Notarial archives, notary Adriaan Zeger 's-Hertoghen, N # 2071, 4 March 1540, 45r-v.
91. De Smedt, *De Engelse Natie*, vol. 2, p. 583.
92. De Smedt, *De Engelse Natie*, pp. 583–5.
93. MPM, Manuscripts, Arch. 681, Journal Herman Janssens, 55r; RAB, Council of Brabant, Lawsuit files Council of Brabant of private individuals, 263, 1557.
94. De ruysscher, *Handel en recht*, p. 242.
95. Postan, *Medieval Trade and Finance*, pp. 49–50.
96. De ruysscher, *Handel en recht*, p. 237.
97. CAA, Privilegiekamer, Natie van Lucca, Pk # 1076, 4 July 1565. Goris, *Etude sur les colonies marchandes*, p. 111; De Smedt, *De Engelse Natie*, vol. 2, p. 582.
98. De Smedt, *De Engelse Natie*, vol. 2, pp. 572–3.
99. CAA, Insolvente Boedelkamer, IB # 788, Journal Daniel de Bruyne, 9v.
100. CAA, Notarial archives, notary Willem Stryt, N # 3133, 217r.
101. 'Als ijmant bij sijnen schuldenaer op eenen anderen wort bewesen, om bij hem betaelt te worden, ende alsoo van handen tot handen voorts tot vier oft vijff persoenen ende meer, die de bewijsinge al aenveerden, indijen hij bij den lesten niet en wort betaelt, heeft tot sijne voldoeninge verbonden alle de gene daerop hij bewesen is', Costuymen Compilatae 1608, part 4, §14. Published in G. De Longé, *Coutumes du pays et duché de Brabant: quartier d'Anvers* (Brussels: Gobbaerts, 1870), IV, p. 380, available at http://www.kuleuven-kulak.be/facult/rechten/Monballyu/Rechtlagelanden/Brabantsrecht/antwerpen/compil4.html [accessed 28 February 2015].
102. G. Malines, *Consuetudo, Vel, Lex Mercatoria or the Ancient Law-Merchant* (London: Redmayne, 1685), p. 100. Such a system was also in place in medieval York: P. Nightingale, 'The Rise and Decline of Medieval York: A Reassessment', *Past & Present*, 206:1 (1 February 2010), pp. 3–42, on p. 6.
103. De Smedt, *De Engelse Natie*, vol. 2, pp. 582–583; Van der Wee, 'Antwerp and the New Financial Methods', pp. 155, nn. 153, 157.
104. CAA, Vierschaar, Sentence books, V # 1249, f 266v-267r. De Bruyne ceded several IOU's by Anthonie Raes. CAA, Insolvente Boedelkamer, IB # 788, Journal Daniel de Bruyne, 42r & 65r.
105. Brulez, *De firma Della Faille*, p. 402; Van der Wee, *The Growth of the Antwerp Market*, vol. 2, p. 348; Van der Wee, 'Antwerp and the New Financial Methods', p. 158.

106. CAA, Gebodboeken, Pk # 915, 120v.

107. CAA, Gebodboeken, Pk # 916, 3v.

108. In Antiquis, p. 598, § XXVII.

109. CAA, Notarial archives, notary Adriaan Zeger 's-Hertoghen, N # 2071, 205v-206r.

110. CAA, Gebodboeken, Pk # 916, 87r.

111. De Smedt, *De Engelse Natie*, vol. 2, pp. 566–7.

112. CAA, Insolvente Boedelkamer, IB # 788, Journal Daniel de Bruyne, 14r, 36r & 52r. Gamel inventory 2 x 1572, and nr 157. De Smedt, 'Antwerpen en de opbloei', vol. 1, pp. 130–2, vol. 2, pp. 20–68.

113. Median values = 9.893.3 grams (with surety) / 8.938.8 (without surety) grams of silver and 5 per cent trimmed mean = 13.183.0 (with surety) / 11.432.6 (without) grams of silver.

114. A crosstable with the identity of debtor and creditor (All foreign, mixed, all native) and whether or not there was a borg principal was drawn. A significant (at 99 per cent level) but very low Cramer's V was found (.036).

115. I found eight bonds between a native guarantor and a native debtor, nine relations between a foreign guarantor and a foreign debtor, two instances between a native debtor and a foreign guarantor and one case of a foreign debtor and a native guarantor.

116. Van der Wee, *The Growth of the Antwerp Market*, vol. 2, p. 349; Kohn, 'Bills of Exchange', p. 27.

117. H. Van der Wee, 'Sporen van disconto te Antwerpen tijdens de XVIe eeuw', *Bijdragen voor de geschiedenis der Nederlanden*, 10 (1955), pp. 68–70.

118. Van der Wee, 'Antwerp and the New Financial Methods', p. 163.

119. Van der Wee, *The Growth of the Antwerp Market*, vol. 2, pp. 350–1.

120. De Smedt, *De Engelse Natie*, vol. 2, pp. 573–4.

121. CAA, Insolvente Boedelkamer, IB # 788, Journal Daniel de Bruyne, 29. The discounting rate is unknown.

122. CAA, Insolvente Boedelkamer, IB # 788, Journal Daniel de Bruyne, 53.

123. CAA, Processen, 7 # 12144, inventory of Jan Spierinck.

124. De Smedt, 'Antwerpen en de opbloei', vol. 2, bonds nr 163, 217.

125. Van der Wee, 'Antwerp and the New Financial Methods', p. 163.

126. Brulez, *De firma Della Faille*, pp. 403–4; Van der Wee, *The Growth of the Antwerp Market*, vol. 2, p. 351.

127. CAA, Gebodboeken, Pk # 216, 1585, 464r.

128. CAA, Gebodboeken, Pk # 216, 1580, 244r.

129. De Smedt, 'Antwerpen en de opbloei', vol. 1, pp. 130. IOUs in inventory, Jan Gamel.

130. Gelderblom, 'Entrepreneurs', pp. 166–7.

131. C. Laurent, J.-P.-A. Lameere and H. Simont, *Recueil des ordonnances des Pays-Bas: 2e série, 1506–1700*, 6 vols (Brussels: Goemaere, 1893–1922), vol. 4, pp. 329–31. In 1520 (27 September) it was declared that the freedom of the fair lasted for six weeks. Laurent, Lameere and Simont, *Recueil des ordonnances*, vol. 2.

132. CAA, Privilegiekamer, Engelse natie, Pk # 1052.

133. Laurent, Lameere and Simont, *Recueil des ordonnances*, vol. 4, pp. 329–31.

134. See chapter one of this book.

135. de Smedt, 'De keizerlijke verordeningen', pp. 22–31; de Smedt, *De Engelse Natie*, vol. 2, pp. 574–81.

136. Text reproduced in H. J. Smit, *Bronnen tot de geschiedenis van den handel met Engeland, Schotland en Ierland* ('s-Gravenhage: Nijhoff, 1928), II, 1, pp. 592–4, n. 594.

137. For a discussion of this request, see: de Smedt, 'De keizerlijke verordeningen'.
138. Explicitly mentioned in the document or deduced from the date of recording of the title and the date of maturity.
139. Van der Wee, 'Antwerp and the New Financial Methods', p. 163.
140. There is a very weak correlation between year and total duration of the IOU in months (-0.126).
141. Very weak correlation between value of the IOU in grams of silver and total duration of the IOU in months (-0.041).
142. Gelderblom and Jonker, 'Completing a Financial Revolution', p. 647. Also for roll-over over loans: H. Kole and C. Van Bochove, 'The Private Credit Market of Eighteenth-Century Amsterdam: Big Money in a Small World', in *Research Group Social Economic History* (Utrecht: Utrecht University, 2011), p. 11.
143. Mostly because Janssens., De Bruyne, De Pape, etc., only seldom mention IOUs with themselves as debtors in their account books.
144. MPM, Manuscripts, Arch. 681, Journal Herman Janssens, 1558, 70r.
145. CAA, Notarial archives, notary Willem Stryt, N # 3133, 153r–154r.
146. CAA, Vierschaar, Sentence books, V # 1239, 1544, 113v.
147. Gelderblom, 'Entrepreneurs', p. 167.
148. CAA, Second Turbeboek, V # 69, 69r-v.
149. A brewer borrows from a colleague and gives the deed of his brewery as surety. CAA, Notarial archives, notary Adriaan Zeger 's-Hertoghen, N # 2071, 94v-95r. Jan Gamel got a dyeworks close to the Hoochbrug and a piece of land as collateral for two bonds. De Smedt, 'Antwerpen En De Opbloei'. Christoffel Pruynen offered Herman Janssens an English warehouse, which Pruynen had constructed together with Jan van Asseliers and Anna Janssens (Herman's sister), as collateral. MPM, Manuscripts, Arch. 681, Journal Herman Janssens, 1570, 108r.
150. MPM, Manuscripts, Arch. 681, Journal Herman Janssens, 1570, 97v.
151. CAA, Insolvente Boedelkamer, IB # 788, Journal Daniel de Bruyne, 2v.
152. CAA, Notarial archives, notary Willem Stryt, N # 3133, 255v–256r.
153. CAA, Vierschaar, Sentence books, V # 1239, 1544, 192r.
154. CAA, Notarial archives, notary Willem Stryt, N # 3133, 61v–62r.
155. CAA, Vierschaar, Sentence books, V # 1240, 6v–7r.
156. Gelderblom, 'The Governance of Early Modern Trade', pp. 627–8; Gelderblom and Jonker, 'Completing a Financial Revolution', pp. 647–8.
157. CAA, Vierschaar, Sentence books, V# 1249, 52v.
158. See 'Molen, Van der, family' in the index.
159. CAA, Insolvente Boedelkamer, IB # 2898, Letter-book Van der Molen, 48r, 84r-v, 89r, 91r.
160. F. Edler, 'The Effects of the Financial Measures of Charles V on the Commerce of Antwerp, 1539–1542', *Belgisch tijdschrift voor filologie en geschiedenis*, 16: 3–4 (1937), pp. 665–73; Van der Wee, *The Growth of the Antwerp Market*, vol. 1, p. 163. 163 CAA, Privilegiekamer, Raeckt den Handel, Pk 1018, piece 8 and the reports by Van der Molen in this period, CAA, Insolvente Boedelkamer, IB # 2898, Letter-book Van der Molen.
161. As can be seen in CAA, Insolvente Boedelkamer, IB # 788, Journal Daniel de Bruyne MPM, Manuscripts, Arch. 681, Journal Herman Janssens.
162. CAA, Vierschaar, Sentence books, V # 1240, 58r.
163. For an example see: de Smedt, *De Engelse Natie*, vol. 2, pp. 560–1.

164. L. Boerner and J. W. Hatfield, *The Economics of Debt Clearing Mechanisms* (Berlin: Free University Berlin, School of Business & Economics, 2010).

165. Van der Wee, 'Antwerp and the New Financial Methods', p. 151, nn. 32, 132.

166. CAA, Insolvente Boedelkamer, IB # 788, Journal Daniel de Bruyne, 17r.

167. Laurent, Lameere and Simont, *Recueil Des Ordonnances*, vol. 4, 4 October 1540. See also: Van der Wee, *The Growth of the Antwerp Market*, vol. 2, pp. 352–4.

168. De Groote, 'De vermogensbalans', pp. 238–9.

169. H. Van der Wee, 'Das Phänomen des Wachstums und der Stagnation im Lichte der Antwerpener und Südniederlandischen Wirtschaft des 16. Jahrhunderts', *Vierteljahr-schrift für Sozial- und Wirtschaftsgeschichte*, 54:2 (1967), pp. 203–49, on pp. 230–2. Van der Wee provides sparse data on interest rates on commercial deposits from fair to fair for the period 1561–84 and on short-term loans to the authorities in the period 1511–55. Annual interests on commercial deposits ranged between 4 per cent and 12 per cent (average of 7.16 per cent): *The Growth of the Antwerp Market*, vol. 1, pp. 525–8. Discussions on the importance of falling interest rates in the late middle ages and the early modern period can be found in: S. R. Epstein, *Freedom and Growth: The Rise of States and Markets in Europe, 1300–1750* (London: Routledge, 2001), pp. 17–29; G. Clark, *A Farewell to Alms: A Brief Economic History of the World* (Princeton, NJ: Princeton University Press, 2007), pp. 167–171; J. L. Van Zanden and M. Prak (eds), *The Long Road to the Industrial Revolution: The European Economy in a Global Perspective, 1000–1800. Global Economic History Series*, (Leiden: Brill, 2009), pp. 22–3; D. Stasavage, *States of Credit: Size, Power, and the Development of European Polities* (Princeton, NJ: Princeton University Press, 2011).

170. Gelderblom, 'The Governance of Early Modern Trade', pp. 629–30; Gelderblom and Jonker, 'Completing a Financial Revolution', p. 663.

171. One hundred and twenty purchases were paid for by a bond, 154 were settled in another way.

172. Foreign creditors: seventy-three bonds and forty-six unregistered debts; native creditors: forty-four bonds and ninety-nine unregistered debts.

173. Average bond owed to a foreign creditor = £55.2 gr. Fl., as opposed to average bond value owed to a native creditor = £53.3 gr. Fl.

174. Expected duration of bond debts = 134.6 days; non-bond debt = 107.8 days. Real duration of bond debts = 174.2; non bond-debts = 144.4.

175. All measured in days. Linear regressions on the de Pape data. The relation between the specified duration of the debt in the bond and its value is equally weak for the entire sample of bonds (not significant, $R^2=0.041$).

176. $R^2=0.528$.

177. Bonds in the upper-third quartile (between £33 and 54 gr. Fl.) were especially likely to be assigned. Pivot tables (debt paid by bond or not as columns paid to original creditor or not as rows) with quartile number as layer. Quartile three (N=81) reports a Cramer's V of 0.269).

178. CAA, Insolvente Boedelkamer, IB # 776, Jaarmarktboek Frans De Pape, 50v.

179. One hundred and twenty-five payments to the original creditor vs. twenty-eight to a third party.

180. CAA, Insolvente Boedelkamer, IB # 776, Jaarmarktboek Frans De Pape, 50v.

181. CAA, Vierschaar, Sentence books, V # 1233, 1504–5 and V # 1238–40, 1544. RAB, Council of Brabant, Sentence books, 589–90. De Smidt et al., *Chronologische lijsten*.

182. De ruysscher, *Handel en recht*, p. 241.

183. De ruysscher, *Handel en recht*, pp. 240–2.

184. De ruysscher, *Handel en recht*, p. 245.

185. Brulez, *De firma Della Faille*, pp. 386–7.

186. Munro, 'English "Backwardness"', p. 144.

187. CAA, Vierschaar, Sentence books, V # 1233, 1504, 48r-v.

188. For example CAA, Notarial archives, notary Willem Stryt, N # 3133, 1540, 339v–340v.

189. RAB, Council of Brabant, Lawsuit files Council of Brabant of private individuals, 315, Supplication of Jeronimus de Moye, 13 June 1540.

190. CAA, Notarial archives, notary Willem Stryt, N # 3133, 1r-3r.

191. CAA, Vierschaar, Sentence books, V # 1239, 1544, 189v.

192. CAA, Notarial archives, notary Willem Stryt, N # 3133, 3r-v.

193. See the debate in: J. Edwards and S. Ogilvie, 'Contract Enforcement, Institutions, and Social Capital: The Maghribi Traders Reappraised', *Economic History Review*, 65:2 (2012), pp. 421–44; A. Greif, 'The Maghribi Traders: A Reappraisal?', *Economic History Review*, 65:2 (2012), pp. 445–69. Graeber also stresses state enforcement and the creation of legal terms. D. Graeber, *Debt: The First 5,000 Years* (New York: Melville House, 2011), p. 54. The embeddedness of private solutions in a wider framework of public institutions is one of the key points in Gelderblom, *Cities of Commerce*, pp. 7–9, 199–200.

194. S. Quinn, 'Money, Finance and Capital Markets', in R. Floud and P. Johnson (eds), *Industrialisation, 1700–1860, The Cambridge Economic History of Modern Britain* (Cambridge: Cambridge University Press, 2004), pp. 147–74, on p. 153.

195. Doehaerd, *Etudes anversoises*, pp. 17–18.

196. Soly, 'De schepenregisters'.

197. De ruysscher, *Handel en recht*, pp. 22–7, 101.

198. CAA, Vierschaar, Sentence books, V 1233, 1504–5 and V1238–40, 1544.

199. M. Oosterbosch, 'Het openbare notariaat in Antwerpen tijdens de Late Middeleeuwen (1314–1531): een institutionele en prosopografische studie in Europees perspectief' (Leuven: KUL, 1992); M, Oosterbosch, '"Van groote abuysen ende ongeregeltheden" Overheidsbemoeiingen met het Antwerpse notariaat tijdens de XVIde eeuw', *Legal History Review*, 63 (1995), pp. 83–101'; J. Van den Nieuwenhuizen, 'Antwerpse maatregelen voor het notariaat in het Ancien Régime', in G. Maréchal (ed.), *Een kompas met vele streken: studies over Antwerpen, scheepvaart en archivistiek, aangeboden aan Dr. Gustaaf Asaert ter gelegenheid van zijn 65ste verjaardag*, Archiefkunde: Verhandelingen aansluitend bij Bibliotheek- en Archiefgids (Antwerp: Vlaamse Vereniging voor Bibliotheek-, Archief- en Documentatiewezen, 1994), pp. 177–183; J. Van Roey, 'Notarissen en Schepenen te Antwerpen in de 16de eeuw', *Kroniek. Organ van Stabuco. Vereniging stadspersoneel Antwerpen*, 1:12 (1950), pp. 49–51.

200. CAA, Notarial Archives, N 2078 & N 3568.

201. De Smedt, 'Antwerpen en de opbloei', vol. 1, pp. 130–2, vol. 2, pp. 20–68; see also the summary article of this thesis: 'De Antwerpse koopman Jan Gamel', *Bijdragen tot de geschiedenis van de Nederlanden*, 56 (1971), pp. 211–24; on Gamel's bonds: De Smedt, 'Antwerpen en de Opbloei', pp. 79–84.

202. CAA, Processen, 7 # 12144, dupliek.

203. CAA, Chamber of Insolvency, IB # 776, Jaarmarktboek Frans De Pape.

204. MPM, Manuscripts, Arch. 681, Journal Herman Janssens, 1550–1570. Soly, 'De Antwerpse onderneemster Anna Janssens'.

205. On Plantin's finances: R. M. Kingdon, 'Christopher Plantin and his Backers, 1575–90. A Study in the Problem of Financing Business During War', in *Mélanges d'histoire économique et sociale en hommage au professeur Antony Babel* (Geneva: Imprimerie de la tribune, 1963); L. Voet, *The Golden Compasses: A History and Evaluation of the Printing and Publishing Activities of the Officina Plantiniana at Antwerp* (Amsterdam: Vangendt, 1969).
206. MPM, Manuscripts, Arch. 98, 116.
207. CAA, Chamber of Insolvency, IB # 788, Journal Daniel de Bruyne.
208. Formsma and Pirenne, *Koopmansgeest te 's-Hertogenbosch*.
209. N. Van Den Brulle, 'De commerciële praktijk in het zestiende-eeuwse Antwerpen aan de hand van registers uit de Insolvente Boedelskamer' (MA thesis, Universiteit Gent, 2010).
210. CAA, Gebodboeken, Pk # 913–29 (1439–1794). Published in: P. Van Setter, 'Index der Gebodboeken', *Antwerpsch Archievenblad*, 1:1 (1864), pp. 120–464.

5 Institutions and the Political Economy of Sixteenth-Century Antwerp Commerce

1. S. Ogilvie and A. W. Carus, 'Institutions and Economic Growth in Historical Perspective', in A. Philippe and N. Durlauf Steven (eds), *Handbook of Economic Growth* (Amsterdam: Elsevier, 2014), ch. 8, pp. 403–513, on p. 429.
2. S. Ogilvie, *Institutions and European Trade: Merchant Guilds, 1000–1800* (Cambridge: Cambridge University Press, 2011).
3. Ogilvie, *Institutions and European Trade*, pp. 32, 101, 211, 307–8; Gelderblom, *Cities of Commerce*, pp. 1–4, 6, 10, 11, 19, 20, 40, 121, 197, 198–200, 205–8.
4. G. Marnef, *Antwerp in the Age of the Reformation: Underground Protestantism in a Commercial Metropolis, 1550–1577* (Baltimore, Md.: Johns Hopkins University Press, 1996), p. 40; K. Wouters, 'Tussen verwantschap en vermogen: de politieke elite van Antwerpen (1520–55): een elite-onderzoek door middel van de prosopografische methode' (Brussels: Free University of Brussels, 2001), p. 135. For the period 1520–55 the foreign merchants (or sons of foreign merchants) Jan de Haro, Alvaro d'Almaras, Fernando de Bernuy, Coenraet del Vaille (Spaniards), Ambrosius Tucher, Melchior Groenenborch (German) and Symon Lhermite (French) became aldermen. Their Antwerp counterparts were slightly less numerous: Jacques de Cordes, Jan, Cornelis and Charles de Renialme, Jan van der Heyden and Pauwels van Dale.
5. Marnef, *Antwerpen in the Age of the Reformation*, p. 40.
6. Marnef, *Antwerpen in the Age of the Reformation*, p. 158.
7. F. Prims, *De kolonellen van de 'Burgersche Wacht' te Antwerpen (december 1577–augustus 1585)* (Antwerp: Standaard, 1942). H. Soly, 'The "Betrayal" of the Sixteenth-Century Bourgeoisie: A Myth? Some Considerations of the Behaviour Pattern of Merchants of Antwerp in the Sixteenth Century', *Acta historiae Neerlandica*, 8 (1975), pp. 31–49, on pp. 44–9.
8. Soly, *Urbanisme en kapitalisme*. Also: H. Soly 'Fortificaties, belastingen en corruptie te Antwerpen in het midden der 16e eeuw', *Bijdragen tot de geschiedenis*, 53 (1970), pp. 191–210.
9. H. Soly, 'The "Betrayal" of the Sixteenth-Century Bourgeoisie: A Myth?'; Wouters, 'Tussen verwantschap en vermogen', pp. 151–2.

10. Gascon, *Grand commerce et vie urbaine*.

11. R. Pike, *Aristocrats and Traders: Sevillian Society in the Sixteenth Century* (Ithaca, NY: Cornell University Press, 1972). I. W. Archer, *The Pursuit of Stability: Social Relations in Elizabethan London* (Cambridge: Cambridge University Press, 1991). G. D. Ramsay, *The City of London in International Politics at the Accession of Elizabeth Tudor* (Manchester: Manchester University Press, 1975).

12. A. Gamberini and I. Lazzarini, *The Italian Renaissance State* (Cambridge: Cambridge University Press, 2012).

13. D. De ruysscher and J. Puttevils, 'The Art of Compromise. Legislative Talks for Marine Insurance Institutions in Antwerp (*c.*1550–*c.*1570)', *Low Countries Historical Review* (forthcoming).

14. G. Wells, 'Emergence and Evanescence: Republicanism and the Res Publica at Antwerp before the Revolt of the Netherlands', in H. G. Koenigsberger and E. Müller-Luckner (eds), *Republiken und Republikanismus im Europa der Frühen Neuzeit* (Munich: Oldenbourg, 1988), pp. 155–68; G. E. Wells, *Antwerp and the Government of Philip II, 1555–1567 S.l.* (Ithaca, NY: Cornell University, 1982); M. Lindemann, *The Merchant Republics: Amsterdam, Antwerp, and Hamburg, 1648–1790* (New York: Cambridge University Press, 2015)

15. See for example the exceptional study: A. van Meeteren, *Op hoop van akkoord: instrumenteel forumgebruik bij geschilbeslechting in Leiden in de zeventiende eeuw* (Hilversum: Verloren, 2006).

16. J. Puttevils, 'The Ascent of Merchants from the Southern Low Countries: From Antwerp to Europe, 1480–1585' (PhD dissertation, University of Antwerp, 2012), pp. 292–7; Gelderblom, *Cities of Commerce*, pp. 104–8.

17. M. Godfrey, 'Arbitration and Dispute Resolution in Sixteenth Century Scotland', *Legal History Review*, 70:1–2 (2002), pp. 109–35; Gelderblom, *Cities of Commerce*, pp. 104–8.

18. Gelderblom, *Cities of Commerce*, p. 107.

19. Kessler, *A Revolution in Commerce*, pp. 60–105.

20. Gelderblom, *Cities of Commerce*, pp. 9, 108.

21. Aldermen assigned to a specific case as judges and arbiters. De ruysscher, *Handel en recht*, pp. 133–5.

22. On the role of arbiters inspecting the evidence such as letters and account books, *Cities of Commerce*, pp. 105–8.

23. The social and economic dimensions of (civil) courts of law have only recently caught the attention of historians. This has been largely a spill-over effect of the increased historiographical interest in criminal history, despite the fact that civil courts have produced much larger collections of source material than criminal justice courts. J. Hardwick, *Family Business: Litigation and the Political Economies of Daily Life in Early Modern France* (Oxford: Oxford University Press, 2009), pp. 5–6; M. Dinges, 'The Uses of Justice as a Form of Social Control in Early Modern Europe', in H. Roodenburg and P. Spierenburg (eds), *Social Control in Europe, 1500–1800* (Columbus, OH: Ohio State University Press, 2004), ch. 9, pp. 159–74; C. Muldrew, 'Credit and the Courts: Debt Litigation in a Seventeenth-Century Urban Community', *Economic History Review*, 46:1 (1993), pp. 23–38; C. Muldrew, *The Economy of Obligation: The Culture of Credit and Social Relations in Early Modern England* (New York: Palgrave, 1998); van Meeteren, *Op hoop van akkoord*; J. Shaw, *The Justice of Venice: Authorities and Liberties in the Urban Economy, 1550–1700* (Oxford: Oxford University Press, 2006); Kessler,

A Revolution in Commerce; M. F. Van Dijck, 'Towards an Economic Interpretation of Justice? Conflict Settlement, Social Control and Civil Society in Urban Brabant and Mechelen During the Late Middle Ages and the Early Modern Period', in M. Van der Heijden, E. Van Nederveen Meerkerk, G. Vermeesch and M. Van der Burg (eds), *Serving the Urban Community: The Rise of Public Facilities in the Low Countries* (Amsterdam: Aksant, 2009), pp. 62–88; J. Bossy, *Disputes and Settlements: Law and Human Relations in the West* (Cambridge: Cambridge University Press, 2003); T. Kuehn, *Heirs, Kin, and Creditors in Renaissance Florence* (Cambridge: Cambridge University Press, 2008); R. L. Kagan, *Lawsuits and Litigants in Castile, 1500–1700* (Chapel Hill, NC: University of North Carolina Press, 1981); M. J. H. A. Lijten, *Het Burgerlijk Proces in Stad En Meijerij Van 'S-Hertogenbosch, 1530–1811* (Assen: Van Gorcum, 1987). For the use of the local court for civil matters by craft guilds in Antwerp, see: H. Deceulaer, 'Guilds and Litigation: Conflict Settlement in Antwerp (1585–1796)', in M. Boone and M. Prak (eds), *Statuts individuels, statuts corporatiefs et status judiciaires dans les villes européennes (Moyen Âge et Temps Modernes): actes du colloque tenu à Gand les 12–14 octobre 1995* (Leuven: Garant, 1996), pp. 171–208.

24. Muldrew, 'Credit and the Courts'; Muldrew, *The Economy of Obligation*; Dinges, 'The Uses of Justice'; J. Shaw, 'Liquidation or Certification? Small Claims Disputes and Retail Credit in Seventeenth-Century Venice', in B. Blondé, P. Stabel, J. Stobart and I. Van Damme (eds), *Buyers and Sellers. Retails Circuits and Practies in Medieval and Early Modern Europe* (Turnhout: Brepols, 2006); B. Willems, *Leven op de pof*, p. 225.

25. D. L. Smail, *The Consumption of Justice: Emotions, Publicity, and Legal Culture in Marseille, 1264–1423* (Ithaca, NY: Cornell University Press, 2003); Dinges, 'The Uses of Justice'; van Meeteren, *Op hoop van akkoord*; Van Dijck, 'Towards an Economic Interpretation of Justice'.

26. Recently, historiography has framed the appeal of cities in terms of the civil services, among which judiciary services, provided by them: M. Prak and J. L. Van Zanden, 'Towards an Economic Interpretation of Citizenship: The Dutch Republic between Medieval Communes and Modern Nation-States', *European Review of Economic History*, 10:2 (2006), pp. 111–45; M. Van der Heijden, E. van Nederveen Meerkerk, G. Vermeersch et al., *Serving the Urban Community: The Rise of Public Facilities in the Low Countries* (Amsterdam: Aksant, 2009); L. Lucassen and W. Willems (eds), *Waarom mensen in de stad willen wonen, 1200–2010* (Amsterdam: Bakker, 2010).

27. Their number fluctuated. In 1490 the magistracy asked Maximilian of Austria for an enlargement of the bench of aldermen from twelve to sixteen aldermen because of the growth of the urban population due to the war and unrest in the Low Countries. In 1556, the number of aldermen increased again to eighteen; in 1577 the number was brought back to sixteen. M. Gotzen, 'Het oud-Antwerps burgerlijk procesrecht volgens de costumiere redacties van de 16e-17e eeuw', *Rechtskundig tijdschrift voor België*, 41 (1951), pp. 291–315, 424–68, on pp. 298–9.

28. But the city government did not recruit intensively from the merchant community: Wouters, 'Tussen verwantschap en vermogen'; H. De Ridder-Symoens, 'De universitaire vorming van de Brabantse stadsmagistraten en stadsfunktionarissen – Leuven en Antwerpen, 1430–1580', *Varia historica Brabantica*, 6–7 (1978), pp. 21–12.

29. More on the bench of aldermen as a court: F. Prims, *Rechterlijk Antwerpen in de Middeleeuwen: de rechterlijke instellingen* (Mechelen: Confraternitas Sancti Yvonis, 1936); Gotzen, 'Het oud-Antwerps burgerlijk procesrecht'; C. Laenens and L. Leemans, *De geschiedenis van het Antwerps gerecht* (Antwerp: Van de Velde, 1953); R. Boumans, *Het*

Antwerps stadsbestuur voor en tijdens de Franse overheersing: bijdrage tot de ontwik-kelingsgeschiedenis van de stedelijke bestuursinstellingen in de Zuidelijke Nederlanden (Brugge: De Tempel, 1965); J. Van den Nieuwenhuizen, 'Bestuursinstellingen van de stad Antwerpen (12de eeuw–1795)', in R. van Uytven, C. Bruneel, H. Coppens and B. Augustyn (eds), *De gewestelijke en lokale overheidsinstellingen in Brabant en Mechelen tot 1795* (Brussels: Algemeen Rijksarchief, 2000), pp. 462–510.

30. De ruysscher, *Handel en recht*, pp. 106–7, 114–22.

31. J. P. A. Coopmans, 'De jaarmarkten van Antwerpen en Bergen op Zoom als centra van rechtsverkeer en rechtsvorming', in M. J. G. C. Raaijmakers, H. C. F. Schoordijk and B. Wachter (eds), *Handelsrecht tussen koophandel en Nieuw BW: opstellen van de vakgroep privaatrecht van de Katholieke Universiteit Brabant bij het 150-jarig bestaan van het WVK* (Deventer: Kluwer, 1988), pp. 1–22; De ruysscher, *Handel En Recht*, pp. 42–5, 134–5.

32. E. Coornaert, *Les Français et le commerce international à Anvers, fin du 15e-16e siècle* (Paris: Rivière, 1961); O Gelderblom, 'The Decline of Fairs and Merchant Guilds in the Low Countries, 1250–1650', *Jaarboek voor middeleeuwse geschiedenis* (2004), pp. 199–238; D. J. Harreld, *High Germans in the Low Countries*; D. J. Harreld 'The Individual Merchant and the Trading Nation in Sixteenth-Century Antwerp', in C. H. Parker and J. H. Bentley (eds), *Between the Middle Ages and Modernity: Individual and Community in the Early Modern World* (Lanham: Rowman & Littlefield, 2007), pp. 271–84.

33. P. Stabel, 'De gewenste vreemdeling: Italiaanse kooplieden en stedelijke maatschappij in het laat-middeleeuwse Brugge', *Jaarboek voor middeleeuwse geschiedenis*, 4 (2001), pp. 189–221; B. Lambert, '"Considéré que lesquels marchans ont souvent question les ungs contre les autres": commerciële conflictbeheersing in het laat-middeleeuwse Brugge', paper presented at the *Sixth European Social Science History Conference* (Amsterdam, 2006), pp. 1–16; B. Lambert, 'De Genuese aanwezigheid in laatmiddeleeuws Brugge (1435–1495): een laboratorium voor de studie van instellingen en hun rol in de econo-mische geschiedenis' (PhD dissertation, Ghent University, 2011).

34. Gotzen, 'Het oud-Antwerps burgerlijk procesrecht', pp. 291–315, 424–68; De ruyss-cher, *Handel en recht*, pp. 100–42. See infra for the Cloth Hall court.

35. Unfortunately the civil sentences in the Vonnisboeken do not provide details on the subdivision which handled the case. If a litigant was not satisfied with the judgment in one of these ancillary courts, he could appeal the matter to the aldermen's court. Several mercantile cases were first brought before the Cloth Hall in 1505 (one case) and 1544 (five cases), involving both local and foreign litigants. These cases dealt with unpaid debts from bills obligatory and unpaid textiles and raw materials for textile production (such as woad). CAA, Vierschaar, Sentence books, V # 1233, 1505, 73r; V # 1238, 1544, 147v, 154r, 162v; V # 1239, 1544, 85v; V # 1240, 1544, 21v.

36. On the Florentine Mercanzia: A. Astorri and D. Friedman, 'The Florentine Mercanzia and its Palace', *I Tatti Studies: Essays in the Renaissance*, 10 (2005), pp. 11–68; Goldth-waite, *The Economy of Renaissance Florence*, pp. 109–14.

37. De ruysscher, *Handel en recht*, pp. 127–8.

38. De ruysscher, *Handel en recht*, p. 101. The recording of criminal verdicts had begun in 1484.

39. De ruysscher, *Handel en recht*, pp. 22–7.

40. CAA, Vierschaar, Sentence books, V # 1233, 1505 and V # 1238–40, 1544.

41. CAA, Processen (7) and Processen supplement (288).

42. CAA, Processen, 7 # 240, 1818 and 11292. CAA, Processen Supplement, 288 # 692,

696, 1266, 1490, 1503, 1577, 1640, 1641, 1657, 1679, 1680, 1685, 3881, 6152, 6157, 8926, 8933, 9479, 9486. See also: De ruysscher, *Handel en recht*, pp. 24–6.

43. CAA, Civil Sentences, V # 1231–57.
44. See infra on the value of the stakes.
45. Hardwick, *Family Business*, p. 58.
46. C. Wollschläger, 'Civil Litigation and Modernization: The Work of the Municipal Courts of Bremen, Germany, in Five Centuries, 1549–1984', *Law & Society Review*, 24:2 (1990), pp. 261–81.
47. J. Van Roey, 'De bevolking', in W. Couvreur (ed.), *Antwerpen in de XVIde eeuw* (Antwerp: Mercurius, 1975), pp. 95–108. We have selected sample years. Not all sentence books have been preserved for every year. Only full years were selected.
48. Hardwick, *Family Business*, p. 58.
49. Muldrew, 'Credit and the Courts'; S. Hindle, *The State and Social Change in Early Modern England* (Basingstoke: Palgrave MacMillan, 2001).
50. Hardwick, *Family Business*, pp. 60–6.
51. I have added the different sums at stake mentioned in the sentences and recalculated the different currencies to pounds Flemish groat using the few exchange rates specified in the sentence and C. Verlinden, *Dokumenten voor de geschiedenis van prijzen en lonen in Vlaanderen en Brabant = Documents pour l'histoire des prix et des salaires en Flandre et en Brabant* (Bruges: Tempel, 1959); H. A. E. van Gelder, *De Nederlandse munten* (Antwerp: Spectrum, 1966). The annuities were computed at 6.25 per cent or the Penning 16. The mean stake value in 1504–5 was £49 gr. FL, that of 1544 £185 gr. Fl. The median stake value in 1504–5 was £12 gr. Fl., that of 1544 £8.5 gr. Fl.
52. I have recalculated these stakes into annual wages for a master mason, so as to have an idea of the value of the stakes in real terms (annual master mason's wage) and to account for the inflation of the forty years between the two sample years. 'Antwerp: Annual Wages and Prices, 1400–1700', available at http://www.economics.utoronto.ca/munro5/AntwerpWage.xls [accessed 28 February 2015]. In 1505, the master mason year wage is estimated at £6.7813 gr. Fl; in 1544, the master mason year wage is estimated at £11.8125 gr. Fl.
53. De ruysscher, *Handel en recht*, p. 112. But most mercantile disputes involved higher stake values.
54. Mean stake value of mercantile cases: £389 gr. Fl.; non-mercantile cases: £37.13 gr. Fl. The difference of means test (t-test) gives a significant difference between the two means (p-value 0.0076 assuming unequal variances). CAA, sentence books, V # 1238–40.
55. Only for the year 1544, since the 1505 data only gave an initial date for ten cases.
56. Mean civil case duration in 1544 in days: mercantile cases: 489 days; non-mercantile cases: 612 days. The difference of means test (t-test) gives a insignificant difference between the two means (p-value 0.3610 assuming unequal variances). AA, sentence books, V # 1238–40.
57. This came out of the bachelor paper of Thomas Feijen (University of Antwerp) who used the following trial files: CAA, Processen Supplement, 288 # 1266, 1689, 9476.
58. Van Dijck, 'Towards an Economic Interpretation of Justice?', pp. 76–8.
59. Interestingly, in a few cases the estimation of these costs took into account the foregone interests on the value of the stake. In the 1538 case of Francois Werner versus Jan de Pape, de Pape had to pay Werner 12 per cent interest 'as if he was a merchant at the Bourse paying interest to another merchant', a rate corresponding with the interest rate

on short-term loans to the government on the Antwerp money market. CAA, Processen Supplement, 288 # 3881, Conclusie, 1v-2r. 'A raison van twelfve ten honderden Tsjaers/ gelyck een coopman den anderen eenren den selven tyt ter voirss voor interest ten minsten gegeven heeft gehat ... ter causen vande intereste dat hy als wesende een coopman ende ter borssen hanterende'. Van der Wee, *The Growth of the Antwerp Market*, vol. 1, p. 526.

60. T. Kuran, 'Judicial Biases in Ottoman Istanbul: Islamic Justice and its Compatibility with Modern Economic Life', *Journal of Law and Economics*, 55/3 (2012), pp. 631–6.
61. Gelderblom, *Cities of Commerce*.
62. Cross table chances of particular plaintiffs and defendants to win their mercantile civil case. Chi^2 = 2.9795, p value = 0.0843, Cramer's V = 0.191. CAA, sentence books, V # 1233, V # 1238–1240.
63. For numbers of merchants see chapter one.
64. The number of Englishmen and Portuguese could be slightly higher, given that it is hard to distinguish Englishmen from the locals, and the Portuguese from the Spanish. Stabel, 'De gewenste vreemdeling'; De ruysscher, *Handel en recht*, pp. 117–21.
65. More 'exotic' merchants – from Spain, Italy and England – were easier to identify than those from France, Germany and the Low Countries.
66. CAA, Vierschaar, Sentence books, V # 1239, 1544, 163v–164r. No references to consular courts were found in the 1505 sample.
67. Four plaintiffs of the sixty-two and five defendants of forty-eight were explicitly described as foreigners, while I could identify five foreign plaintiffs and eight defendants more.
68. Twenty-one plaintiffs were specifically designated as foreigners. I could identify 103 other foreigners. Of the defendants fifteen were mentioned as foreigners, 119 other defendants could be identified as foreigners as well.
69. Greif suggests that in growing markets and communities, origin and allegiance became harder to verify, which led to the decline of the Community Responsibility System. A. Greif, 'Impersonal Exchange and the Origin of Markets: From the Community Responsibility System to Individual Legal Responsibility in Pre-Modern Europe', in M. Aoki and Y. Hayami (eds), *Communities and Markets in Economic Development* (Oxford: Oxford University Press, 2001), pp. 3–41, on pp. 25–7.
70. D. C. North, *Structure and Change in Economic History* (New York: Norton, 1981), p. 24; D. C. North, 'Institutions, Transaction Costs and the Rise of the Merchant Empires', in J. D. Tracy (ed.), *The Political Economy of Merchant Empires* (Cambridge: Cambridge University Press, 1991), pp. 22–41, on pp. 28–9.
71. S. R. Epstein, *Freedom and Growth: The Rise of States and Markets in Europe, 1300–1750* (London: Routledge, 2001), pp. 12–38; Gelderblom, *Cities of Commerce*, pp. 102–4.
72. M. F. Van Dijck, 'Towards an Economic Interpretation of Justice?', pp. 76–82.
73. D. De ruysscher, 'Bankruptcy, Insolvency and Debt Collection among Merchants in Antwerp (*c.*1490–*c.*1540)', in T. M. Safley (ed.), *The History of Bankruptcy: Economic, Social and Cultural Implications in Early Modern Europe* (New York: Routledge, 2013), p. 188. On the importance of royal patents and letters: P. Godding, 'Les lettres de justice, instrument du pouvoir central en Brabant (1430–1477)', *Archief- en bibliotheekwezen in België*, 61 (1990), pp. 385–402.
74. De ruysscher, *Handel en recht*, p. 15. On the Council of Brabant: P. Godding, 'Une justice parallèle? L'arbitrage au Conseil de Brabant', in J. M. I. Koster-van Dijk and

A. Wijffels (eds), *Miscellanea Forensia Historica: ter gelegenheid van het afscheid van Prof. Mr. J. Th. De Smidt* (Amsterdam: Werkgroep Grote Raad van Mechelen, 1988), pp. 123–41; E. Put, *Inventaris van het archief van de Raad van Brabant*, 2 vols (Brussels: Algemeen Rijksarchief, 1999); P. Godding, 'Le Conseil de Brabant sous Philippe le Bon. L'institution et les hommes', in R. Stein (ed.), *Powerbrokers in the Late Middle Ages. The Burgundian Low Countries in a European Context* (Turnhout: Brepols, 2001), pp. 101–14.

75. De ruysscher, *Handel en recht*, pp. 14–16.
76. RAB, Council of Brabant, Sentence books, 589.
77. CAA, Vierschaar, Sentence books, V # 1240, 45r.
78. Brulez, *De firma Della Faille*, pp. 17–21.
79. Casa de Contratación: CAA, Vierschaar, Sentence books, V # 1239, 175r; and the French admiralty court: CAA, Processen Supplement, 288 # 696.
80. Difference of means test (t-test) gives a 0.0442 p-value (significant at 5 per cent level, unequal variances assumed).
81. Mean stake value for Council of Brabant cases: £1,121 gr. Fl. (vs. £390 gr. Fl.). RAB, Council of Brabant, Sentence books, 589–90; for the city court, see supra. This accords with the findings of Maarten Van Dijck who found that the plaintiffs of 's-Hertogenbosch in a case brought to the Council of Brabant were wealthy citizens belonging to the third and fourth fiscal quartile of the city. Van Dijck, 'Towards an Economic Interpretation of Justice', pp. 80–1.
82. Difference of means test (t-test) gives a 0.0358 p-value (significant at 5 per cent level, unequal variances assumed).
83. Godding, 'Une justice parallèle?', pp. 125–6, 129; M.-C. le Bailly, *Recht voor de Raad: rechtspraak voor het Hof van Holland, Zeeland en West-Friesland in het midden van de vijftiende eeuw* (Hilversum: Verloren, 2001), p. 117; Gelderblom, *Cities of Commerce*, pp. 127–8.
84. J. van Rompaey, *De Grote Raad van de hertogen van Boergondië en het Parlement van Mechelen* (Brussels: Paleis der Academiën, 1973), p. 18; J. van Rompaey, 'De Bourgondische staatsinstellingen', in D. P. Blok (ed.), *Algemene Geschiedenis der Nederlanden* (Haarlem: Fibula-Van Dischoeck, 1977–83), pp. 136–55, on pp. 144–7; J. van Rompaey, 'Het ontstaan van de Grote Raad onder Filips de Goede', in H. De Schepper (ed.), *Miscellanea Consilii Magni* (Amsterdam: Universiteit van Amsterdam, 1980), pp. 63–76.
85. C. H. van Rhee, *Litigation and Legislation: Civil Procedure at First Instance in the Great Council for the Netherlands in Malines (1522–1559)* (Brussels: Algemeen Rijksarchief, 1997), pp. 36, 41
86. Gelderblom, *Cities of Commerce*, pp. 127–8. On the Great Council: de Smidt et al., *Chronologische lijsten*; van Rompaey, *De Grote Raad*; L. T. Maes, M. Kocken et. al., *Het Parlement en de Grote Raad van Mechelen, 1473–1797* (Antwerpen: De Vries-Brouwers, 2009). Merchants tended to avoid the Great Council because it acted rather slowly and they preferred quick conflict resolution. In the period 1523–58, first instance cases lasted 976.59 days on average. Van Rhee, *Litigation and Legislation*, pp. 341–2.
87. Gelderblom, *Cities of Commerce*, pp. 129–30.
88. van Rhee, *Litigation and Legislation*, pp. 313–40.
89. Gelderblom, *Cities of Commerce*, p. 128.
90. In 1526 Steven Capelle referred to a precedent case of the Great Council concerning the power held by the bearer of a bill obligatory. One of the officials of the Great Council had even visited the Antwerp Exchange to collect testimonies of this practice. CAA,

294   *Notes to pages 146–8*

Processen Supplement, 288 # 1679, Dupliek Steven Capellen, f22v.

91. De Smidt et al., *Chronologische Lijsten*.
92. Gelderblom, *Cities of Commerce*, pp. 126–33.
93. De ruysscher, *Handel en recht*, pp. 45–7; Gelderblom, *Cities of Commerce*, pp. 135, 137.
94. This part is loosely based on my overview of the debate: J. Puttevils, 'Voor macht en winst. Koopmansgilden en collectieve actie in pre-industrieel Europa, een overzicht', *Leidschrift*, 25:2 (2010), pp 97–114.
95. For a good overview of the history of merchant guilds and the distinction between home merchant guilds and alien merchant guilds: M. Kohn, 'Merchant Associations in Pre-Industrial Europe', 2003, unpublished working paper, available at http://www.dartmouth.edu/~mkohn/Papers/16.%20Associations.pdf [accessed 28 February 2015]; S. Ogilvie, *Institutions and European Trade*, pp. 19–159.
96. O. Gelderblom and R. Grafe, 'The Rise, Persistence and Decline of Merchant Guilds. Re-Thinking the Comparative Study of Commercial Institutions in Pre-Modern Europe', *Journal of Interdisciplinary History*, 40:4 (2010), pp. 477–511.
97. A. Greif, P, Milgrom and B. R. Weingast, 'Coordination, Commitment, and Enforcement: The Case of the Merchant Guild', *Journal of Political Economy*, 102:4 (1994), pp. 745–76. Volckart and Mangels have reached a similar conclusion. Volckart and Mangels argue that, contrary to the late medieval and early modern guilds which functioned as cartels and provided benefits only to the guild members, and were in fact detrimental to the rest of the economy – early merchant guilds of the tenth and eleventh centuries provided protection to merchants through their travelling in groups and mutual assistance in times of need. In doing so, guilds allegedly fuelled the Commercial Revolution. O. Volckart and A. Mangels, 'Are the Roots of the Modern Lex Mercatoria Really Medieval?', *Southern Economic Journal*, 65:3 (1999), pp. 427–50. De Moor has characterized merchant guilds as institutions of corporate collective action. Their aim was to share among their members the risks and uncertainties of the early market economy and to enjoy the scale advantages of acting collectively, for example to obtain the protection necessary for trade. These institutions did so by institutionalizing into clearly defined self-governing organs: they set requirements for membership to keep the benefits of incorporation limited only to members and established their own rules which they enforced through social control. T. De Moor, 'The Silent Revolution: A New Perspective on the Emergence of Commons, Guilds, and Other Forms of Corporate Collective Action in Western Europe', *International Review of Social History*, 53, supplement 16 (2008), pp. 179–212. The theory about the ruler–guild relationship has been verified empirically in Gelderblom and Grafe, 'The Rise, Persistence and Decline of Merchant Guilds', pp. 499–504. This raises doubts about this interpretation of the merchant guild–ruler relationship.
98. For an overview see: Puttevils, 'Voor macht en winst'.
99. Some historians did compare different guilds active in the same city. For example: Stabel, 'De gewenste vreemdeling'; Gelderblom and Grafe, 'The Rise, Persistence and Decline of Merchant Guilds'.
100. Ogilvie, *Institutions and European Trade*.
101. Ogilvie also includes early modern incorporated companies such as the Dutch VOC (East India Company). Many would argue that these companies were fundamentally different, not least because, while they could still restrict who could and did trade on their behalf, a much larger circle of people could be and were shareholders in these companies than were members of guilds. Nevertheless, Ogilvie argues that the

monopolistic practices of these institutions were sufficiently like those of the earlier merchant guilds to allow for a combined analysis of both phenomena (many merchant guilds also continued to exist well into the early modern period). Ogilvie, *Institutions and European Trade*.

102. This is also partially confirmed by the Gelderblom and Grafe's data: Gelderblom and Grafe, 'The Rise, Persistence and Decline of Merchant Guilds', pp. 504–5.
103. Ogilvie, *Institutions and European Trade*, pp. 32, 101, 211, 307–8, 368–70.
104. Gelderblom and Grafe, 'The Rise, Persistence and Decline of Merchant Guilds'.
105. Gelderblom and Grafe, 'The Rise, Persistence and Decline of Merchant Guilds'.
106. Ogilvie, *Institutions and European Trade*, p. 31. This is the main point of Gelderblom, *Cities of Commerce*. See also: M. 't Hart and M. Van der Heijden, 'Stadslucht maakt vrij: autonomie en rivaliteit in de vroegmoderne Noordelijke Nederlanden', in L. Lucassen and W. Willems (eds), *Waarom mensen in de stad willen wonen, 1200–2010* (Amsterdam: Bert Bakker, 2009).
107. Gelderblom and Grafe, 'The Rise, Persistence and Decline of Merchant Guilds', p. 510. Ogilvie does not agree with this line of reasoning: merchant guilds (mainly incorporated companies) continued to exist after 1500, even in those regions with strong states and lively markets. Ogilvie, *Institutions and European Trade*, pp. 38–40. She indicates that merchant guilds became less important in the Low Countries and England because governments had other means of fiscal revenue besides granting privileges to merchant guilds in return for payment. R. Dessi and S. Ogilvie, 'Social Capital and Collusion: The Case of Merchant Guilds', in *Cambridge Working Papers in Economics* (Cambridge: Cambridge University, 2004), pp. 62–3. This line of reasoning is absent in her later monograph.
108. A large dataset on merchant guilds in Bruges, Antwerp and Amsterdam in the later middle ages and the early modern era has recently been collected by Gelderblom from the available and voluminous secondary literature. O. Gelderblom, 'The Decline of Fairs and Merchant Guilds in the Low Countries, 1250–1650', *Jaarboek voor middeleeuwse geschiedenis* (2004), pp. 199–238, and the appendix to Gelderblom and Grafe, 'The Rise, Persistence and Decline of Merchant Guilds', available at http://people.hss.caltech.edu/~jlr/events/Appendix%20to%20Gelderblom%20and%20Grafe.pdf [accessed 28 February 2015].
109. In 1314 John III, or more precisely the ducal regency council (in which the influence of the Brabant cities was particularly strong), announced a market peace. J. Van Gerven,'Antwerpen in de veertiende eeuw. Kleine stad zonder toekomst of opkomend handelscentrum?', *Belgisch tijdschrift voor filologie en geschiedenis*, 76:4 (1998), pp. 907–38, on p. 915; F. Blockmans, 'Van wanneer dateren de Antwerpse jaarmarkten?', *Handelingen van het Vlaamse filologencongres* (1947), pp. 58–9; P. Avonds, *Brabant tijdens de regering van hertog Jan III (1312–1356): De Grote Politieke Krisissen* (Brussels: Paleis der Academiën, 1984).
110. Wool, hides, lead, silver, bacon, grease, butter, honey, iron, wax, almonds, cumin, rice, quicksilver, alum, grain, saffron, ginger, cinnamon, pepper, galangal, zedoaria, cubeb, cloth, furs, steel, copper, linen, amber, fish sauce, tar, ash, beer, meat, salt, thread and clothing accessories are mentioned.
111. K. Höhlbaum, *Hansisches Urkundenbuch*, 8 edn, 6 vols, (Halle: Buchhandlung des Waisenhauses, 1876–99), vol. 2, p. 103.
112. These concerned safe conducts, toll exemptions and the right to elect their own governor and judges and to establish a separate jurisdiction over English merchants. O. de

Smedt, *De Engelse Natie*, vol. 1; M.-R. Thielemans, *Bourgogne et Angleterre: relations politiques et économiques entre les Pays-Bas bourguignons et l'Angleterre, 1435–1467* (Brussels: Presses universitaires de Bruxelles, 1966); De ruysscher, *Handel en recht*, pp. 117–21.

113. A. F. Sutton, 'The Merchant Adventurers of England: Their Origins and the Mercers' Company of London', *Historical Research*, 75:187 (2002), pp. 25–46.

114. Goris, *Etude sur les colonies marchandes,* p. 38; J. Marechal, 'Le départ de Bruges des marchands étrangers (XVe et XVIe siècles)', *Handelingen van het Genootschap voor Geschiedenis: driemaandelijks tijdschrift voor de studie van geschiedenis en oudheden van Vlaanderen*, 88 (1951), pp. 26–74; J. A. Van Houtte, 'Les foires dans la Belgique ancienne', in *La Foire. Receuils de la Société Jean Bodin* (Brussels: Librairie encyclopédique, 1953), pp. 175–207, on p. 193; Gelderblom, 'The Decline of Fairs and Merchant Guilds' and appendix to Gelderblom and Grafe, 'The Rise, Persistence and Decline of Merchant Guilds'.

115. CAA, Privilegiekamer, Raeckt den handel, Pk # 1012, 30 June 1488, Copie vuyten previlegie boeck der stadt van Antwerpen.

116. On the Lucchese in Antwerp: R. Sabbatini, *Cercar esca: mercanti lucchesi ad Anversa nel Cinquecento* (Florence: Salimbeni, 1985).

117. Gelderblom, 'The Decline of Fairs and Merchant Guilds', p. 213.

118. Goris, *Etude sur les colonies marchandes*, pp. 55–70.

119. J.-A.'Turksche kooplieden te Antwerpen in de XVIe eeuw', *Bijdragen tot de geschiedenis*, 14:1 (1922), pp. 30–8.

120. Gelderblom and Grafe, 'The Rise, Persistence and Decline of Merchant Guilds', p. 492.

121. Gelderblom and Grafe, 'The Rise, Persistence and Decline of Merchant Guilds', p. 492.

122. J. D. Harreld, *High Germans in the Low Countries*, pp. 58–9, 69; E. Coornaert, *Les Français et le commerce International*, II, pp. 23–8; G. K. Brunelle, 'Migration and Religious Identity: The Portuguese of Seventeenth-Century Rouen', *Journal of Early Modern History*, 7:3–4 (2003), pp. 283–311, on p. 290; B. Blondé, O. Gelderblom, and P. Stabel, 'Foreign Merchant Communities in Bruges, Antwerp and Amsterdam', in D. Calabi and S. T. Christensen (eds), *Cities and Cultural Exchange in Europe, 1400–1700*, Cultural Exchange in Early Modern Europe (Cambridge: Cambridge University Press, 2007), pp. 154–74, on pp. 166–7. The Venetians, the Milanese and the south Germans (Nuremberg traders), however, enjoyed privileges and the rights to organize a nation in Bruges from the fourteenth century onwards (the Milanese in the fifteenth century). P. Stabel and B. Lambert, 'Squaring the Circle: Merchant Guilds in Bruges', 2006, unpublished paper presented at the Workshop on Mercantile Organization in pre-industrial Europe, Antwerp, 18–19 November 2005; Stabel 'De gewenste vreemdeling'; C. J. F. Slootmans, *Paas- en Koudemarkten te Bergen-op-Zoom, 1365–1565*, 3 vols (Tilburg: Stichting Zuidelijk Historisch Contact, 1985), vol. 2, pp. 525–31, 534–6, 548–52, 594–6, 620–30.

123. Gelderblom, 'The Decline of Fairs and Merchant Guilds'.

124. J. Haemers, '"Ende hevet tvolc goede cause jeghens hemlieden te rysene" Stedelijke opstanden en staatsvorming in het graafschap Vlaanderen (1477–1492)' (PhD dissertation, Ghent University, 2006)

125. Ogilvie, *Institutions and European Trade*, pp. 31, 41.

126. Kohn, 'Merchant Associations in Pre-Industrial Europe'; Gelderblom and Grafe, 'The Rise, Persistence and Decline of Merchant Guilds'; Ogilvie, *Institutions and European Trade*.

127. The Guild of Saint Nicolas which united Low Countries jewellers, tapestry weavers and other craftsmen who sold their products in the Antwerp Dominicans' Pand (first mentioned in 1477) had a membership with a very commercial profile. J. Puttevils, 'The Ascent of Merchants from the Southern Low Countries: From Antwerp to Europe, 1480–1585' (PhD dissertation, University of Antwerp, 2012), pp. 87–9.

128. This is surprising, given the fact that Gelderblom and Grafe did not observe any correlation between increased insecurity and higher levels of control delegated to merchant guilds, i.e., individual merchants empowering their merchant guilds to perform certain tasks on their behalf. Gelderblom and Grafe, 'The Rise, Persistence and Decline of Merchant Guilds', p. 504.

129. H. Soly, 'The "Betrayal" of the Sixteenth-Century Bourgeoisie: A Myth? Some Considerations of the Behaviour Pattern of Merchants of Antwerp in the Sixteenth Century', *Acta historiae Neerlandica*, 8 (1975), pp. 31–49.

130. CAA, Privilegiekamer, Raeckt den Handel, Pk # 1012. Copye vut den ambacht boeck deser stadt van Antwerpe vande incorporatie oft societeyt der cooplieden gemaeckt indt Jaer 1485 opden 5den dach Maye. Published in: J. Denucé, 'De Beurs van Antwerpen: oorsprong en eerste ontwikkeling 15e en 16e eeuwen', *Antwerpsch Archievenblad*, 6 (1931), pp. 81–145, on pp. 96–100. See also: J. Materné, 'Schoon ende bequaem tot versamelinghe der cooplieden: Antwerpens beurswereld tijdens de Gouden zestiende eeuw', in G. De Clercq (ed.), *Ter Beurze: geschiedenis van de aandelenhandel in België, 1300–1990* (Bruges: Van de Wiele, 1992), pp. 50–85, on p. 52. This document has often been incorrectly interpreted as foundation deed of the first Antwerp exchange: J. Marechal, *Geschiedenis van de Brugse beurs* (Bruges: Anjelier, 1949), pp. 40–1; E. S. Hunt and J. M. Murray, *A History of Business in Medieval Europe, 1200–1550* (Cambridge: Cambridge University Press, 1999), p. 214.

131. On the protection of trade: Gelderblom, *Cities of Commerce*, pp. 141–68.

132. During the first elections the members chose eight candidates from which the sheriff selected the four officials.

133. For the Antwerp situation: F. Prims and J. van Roey, *Geschiedenis van Antwerpen* (Brussel: Kultuur en Beschaving, 1977), XVI, pp. 38–69.

134. J. Haemers, *For the Common Good: State Power and Urban Revolts in the Reign of Mary of Burgundy (1477–1482)* (Turnhout: Brepols, 2009); R. Van Uytven, C. Bruneel and A. M. Koldeweij, *Geschiedenis van Brabant van het hertogdom tot heden* (Zwolle: Waanders, 2004), p. 220; W. Blockmans, *Metropolen aan de Noordzee: de geschiedenis van Nederland, 1100–1560* (Amsterdam: Bakker, 2010). pp. 522–32.

135. Marechal, *Geschiedenis Van De Brugse Beurs*, pp. 32–3; Haemers, 'Stedelijke opstanden en staatsvorming', pp. 402–3.

136. Marechal, 'Le départ de Bruges'.

137. Coornaert, *Les Français*, I, p. 80; L. Sicking, *Neptune and the Netherlands: State, Economy and War at Sea in the Renaissance* (Leiden: Brill, 2004), p. 65; Haemers, 'Stedelijke opstanden en staatsvorming', p. 400; Gelderblom, *Cities of Commerce*, pp. 219–21.

138. On this instance of an attempted incorporation: O. de Smedt, 'Het College der Nederlandsche kooplieden op Engeland', *Antwerpsch Archievenblad*, 1:2–3 (1926), pp. 113–20, 321–48, on pp. 116–17; de Smedt, *De Engelse Natie*, vol. 1, pp. 295–8, 314–15; G. D. Ramsay, *The Queen's Merchants and the Revolt of the Netherlands: The End of the Antwerp Mart*, 2 vols (Manchester: Manchester University Press, 1986), vol. 2, pp. 17–33. On the political context of this period: Prims and van Roey, *Geschiedenis van Antwerpen*, XIX, pp. 39–47, XX, pp. 209–225; G. E. Wells, *Antwerp and the Gov-*

ernment of Philip II, 1555–1567 (Ithaca, NY: Cornell University, 1982), pp. 275–306.

139. Van der Wee, *The Growth of the Antwerp Market*, vol. 2, p. 214; de Smedt, *De Engelse Natie*, vol. 1, pp. 206–7. By 1590 Flemish, Italian and Hanseatic merchants had lost all their trade privileges in London. O. Gelderblom, 'The Organization of Long-Distance Trade in England and the Dutch Republic, 1550–1650', in O. Gelderblom (ed.), *The Political Economy of the Dutch Republic* (Farnham: Ashgate, 2009), ch. 9, pp. 223–54, on p. 229.

140. See the recent article by Sutton, 'The Merchant Adventurers'. And Ogilvie, *Institutions and European Trade*.

141. All silks and linens had to be sold to London citizens and re-measured in the English capital by an official, even when they had already been measured and sealed in Antwerp. English merchants were exempt from this procedure and benefited from this measure, since no one would buy the textiles from the Netherlandish merchants which had been opened for re-measuring and were thus no longer in their original folding (the folding acted as an Antwerp quality mark); textiles sold by the English merchants remained still in their original shape. CAA, Privilegiekamer, Engelse Natie, Pk # 1053. The names of the petitioning Antwerp merchants were Loys Frarin, Gherairdt de Velaer, Jan de la Faille, Cornelis van Emden and Nicolaes de Vuecht.

142. De Smedt, *De Engelse Natie*, vol. 1, pp. 238–9. In the same year, a number of Antwerp merchants repeated the same rhetoric: the English were eager to push out Low Countries merchants and had already barred the Hansa. CAA, Privilegiekamer, Engelse Natie, Pk # 1053, 25 July 1555. The merchants were Loys Frarin, Jacques Le Prieur, Gielis Hooftman, Jan Celos, Sebastiaen Danckaert and Niclaes de Voicht.

143. De Smedt, *De Engelse Natie*, vol. 1, pp. 247–51, 258. The Merchant Adventurers had also considered Hamburg and London. The latter was not chosen as the guild's staple since this would attract more foreigners to London, harming the interests of the city's own active trade.

144. De Smedt, *De Engelse Natie*, vol. 1, pp. 269–73.

145. de Smedt, *De Engelse Natie*, vol. 1, pp. 286–93.

146. De Smedt, *De Engelse Natie*, vol. 1, pp. 314, 324, n. 326.

147. De Smedt, *De Engelse Natie*, vol. 1, p. 315.

148. Ramsay, *The Queen's Merchants*, vol. 2, pp. 2, 23.

149. Ramsay, *The Queen's Merchants*, p. 24.

150. Jan Baptista Spinola, Jeronimo Revelasco, Augustijn Lercaro Moneglia, Jeronimo Meyer, Hieronymus Jennis and Antwerp cloth merchants Peter Beck, Hendrick Moons and Rombout Anthonis, silk trader Peter van Eyewerven, spice merchant Hendrik van Onsen and madder traders Gillis and Jozef Smit and Peter Scholyer. CAA, Privilegiekamer, Engelse Natie, Pk # 1059, 30 March 1565, second bundle. Cited in de Smedt, *De Engelse Natie*, vol. 1, p. 298.

151. Herman Pottey, agent of Jan Della Faille in London, and his goods were arrested in 1568; he was released only after posting a £300 sterling bail. W. Brulez, *De firma Della Faille*, p. 565.

152. B. Dietz, *The Port and Trade of Early Elizabethan London Documents* (London: London Record Society, 1972); B. Dietz, 'Antwerp and London: The Structure and Balance of Trade in the 1560s', in E. W. Ives, R. J. Knecht and J. J. Scarisbrick (eds), *Wealth and Power in Tudor England: Essays Presented to S. T. Bindoff* (London: The Athlone Press, 1978), pp. 186–203; A. Pettegree, *Foreign Protestant Communities in Sixteenth-Century London* (Oxford: Publisher, 1986); S. Rappaport, *Worlds within Worlds: Structures*

of Life in Sixteenth-Century London (Cambridge: Cambridge University Press, 1989; I. W. Archer, *The Pursuit of Stability: Social Relations in Elizabethan London* (Cambridge: Cambridge University Press, 1991).

153. De Smedt, 'Het College der Nederlandsche kooplieden'. This merchant guild has not left any of its own documents. Its history was reconstructed from requests and documents of government authorities and from another merchant guild of which a register was preserved. The West traders' guild is documented in O. de Smedt, 'Een Antwerpsch plan tot organisatie van den Nederlandschen zeehandel op het Westen', *Antwerpsch Archievenblad*, 2:2 (1927), pp. 14–30; Puttevils, 'The Ascent of Merchants', pp. 349–55. I will only focus on the England traders in this book.

154. W. E. Lingelbach, 'The Merchant Adventurers at Hamburg', *American Historical Review*, 9:2 (1904), pp. 265–87; Van der Wee, *The Growth of the Antwerp Market*, vol. 2, pp. 237–8.

155. CAA, Rekwestboeken, Pk # 657, 1579–80, 223r.

156. De Smedt, 'Het College der Nederlandsche kooplieden', p. 333.

157. The governor was appointed by the rebelling Estates-General but not approved by king Philip II.

158. The original patent is lost. De Smedt, 'Het College der Nederlandsche kooplieden', p. 118.

159. De Smedt, 'Het College der Nederlandsche kooplieden', p. 119.

160. Appeal to the administrators' judgments could be obtained from the regular, local court of law in these matters. De Smedt, 'Het College der Nederlandsche kooplieden', pp. 321–3. Other rules concerned the appointment of officers who would collect fines and make arrests, the fine on the refusal of assuming office as a headman or councilor and the right of the guild to summon its members at will and at all times.

161. De Smedt, 'Het College der Nederlandsche kooplieden', p. 324.

162. It is unclear whether the college responded to the offer. De Smedt, 'Het College der Nederlandsche kooplieden', p. 332.

163. Ogilvie, *Institutions and European Trade*, pp. 167–70, 175–80.

164. De Smedt, *De Engelse Natie*, vol. 1, p. 436.

165. On this diaspora: Brulez, 'De diaspora'; Gelderblom, *Zuid-Nederlandse kooplieden*.

166. H. J. Smit, *Bronnen tot de geschiedenis van den handel met Engeland, Schotland en Ierland* ('s-Gravenhage: Nijhoff, 1928), II, 2, nr 1451.

167. De Smedt, 'Het College der Nederlandsche kooplieden', pp. 332–6; De Smedt, *De Engelse Natie*, vol. 1, p. 441.

168. E. Lindberg, 'Club Goods and Inefficient Institutions: Why Danzig and Lübeck Failed in the Early Modern Period', *Economic History Review*, 62:3 (2009), pp. 604–28.

169. M. Kohn, 'Merchant Associations in Pre-Industrial Europe', 2003, unpublished working paper, available at http://www.dartmouth.edu/~mkohn/Papers/16.%20Associations.pdf [accessed 28 February 2015], pp. 8–9; Ogilvie, *Institutions and European Trade*, pp. 25, 230–5.

170. For the presence of Low Countries merchants on European markets, see chapter one.

171. On the diaspora: Brulez, 'De diaspora'.

172. See the special issue of the *International Review of Social History* (2001), supplement 9, 'Petitions in social history' on petitions.

173. The privilege texts are dated in 1452, 1503, 1504, 1509, 1511, 1524 and 1589. J. Denucé, 'Privilèges commerciaux accordés par les rois de Portugal aux Flamands et aux Allemands', *Archivo Historico Portuguez*, 7 (1909), pp. 310–19, 377–92.

174. Denucé, 'Privilèges commerciaux', p. 12.

175. Ogilvie, *Institutions and European Trade*, pp. 47, 288–9.

176. E. Stols, 'De Vlaamse Natie te Lissabon (15de–17de eeuw)', in J. Everaert and E. Stols (eds), *Vlaanderen en Portugal: op de golfslag van twee culturen* (Antwerp: Mercator-fonds, 1991), pp. 119–41, on p. 132.

177. Denucé, 'Privilèges commerciaux', p. 12.

178. Ogilvie, *Institutions and European Trade*, p. 319. Gelderblom and Grafe, 'The Rise, Persistence and Decline of Merchant Guilds', appendix.

179. Stols, 'De Vlaamse Natie te Lissabon (15de–17de eeuw)', p. 134.

180. Erasmus Schetz in 1511 and Hans van Pelcquen in 1570. Stols, 'De Vlaamse Natie te Lissabon (15de–17de eeuw)', p. 132. The Portuguese king also granted specific privileges to individual Low Countries merchants, such as the cork export monopoly to Bruges trader Maarten Lem in 1456. Stols, 'De Vlaamse Natie te Lissabon (15de–17de Eeuw)', p. 122.

181. Stols, *De Spaanse Brabanders*, pp. 81–4.

182. Stols, *De Spaanse Brabanders*, p. 86.

183. Stols, *De Spaanse Brabanders*, p. 92.

184. L. Bril, *De handel*; Van der Wee, *The Growth of the Antwerp Market*, vol. 2, pp. 177–83.

185. F. M. Pádron, 'The commercial world of Seville in Early Modern Times', *Journal of European Economic History*, 2:2 (1973), pp. 294–319, on p. 308.

186. Fagel, *De Hispano-Vlaamse wereld*, pp. 263–4.

187. J.-P. Berthe, 'Les Flamands à Seville au 16e Siècle', in H. Kellenbenz (ed.), *In Fremde Kaufleute Auf Der Iberischen Halbinsel* (Köln: Böhlau, 1970), pp. 239–51; Stols, *De Spaanse Brabanders*, p. 82; Fagel, *De Hispano-Vlaamse Wereld*, p. 213; E. Crailsheim, 'Behind the Atlantic Expansion: Flemish Trade Connections of Seville in 1620', *Research in Maritime History*, 43:2 (2010), pp. 21–46.

188. Degryse, *Pieter Seghers*, pp. 30–1.

189. Fagel, *De Hispano-Vlaamse wereld*, p. 213.

190. Stols, *De Spaanse Brabanders*, p. 57.

191. W. Brulez and G. Devos, *Marchands flamands à Vénise* (Brussels: Institut historique belge de Rome, 1965); P. Stabel, 'Venice and the Low Countries: Commercial Contacts and Intellectual Inspirations', in B. Aikema and B. L. Brown (eds), *Renaissance Venice and the North. Crosscurrents in the Time of Bellini, Dürer and Titian* (Milan: Bompiani, 1999), pp. 30–42, on pp. 39–40, 43; P. Stabel, 'Italian Merchants and the Fairs in the Low Countries (12th–16th Centuries)', in P. Lanaro (ed.), *La pratica dello scambio. Sistemi di fiere, mercanti e città in Europa (1400–1700)* (Venice: Marsilio, 2003), pp. 131–160, on pp. 158–60; J. Puttevils, 'A servitio de vostri', pp. 187–94.

192. Brulez, 'De Diaspora', pp. 279–81, 300–5; Brulez and Devos, *Marchands flamands*, I, pp. xix–xxvi.

193. Including Carlo Helman, Francesco Vrins, Giacomo Vanlemens, Giovanni de Cordes, Giacomo Van Castre and Antonio Van Neste. Brulez and Devos *Marchands flamands*, pp. xix–xx.

194. M. Van Gelder, *Trading Places: The Netherlandish Merchants in Early Modern Venice* (Leiden: Brill, 2009), pp. 139–153; M. Van Gelder, 'How to Influence Venetian Economic Policy: Collective Petitions of the Netherlandish Merchant Community in the Early Seventeenth Century', *Mediterranean Historical Review*, 24 (2009), pp. 29–47. The Venetian senate also granted individual privileges to Netherlandish merchants: for example, Marco Manaert obtained an import tax reduction on stockfish and baleen oil

in 1597. Brulez and Devos, *Marchands flamands*, pp. xxii–xxiii. The nation also generated sociability, such as by organizing banquets and religious feasts. Low Countries merchants, mariners and craftsmen could appeal to the poor relief and legal assistance provided by this informal organization. Van Gelder, *Trading Places*, pp. 153–8. On the appointment of a consul after 1609, see Van Gelder, *Trading Places*, pp. 158–69; J Puttevils, 'Middenin het web Van de internationale politiek: Nederlandse diplomaten in Venetië', in M. Boone and P. Stabel (eds), *Fiamminghi a Venezia: Sporen Van De Lage Landen in Venetië* (Brussels: Unibook, 2010), pp. 115–33.

195. M.-C. Engels, *Merchants, Interlopers, Seamen and Corsairs: The 'Flemish' Community in Livorno and Genoa (1615–1635)* (Hilversum: Verloren, 1997).

196. Brulez, 'De diaspora', pp. 299–300; P. Earle, 'The Commercial Development of Ancona, 1479–1551', *Economic History Review*, 22:1 (1969), pp. 28–44. In early seventeenth-century Palermo the Antwerp expatriate Simon le Maire, brother of Isaac le Maire, acted as consul of the 'Flemish', both from the northern and the southern part of the Low Countries. His successor, Henri Dyck, was appointed by both the Brussels and the the Hague governments. C. Tihon, 'Un consulat belge à Palerme au début du XVIIe Siècle', *Bulletin de l'Institute Historique belge de Rome*, 19 (1938), pp. 77–82.

197. All goods of foreigners who died within the realm fell to the Crown.

198. Goods lost at sea which washed ashore were considered the property of the king.

199. For the text see: Z. W. Sneller and W. S. Unger, *Bronnen tot de geschiedenis van den handel met Frankrijk* ('s-Gravenhage: Nijhoff, 1930), pp. 114–17

200. E. Trocmé and M. Delafosse, *Le commerce Rochelais de la fin du 15e siècle au début du 17e siècle* (Paris: SEVPEN, 1952); Craeybeckx, *Un grand commerce d'importation*, pp. 123–6; Brulez, 'De diaspora', pp. 285–7; M. Tranchant, 'Au risque de l'étranger: un sujet majeur de gouvernance à La Rochelle à la fin du Moyen Âge', *Annales de Bretagne et des pays de l'Ouest*, 117:1 (2010), pp. 91–108, on p. 98; J.-P. Poussou, 'Les étrangers à Bordeaux à l'époque moderne', *Annales de Bretagne et des pays de l'Ouest*, 117:1 (2010), pp. 149–64; M. Bochaca, 'Le règlement des litiges commerciaux entre bourgeois et étrangers: les juridictions pour "fait de marchandises" à Bordeaux au milieu du XVe au milieu du XVIe siècle', *Annales de Bretagne et des pays de l'Ouest*, 117:1 (2010), pp. 133–47.

201. P. Benedict, 'Rouen's Foreign Trade during the Era of the Religious Wars (1560–1600)', *Journal of European Economic History*, 13:1 (1984), pp. 29–74; P. Benedict *Rouen during the Wars of Religion* (Cambridge: Cambridge University Press, 2003).

202. They elected two annually changing chairmen, or *Burggrafen*. A council of four of the eldest members was also chosen; two of them would keep the Gesellschaft's administration in order. The guild counted fifty members and charged an entry fee and an annual subscription. Its precise function and goals are unclear; however, this incorporation should be considered within the context of the 1612 revolt, during which the merchants were a powerful group. The revolt failed but the city council permitted the merchants to create new guilds which would have a seat in the city council. Dietz does not mention which privileges this organization received. A. Dietz, *Frankfurter Handelsgeschichte*, 5 vols (Glashütten im Taunus: Auvermann, 1970), vol 2, pp. 83–4.

203. Roughly a third of its membership. Dietz, *Frankfurter Handelsgeschichte*, vol. 2, p. 84.

204. The letter can be found in CAA, Insolvente Boedelkamer, IB # 258, letters Jan Van Immerseel, 19 August 1589. For van Immerseel: Mees, 'Koopman in troebele tijden'.

205. Brulez, 'De diaspora', pp. 293–394.

206. The ritual closely resembles a similar performance depicted in the statue of the two

city virgins, 'Norimbergia' and 'Brabantia', made in 1340 and installed at the Nuremberg Rathaus. The statue represents the annual mission of a Nuremberg messenger to the Episcopal city of Liège and to Brussels. The messenger donated a large sword, a belt, needles and a gold coin to renew the privileges the Nurembergers enjoyed in the duchy of Brabant. H. Boockmann, *Die Stadt im Späten Mittelalter* (München: Beck, 1986), p. 98; E. Mummenhoff and H. Wallraff, *Das Rathaus in Nürnberg* (Nürnberg: J. L. Schrag, 1891), pp. 36–7. Hence, it is possible that the Nuremberg toll exemption privilege was a return favour for the privileges the Nurembergers already enjoyed in the middle of the fourteenth century and which were still in use in the last decades of the sixteenth century.

207. 'Daar de Neerlanders overal benyt worden mits sy negotieren, hetwelcke de borgeryen liever selve souden genieten, en daar de heren des raads hier van principaele cooplieden sijn, diewelcken hetselve oic niet gerne en sien en suecken allen middelen om sulx te beletten, so practiceren sij nu alle nieuwigheden om ons van de gepriviligieerden tol te beroven'. The letter can be found in CAA, Insolvente Boedelkamer, IB # 258, letters Jan Van Immerseel, 19 August 1589. Brulez, 'De diaspora', p. 294.

208. Brulez, *De firma Della Faille*, p. 456.

209. Brulez, 'De diaspora', pp. 294–5.

210. E. Lindberg, 'Club Goods and Inefficient Institutions: Why Danzig and Lübeck Failed in the Early Modern Period', *Economic History Review*, 62:3 (2009), pp. 604–28, on p. 622.

211. P. Dollinger, *The German Hansa* (London: Macmillan, 1970), p. 358.

212. W. E. Lingelbach, 'The Merchant Adventurers at Hamburg', *American Historical Review*, 9:2 (1904), pp. 265–87; E. Lindberg, 'The Rise of Hamburg as a Global Marketplace in the Seventeenth Century: A Comparative Political Economy Perspective', *Comparative Studies in Society and History*, 50:3 (2008), pp. 641–62; Lindberg, 'Club Goods and Inefficient Institutions'.

213. P. Dollinger, *The German Hansa* (London: Macmillan, 1970), p. 356.

214. The contract was renewed in 1615 and 1639. Schulz, *De invloed van het oude Brabant*, pp. 39–41.

215. Schulz, De invloed van het oude Brabant, pp. 48–9.

216. J. Puttevils, 'I mercanti fiamminghi: Nederlandse kooplieden in Venetië', in M. Boone and P. Stabel (eds), *Fiamminghi a Venezia: sporen van de Lage Landen in Venetië* (Brussels: Unibook, 2010), pp. 56–76; C. J. de Larivière, 'Entre gestion privée et contrôle public: les transports maritimes à Venise à la fin du Moyen Age', *Histoire Urbaine*, 12 (2005), pp. 57–68; Van Gelder, *Trading Places*.

217. de Larivière, 'Entre gestion privée et contrôle public'; C. J. de Larivière, *Naviguer, commercer, gouverner. Economie maritime et pouvoirs à Venise* (Leiden: Brill, 2008).

Conclusion

1. J. Wheeler, A Treatise of Commerce (New York: Columbia University Press, 1931), pp. 36–8.

2. See also Gelderblom, 'Entrepreneurs'; S. Ogilvie, M. Küpker and J. Maegraith, 'Household Debt in Early Modern Germany: Evidence from Personal Inventories', *Journal of Economic History*, 72:1 (2012), pp. 134–67.

3. J. Hoock and P. Jeannin (eds), *Ars Mercatoria: Handbücher und Traktate für den Gebrauch des Kaufmanns, 1470–1820: Eine Analytische Bibliographie = Ars Mercatoria:*

Manuels et traités à l'usage des marchands, 1470–1820, 3 vols (Paderborn: Schöningh, 1991).

4. J. Puttevils, 'The Ascent of Merchants from the Southern Low Countries: From Antwerp to Europe, 1480–1585' (PhD dissertation, University of Antwerp, 2012). This chapter from my PhD has been left out of this book. It will be published elsewhere in its entirety. Parts of it are used in 'Sixteenth-Century Antwerp, a Hyper-Market for All? The Case of Low Countries Merchants', in B. Blondé, B. De Munck, G. Marnef, J. Puttevils and M. F. Van Dijck (eds), *Antwerp and the Renaissance* (Turnhout: Brepols, forthcoming).

5. CAA, Privilegiekamer, Engelse Natie, Pk # 1059, fourth bundle. Reproduced in Puttevils, 'Sixteenth-Century Antwerp, a Hyper-Market for All?'.

INDEX